Developing Successful Global Strategies for Marketing Luxury Brands

Fabrizio Mosca
University of Turin, Italy

Cecilia Casalegno
University of Turin, Italy

Rosalia Gallo
Universitat Autònoma de Barcelona, Spain

A volume in the Advances in Marketing, Customer Relationship Management, and E-Services (AMCRMES) Book Series

Published in the United States of America by
    IGI Global
    Business Science Reference (an imprint of IGI Global)
    701 E. Chocolate Avenue
    Hershey PA, USA 17033
    Tel: 717-533-8845
    Fax: 717-533-8661
    E-mail: cust@igi-global.com
    Web site: http://www.igi-global.com

Copyright © 2021 by IGI Global. All rights reserved. No part of this publication may be reproduced, stored or distributed in any form or by any means, electronic or mechanical, including photocopying, without written permission from the publisher. Product or company names used in this set are for identification purposes only. Inclusion of the names of the products or companies does not indicate a claim of ownership by IGI Global of the trademark or registered trademark.
    Library of Congress Cataloging-in-Publication Data

Names: Mosca, Fabrizio, editor. | Casalegno, Cecilia, 1979- editor. |
  Gallo-Martinez, Rosalia, 1964- editor.
Title: Developing successful global strategies for marketing luxury brands
  / Fabrizio Mosca, Cecilia Casalegno, and Rosalia Gallo-Martinez, editor.

Description: Hershey, PA : Business Science Reference, [2021] | Includes
  bibliographical references and index. | Summary: "This book presents the
  most relevant upgraded theoretical frameworks and empirical research
  about the marketing of luxury goods, offering contributions focused on
  contemporary issues affecting luxury industries such as digital
  transformation, sustainable development, changes in luxury consumers'
  behavior, integration between physical and online channels, and the
  development of social media marketing strategies"-- Provided by
  publisher.
Identifiers: LCCN 2020048962 (print) | LCCN 2020048963 (ebook) | ISBN
  9781799858829 (hardcover) | ISBN 9781799868576 (paperback) | ISBN
  9781799858836 (ebook)
Subjects: LCSH: Luxury goods industry. | Luxuries--Marketing.
Classification: LCC HD9999.L852 D48 2021 (print) | LCC HD9999.L852
  (ebook) | DDC 658.8/02--dc23
LC record available at https://lccn.loc.gov/2020048962
LC ebook record available at https://lccn.loc.gov/2020048963

This book is published in the IGI Global book series Advances in Marketing, Customer Relationship Management, and E-Services (AMCRMES) (ISSN: 2327-5502; eISSN: 2327-5529)

British Cataloguing in Publication Data
A Cataloguing in Publication record for this book is available from the British Library.

All work contributed to this book is new, previously-unpublished material. The views expressed in this book are those of the authors, but not necessarily of the publisher.

For electronic access to this publication, please contact: eresources@igi-global.com.

Advances in Marketing, Customer Relationship Management, and E-Services (AMCRMES) Book Series

Eldon Y. Li
National Chengchi University, Taiwan & California Polytechnic State University, USA

ISSN:2327-5502
EISSN:2327-5529

Mission

Business processes, services, and communications are important factors in the management of good customer relationship, which is the foundation of any well organized business. Technology continues to play a vital role in the organization and automation of business processes for marketing, sales, and customer service. These features aid in the attraction of new clients and maintaining existing relationships.

The Advances in Marketing, Customer Relationship Management, and E-Services (AMCRMES) Book Series addresses success factors for customer relationship management, marketing, and electronic services and its performance outcomes. This collection of reference source covers aspects of consumer behavior and marketing business strategies aiming towards researchers, scholars, and practitioners in the fields of marketing management.

Coverage

- Mobile Services
- Online Community Management and Behavior
- Mobile CRM
- Customer Retention
- Telemarketing
- Legal Considerations in E-Marketing
- Text Mining and Marketing
- B2B marketing
- Ethical Considerations in E-Marketing
- Cases on Electronic Services

IGI Global is currently accepting manuscripts for publication within this series. To submit a proposal for a volume in this series, please contact our Acquisition Editors at Acquisitions@igi-global.com or visit: http://www.igi-global.com/publish/.

The Advances in Marketing, Customer Relationship Management, and E-Services (AMCRMES) Book Series (ISSN 2327-5502) is published by IGI Global, 701 E. Chocolate Avenue, Hershey, PA 17033-1240, USA, www.igi-global.com. This series is composed of titles available for purchase individually; each title is edited to be contextually exclusive from any other title within the series. For pricing and ordering information please visit http://www.igi-global.com/book-series/advances-marketing-customer-relationship-management/37150. Postmaster: Send all address changes to above address. © © 2021 IGI Global. All rights, including translation in other languages reserved by the publisher. No part of this series may be reproduced or used in any form or by any means – graphics, electronic, or mechanical, including photocopying, recording, taping, or information and retrieval systems – without written permission from the publisher, except for non commercial, educational use, including classroom teaching purposes. The views expressed in this series are those of the authors, but not necessarily of IGI Global.

Titles in this Series
For a list of additional titles in this series, please visit: www.igi-global.com/book-series

Insights, Innovation, and Analytics for Optimal Customer Engagement
Samala Nagaraj (Woxsen University, India)
Business Science Reference • © 2021 • 334pp • H/C (ISBN: 9781799839194) • US $195.00

New Techniques for Brand Management in the Healthcare Sector
Ana Pinto Borges (European Business School and Research Group, ISAG (NIDISAG), Portugal) and Paula Rodrigues (Lusíada University of Porto, Portugal)
Business Science Reference • © 2021 • 244pp • H/C (ISBN: 9781799830344) • US $225.00

Impact of ICTs on Event Management and Marketing
Kemal Birdir (Mersin University, Turkey) Sevda Birdir (Mersin University, Turkey) Ali Dalgic (Isparta University of Applied Sciences, Turkey) and Derya Toksoz (Mersin University, Turkey)
Business Science Reference • © 2021 • 357pp • H/C (ISBN: 9781799849544) • US $195.00

Building Consumer-Brand Relationship in Luxury Brand Management
Paula Rodrigues (Lusíada University of Porto, Portugal) and Ana Pinto Borges (Instituto Superior de Administração e Gestão, Portugal)
Business Science Reference • © 2021 • 318pp • H/C (ISBN: 9781799843696) • US $225.00

Innovations in Digital Branding and Content Marketing
Subhankar Das (Duy Tan University, Vietnam) and Subhra Rani Mondal (Duy Tan University, Vietnam)
Business Science Reference • © 2021 • 311pp • H/C (ISBN: 9781799844204) • US $195.00

Handbook of Research on Applied AI for International Business and Marketing Applications
Bryan Christiansen (Global Training Group, Ltd, UK) and Tihana Škrinjarić (University of Zagreb, Croatia)
Business Science Reference • © 2021 • 702pp • H/C (ISBN: 9781799850779) • US $295.00

Handbook of Research on Technology Applications for Effective Customer Engagement
Norazah Mohd Suki (Universiti Utara Malaysia, Malaysia)
Business Science Reference • © 2021 • 391pp • H/C (ISBN: 9781799847724) • US $295.00

Leveraging Consumer Behavior and Psychology in the Digital Economy
Norazah Mohd Suki (Universiti Malaysia Sabah, Malaysia) and Norbayah Mohd Suki (Universiti Utara Malaysia, Malaysia)
Business Science Reference • © 2020 • 299pp • H/C (ISBN: 9781799830429) • US $195.00

701 East Chocolate Avenue, Hershey, PA 17033, USA
Tel: 717-533-8845 x100 • Fax: 717-533-8661
E-Mail: cust@igi-global.com • www.igi-global.com

Editorial Advisory Board

Wided Batat, *EM Normandie Business School, France & Metis Lab, France & University of Lyon 2, France*
Stefano Bresciani, *University of Turin, Italy*
Valter Cantino, *University of Turin, Italy*
Francesca Culasso, *University of Turin, Italy*
Philip J. Kitchen, *ICN-Artem School of Business, France*
Alberto Mattiacci, *Sapienza, University of Rome, Italy*
Riccardo Resciniti, *University of Sannio, Italy*
Russell S. Winer, *Leonard N. Stern School of Business, USA*

Table of Contents

Preface xvi

Acknowledgment xxiii

Section 1
Managing Global Luxury Brands in the Era of Digitalisation

Chapter 1
The Evolution of Distribution in the Luxury Sector: From Single to Omni-Channel 1
Fabrizio Mosca, University of Turin, Italy
Elisa Giacosa, University of Turin, Italy
Luca Matteo Zagni, University of Turin, Italy

Chapter 2
Omnichannel Shopping Experiences for Fast Fashion and Luxury Brands: An Exploratory Study 22
Cesare Amatulli, University of Bari, Italy
Matteo De Angelis, LUISS University, Italy
Andrea Sestino, University of Bari, Italy
Gianluigi Guido, University of Salento, Italy

Chapter 3
Examining the Integration of Virtual and Physical Platforms From Luxury Brand Managers'
Perspectives 44
Paola Peretti, The IULM University, Italy
Valentina Chiaudano, University of Turin, Italy
Mohanbir Sawhney, Kellogg School of Management, Northwestern University, USA

Chapter 4
Managing Integrated Brand Communication Strategies in the Online Era: New Marketing
Frontiers for Luxury Goods 62
Fabrizio Mosca, University of Turin, Italy
Cecilia Casalegno, University of Turin, Italy
Giulia Bonelli, University of Turin, Italy
Chiara Civera, University of Turin, Italy

Chapter 5

Investigating the Impact of Luxury Brands' Traditional and Digital Contents on Customer-Based Brand Equity 81
>   *Fabrizio Mosca, University of Turin, Italy*
>   *Philip J. Kitchen, ICN-Artem School of Business, University of Lorraine, France*
>   *Valentina Chiaudano, University of Turin, Italy*

Chapter 6

When Luxury Brands Changed Their Approach to Social Media 101
>   *Fabrizio Maria Pini, MIP School of Management, Politecnico di Milano, Italy*
>   *Dinara Timergaleeva, Wyde – The Connective School, Italy*

Chapter 7

Innovating Luxury Service Experiences Through E-Servicescapes 119
>   *Laura Ingrid Maria Colm, SDA Bocconi School of Management, Bocconi University, Italy*
>   *Stefano Prestini, Bocconi University, Italy*

Chapter 8

Pivots in the Luxury Business: Discovering the New Luxury Consumer Through Social Data 139
>   *Wendy K. Bendoni, Grenoble Ecole de Management, France*
>   *Fabio Duma, School of Management and Law, Zurich University of Applied Sciences,*
>   *Switzerland*

Chapter 9

Luxury Brands and Strategic Management Accounting 157
>   *Peter Clarke, University College Dublin, Ireland*
>   *Edoardo Crocco, University of Turin, Italy*

Section 2
Sustainable Development in the Luxury Industry

Chapter 10

Is Luxury Compatible With Corporate Social Responsibility (CSR)? Models for Sustainable Marketing Strategies 179
>   *Wided Batat, EM Normandie Business School, Paris, France & Metis Lab, France &*
>   *University of Lyon 2, France*
>   *Inas Khochman, American University of Beirut, Lebanon*

Chapter 11

Upcycled vs. Recycled Products by Luxury Brands: Status and Environmental Concern Motives ... 197
>   *Feray Adıgüzel, LUISS University, Italy*
>   *Carmela Donato, LUISS University, Italy*

Section 3
New Trends in Consumer Behaviour

Chapter 12
Generations' Attitudes and Behaviours in the Luxury Sector 214
    Chiara Giachino, University of Turin, Italy
    Bernardo Bertoldi, University of Turin, Italy
    Augusto Bargoni, University of Turin, Italy

Chapter 13
There Is No Such Thing as the Millennial: A Cross-Cultural Analysis of Luxury and Prestige
Perception Among Young People in Switzerland and South Korea 230
    Camilla Pedrazzi, School of Management and Law, Zurich University of Applied Sciences,
        Switzerland
    Fabio Duma, School of Management and Law, Zurich University of Applied Sciences,
        Switzerland
    Maya Gadgil, School of Management and Law, Zurich University of Applied Sciences,
        Switzerland

Chapter 14
Designing Luxurious Food Experiences for Millennials and Post-Millennials 261
    Monica Mendini, University of Applied Sciences and Arts of Southern Switzerland (SUPSI),
        Switzerland
    Wided Batat, EM Normandie Business School, Paris, France & Metis Lab, France &
        University of Lyon 2, France
    Paula C. Peter, San Diego State University, USA

Chapter 15
Influence of Celebrity Endorsement on Mature Female Luxury Cosmetic Consumers 274
    Leonor Alberola Amores, Universitat Jaume I, Spain
    Susana Miquel Segarra, Universitat Jaume I, Spain
    Irene García Medina, Glasgow Caledonian University, UK
    Zahaira Fabiola González Romo, Universitat Internacional de Catalunya, Spain

Compilation of References 296

About the Contributors 341

Index 349

Detailed Table of Contents

Preface xvi

Acknowledgment xxiii

Section 1
Managing Global Luxury Brands in the Era of Digitalisation

Chapter 1

The Evolution of Distribution in the Luxury Sector: From Single to Omni-Channel 1
Fabrizio Mosca, University of Turin, Italy
Elisa Giacosa, University of Turin, Italy
Luca Matteo Zagni, University of Turin, Italy

In today's competitive environment, it is highlighted how the digital channel has over the years become an important distribution channel for goods with a high symbolic value. During its development, it has taken on characteristics very similar to the physical channel with direct distribution models, created through active management of e-commerce sites by luxury brands, and indirectly with the presence of specialized intermediaries by product or multi-brand, often very innovative. Goods that belong to a segment of the luxury market defined as "not affordable" tend to make use of the digital channel more aimed at strengthening the heritage and elite characteristics of the brand. On the other hand, the brands of the "affordable" luxury goods approach the digital channel with a more economically return-oriented perspective, also using intermediaries that allow a higher percentage of market coverage.

Chapter 2

Omnichannel Shopping Experiences for Fast Fashion and Luxury Brands: An Exploratory Study 22
Cesare Amatulli, University of Bari, Italy
Matteo De Angelis, LUISS University, Italy
Andrea Sestino, University of Bari, Italy
Gianluigi Guido, University of Salento, Italy

This chapter explores how luxury and fast fashion brands have been affected by omnichannel strategies, which refer to the opportunity to integrate online and offline channels to create a seamless shopping experience aimed at engaging customers. Through a quali-quantitative research approach, the study examines the potential effects of the implementation of omnichannel activities on the perception of luxury and fast fashion brands. Interestingly, consumers perceive omnichannel strategies as something projected for luxury brands, thus as a way for them to improve the luxury shopping experience. Consequently, when applied to fast fashion brands, omnichannel strategies may lead consumers to perceive such brand as more prestigious, activating a sort of "luxurization." For a luxury company, omnichannel strategies may represent an opportunity because they can increase the perceived luxuriousness of the brand, but also a threat because they may help fast fashion brands to be perceived as luxurious, thus "imitating" luxury companies.

Chapter 3
Examining the Integration of Virtual and Physical Platforms From Luxury Brand Managers' Perspectives 44

> *Paola Peretti, The IULM University, Italy*
> *Valentina Chiaudano, University of Turin, Italy*
> *Mohanbir Sawhney, Kellogg School of Management, Northwestern University, USA*

"The internet dilemma" was the concept used to describe luxury brand companies' initial reluctance to integrate online technologies into their business model. However, over time, luxury brand companies have understood that moving towards digital transformation is the only way to survive on the market and appeal to the new luxury brand consumers. In a few years, digitalisation has become a priority for all luxury brand companies that started to integrate digital and physical platforms to engage consumers through all touchpoints of their shopping journey. In light of the topic's relevance and considering the primary focus of research on consumers, this chapter aims to deepen the digitalisation phenomenon in the luxury market involving the little-explored luxury brand managers' perspective. The authors conducted a longitudinal study to compare the main changes in integrating digital and physical platforms from the managers' perspective between 2014 and 2020. In this endeavour, they also considered how the COVID-19 pandemic had affected luxury brand companies' digitalisation.

Chapter 4
Managing Integrated Brand Communication Strategies in the Online Era: New Marketing Frontiers for Luxury Goods 62

> *Fabrizio Mosca, University of Turin, Italy*
> *Cecilia Casalegno, University of Turin, Italy*
> *Giulia Bonelli, University of Turin, Italy*
> *Chiara Civera, University of Turin, Italy*

After digitalization, both scholars and practitioners found that luxury companies, which have invested in this transformation, not only have increased their revenues, but have also improved customer satisfaction. Luxury companies have reached a greater number of consumers worldwide, but the communication pillars have been preserved. In the near future, luxury companies will have to deal with the effects of COVID-19. Most likely, some of these changes will be a boost of the online shopping; a return to fewer purchases, of valuable items; and the need of an integrated shopping experience. The aim of the chapter is to show how luxury brands have embraced digital channels without losing their pillars. This chapter also aims to show that luxury companies have successfully invested in customer education and that consumers have adapted their behaviour to new touch points with the brand. Finally, this chapter aims to investigate new approaches to integrate the physical and the digital channels and the implications of COVID-19 on the communication strategies of luxury firms.

Chapter 5
Investigating the Impact of Luxury Brands' Traditional and Digital Contents on Customer-Based Brand Equity 81
Fabrizio Mosca, University of Turin, Italy
Philip J. Kitchen, ICN-Artem School of Business, University of Lorraine, France
Valentina Chiaudano, University of Turin, Italy

After a period of initial scepticism, luxury-branded companies now understand the necessity of integrating digital technologies into their marketing actions. Therefore, most luxury companies approach emerging digital tools commencing from communication strategies. The direct consequence is the adoption of social media such as blogs, applications (apps), and social networking as new communication tools alongside and in conjunction with traditional media. The purpose of this chapter lies in seeking to understand the extent to which luxury brand consumers appreciate the contents of luxury brand communications and in comparing digital and traditional ranges. In addition, the chapter investigates the existence of a correlation between the level of satisfaction perceived by luxury consumers and the dimension of customer brand equity according to the Aaker model. In this endeavour, this study is an attempt to provide academics and practitioners with insight about the expectation of luxury brand consumers from contents delivered, comparing digital and traditional platforms.

Chapter 6
When Luxury Brands Changed Their Approach to Social Media 101
Fabrizio Maria Pini, MIP School of Management, Politecnico di Milano, Italy
Dinara Timergaleeva, Wyde – The Connective School, Italy

COVID-19 lockdowns led to a new approach to social media communication by luxury fashion brands. This chapter explores recent pandemic-related changes in the social context and the need for brands to rethink their narrative to engage consumers and influence purchase decisions. The authors selected a panel of 28 fashion luxury brands, both independent and conglomerate-owned, to analyze the paradigm shift in social media communication and content creation. Their findings show that with social media acting as the main touchpoint, luxury fashion brands have effectively produced new communication archetypes, revealing the latent potential of digital platforms as strategic tools.

Chapter 7
Innovating Luxury Service Experiences Through E-Servicescapes 119
Laura Ingrid Maria Colm, SDA Bocconi School of Management, Bocconi University, Italy
Stefano Prestini, Bocconi University, Italy

The digital customer experience is a top priority and major challenge for luxury service companies, who have to connect with their target customers yet strive to remain exclusive and to innovate their core offers while preserving their heritage. After a brief review of the literature on customer experience and virtual environments in luxury service contexts, this chapter focuses on e-servicescapes as a means for innovation and improvement in delivering omnichannel experiences for luxury customers. Adopting Bitner's typology of servicescapes, this chapter is based on a three case vignettes analysis that highlights how luxury service providers can use e-servicescapes to enrich their physical service experiences. Three e-servicescape strategies are identified—integration, amplification, and substitution—that ultimately support companies in renewing and improving their overall luxury propositions.

Chapter 8

Pivots in the Luxury Business: Discovering the New Luxury Consumer Through Social Data 139

Wendy K. Bendoni, Grenoble Ecole de Management, France
Fabio Duma, School of Management and Law, Zurich University of Applied Sciences,
Switzerland

Consumer behavior is continuously evolving, and with it, so is the business of luxury. Besides other societal and economic changes, digital technology and social networks have affected how people search for information, buy products, and relate to luxury brands. As a growing number of people use social networks, an abundance of social data can be analyzed to detect shifts in perception and behaviors, generating insights that can benefit luxury brands. There is a need for theoretical conceptualizations and, based on these, strategy frameworks to help identify relevant sources of social data and derive actionable insights by using social media intelligence in a strategic, structured, and impact-oriented manner. With their conceptual study, the authors aim to close this gap and contribute towards marketing management literature by proposing a conceptual social listening framework. Their framework highlights the benefits of using social data and explains the basic steps of turning data into valuable insights that drive managerial action based on relevant theory and technology.

Chapter 9

Luxury Brands and Strategic Management Accounting 157

Peter Clarke, University College Dublin, Ireland
Edoardo Crocco, University of Turin, Italy

It is generally accepted that the primary objective of the discipline of management accounting is to provide relevant information, financial and non-financial, to business managers in order to assist in their decision making. This discipline evolved during the Industrial Revolution and it was, initially, referred to as cost accounting due to its emphasis on reporting internally-orientated cost information. The purpose of this chapter is to highlight the current techniques of managerial accounting widely used by business organizations all over the world and to describe the managerial implications of said methods when they are utilized by players operating in the luxury sector.

Section 2
Sustainable Development in the Luxury Industry

Chapter 10

Is Luxury Compatible With Corporate Social Responsibility (CSR)? Models for Sustainable
Marketing Strategies 179

Wided Batat, EM Normandie Business School, Paris, France & Metis Lab, France &
University of Lyon 2, France
Inas Khochman, American University of Beirut, Lebanon

Luxury as a field of research has attracted many scholars who examined the potential connections and (in) compatibilities between luxury and corporate social responsibility (CSR). While some studies emphasize the incompatibility between luxury and sustainability, others highlight the important efforts of luxury brands in terms of luxury offerings and sustainable marketing strategies to fit eco-friendly consumers. To foster this research stream, this chapter develops a deeper understanding of the rise and evolvement of CSR in the luxury sector and the major marketing strategies implemented by luxury brands to fit with the needs of today's responsible consumers. The authors will first present a chronological literature review through three key periods, including the underground and advancement stages to the consolidation of sustainable luxury marketing as an established research stream. Then, a framework identifying different luxury CSR strategies will be proposed. Finally, opportunities and futures challenges will be discussed at the end of this chapter.

Chapter 11
Upcycled vs. Recycled Products by Luxury Brands: Status and Environmental Concern Motives ... 197
  Feray Adıgüzel, LUISS University, Italy
  Carmela Donato, LUISS University, Italy

This chapter aims at covering an important gap, contributing to research in the field of luxury markets as well as sustainable consumption, and focuses on new sustainable products by luxury brands. Through an experimental study 3x1 between-subject design in which the product material (upcycled vs. recycled vs. virgin) of a fictitious luxury product was manipulated, the authors investigated which luxury product (upcycled vs. recycled vs. not sustainable) is preferred by consumers in terms of attitude and purchase intentions. Results of this experimental design can inform luxury product managers and designers about whether consumers react more positively towards upcycle vs. recycle products when consumers' status motives and environmental consciousness increase. In addition, they can understand the reasons and emphasize those in their marketing communications to increase demand for those products with this study.

Section 3
New Trends in Consumer Behaviour

Chapter 12
Generations' Attitudes and Behaviours in the Luxury Sector 214
  Chiara Giachino, University of Turin, Italy
  Bernardo Bertoldi, University of Turin, Italy
  Augusto Bargoni, University of Turin, Italy

The luxury sector needs to adapt its strategies to the digital advent, the online purchasing, and new young customers who have different behaviors and attitudes with respect to older generations. Young generations (Millennials and GenZ) signed a deep change for companies and influenced the way of doing business. They tend to gather information online, they share their opinions, and they pay attention to how companies behave. Since they represent a big part of the market, it is fundamental to understand if the luxury sector is relevant for them and how they consider luxury brands, for example, Moncler. Through an online questionnaire, a comparison between young and old generations has been realized.

Chapter 13
There Is No Such Thing as the Millennial: A Cross-Cultural Analysis of Luxury and Prestige
Perception Among Young People in Switzerland and South Korea 230
> *Camilla Pedrazzi, School of Management and Law, Zurich University of Applied Sciences,*
> *Switzerland*
> *Fabio Duma, School of Management and Law, Zurich University of Applied Sciences,*
> *Switzerland*
> *Maya Gadgil, School of Management and Law, Zurich University of Applied Sciences,*
> *Switzerland*

In this chapter, the authors present a cultural comparative study of how millennials in Switzerland and South Korea define and perceive luxury and prestige and how this might influence their luxury consumer behavior. Labels, such as GenX, millennials, GenY, or GenZ, are often used to distinguish cohorts of individuals based on their shared generational experiences and characteristics. However, as previous research shows, mere membership in a generational cohort is not a sufficient explanation for consumption patterns across geographies and cultures. Given the size and importance of the global luxury market and the degree of internationalization of luxury companies, a better understanding of the luxury consumer and the impact of their macro-context is vital. The results of the present study indicate that economic as well as cultural factors have an impact on the definition and perception of luxury among millennials and might also explain differences in consumer behavior.

Chapter 14
Designing Luxurious Food Experiences for Millennials and Post-Millennials 261
> *Monica Mendini, University of Applied Sciences and Arts of Southern Switzerland (SUPSI),*
> *Switzerland*
> *Wided Batat, EM Normandie Business School, Paris, France & Metis Lab, France &*
> *University of Lyon 2, France*
> *Paula C. Peter, San Diego State University, USA*

The relationship between young generations (Millennials and Gen Z), luxury, and food is a current and complex subject. Millennials and Gen Z are the first digital native generations to be very comfortable with technology devices and interested at an early stage in luxury food experiences. By exploring youth food culture and current luxury food experiences and practices, the authors identify three trends (digitalization, extended realities, and cause-related marketing) as key areas food brands and food actors (e.g., restaurants) should capitalize on to educate, facilitate, and promote the adoption of pleasurable, healthy, and sustainable food consumptions. The authors provide an overview of these three new key trends together with examples Millennials and Gen Z consumers are attracted to considering luxurious food consumption and experiences. This chapter contributes to the need to look at contexts of application (food) where sustainability and the digital transformation highlights the present and future for the promotion of luxury goods and experiences.

Chapter 15
Influence of Celebrity Endorsement on Mature Female Luxury Cosmetic Consumers 274
> *Leonor Alberola Amores, Universitat Jaume I, Spain*
> *Susana Miquel Segarra, Universitat Jaume I, Spain*
> *Irene García Medina, Glasgow Caledonian University, UK*
> *Zahaira Fabiola González Romo, Universitat Internacional de Catalunya, Spain*

A 'celebrity endorser' is any individual easily recognisable by the general public who leverages this visibility and goodwill to either appear alongside the product in an ad or endorse the product. This helps cosmetics brands to architect a strong brand image in the eyes of end users, a result due in large to the transference of the endorser's trustworthiness to the brand she/he backs. The study revealed that mature female consumers were more likely to relate to an ad featuring celebrities of similar age as themselves and who are actual users of the product rather than armchair or hands-off endorsers.

Compilation of References 296

About the Contributors 341

Index 349

Preface

The marketing of luxury goods has become progressively significant, and the number of universities and institutions addressing this concept has increased. The global luxury market has grown in value for years, reaching approximately 1.27 trillion euros in 2019, before the 2020 pandemic. This market has always been considered as a recession-proof market, and only the current pandemic had slowed down its rise. However, academics and practitioners agree that luxury market growth will resume gradually by 2022-2023.

The luxury market consists of the sum of niches belonging to different industries of origin. It includes companies specializing in personal goods, such as leather goods and watches or shoes and jewelry goods, cars, hospitality, wines and spirits, gourmet food, fine art, furniture, jet, yachts and cruise. However, when studying the luxury market, we don't focus on each specific industry that belongs to it. On the contrary, we can consider the high symbolic good market as a global market. This fact depends on the particular trait of luxury consumers for which they are transversely uniform in their preferences and buying behaviour regardless of their provenience or area of interest. To simplify this idea, we could assume that Paris' luxury consumers are much more similar to luxury consumers in New York than other French consumers' segments. The existence of a transnational group of consumers who share similar behaviors and are influenced by the same factors implies that luxury companies' marketing strategies can be analyzed without focusing on specific type of good. This fact has facilitated the development of an international presence of luxury brand companies.

More specifically, luxury brand companies have approached both mature and emerging regions where customers with high disposable income are devoted to luxury consumption. If in the beginning, the primary geographic areas in the market for high-symbolic-value goods were Europe, Japan, and North America, then luxury brand companies have extended their area of interest in emerging markets. South-East Asia, South America, Eastern Europe, and Africa have become profitable markets for luxury brand players.

Within this context, luxury firms have adopted strategies aimed at supporting their global presence. These firms have primarily developed hybrid distribution systems, both direct and indirect, but with increasing weight attributed to direct distribution. This growth pertains to the major global players in the luxury market and medium-sized companies that can establish themselves in international markets. These companies increase their attention to using the digital channel to market their products and integrate digital and physical distribution channels; this is a strategy that focuses on acquiring new consumers through social media.

The digital channel has enabled firms to extend their market to new consumers who have different sociodemographic characteristics and are located in emerging countries. In the past decades, high-symbolic-value goods were considered incompatible with the digital channel; even today, some companies that

Preface

maintain extreme brand positioning believe it inappropriate to develop communication or distribution activities. Today, most luxury players have developed a direct presence in the digital space; this strategic distribution option has largely been successful. The digital channel is increasingly integrated with the activities of physical distribution, and this amalgamation makes it possible to enhance the consumer's buying experience, while also maintaining long-term relationships.

Channel integration in luxury goods markets lies, in practice, in the introduction of innovative technologies to points of sale, in the integration between two-way communication activities in social networks, and in the physical channel of distribution. With regard to the first path of integration, the use of technology in luxury-brand stores clearly helps intensify consumers' feelings and stimulates their senses. New technologies make it possible to entertain customers, while enhancing the communication process.

In this market, entry barriers are created with brands and their intangible value. Indeed, it is to underline that to replicate a serially produced high-end good is not difficult nowadays and the quality craftsmanship of the early phases of a firm's development soon gives way to high industrial quality, which is more easily imitated by competitors. Nevertheless, in luxury markets, companies can base their competitive advantage on brand image, which is, in the end, the only real barrier. For companies that want to hold a significant market position, solidifying a brand's image involves developing a global presence and establishing a recognized and distinctive high-value brand.

THE CHALLENGES

In recent years, the advent of new technologies, the concerns about sustainability and the fresh tastes of the youngest generations of luxury consumers have affected the traditional dynamics of the luxury goods markets.

These emerging issues have caused significant changes that request an in-depth exploration by the luxury literature.

According to both scholars and practitioners, digitalisation is a crucial factor that affects luxury companies' business models and strategies. After overcoming the initial scepticism, the digitalisation has become a leitmotiv for all luxury brand companies leading to the integration of digital tools into the distribution and communication strategies. The consequences are the spreading of e-commerce and social media platforms, among most of the luxury brands.

However, in recent time the digitalisation process becomes more complex, requesting more than selling online or communicating online using social media.

It means to rethink the traditional business model to integrate digital processes along the entire shopping journey to meet the new expectations of luxury consumers. Big data, blockchain, omnichannel strategies, and digital customer experience management represent the main digital challenges that luxury brand companies deal with nowadays.

Sustainability is another relevant issue that is reshaping the business model of luxury companies. Sustainable development is not a new practice in the luxury market since governments have been striving for imposing sustainability standards for years. However, luxury companies' real challenge is to overcome the residual CSR perspective to embrace a total integration of environmental, ethical, and social concerns into the corporate strategy. Integrated output and sustainable processes, the introduction of non-financial reporting as operational practice, and a new orientation to circular economy practices are emerging issues that still today request a more in-depth exploration of academic and managerial perspectives.

xvii

Preface

Finally, luxury companies' current challenge is understanding the best way to approach each generation of consumers. The new generations of consumers categorized in Millennials and Z Generations are becoming the leading target group for luxury brand companies. They are different from traditional consumers and ask luxury companies to innovate their offerings, communication and distribution strategies. Moreover, Millennials and Z Generation's concern about sustainability and social issues pushes luxury brands to rethink the end-to-end product life cycle, supply chain management, and unsold stock disposal to become more sustainable.

Despite the relevance of Millennials and Z Generation, luxury companies must consider the elderly consumer. They are still the high spending luxury target group and for this reason, requests particular attention from luxury brand managers.

This book aims to upgrade the most relevant theoretical frameworks and empirical research about luxury goods' marketing, considering the trends above mentioned. For this reason, in this manuscript, we collect contributions focused on contemporary issues affecting luxury industries such as digital transformation of luxury brand companies, sustainable development, changes in luxury consumers' behaviour, integration between physical and online channels, and social media development marketing strategies. The book has adopted a multidisciplinary approach to select contributions from marketing, management, buyer behaviour, and international business. The involvement of contributors affiliated with universities in Europe, the US, and the Far East guarantees to transcend national boundaries.

With regard to the target audience, this manuscript addresses to scholars who need an overview of the emerging issues affecting the luxury market, particularly related to sustainability and digital transformation in the luxury industry. Besides, the book can be a tool for practitioners who manage luxury brands to upgrade their knowledge about sustainability and digital practices. Finally, the book can also be a valuable reference point for local government agencies and public bodies responsible for managing and planning policies for providing incentives in sustainable and digital development.

ORGANIZATION OF THE BOOK

The manuscript is organised into 15 chapters divided into three main sections that follow the new trends impacting the luxury market: digitalisation, sustainability and the new luxury consumers categorised in Millenials and Z Generation.

The first section is about digitalisation and considers this current phenomenon affecting the luxury market paying attention to three main aspects:

- **Digitalisation as omnichannel strategies**. The chapters analyse how luxury companies integrate physical and digital channels to manage cross-channel experiences across all customer journey touchpoints seamlessly.
- **Digitalisation as social media communication.** The chapters deal with how communication strategies include new digital tools such as social media.
- **Digitalisation as innovative digital tools.** The chapters explore the new tools used to monitor consumer behaviour and improve their experiences with the brand.

Preface

In this section, we also propose a chapter about luxury brands and strategic management accounting that provides luxury business managers with Managerial Accounting techniques to assist their decision making in this global and challenger context.

The second section deals with sustainability and includes two chapters that analyse the topic, proposing sustainable marketing strategies and contributing to sustainable consumption research.

The third section concerns the current challenges of luxury brand companies to approach luxury brand consumers, emerging and consolidated market segments. This section encompasses three chapters about Millennials and Z Generation's behaviour and their attitude towards luxury and one chapter that explores the Mature Female Luxury target.

A brief description of each chapter follows.

Chapter 1 aims to highlight how the digital channel has become a relevant distribution channel for high symbolic value goods over the years and describes the integration between digital and physical channel. During the digital channel growth, many innovative digital formats were created: online DOS, digital discounts formats, social commerce activities, multiband indirect digital platforms. The so called "not affordable" luxury goods tend to make use of the digital channel more to strengthen its heritage and elite characteristics. On the other hand, the "affordable" luxury goods brands approach the digital channel with a more profit return-oriented perspective, using intermediaries that allow a higher percentage of market coverage.

Chapter 2 explores how luxury and fast fashion brands have been affected by omnichannel strategies, which refer to the opportunity to integrate online and offline channels to create a seamless shopping experience to engage customers. Through a quali-quantitative research approach, the study examines the potential effects of the implementation of omnichannel activities on the perception of luxury and fast fashion brands. Interestingly, consumers perceive omnichannel strategies as something projected for luxury brands, thus as a way for them to improve the luxury shopping experience. Consequently, when applied to fast fashion brands, omnichannel strategies may lead consumers to perceive such brand as more prestigious, activating a sort of "luxurization". For a luxury company, the omnichannel strategy may represent an opportunity. After all, they can increase the brand's perceived luxuriousness and a threat because they may help fast fashion brands be perceived as luxurious, thus "imitating" luxury companies.

Chapter 3 examines the integration of virtual and physical platforms from luxury brand managers' perspectives. "The Internet Dilemma" was the concept used to describe luxury brand companies' initial reluctance to integrate online technologies into their business model. However, over time, luxury brand companies have understood that moving towards digital transformation is the only way to survive on the market and appeal to the new luxury brand consumers. In a few years, digitalisation has become a priority for all luxury brand companies that started to integrate digital and physical platforms to engage consumers through all touchpoints of their shopping journey. In light of the topic's relevance and considering the primary focus of research on consumers, this chapter aims to deepen the digitalisation phenomenon in the luxury market involving the little-explored luxury brand managers' perspective. We conducted a longitudinal study to compare the main changes in integrating digital and physical platforms from the managers' perspective between 2014 and 2020. In this endeavour, we also considered how the Covid-19 pandemic had affected luxury brand companies' digitalisation.

Chapter 4 analyses how luxury brand companies manage integrated brand communication strategies in the online Era. After the digitalization, both scholars and practitioners found that luxury companies

xix

that have invested in this transformation have increased their revenues and improved customer satisfaction. Luxury companies have reached a more significant number of consumers worldwide, but the communication pillars have been preserved. Shortly, luxury companies will have to deal with the effects of COVID-19. Most likely, some of these changes will be: a boost of the online shopping; a return to fewer purchases, of valuable and items; and the need for an integrated shopping experience. The present chapter aims to show how luxury brands have embraced digital channels without losing their pillars. This chapter also aims to show that luxury companies have successfully invested in customers education and that consumers have adapted their behaviour to new touchpoints with the brand. Finally, this chapter aims to investigate new approaches to integrating the physical and the digital channels and the implications of Covid-19 on luxury firms' communication strategy.

Chapter 5 investigates the impact of luxury brands' traditional and digital contents on customer-based brand equity. After a period of initial scepticism, luxury branded companies now understand the necessity of integrating digital technologies into their marketing actions. Therefore, most luxury companies approach emerging digital tools commencing from communication strategies. The direct consequence is the adoption of social media such as blogs, applications (apps) and social networking as new communication tools alongside and in conjunction with traditional media. The purpose of this paper/chapter lies in seeking to understand the extent to which luxury brand consumers appreciate the contents of luxury brand communications and in comparing digital and traditional ranges. In addition, the paper investigates the existence of a correlation between the level of satisfaction perceived by luxury consumers and the dimension of customer brand equity according to the Aaker model. In this endeavour, this study is an attempt to provide academics and practitioners with insight about the expectation of luxury brand consumers from contents delivered, comparing digital and traditional platforms.

Chapter 6 looks at the changing approach to social media in the global luxury market. COVID-19 lockdowns led to a new approach to social media communication by luxury fashion brands. This chapter offers a more in-dept exploration of recent pandemic-related changes in the social context and the need for brands to rethink their narrative to engage consumers and influence purchase decisions. The authors selected a panel of 28 fashion luxury brands, both independent and conglomerate-owned, to analyze the paradigm shift in social media communication and content creation. Their findings show that with social media acting as the primary touchpoint, luxury fashion brands have effectively produced new communication archetypes, revealing digital platforms' latent potential as strategic tools.

Chapter 7 is focused on innovating luxury service experiences through e-servicescapes. The digital customer experience is a top priority and significant challenge for luxury service companies, who have to connect with their target customers, yet striving to remain exclusive, and to innovate their core offers, yet preserving their heritage. After a brief review of the literature on customer experience and virtual environments in luxury service contexts, this chapter focuses on e-servicescapes as a means for innovation and improvement in delivering omnichannel experiences for luxury customers. Adopting Bitner's typology of servicescapes (1992), this chapter is based on a three case vignettes analysis, that highlights how luxury service providers can use e-servicescapes to enrich their physical service experiences. Three e-servicescape strategies are identified – integration, amplification, and substitution – that ultimately support companies in renewing and improving their overall luxury propositions.

Chapter 8 explores how social data allows luxury companies to discover the evolving luxury consumers. Today the luxury consumer is evolving with new interests, attitudes, and a shift in the way they view the world of luxury. Besides other societal and economic changes, social networks have changed how consumers connect with brands. As an increasing number of consumers use social networks to

Preface

interact with the brand(s), there is an abundance of social data analyzed to detect shifts in perceptions, preferences, and behaviours. At present, there are no satisfying theoretical conceptualizations. A strategy framework is needed to help companies identify relevant social data sources and derive actionable insights for social media intelligence in a strategic, structured, and impact-oriented manner. The authors aim at closing this gap in marketing management literature by proposing a conceptual framework on social listening. A managerial contribution is made by showing the marketing opportunities in using social data and explaining the necessary steps of turning data into insights and data-driven managerial actions based on relevant theory and knowledge about state-of-the-art technology.

Chapter 9 deals with luxury brands and strategic management accounting. It is generally accepted that the primary objective of the discipline of management accounting is to provide relevant information, financial and non-financial, to business managers in order to assist in their decision making. This discipline evolved during the Industrial Revolution and it was, initially, referred to as Cost Accounting due to its emphasis on reporting internally – orientated cost information. The purpose of this chapter is to highlight the current techniques of Managerial Accounting widely used by business organizations all over the world and to describe the managerial implications of said methods when they are utilized by players operating in the Luxury sector.

Chapter 10 proposes models for sustainable marketing strategies. Luxury has attracted many scholars as a field of research examined the potential connections and (in)compatibilities between luxury and corporate social responsibility (CSR). While some studies emphasize the incompatibility between luxury and sustainability, others highlight luxury brands' essential efforts in luxury offerings and sustainable marketing strategies to fit eco-friendly consumers. To foster this research stream, this chapter develops a deeper understanding of CSR's rise and evolution in the luxury sector and the major marketing strategies implemented by luxury brands to fit with the needs of today's responsible consumers. The authors will first present a chronological literature review through three critical periods, including the underground and advancement stages to the consolidation of sustainable luxury marketing as an established research stream. Then, a framework identifying different luxury CSR strategies will be proposed. Finally, opportunities and futures challenges will be discussed at the end of this chapter.

Chapter 11 aims to cover a significant gap, contributing to research in the luxury market and sustainable consumption and focuses on new sustainable products by luxury brands. Through an experimental study 3x1 between-subject design in which the product material (upcycled vs. recycled vs. virgin) of a fictitious luxury product was manipulated, the authors investigated which consumers prefer luxury product (upcycled vs recycled vs not sustainable) in terms of attitude and purchase intentions. This experimental design can help luxury product managers and designers about whether consumers react more positively towards upcycle versus recycling products when consumers' status motives and environmental consciousness increase. Besides, they can understand the reasons and emphasize those in their marketing communications to increase the demand for those products with this study.

Chapter 12 analyses the generations' attitude and behaviours in the luxury sector. The luxury sector needs to adapt its strategies to the digital advent, online purchasing, and new young customers with different behaviours and attitudes regarding older generations. Young generations (Millennials and Gen Z) signed an excellent chance for companies and influenced doing business. They tend to gather information online, share their opinions, and pay attention to how companies behave. Since they represent a big part of the market, it is fundamental to understand if the luxury sector is relevant for them and how they consider luxury brands, such as Moncler. Through an online questionnaire, a comparison between young and old generations has been realized.

xxi

Chapter 13 presents a comparative cultural study of how millennials in Switzerland and South Korea define and perceive luxury and prestige and how this might influence their luxury consumer behaviour. Labels, such as Gen X, millennials, Gen Y, or Gen Z, are often used to distinguish individuals' cohorts based on their shared generational experiences and characteristics. However, as previous research shows, mere membership in a generational cohort is insufficient to explain consumption patterns across geographies and cultures. Given the size and importance of the global luxury market and the degree of internationalization of luxury companies, a better understanding of the luxury consumer and their macro-context impact is vital. The present study results indicate that economic and cultural factors impact the definition and perception of luxury among millennials and might also explain consumer behaviour differences.

Chapter 14 investigates the relationship between young generations (Millennials and Gen Z), luxury, and food. Millennials and Gen Z are the first digital native generations to be very comfortable with technology devices and interested at an early stage in luxury food experiences. By exploring youth food culture and everyday luxury food experiences and practices, the authors identify three trends (digitalization, extended realities, and cause-related marketing) as critical areas food brands and food actors (e.g. restaurants) should capitalize on to educate, facilitate, and promote the adoption of pleasurable, healthy, and sustainable food consumptions. The authors provide an overview of these three new key trends, together with a focus on Millennials and Gen Z. This chapter contributes to the need to look at contexts of application (food) where sustainability and the digital transformation highlight the present and future for promoting luxury goods and experiences.

Chapter 15 examines the influence of celebrity endorsement on mature female luxury cosmetic consumers. A 'celebrity endorser' is any individual easily recognizable by the general public and leverages this visibility and goodwill to either appear alongside the product in an ad or furthermore endorse the product. This fact helps cosmetics brands architect a strong brand image in the eyes of end-users, mainly due to the transference of the endorser's trustworthiness to the brand she/he backs. The study revealed that mature female consumers were more likely to relate to an ad featuring celebrities of similar age as themselves and actual users of the product rather than armchair or hands-off endorsers.

Fabrizio Mosca
University of Turin, Italy

Cecilia Casalegno
University of Turin, Italy

Rosalia Gallo
Universitat Autònoma de Barcelona, Spain

Acknowledgment

The editors would like to the help of all the people involved in this project and, more specifically, to the authors and reviewers that took part in the review process. Without their support, this book would not have become a reality.

First, the editors would like to thank each one of the authors for their contributions. Our sincere gratitude goes to the chapter's authors, who contributed their time and expertise to this book.

Second, the editors wish to acknowledge the reviewers' valuable contributions regarding the improvement of quality, coherence, and content presentation of chapters. Most of the authors also served as referees; we highly appreciate their double task.

Fabrizio Mosca
University of Turin, Italy

Cecilia Casalegno
University of Turin, Italy

Rosalia Gallo
Universitat Autònoma de Barcelona, Spain

Section 1
Managing Global Luxury Brands in the Era of Digitalisation

Chapter 1
The Evolution of Distribution in the Luxury Sector:
From Single to Omni–Channel

Fabrizio Mosca
University of Turin, Italy

Elisa Giacosa
University of Turin, Italy

Luca Matteo Zagni
University of Turin, Italy

ABSTRACT

In today's competitive environment, it is highlighted how the digital channel has over the years become an important distribution channel for goods with a high symbolic value. During its development, it has taken on characteristics very similar to the physical channel with direct distribution models, created through active management of e-commerce sites by luxury brands, and indirectly with the presence of specialized intermediaries by product or multi-brand, often very innovative. Goods that belong to a segment of the luxury market defined as "not affordable" tend to make use of the digital channel more aimed at strengthening the heritage and elite characteristics of the brand. On the other hand, the brands of the "affordable" luxury goods approach the digital channel with a more economically return-oriented perspective, also using intermediaries that allow a higher percentage of market coverage.

INTRODUCTION

Over the years, some countries have developed particular expertise in the luxury sector. Italy and France are examples of places where the luxury goods industry represents a significant share of their GDP, thanks to a strong tradition in the luxury field and high efforts into innovation policy. The luxury market seems to be particularly sensitive to external forces such as socio-demographic, cultural, political, eco-

DOI: 10.4018/978-1-7998-5882-9.ch001

nomic and technological variables. This fact explains why, after the advent of the digital economy luxury companies started to face new challenges and seize new opportunities to maintain their leading role in the national economy. In a globalized digital market, the luxury brand companies must understand how to reshape the traditional marketing mix to better respond to luxury brand consumers' new needs and tastes. Some winning companies permit us to identify successful business models in managing luxury brand companies in the new digitalization era. These companies belong to different luxury sectors, both traditional (fashion, hard luxury, jewellery, perfumes, cosmetics, and cars) and the emerging ones (wines, spirits, gourmet food, furniture, fine art and tourism).

In light of the relevance of the distribution variable in the luxury market, this chapter aims to analyze the evolution of luxury brand companies' distribution strategies in the digitalization era. In this endeavour, the authors highlight trends and strategies concerning the distribution variable, attempting to explain the extent to which luxury brand companies have integrated physical channels with the digital one, moving from a single-channel approach to an omnichannel one. The multi-case studies approach is the methodology used to point out the main strategic differences concerning the luxury market's distribution strategies, considering the difference between "non-affordable", i.e., belonging to exclusive luxury, and "affordable" goods.

The chapter is structured as follows. While the first section offers a theoretical background, the second one outlines the chapter's primary focus discussing distribution strategies in the luxury market. The third section presents future research directions for this topic. Finally, the last one points out the conclusion, implications, and limitations of the study.

BACKGROUND

Over the years, the interest in the luxury goods sector has grown becoming a topic many researchers focus on. An elitist connotation and specific behaviours characterize luxury brand consumers that buy luxury products driven by the primary characteristic of luxury goods: high quality, price, rarity, and creative content (Kim & Ko, 2012; Seo, Buchanan-Oliver, & Cruz, 2015; Kim, Lloyd, & Cervellon, 2016; Seo & Buchanan-Oliver, 2019).

At the beginning of the new Millennium, digital technologies have taken over, bringing new challenges and opportunities for companies in the mass-market and luxury sectors. All companies had to learn to exploit the potential of Web 2.0 to react more effectively to new consumer needs in terms of communication, interactions, and services. The advent of the digital system, which includes distribution, digital communication channels, and User Generated Content has led companies to adopt strategic processes to acquire skills and tools to approach this new digital environment. It is essential to understand that digital innovation does not intend to overcome traditional marketing and its relative strategies but looks to integrate both to evolve the old solution and offer a new and broader approach to the consumer. If a luxury brand would have success in the digital channel, need to give a multisensory experience and a correct and personalized identification (Kapferer and Bastien, 2012).

A significant research area is focused on distribution since it is considered one of the strategic variables in managing the marketing mix for high-symbolic-value goods. The distribution channel is the combination of organizations through which the product moves to the user or end consumer. It plays a key role because it gives consumers access to products and services, putting them in a position to purchase. The goal of a distribution system is to realize the contact between consumers and products

The Evolution of Distribution in the Luxury Sector

effectively. In this sense, as a result of digitization, an evolution that concerns companies' distribution channels has accelerated. This because of two factors: technological development and the contextual growth in consumer behaviour (Grewal et al., 2017). In today's context, integration between the physical and digital channels remains an essential requirement for maintaining competitiveness (Kim & Ko, 2010). The importance of digitization in the distribution channels and their integration with the physical channel consist of companies' ability to collect big data from their consumers. This leads to creating new customer targets, offering customized purchasing solutions, simplifying the purchasing process, and increasing profitability (Grewal et al., 2017). However, the luxury goods sector is characterized by two fundamental elements that distinguish it from the others: exclusivity and rarity. These two aspects go against the digital era trend, allowing consumers to access goods and services more efficiently and at different price ranges. This has resulted in greater caution on luxury brands in implementing digital strategies in distribution, representing one of the most critical variables in the luxury goods marketing mix (Mosca,2016).

In the last decade, the "more traditional" brands belonging to the luxury sector have shown themselves to be afraid of integrating digital channels into their distribution strategies, even though these last ones have increasingly entered into the other business realities. In particular, the Maisons have not immediately ridden the wave of E-commerce. According to previous studies, at the beginning luxury brands used digital channels as a communication tool (Hennigs et al., 2012; Kapferer & Bastien, 2012; Okonkwo, 2009). The motivation is enclosed because distribution strategies strongly influence the perception of the high-end goods' exclusivity and uniqueness: a digital purchasing platform would have led to a lower perception of these two elements by consumers. In contrast, through the physical store, i.e., the boutique, they could perceive them until that moment (Chandon et al., 2016).

Through physical distribution, the brand can recreate a unique shopping experience that brings all the elements of heritage, combined with the sense of exclusivity and rarity also given by the "visual evidence" of the store and its location. However, the technological progress that has led to an increase in the diffusion of various devices, combined with consumers' evolution, has convinced luxury brand companies to integrate digital channels in their distribution strategies to maintain their competitiveness (Corbellini & Saviolo, 2015). Besides, consumers have gradually changed their attitude toward buying luxury goods through the digital channel (Bijmolt, Leeflang, Block, Eisenbeiss, Hardie, Lemmens, and Saffert, 2010). In particular, consumers increasingly use digital channels to interact and purchase through digital channels. In 2018 almost half of the world's luxury consumers belonged to the Millennials generation (1981-1994) and Generation Z (1995-2010). They represent an expenditure that accounted for 35% of the total in 2019 and by 2025 could make up 45% of the market. Between these two generations of consumers, almost half of their purchases are made through digital channels. At the same time, around 75% of the luxury consumers use the digital channel to communicate and purchase (Godey et al., 2016; Kim & Ko, 2012). For these reasons, it is vital for companies to combine these two channels, physical and digital, to approach them through an omnichannel. In today's context, the word "digitalization" does not refer exclusively to e-commerce platforms or communication through social media, but rather to a new approach towards the sector and consumers (Loonam et al.; 2017) luxury firms. This implies an evolution of its business model, which will have to pursue a single channel composed of physical and digital components.

DISTRIBUTION CHANNELS

Distribution is one of the most strategic variables concerning the marketing mix for luxury goods (Borden, 1964; Bruner, 1988; Constantinides, 2006; Dixon & Blois, 1973; McCharty, 1964). The distribution channel is a combination of people and organizations whose aims is transferring products and services from the company to the end-user. Consequently, this channel plays a role of primary importance as it allows the client to access products and services, making their purchase available. The distribution channel's main objective is to make contact between the company and the client as effectively as possible (Winter, Dahar, and Mosca, 2011). It has to represent the luxury brand, as boutiques interpret the brand's concept: consequently, the place of sale is the network between the customers and the luxury universe. The distribution permits to construct of the brand identity since sales bolster or undermine the consumer's dream.

Distribution innovation concerns the types, characteristics, and locations of the sales point and the other distribution channels. The use of multi-sensorial instruments to attract the consumers permits to attract new consumers and strengthen the retention of old consumers and perfect management of the customer relationship (Binz, Hair, Pieper & Baldauf, 2013; Miller & Le Breton-Miller, 2005; Kapferer, 2002; Poza; Ward, 1997). As mentioned above, uniqueness and rarity are the two main elements that characterize the high symbolic value goods sector. These two elements need to be managed according to marketing and brand development goals. On the one hand, the company must preserve and strengthen its brand image and emphasize its rarity and exclusivity characteristics.

On the other hand, the goods must be made available efficiently and effectively in the correct reference place. For these reasons, it is fundamental to select the channel that fits better with the brand's value, in terms of exclusivity and rarity. This was one of the main issues that luxury brands had to face when digital channels were introduced. Since their introduction, the perplexity that brands had regarding undermining the brand image and its main features, has been turned into a digital channel's first approach only as a communication tool (Hennigs et al., 2012; Kapferer & Bastien, 2012; Okonkwo, 2009).

As concerns, luxury goods companies were reluctant to use digital as a distribution channel. They were initially unable to provide consumers with the same shopping experience as in physical shops. This growing importance has led companies to associate the digital channel with the physical channel. To be successful in the digital, globalized market, luxury goods had to be satisfied with the following condition concerns correct and personalized identification and a multisensory experience (Kapferer & Bastien, 2009). After firsts negative impressions, luxury players have increased their presence across a plurality of channels. Companies understood the need to increase the digital channel to satisfy consumers who showed a growing interest in the possibilities for browsing and buying online (Geerts, 2013). In this sense, the digital channel became a hybrid tool of interaction with demand. Through physical or virtual procedures, they play an informative, transactional, and relational role, in an alternatively or simultaneously way.

In a subsequent phase, technology development has made it always more comfortable to ride this digital wave in terms of device and connection. Brands could recreate the atmosphere online, both on the website and social media (Kim et al. 2015). A website is a communication tool, where companies can communicate their heritage, events and present new collection but a virtual shopping place. Some brands have started to introduce e-commerce platforms on their website. From this moment, the digital channel is no longer considered as an additional tool to the physical channel. Instead, it is integrated, giving rise to a single-channel composed of both the physical store and the digital store.

The Evolution of Distribution in the Luxury Sector

Thus, consumers of luxury brands have the opportunity to have a real 360-degree experience called "customer journey". This term refers to a new type of shopping experience, which unlike before is no longer the linear sum of several phases, but a process that involves several points of contact that include both digital and traditional environments (Lemon & Verhoef, 2016). Although the physical retail store still represents a virtual channel in the purchase phase, it is fundamental for luxury brands to have a digital approach to their marketing strategies.

However, in this digital context, the brand's main characteristics and values are communicated through entertainment on the web site and social media. Therefore, it is essential to increase consumers' engagement, which plays an increasingly central role.

Table 1. Distribution strategies in the luxury market

DISTRIBUTION COVERAGE		DIRECT	INDIRECT SHORT	LONG INDIRECT
	EXCLUSIVE	NON AFFORDABLE LUXURY GOODS	NON AFFORDABLE LUXURY GOODS	NOT ADOPTED
	SELECTIVE	NON AFFORDABLE LUXURY GOODS	AFFORDABLE LUXURY GOODS	AFFORDABLE LUXURY GOODS
	INTENSIVE	NOT ADOPTED	NOT ADOPTED	NOT ADOPTED

VERTICAL STRUCTURE OF THE CHANNEL

Both in the physical and digital channel, distribution strategies could be resumed in two kinds: direct and indirect. Companies that pursue the direct option directly manage the distribution and communication channels. On the other hand, the indirect channel requires an intermediary, which can be both physical and digital. Direct distribution in the luxury sector offers several advantages: supporting its own brand identity, deciding on the selling price and the assortment of goods at the point of sale, differentiating the offer from the competition, customizing the relationship with the customer; obtaining greater control and availability of customer information and monitoring the consumer's decision-making process during purchase. The strategic option of indirect, selective, or exclusive distribution is adopted when the company chooses to make its products available to final consumers through intermediaries in the distribution channel. The channel is defined as "long" when there are many intermediaries and "short" in the opposite case. The choice to adopt this distribution channel aims to improve distribution coverage and avoid the risk of an inadequate presence in the market.

THE CHANNEL INTEGRATION IN LUXURY

This chapter's primary focus is to provide evidence of how luxury brands have integrated the physical channels with digital in terms of distribution, thus moving from a single-channel strategy to an omnichannel one. To support our thesis, the authors will complement the theory with business cases, to highlight the main strategic differences in the distribution of luxury goods. In this sense, it is essential to explain two typologies of luxury goods for which different strategies are being implemented in terms of distribution (Chevalier & Mazzalovo, 2008; Giacosa, 2011; Okonkwo, 2007).

Non-Affordable Luxury: t represents highly exclusive luxury products, whose price is very high and affordable only for HNWIs (high net worth individuals). It means that democratization is not for non-affordable luxury. Indeed, the high quality, exclusive distribution, and scarce availability justify the high price; limited editions or, sometimes, single pieces are strongly customized and are linked to the company heritage. Louis Vuitton, Chanel and Hermès for fashion luxury, Ferrari and Rolls Royce for the car sector, Armand de Brignac and Dom Pérignon for wines and spirits, Armani Hotel for travels and holidays, are great examples.

Affordable Luxury: It represents the democratization of luxury. A wider range of product categories, such as accessories, glasses, perfumes, and cosmetics, are inspired by non-affordable luxury, and customers could dream of being part of the luxury universe (Corbellini & Saviolo, 2009). A sort of "trading up" phenomenon happens, for which the customer makes a sort of connection between luxury products and more traditional ones. Generally, companies of non-affordable luxury are not involved in the phenomenon. Tod's, Gucci, Prada, Mercedes, Audi, are examples of affordable luxury. Depending on the type of goods mentioned above, luxury brands can adopt different strategies in terms of distribution channels. They could choose to adopt a direct distribution strategy, an indirect approach, or a combination of both.

HP: The strategies implemented in offline distribution channels for both affordable and non-affordable goods, respectively, have been replicated in digital channels.

The research has been carried out in the following phases to explore the hypotheses:

First Phase: The hypotheses were analyzed by examining the existing literature about the luxury sector and the drivers in the consumption trend, this highlighted a series of variables that impact luxury consumption.

Second Phase: We made a qualitative analysis. In particular, we analyzed the literature on the topic. Also, we analyzed companies' information of 10 non-affordable companies and ten (10) affordable companies by using their websites, journals, and newspaper on them. The purpose is to identify the key drivers within the luxury companies and different considerations in terms of distribution strategy.

In the next chapter, we intend to solve the problem of understanding and identifying successful distribution strategy characteristics for luxury products, both in the digital and physical channels, distinguishing between non-affordable or affordable luxury. To be more exhaustive, we made a comparison between non-affordable and affordable goods.

THE FINDINGS

Non – Affordable Luxury

Concern about non-affordable luxury, distribution has to be distinguished in physical or digital ways to understand the relative strategies. Referred to the physical channel, brands of non-affordable goods have innovated their typology of distribution channels to make it possible to valorize the traditional elements that distinguish the brand, the so-called heritage, and create unique shopping experiences (Mosca, Giacosa, 2016). The direct distribution channel involves contact between manufacturer and consumer that is not mediated by other entities. Direct government of distribution activities favours businesses that sell prestige goods in the achievement of certain benefits. This distribution option for high-symbolic-value goods consists of the direct management of the channel by the manufacturer, without intermediaries, and in the choice of distribution coverage with a limited number of points of sale. First, the quick, direct flow of information from the market to the firm delivers more excellent knowledge of consumer needs and a better ability to grasp new consumption trends even when the signals are still weak and uncertain.

The second advantage for firms that adopt direct distribution is maintaining a strong consistency between the brand image and the style of the point of sale. The brand's attributes and values are represented uniformly in all direct distribution places to maximize their effectiveness in the firm's supply system's communication process. Other advantages of direct distribution in the high-symbolic-value goods market are the uniform level of customer service in all points of sale, training of specialists in the sale of prestige goods, coordinated management of logistics through a centralized warehouse system for each market with real-time supply, higher profit margins for the manufacturer, control of the disposal unsold products, and integration of the sales system in the firm's information system through the computerized management of the order sale-reorder flow. An exclusive direct distribution system is the most extreme form of selective distribution. It favours firms that wish to differentiate their products with a policy of quality and prestige, improving their relationships with customers. The advantages of direct distribution in terms of superior knowledge of the customer, the availability of the best and most reliable information from the market, price control, reduction of intermediation and management margins, brand image consistent with the values offered to the consumer, and control of unsold inventory have facilitated the movement of the strategies of the firms under consideration toward this option. An analysis of a sample of firms' distribution strategies clearly shows a marked acceleration in exclusive direct distribution, particularly for high-end products. The number of sales points owned by firms and the turnover resulting from them increases as a percentage of sales volumes through independent intermediaries. They aimed to stimulate new desires through exclusive and selective direct distribution strategies and attract new young consumers. In this sense, over the years they implemented:

Flagship stores represent single-brand self-owned sale boutique set in famous locations in the most prestigious cities (in terms of tourism, trade, or business) which strengthen the prestige of the brand identity (De Chernatony, 2001; Fabris & Minestroni, 2004; Kapferer & Bastien, 2009; Okonkwo, 2007; Ross & Harradine, 2011). Their dimension is variable: they could have a limited size and commercial offer, but permitting to increase the brand's visibility. Besides, limited series of exclusive customized products are created exclusively for the flagship stores, or the products are only displayed and not offered for sale, almost like a museum (Bruce & Hines, 2007; Fernie, Moore & Lawrie, 1998; Kozinets, Sherry, DeBerry-Spence, Duhacheck, Nuttavuthisi & Storm, 2002; Moore, Doherty & Doyle, 2010). Alternately, they are huge, organized on several floors (Kent, 2007). An example could be given by

Renzo Piano, who projected the Hermès flagship store in Tokyo in the Ginza district, where he created a particular real monument for the brand.

DOS: The DOS format refers to a directly operated single-brand shop which, like the flagship stores, is located in the main cities, but has a smaller sales area. This direct distribution format has a more economic objective compared to the previous form. It guarantees an adequate return on turnover and finds as much information as possible from the reference market. For this reason, it represents a privileged point of contact that allows luxury companies to establish stable and lasting relationships with their customers.

Temporary Stores: They appear suddenly and then close a few months later: they have to test the customers' attraction about a new product idea, a new city or an area of the town probably considered attractive (Giacosa, 2012). The boutique's informal style and a selection of the products (sometimes created for the pop-up stores) vary according to the customers' characteristics and the city where the shop is based (de Lassus & Anido Freire, 2014). When the opening of a pop-up store is an event for the town, it means that the brand has a great attraction. We could remember Hermès pop-up stores in Time Warner Center at Columbus Circle across from Central Park in New York, Louis Vuitton in the Dover Street Market in London, and Marc Jacobs in New York. The benefits of temporary stores are manifold. First, they allow the brand to reinforce the perception of scarcity of the luxury product, by limiting consumers' exposure to it in time and creating a unique and unrepeatable event. The event itself facilitates the customization of the product and the strengthening of the brand image. Temporary stores are also useful distribution formats for gathering information and increasing media visibility. If a brand needs to renovate a store, a temporary store is a solution that allows the companies to boost sales and create movement because of the subsequent re-opening of the flagship store. The advantages of the development of a system of temporary stores are numerous. First, the firm reinforces the brand image, promoting consumers' interaction with the brand in a less formal context.

Besides, temporary stores allow reinforcement of some luxury brands attributes such as scarcity, rarity and uniqueness.

The opening of a temporary store is an event that is important for corporate communication more than distribution, as the media tend to highlight particular circumstances created by a brand. It is also essential to remember that temporary stores allow management to get in touch with those consumers who follow the brand more closely and collect strategic information on new trends in less formal contexts. Finally, a temporary store can also create unique and unrepeatable events, linked to phenomena that combine fashion, culture, and entertainment and support the launch of new products.

As mentioned above, the main issue that luxury players had to consider during the digitalization process, concerned maintaining the characteristics of rarity and exclusivity which have always distinguished the goods belonging to this sector. From this point of view, since the distribution variable is a highly strategic aspect, luxury brands have replicated their distribution method to the digital channel. Therefore, based on the objective that the company intends to pursue, the relative approach is carried out. Each one of them presents a different way of exploiting digital by players.

Direct management digital channel with a communication function: As well as in the physical channel, the flagship store has a purely communicative role, the digital channel can play the same. This channel allows consumers to have a virtual showcase, through which they can learn about the company's mission, activities, brand values, heritage, products (Seringhaus, 2005).

LVMH. The French luxury brand has a showcase site that presents only the information of the Group, the heritage, the various brands, and the relative goods. The website has no option to purchase these goods. Instead, on the website of Louis Vuitton is possible to buy the goods.

The Evolution of Distribution in the Luxury Sector

Table 2. Distribution strategies in the digital direct channel

DISTRIBUTION VIA DIRECT DIGITAL CHANNEL

Direct management digital channel with a communication function

Direct management digital channels integrated with direct physical channels

Directly management digital channel for a full-price luxury brand

Direct management digital channels for marketing products coming to the end of their life cycle

Direct management digital channel aimed exclusively at the intermediary market (B2B)

Direct management digital channel integrated with the direct physical channel: This strategy involves the digital channel being managed directly by the luxury brand and combined with the physical channel. In this case, the consumer has the possibility, for example, to choose a product in the digital channel and to personalize it within the options offered. This strategy involves the digital channel being managed directly by the luxury brand and integrated with the physical channel. The consumer has the possibility, for example, to choose a product in the digital channel with the opportunity to personalize it by concluding the purchase inside the physical store. In this case, the customer is invited to the store to pick up the personalized product. With this strategy, there are no distribution logistics management charges connected to online shipping, and there is no risk of undermining their market share.

CHANEL. The luxury brand has integrated its digital channel with the physical one by creating a showcase section on which consumers can reach some information about goods, as bags, that can be purchased offline. Consumers can not by all collections on the website, but only some categories of products are available.

Directly managed digital channels for a full-price luxury brand: Some luxury players decided to approach the digital channel by developing an e-commerce to sell their full price products directly online. This strategy has led to creating a genuine online store that preserves the digital context's brand values to keep intact the brand's image.

CARTIER. *Cartier may give an example, who does not show their products' prices on the website, but consumers have to do the subscription and ask for information via phone to the sales manager.*

BELL & ROSS. *This is one of the precursory of digital distribution because it was one of the first brands that allowed to purchase their product online. Today all the collection is available except for the limited one.*

Direct management digital channels for making products coming to the end of their life cycle: this kind of approach implicates that the goods are no more available in the physical store or are previous seasons' items. In this case, goods are sold with a price reduction thought an e-commerce site managed by the luxury brand. This model allows to reduce the risk of the uncontrolled spread of unsold items, so this system minimizes the possibility that not authorized individuals make a lower cost purchase and subsequently resale in a physical store. Moreover, it is possible to serve different market segments because it leads to interface with another type of consumer typology that is more price-sensitive, so the elasticity ratio is higher. The emotional intensity during the purchase is lower than physical consumers. This price difference could be explained through the separation of the channel and how the products are sold.

Consumers who make a physical purchase perceive a different offer between online and offline that is not comparable, so there is no price injustice. Direct management digital channel aimed exclusively at the intermediary market: This digital channel management is oriented to wholesalers and retailers. They can place orders online to extend their assortment of brand goods. Luxury brands that control the supply of both direct sales outlets and independent outlets may use this B2B digital channel. The final consumer cannot have access to it.

Affordable Luxury

Even for affordable luxury, distribution has to be distinguished in physical or digital ways to explain the strategies. Concerning the physical channel, the following point-of-sale formats acquire particular importance in indirect distribution: single-brand boutiques, department stores, corners, duty-free shops, and franchised points of sale. The structure of this indirect channel could be defined as "long" or "short", so the complexity depends on the number of intermediaries (Kotler, 2016). The advantage of this strategic approach is that all charges relating to the costs and risks of inter-nationalization are transferred to and borne by the intermediary. The disadvantage lies in the limited control over the foreign market exercisable by the manufacturer. Competition is based on quality in terms of intrinsic characteristics and distribution, permitting the customer retention to achieve an optimal trade-off between the rarity and the volume sold (Catry, 2003; Phau & Prendergast, 2000). This luxury typology abandons exclusive rareness for selective distribution. It increases the number of boutiques and location in which a more comprehensive range of products are sold: a new target is reached through the production and distribution of different merchandise categories (especially accessories) to an affordable price, permitting customers belonging to the luxury universe. A limited number of opportunely selected mono-brand or multi-brand points of sale or specialized corners (their shops or selected boutiques) increase the brand image, favouring the level of customization. An intermediary can lead to a plurality of brands in the same place of sale, both physical and digital, and therefore an overlapping of them. This can confuse the consumer and debase the brand image and consequently, the positioning. Consequently, it becomes fundamental for luxury brands to correctly manage the intermediary and possibly implement a sales policy that aims to sell in or establish collaborative relationships to generate upward information flows on new market trends and customer expectations. In term of physical distribution, affordable luxury brands adopt the indirect channel through the following formats:

Multi-brand point of sale: The multi-brand point of sale is a specialized intermediary by type of merchandise or by customer target. The traditional point of sale has a wide assortment of selected brands, positioned in the highest price ranges, and guarantees personalized customer service.

Luxury department store: The department store is a distribution format characterized by a large surface area with a generalist character, in which prestigious brands for which premium prices are required coexist on the one hand. The offer is more expansive than traditional points of sale, and there are longer opening hours to the public, which increases the attraction to customers. This type of format generates a form of conflict of interest with the distributor concerning the other functions of the distribution channel: brand positioning, how the products are displayed at the point of sale, the quality and quantity of staff available to the customer in the point of sale and the consequent level of service, minimum assortment, product reordering, unsold goods management, payment times. Other new technological distribution channels are also used for affordable luxury: flagship stores and internet websites are some examples. As for non-affordable luxury, flagship stores permit the customer to enjoy an all-enveloping sense of luxury with the sensation of luxury is closely connected to the city where the point of sales is located (Giacosa, 2014). The primary purpose is not a high return on investment (mainly due to the location's cost), but the brand visibility. Also, digital channels, such as internet web site and social networks, are used by affordable luxury firms. For example, Dolce & Gabbana use social media for direct feedback from their customers: thanks to the collaboration with the fashion bloggers, the fashion shows are instantly uploaded on Facebook and Twitter, and the desire for that brand increases. Even in the digital context, affordable luxury players who choose to distribute their products through intermediaries must consider two aspects highlighted in the physical channel. They are the presence of multiple brands in the same place of sale and the conflict between market share and brand positioning and related communication.

Table 3. Distribution strategies in the digital indirect channel

DISTRIBUTION VIA INDIRECT DIGITAL CHANNEL

Pure Internet cut-price multibrand players

Full-price, Pure Internet player

Multi-brand Internet player focused esclusively on the intermediary market (B2B)

Multi-brand pure Internet player integrated with the physical and digital channels

As concerns the indirect digital channel, it is managed by pure Internet players. They are intermediaries who market luxury goods independently on their e-commerce. To achieve a fair market share for affordable goods, companies can choose the indirect channel, on which the players can adopt the following strategies:

Pure Internet cut-price multi-brand players: The logic of this strategy is that of the factory outlet centre. That's means that luxury goods have been sold at a cut-price by an independent intermediary (Chevalier and Mayzlin, 2006).

Full–price, Pure Internet player: As before, also, in this case, there is an independent intermediary who sells luxury goods on his e-commerce. The difference is in price because it consists of a full-price strategy. This means that the intermediary is a real competitor for luxury brand e-commerce and a physical retail store.

NET-A-PORTER.COM. *This intermediary was created by Natalie Massenet and launched with $1.3 million in 2000. It was born as a website where current season clothing, footwear, and fashion accessories have been sold at full prices. Over the years, net-a-porter.com has become the most representative pure internet player for the luxury market, with the UK's highest growth rate. Many sites have been acquired during its growth, enabling net-a-porter.com to increase clients' numbers in the site's database rapidly. This growth was also supported by opening a new distribution centre in New York, which optimized the US's distribution costs and market share. Its website structure seems like a combination of a magazine and a catalogue. In this sense, the logic is to have the same visual impact as a traditional magazine but is consultable as a catalogue. There are many sections in it as an example "Magazine", where consumers can explore the table of contents of a fashion magazine before purchasing the items. The section named "Special" is possible to have more information concerning the style of the products. It is also possible to access various resources such as photographic shootings, representing a focal point of the purchasing process. Consumers can also receive information about the garments they are viewing on the photographs by hovering the mouse over them, after which they can decide whether to buy. Finally, some website areas are developed in collaboration with journalists and stylists from Elle, Vogue, and Marie Claire to keep consumers updated with new fashion events, trends, and products.*

In 2015 become the most significant pure internet player within the luxury brand market, after they merged with Yoox.com. After the acquisition, the Yoox Net-A-Porter Group has a unique business model consisting of multi-brand online stores named, Net-A-Porter, Mr Porter, Yoox, and The Outnet. In addition to its distribution function, the group is also a strategic partner of the leading fashion and luxury brands. In this regard, it designs and manages the various e-commerce sites by creating online flagship stores "Powered by Yoox Net-A-Porter Group", as an example armani.com or valentino.com. In the following years, the YNAP (Yoox Net-A-Porter) group signed numerous partnerships to improve their digital presence worldwide and the innovation in an increasingly focused sector on omnichannel. In particular, in 2016, a joint venture with Mohammed Alabbar was set up to create the leading online luxury retailer in the Middle East. In the following year, in 2017 through an innovative partnership with Valentino, was created "Next Era": it is a new business model focused on omnichannel, intending to provide customers with an integrated experience between the physical and the online stores of the brands. In 2018, Richemont acquired YNAP, one of the largest groups in Switzerland's luxury sector and already a member since 2015. Today the YNAP group has numerous technology and logistics centres in the United States, Europe, the Middle East, Japan, China, and Hong Kong and distributes in more than 180 countries worldwide. The four online multi-brand stores and numerous flagship stores developed on the same logistics and technology platform now reach over 4.3 million customers worldwide.

Figure 1. Net-a-porter.com: lines of business

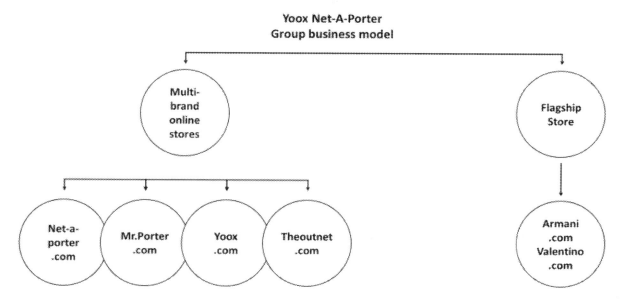

Multi-brand Internet player focused on the intermediary market: In this business model, the independent intermediaries who sell luxury goods are focused on the B2B market. Their offer is not addressed to the final consumer but other physical or digital intermediaries.

Multi-brand pure Internet player integrated with the physical and digital channels: In this case, both digital and physical channels are integrated. The consumer can select the goods directly online and conclude the purchase in the physical store or vice versa can go to the point of sale and then have the product purchased sent home. As is the case for non-affordable goods, the development processes are bidirectional. Luxury brands can start from a physical presence to an online store or, on the contrary, they can bring into the physical channel, a place of digital sales.

CONCLUSION

After the initial hesitation, the luxury sector's competitive environment has changed with the advent of digital.

A few years ago, to increase its brand equity and attract more consumers, the primary source of communication of brand values and messages was considered the company itself. However, in today's competitive environment, companies have to develop their relationships in an innovative way. The development of digital technology and the contextual globalization of markets has led companies to move from a multi-channel perspective to continue operating in international contexts and increasing consumer needs. From this point of view, the digital channel is considered a hybrid tool as it can simultaneously perform an informative function by exploiting both physical and digital contact methods.

The scenario described above shows how the digital channel has developed over the years and how companies in the sector have increasingly integrated it. This channel's development has moved from a

Figure 2. The omnichannel strategy in the luxury market

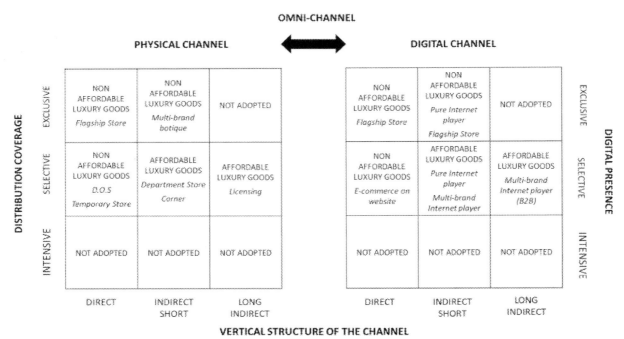

purely informational and liquidation function for unsold products to a strategic driver within the luxury goods distribution channel in today's context.

As far as the physical channel is concerned, luxury brands tend to use mixed distribution. However, there is a clear differentiation between prestige products in the higher price range. The brand's direct selective presence generally prevails, and prestige products in the lower price range, where indirect distribution prevails over direct distribution. However, the simultaneous existence of direct and indirect distribution options has a necessary consequence for the channel's correct management: a clear and defined mission is needed for the different categories of intermediaries. To preserve the brand image and at the same time, reach a particular market share, the digital channel is also composed of similar characteristics. In particular, there are direct and indirect distribution methods. In the first case, there is a management of e-commerce sites by luxury brands.

In contrast, in the second case, the management is entrusted to intermediaries defined as "pure Internet players" who propose a varied offer in terms of luxury goods. Technological development has led to an evolution in digital channels concerning the customer's experience, characterized by uniqueness and positively influences the purchase process (Villanueva & al., 2008). In today's context, luxury brands tend to distribute innovative collections and dedicated products through digital channels. The digital channel's original function is integrated, becoming a part of the supply system characterized by uniqueness and exclusivity at a high price (Cuty & Zang, 2011). The strategic behaviour in the distribution of luxury goods is changeable. It varies about three main dimensions: the multinational extension of the brand, the perceived value, and the brand's image, the economic value of the product category.

The options are described below:

The Evolution of Distribution in the Luxury Sector

Exclusive or selective direct distribution: The leading players in multi-brand luxury goods for some brands in their portfolio of the highest level with inaccessible market positioning and global mono-brand players in the same situation tend to adopt mainly an exclusive direct distribution strategy. Exclusive direct distribution is rarely used because companies are afraid of losing market opportunities due to an excessive restriction of outlets in a given geographical area.

Exclusive or selective indirect distribution: It is mainly adopted by small companies that do not have the economic resources to make direct investments or companies that do not want to be involved in the management of the distribution network because they prefer to focus their efforts on brand image development and communication activities. Selective or exclusive indirect distribution is adopted by companies as a strategy to enter new markets with uncertain macro-environmental scenarios. Many Italian luxury companies that maintain a craft dimension and have not yet developed financial and/or logistical skills do not invest in the development of their shops.

Mixed distribution. Most companies competing in luxury goods markets adopt a hybrid distribution strategy both in digital and physical channels: direct and indirect, selective, and/or exclusive. With this approach, companies can balance the need to achieve sufficient sales volumes and market shares and preserve and strengthen the brand image to sustain premium pricing. In a mixed option, the functions assigned to direct and indirect distribution are well identified. The physical channel activities carried out indirectly managed points of sale to communicate the value of the brand and products and guarantee consumers the shopping experience. The actions of indirect sales outlets mainly aim to ensure a constant flow of adequate revenues and margins. From a digital point of view, luxury brands and their product categories are distinguished by the online channel's function and the level of integration with the physical channel. In today's competitive environment, the best companies are those who, over the years, have been able to integrate these two distribution channels than others. Through this integration, consumers can continuously switch from one channel to another even through various physical retail stores. This also means an increase in the number of touchpoints between luxury brands and consumers, which also have to show a continuous relationship between the physical and the digital channel. The brands of goods characterized by a higher price component, i.e., the non-affordable ones, tend to adopt a direct digital channel strategy and have a higher degree of integration with the physical channel, which is also directly managed. This allows for univocal communication in all areas and gives the luxury consumer a unique experience through both the physical and the digital channel. On the other hand, brands of goods characterized by a lower price component, defined as affordable, are more inclined to adopt an indirect strategy also in the digital channel. In this case, through specialized intermediaries, also known as Internet players, they can reach a significant market share at the expense of non-univocal communication and a lesser consumer experience during the purchase phase.

Finally, it has been found that brands that adopt both strategies tend to use direct channels to promote the latest collections. In contrast, they use e-commerce from specialized intermediaries to sell previous collections remained unsold.

REFERENCES

Allen, M. W., Walker, K. L., & Brady, R. (2012). Sustainability Discourse with a Supply Chain Relationship: Mapping Convergence and Divergence. *Journal of Business Communication*, 49(3), 210–236. doi:10.1177/0021943612446732

Amatulli, C., & Guido, G. (2001). Determinants of purchasing intention for fashion luxury goods in the Italian market: A laddering approach. *Journal of Fashion Marketing and Management*, *15*(1), 123–136. doi:10.1108/13612021111112386

Banathy, H. B. (1996). *Designing social systems in a changing world*. Plenum Press. doi:10.1007/978-1-4757-9981-1

Banister, E., Roper, S., & Potavanich, T. (2020). Consumers' practices of everyday luxury. *Journal of Business Research*, *116*, 458–466. doi:10.1016/j.jbusres.2019.12.003

Batat, W. (2017). *Luxe et expérience client*. Dunod.

Bijmolt, T., Leeflang, P., Block, F., Eisenbeiss, M., Hardie, B., Lemmens, A., & Saffert, P. (2010). Analytics for Customer Engagement. *Journal of Service Research*, *13*(3), 341–356. doi:10.1177/1094670510375603

Binz, C., Hair, J. F. Jr, Pieper, T. M., & Baldauf, A. (2013). Exploring the effect of distinct family firm reputation on consumers' preferences. *Journal of Family Business Strategy*, *4*(1), 4–11. doi:10.1016/j.jfbs.2012.12.004

Borden, N. H. (1964). The Concept of the Marketing Mix. *Journal of Advertising Research*, *24*(4), 7–12.

Bourdieu, P. (1984). *Distinction: A Social Critique of the Judgement of Taste*. Harvard University Press.

Bruce, M., & Hines, T. (2007). *Fashion Marketing. Contemporary Issues*. Elsevier Ltd.

Bruner, G. C. II. (1988). The marketing mix: A retrospective and evaluation. *Journal of Marketing Education*, *10*(1), 29–33. doi:10.1177/027347538801000104

Bruner, G. C. II. (1988). The marketing mix: A retrospective and evaluation. *Journal of Marketing Education*, *10*(1), 29–33. doi:10.1177/027347538801000104

Casaburi, I. (2011). China as a Market: Luxury Brand Consumer Behaviour. *Journal of Marketing Trends*, *1*(6), 47–56.

Catry, B. (2003). The Great Pretenders: The Magic of Luxury Goods. *Business Strategy Review*, *14*(3), 10–17. doi:10.1111/1467-8616.00267

Chailan, C. (2013). The role of Art in Luxury Management. In Proceedings of 6th Euromed Conference of the Euromed Academy of Business, 'Confronting Contemporary Business Challenges through Management Innovation (pp. 569-574). Academic Press.

Chandon, J., Laurent, G., & Valette-Florence, P. (2016). Pursuing the concept of luxury: Introduction to the JBR Special Issue on "Luxury Marketing from Tradition to Innovation". *Journal of Business Research*, *69*(1), 299–303. doi:10.1016/j.jbusres.2015.08.001

Chaudhuri, H. R., & Majumdar, S. (2006). Of Diamonds and Desires: Understanding Conspicuous Consumption from a Contemporary Marketing Perspective. *Academy of Marketing Science Review*, *11*, 1–18.

Chevalier, M., & Mazzalovo, G. (2008). *Luxury brand management*. Franco Angeli.

Choi, T. M. (2011). *Fashion supply chain management: industry and business analysis*. IGI Global.

The Evolution of Distribution in the Luxury Sector

Constantinides, E. (2006). The Marketing Mix Revisited: Towards the 21st Century Marketing. *Journal of Marketing Management, 22*(3), 407–438. doi:10.1362/026725706776861190

Corbellini, E., & Saviolo, S. (2015). *Managing Fashion and Luxury Companies*. ETAS.

Cuty, R. G., & Zhang, P. (2011). Social Commerce: Looking Back and Forward. *Proceedings ASIST*.

De Chernatony, L. (2001). *From Brand Vision to Brand Evaluation. Strategically Building and Sustaining Brands*. Butterworth Heinemann.

De Kerviler, G., & Rodriguez, C. M. (2019). Luxury brand experiences and relationship quality for Millennials: The role of self-expansion. *Journal of Business Research, 102*, 250–262. doi:10.1016/j.jbusres.2019.01.046

De Lassus, C., & Anido Freire, N. (2014). Access to the luxury brand myth in pop-up stores: A netnographic and semiotic analysis. *Journal of Retailing and Consumer Services, 21*(1), 61–68. doi:10.1016/j.jretconser.2013.08.005

Dixon, D. F., & Blois, K. J. (1973). Some Limitations of the 4 Ps as a Paradigm of Marketing. In *Proceedings of the Marketing Education Group* (pp. 92-107). Academic Press.

Duesenberry, J. S. (1949). *Income, Saving and the Theory of Consumer Behaviour*. Harvard University Press.

Eastman, J. K., Goldsmith, R. E., & Flynn, L. R. (1999). Status Consumption in Consumer Behaviour: Scale Development and Validation. *Journal of Marketing Theory and Practice, 7*(3), 41–52. doi:10.1080/10696679.1999.11501839

Erner, G. (2004). *Victimes de la mode?* La Découverte.

Fabris, G., & Minestroni, L. (2004). *Valore e valori della marca*. Franco Angeli.

Fernie, J., Moore, C. M., & Lawrie, A. (1998). A tale of two Cities: An Examination of Fashion Designer Retailing within London and New York. *Journal of Product and Brand Management, 7*(5), 366–378. doi:10.1108/10610429810237637

Geerts, A. (2013). Cluster Analysis of Luxury Brands on the Internet. *International Journal of Management and Marketing Research, 6*(2), 79–82.

Giacosa, E. (2011). *L'economia della aziende di abbigliamento*. Giappichelli.

Giacosa, E. (2012). *Mergers and Acquisitions (M&As) in the Luxury Business*. McGraw-Hill.

Giacosa, E. (2014). *Innovation in Luxury Fashion Family Business*. MacMillan. doi:10.1057/9781137498663

Godey, B., Manthiou, A., Pederzoli, D., Rokka, J., Aiello, G., Donvito, R., & Singh, R. (2016). Social media marketing efforts of luxury brands: Influence on brand equity and consumer behavior. *Journal of Business Research, 69*(12), 5833–5841. doi:10.1016/j.jbusres.2016.04.181

Grewal, D., Roggeveen, A. L., & Nordfält, J. (2017). The future of retailing. *Journal of Retailing, 93*(1), 1–6. doi:10.1016/j.jretai.2016.12.008

Guercini, S., & Ranfagni, S. (2012). Social and Green Sustainability and the Italian Mediterranean Fashion Brands. In *Proceedings of Euromed Congress* (pp. 1-15). Nicosia: Euromed Press.

Guercini, S., & Ranfagni, S. (2013). Sustainability and luxury: The Italian case of a supply chain based on native wools. *Journal of Corporate Citizenship, 52*(52), 76–89. doi:10.9774/GLEAF.4700.2013.de.00008

Guercini, S., & Woodside, A. G. (2012). A strategic supply chain approach: Consortium marketing in the Italian leatherwear industry. *Marketing Intelligence & Planning, 30*(7), 700–716. doi:10.1108/02634501211273814

Hall, E. T., & Hall, M. R. (1990). *Understanding Cultural Differences*. Intercultural Press.

Harrisson, L., & Huntington, S. (2000). *Culture Matters: How values shape human progress*. Basic Books.

Hauck, W. E., & Stanforth, N. (2007). Cohort perception of luxury goods and services. *Journal of Fashion Marketing and Management, 11*(2), 175–188. doi:10.1108/13612020710751365

Hennigs, N., Wiedmann, K.-P., & And Klarmann, C. (2012). Luxury brands in the digital age – exclusivity versus ubiquity. *Marketing Review St. Gallen, 29*(1), 30–35. doi:10.100711621-012-0108-7

Hoecklin, L. (1996). *Managing Cultural Differences: Strategies for Competitive Advantage* (2nd ed.). Addison-Wesley Publishers.

Jones, C., Makri, M., & Gomez-Mejia, L. R. (2008). Affiliate directors and perceived risk bearing in publicly traded, family-controlled firms: The case of diversification. *Entrepreneurship Theory and Practice, 32*(6), 1007–1026. doi:10.1111/j.1540-6520.2008.00269.x

Jones, R. (2002). *The apparel industry*. Blackwell.

Kapferer, J. N. (1997). Managing luxury brands. *Journal of Brand Management, 4*(4), 251–260. doi:10.1057/bm.1997.4

Kapferer, J. N. (1997). Managing luxury brands. *Journal of Brand Management, 4*(4), 251–260. doi:10.1057/bm.1997.4

Kapferer, J. N. (2002). *Ce qui va changer les marques*. Editions d'Organisation.

Kapferer, J. N. (2012). All That Glitters is not Green: The Challenge of Sustainable Luxury. *European Business Review*, (November/December), 40–45.

Kapferer, J. N., & Bastien, V. (2009). *Luxury Strategy*. Franco Angeli.

Kapferer, J. N., & Bastien, V. (2012). *The Luxury Strategy: Break The Rules of Marketing to Build Luxury Brands* (2nd ed.). Kogan Page Ltd.

Kemp, S. (1998). Perceiving Luxury and Necessity. *Journal of Economic Psychology, 19*(5), 591–606. doi:10.1016/S0167-4870(98)00026-9

Kim, A., & Ko, E. (2010). Impacts of Luxury Fashion Brand's Social Media Marketing on Customer Relationship and Purchase Intention. *Journal of Global Fashion Marketing, 1*(3), 164–171. doi:10.108 0/20932685.2010.10593068

Kim, A. J., & Ko, E. (2012). Do social media marketing activities enhance customer equity? An empirical study of luxury fashion brand. *Journal of Business Research, 65*(10), 1480–1486. doi:10.1016/j.jbusres.2011.10.014

Kim, H., Choi, Y. J., & Lee, Y. (2015). Web atmospheric qualities in luxury fashion brand web sites. *Journal of Fashion Marketing and Management, 19*(4), 384–401. doi:10.1108/JFMM-09-2013-0103

Kim, J. E., Lloyd, S., & Cervellon, M. C. (2016). Narrative-transportation storylines in luxury brand advertising: Motivating consumer engagement. *Journal of Business Research, 69*(1), 304–313. doi:10.1016/j.jbusres.2015.08.002

Koivisto, E., & Mattila, P. (2020). Extending the luxury experience to social media – User-Generated Content co-creation in a branded event. *Journal of Business Research, 117*, 570–578. doi:10.1016/j.jbusres.2018.10.030

Kotler, P., & ... . (2016). *Marketing management*. Pearson.

Kozinets, R. V., Sherry, J. F., DeBerry-Spence, B., Duhacheck, A., Nuttavuthisi, K., & Storm, D. (2002). Themed Flagship Brand Stores in the new Millenium: Theory, Practice, Prospect. *Journal of Retailing, 78*(1), 17–29. doi:10.1016/S0022-4359(01)00063-X

Lemon, K. N., & Verhoef, P. C. (2016). Understanding customer experience throughout the customer journey. *Journal of Marketing, 80*(6), 69–96. doi:10.1509/jm.15.0420

Loonam, J., Eaves, S., Vikas, K., & Parry, G. (2017). Towards Digital Transformation: Lessons learned from Traditional Organisations. *Strategic Change.*

McCharty, E. J. (1964). *Basic Marketing: A Managerial Approach* (2nd ed.). Irwin, Homewood.

Miller, D., & Le Breton-Miller, I. (2005). *Managing for the Long Run: Lessons in Competitive Advantage from Great Family Businesses*. Harvard Business Press.

Moore, C. M., Doherty, A. M., & Doyle, S. A. (2010). Flagship Stores as a Market Entry Method: the Perspective of Luxury Fashion Retailing. *European Journal of Marketing, 44*(1(2), 139-161

Mosca, F. (2010). *Il marketing dei beni di lusso*. Pearson Italia.

Mosca, F. (2014). *Distribution Strategies in Luxury Markets: emerging trends*. McGraw-Hill.

Mosca, F. (2017). *Strategie nei mercati del lusso. Marketing, digitalizzazione, sostenibilità*. Egea.

Mosca, F., & Chiaudano, V. (2020). Digital channels and distribution in luxury market. *Marché et organisations, 37*(1), 147-163.

Mosca, F., & Civera, C. (2018). *Digital channels and social media management in luxury markets*. Academic Press.

Mosca, F., & Giacosa, E. (2016), Old and New Distribution Channels in the Luxury Sector. IGI Global. doi:10.4018/978-1-4666-9958-8.ch010

Mulyanegara, R. C., & Tsarenko, Y. (2009). Predicting brand preferences: An examination of the predictive power of personality and values in the Australian fashion market. *Journal of Fashion Marketing and Management, 13*(3), 358–371. doi:10.1108/13612020910974492

Nueno, J. L., & Quelch, J. A. (1998). The Mass Marketing of Luxury. *Business Horizons, 41*(November-December), 61–68. doi:10.1016/S0007-6813(98)90023-4

Nwankwo, S., Hamelin, N., & Khaled, M. (2014). Consumer values, motivation and purchase intention for luxury goods. *Journal of Retailing and Consumer Services, 21*(5), 735–744. doi:10.1016/j.jretconser.2014.05.003

Okonkwo, U. (2007). *Luxury Fashion Branding. New York Palgrave.* Macmillan. doi:10.1057/9780230590885

Okonkwo, U. (2009). Sustaining Luxury Brands on the Internet. *Journal of Brand Management, 16*(5/6), 302–310. doi:10.1057/bm.2009.2

Okonkwo, U. (2010). *Luxury Online.* Palgrave, MacMillan. doi:10.1057/9780230248335

Orton, J., & Weick, K. (1990). Loosely Coupled Systems: A Reconceptualization. *Academy of Management Review, 15*(2), 203–223. doi:10.5465/amr.1990.4308154

Peter, J. P., Donnelly, J. H., Pratesi, C. A., & Aliverti, G. (2018). *Marketing.* McGraw Hill.

Phau, I., & Prendergast, G. (2000). Consuming luxury brands: The relevance of the 'Rarity Principle'. *Journal of Brand Management, 8*(2), 122–138. doi:10.1057/palgrave.bm.2540013

Poza, E. (2007). *Family business* (2nd ed.). Thompson.

Ritzer, G. (1999). *Enchanting and disenchanted world: revolutionizing the means of consumption.* Pine Forge Press.

Ross, J., & Harradine, R. (2011). Fashion value brands: The relationship between identity and image. *Journal of Fashion Marketing and Management, 15*(3), 306–325. doi:10.1108/13612021111151914

Seo, Y., & Buchanan-Oliver, M. (2019). Constructing a typology of luxury brand consumption practices. *Journal of Business Research, 99*, 414–421. doi:10.1016/j.jbusres.2017.09.019

Seo, Y., Buchanan-Oliver, M., & Cruz, A. (2015). Luxury brand markets as confluences of multiple cultural beliefs. *International Marketing Review, 32*(2), 141–159. doi:10.1108/IMR-04-2013-0081

Seringhaus, F. R. (2005). Selling luxury brands online. *Journal of Internet Commerce, 4*(1), 1–25. doi:10.1300/J179v04n01_01

Stokburger-Sauer, N. E., & Teichmann, K. (2013). Is luxury just a female thing? The role of gender in luxury brand consumption. *Journal of Business Research, 66*(7), 889–896. doi:10.1016/j.jbusres.2011.12.007

Taplin, I. M. (2014). Who is to blame? A re-examination of Fast Fashion after the 2013 factory disaster in Bangladesh. *Critical Perspectives on International Business, 10*(1/2), 72–83. doi:10.1108/cpoib-09-2013-0035

Thompson, C. J., Rindfleisch, A., & Zeynec, A. (2006). Emotional branding and the strategic value of the doppelganger brand image. *Journal of Marketing, 70*(1), 50–64. doi:10.1509/jmkg.70.1.050.qxd

Tynan, C., McKechnie, S., & Chuon, C. (2010). Co-creating Value for Luxury Brands. *Journal of Business Research, 63*(11), 1156–1163. doi:10.1016/j.jbusres.2009.10.012

Vigneron, F., & Johnson, L. W. (1999). A review and a conceptual framework of prestige-seeking consumer behavior. *Academy of Marketing Science Review, 9*(1), 1–14.

Villanueva, J., Yoo, S., & And Hanssens, D. M. (2008). The Impact of Marketing-Induced Versus Word-of-Mouth Customer Acquisition on Customer Equity Growth. *JMR, Journal of Marketing Research, 45*(1), 48–59. doi:10.1509/jmkr.45.1.48

Ward, J. L. (1997). Growing the family business: Special challenges and best practices. *Family Business Review, 10*(4), 323–337. doi:10.1111/j.1741-6248.1997.00323.x

Weick, K. (1976). Educational Organizations as Loosely Coupled Systems. *Administrative Science Quarterly, 21*(1), 1–19. doi:10.2307/2391875

Winter, R. S., Dahar, R., & Mosca, F. (2011). *Marketing Management*. Milano Apogeo.

Yeoman, I. (2011). The Changing Behaviour of Luxury Consumption. *Journal of Revenue and Pricing Management, 10*(1), 47–50. doi:10.1057/rpm.2010.43

Chapter 2
Omnichannel Shopping Experiences for Fast Fashion and Luxury Brands:
An Exploratory Study

Cesare Amatulli
https://orcid.org/0000-0002-6296-2569
University of Bari, Italy

Matteo De Angelis
LUISS University, Italy

Andrea Sestino
https://orcid.org/0000-0003-2648-4093
University of Bari, Italy

Gianluigi Guido
University of Salento, Italy

ABSTRACT

This chapter explores how luxury and fast fashion brands have been affected by omnichannel strategies, which refer to the opportunity to integrate online and offline channels to create a seamless shopping experience aimed at engaging customers. Through a quali-quantitative research approach, the study examines the potential effects of the implementation of omnichannel activities on the perception of luxury and fast fashion brands. Interestingly, consumers perceive omnichannel strategies as something projected for luxury brands, thus as a way for them to improve the luxury shopping experience. Consequently, when applied to fast fashion brands, omnichannel strategies may lead consumers to perceive such brand as more prestigious, activating a sort of "luxurization." For a luxury company, omnichannel strategies may represent an opportunity because they can increase the perceived luxuriousness of the brand, but also a threat because they may help fast fashion brands to be perceived as luxurious, thus "imitating" luxury companies.

DOI: 10.4018/978-1-7998-5882-9.ch002

Copyright © 2021, IGI Global. Copying or distributing in print or electronic forms without written permission of IGI Global is prohibited.

INTRODUCTION

Fashion and luxury brands are currently facing new challenges. Walking through the most popular shopping streets, from London's Knightsbridge up to Old Bond Street, from Rome's Via Condotti up to Via del Corso, from Paris' Champs Elysées up to Galeries Lafayette, the shop windows of Burberry, Hermès, Louis Vuitton, and Gucci show their latest creations of refined quality materials and unique craftsmanship. Continuing across near streets, pretty much the same designs at the trendy showcases of H&M, Zara, Top Shop, and Forever 21 could be discovered, although at significantly lower prices and quality: just figure out Via del Corso in Rome, as the main street from which Via Condotti begin. Today, these store perfectly integrate some digital tools (interactive or touch–screen displays, totems, Wi–fi connectivity in the entire store), then extended their traditional presence on online channels (Okonkwo, 2009) (e–commerce, social media, blogs, websites), creating a disruptive digital and technological universe. Luxury brands evoke rarity, heritage of craftsmanship, exclusivity, premium pricing, and superior quality (Amatulli & Guido, 2011; Chevalier & Mazzalovo, 2008). By contrast, fast fashion ensures permanent assortment rotation, low prices, and accessible variety, but with a great aesthetic content, which derives from those brands' ability to imitate the latest luxury fashion brand catwalk offerings (Gabrielli et al., 2013). The evolution of a mass class of wealthy people and the rapid growth of the Internet have allowed consumers to "trade upwards" and purchase luxury items, mixing these luxury products with fast fashion ones, in a way that seems to lead to the so called "democratisation of luxury" (Okonkwo, 2009). The new digital tools, and thus the digitalization, the new tastes of the youngest generations of consumers transformed the dynamics of the luxury goods markets (Batat, 2019; Rios, 2016). Digitalization is a buzzword today: the integration between digital and physical channels, thus between on–line and off–line digital channels, become strictly required to survive and maintain competitiveness (Chaffey et al., 2019). The new marketing strategies enabled by the digital tools are not only limited to e–commerce and social media communication strategies: Digitalization means to rethink the traditional business model to integrate digital processes along the entire value chain (Chaffey & Smith, 2017). The new fast fashion brands have become competitors of luxury brands through the introduction of limited–edition products, celebrity endorsement, high advertisement expenditure, and store openings in prestige retail locations. Additionally, online fashion specialists, through their online e–commerce platforms (e.g. Amazon, Asos, Net–a–porter) easily propose both fast fashion products and luxury products (Brownlie et al., 2013). Differentiating themselves is becoming extremely important for luxury companies, as they have witnessed great changes from their consumers. Indeed, luxury companies are now considering mass brands as a threat. Thus, from a consumer's perspective, in the current scenario, the omnichannel opportunities could contribute to make fast fashion brands perceived as more prestigious, activating a sort of "luxuriation" of such brands. Co–branding strategies have been investigated as a way to bringing together luxury and fast fashion (Amatulli et al., 2016): indeed, luxury brands seem to be near to fast–fashion strategies. Digitalization could additionally make hazy these borders.

For an overview, fashion market revenue is expected to show an annual growth rate (CAGR 2020–2024) of 7.0%, resulting in a market volume of US$149,308m by 2024 (SDMO, 2020), despite the growth will slow to 3 to 4 percent in 2020, slightly below the predicted rate due to the Covid–19 pandemic (McKinsey, 2020). The fashion influence has been propelled by the rise of new designer brands and chains such as Vivienne Westwood, Paul Smith, Stella McCartney, Alexander McQueen, and Alice Temperley and the re–emergence of old luxury brands like Burberry and Mulberry in the UK Market and the historic presence of Gucci, Prada, Dolce & Gabbana, Armani, Versace in the Italian Market (Interbrand, 2020).

High levels of creativity and innovation of product design along with solid entrepreneurial skills in retail and brand management are the keys of success of these luxury brands. Furthermore, digital integrations must be placed in a strategic framework that does not distort corporate history and culture, but become an ally, reaching and full presence.

Considering the current hyper–technological scenario, and the penetrating presence of digital tools in our lives, and shopping experiences, this chapter explores the consumers' reactions to fast fashion and luxury brands, by focusing on the recent omnichannel experiences. The omnichannel experience is instead based on the awareness that consumers travel through different channels (online and offline), also to complete a single purchase (Verhoef et al., 2015); stores begin to offer increasingly integrated environments with a perfect combination of physical and digital presence. Today consumers decide where and when to get in touch with brands, which touchpoints – as the ways with which consumers interact with a company, whether it be person–to–person, through a website, an app or any form of communication (Stein & Ramaseshan, 2016) – to collect information and compare prices and products because of the final purchase choice, by taking advantage during the shopping experience.

Thus, we shed light on how the omnichannel experiences are perceived for the luxury and fast–fashion brands. Interestingly while co–branding strategies led the luxury brands to internalize some strategies of the fast fashion brands, we underline how digital and omnichannel, on the one hand, still, bring the two sectors closer together, but inversely as a "luxurization" of fast fashion brands. Moreover, the chapter also briefly explores the role of privacy concern in omnichannel experiences, suggesting some insights toward digital integration to promote shopping continuity even in the era of social distancing.

THEORETICAL BACKGROUND

Luxury Fashion

A luxury brand can be considered a "coherent system of excellence", a harmonious universe of values, and a perfect system of attributes (Corbellini & Saviolo, 2009). Luxury brands evoke exclusivity, have a well–known brand identity, enjoy high brand awareness and perceived quality, and retain high sales levels and customer loyalty (Phau & Prendergast, 2000). Indeed, a luxury brand can be defined as the sum of feelings and perceptions people have when in contact with a company and its products (Chevalier & Mazzalovo, 2008). Therefore, a luxury company brand lives in consumers' mind and its success or failure is based on how it is positioned in the consumer's mind (Parrott et al., 2015). Indeed, the creation of brand value is crucial in luxury marketing activities; brand value refers to brand equity, which is an indispensable intangible asset for luxury companies and translates into revenues. The brand value is also relevant to consumers, who achieve an immeasurable level of satisfaction from luxury fashion products. The most visible and symbolic aspect of a luxury fashion brand is the brand name (Okonkwo, 2007); this is due to the fact that it is the "brand name" that enchants consumers to a brand and generates a relationship between them and their chosen brand (Chevalier & Mazzalovo, 2008). Luxury brands confer much emphasis on creating high brand awareness and the proper brand image with the objective of achieving a high level of brand loyalty and consequently a steady income stream (Amatulli & Guido, 2012). Therefore, luxury brands generally have the advantage of attaining a higher level of global brand awareness than fast fashion brands (Business of Fashion, 2011). The strategy is conceived to assist in developing the global presence and reputation of the brand, and to leverage its status and awareness.

Luxury and prestige brands have traditionally embraced the premium pricing strategy to highlight their brand exclusivity (Fionda & Moore, 2009), high quality, and the strength associated with luxury goods, and to distinguish them from the fast fashion brands.

The relationship between consumers and a strong brand is a type of bond that begins with a psychological process in the mind of the consumer and is proven through product purchases. Consequently, any luxury brand that attempts to succeed in the competitive luxury market environment needs to understand everything about the luxury consumer (Megehee & Spake, 2012). Thus, considering the consumer's self–concept (Phau & Prendergast, 2000) and wearing luxury goods is a way to raise the value of the self (Megehee & Spake, 2012). The reason for the purchase of luxury goods is mainly their symbolic value in fulfilling consumer needs and desires. However, research has acknowledged that two main purchasing motives may be identified in luxury consumption: "luxury for others" and "luxury for oneself" (Kapferer & Bastien, 2009; Kastanakis & Balabanis, 2014). Therefore, luxury goods can be purchased for status symbols (i.e., for social statements) or to express an individual style (i.e., for personal pleasure). Vigneron & Johnson (2004) highlighted that the meaning of luxury is determined by a consideration of "interpersonal" versus "personal" perceptions and motives. Amatulli & Guido (2011, 2012) introduced the conceptualization of "internalized" versus "externalized" luxury consumption – the former based on the aim of expressing an individual style and the latter based on the aim of showing off a social position. For luxury companies the latter is important to support, given the fact that there should be more people aware of the brand than those who can truly afford to purchase it. If somebody is observing another person and doesn't identify the brand they're wearing, then part of the brand value is lost (Okonkwo, 2007). The luxury brand must be well known and accredited in order to be desired (Chevalier & Mazzalovo, 2008). Luxury consumers are less price sensitive and they buy a complete package of experiences, feelings, and identities, made up of the product and the brand characteristics (Phau & Prendergast, 2000). Luxury consumers acquire their products chiefly in physical stores in order to benefit from a whole product selection and delight in the luxury retail atmosphere. As mentioned by Okonkwo (2007) there are currently two major segments of the luxury consumer population. The first is the "traditional luxury consumer" who still venerates entrenched brands like Hermès and Christian Dior; and the second segment comprises a considerable proportion of luxury consumers known as the "new luxury consumer" population. This new consumer group is no longer attracted by only brand names but also appreciates a full package of products and services that offer stable value through innovation and an extraordinary experience in every element of brand (Megehee & Spake, 2012), including new fruition channels such as digital ones (Mosca & Civera, 2017) The current luxury consumer is highly sophisticated, stylish, brand literate, fashionable, and aware of their tastes and preferences (Amatulli et al., 2011). They have strong values and principles (Schiffman et al., 2008).

Fast Fashion

Fast fashion concerns a consumer–driven approach (Barnes & Lea– Greenwood, 2010), a business strategy which is intended at decreasing the number of processes involved in the buying cycle and lead times for getting new fashion product into stores, in order to satisfy consumer demand (Joy et al., 2012). The term "fast fashion" was first invented by retailers to indicate how fashion styles and trends change rapidly from the catwalk to the store (Brooks, 2015). The aim of fast fashion is the ability to react quickly to ever–changing fashion trends and consumer demands in order to gain competitive advantage (Barnes & Lea– Greenwood, 2010). Mass retailers such as Zara and H&M have adopted this business strategy and have become recognized for steadily refreshing their product range with new fashion styles, capturing the attention of media and driving customers to visit their stores on a frequent basis (Rosenblum, 2015). As this phenomenon has expanded within the fashion industry, rather than being concerned to mass retailers they have become known as fast fashion brands (Bhardwaj & Fairhurst, 2010). What characterize these brands are the trendy inexpensive clothes, cheaply made designer knockoffs, rapid speed, stylish and up–to–date fashions garments which lure consumers into paying full price now rather than deferring gratification until the year–end sales arrive (Joy et al., 2012; Rosenblum, 2015). Fast fashion replaces exclusivity, glamour, originality, and luxury with "mass–exclusivity" "massluxe" or "masstige" (Toktali, 2008), by producing products in smaller volumes that usually are not restocked, in order to minimize the risk of inaccuracy and being out of date. As a result, the fashion items change every few weeks. Collections are small and often sell out, creating an air of exclusivity and cutting down on the need for markdowns. According to Barnes & Lea–Greenwood (2010) the fast fashion brands' decisions in producing their products take a lead from luxury fashion brands. What has changed today is not the speed of imitating, but the low cost and large scale at which copies are being made. Fast fashion imitations threaten the innovation process and move the focus of innovation from expressive aspects towards status aspects (Hemphill & Suk, 2009). Fast fashion is a consumer–driven approach and its persistent demand for novelty is its central force (Bhardwaj & Fairhurst, 2010). Hence, the objective of the fast fashion model is to meet consumer demand by speedily designing, producing, and delivering highly fashionable garments in the shortest possible time (Ertekin & Atik, 2015). Fast fashion' customers expect stylish and fresh offerings which result in a high periodicity of fashion turnover and produces a "buy now because you won't see this later" scarcity mentality (Miller, 2013). Updated looks, greater variety and choice, well–designed and limited editions, along with the speed of their availability, have made this industry very attractive to many consumers – the initial appeal having been to the young but now attracting mature consumers too (Joy et al., 2012). Refined and well–informed consumers, in search of an individual look, have moved towards consumption behaviours such as "mix and match" (Feitelberg, 2010; Yeoman, 2007). Fast fashion allows dreams of luxury to come true. Many consumers will fantasise and dream about owning, wearing and acquiring replicas of catwalk looks or celebrity couture fashions (Miller, 2013).

Fast Fashion vs. Luxury Fashion Brands: Co–Branding Strategies and New Scenarios

The success of fast fashion has affected consumers' perception as they are no longer regarded as simply "fast fashion" brands but are now "fast premium fashion" brands or, in some cases, "high–end" brands (Bhardwaj & Fairhurst, 2010). Although they remain focused on a mass–market target, it is no longer pertinent to consider these brands as low–end fast brands (Joy et al., 2012). The fast fashion brands have developed new marketing mix strategies and retail tactics that are comparable to those of luxury fashion brands, thus developing a "luxurious appeal" at a better price–value balance (Joy et al., 2012). For fast fashion companies, one of the results of these strategies is the significant rise of their brand asset value. To illustrate, in 2019, Zara featured for the first time on the list of the 100 Best Global Brands (Interbrand, 2020). Indeed, Zara was ranked number 29, much higher than the value of luxury brands like Dior, Gucci, Burberry, Prada, and Tiffany. Similarly, H&M was ranked immediately after Zara number 30, confirming its prominences compared to the major luxury brands. Consequently, L'Avenue des Champs Elysées in Paris, or Via Condotti and the near Via del Corso in Rome, which are considered as the epitome of a luxury location, currently has stores representing non–luxury brands such as Zara, H&M and alongside Louis Vuitton, Gucci, and Cartier, and several other fast fashion brands (Bhardwaj & Fairhurst, 2010). The phenomenon of "mix and match" brings together the ideas of luxury and mass–market consumerism (Corbellini & Saviolo, 2009), combining items of fast fashion and luxury fashion, thus bringing fast fashion "closer" to the luxury concept. Increasingly consumers of middle– or lower–class origin are being associated with this phenomenon. Accessories are typically purchased from the luxury brand market, as the price of these longer lasting items is perceived as more affordable (Atwal & Williams, 2017). Garments, however, as they are being purchased more frequently, are bought from fast fashion companies (Brown, 2011). Mix and match allow the opportunity of creating a more affordable luxury lifestyle and gives the consumer the possibility of gaining a higher prestige within their peer group. Considering the current digital scenario and the large availability of online multi–brand platform, in which both luxury and fast fashion products are offered to consumers, mix–and–match become more easily: a click is required to insert your favourite purchases in the cart and create your own outfit. Like fast–fashion retail strategies, some brands like Dolce & Gabbana, Chanel, Versace and Prada have adopted this strategy to reduce seasonality risk. In 2013 Louis Vuitton introduced bold new looks creating an entire Mix & Match Spring/Summer Collection between the Cruise and Icon lines with their own unique styles. Burberry's invested in its supply chain to react rapidly to sales trends and capitalize on bestsellers (Business of Fashion, 2011). Luxury fashion brands have also created more reasonable lower priced diffusion lines mixing haute couture with ready–to–wear such as Giorgio Armani: the stylist developed the Emporio Armani line, a diffusion line aimed at targeting the young adult market. These diffusion lines are mass–produced and designed to appeal to the younger consumer (Armani, 2015). A recent strategy by fast fashion brands is to develop collaborations with luxury brands in order to reach new potential consumers, elevate their brand status (Okonkwo, 2007) and create unique products (Griffioen, 2011), moreover accessing digital channels (Ozuem & Azemi, 2017). Indeed, co–branding has been recognized as the first branding strategy that pairs two separate well–known brands together for a unique, collaborative project (Sreejesh, 2012). This could include new or revived products, services or ventures as well as advertising or distribution outlets. Due to the high level of competition and brand protection among luxury brands, the phenomenon of co–branding has been rare in the luxury goods sector. If a co–branding strategy is well managed by combining elements between two brands such as values, visions and wills to generate real synergies, it presents an interesting path towards creating strong brand reputation and differentiation (Rollet et al., 2013). Brands may embrace co–branding for various reasons, depending on whether they are luxury brands or fast fashion brands. If co–branding strategy is based on consistency and integration between elements of the two brands (e.g., visions and values), it presents an interesting and effective strategy for creating sustainable brand reputation and differentiation for fast fashion brands (Hoffmann & Coste–Manière, 2012). However, advertising co–branded luxury goods in a fast fashion store provides a gateway for fast–market customers to penetrate the luxury goods arena. This strategy brings credibility to fast fashion brands, increasing sales revenues, consumer perceived quality and value, as well as high media exposure, differentiation from other fast fashion brands and the positioning of the brand in consumers' mind as more premium (Okonkwo, 2007).

Fast Fashion vs. Luxury Fashion Brands: Rom Online to Omnichannel Strategies

The luxury consumption is based on two areas of motivation, a personal level aimed at achieving their satisfaction and the other interpersonal level, focused on ostentation and time to look for a status symbol: Luxury products are used for both a social recognition in its externalizing (Amatulli et al., 2011) or for a hedonistic and pleasure–seeking purpose (Novak & MacEvoy 1990; Vigneron & Johnson 1999; 2004). Luxury consumers are looking for self–expression and social representation, which is the desire to receive approval from other individuals (Eastman & Eastman, 2011). Two fundamental characteristics for which a consumer chooses a luxury product are the high quality and hedonistic benefits sought. Luxury goods are considered a tool to satisfy their well–being, whose purchasing behaviour is not led by functional motivations, but by sensory pleasures and aesthetic beauty (Amatulli & Guido, 2011). The goal of luxury brands is to generate around their products a strong, decisive, and clear image in the mind of potential consumers, thus establishing a long–term relationship with them. It is equally essential that their advertisements are disseminated through channels that contribute to enriching the meaning of the message of exclusivity, prestige, and uniqueness. The main communication channels of luxury companies have always been the press, fashion magazines, television, and fashion shows. Today, both luxury and fast fashion brands could take advantage by their online and offline presence, by leveraging on such disruptive digital strategies enabled by new technologies: From the simplest social networks, web, e–commerce, blogs, up to exploitation of Big Data collected for profiling or predicting the behaviour of purchase, by leveraging from in–store technology, artificial intelligence, and smart objects (Sestino et al., 2020a). Additionally, luxury and fashion brands could find an advantage by exploiting online channels through the Influencers, Bloggers, Instagrammers, and Youtubers to influence consumers' perceptions of their brands, thus increasing their emotional involvement (Evans et al., 2017; Lou & Yuan, 2019). Furthermore, from the offer perspective, digital strategies generate a series of advantages for businesses (Kalakota & Whinston, 1997; Turban et al., 2017), and although new technologies like smart objects might be useful to improve luxury consumption experiences, some research (i.e., Sestino et al., 2020b) suggest that consumers' status consumption orientation could influence consumers' perceived usefulness of new technological tools, and marketers should be able to preliminary segment their markets on the basis of such consumers related characteristics. Digital can contribute to the expansion of markets, extending them beyond any geographical limit without having to make investments in physical distribution structures: the costs of accessing virtual stores are lower and independent of distance (Kaur, 2011). Businesses can also establish relationships with consumers by exploiting the interactivity of digital channels by developing direct two–way communications in real–time (Barlow et al., 2004). The shopping experience can be constantly guaranteed, because the digital channel makes a sale not tied to a specific moment, thus overcoming the obstacles and barriers of physical time of offline distribution (Dholakia & Uusital, 2002). Internet technologies and online marketing tools as a part of digital transformation (Chaffey & Smith, 2017) offer several competitive advantages such as agility, selectivity, individuality, and interactivity (Shim et al., 2012). The reference scenario about the use of the digital channel for luxury and fashion goods, however, seems to have changed over the last years. For consumers, however, digital tools are considered an opportunity to make increasingly aware and accurate decisions that allow them a greater probability of satisfaction and loyalty (Remy et al., 2015. Today's luxury and fashion consumers are increasingly turning to the information sources available on websites (Rios, 2016). Over the years, luxury and fashion brands had an attitude of the extreme

Omnichannel Shopping Experiences for Fast Fashion and Luxury Brands

reluctance of the digital world, which put them in a position to show a significant delay regarding the use of these tools for business purposes, when compared to companies from other sectors (Okonkwo, 2009). The main reason for this diffidence concerns the real essence of the changes brought about by the diffusion of digital: luxury companies always tried to build their image as made of tradition and exaltation of the past and therefore encountered first difficulties in combining these characteristics with a world of continuous innovation like that of the digital. Since the beginning, the web also showed its extremely popular tool and opportunities, promising anyone free access and the chance to get in touch with anyone. Luxury companies, at first, saw in this aspect a real threat to their branding policies, only recently recognizing the benefits (Bjorn–Andersen & Hansen, 2011). Only over time, they began to understand that the advantages brought by digital tools could be exploited to their advantage even by luxury and fashion brands: one of the knots to be resolved, however, remains the question of exclusivity (Hennigs et al., 2012). Exclusivity is one of the characteristics that luxury goods must possess and which, therefore, must be manifested in all the brand's touchpoints (Atwal & Williams, 2017). In the offline world, the sense of exclusivity can be conveyed through a wise choice of commercial locations and places (such as the stores), the arrangement of products in an appropriate manner and through the behaviour of the sales staff, who can contribute to making the shopping experience unique (Schüller et al., 2018), sometimes accosting luxury and fashion stores to art galleries and museums (Joy et al., 2014) due to their position, or palace in which store are located. The sense of exclusivity is also created through communication and advertising, which have the task of making luxury products perceived as accessible to a few, but desirable for everyone. (Kim et al., 2016). Digital can confirm to be a particularly suitable tool in this sense, given that it can be exploited to create a sense of desirability, through the contact of the brand with many potential consumers (Ahuja, 2014; Brun et al., 2015). Online presence proves to be a valid strategy to amplify the sense of omnipresence of the brand. One of the characteristics that consumers associate with luxury brands is their global character and, thanks to the use of social media, luxury brands can ensure a widespread presence everywhere, and potentially at any moment of consumers' life. The brand is not diminished by the fact of being present in a context, such as that of the web, apparently dissonant, given that modern customers consider it normal and, indeed, expect this to happen (Kozlova et al., 2017; Stephen, 2016). The goal that luxury brands are pursuing today is to design a digital experience that reflects the attributes of luxury as it is traditionally understood (Hennigs et al., 2012). The expression "digital luxury experience", embodies this phenomenon (Achille, 2017): luxury players have understood the new needs of their customers and aim to satisfy them by trying to offer them added value also in digital touchpoints (Heine & Berghaus, 2014).

After a prolonged period of store openings in the main city streets on a global level, the current challenge for luxury and fashion brands, is to grab newer spaces: virtual ones or integrating digital technologies in their traditional stores. The online channel has been developing at great speed, becoming increasingly important within corporate strategies. Indeed, the Internet and the new digital technologies, help luxury, and fashion brands to create better interaction and relationships with the consumer, realizing unique shopping experiences. The digital experiences and physical experiences that the consumer lives are more integrated and connected: it is essential to make the technology applied to the retail channels functional and usable, to create additional support for the purchasing process (Okonkwo, 2010). The key to success was recognized in the perfect balance between offline and online, by implementing omnichannel strategies (Lawry & Choi, 2013; Ozuem & Azemi, 2017). To survive in an increasingly competitive environment, most brands attempt to adopt integrated online–offline customer relationship management (Frasquet & Miquel, 2017). At the physical size of the store, brands are gradually adding digital tools, moving from the world of web and e–commerce platforms, up to and of social media, and finally redesign the in–store experiences (Aiolfi & Sabbadin, 2019; Lawry & Choi, 2013; Thamm et al., 2016). The modern digital consumers prove to be a flexible buyer, particularly able to extricate himself between different channels and devices during the evaluation phase and, consequently, the boundary between traditional economy and digital economy is, for him, extremely blurred. Therefore, it becomes strategic for brands to know and capitalize on the wealth of information that gravitates around the consumers' decision–making process, intending to transform it into a competitive advantage: The orientation towards this type of consumers requires the omnichannel strategy (Payne et al., 2017). The digitalization of the tools used by consumers has thus projected retailers towards new ways of managing their marketing activities based on their centrality and technological innovation as critical success factors for the achievement of the competitive advantage (Verhoef et al., 2015). Indeed, Rigby (2011) defined this omnichannel strategy as dominant approaches for retailers. This corresponds to the synergic, integrated and hybrid management of all channels available to retailers to interact with consumers and is aimed at offering them a seamless shopping experience, that is, without friction along the entire customer journey (Verhoef et al., 2015). Thus, the use of the Internet and the rapid growth of digital tools offered the opportunity to create new values even in offline stores (Frasquet & Miquel, 2017). Consumers' shopping behaviour can be encouraged and influenced by a wide variety of inherent factors such as external stimuli in the sales environment such as store characteristics, sensory stimuli, promotions, advertising, retail technologies (Holbrook & Anand, 1990). Thus, the omnichannel consists of giving the possibility to these new flexible consumers, to get in touch with the brand in any way he wishes, without making any division between what happens in the physical space and what happens online, through new digital technologies (Mosquera et al., 2018). Luxury and fashion retailers could trigger purchasing behavior by encouraging the use of digital also thanks to the use of new in–store technologies, thus promoting innovative direct marketing practices based on proximity: self–service technologies, contactless technologies, display interactive technologies (Willems et al., 2017). Thus, the stimuli included in the offline shopping environment, together with the new digital marketing activities practiced by the retailer, could influence the emotional states of the consumer, overstimulating them enriching the traditional luxury and fashion shopping experience, using digital in their favour as well in addition to their online presence (Aiolfi & Sabbadin, 2019; Lynch & Barnes, 2020; Kent et al., 2016). If on one hand new way of shopping by an increasingly evolved consumer is emerging, on the other hand, companies must involve them differently, satisfying increasingly demanding requests for customization. In this new scenario, digital does not necessarily replace offline but completes it, creating a harmonious customer experience along with all possible points of contact between the brand and the customer through multiple channels, "integrating bricks with clicks" (Herhausen et al., 2015). Consumers ask for omnichannel experiences, and the fashion brands must create as many touchpoints as possible between their brand and the consumers. In this omnichannel direction, even the luxury players have started to stand out. Tommy Hilfiger has introduced smart mirrors in its dressing rooms, as mirrors equipped with RFID (radio frequency identification) sensors that recognize the clothes brought into the dressing room and are equipped with a touchscreen that allows personalized navigation within the shop (Pantano & Dennis, 2019). Moreover, to launch a new sneaker in an attempt to reach the target of Millennials, Lacoste has commissioned Engine Creative to produce a global augmented reality communication campaign, developing an application that combines the 3D scanning of products with virtual reality, and it is used in–store (Scholz & Smith, 2016): consumers can see what the model would look like on their foot without having to try it. It is no longer a matter of choosing between the physical experience of the store and the dematerialized experience of e–commerce because technological development will help more and more to reproduce the conviviality of shopping.

METHODOLOGY

The aim of study was to highlight how omnichannel activities are perceived in general and in the different context of luxury and fast fashion, through an exploratory research design, based on a quali–quantitative approach. Using both qualitative and quantitative data give the research a more comprehensive angle, and this could be used to answer if both the perception in the mind of the consumer has altered but also why luxury fashion brands have inclined towards the fast fashion model with its associated consequences. We created an electronic semi–structured questionnaire through SurveyMonkey and collect data through the online platform of Amazons' Mechanical Turk, which is widely used in academic studies for its ease of access, speed of data collection and reasonable costs (Aguinies et al., 2020). Data were collected through an online questionnaire and answers were classified into different categories based on the way consumers perceived omnichannel, and then the differences between the luxury fashion and fast–fashion brands. As a part of our exploratory research design we used in–depth qualitative analysis, investigating perceptions of the new sales environment. The insights are then analysed following the abductive research logic (Blaikie, 2009) and the guidelines of the grounded analysis (Easterby–Smith et al., 2008).

The questionnaire was divided into three main sections. In the first one, we briefly provide a definition of omnichannel shopping experiences, then proposing a 2–minute video as a marketing stimulus to watch, in which a consumer was shopping in a store, driven by new digital tools and technologies (smartphones, beacons, mirrors, augmented reality, and in general self–service technologies). The second section featured some items to investigate their knowledge about omnichannel experiences and their shopping habits. Then, we asked through open–ended questions, their perception about omnichannel shopping experiences in general, and then to imagine it integrated both in luxury and fast fashion brand stores. The final section collected socio–demographic data related to gender, employment, age, education level, and marital status.

RESULTS AND DISCUSSION

We received a total of 135 questionnaires. The sample includes 70 (52%) men and 65 (48%) women. The age of the respondents ranged between 20 and 67 years (M= 34.93; SD= 8.88).The sample consists of 74 (55.05%) of those with a university degree, and 36 (26.6%) higher (Ph.D.), while the remaining 25 (18.35%) of the sample is made up of those with a lower academic qualification. Considering the sample, 11,10% usually do shopping every–day and 38.55%, 2–3 times per week. Only the 6.55% declared to rarely do shopping. The remaining 43.12% declared to do shopping less then every week (specifically, 29.05% declared to do shopping 2–3 times per month, and 14.07%, once per month). Moreover, we asked for the preferred retail channels mainly used in their shopping experiences. Interestingly, a greater use of online digital channels such in brands' websites and e–commerce sections emerged (38,55%), and multi–brand e–commerce platforms such as Amazon, Asos, Net–a–Porter (35.50%), reaching a total of 74.05% respondents. Otherwise, only the 21,45% still prefer retailers' store and traditional physical channel. We also asked for consumers' intention to use of traditional catalogue channels, demonstrating how it is now considered as obsolete (no respondent choice this channel). Finally, only the 4.4% generally use mobile app for smartphone to do shopping (such as Wish). Considering the proposed new hybrid environment, and the mix between on–line and off–line in the store described in the scenario and in the video–stimulus provided, most of the respondents had already heard and knew the meaning of omnichannel (71.23%). Otherwise, only a fifth did not know about it (27.95%). The qualitative analysis has shed light on three relevant topics: increased perceived shopping experiences; fast–fashion brand "luxurization"; and – not surprisingly – shopping privacy concern. Interestingly, considering the current historical moment we are living, results also shed light on omnichannel experiences in shopping experiences, perceived as a way to react to social distancing policies introduced after the COVID–19 pandemic. We report the most important content to justify the insights found, as shown in the Tab. 1 below.

Table 1. Main insights from the qualitative study

Omnichannel experience for luxury and fast–fashion brands	
Increased perceived shopping experience	Omnichannel is perceived as a way to enrich consumers' interactions, through a synergic, integrated and hybrid management of all channels available to retailers to interact with consumers and is aimed at offering them a seamless shopping experience.
Fast–fashion brands' "luxurization"	Omnichannel–oriented initiatives may represent a threat for a luxury company because they may help fast fashion brands to imitate luxury brands and to be perceived as luxurious.
Shopping privacy concern	Consumers are concerned about how the data generated and gathered by their interactions during their whole shopping experience can be exploited.
COVID-19 related opportunities to sustain consumption	Omnichannel strategies could be implemented both from luxury and fast-fashion brands, by considering their technical characteristic compliant with the social-distancing policies imposed by the diffusion of the COVID-19, and because consumers could perceive such strategies as useful to maintain their shopping consumption habits.

Increased Perceived Shopping Experience

When asked about their knowledge of the increasing influence of omnichannel strategies in the shopping environment (both in luxury and fast fashion) the interviewees were quite unanimous in their response that in the actual economic situation, omnichannel strategies is a growing entity shopping environment, in emphasizing their experiences. The general opinion of the interviewees on how the fast fashion and luxury brands have started to internalize omnichannel strategies, agreed on the theme that this has improved significantly in recent years, simplifying their shopping activities, thus increasing their experiences (Demirkan & Spohrer, 2014).

"The experience seems great, having everything connected makes it simple and easy" (F, 28).

Most of the interviewees confirmed that the transformation of the shopping environment by integrating more digital components should have been more typical of luxury brands, considering that their purpose is to offer a totalizing experience to the consumer. Interestingly, respondents underline that omnichannel shopping initiatives are consistent with the role that time have in luxury. Indeed, time is important in luxury not only for the companies that must create high quality and artisanal products, which require time, but also for the consumers. Indeed, luxury consumers typically need time to find the right luxury

Omnichannel Shopping Experiences for Fast Fashion and Luxury Brands

item and to enjoy it or luxury services, thus most of luxury purchasers usually have time to spend in shopping. Importantly, the role of time seems to make omnichannel strategies more in line with the luxury business because luxury consumers seem to be more willing, than consumers of fast fashion, to spend their time in activities that require time, such as those related to omnichannel activities. Such insight is, for instance, underline by the following statement:

"I think it makes way more sense for luxury brands than it does for fast fashion since people willing to spend money on luxury products tend to also be willing to spend their time" (F, 25).

Indeed, during the shopping experience, consumers can be influenced by five situational variables (Belk, 1975; Spence et al., 2014), such as the physical setting (physical and spatial aspects of the environment), the social setting (the people with whom it interacts), the temporal perspective (the availability of time to complete the purchase and consumption processes), the definition of the task (the reasons that induce the need to purchase), and finally the antecedent states of the consumer (physiological states or temporary and the moods that characterize the consumer). Considering the physical environment as the set of physical and spatial aspects of the environment in which the consumer activities take place, the atmosphere of the store, the structure, the materials, the layout, the technological elements, they contribute as purely sensorial stimuli to modify the behaviour of the consumer, acting both on the level of knowledge and on his mood (Kotler, 1973). Therefore, there is a strong link between the perception of the atmosphere of the store, of which today, the omnichannel interactive technologies are an integrant part, and consumers' behaviour: consumers are led to spend more money, and stay longer in the stores rather how much they planned, when in a stimulating shopping environment that arouses involvement and awareness feelings (Donovan & Rossiter, 1982). Indeed, considering the luxury characteristics (Phau & Prendergast, 2000), the introduction of deeper omnichannel shopping experiences in the physical stores, is mainly expected in luxury brands':

"I imagine the luxury brands will be the first to bring this experience live" (M, 47).

The expectations of the interviewees for the future development of the omnichannel in fast–fashion and luxury, in general, were optimistic. All the interviewees expressed the confidence that the presence of fast fashion brands will increase, together with its success, however observing how the propensity to digital is a factor not to be overlooked. As the consumer grows to interact and make new digital technologies his own (such as in digital natives), the experience they benefit from will be maximized (Brown, 2011; Lissitsa & Kol, 2016), including shopping as well.

"The thinking is that as customer become more technological savvy. An omnichannel retail strategy improves the customer experience and provides more channels for customer purchase, whether it is on mobile, web, or in stores" (M, 25).

In summary, the respondents were generally positive towards the omnichannel in the shopping experience and said that their opinions on the fast fashion and luxury brands have changed thanks to the perceived role of digital in the sales environment, strengthening awareness and consumer perception, and the value of both brands.

"I think that omnichannel is a good step forward in having a seamless combination of online and in–person retail" (M, 20).

Specifically, when suitably integrated with a correct balance between technology and physical presence, the omnichannel is perceived as the best possible strategy. This intuition is consistent with Rigby (2011) which defines the omnichannel strategy as a focal point for retailers and Verhoef et al., (2015), which emphasized the synergic, integrated and hybrid management of all available channels in order to interact with consumers, offering them an uninterrupted and frictionless shopping experience along the entire shopping journey.

Fast Fashion Brand Luxurization

Today's fashion clients are highly involved in the consumption process, they know about brands trends, products – the Internet and social media offers them an unlimited source of information. Evans (2017) and Tungate (2005) argued that the days when consumers were loyal to brands are long gone. Among other strategies, fast fashion brands have tried to enter into new seasonal co–branding collaboration with different designers and celebrities in order to impress their target group of consumers. This results in special and limited collections that generate buzz in a distinctive way. The very first collaborations started in 2004 between H&M and the iconic Chanel designer Karl Lagerfeld, followed by other luxury brands such as Stella McCartney (2005), Viktor & Rolf (2006), the Italian brand Roberto Cavalli (2007), and the Japanese fashion house Comme des Garçons (2008).

When asked about their feelings towards co–branding collaboration with fast fashion brands, the interviewees were in general positive arguing that the fashion industry has been affected by co–branding activities in more than one way. Combining every–day garments with the exclusivity of high–end designer items will result in the development of "mass–exclusivity", "massluxe" or "masstige" collaborations (Tungate, 2005). Mass brands are changing people's views about variety and speed at which this variety changes and that consequently trendy items can be purchased at lower prices. Interestingly, considering the expected price in the fast–fashion environment and the massifications to the digitalization and the wide range of proposed products and information's, online accessible, digitalization strategies such as omnichannel shopping experiences has been recognized as a way to promote discount. To illustrate, a respondent argued that:

"I imagine the experience would be more prominent in fast fashion as there would be more information about discounts, and so on" (F, 30).

Interestingly, while certain strategies such as co–branding have brought luxury brands closer to those of fast fashion, in order not to be expelled from the markets, digital strategies showed an inverse trend.

Specifically, an enrichment of shopping environments with technological stimuli is expected more in the luxury brands' as shown below:

"I imagine the technology would be more personally tailored for a luxury brand than a fast fashion brand" (F, 24).

Omnichannel Shopping Experiences for Fast Fashion and Luxury Brands

However, this strategy would also be welcome in fast–fashion, and indeed it is perceived by the final consumer as a way of increasing the value of fast–fashion products, of enriching the shopping experience, therefore aimed at a fast–fashion brand "luxurization", due to the increase in the whole experiences rather than the simple products desired.

"I think the omnichannel experience is a way for fast fashion to feel more luxurious. But the items themselves are not luxurious. There is still a difference between the quality of the item versus the quality of the experience" (F, 27).

Thus, omnichannel strategies seem to activate a sort of "luxurization", showing an inverse trend of fashion strategies such as the co–branding one, who allowed luxury brands to exploit the typically of the fast fashion brands. Nevertheless, this statement requires some considerations: while from a fast fashion perspective this could be recognized as an opportunity, from a luxury brand perspective, this represent a threat, when fashion brands are perceived luxurious as luxury brands.

Shopping Privacy Concern

As in any environment pervaded by new technologies, the management of personal data, and the privacy concern are ever present and relevant variables. Consumers are concerned about how the data generated by their interactions can be exploited. In a hyper–technological context characterized by the maximum integration between offline and online channels such as the omnichannel one (Verhoef et al., 2015) the problem is amplified. The personalization of marketing messages, purchase suggestions, online interactions in the offline environment is highly sought after by consumers, who however are still afraid of how the data from which marketers draw to provide them with solutions consistent with their expectations, are manged. The combination of online and offline retailer channels during a customer journey, incorporating digital devices in retail stores, allows retailers to better observe customer behaviour, collect customer data, analyse their needs and provide personalized services. Indeed, some respondents declared:

"It makes me feel like my data may be exposed too much, however, I can see it being useful for people who shop often" (F, 28)

Such personalization can provide additional value for customers but can also lead to privacy issues. Indeed, the literature has shown that personalized services cause higher privacy concerns than non–personalized services and that one of the factors that can decrease the intention to adopt digital services has decreased in scenarios with personalized services, both online and offline (Shi et al., 2020) Furthermore, further studies (Wetzlinger et al., 2017 have shown how the intention to adopt personalized services is generally lower in retail stores (with digital elements of the sale omnichannel retail), when compared to the online store. These insights are also confirmed in our research.

COVID-19 Related Opportunities to Sustain Consumptions

The results of our research have highlighted results consistent with the historical period in which this study was conducted. Given the policies of social distancing imposed to limit the spread of COVID–19 contagion (Lewnard & Lo, 2020), omnichannel shopping strategies have been recognized as a solution to ensure almost unchanged shopping experiences. The Coronavirus emergency is showing that business strategies must be rethought by focusing on a complete use of digital technology through e–commerce, mobile apps, automation, augmented reality, communication via social networks (McKinsey, 2020).

"I think it is interesting and is a good thing especially during this COVID–19 pandemic. It can offer different options as to how people shop" (F, 50)

"The omnichannel experience is something I would find interest in during this pandemic as I like to have many options available" (F, 29)

As in the statements above, the pandemic, forcing individuals to social distancing, has thus led to a change in the perception of the usefulness of technology and also of the habits of the world population: despite the privacy concern, integrating technologies has been recognized a right way to maintain and assure similar lifestyle habits compared to the pre–pandemic world.

CONCLUSION

Omnichannel strategies have become increasingly important in determining the strategies of global luxury and fast fashion brands. From our contribution emerges the relevance for brands to adapt their strategies to the new idea of conceiving the entire consumers' experience (Verhoef et al., 2015), in an integrated and coherent manner, through all the touchpoints involved. As highlighted in this chapter, technology firstly acted as an enabling element for the adoption of new marketing strategies, leading to multichannel and physical and digital coexistence according to two parallel and separate paths, then evolving towards omnichannel, whose the real innovative aspect is the shifting of the focus on the consumers' renewed needs, and on the value offered to them throughout the shopping experiences, and the hybrid co–existence of the channels. Omnichannel is both an opportunity and complex challenge for luxury and fast fashion marketers today, in reinforcing situational variables in consumers shopping experience (Belk, 1975; Spence et al., 2014): this radical change in the planning of online and offline activities implies the adoption of a mentality oriented to guarantee a seamless and coherent experience for the customer, definitively overcoming the barriers between the physical world and digital world. Undoubtedly, an omnichannel business represents an opportunity for retailers to leverage the synergies offered by each channel, by synchronizing their interactions with those of consumers, through multiple touchpoints: however, omnichannel is not a certainty, but a continuous challenge. This can be truthful valid for companies operating in fashion retailing who are obliged to undertake managerial innovation and digital transformation paths in order to promptly seize trends and opportunities with new business models, adapting to market expectations. This new shopping environment based on the combination of online and offline purchases (Verhoef et al., 2015) can be positively perceived by consumers, increasing the overall level of awareness of both luxury and fashion brands; more specifically by reinforcing the luxury brands' presence in consumers' minds and by activating a sort of brand "luxurization" for fast fashion brands.

With regard to limitations, we acknowledge that a weakness of this chapter could be represented by the small number of collected answers that could reduce the scalability of the findings to a wider population, even if fitting with a qualitative research approach. Thus, future research could improve the sample of consumers to be involved. Moreover, future studies may involve projective tasks, fairy tales and collages (Belk et al., 2012). Summarizing, our findings emphasize that omnichannel–oriented initiatives may represent an opportunity for luxury companies because they may increase the perceived luxuriousness of luxury brands, despite, omnichannel–oriented initiatives may represent a threat for them, because they may help fast fashion brands to imitate luxury brands, and to be perceived as luxurious.

REFERENCES

Achille, A. (2017). *Digital Luxury Experience 2017*. Altagamma–McKinsey Online Observatory.

Aguinis, H., Villamor, I., & Ramani, R. S. (2020). MTurk Research: Review and Recommendations. *Journal of Management*. Advance online publication. doi:10.1177/0149206320969787

Ahuja, V. (2014). Louis Vuitton: Using Digital Presence for Brand Repositioning and CRM. In Handbook of Research on Effective Marketing in Contemporary Globalism (pp. 315–324). IGI Global.

Aiolfi, S., & Sabbadin, E. (2019). Fashion and New Luxury Digital Disruption: The New Challenges of Fashion between Omnichannel and Traditional Retailing. *International Journal of Business and Management, 14*(8), 41. doi:10.5539/ijbm.v14n8p41

Amatulli, C., & Guido, G. (2011). Determinants of Purchasing Intention for Fashion Luxury Goods in the Italian Market: A Laddering Approach. *Journal of Fashion Marketing and Management, 1*(15), 123–136. doi:10.1108/13612021111112386

Amatulli, C., & Guido, G. (2012). Externalised vs. internalised consumption of luxury goods: Propositions and implications for luxury retail marketing. *International Review of Retail, Distribution and Consumer Research, 22*(2), 189–207. doi:10.1080/09593969.2011.652647

Amatulli, C., Guido, G., & Caputo, T. (2011). Strategic Analysis through the General Electric/McKinsey Matrix: An Application to the Italian Fashion Industry. *International Journal of Business and Management, 5*(6), 61–75. doi:10.5539/ijbm.v6n5p61

Amatulli, C., Mileti, A., Speciale, V., & Guido, G. (2016). The Relationship between Fast Fashion and Luxury Brands: An Exploratory Study in the UK Market. In *Global marketing strategies for the promotion of luxury goods* (pp. 244–265). IGI Global. doi:10.4018/978-1-4666-9958-8.ch011

Armani. (2015). *40 Years of Armani*. Retrieved June 15, 2015, from http://atribute.armani.com/it/atribute–to–history/

Atwal, G., & Williams, A. (2017). Luxury brand marketing–the experience is everything! In *Advances in luxury brand management* (pp. 43–57). Palgrave Macmillan. doi:10.1007/978-3-319-51127-6_3

Barlow, A. K., Siddiqui, N. Q., & Mannion, M. (2004). Developments in information and communication technologies for retail marketing channels. *International Journal of Retail & Distribution Management, 32*(3), 157–163. doi:10.1108/09590550410524948

Barnes, L., & Lea–Greenwood, G. (2010). Fast fashion in the retail store environment. *International Journal of Retail & Distribution Management, 10*(38), 760–772. doi:10.1108/09590551011076533

Batat, W. (2019). *Experiential Marketing: Consumer Behavior, Customer Experience and The 7Es.* Routledge. doi:10.4324/9781315232201

Belk, R. W. (1975). Situational variables and consumer behavior. *The Journal of Consumer Research, 2*(3), 157–164. doi:10.1086/208627

Belk, R. W., Ger, G., & Askegaard, S. (2003). The fire of desire: A multisited inquiry into consumer passion. *The Journal of Consumer Research, 30*(3), 326–351. doi:10.1086/378613

Bhardwaj, V., & Fairhurst, A. (2010). Fast fashion: Response to changes in the fashion industry. *International Review of Retail, Distribution and Consumer Research, 1*(20), 5–173. doi:10.1080/09593960903498300

Bjørn–Andersen, N., & Hansen, R. (2011). The adoption of Web 2.0 by luxury fashion brands. *Proceedings of CONFIRM, 34.*

Brooks, A. (2015). *Clothing Poverty: The Hidden World of Fast Fashion and Second–hand Clothes.* Zed Books Ltd. doi:10.5040/9781350219243

Brown, T. (2011). Are you a digital native or a digital immigrant? Being client centred in the digital era. *British Journal of Occupational Therapy, 74*(7), 313–314. doi:10.4276/030802211X13099513660992

Brownlie, D., Hewer, P., & Stewart, R. (2013, July). Keeping fashionable company: ASOS and the collective logic of online spaces. *Academy of Marketing Conference 2013.*

Brun, A., Castelli, C. M., Kluge, P. N., & Fassnacht, M. (2015). Selling luxury goods online: Effects of online accessibility and price display. *International Journal of Retail & Distribution Management, 43*(10-11), 1065–1082.

Business of Fashion. (2011). BoF Exclusive: Getting The Luxury Fashion Business Model Right. *The Business of Fashion.* Retrieved September 15, 2013, from http://www.businessoffashion.com/2011/01/bof–exclusive–getting–the–luxury–fashion–business–model–right.html

Chaffey, D., Hemphill, T., & Edmundson–Bird, D. (2019). *Digital business and e–commerce management.* Pearson.

Chaffey, D., & Smith, P. R. (2017). *Digital marketing excellence: planning, optimizing and integrating online marketing.* Taylor & Francis. doi:10.4324/9781315640341

Corbellini, E., & Saviolo, S. (2009). *Managing Fashion and Luxury Companies.* Etas.

Demirkan, H., & Spohrer, J. (2014). Developing a framework to improve virtual shopping in digital malls with intelligent self–service systems. *Journal of Retailing and Consumer Services, 21*(5), 860–868. doi:10.1016/j.jretconser.2014.02.012

Dholakia, R. R., & Uusitalo, O. (2002). Switching to electronic stores: Consumer characteristics and the perception of shopping benefits. *International Journal of Retail & Distribution Management, 30*(10), 459–469. doi:10.1108/09590550210445335

Donovan, R. J., Rossiter, J. R., Marcoolyn, G., & Nesdale, A. (1994). Store atmosphere and purchasing behavior. *Journal of Retailing, 70*(3), 283–294. doi:10.1016/0022-4359(94)90037-X

Eastman, J. K., & Eastman, K. L. (2011). Perceptions of status consumption and the economy. *Journal of Business & Economics Research*, *9*(7), 9–20. doi:10.19030/jber.v9i7.4677

Ertekin, Z. O., & Atik, D. (2015). Sustainable Markets: Motivating Factors, Barriers, and Remedies for Mobilization of Slow Fashion. *Journal of Macromarketing*, *35*(1), 53–69. doi:10.1177/0276146714535932

Evans, N. J., Phua, J., Lim, J., & Jun, H. (2017). Disclosing Instagram influencer advertising: The effects of disclosure language on advertising recognition, attitudes, and behavioral intent. *Journal of Interactive Advertising*, *17*(2), 138–149. doi:10.1080/15252019.2017.1366885

Feitelberg, R. (2010). Mix and match. Sportswear houses are playing the versatility card. *Women's Wear Daily*, *2*, 10.

Fionda, A. M., & Moore, C. M. (2009). The anatomy of the luxury fashion brand. *Journal of Brand Management*, *5*(16), 347–363. doi:10.1057/bm.2008.45

Frasquet, M., & Miquel, M. J. (2017). Do channel integration efforts pay–off in terms of online and offline customer loyalty? *International Journal of Retail & Distribution Management*, *45*(7/8), 859–873. doi:10.1108/IJRDM-10-2016-0175

Gabrielli, V., Baghi, I., & Codeluppi, V. (2013). Consumption practices of fast fashion products. *Journal of Fashion Marketing and Management*, *17*(2), 206–224. doi:10.1108/JFMM-10-2011-0076

Griffioen, A. (2011). *Creating Profit Through Alliances: How collaborative business models can contribute to competitive advantage.* Retrieved October 10, 2013, from http://www.allianceexperts.com/images/documents/creating–profit–through–alliances–sq.pdf

Guido, G., Amatulli, C., Peluso, A. M., De Matteis, C., Piper, L., & Pino, G. (2020). Measuring internalized versus externalized luxury consumption motivations and consumers' segmentation. *Italian Journal of Marketing*, 1–23.

Heine, K., & Berghaus, B. (2014). Luxury goes digital: How to tackle the digital luxury brand–consumer touchpoints. *Journal of Global Fashion Marketing*, *5*(3), 223–234. doi:10.1080/20932685.2014.907606

Hemphill, C. S., & Suk, J. (2009). The Law, Culture, and Economics of Fashion. *Stanford Law Review*, 61.

Hennigs, N., Wiedmann, K. P., & Klarmann, C. (2012). Luxury brands in the digital age–exclusivity versus ubiquity. *Marketing Review St. Gallen*, *29*(1), 30–35. doi:10.100711621-012-0108-7

Herhausen, D., Binder, J., Schoegel, M., & Herrmann, A. (2015). Integrating bricks with clicks: Retailer–level and channel–level outcomes of online–offline channel integration. *Journal of Retailing*, *91*(2), 309–325. doi:10.1016/j.jretai.2014.12.009

Hoffmann, J., & Coste–Manière, I. (2012). *Luxury Strategy in Action.* Palgrave Macmillan. doi:10.1057/9780230361546

Holbrook, M. B., & Anand, P. (1990). Effects of tempo and situational arousal on the listener's perceptual and affective responses to music. *Psychology of Music*, *18*(2), 150–162. doi:10.1177/0305735690182004

Interbrand. (2020). *Best Global Brands 2019.* Retrieved at: https://www.interbrand.com/best–brands/

Joy, A., Sherry, J. F. Jr, Venkatesh, A., Wang, J., & Chan, R. (2012). Fast Fashion, Sustainability, and the Ethical Appeal of Luxury Brands. *Fashion Theory*, *3*(16), 273–296. doi:10.2752/17517411 2X13340749707123

Joy, A., Wang, J. J., Chan, T. S., Sherry, J. F. Jr, & Cui, G. (2014). M (Art) worlds: Consumer perceptions of how luxury brand stores become art institutions. *Journal of Retailing*, *90*(3), 347–364. doi:10.1016/j. jretai.2014.01.002

Kalakota, R., & Whinston, A. B. (1997). *Electronic commerce: a manager's guide*. Addison–Wesley Professional.

Kapferer, J. N., & Bastien, V. (2009). The specificity of luxury management: Turning marketing upside down. *Journal of Brand Management*, *16*(5-6), 311–322. doi:10.1057/bm.2008.51

Kastanakis, M., & Balabanis, G. (2012). Between the mass and the class: Antecedents of the "bandwagon" luxury consumption behavior. *Journal of Business Research*, *65*(10), 1399–1407. doi:10.1016/j. jbusres.2011.10.005

Kaur, G. (2011). Traditional Commerce Vs. E–Commerce. *International Research Journal of Management Science and Technology*, *2*(3), 334–340.

Kent, A., Vianello, M., Cano, M. B., & Helberger, E. (2016). Omnichannel fashion retail and channel integration: The case of department stores. In *Handbook of research on global fashion management and merchandising* (pp. 398–419). IGI Global. doi:10.4018/978-1-5225-0110-7.ch016

Kim, J. E., Lloyd, S., & Cervellon, M. C. (2016). Narrative–transportation storylines in luxury brand advertising: Motivating consumer engagement. *Journal of Business Research*, *69*(1), 304–313. doi:10.1016/j. jbusres.2015.08.002

Kotler, P. (1973). Atmospherics as a marketing tool. *Journal of Retailing*, *49*(4), 48–64.

Kozlova, O. A., Sukhostav, E. V., Anashkina, N. A., Tkachenko, O. N., & Shatskaya, E. (2017, December). Consumer model transformation in the digital economy era. In *Perspectives on the use of New Information and Communication Technology (ICT) in the Modern Economy* (pp. 279–287). Springer.

Lawry, C. A., & Choi, L. (2013). The Omnichannel luxury retail experience: Building mobile trust and technology acceptance of quick response (QR) codes. *Marketing ZFP*, *35*(2), 144–154. doi:10.15358/0344-1369_2013_2_144

Lewnard, J. A., & Lo, N. C. (2020). Scientific and ethical basis for social–distancing interventions against COVID–19. *The Lancet Infectious Diseases*.

Lissitsa, S., & Kol, O. (2016). Generation X vs. Generation Y–A decade of online shopping. *Journal of Retailing and Consumer Services*, *31*, 304–312. doi:10.1016/j.jretconser.2016.04.015

Lou, C., & Yuan, S. (2019). Influencer marketing: How message value and credibility affect consumer trust of branded content on social media. *Journal of Interactive Advertising*, *19*(1), 58–73. doi:10.108 0/15252019.2018.1533501

Lynch, S., & Barnes, L. (2020). Omnichannel fashion retailing: Examining the customer decision–making journey. *Journal of Fashion Marketing and Management, 24*(3), 471–493. doi:10.1108/JFMM-09-2019-0192

McKinsey. (2020), *It's time to rewire the fashion system: State of Fashion coronavirus update.* McKinsey and Company. https://www.mckinsey.com/industries/retail/our–insights/its–time–to–rewire–the–fashion–system–state–of–fashion–coronavirus–update

Megehee, C. M., & Spake, D. F. (2012). Consumer enactments of archetypes using luxury brands. *Journal of Business Research, 65*(10), 1434–1442. doi:10.1016/j.jbusres.2011.10.009

Miller, K. (2013). Hedonic customer responses to fast fashion and replicas. *Journal of Fashion Marketing and Management, 2*(17), 160–174. doi:10.1108/JFMM-10-2011-0072

Mosca, F., & Civera, C. (2017). *Digital channels and social media management in luxury markets.* Routledge. doi:10.4324/9780203702048

Mosquera, A., Olarte–Pascual, C., Ayensa, E. J., & Murillo, Y. S. (2018). The role of technology in an omnichannel physical store. *Spanish Journal of Marketing–ESIC.*

Novak, T. P., & MacEvoy, B. (1990). On comparing alternative segmentation schemes: The list of values (LOV) and values and life styles (VALS). *The Journal of Consumer Research, 17*(1), 105–109. doi:10.1086/208541

Okonkwo, U. (2007). *Luxury Fashion Branding: Trends, Tactics, Techniques.* Palgrave Macmillan. doi:10.1057/9780230590885

Okonkwo, U. (2009). Sustaining the luxury brand on the Internet. *Journal of Brand Management, 16*(5–6), 302–310. doi:10.1057/bm.2009.2

Okonkwo, U. (2010). *Luxury online: Styles, systems, strategies.* Springer. doi:10.1057/9780230248335

Ozuem, W., & Azemi, Y. (Eds.). (2017). *Digital Marketing Strategies for Fashion and Luxury Brands.* IGI Global.

Pantano, E., & Dennis, C. (2019). The Case of Tommy Hilfiger. In *Smart Retailing* (pp. 91–97). Palgrave Pivot. doi:10.1007/978-3-030-12608-7_8

Parrott, G. R., Danbury, A. H., & Kanthavanich, P. (2015). Online behavior of luxury fashion brand advocates. *Journal of Fashion Marketing and Management, 19*(4), 360–383. doi:10.1108/JFMM-09-2014-0069

Payne, E. M., Peltier, J. W., & Barger, V. A. (2017). Omni–channel marketing, integrated marketing communications and consumer engagement. *Journal of Research in Interactive Marketing.*

Phau, I., & Prendergast, G. (2000). Consuming luxury brands: The relevance of the Rarity Principle. *Journal of Brand Management, 2*(8), 122–138. doi:10.1057/palgrave.bm.2540013

Remy, N., Catena, M., & Durand–Servoingt, B. (2015). *Digital inside: Get wired for the ultimate luxury experience.* McKinsey & Company.

Rigby, D. (2011). The future of shopping. *Harvard Business Review*, *89*(12), 65–76.

Rios, A. E. (2016). The impact of the digital revolution in the development of market and communication strategies for the luxury sector (fashion luxury). *Central European Business Review*, *5*(2), 17–36. doi:10.18267/j.cebr.149

Rollet, M., Hoffmann, J., Coste–Manière, I., & Panchout, K. (2013). The concept of creative collaboration applied to the fashion industry. *Journal of Global Fashion Marketing*, *1*(4), 57–66. doi:10.1080/2 0932685.2012.753337

Rosenblum, P. (2015). Fast Fashion Has Completely Disrupted Apparel Retail. *Forbes*. Retrieved June 30, 2015, from http://www.forbes.com/sites/paularosenblum/2015/05/21/fast–fashion–has–completely–disrupted–apparel–retail/

Schiffman, L. G., Hansen, H., & Kanuk, L. L. (2008). *Consumer Behaviour: A European Outlook*. Prentice Hall FT.

Scholz, J., & Smith, A. N. (2016). Augmented reality: Designing immersive experiences that maximize consumer engagement. *Business Horizons*, *59*(2), 149–161. doi:10.1016/j.bushor.2015.10.003

Schüller, S., Dietrich, D., & Spielmann, L. (2018). The Future Role of Physical Touchpoints in Luxury Retailing. *Marketing Review St. Gallen*, *35*(6).

Sestino, A., Amatulli, C., Peluso, A. M., & Guido, G. (2020b). *New technologies in luxury consumption experiences: The role of individual differences*. Conference Italian Society of Marketing, LIUC University of Castellanza. Retrieved at: https://www.researchgate.net/publication/344994033_New_technologies_in_luxury_consumption_experiences_The_role_of_individual_differences

Sestino, A., Prete, M. I., Piper, L., & Guido, G. (2020a). Internet of Things and Big Data as enablers for business digitalization strategies. *Technovation*, *98*, 102173. doi:10.1016/j.technovation.2020.102173

Shi, S., Wang, Y., Chen, X., & Zhang, Q. (2020). Conceptualization of omnichannel customer experience and its impact on shopping intention: A mixed–method approach. *International Journal of Information Management*, *50*, 325–336. doi:10.1016/j.ijinfomgt.2019.09.001

Shim, B., Choi, K., & Suh, Y. (2012). CRM strategies for a small–sized online shopping mall based on association rules and sequential patterns. *Expert Systems with Applications*, *39*(9), 7736–7742. doi:10.1016/j.eswa.2012.01.080

Spence, C., Puccinelli, N. M., Grewal, D., & Roggeveen, A. L. (2014). Store atmospherics: A multisensory perspective. *Psychology and Marketing*, *31*(7), 472–488. doi:10.1002/mar.20709

Sreejesh, S. (2012). Consumers' Evaluation of Co–Brand Extensions: The Effects of Concept Congruity on the Evaluation of Co–Branded Products, Analyzing the Moderating Role of Task Involvement. *International Management Review*, *1*(8).

Statista Digital Market Outlook. (2020). *Fashion eCommerce Report 2020*. Stastista. Retrieved at: https://www.statista.com/study/38340/ecommerce–report–fashion

Stein, A., & Ramaseshan, B. (2016). Towards the identification of customer experience touch point elements. *Journal of Retailing and Consumer Services*, *30*, 8–19. doi:10.1016/j.jretconser.2015.12.001

Stephen, A. T. (2016). The role of digital and social media marketing in consumer behavior. *Current Opinion in Psychology*, *10*, 17–21. doi:10.1016/j.copsyc.2015.10.016

Thamm, A., Anke, J., Haugk, S., & Radic, D. (2016, July). Towards the omni–channel: Beacon–based services in retail. In *International Conference on Business Information Systems* (pp. 181–192). Springer. 10.1007/978-3-319-39426-8_15

Toktali, N. (2008). Global Sourcing Insights from the Clothing Industry: The Case of Zara, a Fast Fashion Retailer. *Journal of Economic Geography*, (8), 21–38.

Turban, E., Outland, J., King, D., Lee, J. K., Liang, T. P., & Turban, D. C. (2017). *Electronic commerce 2018: a managerial and social networks perspective*. Springer.

Verhoef, P. C., Kannan, P. K., & Inman, J. J. (2015). From multi–channel retailing to omni–channel retailing: Introduction to the special issue on multi–channel retailing. *Journal of Retailing*, *91*(2), 174–181. doi:10.1016/j.jretai.2015.02.005

Vigneron, F., & Johnson, L. W. (1999). A review and a conceptual framework of prestige–seeking consumer behavior. *Academy of Marketing Science Review*, *1*(1), 1–15.

Vigneron, F., & Johnson, L. W. (2004). Measuring perceptions of brand luxury. *Journal of Brand Management*, *11*(6), 484–506. doi:10.1057/palgrave.bm.2540194

Wetzlinger, W., Auinger, A., Kindermann, H., & Schönberger, W. (2017, July). Acceptance of personalization in omnichannel retailing. In *International Conference on HCI in Business, Government, and Organizations* (pp. 114–129). Springer. 10.1007/978-3-319-58484-3_10

Willems, K., Brengman, M., & Van De Sanden, S. (2017). In–store proximity marketing: Experimenting with digital point–of–sales communication. *International Journal of Retail & Distribution Management*, *45*(7/8), 910–927. doi:10.1108/IJRDM-10-2016-0177

Yeoman, I. (2007). Pricing trends in Europe's fashion industry. *Journal of Revenue and Pricing Management*, *6*(4), 287–290. doi:10.1057/palgrave.rpm.5160099

Chapter 3
Examining the Integration of Virtual and Physical Platforms From Luxury Brand Managers' Perspectives

Paola Peretti
The IULM University, Italy

Valentina Chiaudano
University of Turin, Italy

Mohanbir Sawhney
Kellogg School of Management, Northwestern University, USA

ABSTRACT

"The internet dilemma" was the concept used to describe luxury brand companies' initial reluctance to integrate online technologies into their business model. However, over time, luxury brand companies have understood that moving towards digital transformation is the only way to survive on the market and appeal to the new luxury brand consumers. In a few years, digitalisation has become a priority for all luxury brand companies that started to integrate digital and physical platforms to engage consumers through all touchpoints of their shopping journey. In light of the topic's relevance and considering the primary focus of research on consumers, this chapter aims to deepen the digitalisation phenomenon in the luxury market involving the little-explored luxury brand managers' perspective. The authors conducted a longitudinal study to compare the main changes in integrating digital and physical platforms from the managers' perspective between 2014 and 2020. In this endeavour, they also considered how the COVID-19 pandemic had affected luxury brand companies' digitalisation.

DOI: 10.4018/978-1-7998-5882-9.ch003

Examining the Integration of Virtual and Physical Platforms From Luxury Brand Managers' Perspectives

1. INTRODUCTION

During the last two decades, the Internet revolution has changed the way of doing business. The new digital technologies like artificial intelligence, virtual reality (VR), sharing economy, IoT, and social commerce app have empowered consumers from a market target to become companies' innovation partners (BCG, 2020; Reinartz et al., 2019; Solis, 2013).

Among this interconnected ecosystem, we concentrate our attention on the virtual relationship platforms (online and mobile) that act as a powerful tool to engage customers towards their shopping journey. The main strength of virtual relationship platforms is their ability to switch from the top-down relationship to a bottom-up one, where customers play a leading role. Moreover, according to Bolton et al., 2018, digital platforms with physical ones (stores) enhance customer experience and improve employee performance.

Even if academic studies and reports confirmed the positive effects of virtual relationship platforms on marketing strategies, luxury brand companies long remained sceptics about the opportunities provided by the integration between physical and digital tools. Most companies have chosen to support the traditional point of view for which new technologies could represent just a limited part of the customer journey experience. Particularly, deeper integration between virtual and digital platforms was perceived as an off chance for different reasons. In general, the main concerns were related to the evident incompatibility between digital technologies and the nature of luxury brands (Dall'Olmo Riley & Lacroix, 2003). On the one hand, Internet-based technologies promoted free access and a low level of physical contact.

On the other hand, luxury brands companies aimed to preserve their status of exclusivity and rarity. Physical contact is another controversial variable since it is an essential trait of the luxury brand experience that digitalisation strongly affected (Chevalier & Mazzalovo, 2012). Finally, from an internal point of view, the integration between virtual and physical tools generated a resistance due to the expected efforts in reallocating resources and improving traditional know-how of luxury brand managers with the new digital skills.

However, over time luxury brand companies have understood that moving towards digital transformation was necessary. Furthermore, luxury brand consumers who demanded more tailored and interactive experiences require integrating new digital tools into luxury brand marketing strategies.

Reports from the most relevant consultancy agencies pointed out how luxury brand companies have ridden the digital wave in recent times, and the pandemic was one of the leading accelerators (BCG, 2019; Deloitte, 2019). Digital transformation has become a priority in the luxury industry. So, in a few years, luxury brand companies have moved from a digital embryonic stage to deeper integration between digital and physical platforms. Today, the integration of digital technologies such as Artificial Intelligence (AI), Big Data and e-commerce with the physical channel (stores) to support luxury brand companies in redesigning customer engagement through data analytics is the priority for all luxury brand companies (BCG, 2019; Deloitte, 2019).

Currently, we can find some articles on the topic of digitalisation in the luxury market. However, most of them are mainly focused on the impact of new digital technologies on the enhanced experience from the consumers' perspective. These studies deal with how consumers perceive the integration between digital and physical platforms towards their shopping journey and how that integration impacted brand equity, loyalty, willingness to pay, or buy (Guercini et al., 2020; Taube & Warnaby, 2017).

In light of the relevance of the topic and considering the primary focus on consumers, we aim to deepen the digitalisation phenomenon in the luxury market involving the little-explored perspective of luxury brand managers. We conduct a longitudinal study to compare the main changes from the managers' perspective and the new way luxury brand managers create value for their consumers.

Also, we looked at the current drivers that accelerate the digital transformation of luxury brand companies due to Covid-19 (McKinsey, 2019).

2. BACKGROUND

2.1 When Luxury Meets Digital

Not long after the advent of the Internet, most mass-market companies have mastered digital technologies. On the contrary, for several years, luxury brand companies remained sceptics about the digitalization questioning the opportunity to develop an online presence and how to digitize without diluting the brand image. The common questions among academics and practitioners were: "How can luxury companies maintain their ability to sell a dream while having an online presence? How can the luxury companies protect the brand image in the long run?". The literature offered several reasons to support the incompatibility between luxury and Web 2.0. Some authors agreed that the core attributes of luxury like exclusivity, premium price, prestige, scarcity appeared undoubtedly in contrast with the principles of the Web 2.0 whose main goal was being accessible to everyone (Chevalier & Mazzalovo, 2012; Okonkwo, 2010). Other authors explain how, in the online environment, the lack of physical interaction and the absence of multi-sensory experiences represent barriers to digitalization (Arrigo, 2018). Furthermore, most luxury companies were concerned with the variety and complexity of managing digital channels.

However, digitalization has quickly become an inevitable choice for luxury brand companies. "Digitalize or Die: the choice of luxury brands" was the title of a brilliant report published by BGC in September 2016. It clearly explained that embracing digital technologies was the only option for luxury brand companies to remain on the market and appeal to new luxury consumers (Abtan et al., 2016), that has become a real driver for digitalization. Over time, luxury consumers expected more than buying luxury products online. They asked to engage with superior online experiences on social media and multiple channels to actively interact with brands (Kapferer, 2014). Luxury brand consumers were ready for omnichannel interactions and requested a digital experience seamlessly integrated across all touchpoints of the customer journey (Kim, 2019; Passavanti et al., 2020). In addition to creating showcase sites and sales channels, luxury brand companies worked harder to design new business models that integrate digital and physical tools (Mosca & Chiaudano, 2020) and embrace customer-centricity as the dominant principle. In recent times, most luxury companies have demonstrated the ability to engage consumers with immersive "phygital" experiences that refer to hybrid experiences that merge both the digital and physical world (Batat, 2019; Belghiti et al., 2018, Magnelli et al., 2020).

Designing and offering a "phygital" approach is not an easy task for luxury brand managers whose efforts have become more than implementing marketing campaigns to sustain the brand image. At this digitalization stage, luxury brand managers need to offer consumers something extraordinary, creating tailored and personalized experiences that engage consumers in all touchpoints of the customer journey across digital and physical channels (Cailleux et al., 2009). The relationship platforms assist luxury brand companies in this effort. As the relationship platforms map the customer journey and manage the interactions with consumers, they allow luxury brand companies to understand the level of brand awareness, engagement and loyalty and effectively build the long-term relationship with consumers.

2.2 Physical and Virtual Relationship Platforms in the Luxury Market

Traditionally, stores are the leading platforms through which consumers experience the brands, places where products can be distributed and sold and, at the same times, where companies can create a superior customer experience. After being solely sales and distribution hubs, stores have become marketing tools used to influence the brand image and guarantee a unique experience to consumers engaged with sensory and emotional stimuli (Magnelli et al., 2020). They act as "relationship platforms" where it is possible to represent the brand and manage interactions with consumers. The relational function of stores is particularly relevant in the luxury brand market where endogenous factors, subconscious, and instinct strongly influence luxury brand consumers' decision-making process (Magnelli et al., 2020; Mosca & Civera, 2017)

In the era of Web 2.0, with the spreading of e-commerce platforms and digital technologies, luxury brand companies need to create relationships with consumers in a new context (Kim & Ko, 2010). Consumers are more informed and requested to be engaged with personalised and multisensory experiences that involve physical channels and digital ones. So, luxury brand companies are asked to develop omnichannel experiences that offer seamless experiences, whether online from a desktop and mobile device or offline in a physical store (Baker et al., 2018).

The introduction of the virtual relationship platforms to enforce the physical ones (stores) give luxury brand companies the opportunity to effectively build and manage consumers' interactions (Loureiro et al., 2018). The main strength of virtual relationship platforms is their ability to switch from the top-down relationship to a bottom-up one, where customers play a leading role (Okonkwo, 2009). These new marketing tools can communicate and engage with various consumers who are heterogeneous and much more aware and informed before the purchase. Moreover, since the virtual platforms can capture critical information generated in each customer journey touchpoint, they allow luxury brand companies to meet the consumer's expectations and capture customer attention, creating a higher level of relations.

In recent times when the pandemic has accelerated the digitalisation of luxury brand companies, the adoption of virtual relationship platforms and their integration with the physical ones has become a leitmotiv for all companies (Klaus & Manthiou, 2020; The State of Fashion, 2021). Once again, this scenario will require another effort from luxury brand managers. With the beginning of the pandemic era, luxury companies needed quickly to identify the right formula of integration between physical and digital platforms to have a high level of consumer engagement and advocacy, but, at the same time, to protect the unique dimension of a luxury brand (D'Arpizio et al., 2020).

Luxury brand managers are requested to rethink the supply chain, inventory, and delivery systems to become more effective in satisfying consumers' needs (Roggeveen & Sethuraman, 2020). Flexibility, agility, and digital presence are necessary to manage a business during an uncertain situation and to maintain consumer interactions.

Some academic contributions and consultancy reports deal with the topic of digitalisation in the luxury market; however, the focus is on how consumers perceive the integration between digital and physical towards their shopping journey and how integrating virtual and physical platforms impacted consumers' experience with luxury brands (Guercini et al., 2020; Taube & Warnaby, 2017). On the contrary, no more literature is focused on the phenomenon of digitalisation in the luxury market from the managers' perspective. Our chapter aims to understand the motivation for digital integration, how the integration has evolved and how the ongoing pandemic has accelerated the process of digitalisation in the luxury brand marketing explaining the phenomenon from managers' point of view. The main research questions that arise concerning the analysis are as follows:

- **Motivation:** What reasons have led to the need to combine traditional and virtual platforms according to the managers' point of view?
- **Progression and Resources:** How has the progression of integration been? What share of the marketing budget is dedicated to offline vs online?
- **Evolution and Covid 19:** What is the direction of evolution? How has Covid-19 impacted on digitalisation?

3. METHODOLOGY: SAMPLE, MEASURES AND ANALYSIS

Authors conduct a longitudinal study to compare the main changes from the managers' perspective and the new way luxury brand managers create consumers' value after the pandemic. As this is a longitudinal study, the same group received the questionnaire twice: luxury brand managers with a time lag separating the different information-gathering methods. The differences between lagged data are the raw data used for elaboration, without aggregating them. In this way, our study provides academics and practitioners an overview of the things that have changed (Ricciardi & Rossignoli, 2016).

Data collection for this article began in 2014 and ended in 2020. Personal invitation to answer the questionnaire is a sole source of primary information to update the database.

Authors collected the data from two consistent samples of Italian luxury brand managers.

The first survey delivered in 2014 aimed to collect data about managers' initial perceptions regarding the possible integration of digital technologies with the physical ones. The sample consists of 35 Italian marketing managers, who work in the luxury industry from different companies. The respondents received via e-mail the semi-structured questionnaire and authors promised them anonymity.

Authors repeated the data gathering twice in 2020 to identify the evolution in managing digital platforms and future trends. In this case, the database includes 26 respondents that were promised anonymity by the authors.

The study was divided into three areas to carry out the analysis, which corresponded to integrating the digital platforms with the physical ones: early-stage, maturity, and future development. For each of these areas, researchers carry out the analysis by using various techniques to measure and represent the results.

The data collected are of an ordered qualitative nature. Fundamental descriptive statistical analysis is the statistical technique used to analyse the data collected.

4. RESULTS

As previously mentioned, this chapter aims to investigate how the integration of virtual and physical platforms has evolved and how the ongoing pandemic has accelerated the digitalisation of luxury brand companies.

In the next paragraphs, we showed study 1 focused on the early stage of integration of virtual and physical platforms and then the study 2 whose aim is to examine the maturity stage and the future development of integration.

Figure 1. Structure for analysis of luxury managers' surveys
Source: Authors' personal elaboration (2020)

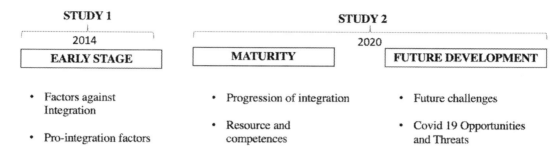

Specific assumptions were developed on the basis of the analysis of literature and the objective of this empirical investigation is to analyse them in detail trying to understand what is happening, particularly concerning Italian luxury brand managers.

4.1. Study 1: The Early Stage of Integration

As emerged by our study, in 2014, integration of virtual platforms was still at an early stage. We can assess that 54.3% of luxury brand managers confirm that technologies are evolving enabling luxury brands to get closer to their consumers. "The corporate website is the best virtual platform to convey the brand's image, and social networks are places where we can build a different experience, still unique but more personal", asserted one interviewed marketing manager.

Therefore, in confirmation of the route taken, it can be shown how the managers moved from the Internet to social platforms trying to follow a path that may remain consistent with the touchpoints used off-line (points of sale and the use of traditional means of communication). However, we are still in a phase where the need of testing new marketing methods is highlighted (Strongly Agree, 46.7% in terms of promotion, and integrated with 4P, Strongly Agree 37.1%).

Concerning the effectiveness of traditional communication methods, 44% of the managers interviewed agreed (Strongly Agree/Agree) that are not effective anymore.

Going even more in detail in the following paragraphs, we discover the main factors favoring and against digitalization. In fact, there are still many doubts about digital and its fit with the luxury market at this stage.

4.1.1 Factors Against the Integration

We identified some factors that hinder the natural integration of offline and online relationship platforms. The analysis initially reveals the need to review the allocation of resources towards virtual relationship platforms not to lose effectiveness.

Another factor that acts as a deterrent for virtual platforms is the unique dimension of luxury brands (Strongly Agree 53.8%, Agree 37.5%). In particular, a situation emerges: there is a desire to find a tricky balance between a "top-down" approach to communication and a "bottom-up" one that starts with a dialogue with consumers. Being consistent is the challenge that appears the most complex (71%), together with the fear of losing control (54.3%). Some examples of quotes taken from the open questions present in this questionnaire, confirm the trend described above:

- "Reach the compromise between the democratization imposed by social networks and the exclusivity of the brand".
- "Find the right marketing mix between virtual and physical and how to find in both channels the most appropriate tone of voice".
- "Luxury brands should be online, but they don't believe in social commerce especially within certain platforms (e.g., Facebook) because it is a must for us to maintain our heritage, exclusivity, quality and personality".

The need to acquire new skills is clearly understood, together with a review of marketing processes and the implications that this may have from an organization point of view (82%). Also, luxury managers need to understand how virtual platforms may help brands to grow. An exciting piece of information concerns that 62% of them declare that there are luxury brands that, thanks to a strategic and integrated use of virtual relationship platforms, have acquired a competitive advantage. They cite Burberry, Tiffany, Gucci and Coach.

4.1.2 Pro-Integration Factors

Grouping together various items in the questionnaire, we also identified the four macro factors that may facilitate integrating physical and virtual relationship platforms: technological evolution, new marketing tools, new consumers' behaviour and the crisis of traditional media.

4.1.2.1 Technological Evolution (e.g., e-Commerce, Social Media, etc.)

Technological evolution is crucial, and it is seen as a way to integrate luxury brand experience:

- "Technology will evolve quickly, and all luxury brands will have to adapt and be present, in a rigorous way, to keep meeting expectations and the "social" needs of a digitally mature audience".
- "Virtual platforms, like Facebook, maybe one day, will also become transaction channels. But by definition, it would be important for us to guarantee our presence but for now they remain a mass type platform, not suitable for selling our luxury brands where exclusivity is everything".
- "Unless it becomes highly customizable, I do not think that possible forms of e-shop, on mobile, for example, will ever be important for luxury brands unless we can integrate them with our shops".

Technological evolution is an element that has triggered the requirements to adapt the choice of relationship platforms through which consumers can be reached, not without some resistance. It is precisely the new technologies that have brought luxury brands closer to their consumers, encouraging marketers to use them, although with great caution and fear. The limits that seem to prevail, in using virtual relationship platforms, are the ones that, on the one hand, protect the dimensions of the luxury brands and, on the other hand, support the marketers' requirement to control the experience.

4.1.2.2 New Marketing Tools

"Find the right balance between "do-not-interact" with the audience, just releasing institutional messages and real engagement with them."

According to managers of luxury brands, the second factor that has led to virtual relationship platforms alongside physical ones is the desire to test and use new tools from a marketing point of view. "Surely, Facebook is currently the most crucial virtual platform: it is the most used and widely spread. However, we are trying different forms of marketing tools within the digital space like online media, video channels and social networks like Facebook and Twitter". Sentences, as the above mentioned, reveal that the leading virtual platform used in the early stage of integrations are:

- *Social Networks:* Facebook proves to be the most transverse (87.9% (29), Total cases: 33) followed by other social networks such as Twitter and Pinterest (76.5% (26), Total points: 34). To these, managers add video delivering platforms like YouTube. This kind of medium act for directing specific communication campaigns (61.8% (21), Total cases: 34).
- *Online and offline integration:* in particular they are an example of the involvement of influencers (e.g., bloggers) within events at points of sale (73.5% (25), Total cases: 34), and the insertion of digital devices (e.g., iPads, touch screens) within flagship stores (55.9% (19), Total cases: 34) to improve and enrich the customer experience.
- *E-commerce:* a significant piece of information is the launch of an e-commerce site dedicated to a luxury brand (64.7% (22) – Total cases: 34).
- *Online Media:* the placing of offline media alongside online Media is already occurring, in fact, 47.1% (16) state that they have planned paid-for visibility activities on virtual relationship platforms (e.g., sponsored links on Facebook and Google).
- *Mobile:* this platform is at the embryonic stage in terms of growth. Mobile activities in terms of marketing were used last year, in 26.5% (9) of cases.

In confirmation of this trend in which the virtual space is growing and transforming, it has emerged that managing virtual platforms request companies to place new professional profiles entirely dedicated to virtual platforms (67.7% (23), Total cases: 34). Also, 57.6% of interviewees declared that they systematically carry out analyses dedicated to online reputation and sentiment.

4.1.2.3 New Consumers' Behaviour

"For some luxury goods, even Facebook may become an important transactional platform for purchases not exceeding € 2,000/3,000."

It emerges from the study that luxury brand consumers have changed their behavior following technological innovation. They have expectations targeted about using technology that is leading them towards a natural online and offline convergence. Although initially, within the experience of consumption of luxury brands, relationship platforms could have a crucial role in generating awareness during the discovery and involvement phase, now the inclination towards online purchase and via mobile seems to be increasing.

51% of the interviewees maintained that relationship platforms influence purchases made by luxury consumers. In comparison, 17% do not know (a sign that further studies in this area still have no clear evidence). Therefore, 31% who disagree are clearly in the minority.

It is also interesting to note that managers essentially consider luxury consumers, particularly loyal ones, ready to purchase both online and offline without any problem. Other relevant aspects that emerged from the survey are the following ones:

- The awareness and discovery stages are essentially online;
- Luxury consumers seem to be more interested in niche brands than in the past; they are open to online purchasing. They want to interact with designers and find out more about the business that produces the brand in question.

4.1.2.4 Crisis of Traditional Media

Traditional communication methods are in crisis, and they do not help to sell as in the past (51.4%), and indeed, the evolution of the Internet has made communication complex (47.1%). Therefore, the perception is that consumers' attention towards offline media has diminished, for 17% quite a lot and a lot for 54%.

Figure 2. Pro-integration factors and factor against the integration
Source: Authors' personal elaboration (2020)

Factors against integration	Pro-integration factors
• Allocations of resources • New skills • Unique dimension of luxury brands • Find the right marketing mix	• Technological evolution • New marketing tools • New consumers' behaviour • Crisis of traditional media

4.2. Study 2: Maturity and Future Development

The second study aims to explore the maturity stage of integration between digital and physical platforms to answer the following questions: "How has the progression of integration been? What share of the marketing budget is dedicated to offline vs online?".

With this study conducted in 2020, the authors confirmed that luxury brands managers are now more confident with technological innovation. At this stage, digitalisation has become more than replicating online the offline experience. All respondents expressed that digital technology has empowered luxury companies through new tools that better consumer expectations. Among digital platforms, the evolution of social media is an opportunity for luxury brands to create further promotional actions to integrate with the traditional ones (85%). Also, e-commerce plays a leading role in luxury brand strategy, and it will undoubtedly grow in the next future (73%) also pushed by Covid 19 consequences.

4.2.1 Progression of Integration, Resources and Competencies

In recent times, luxury brand consumers have increasingly invest on their branded websites (69.23%) with an increasing focus on offering omnichannel services (e.g. buy online and pick up in store, etc).

These conditions have pushed luxury brand companies to consider virtual platforms as a must to have if they do not want to lose their relationship with consumers. However, given the complexity of the luxury organization, managers have approached virtual platforms cautiously and consistently (53% Strongly agree; 34% Agree) to manage the integration with all 4Ps. Caution and accuracy have led luxury brand companies to succeed: the use of virtual platforms allows luxury companies to reach a global target of consumers (72% Strongly agree; 31% Agree) and create a space where consumers can share opinions and interact with brands (61% Strongly agree; 34% Agree).

The main activities implemented in the last twelve months have involved four main initiatives:

- Online payment platforms like Google Adwords; Facebook or Instagram Ads (77%)
- Digital devices in the points of sale to enhance the shopping experience (65%)
- Engagement of influencers (bloggers, fans, communities) for events or to sponsorize online the brand (88%)
- Video channel campaigns (88%)

Differently from the first stage of digitalisation when the budget dedicated to the online activities accounted for less than 30% of the total marketing strategies, in 2020 the percentage of funding dedicated to the online activities has grown. As observed by Figure 3, 50% of the managers interviewed stated that they invest more money in online activities (between 50% -70% of the budget). These funds also include the placement of new professionals to understand better how the Internet can help them grow and meet consumers expectations. In fact, 96% of respondents have declared that the luxury company they work for has employed new professionals to manage digital marketing and social media activities.

Figure 3. Percentage of the budget dedicated to online activities
Personal elaboration (2020)

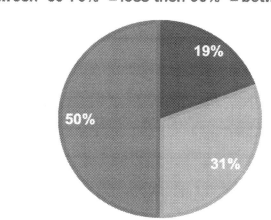

However, in spite of an increasing amount of funds for online activities, a fully integrated budget allocation between digital and offline activities has not yet been shared among luxury brands. Figure 4 shows that the investments in communication through digital represent a new budget item for the company and are not integrated with the one dedicated to traditional media. Only 27% of the sample declared that the account for conventional marketing tools and the digital ones are totally integrated. For another 73% of the sample, a budget dedicated to online activities is separated from the offline activities. This fact means that despite the maturity stage of integration, luxury brand companies cannot create an integrated budgeting allocation for managing digital and physical activities together.

Figure 4. Integration between digital and traditional communication tools
Personal elaboration (2020)

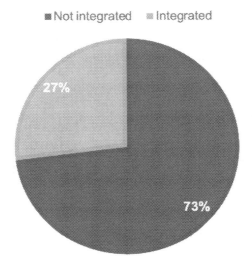

Considering the role of physical platforms, 53% of managers agree that conventional media are in crisis because luxury consumers perceive the physical platform as less attractive. However, as it emerged from our study, the main sales point for luxury brands is still the flagship stores (73%) and multi-brand shops. So, despite the spreading of e-commerce, the physical stores will preserve their position as places where products can be distributed and sold.

4.2.2 Future Challenges and Covid 19 Effect on Luxury Industry

Finally, what are the challenges that luxury brand managers have to face and in particular what is their overall attitude towards digital integration?

According to luxury brand managers, in the next future luxury brand companies will cope with the following challenges:

- The maintenance of a premium image by ensuring that it is coherent online and offline.
- The effective protection of the luxury brand against counterfeiting products which are increasingly common online.
- The need to create integrated marketing programs that involve online and offline channels to enhance the quality of products and services and offer unique shopping experiences to consumers.

The last point is particularly complex for luxury brand companies. We ask the luxury manager the most difficult aspect for those who have to deal with the marketing of a luxury brand today. Quality of experience across all channels and identifying a customer journey that meets expectations in terms of experiences and needs have emerged as the main struggling points for those who operate in the luxury brand market nowadays.

Concerning the next future, the effects of Covid 19 play a crucial role. The current study demonstrated that not all managers know about the market resilience of the luxury brand after the pandemic crisis. If someone agreed that the luxury brand market would be more crisis-proof, others instead believe that the luxury industry would not be exempt from a struggling situation (mean= 3,4). Unlike the previous crisis affecting the luxury market (2002–03 SARS outbreak, 2008–09 global financial crisis), the current turmoil impacted the real economy with job losses, GDP decline, and store closure due to the lockdown measures. The consequences are lost sales and less return for luxury brand companies.

However, the pandemic positively impacts the luxury industry if we consider the digitization process. All managers interviewed agreed that the pandemic is an accelerator factor for digital transformation (mean= 3,8) and online purchases of luxury brands (mean=3,7). The booming of the second-hand market is another potential effect of Covid 19 that luxury brand managers agree with (mean= 3,4).

Despite Covid 19, luxury is not perceived as less critical by luxury brand consumers (mean= 2,07), and luxury brand companies will not cut their budget in PR and communication.

Table 1. The Long-Term Effects of Covid-19

Long term effect of COVID 19	Means (1- 4)	Variance
Second-hand market booming	3,384615385	0,406153846
Budget cutting in PR and communication	2,461538462	0,498461538
A consolidation of the luxury sector	2,615384615	0,406153846
Acceleration of the digitization process	3,769230769	0,177514793
Acceleration of online purchase	3,730769231	0,273668639
Less about seasonal trends and more about timeless pieces	3,153846154	0,668639053
Luxury companies with a weak market position will disappear	2,730769231	0,658284024
The luxury industry will also not be exempt from the crisis	3,346153846	0,610946746
Thinking different is the new leitmotiv of luxury brand consumers	3,269230769	0,735207101
Change in purchasing strategies (more traditional)	2,846153846	0,74556213
Luxury is perceived as less important	2,076923077	0,455621302
More human communication/tone of voice	3,115384615	0,563609467
Feeling closer to brands of fans	3,269230769	0,735207101

Personal elaboration (2020)

5. DISCUSSION

This chapter aims to contribute to the luxury market literature concerning the digitalisation of luxury brand companies. Significantly, the chapter deals with the integration between digital and physical platforms from the early stage of integration to the current evolution from the managers' point of view.

As emerged from the beginning, luxury brand managers agree they are in a period of fundamental change that requests a great deal of effort. The study has grouped the factors that lead to digitalisation into four main macro-areas: technological evolution, new marketing tools, new consumers' behaviour, and traditional media crisis. Therefore, both exogenic factors (e.g. new technologies) and endogenic factors (e.g. the need to adopt marketing strategies that require more effective tools) have driven the digitalisation of luxury brands.

However, the study also reveals that digitalization is still generating quite a bit of internal resistance at an early stage. Loss of control and the opening up to direct communication with consumers through virtual platforms is seen as a necessity and not necessarily as an opportunity. In other words, the digitalisation mainly consists of replicating physical experiences, while protecting the luxury brand's dimensions as far as possible, trying to offer content that reinforces brand awareness without going beyond that. The majority of luxury brands consider virtual relationship platforms (in particular social media) a natural extension of physical media, without in any case having a precise role in the construction of a relational marketing strategy with consumers. In building these platforms, the objective is to partially replicate the "offline" experience without considering consumers' behaviour online and the interaction opportunities offered by new technologies.

The second study set in 2020 shows that the situation has changed. Most luxury brand companies have launched many digital initiatives integrating virtual platforms into their business model. Even those more "traditionalist" with an "old fashioned" marketing approach, consider virtual platforms necessary and the most effective tools to interface with consumers. Unlike in the past when the digital channels replicate the "offline experience", now luxury brands are trying to offer consumers the opportunity to interact through all the platforms (both digital and physical) in a very fluid way. Therefore, luxury companies now guarantee omni-channel interactions seamlessly integrated across all touchpoints of the customers' journey.

Finally, advancing digital skills thanks to the introduction of new employees' training and important investment in technology attested luxury brand companies' significant efforts in the digitization process.

Despite the remarkable improvements in integrating the virtual platform into the business model, from this article emerge some areas for improvements:

- **A full integration of budget allocation between digital and offline activities**

Investments in digital activities are not integrated with the one dedicated to traditional channels and in most cases represent a new budget item.

In the next future, the luxury brand managers' effort consists of matching investments decisions and priorities with marketing strategies considering both platforms together (digital and physical) and new processes that involve the use of virtual platforms combined with the physical ones across the entire customer experience.

For this purpose, luxury brand companies will rethink the role and the structure of the marketing function and how it interacts with other functions. Moreover, new parameters for measuring the performance of the digital integrated business model will be defined.

- **Managing customer experience using Big Data**

"More attention to customers' expectations" is a statement from most of the interviewed managers. In response to the needs of consumers, luxury companies need to offer more personalised and one to one experience. The improvement in Big Data management is a crucial activity that concurs to the goal. It consists of the introduction of virtual platforms that track customer experiences in all phases of the shopping journey to gain information essential to develop personalised customer experience.

- **Keeping up omnichannel experiences in stores**

As emerged from the study, flagship stores and, multi-brand shops remain the main sale points for luxury brand consumers. Adopting the latest digital technologies within the stores (mobile marketing, QR Code, App, touch screen, virtual reality, etc.) is essential to maintain a high engagement level with consumers. From the first digitalisation stage to maturity, the number of luxury companies that use technological devices has grown (+41%). However, considering the rapid development of technologies and consumer behaviour, luxury brand companies have always to update to keep up.

- **Learn best practices from the crisis context**

"The pandemic allowed brands to understand the importance of digital in a situation of repeated closure of physical stores and consequently has accelerated the integration process between offline and online that must be as seamless as possible."

"During the closure, we have the opportunity to develop or enhance online platforms to educate boutique sellers about new collections."

"The lockdown give us the opportunity to carry out some experiments with innovative technologies."

Without a doubt, the pandemic has negatively affected sales and growth of luxury brands. However, the crisis context offered luxury brands the opportunity to learn more about the integration of platforms. As the quotes show, some luxury brands have innovated digital technologies or proposed omnichannel ways to buy and preserve the pleasure of shopping while keeping consumers safe during the lockdown.

For example, some luxury brands allowed consumers to make in-store purchases directly from home. How did the process work? Consumers access digital catalogues of store items from Whatsapp or email. Then they are involved in one-to-one relationships with sale representatives and virtual tours that end with the home delivery of the purchased items. The catwalks organised during the pandemic are other examples of how Covid-19 has accelerated the digitalisation process in the luxury market with innovation that will have a long term horizon.

6. RESEARCH LIMITS AND FURTHER RESEARCH DIRECTIONS

This research attempts to analyse the current integration between digital and physical platforms identifying actual and future challenges.

However, the study conducted has the following limitations:

- **Primary focus on the Italian market**

Italy is the primary market for luxury studies in terms of the number of players and market share. According to Deloitte (2020), 20% of high performer players in the Top 100 increases in 2019 are Italian luxury brand companies. Moreover, 12,4% of luxury brand sales depend on Italy's companies (Deloitte; 2020).

Despite the relevance of the Italian market, the primary focus on luxury brand companies located in Italy is partially representative of the global luxury brand market. For this reason, other researchers could extend the study to other relevant markets such as France, Switzerland or the United States that host the most comprehensive number of luxury brand companies.

- **A limited sample of managers**

Our study collected 35 interviews in the first attempt and 26 interviews in the second. Future research could be expanded by widening the sample. Moreover, this study could be extended to retail managers to better understand how traditional points of sales can be integrated with digital platforms in order to enhance the customer experience.

REFERENCES

Abtan, O., Barton, C., Bonelli, F., Gurzki, H., Mei-Pochtler, A., Pianon, N., & Tsusaka, M. (2016). *Digital or Die: The Choice for Luxury Brands*. Retrieved from: https://www.bcg.com/it-it/publications/2016/digital-or-die-choice-luxury-brands

Arrigo, E. (2018). Social media marketing in luxury brands: A systematic literature review and implications for management research. *Management Research Review*, *41*(6), 657–679. doi:10.1108/MRR-04-2017-0134

Baker, J., Ashill, N., Amer, N., & Diab, E. (2018). The internet dilemma: An exploratory study of luxury firms' usage of internet-based technologies. *Journal of Retailing and Consumer Services*, *41*, 37–47. doi:10.1016/j.jretconser.2017.11.007

Batat, W. (2019). *The New Luxury Experience: Creating the Ultimate Customer Experience*. Springer International Publishing. doi:10.1007/978-3-030-01671-5

BCG. (2019). *2019 True-Luxury Global Consumer Insight*. Retrieved from: http://media-publications.bcg.com/france/TrueLuxury%20Global%20Consumer%20Insight%202019%20-%20Plenary%20-%20vMedia.pdf

BCG. (2020). *Transform customer journeys at scale—and transform your business*. Retrieved from: https://image-src.bcg.com/Images/BCG-Transform-Customer-Journeys atScale%E2%80%94and-Transform-Your-Business-Nov-2019_tcm9-233853.pdf

Belghiti, S., Ochs, A., Lemoine, J. F., & Badot, O. (2018). The Phygital Shopping Experience: An Attempt at Conceptualization and Empirical Investigation. In P. Rossi & N. Krey (Eds.), *Marketing Transformation: Marketing Practice in an Ever-Changing World. AMSWMC 2017*. doi:10.1007/978-3-319-68750-6_18

Bolton, R. N., McColl-Kennedy, J. R., Cheung, L., Gallan, A., Orsingher, C., Witell, L., & Zaki, M. (2018). Customer experience challenges: Bringing together digital, physical and social realms. *Journal of Service Management, 29*(5), 776–808. doi:10.1108/JOSM-04-2018-0113

Braccini, A. M., & Spinelli, R. (n.d.). *Empowering Organizations* (Vol. 11). Springer International Publishing. doi:10.1007/978-3-319-23784-8_23

Cailleux, H., Mignot, C., & Kapferer, J.-N. (2009). Is CRM for luxury brands? *Journal of Brand Management, 16*(5–6), 406–412. doi:10.1057/bm.2008.50

D'Arpizio, C., Levato, F., Fenili, S., Colacchio, F., & Prete, F. (2020). *Luxury after Covid-19: Changed for (the) Good?* Bain & Company. Retrieved from: https://www.bain.com/insights/luxury-after-coronavirus/

Dall'Olmo Riley, F., & Lacroix, C. (2003). Luxury branding on the Internet: Lost opportunity or impossibility? *Marketing Intelligence & Planning, 21*(2), 96–104. doi:10.1108/02634500310465407

Deloitte. (2019). *Global Powers of Luxury Goods 2019 Bridging the gap between the old and the new*. Retrieved from: https://www2.deloitte.com/content/dam/Deloitte/ar/Documents/Consumer_and_Industrial_Products/Global-Powers-of-Luxury-Goods-abril-2019.pdf

Guercini, S., Ranfagni, S., & Runfola, A. (2020). E-commerce internationalization for top luxury fashion brands: Some emerging strategic issues. *Journal of Management Development*. ahead-of-print. doi:10.1108/JMD-10-2019-0434

Kapferer, J.-N. (2014). The future of luxury: Challenges and opportunities. *Journal of Brand Management, 21*(9), 716–726. doi:10.1057/bm.2014.32

Kim, A. J., & Ko, E. (2010). Impacts of Luxury Fashion Brand's Social Media Marketing on Customer Relationship and Purchase Intention. *Journal of Global Fashion Marketing, 1*(3), 164–171. doi:10.1080/20932685.2010.10593068

Kim, J.-H. (2019). Imperative challenge for luxury brands: Generation Y consumers' perceptions of luxury fashion brands' e-commerce sites. *International Journal of Retail & Distribution Management, 47*(2), 220–244. doi:10.1108/IJRDM-06-2017-0128

Klaus, P., & Manthiou, A. (2020). Applying the EEE customer mindset in luxury: Reevaluating customer experience research and practice during and after corona. *Journal of Service Management, 31*(6), 1175–1183. doi:10.1108/JOSM-05-2020-0159

Loureiro, S. M. C., Maximiano, M., & Panchapakesan, P. (2018). Engaging fashion consumers in social media: The case of luxury brands. International Journal of Fashion Design. *Technology and Education, 11*(3), 310–321. doi:10.1080/17543266.2018.1431810

Magnelli, A., Pizziol, V., & Manzo, M. (2020). Innovative in-store ICT marketing solutions for an enhanced luxury shopping-experience. *Marche et organisations, 37*(1), 165–183.

McKinsey. (2020). *The luxury industry during—And after—Coronavirus.* Retrieved on 31st July 2020, Retrieved from: https://www.mckinsey.com/industries/retail/our-insights/a-perspective-for-the-luxury-goods-industry-during-and-after-coronavirus

Mosca, F., & Chiaudano, V. (2020). Digital channels and distribution in luxury market. *Marchè et organisations, 37*(1), 147–163.

Mosca, F., & Civera, C. (2017). *Digital Channels and Social Media Management in Luxury Markets.* Routledge. doi:10.4324/9780203702048

Okonkwo, U. (2009). Sustaining the luxury brand on the Internet. *Journal of Brand Management, 16*(5–6), 302–310. doi:10.1057/bm.2009.2

Okonkwo, U. (2010). *Luxury Online: Styles.* Systems, Strategies. doi:10.1057/9780230248335

Passavanti, R., Pantano, E., Priporas, C. V., & Verteramo, S. (2020). The use of new technologies for corporate marketing communication in luxury retailing: Preliminary findings. *Qualitative Market Research, 23*(3), 503–521. doi:10.1108/QMR-11-2017-0144

Reinartz, W., Wiegand, N., & Imschloss, M. (2019). The impact of digital transformation on the retailing value chain. *International Journal of Research in Marketing, 36*(3), 350–366. doi:10.1016/j.ijresmar.2018.12.002

Ricciardi, F., & Rossignoli, C. (2016). Research Methods in the itAIS Community: Building a Classification Framework for Management and Information Systems Studies. In T. Torre, A. M. Braccini, & R. Spinelli (Eds.), Empowering Organizations (vol. 11, pp. 297–315). Springer International Publishing. doi:10.1007/978-3-319-23784-8_23

Roggeveen, A. L., & Sethuraman, R. (2020). How the COVID-19 Pandemic May Change the World of Retailing. *Journal of Retailing, 96*(2), 169–171. doi:10.1016/j.jretai.2020.04.002

Solis, B. (2013). *WTF? What's the Future of Business? Changing the Way Businesses Create Experiences.* John Wiley & Sons.

Taube, J., & Warnaby, G. (2017). How brand interaction in pop-up shops influences consumers' perceptions of luxury fashion retailers. *Journal of Fashion Marketing and Management, 21*(3), 385–399. doi:10.1108/JFMM-08-2016-0074

The State of Fashion. (2021) Retrieved from: https://www.mckinsey.com/~/media/McKinsey/Industries/Retail/Our%20Insights/State%20of%20fashion/2021/The-State-of-Fashion-2021-vF.pdf

KEY TERMS AND DEFINITIONS

Customer Engagement: The concept of customer engagement is related to the customer's behavioural manifestations towards a luxury brand.

Customer-Centricity: Customer centricity means creating the right context to manage customer experience towards the entire shopping journey.

The marketing must take care of it: but the whole organization needs to be reshaped to meet consumers' expectations, intervening on the organization, processes and financial metrics.

Omnichannel Experience: Omnichannel experience removes the limits between different sales and marketing channels to create a unified, integrated experience. The distinctions between digital channel - website, social, mobile, email - and physical one (shop), disappear as a single experience of commerce emerges.

Virtual Relationship Platforms: The virtual relationship platforms (online and mobile) are powerful tools to engage customers in their shopping journey. The main strength of the virtual relationship platforms is their ability to switch from the top-down relationship to a bottom-up one, where customers play a leading role.

Chapter 4
Managing Integrated Brand Communication Strategies in the Online Era:
New Marketing Frontiers for Luxury Goods

Fabrizio Mosca
University of Turin, Italy

Cecilia Casalegno
University of Turin, Italy

Giulia Bonelli
University of Turin, Italy

Chiara Civera
University of Turin, Italy

ABSTRACT

After digitalization, both scholars and practitioners found that luxury companies, which have invested in this transformation, not only have increased their revenues, but have also improved customer satisfaction. Luxury companies have reached a greater number of consumers worldwide, but the communication pillars have been preserved. In the near future, luxury companies will have to deal with the effects of COVID-19. Most likely, some of these changes will be a boost of the online shopping; a return to fewer purchases, of valuable items; and the need of an integrated shopping experience. The aim of the chapter is to show how luxury brands have embraced digital channels without losing their pillars. This chapter also aims to show that luxury companies have successfully invested in customer education and that consumers have adapted their behaviour to new touch points with the brand. Finally, this chapter aims to investigate new approaches to integrate the physical and the digital channels and the implications of COVID-19 on the communication strategies of luxury firms.

DOI: 10.4018/978-1-7998-5882-9.ch004

Copyright © 2021, IGI Global. Copying or distributing in print or electronic forms without written permission of IGI Global is prohibited.

Managing Integrated Brand Communication Strategies in the Online Era

INTRODUCTION

Spaces and environments are places of consumption, but they also provide communication opportunities to the consumer who, in turn, uses consumption as a communication system that is expressed through a variety of languages (Mosca et al., 2013).In the luxury sector, it must be considered that products encompass intangibles values that go beyond their functions and are often the main reason for purchases (Mosca, 2017). Academics and practitioners agree on the multidimensional concept of Luxury (Chandon et al., 2016; H. Kauppinen-Raisanen et al., 2019), that determines different motivations to buy this type of products and, moreover, a variety of interpretations depending on the consumer. Of course, there are certain factors which are known to affect the willingness to buy a luxury product and the purchasing behaviour: people culture, education, financial resources and social status are some examples. On the other hand, luxury goods are able to convey inner and personal expressions. Therefore, the value of the Brand is partly defined by the consumer creative role, who takes the brand meanings and personalizes them (Seo & Buchanan-Oliver, 2017). The result is that both the management and the final consumer participate in communicating the concept of the Brand. This is particularly true for luxury goods which are sold in markets that are difficult to define, but which is possible to find various layers of media attitudes. In fact, it is possible to say that the traditional consideration whereby business serves as the exclusive source of communication massages and brand-related content, design to influence the behaviour of the consumer and create brand equity is overtaken. This is due to the fact that marketing and communication strategies, together with the instruments and actors involved in their planning processes, need to take into account the evolution of technology, the transformation of consumer behaviour and media attitudes, the fact that stakeholders constantly communicate each other and this kind of communication is difficult to manage. The communication works in attracting people interest toward a certain brand, but, at the same time, it works as a shield for the corporate reputation and a springboard for spreading corporate values. It is important to underline that technological evolution has been leading mass media to a decline in their ability to attract people's (audiences') attention. It should be considered that attitudes toward the media have changed, together with the growing interest in new media content generated by people – the so-called user-generated content (UGC) – such as blogging, podcasting, online videos, and social networking. Across all the social media platforms, Instagram and Facebook are the most common in the luxury sector. More than the 80% of members of most the luxury categories have an account on Instagram and on Facebook (Altagamma& Accenture, 2020). In 2019, another interesting social network became widely used among young individuals: TikTok. The majority of luxury brands are still discovering this channel, in fact, less than the 20% are currently present on TikTok, but we already have a practical and successful example: Gucci (Altagamma& Accenture, 2020). It is evident that the digitalization has led to a real change in the luxury industry where companies have finally accepted and leveraged the coexistence of both offline and online channels. In order to respond to the aforementioned trends, organizations are generally dealing with developing a communication plan that can integrate all those tools with which they intended to interface with their stakeholders (Schultz, Tannenbaum &Lauterborn, 1993; Krugman et al., 1994; Duncan &Mulhern, 2004; Belch & Belch, 1998, 2009; Baker et al., 2018; Park et al., 2018; Knowledge@Wharton, 2020; Lee at al., 2020; Ryu, 2020).

The evolution of technology and the change of media employed to communicate with the audience have made it possible for consumers to screen brands' messages. Therefore, it is harder for the Brand to be relevant in the eyes of clients. To be truly relevant, luxury brands have to implement interactive marketing strategies that embrace both proper content and UGC. Thus, consumers are willing to pay attention to messages, to get involved with communication and, then, to share their sentiment towards the Brand through their network. To reach their target audience, the concept of integrated communication becomes inseparable from common value sharing with stakeholders; people are more worried about values and how responsible a given firm is. Of course luxury brands have to invest in communication promoting their products, but in such industry it is equally necessary to discuss inclusion, diversity, sustainability and philanthropic topics. Indeed, an interesting example is the recent campaign of Armani Fragrances, "My Way", that tells about different women stories, coming from different cultures, revealing their backgrounds that turned them into stronger and determined women. Another example of inclusivity in communication, comes from Gucci. The Brand has been pioneering in choosing Ellie Goldstein as one of its model, a young girl with the Down syndrome who can represent all those people that has a dream and to whom the Brand wants to communicate: this dream can come true.

Globalization, the environmental crisis, economic disparities and ultimately the healthcare crisis due to Covid-19 in 2020, represent some of the primary factors that have contributed to the increase in stakeholders' expectations and their awareness towards goods and services. Customers, above all, feel more involved in purchases; they pay attention to the production process, when they can, and they want to be notified about everything concerning the firm through which they are buying products. As a consequence, companies have to rethink their offers, as well as their social and environmental impacts and built a new system of values that responds to the reference community and society at large. In recent years, there has been talking about sustainability awareness introduced by younger luxury consumers and market research has shown that the most environmentally conscious are Generations Z and Millenials (BCG & Fondazione Altagamma, 2019). Furthermore, there is new academic evidence according to which Millenials are not more sensitive to sustainability aspects than older generations when buying a luxury product. It seems that Millenials are willing to react emotionally if the Brand misbehaves, but somehow they believe that luxury and sustainability are contradictory (Kapferer&Michaut-Denizeau, 2020). If mature luxury consumers are now environmentally-friendly, it indicates that sustainability and social responsibility in general have become a wider opportunity in the luxury industry. Hence, luxury brands should include their social and environmental commitment in communication to enhance their expression, but they also should take into consideration that the customer might not pay a premium price for a product only because of its sustainable production process (Diallo et al., 2020).

Turning to the change made in technology, as well as taking into account the micro-environment factors considered above, we discover that stakeholders (from the luxury goods and players' perspectives) are willing to share values and they want to participate in the content generation of every firm's story. They aim to be a part of an exclusive group; this sentiment has been stronger, especially since these individuals have lived in a period of crisis. Moreover, the boundaries of the luxury market have opened to new economies and generations, that are often eager to engage with high symbolic value brands. The so-called "conspicuous consumption" has represented both an opportunity and a threat for companies, which thus has rethought the strategy behind their uniqueness and have defined the so-called "*artificial rarity*" (Kapferer, 2017). The latter can be reached through different marketing actions which engage the luxury consumer, such as crafting stories (Kim et al., 2016; Hughes et al., 2016; Nambiar, 2018; Gurzi et al., 2019), launching limited editions, creating extraordinary and omnichannel experiences (Koivisto&Mattila, 2018; Holmqvist et al., 2019) and combining luxury with the art (Chailan, 2018; Grassi, 2019; De Angelis et al., 2020).In the digital age, their success can come if two conditions are fulfilled: personalized identification and provision of a multi-sensory experience. The response to these conditions has led luxury companies to take to online strategies, without forgetting that the concept of a traditional store always plays a major role in the experience of buying luxury goods.

Since the spread of digital environments has certainly helped to broaden the spectrum of possibilities to managing channels, while offering new areas for competitive confrontation, it is possible to assume that new technologies have contributed in defining a hybrid environment in which, finally, pre-and post-digital revolution habits coexist. The first research question that this chapter seeks to answer is the following: Can we still talk about a certain type of "reverse multichannel marketing"? The aim, indeed, is to present which are the latest evidence of the management of this kind of hybrid distribution and communication channel and how it can be used in the future to reach business and branding goals in luxury market.

Considering the particular sector that the present chapter wishes to analyze, the concept of multichannel marketing has been translated into physical and digital channel integration, with the aim of enhancing consumer and audience engagement. We proved that multichannel marketing is not just a fad, but it represents a new strategy. However, is this strategy intended to last and which new facets are going to arise? This is the other research question that the present chapter seeks to answer, also providing some case analysis. If the multichannel marketing strategies are meant to consolidate, thus they will be affected by the impact of Covid-19 on the luxury market.

Moreover, this chapter wants to emphasize the importance of the concept of consistency, since, in every marketing book, authors say that luxury market players follow different rules than their competitors in terms of consumer goods. Luxury companies have assumed different roles in communication, that is equally important. We talk about communicative coherence and the ability of companies to decline to provide such consistency across all those channels at their disposal to reach their intended audience, considering that, for luxury goods above all, the selling point has always been the first way to communicate the Brand's identity and its real essence. Is this consistency reached even if luxury players are mixing their classical channels with those channels that are always exploited by players in every kind of market?

COMMUNICATION AND DISTRIBUTION INTEGRATION AS A LOGICAL MULTICHANNEL LAST STEP

The real challenges for every company relate to new communication trends on the one hand, and changing buyers' attitudes on the other. Nowadays, one of the most important marketing paradigms refers to the fact that the more consumers perceive that the firm's values are closely aligned with what they think, trust in, and feel, the more they are likely to buy. Once the customer, who has become informed and constantly connected through online channels, find a meaningful brand for oneself then he/she will be willing to decline that Brand on different aspects of his/her lifestyle. Conscious of this mechanism, some fashion luxury brands try to expand their offer in order to reach more consumer through their products and services. For example, in 2019 Gucci decided to enter in the cosmetics market launching a lipstick line and today has expanded its beauty product offering, that is sold both online and offline. In the latter case, the consumer also has the possibility to book – via website – an appointment in-store, was to have a dedicated experience and service. Stakeholders of the luxury companies are more informed and they want to know everything about the organization in which they are involved. This is particularly true in highly symbolic value goods markets. Furthermore, using digital channels to connect with their favourite brands, luxury consumers provide a lot of information and insights to companies which, in turn, can improve their CRM strategies.It is not only the online environment that helps luxury companies to learn more about their clients. Luxury stores still being a fundamental touchpoint where consumers look for a unique multi-sensory experience and extraordinary personalized services to engage with the Brand and play an active role in the brand universe (Kauppinen – Raisanen et al., 2020). According to BCG &Altagamma (2020) one of the main trend in the luxury industry,that will be accelerated by COVID-19 crisis, is the leveraging of data by firms in order to strengthen a seamless relationship with clients both online and offline. The so-called *"clienteling 2.0"* (digital and personalized) will be more appreciated than before from 46% of luxury consumers worldwide, and it will be even more relevant for the 57% of Italian luxury consumers (BCG &Altagamma, 2020).

At the same time, the continuous compression of the product life cycle reinforces new consumption mechanisms that will be focused not only on the possession of the product, but on the sharing on wealth and consumption experiences. Moreover, in recent years, research and managers have found that various consumption forms exist together in luxury markets and have identified two different perspectives behind the consumer motivation in buying a luxury good: the personal and the social ones (Coehlo, Rita & Santos, 2018). A recent implication of the luxury market growth is that luxury products are becoming a medium through which create a social hierarchic (Kapferer, 2017) instead of being an outcome of social stratification. Today the traditional luxury consumer still exist and demand unique heritage brands and products, which can differentiate them from others. This kind of consumer, follow the more traditional buying behaviour (well described in the Conspicuous Consumptions Veblen Model). At the same time, the fragmentation of luxury (Turunen, 2018) gave rise to the consumer of the *"new luxury"*. This type of luxury is not based on exclusivity, rather on the emotion and the lifestyle that it can convey.

The aforementioned findings highlight that a lot of the traditional marketing logic has changed in these last few years. Even if the concept of "multichannel marketing" is not new, here we can find the roots of another trend: the integration of distribution and communication platforms. This is due to the increase in the penetration of digital environments, which feed customers' associations of new activities when compared to the more traditional rituals of consumption. It is a common practice to look information about a product through blogs, social networking pages, and online groups before making a buying decision; people want to understand from other people how good a certain brand is, where to buy a certain product, and how long-lasting the materials or textiles of a certain good are. There is also recent evidence that influencers, especially micro-influencers, which have a strong social presence on social media like Instagram are perceived as a trustworthy source of information when promoting a luxury brand (Venus Jin et al., 2018). As a result, it is possible to observe that the same consumer buys a product by using more than one channel, depending on the product and its availability, price, time, and service (Venkatesan et al., 2007; Klaus, 2020).

When we talk about multichannel marketing, we refer to a strategy concerning the use of more than just one channel for placing information and product/services on the market – even in the aftermarket – and the results is a major public commitment and a higher degree of customer engagement (Rangaswamy& Van Bruggen, 2005). Customers, regardless of the luxury targets, are conscious of their relevant role within the brand communication strategy. Customers, in particular, perceive that they have the chance to interact with brands; they can generate content, and they can ultimately affect the future of a certain brand(Osmonbekov et al., 2009).

Managers can exploit the advantages of stemming from multichannel marketing strategies; they can increase the customer perception of brand equity through concrete actions associated with client retention.A firm that uses multichannel marketing is able to segment and manage the increasing variety

Managing Integrated Brand Communication Strategies in the Online Era

of demand; in this way, it is aided by digital innovation. Market management can be easier, and there is a major opportunity to augment the awareness of a corporate brand (Mosca, 2014). Specifically, there are no geographical barriers when we talk about online strategies and, at the same time, the integration of communication and distribution channels (online and offline) is possible. Moreover, by leveraging the digital environment, it is possible to collect data surrounding consumers habits and fads, both new and uncommon, and this can offer the ability to make a decisive contribution to the acquisition of other geographical markets. Since one of the so-called "lost opportunities" (Kotler et al., 2009) is represented by the impossibility of finding a product in a local market, the online distribution provides companies with a chance to exploit brand communication to sell more products and at a lower cost (Osmonbekov et al, 2009). At the same time, firms can benefit from the results coming from customer relationship management (CRM) when they carefully handle channels.

The arrival of online and social platforms has created another profound change: the upside-down use of communication and distribution strategies. More precisely, when considering the term "social media"– which gained popularity in 2005 – it has been used to describe different types of digital content that have been developed for interactive advertising; this offers audience members the possibility to generate content around a specific brand. Here, we talk about *user-generated contents* (UGC), as argued by Kaplan and Haenlein in 2010, and as more recently investigated by researchers in the luxury sector (Agarwal, 2020; Hasbullah et al., 2020). Consumers become leading actors, and firms can develop measures of engagement and take advantage of word of mouth referrals with a proactive and dynamic approach. This dynamic approach indicates that another trend is becoming important: online selling through mobile channels. Luxury players are moving to mobile and can definitely benefit from this channel, considering that in recent years the time spent by costumers on mobile has rapidly increased and already in 2018 the 98% of luxury customers had a smartphone (McKinsey & Company, 2018). Given that authors have previously talked about the integration of channels, we must now point out that the instruments have traditionally been used for distribution, they are now being used and designed to achieve the objectives of establishing competence, which has previously been assigned to communication functions. Vice versa, web and mobile, designed to spread the communication at the beginning, are now becoming the main distribution channels.

Considering what was described above, managers have to approach new strategies through the understanding of how customers use different platforms, after having analyzed them through a new demand segmentation model, as represented in Table 1. This table provides an output of previous researches(Mosca *et al.,* 2013, 2014). The considered dimensions (empathy, expression, and enhancement, which originated from the study of people's attitudes toward online and offline media) are valid for every kind of market, but the interesting thing is that they are also valid for luxury goods (in mature markets). By matching these dimensions with new customer/audience attitudes toward media, it is possible to outline new profiles. Table 1 illustrates a scheme that can be helpful when determining the best method through which to integrate distribution and communication channels; it provides a complete overview of customer behaviours. It is possible to highlight three types of profiles: the *Traditionalist*, the *Multimedia lover* and the *Eager about social media*. Every profile presents, as it is possible to see in the table, a different tendency in using the web and the other screens and a specific reason driving his/her interaction with brands.

The research questions that were posited in the present chapter now have their first answers. We are talking about the definition of a strategy that concerns the integrated use of communication and distribution channels, which is the answer that players are giving to markets changes. We are not talking about

Table 1. Online users' profiles (mature markets) (Mosca et al., 2013)

	Traditionalist	Multimedia Lover	Eager about Social Media
	He/she lives the brand communication primarily through its above the line (ATL) media effectiveness. He/she prefers printed paper and specialized magazines as tools through which to enjoy communication and to find information on product sand luxury brands.	The ATL advertisement triggers a mechanism that sees this individual interacting with the Brand and its products through the use of multiple screens. He/she spontaneously remember integrated communication campaigns, becoming–in some cases–means of communication him/herself by sharing content(institutional or not) such as videos, photos, and articles.	Actively contributes to the promotion of messages and information, often becoming an active user not only in the process of diffusion, but also in the process of content creation through the use of comments, links to external sites, or providing additional information through blogs, etc. These individuals are major users of exclusive content made available by companies.
Empathy	✓	✓	✓
Expression	✗	✓	✓
Enhancement	✗	✗	✓

a "fad" or a quick trend; rather, we are talking about a strategy that gains the confidence of the target audience. This phenomenon had its birth in 1994, and it has become viral in recent years, thanks to the increased sales in mobile devices. The first example of such "reverse multichannel marketing" comes from the mass market. In fact, it is possible to analyze a particular case study: Made.com. In early2015, the UK furniture selling Web site opened its fourth showroom in Soho. The aim of this strategy was to enable people to have hands-on experiences. As is already known, the biggest bug in online selling revolves around the impossibility of trying or touching goods prior to purchase. Made.com can avoid this problem by offering physical places in which nothing is for sale, but where people can test a product, see its real colours, view textiles, and assess their dimensions. As such, we are talking about a space that is not a shop – no cash is exchanged on the way out; rather, this space offers a sort of physical complement to the online purchasing experience. The outfit features 1:1 goods projections to show how possible combinations can be realized when requested by customers. Visitors are equipped with tablet to gather information on specific products. They can also project their place's spaces, create wish lists, and buy desired products. This case illustrates how some important elements are fundamental when effectively integrating distribution and communication channels:

- People are encouraged to constantly use screens; they want to optimize the free time they have through screen technology;
- People are willing to make purchases, but only when they know the materials, textiles, and dimension of the goods they want to try;
- Since technology can help managers in this way, the interaction between communication and distribution channels can bring about positive results, but it is possible to sell only when people perceive that a certain degree of consistency exists among the various channels used;
- A customer may decide to make an online purchase via a physical point of sale if the technology experienced in the physical place can lend value to the purchase itself;
- The audience and possible customers never "go to sleep"; this refers to the idea that the Web and the marketing strategy must consider that this platform does not have geographical barriers;

Managing Integrated Brand Communication Strategies in the Online Era

- The integration of virtual and physical channels has been reinvented with upside-down logic: the online channel is not additional or an accessory to the physical one; rather, both channels are part of the same process. The physical place is the communication channel and the online space is the selling one.

The above case shows that the spread of digital environments has helped broaden the spectrum of channel possibilities, and this can serve as a new area of competition. If we think that technology and its new horizons have redefined something, it is possible to refer to this as a hybrid exchange environment in which managers can study the coexistence of well-established and growing habits. To give a more recent example of how luxury companies can benefit from the channels integration, we can refer to the department store GaleriesLaFayette. During the lockdown due to COVID19, that strongly affected France, LaFayetteimplemented a remote but personalized live shopping experience. Using an online video platform, customers could stay at home and shop like they were in store thanks to the personalized shopping experience recreated online, given by consultants and personals shoppers (BCG &Altagamma, 2020). Moreover, the increasing synchrony between distribution and communication channels can enhance the reassurance felt by customers and, as a consequence, it can further bolster client loyalty (Berger, 2006; Yazdanian et al., 2019). When a firm is able to surround its target market, the result will be engagement and long-range profit.

ONLINE AND OFFLINE INTEGRATION ENHANCEMENT: HOW LUXURY FIRMS EXPLOIT THE CONCEPT OF MULTICHANNEL MARKETING

The luxury market's competitive landscape in recent years has been changing, primarily due to the rise in user-generated content. Firms have to revise their strategies to implement a "hold" concept: multichannel marketing is increasing in importance, as international media trends are operated by an ever-more demanding and informed audience.

International research initiatives have probed into the situation that luxury firms are facing a high degree of success: a phenomenon that is known as the "digital challenge". These firms try to integrate both online and offline communication tools and, as a result, they recourse to a plurality of channels that are used to sell, but that is also primarily implemented to tell a story, to enhance the perception of product quality. This is interesting if we think that brands like Burberry, Chanel, Bottega Veneta, Gucci, and Ferrari are using the same channels (digital ones) that mass-market firms are using. However, digital channels are a necessity even for luxury goods, since the most frequently used exchange platforms are currently online. Again, is this just a passing trend or a real competitive strategy? The integration of different platforms in contemporary times revolves around the Web. The age of 2.0 has led the luxury goods players, as will be discussed below, to adopt the same strategies and tactics taken by the actors in mass markets; this has been a revolution, especially if you think that traditional marketing has always considered luxury and mass markets as two competitive environments with totally different mixed marketing strategies. Yet, the Web is able to bridge these two worlds without upsetting them and without having the various players fail their promise of consistency. Data relating to social media serve as examples of what was said earlier: in the middle of 2013, social media was compared (Mosca et al., 2013) between a number of brands (like Chanel) and more famous brands to the consumer (such as Benetton). It turned out that the number of likes and shares for the luxury fashion player was twice that of those in the mass market. This finding is as relevant as ever, as it indicates the short amount of time it took for brands like Chanel to develop their own social presence online. Considering the necessity of using digital platforms to reach and engage people as a standpoint, it is useful to underline that digital channels are a way better method through which to interact with the audience. Consequently, digital platforms take on a double connotation: a digital channel is a tool through which to inform and persuade individuals, like other older media; at the same time, it represents a way through which to sell a product, using both physical and virtual contact modes. According to this idea, it is possible to say that the benefits coming from online and offline integration strategies interest both luxury firms, as well as their audience members. First of all, the public's attention can be easily captured through the interactions caused by the nature of Web 2.0; this pertains to UGC, which was previously discussed, and its power to enhance people's engagement. Moreover, pushing the simultaneous use of different screens – which is called "interactive multimedia" (Casalegno, Li, 2012) – provides luxury firms with some advantages, including the following: long-lasting customer loyalty, especially since the audience is surrounded by a certain message from the firm; the pulse of customer's experience as the result of the interaction; sales increase given that the more a customer has confidence in a brand, the more he or she is going to buy it; and employee retention, since the first customer of a firm is the employee him/herself. On the other side, even customers can benefit from a multichannel strategy; they can customize the product they want by providing feedback to firms, they save time when comparing products and during the purchase process, they feel involved in the exchange process, and they can receive the product in a shorter amount of time through online purchasing. According to this perspective, even the development of a digital channel for luxury players has to consider integration with the traditional distribution channel; it is not to be viewed as a standalone distribution channel, but as one that complements the physical channel, as will be argued below, and as various examples in the text can show. Traditional and physical stores always play a major role in the experience of buying luxury goods, but the huge success of the digital channel turns it into an inescapable variable for players in the market for highly symbolic value goods. Nowadays, a Web strategy is essential for a luxury brand (Mosca et al., 2013, 2014). In order to provide a clearer idea of how powerful the method of selling online is becoming, one must consider the Luxury Goods Worldwide Market Study (Fall–Winter 2019). The results of this research project – developed by Bain & Company for Fondazione Altagamma – show that considering the overall luxury market, which value is estimated at €1.3 trillion globally, the online sales of luxury product account for 12% of the market (in 2019) growing at 22% exchange rate. In 2019, globally 75% of luxury goods transaction were influenced by the online channel, with the 20% to 25% of purchases made possible thanks to the digital (Bain & Company, 2019). This shows that Web channels today can no longer be regarded as virtual spaces in which consumers hunt for bargain purchases. Luxury customers are involved in services and the breadth of offering, as they are when they buy products in a physical place. Another important finding is that the online will keep growing and that the old ROPO[1] the model will progressively fade. According to the research True-Luxury Global Consumer Insights 7th Edition – developed by Altagamma and BCG – in the past 50% of True-Luxury consumers started their journey searching products and inspirational contents online; meanwhile the 80% of True-Luxury consumers carried out their purchases in-store (of which 39% had previously researched the product online). In the future, the luxury consumer expects to find online the same offline intimate relationship with the Brand and the online penetration is expected to grow up to 20% of luxury sales in 2022 (Altagamma and BCG, 2020). Especially in this particular competitive environment, consumers are looking for a deep and intimate relationship with brands that emphasize recognition, respect, dialogue, and collaboration with their costumers (Mosca et al., 2013).

Managing Integrated Brand Communication Strategies in the Online Era

On the other hand, costumes tend to reject those brands that do not regard their involvement, nor that provide the attention they require. So, they tend to abandon those firms that are not able to convey their experiences, values, and excellent product concepts in a way that is consistent between the real world and the online environment. From this perspective, integrated communication has gained importance in the management of luxury brands. These brands have already exploited their online potential in communication, and they are approaching the Web as a means through which to sell products by leveraging their unique values. Table 2 summarizes the shared content belonging to the most major luxury firms in the past year (2014).

Table 2. Online/social shared luxury firms' contents (analysis conducted by the authors)

	Heritage	Storytelling	Events & Celebrities	Entertainment
Automotive	25%	35%	20%	20%
Fashion	15%	30%	40%	15%
Wine and spirits	40%	10%	15%	35%
Jewellery and watchmaking	35%	20%	30%	15%
Perfumery and cosmetics	35%	15%	15%	35%

Focusing attention on the third research question, it is necessary to consider the ways in which luxury players can maintain consistency in their Brand's identity, the new communication and distribution channels that are adopted, and the efforts to reach a certain brand positioning. In this scenario, which is dominated by a stronger relationship between people and technology, communication, and the Web, the marketing of luxury goods requires a new communication model based on the 7Es (4Es + 3Es): Experience, Exclusivity, Engagement, and Emotion, in addition to the other 3Es that have arisen from the opportunities that the Web affords. In particular, the 3Es that have emerged from the social Web has brought the following to communication: Expression, Enhancement and Empathy. This strategy is described below.

THE "7ES" STRATEGY FOR A MAJOR BRAND'S CONSISTENCY: OUTFITS AND RESULTS

The 7Es strategy was already considered in previous researches (Mosca et al, 2013, 2014), but the interesting thing is that these seven elements are still being considered, and the channels through which luxury players market their products has been based on this model in the last four years to enhance their positioning and the consistency of their Brand's identity. As has already been argued, it is very uncommon for luxury players to employ marketing and communication strategies using the same communication and distribution channels already used by mass-market firms. One must examine what it is about the "sense of elite" that comes from the unique experiences of a customer, and how this could be received from a selling point. What about the services given by shops and showroom employees? What about the rules that were already studied and applied by managers until a few years ago? Consistency, "sense of elite", and brand engagement can be enhanced through Web communication and online selling if luxury firm managers consider the following elements.

Experience. During the recession and post-recession, and unlike in other markets, the traditional luxury goods customer has not significantly limited his or her consumption. As a result, luxury goods markets have not been heavily affected by the crisis; rather, it can be highlighted that purchasing trends have shown the opposite pattern. While the luxury market and spending on luxury goods has grown, on the other side, luxury consumers have become more selective, informed, and a little bit more cynical. Today, the luxury consumers' purchasing decisions revolve around the question, "Is it worth it?". This question will probably be even more common considering the historical period of health crisis we are living, that is going to have consequences on the global economy, including the luxury sector. In this difficult scenario, luxury companies have to provide unique and engaging experiences. Some authors have observed how experience is central for the luxury consumer. Attention is no longer paid to what you buy, but how you buy. This stems from the fact that the selling point has become the focus of a luxury brand's marketing strategies, and it now constitutes a central element in the process of integrated communication, which is capable of influencing, through its tangible and intangible elements, the Brand's image. It also ensures that the consumer is provided with a unique and engaging experience.

Gucci – Gucci Garden

Gucci Garden – inaugurated in January 2018 – is a unique place designed by the creative director of the *Maison*, Alessandro Michele, and located in the heart of Florence in the historical building called "Palazzo della Mercanzia". Gucci Garden offers to the visitor a completely immersive brand experience: a boutique where to shop unique pieces of the Brand (available only in this location); the Gucci restaurant "Osteria da Massimo Bottura" where to enjoy a Michelin-starred dinner; and the "Gucci Garden Galleria" an art gallery curated by Maria Luisa Frisa. In this location, the physical experience of visitors is seamlessly integrated with digital devices, like the video installations that are placed in the Gallery to tell the story of the house. The museum is divided in thematic areas (as "Guccification", "Détournement" or "Cosmic Colors"), that lead to the "*Chamber cinema*", a small auditorium with soft lighting and a screen for experimental movies. The *main* museum is nonconformist: it starts from the classic museum's iconography, but it adds the flair of the fashion house's innovative vision, leading the visitors into a hypnotic and fascinating space, as seen by the symbolic Gucci Eye. This place wants to be a tribute to Gucci iconic campaigns, vintage flavour and craftsmanship. The Gucci Garden is open to everyone and half the ticket price to enter into the Galleria is donated by the Brand to restoration projects in Florence.

Burberry

In 2020 this fashion luxury player invested in the AR (augmented reality) through Google Search, to improve the digital customer experience while shopping online. Burberry has decided to invest gradually in this tool, that is currently operating in the US and UK. Consumers when searching for Burberry's items in Google through their smartphones, will be able to see the 3D image of the product as it was the real one. Indeed, products are displayed embedded in the environment around them, as they actually were in the boutique. Burberry wants to enhance the shopping experience and personalized luxury commerce, considering that looking for inspiration is one of the main phases of the decision process in purchasing a luxury good. The Brand has been a pioneer in the introduction of technology in its physical stores, as

Managing Integrated Brand Communication Strategies in the Online Era

in the case of the flagship store inaugurated in London in 2012. Recently, during the opening of the new Burberry flagship store in Ginza, the Brand has used the AR technology to involve visitors in a unique AR experience activated only through QR codes on pistachio Thomas Burberry flags on Ginza Chuo-Dori. Visitors could activate an Artificial Reality lens to discover hidden Burberry deer on the streets of Ginza, and after finding a deer, share it on their social media profiles. Moreover, In December 2019, Burberry launched a new digital in-store experience, in London, powered by Google Lens: users could see a live aerial feed of themselves on their phone, surrounded by a herd of Burberry deer. (www.burberry.com).

Exclusivity. In marketing, exclusivity is considered to arise from the second P of the marketing mix: price. Exclusivity, however, has always been the cornerstone of a luxury firm's strategies, and no concept has ever been more intensely protected. Is widely believed that the use of digital marketing in luxury marketing strategies could "put in jeopardy the exclusivity of the brand"; however, on the contrary, it could offer a real opportunity and an elegant way through which to control and develop such exclusivity, simultaneously increasing the visibility of a brand. As a result, the players of the luxury market have created exclusive platforms for consumers, as for instance the virtual community. This expedient has been used, for example, by Burberry for its "Art of Trench". In fact, each *Maison* has a special icon that distinguishes one from the other – similar to, for instance, the Hermès Kelly. For Burberry, this icon is its trench coat. As its symbolic garment, Burberry's ex-creative director, Christopher Bailey, has created a real fashion social network that collects photoshoots of characters, famous and not, who wear the company's icon. The British *Maison* had developed a platform that combines high-quality content produced by the Brand with those of its users by allowing users to communicate with the company and with one another. To launch the project, Christopher Bailey had hired Scott Schuman, the world-famous photographer, to take the first hundred pictures; later, users have responded to the initiative by uploading thousands of their own photos.

Engagement. In the realm of luxury goods, engagement is granted and often evoked by one thing: the story. Any video, online experience, or a simple post on Facebook, which is equipped with engaging content, constitutes a story that arouses emotions and involves the viewer in a unique experience. Today, in the luxury market, convincing the consumer to buy is not sufficient. Convincing them, however, to participate in an exclusive trip with and within the Brand is the key to success, and that is what stories achieve. In addition, it is known that these stories "sell".

Tiffany

The jeweller reported a significant increase in sales after the public and the press enthusiastically greeted the microsite developed by the Brand, What Makes Love True. What Makes Love True offers videos, stories, and content from Web users/customers that follow the stages of how the main characters of the stories met and fell in love in a mix that also involves film and romantic songs. Another engaging marketing and selling activity recently launched by the Brand has been the "Engagement Ring Finder". The app allowed consumers to try – on Tiffany engagement rings and share their photos on social networks.. These two actions of digital marketing conveyed the powerful and engaging history of the Tiffany brand in achieving true love. Tiffany has decided not to focus only on selling products, but on an entire way of life. This is clearly demonstrated in the Brand's campaigns, "Will You?", launched in 2015. In the campaign different real-life couples were represented, including same-sex ones. This was a powerful message of inclusivity, by one of the main players of the luxury jewellers. The story told by the official campaign video, was about couples being separated for a time, looking forward to being reunited by love and, of course, by Tiffany jewellery. The campaign aimed to communicate emotion, love and romance, making people feel personally involved in the story. The video became viral, reaching millions of views on YouTube and generating a huge stream of eWOM on social media.

La Mer

In 2019, the luxury skincare brand La Mer launched an engaging digital campaign especially focused on the Gen Y and Z target. The campaign was aimed to promote the exclusive crème La Mer Blue Heart (sold at 435 €) and to tell the brand mission towards the marine habitat conservation. La Mer dedicated a specific section of its website to this educational initiative: there, the user could find the campaign's video where a young girl talks about oceans and invites the audience to join La Mer mission to protect the sea. At the end of the page, the user could proceed with the purchase and read a detailed description of the product together with the explication of its charity purpose. It was interesting to notice that, in this same section, the user also had the possibility to contact the Brand to have more information. An image gallery labelled with the hashtag #LaMerBlueHeart allowed users to browse through photos made by consumers that bought the crème and decided to share their experience. This gallery, made the page more editorial and created a connection between UGC and brand contents, posted on the website and on social networks. In this case, there was a clear *call to action* towards clients, to invite them to be firsthand involved in the project: for every post shared, La Mer donated 25$ to preserve the ocean.

Emotion. The combination of the 3Es described above takes the fourth element of luxury marketing into account: emotion. Without the proper application of this key variable, the success of luxury brands is not sustainable in the long run. The reason is simple: luxury firms have consumers that can buy almost anything they want. In this context, the physical product acquires secondary importance in favour of what luxury consumers are really looking for: a more personal experience or an engaging story that will evoke in them a particular emotion. With respect to these basic Es, which have been identified through a literature review (Luan, 2008; Okonkwo, 2010; Kapferer & Bastien, 2014), it is evident that in order to complete the model, it is necessary to add the 3Es that are linked to consumer empowerment (Mosca et al., 2013).

Enhancement. This is the enrichment of luxury content through the provision of exclusive content; this content could be shared, but it is used to increase the consumer's experience.

Expression. The Internet provides consumers with the opportunity to manage the amount of time they communicate. This has given way to a communication style that is more charming, elegant, and dream-like, and that is able to reach a specific target market which, until now, was not possible with only above the line media.

Cartier

The first luxury brand to use a social network in its marketing strategy was Cartier which, in 2008, created its first official page on MySpace to advertise one of its brands (Love) and its charity campaign. From 2008 onward, Cartier has leveraged the power of the Web, creating opportunities through which to enhance the Brand's expression. Over the years, Cartier has evolved its marketing strategies using even more the Web and social networks as a communication and selling point. One of the most popular social network for this Brand is WeChat, on which Cartier has an online shop. In 2017 the French *Maison,* part of the Swiss Group Richemont, launched a digital campaign for Valentine's Day. A pink gold bracelet,

Managing Integrated Brand Communication Strategies in the Online Era

specifically designed for the campaign was launched on the online WeChat store. However, the shopping experience was not completely digital: the first 88 bracelets sold were "physically" delivered by smartly dressed boys straight to the client's doorstep. This was a valuable service that on a special occasion like Saint Valentine made the shopping experience unique and the customer feels special. Another successful communication strategy of the Brand was designed in 2019, to launch the new modern collection "Clash de Cartier". This collection was distributed both online, including on WeChat e-shop and in brick-and-mortar stores. The pieces were designed to meet the diverse jewellery needs of younger generations and to be for an everyday style, but at the same time to allow consumers to express their individuality. The Clash de Cartier was cool and the value of the collection was embedded by the young British actress Kaya Scodelario, who starred in the campaign film representing the duality of young generations. In addition to the long video format, Cartier chose to convey a series of multiple facets of personality through social media, that could resonate between the target audience. Again Cartier decided to create a seamless user experience that went from online to offline and vice versa. A six-day jewellery exhibition, open to the public, was organized in Shangai. The event consisted in different interactive spaces and installations, including mirror walls with sound and colour alteration or art wall with interactive sensor effects and a mysterious cafe which can only be accessed with a "secret" switch. On the other hand, a mini-program on WeChat was created as a key part of the exhibition interaction. Users could make some active action to join the exhibition, like download the exhibition maps and make appointments for new product fitting. Moreover, users could upload their selfies to the mini-program to see their photos on the screen wall installed in the physical space.

Empathy. UGC media are able to provide luxury firms with personal information about their customers, allowing companies to establish a more intimate relationship with their clients. This practice is in line with the inversion of the traditional communication scheme that has influenced the current scenario in almost all markets.

Chanel

Although Chanel has already been mentioned as being very active in social networks, this famous player has not offered sales channels online to date. The company's online presence has been developed to attract customers to its traditional stores. Why? Chanel says that if you do not try on clothes, you cannot buy them. The online catalogue is not used to sell products through the Web; rather, it serves as a tool through which to push its in-store sales. Finally, the company's online and social presence was established to create a sense of empathy, which was already explained. The Brand aims to tell a story: the story of Madame Coco and what makes her an icon. For this reason Chanel has created the *Inside Chanel* contents, a series of videos conveyed through its digital channels to transport the audience inside the history of the iconic Brand and revealing anecdotes, like the importance of *The Camellia,* the flower icon of the Brand. Those stories can affect people, and this is an effective way through which to establish a more intimate relationship with the customer. In this instance, we are talking about a case of integrating online and offline channels, of course, but the two platforms, the distribution as well the communication one, are not changing their rules, at least so far.

FUTURE DIRECTIONS: BENEFITS AND RISKS FOR CONSUMERS

The potential impact of online stores on a customer's purchase behaviours represents an interesting area of discussion. Are people changing their habits and attitudes in such a way that pushes every luxury firm to consider online selling? So far, as has already been shown, some luxury players have not decided to sell online. The number of luxury brands that have embraced the digital channel has increased, but there are some "traditionalists" that still won't sell their exclusive products online, like Chanel. However, what about tomorrow? Managers can try to provide solutions to the aforementioned questions by considering that online selling features risks and benefits. On the one hand, an online shop can augment the 7Es, and the 7Es can be exploited to encourage people to buy online.

Moreover, some researchers (like the "True Luxury Consumer Insight" by BCG and Altagamma) are advising about trends that may arise in the luxury market due to the impact of COVID-19 on people behaviour and preferences. It is expected that between 2020-2021, experiential luxury will drop between 40% and 60%, while for personal luxury goods the drop is expected to be around -25% and -45%. However, there is evidence that the majority of luxury consumers that had invested in experiential luxury before the pandemic outbreak, are more likely to do the same after COVID-19. At the moment, Chinese luxury consumers seem to be more optimistic about recovery, but they are not so willing to travelling again for luxury shopping in the short term. European and Russians seem to be more. During the emergency, luxury companies have cancelled their event and have undertaken solidarity actions to help the worldwide community. Luxury brands have used the communication to reassure customers, stay close to their audience and for entertaining, sharing special content on their social networks (Altagamma Social Luxury Index by Altagamma and Accenture). However, how all these upcoming changes will be faced by luxury companies? And how their communication and marketing strategies will change in the upcoming future?

It is also worth considering that in the future, generations Y and Z will represent the luxury target market, and studies on their attitudes toward buying and media are showing a strong predilection for online tools (both for buying and for gathering information). Moreover, we have already considered that customers can benefit from online purchasing methods (they can customize their future purchases, they can experience the Brand, and they can interact with and gather major information about the firm itself); in addition to these benefits, customers are also able to monitor online product stocks (usually when a certain product is scarce, people know).

On the other side, online sales still feature risks. From a customer's perspective, the first risk is linked to the nature of the online environment: you cannot try to think, you cannot see the clothes or purses live, and sometimes the screen on your laptop/PC can provide you with a poor image resolution. Moreover, if the value of a luxury product is high, given its selective distribution, how does the online environment change this – especially since Web pages have no barriers? Eventually, from the firms' perspective, the online environment can create conflict among distribution channels. Finally, managers need to face the pros and cons of online strategies and, consequently, they have to consider if their target market is ready to accept online products. At the same time, they need to consider that people love, above all, to experience products in luxury markets.

CONCLUSION

Digital technology has brought about a radical change in the dynamics of marketing, and it has become increasingly important. The spread of social media and mobile media offers firms new business opportunities; these firms have the potential to create viral communication campaigns and to reach, thanks to the potential of new media, multiple market segments, providing the ability to customize messages. While the Web experience is based on exchange, sharing, and collaboration, consumers of luxury goods in mature markets are certainly not immune to this revolution. Hence, firms need to have an online presence, not only through Web sites, but they should also provide content and services to the expanding virtual community. All businesses, including those operating in the field of luxury goods, are conscious that in order to be on the Internet, "showcase Web sites" are being overtaken by the real leading players in the creation and exchange of information and experiences, offering dedicated spaces, content, and additional services to users and fans of the Brand.

Luxury firms thus address their system of offerings to consumers with a view of producing any number of functional benefits. With this in mind, the physical quality of the goods, while important, is instrumental in the creation of the emotions that are sought and shared. This can enhance a new concept called "reverse multichannel marketing". What has primarily been a communication platform thus far is now transforming into a selling place, while what has always been a selling platform is now becoming a "showcase" where people can gather information on and experiment the values of the Brand. The consumer journey in the luxury industry is quickly shifting to the online and brands are showing evidence of their ability to be present on this channel, maintaining their exclusive appeal. This represents an interesting and fruitful area for future research for both academics and managers.

REFERENCES

Agarwal, M.V. (2020). *Importance of User Generated Content as a part of Social Media Marketing that drives Customer's Brand Awareness and Purchase Intentions.* doi:10.13140/RG.2.2.33503.61609

Altagamma & Accenture. (2020). *Altagamma Social Luxury Index 2020.* Author.

Bain & Company. (2020). *Eight Themes That Are Rewriting the Future of Luxury Goods.* Luxury Goods Worldwide Market Study, Fall-Winter 2019.

Baker, J., Ashill, N., Amer, N., & Diab, E. (2018). The internet dilemma: an exploratory study of luxury firms' usage of internet-based technologies. *Journal of Retailing and Consumer Services, 41,* 37-47. doi: 10.1016 /j.jretconser.2017.11.007

BCG & Altagamma. (2020). *True-Luxury Global Consumer Insight.* Author.

Casalegno, C., & Li, Y. (2012). *Tendenze evolutive in atto: la comunicazione integrata.* Academic Press.

Chailan, C. (2018). Art as a means to recreate luxury brands' rarity and value. *Journal of Business Research, 84,* 414–423. doi:10.1016/j.jbusres.2017.10.019

Chandon, J. L., Laurent, G., & Valette-Florence, P. (2016). Pursuing the concept of luxury: Introducing to the JBR Special Issue on "Luxury Marketing from Tradition to Innovation". *Journal of Business Research, 69*(1), 299–303. doi:10.1016/j.jbusres.2015.08.001

Coelho, P. S., Rita, P., & Santos, Z. (2018). On the relationship between consumer-brand identification, brand community, and brand loyalty. *Journal of Retailing and Customer Services, 43*, 101–110. doi:10.1016/j.jretconser.2018.03.011

De Angelis, M., Amatulli, C., & Zaretti, M. (2020). The Certification of Luxury: how art can affect perceived durability and purchase intention of luxury products. *Sustainable Luxury and Craftsmanship,* 61-84. doi:10.1007/978-981-15-3769-1_4

Diallo, M. F., DahmaneMouelhi, N.B., Gadekar, M., & Schill, M. (2020). CSR actions, brand value, and willingness to pay a premium price for luxury brands: Does long-term orientation matter? *Journal of Business Ethics*. Advance online publication. doi:10.100710551-020-04486-5

Duncan, T., & Mulhern, F. (2004). *A White Paper on the Status, Scope and Future of IMC*. New York: McGraw-Hill.

Grassi, A. (2020). Art to enhance consumer engagement in the luxury fashion domain. *Journal of Fashion Marketing and Management, 24*(3), 327–341.

Gurzki, H., Schlatter, N., & Woisetschlager, D. M. (2019). Crafting extraordinary stories: Decoding luxury brand communication. *Journal of Advertising, 48*(4), 401–414. doi:10.1080/00913367.2019.1641858

Hasbullah, N. N., Sulaiman, Z., & Mas'od, A. (2020). User-Generated Content Sources: The Use Of Social Media In Motivating Sustainable Luxury Fashion Consumptions. *International Journal of Scientific & Technology Research, 9*(3), 5208-5214.

Holmqvist, J., Diaz Ruiz, C. A., & Penaloza, L. (2019). Moments of luxury: Hedonic escapism as a luxury experience. *Journal of Business Research, 116*, 503–513. doi:10.1016/j.jbusres.2019.10.015

Hughes, M. U., Bendoni, W. K., & Pehlivan, E. (2016). Storygiving as a co-creation tool for luxury brands in the age of internet: A love story by Tiffany and thousands of lovers. *Journal of Product and Brand Management, 25*(4), 357–364. doi:10.1108/JPBM-09-2015-0970

Kapferer, J. N. (2017). *Lusso. Nuove sfide, nuovi sfidanti*. Franco Angeli.

Kapferer, J. N., & Michaut-Denizeau, A. (2020). Are millennials really more sensitive to sustainable luxury? A cross-generational international comparison of sustainability consciousness when buying luxury. *Journal of Brand Management, 27*, 35–47. doi:10.105741262-019-00165-7

Kaplan, A. M., & Haenlein, M. (2010). Users of the world, unite! The challenges and opportunities of Social Media. *Business Horizons, 53*(1), 59–68. doi:10.1016/j.bushor.2009.09.003

Kauppinen-Raisanen, H., Gummerus, J., VonKoskull, C., & Cristini, H. (2017). The new wave of luxury: The meaning and value of luxury to the contemporary consumer. *Qualitative Market Research, 12*(3), 229–249. doi:10.1108/QMR-03-2016-0025

Kennedy, E., & Guzman, F. (2017). When perceived ability to influence plays a role: Brand co-creation in Web 2.0. *Journal of Product and Brand Management, 26*(4), 342–350. doi:10.1108/JPBM-04-2016-1137

Kim, J.-E., Lloyd, S., & Cervellon, M.-C. (2016). Narrative transportation storylines in luxury brand advertising: Motivating consumer engagement. *Journal of Business Research, 69*(1), 304–313. doi:10.1016/j.jbusres.2015.08.002

Klaus, P. P. (2020). The end of the world as we know it? The influence of online channels on the luxury customer experience. *Journal of Retailing and Consumer Services, 57*. Advance online publication. doi:10.1016/j.jretconser.2020.102248

Knowledge@Wharton. (2020). *Can Luxury Retail Attract a New Generation of Shoppers?* Author.

Koivisto, E., & Mattila, P. (2018). Extending the luxury experience to social media – User-Generated Content co-creation in a branded event. *Journal of Business Research, 117*, 570–578. doi:10.1016/j.jbusres.2018.10.030

Kotler, P., Adam, S., Denize, S., & Armstrong, G. (2009). *Principles of Marketing* (4th ed.). Pearson Education.

Krugman, D. M., Reid, L. N., Dunn, S. W., & Barban, A. M. (1994). *Advertising: Is Role in Modern Marketing*. Dryden Press.

Lee, H., Rothenberg, L., & Xu, Y. (2019). Young luxury fashion consumers' preferences in multichannel environment. *International Journal of Retail & Distribution Management, 48*(3), 244–261. doi:10.1108/IJRDM-11-2018-0253

Mosca, F. (2017). *Strategie nei mercati del lusso. Marketing, digitalizzazione, sostenibilità*. Egea.

Mosca, F., Casalegno, C., &Feffin A. (2013, October). *Nuovi modelli di comunicazione nei settori dei beni di lusso: un'analisi comparata*. Paper X Convegno della Scuola Italiana di Marketing, Milano.

Mosca, F., Casalegno, C., & Feffin, A. (2014, September). Last Marketing Communication Challenges In Luxury Brand Markets: A Comparative Analysis. *7th Annual Conference of the EuroMed Academy of Business*.

Nambiar, R. (2018). Storytelling long-format Ads – A better way for effective consumer engagement. *International Journal of Research and Scientific Innovation, 5*(3), 8–13.

Okonkwo, U. (2010). *Luxury Online. Styles, Systems, Strategies*. Palgrave Macmillan. doi:10.1057/9780230248335

Osmonbekov, T., Bello, D. C., & Gilliland, D. I. (2009). The impact of e-business infusion on channel coordination, conflict and reseller performance. *Industrial Marketing Management, 38*(7), 778–784. doi:10.1016/j.indmarman.2008.03.005

Park, M., Im, H., & Kim, H.-Y. (2018). "You are too friendly!" The negative effects of social media marketing on value perceptions of luxury fashion brands. *Journal of Business Research, 117*, 529–542. doi:10.1016/j.jbusres.2018.07.026

Rangaswamy, A., & Van Bruggen, G. (2005). Opportunities and challenges in multichannel marketing: An introduction to the special issue. *Journal of Interactive Marketing, 19*(2), 5–11. doi:10.1002/dir.20037

Ryu, S. (2020). Online luxury goods with price discount or onsite luxury goods with luxury services: Role of situation-specific thinking styles and socio-demographics. *Journal of Retailing and Consumer Services, 57*. Advance online publication. doi:10.1016/j.jretconser.2020.102253

Schultz, D. E., Tannenbaum, S. I., & Lauterborn, R. F. (1993). *Integrated Marketing Communications.* NTC Business.

Seo, Y., & Buchan-Oliver, M. (2017). Constructing a typology of luxury brand consumption practices. *Journal of Business Research, 99*, 414–421. doi:10.1016/j.jbusres.2017.09.019

Turunen, L. L. M. (2018). *Interpretations of Luxury. Exploring the customer perspective.* Palgrave Advances in Luxury.

Venkatesan, R., Kumar, V., & Ravishanker, N. (2007). Multichannel Shopping: Causes and Consequences. *Journal of Marketing, 71*(2), 114–132. doi:10.1509/jmkg.71.2.114

Venus Jin, S., Muqaddam, A., & Ryu, E. (2019). Instafamous and social media influencer marketing. *Marketing Intelligence & Planning, 37*(5), 567–579. doi:10.1108/MIP-09-2018-0375

Voyer, B., & Tran, V. (2013). *Risks and benefits in selling luxury goods online: should Chanel, the icon of timeless fashion, open an e-boutique?* ESCP Europe, case study 3. Retrieved from www.casecenter.org

Yazdanian, N., Ronagh, S., & Laghaei, P. (2019). The mediation roles of purchase intention and brand trust in relationships between social marketing activities and brand loyalty. *International Journal of Business Intelligence and Data Mining, 15*(4), 371–387. doi:10.1504/IJBIDM.2018.10008661

ENDNOTE

[1]   ROPO: Research online; purchase offline.

Chapter 5
Investigating the Impact of Luxury Brands' Traditional and Digital Contents on Customer–Based Brand Equity

Fabrizio Mosca
University of Turin, Italy

Philip J. Kitchen
ICN-Artem School of Business, University of Lorraine, France

Valentina Chiaudano
University of Turin, Italy

ABSTRACT

After a period of initial scepticism, luxury-branded companies now understand the necessity of integrating digital technologies into their marketing actions. Therefore, most luxury companies approach emerging digital tools commencing from communication strategies. The direct consequence is the adoption of social media such as blogs, applications (apps), and social networking as new communication tools alongside and in conjunction with traditional media. The purpose of this chapter lies in seeking to understand the extent to which luxury brand consumers appreciate the contents of luxury brand communications and in comparing digital and traditional ranges. In addition, the chapter investigates the existence of a correlation between the level of satisfaction perceived by luxury consumers and the dimension of customer brand equity according to the Aaker model. In this endeavour, this study is an attempt to provide academics and practitioners with insight about the expectation of luxury brand consumers from contents delivered, comparing digital and traditional platforms.

DOI: 10.4018/978-1-7998-5882-9.ch005

Copyright © 2021, IGI Global. Copying or distributing in print or electronic forms without written permission of IGI Global is prohibited.

1. INTRODUCTION

At the end of the twentieth-century, luxury branded companies were faced with the Internet dilemma (Chandon et al., 2016; Kapferer & Bastien, 2012). While most mass-market companies immediately exploited Internet-based technologies in an attempt to improve their marketing and communication strategies, luxury companies were hesitatant (Baker et al., 2018). Luxury brand managers believed the Internet and its features were a threat to luxury brand positioning. The Internet, by its very nature, seemed to be in stark contrast to exclusivity, rarity, scarcity and elitism associated with luxury brands (Chevalier & Gutsatz, 2012; Okonkwo, 2010). Internet-based technologies generally observe the same rules of mass media such as the pull marketing approach, the lack of physical contact and free access. These characteristics of digital tools are inconsistent with core attributes of luxury brands that have been traditionally preserved by selective communication, exclusive distribution and in-store physical contact (Dall' Olmo Riley & Lacroix, 2003; Baker et al., 2018).

At first, not only managers but also consumers agreed with the inconsistency between digital technologies and luxury brands. Some studies revealed that consumers preferred the in-store experience rather than the one on the Web site of luxury brands. Consumers argued that e-shopping caused a loss of quality since the online experience prevented the pleasure of touching products and limited physical contact. The risk of online counterfeiting is another deterrent to buying luxury products online (Seringhaus, 2005; Morra et al., 2018).

However, it was not long before luxury companies took up the challenge of digitalisation. The first to overcome the initial scepticism about the Internet were big luxury players such as Gucci and Louis Vuitton. They realised that Internet-based tools were an opportunity to engage consumers that proved an increasing estimation of web interactions with luxury brands in each phase of the customer journey (Liu et al., 2019; Loureiro et al., 2018).Over time, an increasing number of luxury brand companies gradually integrated new digital technologies into their marketing strategies (Kim & Ko, 2012; Bazi et al., 2020). The growth of luxury e-commerce platforms and the adoption of more than one social media as marketing tools attested the commitment of luxury brand companies in improving their online presence (Mosca & Civera, 2017;Guercini et al., 2020).

Among digital tools used by luxury brands, the adoption of social media has attracted the attention of both academics and practitioners.

Social media are online platforms used to deliver information about products, services, and all kinds of topics. Different from traditional communication media such as television and radio, social media allows users to collaborate, share and interact (Mangold & Faulds, 2009). Based on a dual way communication form, social media empower users from being passive targets of advertising to become active participants in conversations. The use of social media helped luxury companies to improve the buying experience of consumers and to favour the creation of communities around a specific brand (Godey et al., 2016; Dwivedi & McDonald, 2020). The members of online communities have strong market potential as they often act as brand advocates that direct other consumers toward or away from specific luxury products, brands and services.

Even if social media now play an increasingly crucial role in the communication strategy, they have not entirely replaced traditional communication tools. On the contrary, luxury brand companies continued to take into account traditional media, such as television, billboards, fashion magazines and product-placement.

For this reason, the current issue for luxury brand companies is identifying an effective combination of digital and physical tools to attract, satisfy and to interact with the audience (Schivinski et al., 2016).

The literature provides some contributions about the use of social media in the luxury market and their impact on consumer behaviour and brand equity (Brogi et al., 2013; Godey et al., 2016; Park et al., 2018; Schivinski et al., 2016; Zollo et al., 2020; Bazi et al., 2020). However, a study that analyses the impact of luxury brand communication comparing the digital and traditional contents does not exist. The current paper aims to address this gap by seeking to understand the value created by digital and conventional contents from the luxury customer perspective.

To achieve this objective, we use the Aaker (1996) model that considered three dimensions to measure brand equity: perceived quality, brand loyalty and brand awareness relative to the brand association.

Results of this study extends the existing research on luxury brand communication by investigating the integrated communication strategies of luxury brand companies and clarifying how different contents impact on luxury brand consumers' perception. In this endeavour, we provide academics and practitioners with some insight into how to communicate effectively with luxury brand consumers.

2. LITERATURE REVIEW

2.1 The Definition of Social Media and the Main Classifications

The Web 2.0 revolution favoured the spreading of social media as tools of daily life for both consumers and companies.

Social media as online tools can be used to deliver information about products, services, and all kinds of topics. Different from traditional communication media like television and radio, social media allow users to collaborate, share and interact (Mangold & Faulds, 2009). As confirmed by Xiang & Gretzel (2010), social media are the first Internet-based tools that offer consumers the opportunity to create and deliver information. Social media empowered consumers from being a target of a message to participate in the creation of content. As explained by Kaplan & Haenlein (2010), social media are Internet-based devices that favoured the spreading and sharing of user-generated contents that refer to online contents directly created and delivered by consumers. Another innovation of social media concerns their ability to target the audience effectively. In this way, companies can improve exchange of information and feedback with consumers whose satisfaction may increase, and where their online experience improves.

The literature provides several classifications of social media that look at different variables. Zafarani et al., (2014) identify seven categories of social media that depend on the half time of information which is the range of time until the content is no longer attractive to the audience. This classification includes blogs, media sharing, microblogging and social bookmarking.

The model POE classifies social media in three categories considering the way to control and manage the digital platforms. POE is the acronym of paid media, owned media and earned media.

- Paid media refers to digital platforms that involve a paid placement. Banners and Google AdWords are examples of paid media since companies usually paid to created campaigns on these platforms.
- Owned media identify digital platform directly owned by the company that has full control on contents posted. Websites and the company's accounts on social networks are examples of owned media.

- Earned or Organic media are digital platforms where companies post contents without a paid promotion. On earned media, the company does not control the interactions among users who mention, recommend or post images of products on their initiative. For this reason, the presence of the company via earned media depends on the ability of the company's ability to engage consumers and trigger digital word-of-mouth.

Another classification of social media considers who created the contents than can be firm-created or user-generated (Schivinski et al., 2016).

Firm-created content is any content directly posted by the company on its social media profile whose aim is building one-on-one relationships with consumers.

User-generated content is any content created by the audience. Specifically, the user-generated contents are contents posted on the Web by the users rather than advertising agencies (Daugherty et al., 2008). This was founded by the OECD in 2007 to define those contents with a high level of creativity and not for commercial purpose. The growth of user-generated contents generated the development of community and strengthened consumer-consumer relations.

2.2 The Apparent Oxymoron: Social Media and Luxury Brands

Despite the great potential of social media, at first sight, luxury brand companies were not interested in using social media or any other Internet-based platforms. Social media and all online platforms observe the same rules of the Internet that make them more inclusive and democratic tools to preserve the exclusivity and elitism of luxury brands. Some aspects of social media, such as the pull marketing approach, the lack of physical contact, and free access initially seemed inconsistent with the principles of luxury (Jahn et al., 2013).

Not only managers but also academics agreed to consider social media in contrast with exclusivity, scarcity, uniqueness of luxury brands (Dall' Olmo Riley & Lacroix, 2003). The dual-way communication and the resulting lack of control on contents posted by luxury brand consumers implies difficulties in preserving the luxury brand aurea.

Table 1 developed by Larraufie & Kourdoughli (2014) offers an overview of the main reasons that validate the inconsistency between luxury and social media. The first aspect is related to the mass media nature of digital contents whose consequence is free accessibility, that is considered a real risk for the preservation of luxury brand prestige, exclusivity and rarity. Another challenge for integrating social media in the communication strategy of luxury brands concerns the difference in term of the core value. If social media are synonymous of modernity, luxury brands prefer to remain anchored to the past and their assumed heritage value. Finally, the possibility to consume contents delivered by social media in an unlimited way is another aspect in apparent breach of the rarity of luxury brands.

However, luxury brand company managers gradually understood that Web 2.0 and digital tools are not a threat to luxury brands but an opportunity. Social media represent the perfect key both to reach new consumers and improve long term relations with actual consumers (Angella J. Kim & Ko, 2012; Mandler et al., 2020). The new ways to interact with luxury brand consumers using social media allow luxury brand companies access to interesting information about their targets' preferences (Vithayathil et al., 2020; Wang, 2020).

The Impact of Luxury Brands' Traditional and Digital Contents on Customer-Based Brand Equity

Table 1. Conditions of inconsistency between luxury and social media

CHARACTERISTICS OF LUXURY	CHARACTERISTICS OF SOCIAL MEDIA
Elitism and prestige	Mass media nature
Core value: tradition and heritage	Core Value: modernity
Exclusivity	Open access
Rarity	Unlimited consumption

Source: personal elaboration from Larraufie & Kourdoughli (2014)

Recognising the potential of the digital platforms, big players started to embrace Internet-based technologies and to include social media in their communication and marketing strategies from 2009. For example, Gucci created a micro-website "Guccieyeweb.com" to sell a limited edition of sunglasses that were only available online. Burberry developed a microsite "Artoftrench.com" whose aim was to sponsor the iconic value of Burberry and its associated values. Dolce & Gabbana is a good case of implementation of user-generated contents. It invited young fashion bloggers to its catwalks asking them to share live contents on their social profiles. Since young generations of luxury brand consumers are digitally savvy, this practice seemed an easy way to engage other young consumers.

The number of luxury brands that use digital practices exponentially grew year by year (Bazi et al., 2020). Today all luxury brands from the most famous to the emergent have created a website and offer at least a profile via social media. Jiyoung, Kim & Ko (2010) were first who attempted to theorise the activities of social media platforms. They identified five more functions that help luxury brands to improve customers' relationships through social media. They are entertainment, interaction, trendiness, customisation and E-Wom.

- Entertainment refers to the ability of social media to hold the attention and interest of users or to guarantee them pleasure.
- Interaction is a direct consequence of dual-way communication of social media that allows companies to create interactive relationships with consumers. Luxury brand companies involve consumers in an engaging exchange of information and feedback.
- Trendiness is a function related to the ability of social media to provide the latest news about luxury brands.
- Personalisation regards the creation of tailored made contents that better satisfy the luxury brand audience.
- Finally, E-WOM refers to the passing of information from users to user thought digital tools. This process allows consumers to share information and feedback about specific products, brands, and services to help other consumers during the buying process (Hawkins et al., 2004).

The Altagamma Social Luxury Index (2020) confirmed luxury brand managers became increasingly aware of the relevance of social media as communication and distribution tools in the current ongoing pandemic (Kitchen et al, 2020). Indeed, the pandemic has influenced the social communication of all brands, leading them to reshape content and tones in their dialogue with users. For example, in the period between January and May 2020, luxury brand companies registered an increase in social interactions with users compared to the same period in 2019: event cancellations, emergency (production reconversion and special measures adopted), reaction and solidarity, and restart are the main topics of discussion (Altagamma & Accenture, 2020). These will undoubtedly continue well into the second wave if the pandemic at the end of 2020.

2.3 Luxury Brand Communication: When Traditional Media Meet Social Media

As we mentioned before, multiplication of media is one area in which technological innovation has impacted. With the Internet revolution, marketing managers need to integrate traditional media like television, radio, magazines and billboards, with the emerging digital tools. However, one does not necessarily supplant or replace the other.

This emerging integration between digital and conventional media led managers to face the challenge of integrated marketing communication (IMC). This concept refers to the creation of coordinated and consistent messages across various channels of communication to transfer a single and unique image to consumers (Kitchen et al., 2004; Kitchen, 2017). Even if pursuing integrated marketing communication strategies is essential for all kind of companies, it is also necessary for luxury companies. Messages conveyed by companies operating in the luxury market need to be capable of transferring to consumers the core attributes of the luxury product concept that are heritage, high quality, preciousness, rarity and craftsmanship. These attributes are crucial to sustaining the luxury positioning of a brand.

Figure 1 summarises the traditional and digital media that luxury brand managers integrate into their communication strategies. That said, they are no longer exist in separate silos. For example, virtually all the traditional media are available online as offline.

Figure 1. Traditional and Social media in the luxury market

2.3.1 Traditional Media in the Luxury Market

Before the digital revolution, companies interacted with consumers only using one-way communication. In this case, information is transferred in one direction, from sender to receivers. There was little or no opportunity for receivers to give feedback to the sender since the audience is unable to interact directly with the source of information. Hence, traditional media are communication channels that deliver messages through one-way communication to the widest audience possible.

The Impact of Luxury Brands' Traditional and Digital Contents on Customer-Based Brand Equity

Even if social media played an increasingly crucial role in the communication strategy, they have not entirely replaced traditional communication tools and nor are they expected to do so. On the contrary, luxury brand companies continued to take into account traditional media that are magazines, television and radio, billboards, PR, Events, Product placement, Testimonials, Catwalks and Word of mouth (Figure 2). A type of co-mingling of offline and online communication, where choice is governed by understanding of market dynamics.

2.3.2 Social Media in the Luxury Market

The advent of the Web allowed companies to transition from one-way to two-way communication. It occurs when the receiver is not only the target of communication but has the potential to become an active participant in the communication process. With social media, communication between a business/brand and its customers can become a dialogue or an exchange of information.

Figure 1 shows the social media adopted by luxury brand companies: blog, social network and applications. The adoption of these digital tools allows luxury companies to improve relations with luxury brand consumers. With the adoption of digital technologies, websites are no longer platforms closed to external editing, but become participation-based platforms, as consumers become content creators. Moreover, social media encourage active consumer participation, favour the aggregation of consumers and promote the spreading of user-generated content (Sashi, 2012).

In this context, online brand communities (OBCs) were born. The concept of online brand community was theorised for the first time by Muniz & O'Guinn, (2001) as "a specialised, non-geographically bound community, based on a structured set of social relationships among admirers of a brand". So, the main elements that characterise online brand communities are:

- Members who share rituals and moral responsibility to the brand;
- The relations among the users;
- The common interest of the members for a specific brand, towards which they feel sympathy and admiration.

Brand communities can be classified into two types based on their origin:

- the official OBCs identify online brand communities created and sponsored by luxury brand companies to improve the exchange of information of users and awareness of the brand.
- the spontaneous OBCs, indicate the communities that depend on the automatic aggregation of fans of a particular brand.

The second type of community is the one luxury companies should pay more attention to since include consumers are strongly attracted to the brand.

Brogi et al. (2013) showed that online brand communities have a positive impact on brand equity and in particular on brand loyalty.

Communities represent a tool to improve the experience of luxury brand consumers. First of all, they allow luxury brand companies to understand the perception of consumers towards products and services offered by the company.

Secondly, online brand communities favour the affirmation of common behaviours among members which monitored, can allow companies to implement ad hoc strategies to fit luxury consumers.

2.3.2.1 Blog

The word blog comes from weblog that means online journal. It is a digital platform on which creators share different types of contents such as videos of fashion shows, pictures of new products, recommendations and news about luxury brands. These types of contents aim to attract luxury brand users addicted with a specific interest in luxury fashion, lifestyle or gourmet food.

We can differ blogs by considering two main factors:

- Blog creator that refers to a person that create and manage a blog.
- Prevailing contents posted on social media that concerns the kind of communication format prevailing on the blog.

Jin & Cedrola (2017) identified two kinds of creators for luxury blogs:

- Luxury industry insiders: They are experts in the luxury sector since they have developed a deep knowledge of luxury thanks to their previous careers in a luxury company or as writers in a luxury magazine. Annadellorusso.com is an example of the luxury industry insider. Her jobs as editor and fashion consultant for Vogue Japan.
- Independent bloggers: They are people that gained credibility in the world of luxury consumers thanks to the recommendations, opinions and feedback about luxury brands posted on personal blogs. The Blond Salad is a famous example of this kind of blog. It was founded in 2009 by the collaboration between Chiara Ferragni and Riccardo Pozzoli. It was born as a fashion and travel blog since Chiara Ferragni posted on it both outfit and travel tips.

Mosca & Civera (2017) define social media according to the form of prevailing contents that can be:

Plog if contents posted on the blog are mostly images.
Vlog if contents posted on the blog are mostly videos.
Mlog if contents posted on the blog are mostly musical tracks.

2.3.2.2 Social Networks

Social networks are the most popular social media. They are platforms that allow consumers with the following activities:

- creating a public profile which is made accessible to other users of the social network;
- defining of a list of users with whom to get in touch and share content;
- analysing the characteristics of their network of contacts using analytics

According to consumers, staying in touch with friends, obtaining information, entertainment and sharing contents with other people are the main reasons to create a personal profile on social media (Loureiro et al., 2018).

The Impact of Luxury Brands' Traditional and Digital Contents on Customer-Based Brand Equity

Initially, luxury brand companies did not exploit the potential of social networks, since their nature of mass media is risking for uniqueness and exclusivity of luxury brands. However, once luxury brand companies created their business profile on social networks, the number of users that followed them increased exponentially.

Among the social networks, Facebook, Instagram and YouTube are the most common in the luxury market (Altagamma & Accenture, 2020).

2.3.2.3 Apps

Among the mobile marketing tools, smartphones and tablets play a leading role since their degree of penetration is very high both in mature countries and in emergent ones such as India and China (Altagamma & Accenture, 2020).

As regards the situation of the luxury goods market, 98% of worldwide luxury brand consumers have mobile devices whose use is four times higher than desktop devices (We are social, 2020).

Furthermore, the BCG report (2019) found that the use of smartphones has involved all generations of luxury brand consumers from younger generations to elderly consumers. Baby Boomers that are consumers over the age of 50 have more than three devices on which they spend an average of 16.4 hours a day.

The increasing use of mobile devices among luxury brand consumers convinced luxury brand companies to develop mobile applications to engage and interact with consumers.

The creation of mobile apps helped luxury brand companies in terms of:

- strengthen brand awareness, through the use of contents that support heritage as Gucci Places;
- strengthen brand loyalty;
- intensify the brand experience through the use of apps that allow consumers to live experiences related to the universe of the brand (Louis Vuitton City Guide);
- Influence purchase intention of luxury brand consumers;
- Optimise the service offered to luxury brand consumers.

3. THE GAP IN THE LITERATURE

We can find some studies about the use of social media in the luxury market and their impact on consumers behaviour and brand equity (Brogi et al., 2013; Godey et al., 2016; Angella J. Kim & Ko, 2012). However, studies that analyse the impact of luxury brand communication comparing contents provided by the digital and traditional tools do not exist. The current article aims to cover this gap. This study tries to understand the value created by digital and conventional means from the luxury customer perspective. To define the value perceived by luxury consumers, we borrowed the model of customer-based brand equity from Aaker, (1996). This model measures the value of the brand from the consumers' points of view as the differential effect that brand knowledge has on consumers response to the marketing of that brand. In other words, a brand has positive brand equity when consumers react positively to its promotional actions rather than to an unbranded version of the same product. Aaker model is a multidimensional construct that comprises five dimensions: brand awareness, brand association, perceived quality, brand loyalty and other proprietary brand assets (Aaker 1996). In our study, we prefer to include only three dimensions of brand equity: brand awareness with the brand association, perceived quality and brand loyalty. Even if brand awareness and brand association seem different concepts, some authors suggest combining them into a single dimension and propose empirical evidence to support their thesis (Washburn et al., 2004; B. Yoo et al., 2000; Boonghee Yoo & Donthu, 2001). With regards to the last dimension "other proprietary brand assets", it does not refer to a perceptual, behavioural or attitudinal nature since it consists of patents, trademarks and other intangible assets. For this reason, we decided not to include this dimension in our paper.

Considering contents, we classify digital contents as firm-created contents (FCC) and user-generated contents (UGC) as proposed by Schivinski et al (2016).

As mentioned before, firm-created content is any content directly posted by the company on its social media profile whose aim is building one-on-one relationships with consumers.

On the contrary, user-generated content is any content created by the audience. The user-generated contents are the ones posted on Web by the users rather than advertising agencies (Daugherty et al., 2008).

Leveraged on the brand equity model proposed by Aaker and the classification of contents of Schivinski et al., (2016) with our paper, we aim to respond to the following research questions:

What kind of contents generates greater satisfaction for luxury consumers?
What is the correlation between satisfaction of luxury consumers and brand loyalty, quality perceived and brand awareness?
What is the correlation between satisfaction provided by FCC and brand loyalty, brand quality and brand awareness?
What is the correlation between satisfaction provided by UGC and brand loyalty, brand quality and brand awareness?
What is the correlation between satisfaction provided by traditional contents and brand loyalty, brand quality and brand awareness?

Figure 2. Model to study the correlation between satisfaction perceived from each kind of contents and brand loyalty, quality perceived and brand awareness.
Source: Personal elaboration

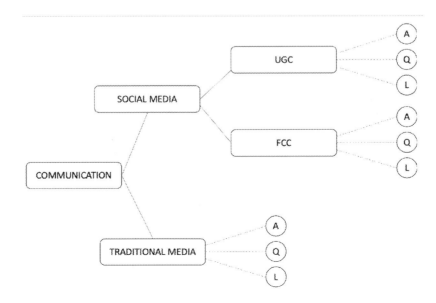

The Impact of Luxury Brands' Traditional and Digital Contents on Customer-Based Brand Equity

4. METHODOLOGY

After the review of literature, we developed a semi-structured questionnaire to achieve the following goals:

- Describe the demographic characteristics of our sample.
- Evaluate which kind of content generates the most satisfaction considering the opinions of Italian luxury brand consumers.
- Study the correlation between satisfaction perceived by each kind of content and three dimensions of Brand Equity theorised by Aaker model (quality, loyalty and brand awareness).

The inception of the questionnaire provides respondents with a disclaimer as indicated by Boonghee Yoo & Donthu, (2001): "There are no right or wrong answer; only your opinions matter. The goal of this study is to understand how to manage a successful luxury brand. To guarantee valid and meaningful results, we need your help!". The disclaimer aims to minimise any possible bias.

About the luxury brands involved in this study, we selected luxury brands whose core business consists of personal luxury goods sector (bags, shoes, clothing, watches, perfumes and cosmetics) and based on their active presence on social media. Brands chosen are involved not only on the traditional channels such as television, magazines or billboards but also on the digital track both with contents created and controlled by the company (firm created contents) and with those posted by consumers (user-generated contents).

Figure 3 can represent the brands chosen for our research in a positioning matrix according to two variables: the level of craftsmanship and the nationality of the brand, (Italian or international brand).

We chose these variables following the importance they play in the luxury goods market. 'Made In' is one of the main factors that influence consumers' purchasing behaviour as it is a guarantee of quality and benefits (Kapferer & Bastien, 2012) while craftsmanship transmits the heritage of the brand and increases the value of the product (Gardetti, 2020).

Figure 3. Matrix of brand analysed
Source: Personal elaboration

The sample of consumers includes 201 followers of at least one of the luxury brands represented in the table (Table 2). We reached the respondents in two main ways:

- we posted the link of the questionnaire weekly on blogs, forums or Italian groups focused on luxury brands on Facebook (Ladies Tiffany, Tiffany what a passion, Michael Kors Addict), Linkedin or independent blogger focused on fashion;
- we sent the link of the survey to Instagram users who are followers of al at least one of the luxury brands selected for our study. The choice of Instagram depends on the growing importance that Instagram plays in the luxury goods market. According to Altagamma & Accenture, 2020, Instagram represents the leading social network for posting photos and videos since it is a beneficial communication channel to transmit luxury brand attributes.

Based on items used in the literature and the definitions established in our research, we generated a pool of items to measure Brand Equity and satisfaction perceived by each communication content (firm created content, user-generated content and traditional content). We measured all items on 7-point Likert-type scales, with anchors of 1 = strongly disagree and 7 = strongly agree.

Basic descriptive statistical analysis is the methodology used to analyse the questionnaire items related to the satisfaction perceived by each kind of contents. We calculate the arithmetic means of the level of satisfaction perceived by luxury brand consumers from each communication channel (FCC, UGC, traditional) for each selected brand to identify the preferred communication channel for luxury brand consumers. Moreover, to evaluate the relationship between each component of the brand equity (brand awareness, brand loyalty and quality perceived) and the level of satisfaction, we used the correlation method.

5. ANALYSIS AND RESULTS

The demographic characteristics of the sample are presented in Table 2. The sample consists of 201 luxury brand consumers (141 women and 60 men). The nationality is Italian since the research was conducted through a survey exclusively focused on Italian luxury brand consumers. As asserted by Godey (2016), Italy is a historical and conventional luxury markets characterized by sophisticated tastes and preferences.

From education, it should be emphasised that 60% of the sample is made up of graduates. Considering the segmentation by age, most of the respondents aged from 23 to 34 years old belong to Generation Z and Millennials. The BCG report identified these youngest generations of consumers as the ones who most frequently use social media to interact with luxury brands (BCG, 2019). Moreover, Millennials and Generation are the most important generations in the luxury brand industry because they at as the key driver of the growth of the luxury market (Mundel et al., 2017).

- *What kind of contents generates greater satisfaction for luxury consumers?*

As we mentioned before, to define the satisfaction of each communication channel, we calculate the means of consumer perceptions for each type of content (Table 3).

For all the luxury brands, except Dolce & Gabbana, the firm created contents result as contents are perceived as the most effective. In many cases, the mean of answers results as higher than 5. The user-generated contents that are contents posted on the Web by users are considered significant by most consumers, even if this kind of contents registered a mean less high than firm created contents. Finally, contents delivered through traditional media like billboards, television, magazines, are the ones that

The Impact of Luxury Brands' Traditional and Digital Contents on Customer-Based Brand Equity

generally generate less satisfaction. Only offline contents provided by Dolce&Gabbana satisfy the luxury brand followers more than digital contents. Dolce&Gabbana, more than other brands, are famous for its advertising campaign on television or communication in the shop. Moreover, from the results emerges as in general for the category of Italian brands with a low level of craftsmanship, traditional contents are still able to generate a particular satisfaction among luxury brand consumers.

Table 2. Demographic characteristics of the sample

GENDER		EDUCATION		AGE		SOCIAL STATUS	
Female	141	Phd	3	Gen Z	67	Single	96
Male	60	Post Graduate Certificate	10	Millennials	106	Engaged	67
		Master Degree	113	Gen X	25	Married	20
		High School Degree	72	Baby Boomers	2	Others	18
		Middle School Graduated	3				
Tot	201		201		201		201

Source: Personal elaboration

Table 3. Contents and satisfaction

BRAND	FIRM CREATED CONTENT (FCC) Mean	USER GENERATED CONTENT (UGC) Mean	TRADITIONAL COMMUNICATION Mean
ARMANI	5,08	4,9	4,9
DOLCE E GABBANA	5,66	5,27	5,71
CUCINELLI	4,64	3,55	3,45
FRRAGAMO	4,84	4,55	3,68
MARINELLA	5,8	5	4,6
MICHAEL KORS	5,19	4,69	4,19
TIFFANY	5,41	5,03	3,78
BURBERRY	4,7	4,59	4,24
LOUIS VUITTON	5	4,78	4,16

- *What is the correlation between satisfaction generated by each kind of content and brand loyalty, brand quality and brand awareness?*
  a. What is the correlation between satisfaction provided by FCC and brand loyalty, brand quality and brand awareness?

As shown by Table 4, in most cases, it emerges that there is a very low correlation between satisfaction provided by FCC and brand quality. Only about Burberry, does the correlation exceed the threshold of 0,5. In particular, Burberry registered a positive correlation between FCC satisfaction and all dimensions of Brand Equity. This is a direct consequence of Burberry efforts in developing digital campaigns: Burberry was the first brand to integrate digital and traditional communications, and it is now considered as a digital champion thanks to the effectiveness of digital campaigns promoted both online and in-shop.

On the contrary, as regards Louis Vuitton, which is another digital champion as Burberry, a very low correlation emerges between the level of satisfaction of firm created content and components of the Equity brand.

If we consider the correlation between satisfaction perceived by FCC contents and brand loyalty and awareness, results depend upon the considered brand. For example, in the case of Armani, there is a high correlation between the satisfaction of FCC and brand loyalty and awareness. On the contrary, in the case of Ferragamo, the correlation is negative. So, a general rule does not emerge from the study.

Table 4. Correlation between the level of satisfaction perceived by FCC contents and dimensions of Brand Equity.

Brand	Quality	Loyalty	Brand awareness
ARMANI	0,28	0,65	0,64
DOLCE&GABBANA	0,08	0,2	0,363
MICHAEL KORS	0,26	0,25	0,37
TIFFANY	0,5	0,14	0,44
CUCINELLI	-0,45	0,04	0,04
FERRAGAMO	0,01	-0,1	-0,11
MARINELLA	0,07	0,08	0,05
BURBERRY	0,6	0,47	0,58
LOUIS VUITTON	0,37	0,35	0,33

b.   What is the correlation between satisfaction provided by FCC and brand loyalty, brand quality and brand awareness?

As shown by Table 5, the correlation between satisfaction perceived and brand quality is low. The correlation between satisfaction perceived by luxury consumers and quality does not reach a peak of 0,4 for most of the brands included in our study. In the case of Tiffany and Dolce and Gabbana, the correlation between the variables analysed is near to 0. Moreover, if we consider Marinella, the correlation is negative. Results suggest that luxury brand companies should not leverage on user-generated contents to increase the quality perceived of the brand.

The Impact of Luxury Brands' Traditional and Digital Contents on Customer-Based Brand Equity

Table 5. Correlation between the level of satisfaction perceived by UGC contents and dimensions of Brand Equity.

Brand	Quality	Loyalty	Brand awareness
ARMANI	0,4	0,57	0,65
DOLCE&GABBANA	0,24	0,23	0,36
MICHAEL KORS	0,21	0,28	0,14
TIFFANY	0,02	0,1	0,05
CUCINELLI	0,01	0,67	0,22
FERRAGAMO	0,34	0,25	0,15
MARINELLA	-0,45	0,16	0,6
BURBERRY	0,44	0,48	0,4
LOUIS VUITTON	0,37	0,41	0,43

c.   What is the correlation between satisfaction provided by contents provided by traditional media and brand loyalty, brand quality and brand awareness?

Concerning traditional media, Table 6 reveals the positive correlation between satisfaction perceived by the content delivered by traditional communication channels and luxury brand loyalty. This fact suggests luxury companies should concentrate their efforts on improving contents provided by traditional media like magazines, billboards or television to increase the loyalty of their fans. It is particularly true for Italian brands Ferragamo, Marinella that are famous for their craft production.

Table 6. Correlation between the level of satisfaction perceived by traditional contents and dimensions of Brand Equity.

Brand	Quality	Loyalty	Brand awareness
ARMANI	0,25	0,46	0,46
DOLCE&GABBANA	-0,17	0,27	0,28
MICHAEL KORS	0,11	0,16	0,02
TIFFANY	0,05	-0,05	0,04
CUCINELLI	-0,26	0,31	-0,11
FERRAGAMO	0,12	**0,6**	0,2
MARINELLA	0,6	**0,6**	0,6
BURBERRY	0,45	0,27	0,26
LOUIS VUITTON	0,22	0,45	0,19

6. CONCLUSION AND FURTHER RESEARCH

With the advent of the Internet, luxury brand companies were initially sceptical about the chance of integration between digital and physical channels. The key motivation militating against adoption of Web 2.0 technologies concerned their open access that seemed to be inconsistent with some core attributes of luxury like exclusivity, elitism and rarity. However, after some hesitation, luxury brand companies understood that the Internet was not a threat but a real opportunity. Digital technologies then seemed to be a golden key to satisfy the new needs of luxury consumers. Luxury brand consumers influenced by the youngest generations of digital native (Mundel et al., 2017), started to seek increasing digitalisation in terms of communication and distribution strategies. Therefore, some luxury companies decided to approach the emerging digital tools starting from communication strategies. The direct consequence was the integration of social media as new communication tools alongside traditional media such as television, magazines and billboards. Most luxury brands started to open profiles on social networks and to sponsor their Vlog on YouTube. Among social media, Instagram Facebook achieved a leading role in becoming the most critical touchpoint between luxury companies and consumers.

With the integration of social media, the main challenge of luxury brand companies was developing an integrated marketing strategy that refers to the creation of coordinated and consistent messages across various channels of communication to transfer a single and unique image to consumers.

However, when luxury brand companies are choosing a platform for their campaign, they need to take into account the expectation of luxury brand consumers from contents delivered by specific communication platforms. For example, luxury brands are asked more informative contents on Facebook, and photographs or images about catwalks or stars on Instagram. So, we can assess that an emerging issue for luxury brand companies is understanding how to create useful contents to satisfy luxury consumers across different social platforms.

This study is an attempt to understand how luxury brand consumers perceive luxury brand communication comparing traditional and digital contents distinguish firm created content from user-generated contents.

We demonstrate that digital contents are more appreciated than the traditional ones. Particularly, firm-created contents that are contents directly posted and controlled by luxury brand companies are perceived as the most effective by consumers points of view. Moreover, we find that also user-generated contents, i.e., content created by other users are perceived as better than traditional contents.

The positive opinion about digital contents confirms how customisation, greater interactivity and quality of digital content help luxury companies to establish a better relationship with luxury consumers.

Finally, we deepen the perception of luxury brand communications investigating the impact of digital and traditional contents on dimensions of customer-based Brand Equity.

Results revealed a positive correlation between contents delivered by traditional media and loyalty. This fact suggests that even if traditional contents are perceived as less attractive by luxury brand consumers, they still play a relevant role in preserving the value of the brand. Media like magazines, billboards or television are the best tools to increase loyalty.

Moreover, another relevant result is the low correlation between user-generated content and quality. This result implies that contents posted on social media or shared among communities' members are not significant on quality perception.

The study conducted and presented in this research is an attempt to deepen the integration between digital and traditional communications tools, but there are some limitations:

- *Exclusive focus on Italian Market.* As explained in the methodology section, we chose Italy as a target market since it is a historical and conventional luxury markets characterized by sophisticated tastes and preferences. However, researchers could extend further analysis to other essential luxury markets such as France, China, or India. While French consumers are similar to the Italian ones considering their tastes and behaviours, China and India consumer are emerging luxury consumers with new needs and tastes.
- *Limited cluster of brands* In our research, we chose a limited cluster of brands considering two main variables that define luxury brands that are Made In and level of craftmanship. Further research could include a more massive cluster of luxury brands to generalise the results better. Moreover, researchers could add the prominence in social media interactions and the numbers of followers as other variables used to select the brands.

REFERENCES

Aaker, D. A. (1996). *Building Strong Brands.* Free Press.

Accenture. (2020). *A., & Accenture.* Altagamma Social Luxury Index.

Baker, J., Ashill, N., Amer, N., & Diab, E. (2018). The internet dilemma: An exploratory study of luxury firms' usage of internet-based technologies. *Journal of Retailing and Consumer Services, 41,* 37–47. doi:10.1016/j.jretconser.2017.11.007

Bazi, S., Filieri, R., & Gorton, M. (2020). Customers' motivation to engage with luxury brands on social media. *Journal of Business Research, 112,* 223–235. doi:10.1016/j.jbusres.2020.02.032

BCG. (2019). *2019 True-Luxury Global Consumer Insight.* BCG.

Brogi, S., Calabrese, A., Campisi, D., Capece, G., Costa, R., & Di Pillo, F. (2013). The Effects of Online Brand Communities on Brand Equity in the Luxury Fashion Industry. *International Journal of Engineering Business Management, 5,* 32. doi:10.5772/56854

Chandon, J.-L., Laurent, G., & Valette-Florence, P. (2016). Pursuing the concept of luxury: Introduction to the JBR Special Issue on "Luxury Marketing from Tradition to Innovation". *Journal of Business Research, 69*(1), 299–303. doi:10.1016/j.jbusres.2015.08.001

Chevalier, M., & Gutsatz, M. (2012). *Luxury retail management: How the world's top brands provide quality product and service support.* Wiley. http://public.eblib.com/choice/publicfullrecord.aspx?p=818410

Cuomo, M. T., Mazzucchelli, A., Chierici, R., & Ceruti, F. (2020). Exploiting online environment to engage customers: Social commerce brand community. *Qualitative Market Research, 23*(3), 339–361. doi:10.1108/QMR-12-2017-0186

Dall'Olmo Riley, F., & Lacroix, C. (2003). Luxury branding on the Internet: Lost opportunity or impossibility? *Marketing Intelligence & Planning, 21*(2), 96–104. doi:10.1108/02634500310465407

Daugherty, T., Eastin, M. S., & Bright, L. (2008). Exploring Consumer Motivations for Creating User-Generated Content. *Journal of Interactive Advertising, 8*(2), 16–25. doi:10.1080/15252019.2008.10722139

Dwivedi, A., & McDonald, R. E. (2020). Examining the efficacy of brand social media communication: A consumer perspective. *Journal of Marketing Theory and Practice*, 28(4), 373–386. doi:10.1080/106 96679.2020.1768870

Gardetti, M. A. (2020). The Basic Aspects of Luxury and Its Relations with Sustainability. In *Sustainability: Is it Redefining the Notion of Luxury?* (pp. 17–64). Springer. doi:10.1007/978-981-15-2047-1_2

Godey, B., Manthiou, A., Pederzoli, D., Rokka, J., Aiello, G., Donvito, R., & Singh, R. (2016). Social media marketing efforts of luxury brands: Influence on brand equity and consumer behavior. *Journal of Business Research*, 69(12), 5833–5841. doi:10.1016/j.jbusres.2016.04.181

Guercini, S., Ranfagni, S., & Runfola, A. (2020). E-commerce internationalization for top luxury fashion brands: Some emerging strategic issues. *Journal of Management Development*. ahead-of-print. doi:10.1108/JMD-10-2019-0434

Hawkins, D. I., Best, R. J., & Coney, K. A. (2004). *Consumer Behavior: Building Marketing Strategy*. McGraw-Hill Irwin.

Jahn, B., Kunz, W. H., & Meyer, A. (2013). The Role of Social Media for Luxury-Brands – Motives for Consumer Engagement and Opportunities for Businesses. SSRN *Electronic Journal*. doi:10.2139srn.2307106

Jin, B., & Cedrola, E. (2017). *Fashion Branding and Communication: Core Strategies of European Luxury Brands*. Springer. doi:10.1057/978-1-137-52343-3

Kapferer, J.-N., & Bastien, V. (2012). *The Luxury Strategy: Break the Rules of Marketing to Build Luxury Brands*. Academic Press.

Kaplan, A. M., & Haenlein, M. (2010). Users of the world, unite! The challenges and opportunities of Social Media. *Business Horizons*, 53(1), 59–68. doi:10.1016/j.bushor.2009.09.003

Kim, A. J., & Ko, E. (2010). Impacts of Luxury Fashion Brand's Social Media Marketing on Customer Relationship and Purchase Intention. *Journal of Global Fashion Marketing*, 1(3), 164–171. doi:10.108 0/20932685.2010.10593068

Kim, A. J., & Ko, E. (2012). Do social media marketing activities enhance customer equity? An empirical study of luxury fashion brand. *Journal of Business Research*, 65(10), 1480–1486. doi:10.1016/j.jbusres.2011.10.014

Kitchen, P. J. (2017). Integrated Marketing Communications: Evolution, Current Status, Future Developments. *European Journal of Marketing*, 51(3), 394–405. doi:10.1108/EJM-06-2016-0362Kitchen, P. J., Tourky, M. E. A., Petrescu, M., & Rethore, C. (2020). (in press). Globalisation, Marketing, Sustainability, Tourism and the Hand Mirror of COVID-19. *Academy of Business Research*.

Kitchen, P. J., Brignell, J., Li, T., & Jones, G. S. (2004). The Emergence Of IMC: A Theoretical Perspective. *Journal of Advertising Research*, 44(1), 19–30. doi:10.1017/S0021849904040048

Larraufie, A.-F. M., & Kourdoughli, A. (2014). The e-semiotics of luxury. *Journal of Global Fashion Marketing*, 5(3), 197–208. doi:10.1080/20932685.2014.906120

Liu, X., Shin, H., & Burns, A. C. (2019). Examining the impact of luxury brand's social media marketing on customer engagement: Using big data analytics and natural language processing. *Journal of Business Research*. Advance online publication. doi:10.1016/j.jbusres.2019.04.042

Loureiro, S. M. C., Maximiano, M., & Panchapakesan, P. (2018). Engaging fashion consumers in social media: The case of luxury brands. International Journal of Fashion Design. *Technology and Education*, *11*(3), 310–321. doi:10.1080/17543266.2018.1431810

Mandler, T., Johnen, M., & Gräve, J.-F. (2020). Can't help falling in love? How brand luxury generates positive consumer affect in social media. *Journal of Business Research, 120*, 330–342. doi:10.1016/j.jbusres.2019.10.010

Mangold, W. G., & Faulds, D. J. (2009). Social media: The new hybrid element of the promotion mix. *Business Horizons*, *52*(4), 357–365. doi:10.1016/j.bushor.2009.03.002

Morra, M. C., Gelosa, V., Ceruti, F., & Mazzucchelli, A. (2018). Original or counterfeit luxury fashion brands? The effect of social media on purchase intention. *Journal of Global Fashion Marketing, 9*(1), 24–39. doi:10.1080/20932685.2017.1399079

Mosca, F., & Civera, C. (2017). *Digital Channels and Social Media Management in Luxury Markets*. Routledge. doi:10.4324/9780203702048

Mundel, J., Huddleston, P., & Vodermeier, M. (2017). An exploratory study of consumers' perceptions: What are affordable luxuries? *Journal of Retailing and Consumer Services, 35*, 68–75. doi:10.1016/j.jretconser.2016.12.004

Muniz, A. M. Jr, & O'Guinn, T. C. (2001). Brand Community. *The Journal of Consumer Research*, *27*(4), 412–432. doi:10.1086/319618

Okonkwo, U. (2010). *Luxury Online: Styles*. Systems, Strategies., doi:10.1057/9780230248335

Park, M., Im, H., & Kim, H.-Y. (2018). "You are too friendly!" The negative effects of social media marketing on value perceptions of luxury fashion brands. *Journal of Business Research*. Advance online publication. doi:10.1016/j.jbusres.2018.07.026

Report Digital 2020: I dati global. (2020). *We Are Social Italia*. https://wearesocial.com/it/blog/2020/01/report-digital-2020-i-dati-global

Sashi, C. M. (2012). Customer engagement, buyer-seller relationships, and social media. *Management Decision*, *50*(2), 253–272. doi:10.1108/00251741211203551

Schivinski, B., Christodoulides, G., & Dabrowski, D. (2016). Measuring Consumers' Engagement With Brand-Related Social-Media Content: Development and Validation of a Scale that Identifies Levels of Social-Media Engagement with Brands. *Journal of Advertising Research*, *56*(1), 64–80. doi:10.2501/JAR-2016-004

Seringhaus, F. H. R. (2005). Selling Luxury Brands Online. *Journal of Internet Commerce*, *4*(1), 1–25. doi:10.1300/J179v04n01_01

Vithayathil, J., Dadgar, M., & Osiri, J. K. (2020). Social media use and consumer shopping preferences. *International Journal of Information Management, 54*, 102117. doi:10.1016/j.ijinfomgt.2020.102117

Wang, T., & Lee, F.-Y. (2020). Examining customer engagement and brand intimacy in social media context. *Journal of Retailing and Consumer Services, 54*, 10. doi:10.1016/j.jretconser.2020.102035

Washburn, J. H., Till, B. D., & Priluck, R. (2004). Brand alliance and customer-based brand-equity effects. *Psychology and Marketing, 21*(7), 487–508. doi:10.1002/mar.20016

Xiang, Z., & Gretzel, U. (2010). Role of social media in online travel information search. *Tourism Management, 31*(2), 179–188. doi:10.1016/j.tourman.2009.02.016

Yoo, B., & Donthu, N. (2001). Developing and validating a multidimensional consumer-based brand equity scale. *Journal of Business Research, 52*(1), 1–14. doi:10.1016/S0148-2963(99)00098-3

Yoo, B., Donthu, N., & Lee, S. (2000). An Examination of Selected Marketing Mix Elements and Brand Equity. *Journal of the Academy of Marketing Science, 28*(2), 195–211. doi:10.1177/0092070300282002

Zafarani, R., Abbasi, M. A., & Liu, H. (2014). *Social Media Mining: An Introduction.* Cambridge University Press. https://books.google.it/books?id=fVhzAwAAQBAJ doi:10.1017/CBO9781139088510

Zollo, L., Filieri, R., Rialti, R., & Yoon, S. (2020). Unpacking the relationship between social media marketing and brand equity: The mediating role of consumers' benefits and experience. *Journal of Business Research, 117*, 256–267. doi:10.1016/j.jbusres.2020.05.001

KEY TERMS AND DEFINITIONS

Customer-Based Brand Equity (CBBE): CBBE measures the value of the brand from the consumers' points of view as the differential effect that brand knowledge has on consumers response to the marketing of that brand.

Firm-Created Content (FCC): Firm-created content is any content directly posted by the company on its social media profile whose aim is building one-on-one relationships with consumers.

Online Brand Community (OBC): A specialized, non-geographically bound community, based on a structured set of social relationships among admirers of a brand.

User-Generated Content (UGC): User-generated content is any content created by the audience. The user-generated contents are contents posted on the Web by the users rather than advertising agencies.

Chapter 6
When Luxury Brands Changed Their Approach to Social Media

Fabrizio Maria Pini
MIP School of Management, Politecnico di Milano, Italy

Dinara Timergaleeva
Wyde – The Connective School, Italy

ABSTRACT

COVID-19 lockdowns led to a new approach to social media communication by luxury fashion brands. This chapter explores recent pandemic-related changes in the social context and the need for brands to rethink their narrative to engage consumers and influence purchase decisions. The authors selected a panel of 28 fashion luxury brands, both independent and conglomerate-owned, to analyze the paradigm shift in social media communication and content creation. Their findings show that with social media acting as the main touchpoint, luxury fashion brands have effectively produced new communication archetypes, revealing the latent potential of digital platforms as strategic tools.

INTRODUCTION

Luxury fashion brands can be described as latecomers to marketing strategies for digital media—long regarded as incompatible with their image of exclusivity and uniqueness (Heine & Berghaus, 2014). The main reason for this lack of interest was the assumption that digital media was better suited to mass-market products, with their e-commerce websites and low-priced merchandise. Luxury fashion consumers, on the other hand, were traditionally perceived as an elitist group demanding a personal touch and a rich, multi-sensory experience that could only be provided through physical touchpoints (Dell'Olmo, Riley & Lacroix, 2003).

Only in recent years have luxury fashion brands gained a new perspective on digital and social media, and they have done so because of an evolution in their customers' shopping habits. The growing relevance of millennials as the core customer segment, along with their extensive use of social media and participation in groups and communities, has forced luxury brands to adopt new communication

DOI: 10.4018/978-1-7998-5882-9.ch006

Copyright © 2021, IGI Global. Copying or distributing in print or electronic forms without written permission of IGI Global is prohibited.

strategies, such as increasing their presence in social media and partnering with influencers to reach and engage customers. Involvement in social media content and participation in groups and communities affect customers' brand-perception and motivation to buy luxury fashion goods, and may eventually lead to an offline purchase. Luxury fashion shoppers generally access social media platforms to become acquainted with a brand's lifestyle, collections, and iconic products. Consumers' attitude towards brand engagement is more reactive than proactive (Mosca & Casalegno, 2017; Pini & Pelleschi, 2017) and related to the consumption of visual content as a source of inspiration and sense of belonging (Kapferer & Bastien, 2012). In this sense, the interaction between customers, fans, and luxury brands still retains some of the traditional perception of luxury brands as detached from customers and dictating standards, trends, and tastes (Remuary, 2004).

The social and economic crisis brought by the COVID-19 pandemic and the ensuing lockdowns across the world have led to a very different set of circumstances, created by consumers' new communication needs and demand for deeper, more personal engagement with brands. These events have brought a radically new perspective to social media content creation and management, and a new engagement model that may affect the relationship between consumers and luxury brands over the long term, as well as carrying some interesting implications for future social media marketing efforts.

In order to analyze this paradigm shift in social media communication and content creation, the authors selected a panel of 28 luxury fashion brands, both independent and conglomerate-owned. The research aimed to answer the following questions: How have luxury fashion brands reacted to lockdown measures? Did their narratives undergo an evolution or change? Did any archetypical brand narrative approaches emerge during the crisis? A grounded research exploratory method was adopted (Glazer et al., 2006) to answer the research questions, with an ethnographic approach based on artifact analysis (Hine, 2015; Rose, 2012). Special focus was given to brand communication artifacts (frequency, layout, tone of voice, object of communication, communication details) published on Facebook, Instagram, and LinkedIn over a time span encompassing: (i) the month before the crisis hit Europe; (ii) the onset of the crisis and subsequent lockdowns; (iii) the first easing of lockdown measures.

The remainder of this chapter is organized as follows. First, drawing upon data from a wide variety of sources, the authors provide a historical perspective on the evolution of communication strategies in the luxury fashion industry (Howell and Prevenier, 2001), highlighting different phases as well as social and economic determinants. The next section outlines research design and methods used in assessing luxury fashion brands' communication approach at the onset of the pandemic. Finally, the authors describe the main findings from the research and offer recommendations for management that will likely prove beneficial to social media marketers in the luxury fashion industry.

1. COMMUNICATION PRACTICES AND STRATEGIES IN THE LUXURY FASHION INDUSTRY: A HISTORICAL PERSPECTIVE

Luxury fashion brands' narratives and meanings have evolved over time, becoming the portal through which customers and fans could "enter the legend" (Remaury, 2004; Mosca & Casalegno, 2020) and transform themselves into the heroes of the myths that are constructed and disseminated by brands[1] (Sachs, 2011).

The role of modern brands in customers' lives has its origins in the changed perception of products brought by the separation of consumers and producers as a result of mass production and distribution

When Luxury Brands Changed Their Approach to Social Media

models (Remuray, 2004; Bastos and Levy, 2012). No longer intimately associated with the unique characteristics that defined their function, such as the name and skills of the craftsmen that made them or the place where they were bought, consumer products have become anonymous, standardized, and machine-made, often in remote parts of the world. As a result, the value attached to consumption, especially of luxury goods, risked decreasing and products needed to have their own personality and identity in the market to compensate for this loss of meaning. The evolution of branding is closely tied to the birth and diffusion of mass media in the early nineteenth century and the role it played in broadcasting brands' new meaning and image (Moore and Reid, 2008, p. 429). This is often associated with the "meaningful purchase" experience where customers are brand enthusiasts wishing to immerse themselves in the world and narrative of the brand. Only brands that can tell a story—brands that actually have something to say—can succeed in making meaning and delivering a customer experience that is based on shared values, thus establishing a deeper relationship with their customer base. Much of a brand's real value, then, lies not in the products it offers but in the memories it creates (Kapferer, 2008).

This process of meaning-creation is generally associated with the development of the luxury fashion industry in the aftermath of World War II. In the following pages, the authors will describe the evolution of luxury fashion brands and their communication strategies and policies. Their description takes into consideration the economic and social determinants of this evolution.

1.1 The Maison Era: The Creator and The Role of the Atelier

According to fashion historians, the origins of haute couture can be traced back to Queen Marie Antoinette and her personal dressmaker Rose Bertin's stunning creations (Langlade,1913). However, the English couturier Charles Frederick Worth, who established his Maison in Paris in 1858 (Neto, 2018), is generally credited with turning haute couture into a full-fledged industry. Other haute couture designers soon followed suit: Gabrielle "Coco" Chanel opened her first shop in 1910, and Cristóbal Balenciaga in 1919 (Miller, 1993). Nevertheless, the late 1940s–60s can be reasonably considered as the golden age of haute couture, when the majority of brands that are today at the pinnacle of the luxury fashion industry established their businesses (Assouly and Bergé, 2005). The starting point of this golden age may be dated to 1947, when Christian Dior presented his debut "New Look" collection, incorporating in his designs the winds of change blowing through society (Olds, 2001; Jones and Pouillard, 2009). Haute couture clothes responded to the members of the elite's need for defining (and signaling to others) the social group to which they belonged to, while at the same time differentiating themselves from the masses (Fukai, 2002). Christian Dior's lavish styles, soon imitated by other couturiers, were reminiscent of the Belle Epoque, a period characterized by optimism and progress as well as dramatic social inequality and stratification (Turner, 2011). The haute couture designers of the time dictated fashion trends, establishing their own vision of beauty as representatives of their Maison, without any noticeable interaction with the clients (Steele, 2017).

1.2 The Prêt-à-Porter Era: The Birth of Luxury Fashion Brands

After the death of Christian Dior, 21-year-old Yves Saint Laurent took the helm of Maison Dior. The young designer's appointment, the first-ever case of "succession" in the world of Maisons, not only marked the emergence of a new figure in haute couture—the creative director—but also led to dramatic changes in the fashion system as a whole.

Although Saint Laurent followed in the stylistic footsteps of Maison Dior, his young age allowed him to be particularly in tune with the evolving trends in society and among his customer base. Indeed, while haute couture was still relevant, women were no longer as amenable to its dictates as they had been in the past, and by the end of the 1950s, the whole concept had started to become obsolete. Women wanted to be free, dress up affordably and comfortably and make their own decisions. The shift from haute couture to prêt-à-porter (ready-to-wear) was swift, and brands that had reached their peak needed to react quickly (Settembrini, 1994). One of the reasons for this shift was the emergence of the jet set, a new wealthy social group whose luxury lifestyle was enabled by the democratization of air travel, which replaced cruise ships as the main means of transport for transoceanic travel in the 1960s (Stadiem, 2014). Democratization in this context did not equate to affordability but rather to the increased ease of travelling by plane. Bulky, heavy trunks, more suitable for ship travel than airplanes, necessarily gave way to lighter, flexible suitcases that were simply inadequate to accommodate haute couture's highly elaborate outfits. At the same time, ready-to-wear clothes were easier to buy and more versatile, as well as allowing more freedom in terms of self-expression.

Last but not least, the counterculture era that shaped the ready-to-wear revolution also saw the emergence of the media as a tool for consumer engagement: television and cinema became cultural forces that, along with fashion magazines and photos of celebrity outings, could help trends spread rapidly and globally. The actress Audrey Hepburn and the designer Hubert de Givenchy were the epitomes of this revolution: their collaboration on the costumes for *Breakfast at Tiffany's* radically transformed the way fashion and fashion brands were promoted. Fashion became more affordable and lost its air of exclusivity (Smith, 2002).

The shift from haute couture's promise of absolute luxury to the concept of ready-to-wear meant sweeping changes to the operational management of luxury fashion houses, which moved from one-of-a-kind bespoke designs to industrial manufacturing. To provide customers with a broader assortment of merchandise and product lines, the Maisons developed the system of licensing.

1.3 Less is More: Feeding Meaning Into Luxury Fashion Brands

The next phase in the development of the luxury fashion industry was mainly characterized by attempts to overcome the drawbacks of licensing and a proliferation of product lines.

From an operational standpoint, licenses were ruling the luxury fashion business. Although for a time the licensing model had helped companies meet demand and ease the transition from haute couture to ready-to-wear, the transitional period itself ended up being extremely short, leaving no time to address the impact of licensing on supply chains and on the communication of brand values. The use of intuitive decision-making by management led to a widespread identity crisis among luxury brands in the early 1990s, brought by the gradual dilution of brand values in favor of licensing processes.

Fashion houses predominantly reacted to brand value dilution by taking a "less is more" approach. Although the approach is often associated with stylistic changes and a focus on minimalism, in this case it encompassed all aspects of business, as luxury fashion brands found themselves drowning in a sea of licensed products. Licensing arrangements needed to undergo a complete overhaul, which was carried out through a series of steps aimed at taking back control of production and the brand itself. Applying the "less is more" approach to production required a fundamental change in organizational management, and indeed the late 1980s and early 1990s saw the emergence of brand conglomerates (Donzé, 2018). Further, by buying back their licenses, brands were able to focus on in-house production and cut product

When Luxury Brands Changed Their Approach to Social Media

ranges. To reinforce brand image and provide customers with a clear definition of what luxury fashion brands stand for, a large investment in flagship stores was undertaken at this time. The new emphasis on brand identity as a core asset required large investments in experiential touchpoints, allowing customers to enjoy a multi-sensory brand experience an access the whole range of collections under one roof (Hagtvedt and Patrick, 2009). Together with global retail expansion, large investments were devoted to advertising timeless iconic pieces so as to differentiate from competing brands.

1.4 The Rise of Fast Fashion and Its Impact on Collections and Brand Presence

One of the most significant developments of the 2000s was the rise of fast fashion (Giertz-Mårtenson, 2012). In April 2000, H&M opened its first store in the United States and *The New York Times* reported that "[…] in the late 1990s and early 2000s, it became increasingly more acceptable to flaunt one's love for low-cost fashion and seen as especially savvy to be able to mix high and low fashion with aplomb. The retailer had arrived at the right time as consumers had just recently become more likely to hunt for bargains and dismiss department stores, stating that it was now 'chic to pay less'" (La Ferla, 2000).

Comparing value propositions in fast fashion and luxury markets seemed an exercise in futility at the time. Nevertheless, the influence of fast fashion did grow steadily, and over the past 10 years consumers have come to expect a quick turnaround of trends. Traditionally, the arrival of new haute couture and luxury ready-to-wear collections in stores followed a bi-annual schedule (Sproles, 1981). Since the advent of fast fashion, however, with retailers delivering new products to the stores every two weeks, luxury brands have had to step up their game, introducing new resort or cruise and pre-fall collections. This has led to an overhaul of the fashion calendar, which nowadays requires luxury brands to present at least four collections yearly—two for the Maisons registered to the Chambre Syndicale de la Haute Couture. Under the increasing pressure of fast fashion, they have had to improve manufacturing and supply chain processes to be able to meet customers' needs. The recent attempt by some luxury brands to adopt a "see now, buy now model"—basically a fast fashion approach to the delivery process—marked the culmination of the fast chain supply model (Brun et al, 2016).

Not only has the acceleration of fashion cycles influenced luxury companies' supply chains but also the way collections are distributed. Flagship stores have become ever more crucial to brand success and the ability to provide customers with a branded luxury experience. The need for mono-brand boutiques carrying multiple collections yearly across the globe has progressively shifted costs from manufacturing to distribution processes, with stores and labor making up the main costs.

1.5 The Hype Phenomenon and the Rise of Social Media: Luxury Fashion Brands Meet Millennials

A strong influence of street style and the rapid growth of the Chinese market for luxury fashion marked the period that has come to be known as the Mayfly era, also characterized by the rise of "hype brands" and the repositioning of old luxury fashion houses, with a focus on delivering ultra-trendy clothes (Rovai, 2014). The main problem with this approach, however, is that brands must always be "talked about". This type of brand repositioning (or more appropriately, a revolution in style codes) is best illustrated by Demna Gvasalia's appointment at Balenciaga, or Alessandro Michele's at Gucci, Riccardo Tisci's at Burberry, Virgil Abloh's at Louis Vuitton, and Kim Jones' at Christian Dior, whose designs are heavily influence by street-style culture and celebrity endorsements (Friedman, 2015; Sepe and Anzivino, 2020).

There are several factors at play that might explain the reasons behind the adoption of this novel approach by luxury fashion brands. The first relates to a shift in the age of luxury fashion consumers. So-called millennials—keen on innovation in design and unique products that let them express their identity and signal their values—expect luxury brands to look beyond tradition for new ideas and interpretations of luxury. Their expectations have led luxury fashion brands to embrace collaboration with street-style brands and celebrities (Dimitrova et al, 2018). Among the most successful collaborations were the pairings of Yeezy and Adidas, Louis Vuitton and Supreme, and Chanel and Pharrell Williams. This had an enormous impact on the way products are presented, with a mushrooming of limited editions, drops, and other forms of exclusive access to products. When it comes to collaborations, usually the history of the brand and its heritage have little to no relevance. It is all about the logo and attracting new customers.

Strong social media engagement is another key factor (Gallaugher and Ransbotham, 2010). The importance of influencers who reach their audiences exclusively through social media platforms is incredibly high. Since millennials are their main target, luxury fashion brands need to be present on these platforms as well, collaborating with influencers and adjusting their approach to communication in order to reach new customers. The need to engage millennials on social media platforms while at the same time exploring new storytelling approaches has triggered a wave of experimentation in digital communication. In 2013, Louis Vuitton's creative director, Marc Jacobs, designed tour costumes for Hatsune Miku's virtual avatar. Miku, a sixteen-year-old Japanese singer, performs onstage as an animated hologram and has collaborated with Lady Gaga and Pharrell Wiliams. Riccardo Tisci, during his tenure as creative director of Givenchy, also designed an exclusive haute couture gown for Miku, who modeled alongside Tisci at Givenchy's Paris studio for US Vogue's May 2016 issue. Most recently, Louis Vuitton enlisted the fictional video game character Lightning, a pink-haired avatar from the "Final Fantasy" video game series, for its SS16 advertisement campaign (Pini & Pelleschi, 2017).

The third factor in fashion's new, faster cycles is e-commerce (Popomaronis, 2017). The luxury fashion industry was a very late adopter of the e-retail model for several reasons. First, there was surely a fear that easy accessibility would jeopardize customer perceptions of exclusivity. Accordingly, the democratization of luxury fashion was seen as a negative factor. Furthermore, delivering brand values through digital platforms without compromising on exceptional customer experiences is a complex task. For these reasons, luxury e-commerce has a very recent history and is still in the growth stage of its development. In 2017, only 40% of luxury brands sold their merchandise online (Blackden, 2016; Danziger, 2018).

1.6 The COVID-19 Crisis and the Challenges for Luxury Fashion Brands

As discussed above, luxury fashion brands have undergone a significant evolution over the last decades. The impact on the role and significance of brands, their value proposition and, more interestingly for the purposes of this chapter, the way they communicate with their ever-changing customers has been enormous. Over the years, luxury fashion brands have modified their role in supporting value creation, as well as the way in which they establish relationships with customers and communicate their identity (Donzé and Wubs, 2019). From a "creator-centric" environment, where ateliers and Maisons were the center of value-creation processes while customers obediently followed the whims of the moment, luxury fashion brands have progressively evolved to different roles and a newfound relevance. Ready-to-wear drew a separation between brands and creators or Maisons, allowing products to move across social boundaries and product categories through licensing agreements and indirect distribution. Brand image, broadcast and magnified by television and in films, reached a large and growing audience of potential

When Luxury Brands Changed Their Approach to Social Media

customers. The "less is more" period saw strong efforts by luxury fashion brands to re-establish their identity after years of progressive dilution—namely, a focus on direct distribution and smaller product lines meant the possibility of having an impact on customers with a coherent and meaningful brand. The fast fashion revolution forced luxury fashion brands to turn stores into hubs for the large number of collections hitting the market all year round. Communication was aimed at establishing a long-lasting relationship with the customer base, using brand identity as a durable asset capable of generating loyalty despite the fast turnover of collections and styles. The Mayfly period and the advent of the Millennial generation put strong pressure on luxury brands to innovate communication by engaging celebrities and influencers in the process, as well as increasing their presence on social media platforms. Unique products, drops, and collaborations are at the core of the communication effort to attract the attention of a consumer that is in constant search of innovation (Barron, 2019). The proliferation of social media platforms and their enormous success (they reach two-thirds of all Internet users worldwide) ushered in a completely new era, especially in terms of luxury brands' approach to communication, customer engagement (Gallaugher & Ransbotham, 2010; Kozinets, de Valck, Wojnicki, & Wilner, 2010), and brand reputation building (Correa, Hinsley, & De Zúñiga, 2010; Spillecke & Perrey, 2012). Luxury consumers use different social media differently, depending on the platform and its functionalities. While Twitter is often used to learn about or comment on live events in real time, Facebook is accessed to acquire deeper knowledge of products and brands, and Instagram is the source of inspiration for outfits, new products, or engaging lifestyles.

The COVID-19 crisis and the ensuing lockdowns in several countries hit luxury fashion brands at a time of euphoria characterized by the strong relevance of social media, influencers and celebrity engagement, and an approach to communication strongly focused on product uniqueness and exclusivity as well as the representation of an emerging global elite capable of inspiring Millennials. Products and big logos were central in shaping consumers' identities, with Instagram feeds flooded with the hashtag #ootd (outfit of the day) and other displays of belonging and excess. Lockdown and isolation were the moment of disruption in that model of communication and brand engagement: showing off was suddenly impossible, boutiques and flagship stores were shut down, and catwalks were cancelled or downgraded. All this has placed brands in a completely new landscape. In the next pages, the authors will present the findings of a research aimed at identifying changes in the social media presence of luxury fashion brands during lockdowns. The aims of this work are: identifying different approaches adopted by brands; describing shifts in the narrative models adopted; and providing some insight into long-term implications for customer relationships.

2. RESEARCH DESIGN AND METHODS

As stated earlier, the authors' intent was to analyze how luxury fashion brand narratives were affected by the COVID-19 pandemic and by the public health measures taken to curb its spread. Accordingly, the main research aims were to:

(i) describe social media communication practices at the onset of the COVID-19 crisis and during the lockdown period;
(ii) identify possible crisis-induced changes in brand narratives on social media platforms;

(iii) investigate the existence of communication "archetypes", i.e., social media communication models adopted by luxury fashion brands for content creation during the crisis;

(iv) provide insights into possible long-term consequences of these changes for social media communication strategies and the way customer relationship is built and maintained.

In order to answer the research questions, the authors identified a panel of 28 luxury fashion brands (Table 1) and analyzed communication artifacts on their pages and profiles on social media platforms (namely, Instagram, Facebook and LinkedIn) over a period of time encompassing (i) the month before the COVID-19 crisis hit Europe; (ii) the onset of the crisis and subsequent lockdowns; (iii) the first easing of lockdown measures.

A grounded research exploratory method was selected (Glazer et al. 2006). Given the abnormal environment and research conditions, as well as the significant number of variables taken into consideration, a mixed method research design was adopted, based on a multiple longitudinal case study approach.

In case study methodology, data collection may be regarded as a critical issue in research design; therefore, research is supported by content analysis of visual and textual materials. Digital communication artifacts, and the way they are accessed through several devices and platforms, carry specific implications for image analysis. The analysis of digital visual images requires an approach that takes into consideration the fact that there are two "sites", or stages, at which meaning is made. The first is the site of production, where luxury fashion brands create their own visual content. The second is the social media platform, where the image is published and seen by the audience. The importance of such diversification within research design lies in the nature of social media strategies for luxury fashion brands, since the same images might lead to a different consumption of meaning depending on the nature and characteristics of the social media platform supporting the content. Such characteristics, including context of use, nature of the audience and level of engagement, may affect the sense and meaning of the image. Accordingly, both original content for a single social media platform and content replication were considered in the data collection phase of the research process. The stage of correspondence of visual and textual content analysis is crucial in research, especially when the object of the analysis is Social Media, where there is a direct relationship between images or videos and textual content. Every stage of content analysis entails decisions about meaning and significance.

Content analysis was implemented through content coding, using the following categories: layout, frequency, tone of voice, communication details and communication objectives. These characteristics provide an immediate interpretation and are directly connected to the research questions (Luz and Collins, 1993). After all data was collected, a pattern-matching technique (Yin, 2003; Trochim, 1989) was applied to compare empirical patterns with predicted ones.

In order to provide a comprehensive answer to the research questions, particular attention was paid to the preparation of data collection through the analysis of secondary sources. This phase involved the selection of data and reliable sources to: (i) provide a general overview of the luxury fashion market, industry, and context before the pandemic. Main industry resources, such as *Women's Wear Daily*, *The Business of Fashion*, *Vogue*, etc., were analyzed to confirm brands' historical presence and the emergence of new ones that could be the object of research; (ii) select the key players in the panel; (iii) screen pages and profiles to determine whether brands were active on social media, the quantity of followers and fans, and the level of engagement—on the basis of which cases were selected for in-depth analysis.

The COVID-19 pandemic and the ensuing lockdowns had dramatic consequences that may be compared to those of a global war. Therefore, to gain a better picture of the event and its impact, the data preparation process included correlation of secondary sources not directly related to the fashion industry, such as publications by the World Health Organization (WHO), local and worldwide news reports, and financial reports. For example, brands' reactions to the announcement of blanket lockdowns across Europe were analyzed. The news seemingly took many by surprise, as suggested by disruptions in social media activity that for brands such as Fendi, Moncler, Thomas Pink, etc. lasted well over 10 days after the first lockdowns were announced.

The process of data collection began with sample selection. In light of the multifarious nature of the luxury fashion market, and its different kinds of customer profiles and creative concepts, the authors decided to include a relatively large number of brands in the study, focusing on an intentionally diverse sample. Twenty-eight luxury fashion brands were selected, from heritage luxury fashion brands Dior, Chanel, and Hermes, to edgy and fashionable brands such as Gucci and Balenciaga and niche brands such as Jil Sander and Thomas Pink. An effort was made to include both independent and conglomerate-owned brands. The latter included brands owned by the LVMH group (10 brands), the Kering Group (4 brands), Mathoola (2 brands) and OTB (1 brand). The remaining brands in the study were considered as independent. Brand extensions and sub-brands (e.g., Miu Miu by Prada or Armani Exchange by Giorgio Armani) were not included in the panel.

After selecting the cases for analysis, the next step focused on social media platforms. Digital platforms were examined with the help of secondary sources, and Instagram, Facebook and LinkedIn were selected as the most relevant for the purpose of the study.

More specifically, Instagram turned out to be luxury fashion brands' preferred social media channel to engage and interact with audiences. Generally speaking, fashion is a visual industry, and the opportunity to extensively showcase a brand's identity is crucial. Instagram combines several interrelated, interactive visual tools that facilitate the process of delivering information to the marketplace, as well as allowing brands to make use of different patterns, layouts, color combinations and textual content to maintain a strong and consistent brand identity.

Facebook seems to offer more potential for delivering informative content. As the content flow does not create a distinct visual profile, information can be delivered randomly without the risk of damaging overall visual quality.

LinkedIn was included in the study as the platform used by many luxury brands for professional communication during lockdowns. As such, it offered insights into the way fashion brands and their parent companies dealt with the crisis.

In addition to the three social media platforms at the core of the analysis, brand communication on TikTok was also examined. The platform was included in the study in light of the fact that several brands apparently discovered it during lockdowns as the new tool for connecting with younger generations. However, since the platform's social media strategy went through extensive and rapid changes during the selected time frame, a robust analysis for research purposes was not possible.

The analysis focused on digital communication by luxury fashion brands over a 4-month time frame divided into 3 periods corresponding to: (i) communication in the month preceding lockdowns, in order to assess social media presence and content management under normal conditions; (ii) communication during lockdowns; and (iii) communication after lockdown measures were lifted, to examine social media content during the phase of recovery and return to relatively normal conditions. While it may at first be considered a drawback, the apparent time frame volatility can be explained by the fact that various countries and markets entered lockdowns at different times. In Italy and France, for example, lockdowns were officially announced on 10 March 2020 and 17 March 2020, respectively. Therefore, these dates were taken as reference points for Italian and French brands. The same logic was applied to the end of the lockdown period, albeit with additional peculiarities. After being forced by lockdowns to reshuffle their social media presence, luxury fashion brands did not find returning to normal content strategies an easy task, after all. For this reason, the overall time frame is variable but clearly specified in each case.

During the analysis stage of research, visual methodologies were used to provide evidence for the research questions. Communication artifacts were examined through visual images and videos posted by luxury brands on social media pages and their evolution within the time frames specified above. Together with page layout, the main artifacts in this review process were the images themselves. (This is especially true for Instagram due to the platform's features.) All visual content was coded using categories such as general tone of voice of the page, frequency of publication, object of the specific communication (e.g., product, event, testimonial, designers, etc.), and information on the level of engagement it generated. Therefore, this was not a purely visual content analysis. Rather, it consisted of a mixed technique that took into account the framing of single visual artifacts in the wider context of approach to social pages and social media strategy, engagement, and reactions to the content itself. It is worth noting that Instagram was the most significant source in the analysis, since it provides a general view of the page and, at the same time, all pictures can be accessed one by one. All images collected during observation were clustered and coded according to: (i) layout, (ii) frequency, and (iii) genre.

The coding process allowed the authors to develop a better understanding of the major changes that occurred during lockdown periods. For example, relevant differences in the approach to social media communication and brand narratives at different phases of the research timeline emerged clearly from the analysis of page layouts. Visual communication layouts in the month preceding lockdowns may be grouped as follows: (i) 3–6 pictures with the same theme (new product, brand ambassadors, events) and color compliance; (ii) chessboard layout (with emphasis on certain colors or on the product); (iii) abstract aesthetics, with a single color palette. During lockdowns, the visual elements of the page were reconsidered. Content was still accurate in most cases, but in a more random way. This could be partially explained by the fact that luxury fashion brands had to react rapidly, especially as regards COVID-19–related activities. Some, for example, started posting pictures of hospitals and health-related topics because they were involved in fundraising projects. Others, like Gucci for instance, completely abandoned layout maintenance during the lockdown period. Their photo selection can hardly be called curated, the final effect being somehow intentionally unprofessional. After lockdown restrictions were lifted, most gradually went back to pre-crisis layouts, showing 3 pictures with the same theme.

3. MAIN FINDINGS AND RESEARCH LIMITATIONS

The research focus was on social media communication of luxury fashion brands, which mainly use platforms to engage with existing or future customers and influence purchase decision. Lockdowns brought significant changes to people's habits, which also affected their usage of social media platforms. As far as luxury fashion is concerned, several key changes may have been determined by the impossibility for customers to "go out and show off". Changes in the social context and individual situations generated a sudden need for luxury fashion brands to develop new forms of narratives to engage consumers and push them towards some form of purchase behavior. Appellation, as Williamson (1978) has called it, is especially relevant to describing such changes. The concept suggests that when viewers encounter an ad, they create their own meaning for the product they are offered by making connections between signs and,

When Luxury Brands Changed Their Approach to Social Media

Table 1. Panel composition

Conglomerate-owned Brands		Independent Brands
Conglomerate	**Brands**	
Kering	Balenciaga, Bottega Veneta, Brioni, Gucci	J.W. Anderson, Chanel, Giorgio Armani, Hermes, Lanvin, Jacquemus, Jil Sander, Missoni, Moncler, Prada
LVMH	Berluti, Celine, Dior, Fendi, Givenchy, Kenzo, Loro Piana, Lowe, Patou, Thomas Pink	
Mayhoola	Balmain, Valentino	
OTB	Marni	

in the same way, they give meaning to themselves. That is the reason why many luxury fashion brands during lockdowns "pushed" images of beauty and care products in particular environments. Chanel's series focused on an entertaining beauty narrative ("Bold-Blue Monday," "Red-Lips-Only Thursday") that placed beauty products in the familiar critical environment of lockdown, so as to let viewers associate the images with themselves and easily visualize the product within their own setting.

Furthermore, data elaboration highlighted major changes in luxury brands' narratives during lockdowns. Among the most evident effects of lockdowns was a complete reshuffle of editorial calendars, with a sharp increase in real-time content production and fully redesigned narrative approaches. In terms of general findings, some key aspects emerged clearly: (i) luxury brands devoted huge efforts to providing consumers with content related to activities not traditionally covered by their narratives (e.g., yoga classes with Missoni, Alicia Keys' concert for Valentino on Instagram, or podcasts and conversations about general and fashion-related topics with key actors in the industry); (ii) brand pages looked more and more like personal pages, with spontaneity and informality taking the place of that sense of elitism so often associated with luxury brand narratives, and this had an impact not only on content but also on layouts and tone of voice; (iii) brands devoted time to opening themselves up to consumer engagement, placing a strong emphasis on heritage and know-how (as in the case of Brioni's #tailoringlegends or Dior's #DiorHeritage); (iv) product promotion was subtler and less central, with a large use of editorials and a focus on iconic products (usually less central in social media communication, which is more focused on present collections) or affordable luxury items (easier to purchase online).

Another relevant change in communication patterns was evident in the gradual receptiveness to co-creation, which reached unexpected, innovative peaks, such as with Marc Jacob's co-creation of branded fashion outfits for the Animal Crossing gaming platform. Lockdowns forced luxury brands to develop new creative approaches that led to less refined and more spontaneous brand image management: a prime example of this was Versace's creative director's grandmother modelling on a FaceTime Vogue photoshoot.

Not all social media platforms have been affected by these changes in the same manner. Different levels of intimacy and creativity were possible on different platforms. Instagram was the top choice for most fashion luxury brands, and the one that offered the best possibilities for creativity. Facebook offered fewer opportunities for engaging with consumers and creating emotional bonds, and some brands even had "empty" pages. The virus and the events surrounding the pandemic were rarely mentioned on LinkedIn, where brands are seen as part of a conglomerate as opposed to other social media where they have stand-alone profiles.

Four main brand narrative archetypes were identified during this phase of research, depending on brands' response to the COVID-19 crisis:

The Patrician Brand: Before lockdowns, luxury fashion brands in this group used social media platforms and profiles as online magazines where they would visually showcase new products and the brand's heritage, maintaining a distant and aloof communication style and no engagement with their audience. Although their communication style changed significantly when lockdown measures were introduced, it still centered around emphasizing brand heritage and know-how. Traditional product promotion was replaced by extensive editorial content, which nevertheless included product mention. The lifting of lockdowns was not accompanied by any particular announcement; therefore, the return to pre-COVID social media strategies was barely noticeable.

The Friendly Brand: The communication style used by brands in this group before lockdowns were introduced was characterized by limited content, traditionally tied to product launches/promotion. Yet their level of engagement with their audiences dramatically increased during lockdowns, with prompt replies to comments and deeper interaction overall compared to other archetypes, revealing a marked shift in social media and content strategies. Brands in this group offered entertaining and engaging content such as live performances, yoga sessions, and livestreaming DJ sets, or used their social media pages to provide educational content—hosting artists and craft workshops as well as environmental podcasts. In most cases, there was no mention of the product(s). When lockdowns were lifted and the time came to revisit their narrative, brands within this archetype chose one of two communication approaches: either (1) thanking the community for the time spent together and promptly removing all references to COVID-19 from their new content; or (2) continuing to post engaging COVID-19–related content alongside regular advertisements and product promotions.

The Socially Conscious Brand: In the month before lockdowns became widespread, brands in this group showed a friendly yet "relaxed" attitude toward engaging with customers in social media. Most of their content during lockdown revolved instead around the COVID-19 pandemic, safety tips and precautions, donations to coronavirus relief efforts, and providing support and visibility to small businesses affected by the restrictions. In fact, some used their pages to popularize the issue of staying-at-home and emphasize the seriousness of the pandemic. Gucci, for instance, contributed its Instagram pages to spreading messages from the World Health Organization from the very onset of the COVID-19 outbreak, helping to share public service information. Any move by these brands towards classic marketing strategies after lockdowns ended was evident and noticed by the audience.

The Static Brand: A relatively significant number of luxury fashion brands did not change their communication techniques during lockdowns. However, it should be noted that, even before then, they seemingly favored a static and traditional approach to social media content creation—with carefully curated images and fixed layouts making their social profiles look like photo galleries. Having treated communication during lockdown as a perfunctory exercise, with no real changes in content, the brands in this group seamlessly resumed their traditional methods as soon as restrictions were lifted.

The exploratory nature of this research places limitations on generalizing its findings, mainly because of the methods used and case study selection criteria. Indeed, case studies were selected for their relevance to the research aims and ability to show, at a very high level of visibility, changes in the nature of brand narratives that where the object of observation. The presence of similar patterns in luxury fashion brands that operate with a lower intensity of investment in communication through social media platform is yet to be explored.

When Luxury Brands Changed Their Approach to Social Media

Furthermore, a relationship between lockdown phases and alternative brand narrative activation was established in a comprehensive model, although the organizational conditions enabling shifts in communication strategies, and how these can be turned into explicit processes to support digital marketing communication in times of crisis, should be studied in greater detail. These limitations, then, provide the opportunity to further investigate the topic.

What are the organizational determinants of change in luxury fashion brand narratives? The organizational processes supporting digital media strategies have led to different patterns of response to the crisis brought by lockdown measures. Such processes involve not only actors within the company but also the external network of suppliers and consultants.

Can brand communication archetypes such as those highlighted in the findings be generalized? A quantitative research with a larger representative sample may help to further investigate the subject.

4. IMPLICATIONS FOR MANAGEMENT

Despite the exploratory nature of the study, several implications for management can be drawn from the findings, especially as regards brand narratives and social media communication. A brand narrative approach that is coherent with new scenarios and rapid shifts in consumption patterns can have a significant impact on customer engagement and brand loyalty. The success of the turnaround plan is very much dependent on the activation of new patterns of social media communication. Findings from this study can help foster discussion and prompt further research into key managerial issues that may be summarized as follows:

The open question at this stage is whether a return to classical marketing approaches is possible after laying bare the brand's soul. The obvious risk is that customers perceive going back to a less personal and "intimate" connection as unfair. In the current context, brands should embrace more flexible, balanced ways of communicating with customers—e.g., by favoring real "social media" pages, audience engagement, and content co-creation over digital magazines on Instagram and other platforms.

The way in which luxury fashion brands are reacting to the crisis seems to be related to the archetype they belong to in terms of brand narrative. Thus, a deeper understanding of the nature of brand storytelling and its ability to evolve may help management plan for the required investment and actions needed to increase brand equity over time.

New patterns of social media communication that started to emerge during lockdowns revealed Instagram's latent potential. The lockdown during the Milan fashion week in February 2020 forced many brands to revise their calendars and rethink their approach to catwalks. Many used Instagram as the main platform for showing the new collections. Since social distancing rules made it impossible for buyers and PRs to physically attend the fashion shows, the industry "filter" was to all extents removed. By exclusively showing their collections on Instagram, designers allowed consumers to be more directly involved, while naturally moving towards a direct-to-consumer business model. Not only was Instagram used to showcase products but also to gauge consumers' reactions without the influence of third-party opinions.

An important implication for luxury fashion brands, especially the younger ones, is that customers' insights may be obtained at the initial launching phase of new collections. Further, Instagram may be exploited not only as an additional tool, but also as a way to cut costs. Digital avatars and digital prototypes of the collection may be effectively used in uncertain times. Finally, there is room for new ways of engaging with audiences without the added expense of PR campaigns, sample products and celebrities, and endorsements by influencers.

Once again, the unexpected changes to the way brands can deliver their identity through social media and fashion shows make it difficult not to question the role of influencer marketing in a direct-to-consumers reality. As mentioned elsewhere in this chapter, audience engagement and openness to co-creation, especially when brand-initiated, allow consumers and brand enthusiasts to perceive the more sincere side of luxury fashion brands. Therefore, agents and intermediaries that help customers feel a closer connection to brands may be perceived as redundant.

Finally, it may be concluded that a "friendlier," more open approach to customer relationship management carries with it several implications, also in terms of organizational roles and company practices. First, the role of creative director is further strenghened. As highlighted in the case of Alessandro Michele, who shared his personal diary on Instagram the central role of the creative director in brand communication on social media platforms is key to showing brand authenticity and the degree of openness towards customers. Editorial calendars become less anchored to product promotion and more open to incorporating real-time content—with on-the-fly, less polished stories that nonetheless create a more inclusive and "intimate" feel. This affords digital communication teams the opportunity of operating within a framework that is more strategy-oriented, as well as allowing greater freedom and discretion as to how to respond to consumer needs and external influences. The opportunities offered by a more sophisticated use of social media (and other platforms too, as in the case of Animal Crossing for Marc Jacobs, or Valentino) pave the way for interesting new approaches to the promotion and development of high-fashion collections. Traditional runway shows may soon lose their centrality, with significant benefits in terms of reducing promotional costs. Additionally, new and innovative approaches to customer engagement may be developed, and new opportunities may be offered by the use of big data to assess customer engagement and response to new collections. In the case of luxury brands, such integration between digital communication and other aspects of the supply chain may lead to greater integration of value creation processes and got-to-market strategies, and, overall, to redesigning business models and reconfiguring some of their key elements.

REFERENCES

Assouly, O., & Bergé, P. (2005). *Le luxe: essais sur la fabrique de l'ostentation. Institut français de la mode*. Editions du regard.

Barron, L. (2019). The Return of the Celebrity Fashion Muse: Brand Endorsement, Creative Inspiration and Celebrity-Influenced Design Communication. *Fashion Theory*, 1–20. doi:10.1080/136270 4X.2019.1656946

Bastos, W., & Levy, S. J. (2012). A history of the concept of branding: Practice and theory. *Journal of Historical Research in Marketing*, 4(3), 347–368. doi:10.1108/17557501211252934

Blackden, E. (2016). 6 key luxury trends that will make or break brands in 2016. *Luxury Society*. Retrieved April 25, 2020, from https://www.luxurysociety.com/en/articles/2016/01/6-key-luxury-trends-that-will-make-or-break-brands-in-2016/

When Luxury Brands Changed Their Approach to Social Media

Brun, A., Castelli, C., & Karaosman, H. (2016). See now buy now: A revolution for luxury supply chain management. In R. Rinaldi & R. Bandinelli (Eds.), *Business Models and ICT Technologies for the Fashion Supply Chain* (pp. 33–46). Springer.

Correa, T., Hinsley, A. W., & De Zúñiga, H. G. (2010). Who interacts on the web? The inter-section of users' personality and social media use. *Computers in Human Behavior, 26*(2), 247–253. doi:10.1016/j.chb.2009.09.003

Dall'Olmo Riley, F., & Lacroix, C. (2003). Luxury branding on the Internet: Lost opportunity or impossibility? *Marketing Intelligence & Planning, 21*(2), 96–104. doi:10.1108/02634500310465407

Danziger, P. N. (2018). 4 Mega-Trends ahead for the luxury market in 2019: expect turmoil and slowing sales. *Forbes*. Retrieved April 25, 2020, from https://www.forbes.com/sites/pamdanziger/2018/12/18/whats-ahead-for-the-luxury-market-in-2019-expect-turmoil-and-slowing-sales/#35352dd86578

Dimitrova, L. I., Björck, L., & Fregne, A. (2018). Limited edition: Collaborations between luxury brands. *LBMG Strategic Brand Management-Masters Paper Series*.

Donzé, P. Y. (2018). The birth of luxury big business: LVMH, Richemont and Kering. In P. Donzé & R. Fujioka (Eds.), *Global Luxury* (pp. 19–38). Palgrave. doi:10.1007/978-981-10-5236-1_2

Donzé, P. Y., & Wubs, B. (2019). Storytelling and the making of a global luxury fashion brand: Christian Dior. *International Journal of Fashion Studies, 6*(1), 83–102. doi:10.1386/infs.6.1.83_1

Friedman, V. (2015). Balenciaga Names Demna Gvasalia, Vetements Designer, as Artistic Director. *New York Times*. Retrieved April 25, 2020, from https://www.nytimes.com/2015/10/08/fashion/balenciaga-names-demna-gvasalia-vetements-designer-as-artistic-director.html

Fukai, A. (2002). *Fashion: the collection of the Kyoto Costume Institute: a history from the 18th to the 20th century*. Taschen.

Gallaugher, J., & Ransbotham, S. (2010). Social media and customer dialog management at Starbucks. *MIS Quarterly Executive, 9*(4), 197–212.

Giertz-Mårtenson, I. (2012). H&M–documenting the story of one of the world's largest fashion retailers. *Business History, 54*(1), 108–115. doi:10.1080/00076791.2011.617203

Glaser, B., Bailyn, L., Fernandez, W., Holton, J. A., & Levina, N. (2015). What Grounded Theory Is...A Critically Reflective Conversation Among Scholars. *Organizational Research Methods, 18*(4), 581–599. doi:10.1177/1094428114565028

Hagtvedt, H., & Patrick, V. M. (2009). The broad embrace of luxury: Hedonic potential as a driver of brand extendibility. *Journal of Consumer Psychology, 19*(4), 608–618. doi:10.1016/j.jcps.2009.05.007

Heine, K., & Berghaus, B. (2014). Luxury goes digital: How to tackle the digital luxury brand–consumer touchpoints. *Journal of Global Fashion Marketing, 5*(3), 223–234. doi:10.1080/20932685.2014.907606

Hine, C. (2015). *Ethnography for the internet: Embedded, embodied and everyday*. Bloomsbury Publishing.

Howell, M., & Prevenier, W. (2001). *From Reliable Sources: An Introduction to Historical Methods*. Cornell University Press.

Jones, G. G., & Pouillard, V. (2009). Christian Dior: A New Look for Haute Couture. Harvard Business School Case no. 809-159. Harvard Business School Publishing.

Kapferer, J. N. (2008). *The new strategic brand management: Creating and sustaining brand equity long term.* Kogan Page Publishers.

Kapferer, J. N., & Bastien, V. (2012). *The luxury strategy: Break the rules of marketing to build luxury brands.* Kogan Page Publishers.

Kozinets, R. V., de Valck, K., Wojnicki, A. C., & Wilner, S. (2010). Networked narratives: Understanding Word-of-Mouth Marketing in Online Communities. *Journal of Marketing, 74*(2), 71–89. doi:10.1509/jm.74.2.71

La Ferla, R. (2000). Cheap Chic'Draws Crowds on 5th Ave. *New York Times.* Retrieved April 25, 2020, from https://www.nytimes.com/2000/04/11/style/cheap-chic-draws-crowds-on5thave.htmUpagewanted=all

Langlade, É. (1913). *Rose Bertin: The Creator of Fashion at the Court of Marie-Antoinette.* Charles Scribner's Sons.

Lutz, C. A., & Collins, J. L. (1993). *Reading National Geographic.* University of Chicago Press.

Miller, L. E. (1993). *Cristóbal Balenciaga.* Batsford.

Moore, K., & Reid, S. (2008). The birth of brand: 4000 years of branding. *Business History, 50*(4), 419–432. doi:10.1080/00076790802106299

Mosca, F., & Casalegno, C. (2020). Managing Integrated Brand Communication Strategies in the Online Era: New Marketing Frontiers for Luxury Goods. In Global Branding: Breakthroughs in Research and Practice (pp. 227–242). IGI Global.

Mosca, F., Casalegno, C., & Rosso, C. (2017). *Luxury Brands and Social Media: Implications around New Trends in Selling Luxury Products. A study across different product categories.* Global Fashion Management Conference at Vienna 2017, Vienna, Austria. 10.15444/GFMC2017.01.01.01

Neto, M. J. P. (2018). Charles Frederick Worth and the birth of Haute Couture: Fashion design and textile renewal in the times of conspicuous consumption. In G. Montagna & C. Carvalho (Eds.), *Textiles, Identity and Innovation: Design the Future: Proceedings of the 1st International Textile Design Conference.* CRC Press.

Olds, L. (2001). World War II and fashion: The birth of the new look. *Constructing the Past, 2*(1), 47–64.

Parry, Z. (2018). *From hood to haute: the luxurification of streetwear* [Unpublished doctoral dissertation]. Hogeschool van Amsterdam.

Perrey, J., & Spillecke, D. (2012). *Principles of successful brand management: art, science, craft. Retail Marketing and Branding: A Definitive Guide to Maximizing ROI.* John Wiley & Sons.

Pini, F. M., & Pelleschi, V. (2017). Creating a Seamless Experience for Luxury Consumers Integrating Online and Offline Communication. In E. Rigaud-Lacresse & F. Pini (Eds.), *New Luxury Management* (pp. 217–237). Palgrave Macmillan. doi:10.1007/978-3-319-41727-1_12

When Luxury Brands Changed Their Approach to Social Media

Popomaronis, T. (2017). Luxury Brands Are Becoming Big Players In The E-Commerce Game. *Forbes*. Retrieved April 25, 2020, from https://www.forbes.com/sites/tompopomaronis/2017/02/28/luxury-brands-are-becoming-big-players-in-the-growing-ecommerce-game/#4fb635d22079

Remaury, B. (2004). *Marques et récits: La marque face à l'imaginaire culturel contemporain*. Institut Français de la Mode-Editions du Regard.

Rose, G. (2012). Visual methodologies: An introduction to researching with visual methods. *Sage (Atlanta, Ga.)*.

Rovai, S. (2014). The evolution of luxury consumption in China. In G. Atwal & D. Bryson (Eds.), *Luxury Brands in Emerging Markets* (pp. 130–134). Palgrave Macmillan. doi:10.1057/9781137330536_12

Sachs, J. (2012). *Winning the Story Wars*. Harvard Business Review Press.

Sepe, G., & Anzivino, A. (2020). Guccification: Redefining Luxury Through Art—The Gucci Revolution. In M. Massi & A. Turrini (Eds.), *The Artification of Luxury Fashion Brands* (pp. 89–112). Springer International.

Settembrini, L. (1994). *From haute couture to prêt-à-porter*. Guggenheim Museum.

Smith, K. E. (2002). *The influence of Audrey Hepburn and Hubert de Givenchy on American fashion, 1952–1965* [Unpublished master's thesis]. Michigan State University.

Spillecke, D., & Perrey, J. (2012). *Retail Marketing and Branding: A Definitive Guide to Maximizing ROI*. Wiley.

Sproles, G. B. (1981). Analyzing fashion life cycles—Principles and perspectives. *Journal of Marketing, 45*(4), 116–124.

Stadiem, W. (2014). *Jet Set: The People, the Planes, the Glamour, and the Romance in Aviation's Glory Years*. Ballantine Books.

Steele, V. (2017). *Paris fashion: a cultural history*. Bloomsbury Publishing. doi:10.5040/9781474269711

Trochim, W. M. (1989). Outcome pattern matching and program theory. *Evaluation and Program Planning, 12*(4), 355–366. doi:10.1016/0149-7189(89)90052-9

Turner, N. (2011). Deprivation Fashion. *Duck: Journal for Research in Textiles and Textile Design, 2*.

Vigneron, F., & Johnson, L. W. (2004). Measuring perceptions of brand luxury. *Journal of Brand Management, 11*(6), 484–506. doi:10.1057/palgrave.bm.2540194

Williamson, J. (1978). *Decoding advertisements: ideology and meaning in advertising*. Marion Boyers.

Yin, R. K. (2003). *Design and methods. Case study research*. Sage.

ENDNOTE

[1] Emotional assets are becoming ever more significant for brand differentiation, due to the increasing relevance of symbolic consumption and consumers' propensity to choose a product because of a"consonance" between its symbolic personality and their own (Vigneron and Johnson, 2004).

Chapter 7

Innovating Luxury Service Experiences Through E–Servicescapes

Laura Ingrid Maria Colm
SDA Bocconi School of Management, Bocconi University, Italy

Stefano Prestini
Bocconi University, Italy

ABSTRACT

The digital customer experience is a top priority and major challenge for luxury service companies, who have to connect with their target customers yet strive to remain exclusive and to innovate their core offers while preserving their heritage. After a brief review of the literature on customer experience and virtual environments in luxury service contexts, this chapter focuses on e-servicescapes as a means for innovation and improvement in delivering omnichannel experiences for luxury customers. Adopting Bitner's typology of servicescapes, this chapter is based on a three case vignettes analysis that highlights how luxury service providers can use e-servicescapes to enrich their physical service experiences. Three e-servicescape strategies are identified—integration, amplification, and substitution—that ultimately support companies in renewing and improving their overall luxury propositions.

1. INTRODUCTION

A recent report by Euromonitor International (2019) revealed that digital has been one of the most transformative innovations in the luxury industry, with connectivity being the "new normal" for many luxury customers and a major game-changer for players in the luxury landscape. Thus, the digital customer experience is a top priority and a major challenge for luxury companies, who have to connect with their target customers, yet striving to remain exclusive (Blasco-Arcas et al., 2016; Baker et al., 2018).

This tendency is even more crucial for luxury service providers, who have to convey and "tangibilize" the experience offered in their physical environment also through their e-servicescapes (the service's online

DOI: 10.4018/978-1-7998-5882-9.ch007

environment), in order to involve especially the younger generations, who are not only online channels' main users (Mangold & Smith, 2012) – having grown up in a digital world (Deloitte, 2017; Danzinger, 2019) – but are also looking increasingly for customized, co-created and intimate customer-company experiences (McKinsey & Company, 2018). In addition, such innovations become even more relevant from a strategic standpoint in a moment in time in which access to the physical service environment can be difficult, limited or even impossible due to the exogenous shock caused by the Covid-19 pandemic.

After a brief review of the literature on customer experience, digital experiences and digital environments in luxury service contexts, this chapter focuses on e-servicescapes as a means for innovation and improvement in delivering omnichannel experiences for luxury customers. In fact, e-servicescapes are a relevant source of competitive advantage, if the company is capable to incorporate customers' needs and wants into its design (Parasuraman et al., 2005; Sonmath et al., 2008). Thus, this chapter investigates and focuses on how e-servicescapes can play the role of facilitators in the interaction between a service provider and its customers, spurring a favorable company image in the customer's mind (Fisk et al., 2000) – a particularly salient aspect for luxury firms, who need to sustain their unique positioning in the long-term.

Three case vignettes, selected according to Bitner's typology of servicescapes (1992) and focusing in particular on elaborate interpersonal services, are used to shed light on how luxury service providers can use e-servicescapes to enrich their customers' physical experiences, ultimately innovating their service offer and overall value proposition.

From an academic standpoint our findings contribute to a better understanding of e-servicescapes' and digital environments' roles in innovating effectively luxury service providers' offerings. The results also speak to luxury service managers who need to constantly update their high-end offers from a technological standpoint, keeping them relevant for their demanding customer base. Thus, e-servicescapes can play an important role in fostering customers' active involvement, renewing a company's business model and making it more resilient to exogenous shocks (like the one caused by the Covid-19 pandemic), as well as improving the brand's overall omnichannel strategies.

2. CUSTOMER EXPERIENCE IN LUXURY SERVICE CONTEXTS

The concept of *customer experience* grounds its roots in the 1980s, when the literature on consumer behavior was rapidly growing, and offered a new, original view of customers as feelers and emotional human beings, beyond just rational decision-makers only caring about a product's functional benefits. Customer experiences thus encompass the role of emotions in consumption behavior and can be defined as a subjective state of consciousness with "a variety of symbolic meanings, hedonic responses, and aesthetic criteria" (Holbrook & Hirschman, 1982, p. 132).

The concept became more prominent a decade later in the marketing field, when Pine and Gilmore coined the term *experience economy* (Pine & Gilmore, 1999), referring to a new category of economic offering, which requires companies to conceive and deliver memorable events for their customers. Along with that, Schmitt (1999) developed a conceptual framework for experiential marketing, distinguishing among five types of experiences that companies can craft for to their customers: sense, feel, think, act and relate. Several contributions followed in the marketing and management disciplines, emphasizing the role of customer experiences as value generators for both firms and customers (see for instance Addis & Holbrook, 2001; Carù & Cova, 2003; LaSalle & Britton, 2003). Indeed, customers are keener to soak in delightful experiences, which last longer in the customer's mind, and thus stimulate a virtuous circle in terms of competitive advantage for the firm (Rather, 2020).

Due to its interactive nature, customer engagement gains special significance for services, since they are characterized by intense exchanges between provider and customers (e.g., Hollebeek et al., 2019). Indeed, the concept of *service experience* – the interaction between firm and consumer when a service is provided – is a construct that has been acknowledged as central for the design and offering of the service (Zomerdjik & Voss, 2010). This aspect is particularly relevant in the light of the co-created nature of services, which are the result of a joint effort between company and customers (Prahalad & Ramaswamy, 2004).

In 2011 Helkkula offered a systematic literature review of service experience in marketing research, with the aim of characterizing the concept. She ultimately identified three categories: the phenomenological, the process-based, and the outcome-based service experience. The first category of literature goes back to the origins of customer experience and is adopted by researchers following the original definition provided by Holbrook and Hirschman (see Schembri, 2006; Vargo & Lusch, 2008). According to this understanding, a service experience is a subjective, internal phenomenon for each individual. Moreover, since customers are often times in a collective setting during the service experience, the latter can also be labelled as relational, social and intersubjective, since a joint sensemaking process takes place (Pullman & Gross, 2004). The process-based category views service experience as a process, hence focusing on the actions, phases, or steps making up such process (Toivonen et al., 2007). Finally, the outcome-based service experience category focuses on service experience as one element in models linking a number of variables or attributes to various outcomes.

it can be assessed that customer experiences are manifold, since they are composed by different elementary components, but at are experienced as a whole (Gentile et al., 2007). For this reason, companies should strive to offer smooth service experiences, able to convey a consistent omnichannel company image.

The latter aspect is particularly salient in the context of luxury services, since "managing luxury consists in managing the aura of the brand over time" (Dion & Arnould, 2011) to maintain and sustain the unique positioning of the brand. This cannot be successfully accomplished without an ongoing delivery of seamless service experiences through all touchpoints between the company and its customers (be it a retail store, trade show, website, etc.). Indeed, to justify its prestigious positioning in the customers' eyes, a luxury service provider must ensure that the delivered experiences always meet three criteria.

First, luxury service providers should always ensure the experiences are of high quality, since luxury offerings are traditionally associated with exclusivity and status (Atwal & Williams, 2009). Luxury service experiences thus have to reflect the heritage of the company, signal the values of the brand, and justify the offer's high price. For this reason, luxury brands need to strictly control all elements of the service encounter – including back-office organization, frontline employees' selection, and employees' interaction with customers (Dion & Borraz, 2017; Tynan et al., 2010). This involves the provider taking an active role in "orchestrating" the delivery of extraordinary experiences (Arnould & Price, 1993), as the example of The Spa at Mandarin Oriental in Guangzhou (China) shows. There, the five-starred spa experience has been organized as a structured ritual, from the first consultation with the therapist to the after-treatment activities. Upon arrival, the guest is escorted into a stylish private pod and offered a cup of tea. Then, a complimentary tian quan, a calming Chinese bathing ritual, follows. All these activities take place before the guest even starts the scheduled treatment (Kester, 2018).

Second, luxury service experiences should always be personalized. In the past, customization has mainly characterized the product-sphere, with luxury buyers dreaming about "accumulating" unique possessions. This trend has now also spilled over to services, stimulating the desire of spending quality time while living unique experiences. So, luxury service brands need to deliver personalized offers corresponding to their brand image, in order to maintain and sustain their unique positioning in the marketplace (Kapferer & Bastien, 2009). An example of such customization is provided by the renowned multi-Michelin starred chef Gordon Ramsey, who organizes private dining events, where guests can choose venue and menu options.

Lastly, co-creation plays a particularly significant role in this context, since customers are increasingly appreciating – and also expecting – to be involved in the service design and delivery process previously managed uniquely by the provider (McKinsey & Company, 2018; Prahalad & Rawaswamy, 2004). This implies designing experiences in such a way that the customer is always involved actively, like the international wedding planner Colin Cowie is doing, who is constantly interacting with the future spouses for detailed consultations.

3. CHALLENGES AND OPPORTUNITIES OF DIGITAL ENVIRONMENTS IN LUXURY SERVICES

Literature has acknowledged the widening gap between luxury market complexity and organizations' ability to understand and respond to these new conditions. Digital marketing and the digitalization process have led to a growing diffusion of *digital environments*, which are settings or "places" produced through computer technology – including websites, mobile applications, social media, audio and video content, and other web-based resources – that allow social interaction (Andrade Braga, 2009). Such interactions take place among individuals, but also between individuals (customers) and companies, since "as customers spend more time in digital environments, brands are moving into digital services" (Chung et al., 2020, p. 587).

However, not all industries are entering digitalization with the same pace, and in some cases the adoption of new digital technologies is rather slow. Indeed, luxury brands belong to those not yet having fully embraced the Internet (Euromonitor International, 2019). Such reluctancy depends in the first place on luxury being the embodiment of heritage and tradition, which requires bridging the gap between past and future prudently. It also involves adopting a long-term vision, in order to "follow" trends only selectively and to find a credible balance between presence and absence (Holmqvist et al., 2020; Kapferer, 2013). Against this backdrop, e-commerce has been typically considered inappropriate for luxury companies (Wiedmann et al., 2009), which is why this sector is behind others also with respect to online transactions (Díaz et al., 2016). An example of controlled digitalization in luxury environments is the case of Chanel, the iconic luxury fashion company, that does not sell its exclusive garments through digital platforms. So far, consumers can only purchase fragrances and cosmetics through the branded e-commerce.

In addition to this, the innovations introduced by the so-called digital revolution, were not created for luxury brands, but instead for big, mass corporations. As Kapferer (2013) explains, when it comes to digital "everything is big: big data, large numbers of fans on Facebook, most-searched products on the Internet, most-viewed pieces of brand content on YouTube, highest of visitors and so on" (p. 37). This is exactly the contrary of the exclusivity that characterizes luxury brands and their sources of competitive advantage. Accordingly, literature strongly recommends caution when luxury companies plan to adopt strategies from non-luxury contexts, in order to avoid undermining the luxury service experience (Holmqvist et al., 2020). This is all the more so, as introducing digital innovations necessarily requires

Innovating Luxury Service Experiences Through E-Servicescapes

companies to revise their business models (Leeflang et al., 2014), thus involving radical changes to the company's DNA.

Another reason for luxury companies' skepticism towards being present in digital environments is linked to the web's tendency to shorten distances between actors, while a luxury brand's positioning is built on keeping distance and creating a sense of aspiration. The web also creates "democratization", while luxury providers need to stretch the distance between potential and actual customers (Kapferer & Bastien, 2009). As a consequence, finding growth opportunities through digital environments yet remaining rare, is a critical issue that luxury companies are confronted with.

These issues are particularly challenging for luxury service providers, since such companies are based on selling the "intangible". At the same time, despite of the manifold difficulties connected to adopting digital innovations, a presence in digital environments is mandatory for luxury firms, since it allows to seize several opportunities.

In the first place, one third of all luxury customers in 2019 were Millennials or younger generations, and these targets rely intensively on Internet usage. This figure is expected to breach 50% by 2024, making a company's strong online presence a huge opportunity for establishing long-lasting relationships with a relevant, growing target (Thomsen et al., 2020).

Second, digital sales grew by 59% between 2013 and 2018, also thanks to mobile connectivity, which gives luxury customers instant access to everything from everywhere (Euromonitor International, 2019). Moreover, according to McKinsey & Company (2018), more than 80% of luxury sales are influenced by digital devices, as well as online user-generated content (see Chen et al., 2011; Mangold & Faulds, 2009). For instance, social media and peer reviews play a particularly crucial role in the context of services, since they allow to partially pre-assess the service that is going to be fully discovered only during the experience phase. Thus, investing in e-commerce, web-based services, as well as website and mobile application's design can have a strong, favorable impact on a luxury brand's reputation.

Lastly, it would be important for luxury companies to earn an established position in digital environments earlier than their direct competitors. This can help "defending" the own image and distinctiveness through a credible and recognizable positioning, able to capture web users' scarce attention (Kapferer, 2013) and contrast volatile relationships (see for instance Kim & Kim, 2020).

To seize the opportunities offered by digital innovation, luxury firms need to be driven by forward-looking and well-conceived digital strategies, able to determine to whom to talk and how, where (not) to go, and what to do there. Such digital strategies' main goal should be ensuring a streamlined omnichannel presence to luxury service providers. Indeed, it is crucial that both offline and online luxury service experiences are always advanced from a technological standpoint. Indeed, luxury research recognizes that perfect levels of service require the involvement of modern information technology, because customers are themselves tech-savvy and thus have high expectations also from luxury brands (Euromonitor International, 2019; Kapferer, 2013). So, service providers should fully leverage digital technology's potential and be credible trend-setters in the eyes of their demanding customers.

4. E-SERVICESCAPES AS A MEANS OF INNOVATION FOR LUXURY SERVICE PROVIDERS

In literature the setting or ambience in which the service is delivered and in which the service experience together with the relations between provider and customer take place, has been labeled as *servicescape*.

Booms and Bitner (1981) provided a first definition, describing a servicescape as "the environment in which the service is assembled and in which the seller and customer interact, combined with tangible commodities that facilitate performance or communication of the service" (p.36). Bitner (1992) further developed the concept and synthetized a servicescape as the physical environment in which a service process takes place. In this context both customers and employees are exposed to three different categories of stimuli, that – intentionally or accidentally – provide information about the setting: signs (environmental objects acting as explicit communicators, such as entrance/exit signs or labels indicating the brand name or rules of conduct), symbols (environmental objects communicating through implicit cues and shared meanings, such as white cloths signaling a restaurant's high-end positioning) and artifacts (environmental objects holding some cultural, historical or social interest for customers, acting as mementos of a pleasant experience, such as souvenirs or merchandise). These characteristics highlight that servicescapes are interactive settings, in which the service experience is created jointly and through the exchanges between provider and its customer(s). In this light, firms are constantly trying to improve servicescapes in order to offer unique, immersive, and interactive experiences (Cearley et al., 2017). This can be obtained also thanks to the strategic employment of digital technologies – both in store and virtually. Hence, servicescapes represent strategic assets with a strong innovation potential for companies, since they allow to address the dynamic nature of service experiences, adapting to and anticipating demand's continuously evolving needs and wants.

In the light of the increasing role of technology in shaping the customer experience, recent literature has started to focus also on servicescapes in relation to new, virtual contexts. Many terms have been employed to define the digital servicescape: e-scape (Koering, 2003), cyberscape (Williams & Dargel, 2004), bricks-and-clicks setting (in contrast to bricks-and-mortar) or clicks-only setting (Tuzovic, 2008), or virtual servicescape (Mari & Poggesi, 2013). However, the term that has become more common is *e-servicescape* (first introduced by Hopkins et al., 2009), defined as "the online environment factors that exist during service delivery" (Harris & Goode, 2010, p. 231). Such literature has focused on delineating the digital dimension of the servicescape and highlights in particular how the underlying logics of the servicescape's design apply not only to physical but also to online environments – as for instance, to the company's website, app or social media accounts. The ultimate goal is understanding the e-servicescape's role in the firm's overall value creation process and how to integrate it into existing business models effectively (Nilsson & Ballantyne, 2014). Indeed, e-servicescapes represent powerful instruments that service providers can leverage for renewing their offers and delivering enhanced and streamlined holistic experiences, both online and offline – e.g., with the aid of virtual tools such as interactive mirrors, touchscreens, or digital showrooms (Duncan et al., 2016).

So, e-servicescapes have the task to modernize the service offer's current features while safeguarding the luxury brand's heritage and exclusive positioning (Kapferer, 2013). This means that any innovation concerning the online servicescape's dimension must necessarily accommodate the tension between being perceived as contemporary and timeless. In addition, e-servicescpes should capitalize on the multisensory, sometimes opulent, experience typically delivered in the physical setting, ensuring to recreate the feeling of escapism that distinguishes luxury service experiences from ordinary ones. This feeling of elevation and exclusivity, and the associated rituals, can be challenging to convey in a digital setting (Kapferer & Bastien, 2009).

However, investing into innovative e-servicescapes ensures numerous benefits. For instance, they allow for a higher control over the delivered experience. Traffic and interactions over the web, and especially through social media, are tracked and can be analyzed by the company, thus gaining a better knowledge

Innovating Luxury Service Experiences Through E-Servicescapes

of the critical areas in the customer journey. This can lead not only to a higher customer satisfaction – indicated by customers' choice to continue using a given website or online service (Chung et al., 2020) – but also help to "tangibilize" the created online experience and even contribute to "humanizing" the brand, since it becomes more responsive to customers' preferences (Thomsen et al., 2020).

Indeed, a more intense interaction between company and customer thanks to the e-servicescape stimulates customer participation and feedback. For example, social media give the possibility to build causal interactions with customers (Kim & Ko, 2012), making those exchanges more comparable to the real-world ones, occurring through human agents, who typically provide support for purchase decisions, gathering information, etc. (Holzwarth et al., 2006).

This allows providers to incorporate customer reactions into both their online and offline environments, crafting more customized offers and spurring omnichannel strategies inspired by data and relevant first-hand information. In some cases, exchanges can even occur real time, e.g., through videocalls or chatbots, which favor customer engagement and co-creation (Chung et al., 2020). As a result, such initiatives create a virtuous circle, with positive reverberations on the establishment of long-lasting relationships and customer trust, thus stimulating re-purchase behavior and loyalty (Harris & Goode, 2010).

For some luxury services (as for instance luxury hotels, spas or restaurants) e-servicescapes also present e-commerce opportunities. The actual offer is still going to be experienced offline, but the various digital properties can act as further sales channels to buy or book the service in advance (e.g., via application). This does not only lead to additional sales opportunities, but also allows the service provider to better manage peaks and valleys, ultimately offering less crowded and more personalized offline experiences. In some other cases (e.g., luxury make-up classes or ad hoc consultancies) the e-servicescape can also be an alternative to the physical experience, thus representing a source of business model innovation.

Against this backdrop, another relevant and steadily growing category that benefits from integrating e-servicescapes into their settings are personal luxury companies. In fact, services play an increasingly important role in emphasizing the unique properties of luxury goods and can help improving the positioning and overall brand value (see Vargo & Lusch, 2008). As the personal luxury market (including luxury jewelry, timepieces, beauty, designer apparel, spirits, etc.) has showcased continuous growth across the years (Euromonitor International, 2019) also thanks to technological advances that have strongly influenced how consumers browse and buy luxury goods, e-servicescapes play a pivotal role. Indeed, they represent powerful means of innovation for such product-centric luxury businesses, since they are striving to convey exclusive, more relatable, customized, and interactive experiences. For instance, Burberry's – already a fashion-pioneer in bringing digital into their luxury in-store experiences – recently introduced an in-app messaging function called "R Message" that allows selected customers to directly interact with sales assistants. Among others, R-Message allows them to book in-store appointments, make product requests, or simply facilitate purchases by sending pictures. Similarly, Chanel Beauty has launched its own virtual makeover called "Chanel Try On" in Spring 2020, which allows customers to try the brand's iconic lipsticks in a wide range of versions. To fully exploit the benefits offered by virtual reality, Chanel Beauty has developed a tool that works on desktop as well as mobile, with the aim of catering also to the younger target's needs. In addition to modernizing the personal luxury provider's offer, digital service environments can also support businesses in better conveying their heritage and ensuring alignment between the customers' and the brand's corporate values. In this light, Cartier has developed the series of short films "L'Odyssée de Cartier" that can be viewed on their website, which retrace the maisons's milestones in the jewelry industry over time (e.g., the origins of the iconic panther or the Russian influence on jewels' design). This way, the brand's heritage can be better conveyed also during the in-store experience.

In conclusion, if the digital e-servicescape strategy matches effectively the offline servicescape and is fully integrated into the overall customer journey, luxury brands can close the gap between virtual and physical world and build robust and powerful service experiences, positively impacting their revenues, financial performance, unique selling proposition, and exclusive positioning.

5. THE ROLE OF E-SERICESCAPES IN THE INNOVATION OF LUXURY SERVICE EXPERIENCES: A MULTIPLE CASE VIGNETTES ANALYSIS

The following section focuses on how e-servicescapes can represent effective means to innovate luxury service experiences. More specifically, with the aid of three successful examples it aims at shedding light on the servicescape's digital sphere can contribute to innovating the physical and thus the overall service experience, generating pleasant, holistic luxury experiences for the final customer.

Adopting Bitner's typology of servicescapes (1992), this chapter is based on a three case vignettes analysis, that highlight how luxury service providers can use e-servicescapes to enrich and improve their customers' physical experiences.

Bitner categorized services basing on two dimensions: the types of service organization (depending on who performs the activities within the servicescape, that is, the customer, the employee, or both), and the physical complexity of the servicescape (which can be lean – in the case of simple environments, or elaborate – in the case of richer and more complex servicescapes). This chapter focuses in particular on elaborate interpersonal services from the luxury sector.

Through a multiple case vignettes approach (Holland & Naudé, 2004), examples of luxury service providers from different industries – hospitality, real estate, and fitness – are selected to highlight how e-serivcescapes can become effective innovation tools for luxury service experiences – with reverberations both online and offline. For each case a detailed account is provided of what occurs in each service setting and during each service experience, emphasizing the impact and relevance of the innovation introduced through the e-servicescape. More specifically:

- The first case vignette deals with the luxury resort *Forte Village* located in Sardinia, Italy, who allows their guests to create their own "Perfect Day" through an interactive branded video-content, making them compose their physical experience by choosing the activities to perform from several possible virtual video-options.
- The second case vignette is about the auction house *Sotheby's International Realty*, who has been the first luxury real estate brand to introduce 3D and Augmented Reality (AR) Tours through an app, allowing their customers to virtually explore homes and thus fully immersing themselves in the home-search experience.
- The third case vignette features the New York-based luxury health and fitness club *Mercedes Club*, who introduced the "Mercedes Zoom Club", offering exclusive virtual fitness classes, led by professional instructors, in order to overcome the problem of having to close their facilities because of the Covid-19 pandemic.

Innovating Luxury Service Experiences Through E-Servicescapes

5.1 Forte Village's "A Perfect Day" Initiative: How to Integrate the Customer Experience Through Video-Content

Luxury hospitality facilities offer by definition hedonic, pleasurable experiences to their hotel guests (Holbrook & Hirschmann, 1982). But precisely because of this, such organizations put particular effort into continuously innovating their value proposition, with the aim of making it unique. Despite having been nominated World's Leading Resort for more than twenty years in a row by the World Travel Awards jury, the luxury resort *Forte Village*, located in southern Sardinia (Italy) recently invested more than € 50 million into a complete restyling of its own facilities.

Their goal was to become a "destination in the destination", chosen by its guests because of the avant-garde experiences offered in the resort's fifty hectares' park, which includes eight hotels, forty suites, and thirteen villas, as well as more than twenty restaurants, some of them led by starred chefs. Also all other services are driven by the mantra of offering exclusive yet truly Made in Italy holidays, leveraging on Sardinia's beautiful landscape: the deluxe spa with dedicated medical team and thalassotherapy surrounded by untouched nature, the award-winning sports academy including wellness and fitness trails along the sea, and the various concerts and shows performed by international artists in an Italian-style piazza.

In order to make current and potential customers fully aware of the renewed resort experience – informing them about the large number of activities that can be performed during the stay and stimulating their curiosity before arrival – Forte Village's management decided to exploit the potential of innovative digital solutions. The ultimate goal was allowing customers to live the beauty of the Forte Village-experience even before and after their holidays, "stretching" it beyond the actual period of stay, thanks to tailor made, high quality video-content. In this light the *"A Perfect Day"* initiative was born: an initiative allowing the guests to create their own ideal day in the resort through an interactive branded video-content, making them compose their physical experience, by choosing the alternative activities from several possible virtual video-options. Customers have the chance to craft what they believe is a "perfect day" for them, according to their tastes, sought benefits and desires. For each moment of the day, guests can choose between two alternative activities to perform (e.g., the sports academy or the spa, entertaining shows or cooking classes, etc.). According to the own choice, each user is shown a simulation of the selected experience. All possible combinations of experiences are linked to each other through a storytelling approach, with professional actors personifying the guests during the different leisure activities. Such customized storytelling helps discovering the rich offer of luxury services that distinguishes the Sardinian resort from other competitors in the luxury hospitality industry, as well as fostering customers' engagement. Indeed, the "A Perfect Day" website platform also allows to share the own video experience on social media, invite other people to create their own ideal day, and eventually, collect more information on the resort's website in order to plan transforming the digital experience into an actual one.

In addition to receiving customers' appreciation, the initiative was also awarded the Telly Awards prize in 2019 (for video and television content) as Bronze Winner in two categories (Non-Broadcast General-Lifestyle and Non-Broadcast General-Travel/Tourism). In fact, "A Perfect Day" allowed Forte Village to reach a higher level of interaction with luxury travelers, also speaking to new customer segments (e.g., Millennials). This stronger engagement is especially important in the "information seeking" and "intent" phases of the customer journey, where such an interactive video-experience can persuade the user to actually choose Forte Village, thus impacting reservations positively.

The initiative has proven effective, but the resort decided not to replicate it in the future – exactly because of its success: the management does not aim at establishing a specific e-servicescape model, but instead at continuously innovating, surprising customers with new ways to improve the service experience, both offline and online. The aim is to develop more and more immersive digital experiences that can convey the uniqueness of the luxury resort's offer over time.

Table 1. Forte Village: Main Information

Company and E-Servicescape Strategy Information	
Industry	Luxury hospitality
Location	Southern Sardinia, Italy
Core offer	Luxury resort with a fifty hectares park, eight hotels, forty suites, thirteen villas, over twenty restaurants (some led by starred chefs) and a spa
Brand Positioning/Mission	Be a "destination in the destination"
Revenues	About USD 104 Million (2019)
Number of Employees	About 1000 (1200 including external collaborations, e.g., artists)
E-Servicescape Strategy ("A Perfect Day" Initiative)	Allow customers to create their own "Perfect Day" at the resort before arrival with the aid of digital technologies, making them compose their physical experience by choosing the activities to perform from several possible virtual video-options

5.2 Sotheby's International Realty's Virtual Home Tours: How to Amplify the Customer Experience Through Augmented Reality

An outstanding case that helps shedding light on how luxury services can successfully implement robotics and advanced technology (Wirtz et al., 2020), taking the physical service experience to "the next level", is provided by the international company *Sotheby's International Realty*. Founded in 1976, Sotheby's International Realty Affiliates LLC is one of the highest-level players in the real estate industry, and a subsidiary of Realogy Holdings Corp., a worldwide leader in real estate franchising and a provider of real estate brokerage, relocation and settlement services. With more than a thousand offices in seventy countries worldwide, one of the company's strengths is its widespread presence on the local territory.

From the very beginning, its mission has been to create a link between the most prestigious, independent real estate firms, and the finest clientele in the world. To do so, Sotheby's International Realty is characterized by a full franchise system, which is subject to rigorous rules and continuous control in order to safeguard service excellence. Indeed, affiliations are constantly reviewed, and only brokerages and individuals that meet strict qualifications are accepted. At the same time, Sotheby's International Realty ensures maximum support to its affiliates, providing them with a wide array of resources – spanning from marketing and operations to education and recruitment, including also business development.

With the aim of enhancing the customers' perceived service quality in an original and unconventional way for the luxury real estate industry, in 2018 Sotheby's International Realty's management decided to take advantage from the strong development of AR. Already back in 2016, Goldman Sachs (see Bellini et al., 2016) had predicted that the AR market in real estate could top $ 2.6 billion by 2025. Yet, such opportunity is still underexploited, and as a matter of fact Sotheby's International Realty became the first real estate brand to launch and implement a virtual staging, AR-application for the homebuying

Innovating Luxury Service Experiences Through E-Servicescapes

experience: *Curate by Sotheby's International Realty*. This mobile app offers customers the possibility to see a home's virtual staging images through an immersive, tridimensional AR-representation. One main advantage is the positive effect on the customer journey, which becomes more personal, shifting the focus from the concept of "house" to "home". Thanks to digital technology, customers can also swap among several possible interior design styles, comparing and contrasting them in real time – a function that physical staging could never accomplish.

The main features embedded in such digital platform include: visualization (any property can be transformed through selection of AR furnishings), recollection (thanks to the screenshot function embedded in the app, viewers can capture their favorite combinations of AR furnishings), and shop (additional information about the displayed AR furnishings are also available, including external links to retailer websites). Moreover, the virtual furniture is truthful and shown to scale, perfectly matching the visited house's spaces, which strongly simplifies homebuyers' relocation experience.

Sotheby's International Realty's example shows how e-servicescapes can help to completely rethink, renew and expand a very "traditional" experience, like the luxury homebuying one, providing tangible advantages to both buyer and seller. The former can showcase properties in several, different ways, adapting to the potential customer's taste, while minimizing the need to physical staging. The latter can see, and thus better imagine, the house being visited without any visualization barrier, avoiding complex on-site estimations and measurements (that can also hamper the visit's experience itself), while facilitating the later move-in and home furnishing phases.

Table 2. Sotheby's International Realty: Main Information

Company and E-Servicescape Strategy Information	
Industry	Luxury real estate
Location	Global presence (with 990 offices in 72 countries)
Core offer	Operates as a franchise focusing on brokering and marketing of residential luxury homes and real estate
Brand Positioning/Mission	"Find a home that suits your lifestyle"
Revenues	USD 114 Billion (2019, global sales volume)
Number of Employees	More than 19,000 sales associates worldwide
E-Servicescape Strategy (Virtual Home Tours)	Allow customers to virtually explore houses by engaging in 3D and AR Tours through an app, with the aim of providing a full-immersion in the home-search experience

5.3 Transforming the Mercedes Club into the "Mercedes Zoom Club": How to Substitute a Physical With a Virtual Customer Experience

Luxury fitness and wellness clubs are known as places where people can train, relax and eat healthy, while benefitting from the wide array of services delivered by such providers in an exclusive location. At the same time, socializing, networking and feeling part of a community they can identify with is also important for club members (Healy & McDonagh, 2013).

The luxury health and fitness club *Mercedes Club*, located in Manhattan, New York City, has positioned the own offer exactly at the intersection of these characteristics. In 2019 the club counted more than 2500 members, paying a monthly fee ranging from \$100 to \$199 (depending on the included services) and a \$300 entry fee. It provides a combination of modern design, high-level amenities (such as an outdoor movie theater, rooftop decks, and a resort-style swimming pool) and latest equipment in the very heart of one of the world's most vibrant cities. The quality of the service is integrated by more than seventy weekly group exercise classes, and more than one-hundred employees, including elite personal trainers. At its onset, the Mercedes Club started as an exclusive place, only open to the residents of the surrounding 900 high-class apartments. But then, given the club's huge dimensions and the appeal of the offered experience, the management decided to open up to the general public.

All of a sudden, in Spring 2020, the club had to stop its successful business activity because of the outbreak of the Covid-19 pandemic, with the subsequent lockdown of New York City. This interruption did not only affect all offered classes and activities, but also prevented club members from accessing the facilities, thus temporarily blocking the whole mechanisms characterizing the Mercedes Club community and business model. To avoid this, and in order to keep the club's activities running, the Mercedes Club management, reacted quickly and decided to switch to the distance-modus, offering personal training, group fitness and sports classes over the virtual platform Zoom. This way, the *Mercedes Zoom Club* was created. The hardest challenge was to deliver the same service quality and service experience of the physical location over a digital platform. Nonetheless, only one week after New York City's lockdown the club was – virtually – up and running again, offering all substitutive activities for free, without having to pay the membership fee. This was meant to be not only a strategic move, to prevent losing members, but also a sign of commitment towards the community, who was facing an unexpected and severe crisis situation.

Members were impressed by the initiative: not only by its high quality standards, but also because it allowed them to have an enjoyable distraction while being forced to spend their times at home, and it was offered for free (in contrast to the majority of the fitness and wellness clubs in the City). To further stimulate the sense of being a community, during the lockdown period also non-members were admitted to virtual classes they were normally not enrolled in. This also helped to create word-of-mouth about the Mercedes Club's activities.

The Mercedes Zoom Club turned out to be a success beyond expectations, thus making the management consider keeping the virtual classes in addition to the physical ones in the future "new normal" scenario. The club wants to further invest into this new offer typology, substituting the Zoom platform with a proprietary software, and buying high-quality video cameras, additional lights and supplements, in order to make more professional recordings of the streamed classes. Since an enhanced offer justifies a (higher) price, such e-servicescape-based classes will be only offered for free to regular members and club-goers, while online-only subscribers will have to pay a reduced fee to join the virtual classes.

This example highlights how the e-servicescape can be not only a source of innovation for the company's current business model, but also a viable alternative to the traditional, physical offer when this cannot be delivered.

Innovating Luxury Service Experiences Through E-Servicescapes

Table 3. Mercedes Club: Main Information

Company and E-Servicescape Strategy Information	
Industry	Luxury fitness and wellness
Location	Manhattan, New York City
Core offer	Luxury health and fitness club, offering latest equipment and exclusive classes in a downtown location, in addition to a great variety of high-level amenities (e.g., outdoor movie theater, rooftop decks, resort-style swimming pools, restaurants)
Brand Positioning/Mission	"If it doesn't challenge you, it doesn't change you"
Revenues	About USD 1 Million (2019)
Number of Employees	About 118 (reduced to 50 during the acute phase of the Covid-19 pandemic in Spring 2020)
E-Servicescape Strategy (Mercedes Zoom Club)	Allow customers to enjoy high-end, exclusive virtual fitness classes, led by professional instructors, while gyms and fitness studios were closed because of the Covid-19 pandemic

6. MAIN EVIDENCES FROM THE EXAMINED CASE VIGNETTES: INTEGRATION, AMPLIFICATION, AND SUBSTITUTION AS LUXURY E-SERVICESCAPE STRATEGIES

The cases presented in this chapter belong all to the category of elaborate interpersonal services (Bitner, 1992) within the luxury sector, yet draw on three different industries (hospitality, real estate, and fitness). Each vignette highlights the example of a service provider that has managed to strengthen the own service offer through an innovative usage of the e-servicescape dimension at the customer experience level. In fact, the main findings emerging from the cases analyzed, underline the fundamental contribution of well-conceived, avant-garde e-servicescapes to a company's luxury positioning and overall value proposition. Evidence points to the identification of three different *e-servicescape strategies* that luxury firms can employ to innovate their holistic service experiences, making them seamless and consistent from an omnichannel perspective.

The hospitality industry is a context in which the digital environment is typically leveraged to support the core service but is seldomly considered as an additional channel through which the experience – or at least a part of it – can be delivered. The Forte Village case offers an example of how e-servicescapes can be used as a powerful instrument to effectively integrate the luxury provider's physical experience with the aid of digital technology. Thus, this strategy can be labelled as *integration* and provides a series of benefits to the company adopting it. Indeed, through the "A Perfect Day" initiative customers have the opportunity to live part of the experience in advance – something that would not be possible without the involvement of virtual tools. This is particularly important for luxury services, where the duration of the experience is often limited in time or rather short. Guests are confronted with the question of which activities they would like to perform, weeks or even months ahead of their vacation (and maybe even before having actually booked). This has a positive impact on customer engagement and stimulates customer participation from the onset, ultimately resulting in higher customer-brand interactions (Hollebeek et al., 2019). Interactions are also fostered "among peers", since customers can share the composed vides on their social media accounts, which generates high-end word of mouth both about the "A Perfect Day" initiative and the Sardinian resort. In addition, this strategy concretely leverages on customer co-creation (Prahalad & Ramaswamy, 2004) – an aspect that is particularly important in the light of generating a higher involvement of the younger generations in luxury settings. In fact, guests are asked to create their

131

own ideal (holi)day using an interactive video-content tool to craft their physical experience the way they would like to live it. This provides benefits for both parties involved: it helps "tangibilizing" the offer (Thomsen et al., 2020) and increases customers' familiarity with the resort before they arrive, and at the same time it allows the provider to see in advance which activities spark more interest. Thus, through this e-servicescape-based initiative, Forte Village does not only improve the own image and positioning in both the real and the virtual world, but it can also control for possible peaks and organize the resort's activities accordingly in a timely manner, to further improve its image of exclusivity.

In the case of Sotheby's International Realty's AR application, the strategic function of the e-servicescape was different. Here, the e-servicescape's role is not to serve as a catalyst between the offline and online experience, but instead to expand the offline experience beyond its physical boundaries. Indeed, the Curate by Sotheby's International Realty app is an example of an e-servicescape strategy based on *amplification*. This strategy implies leveraging on digital environments in order to innovate the current service experience by augmenting it. In this sense, the real estate's company mobile app offers a challenging opportunity: customers have the possibility to see the houses they are visiting in a so far unimaginable way, de facto transforming a very traditional and low-engagement activity into an almost futuristic and intensely co-created one. This is particularly interesting, since co-creation might be a risky option for "luxury service encounters where customers may want to take a backseat and be pampered" (Wirtz et al., 2020, p. 38), like it is the case for the very traditional homebuying industry. Indeed, in this context customers typically live a rather passive experience: the sales agent guides the potential buyer through the house and explains its features and peculiarities, while the customer observes and listens. The AR app "forces" customers to actively participate in the experience, contributing to its success through their imagination and preferences. So, a series of tangible advantages is offered to the customer who accepts to play the new, digitally enabled role in the service offer: a more appealing and memorable visit, an easier relocation experience, and avant-garde design inspirations. In addition to this, the application's high quality (e.g., with to-scale virtual furniture matching perfectly the home's spaces) generates a sort of "wow-effect" in the user, that contributes to the promotion of the provider's luxury positioning (Atwal & Williams, 2009).

If the first two case vignettes are driven by e-servicescape strategies with integration and amplification purposes, the Mercedes Club with its "Mercedes Zoom Club" is led by a different motivation. In this case, the exogenous shock caused by the Covid-19 pandemic forced the luxury fitness club located in New York to close its facilities from one day to the other. To avoid stopping all activities and weakening the sense of belonging to a cohesive elite community – one of the main reasons for members to join the club – the management decided to replace physical with online fitness classes. Thus, the Mercedes Club adopted a *substitution* strategy to navigate the lockdown, i.e. using the e-servicescape dimension as a service delivery channel instead of the physical one. Indeed, e-servicescapes can act as facilitators in the interaction between a service provider and its customers (Fisk et al., 2000), to the point of becoming enablers when no other option is possible. In addition to the activities, also community interactions were transferred to the digital environment: users met online and interacted with each other during the streamed classes, in fact co-creating the joint experience. This is another important aspect since online communities can provide different kinds of value to their members: intellectual value, cultural value, and social value (Seraj, 2012). In this case, the e-servicescape played a particularly important role in fostering the latter, by recreating an interactive environment for building relationships. In the end, the experience turned out to be so appreciated by customers, that the temporary substitution was transformed into a partially permanent one, keeping some fitness courses in the streaming modus also once the Covid-19 restrictions will be removed. This successful business model revision would not have been possible if the company had not introduced and experimented such digital innovation in the context of an unpredictable situation (Leeflang et al., 2014). The three above-depicted e-servicescape strategies are visually summarized in Figure 1.

Summing up, the three examined case vignettes allow to shed light on different strategic functions of e-servicescapes in the context of luxury service experience innovation: integration, amplification, and substitution. Luxury service managers should consider which kind of e-servicescape strategy suits their case best, according to the specific situation they are confronted with, and depending on the goals they want to achieve – i.e., better blending the offline and online servicescape dimensions, extending the service experience beyond current boundaries, or replacing the physical with the virtual delivery mode. It is worth highlighting, that the latter strategy can also substitute the existing service experience only temporarily (e.g., in a crisis situation) or in part – for instance, making the e-provision available only for a specified timeframe, or delivering only some limited portions of the luxury experience over the web. At the same time, there are also two aspects that all strategies have in common and which represent essential elements for an effective luxury experience innovation based on digital environments. First, all three cases rely heavily on co-creation and on active customer involvement. Technology favors customer engagement and co-creation (Chung et al., 2020), but according to the examined case vignettes, it also seems to be the other way around: co-creation favors the implementation of technology-driven strategies. Indeed, co-creation represents a fundamental building block for innovating luxury service experiences through digital instruments, since customers appreciate to participate in the creation process of something unique. Second, in all three cases the service provider's key to successful e-servicescape innovation was the consideration of the customer's main underlying needs: i.e., the desire and impatience to spend holidays in an exclusive location; the dream to transform what is "just" a luxury house into one's unique home; and the need to be part of a selected elite community. So, putting the customer at the very center, and investigating the possibilities through which digital tools can contribute to improving the company's response, seems to be the optimal way for delivering all-encompassing luxury service experiences. In fact, the three above-presented strategies are not necessarily alternatives but can also be implemented simultaneously by the same company, if this matches the target customers' needs.

Figure 1. The Three E-Servicescape Strategies

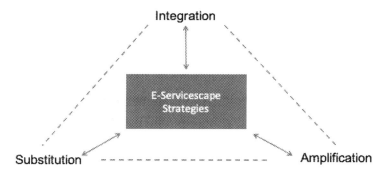

7. CONCLUSION

The development of avant-garde, exclusive, and appealing service experiences represents a main challenge for luxury service providers, especially in the light of digital technologies' growing role in this process. Indeed, they need to continuously maintain a balance between two tensions: establishing a direct contact with the own target, while keeping enough distance to be perceived as exclusive; and regularly renewing their own core offer, while preserving the brand's heritage and timeless aura. The digital dimension can contribute in several ways to effectively addressing such tensions while improving the luxury service experience, as previously depicted in the three case vignettes: through integration (integrating the physical experience with the digital one), amplification (including additional functions into the experience), and substitution (replacing the physical experience with a digital one). For this reason, such digital, service-based strategies can also be attractive for product-centric businesses (like personal luxury brands), that can enhance and innovate their offerings through such initiatives. However, a "prerequisite" for making these strategies work in practice, is developing a full-fledged digital orientation. Managers should not simply consider technology as an add-on or fringe to the physical experience but try to insert it with a protagonist role into their existing luxury strategies, in order to develop holistic, omnichannel experiences. This represents a relevant step towards providing a better understanding of luxury services – a topic that is still little considered (Wirtz et al., 2020) – and of how advanced technology can enhance companies' core offerings, their exclusive experiences and the brand's competitive advantage in the long run.

REFERENCES

Addis, M., & Holbrook, M. B. (2001). On the conceptual link between mass customisation and experiential consumption: An explosion of subjectivity. *Journal of Consumer Behaviour*, *1*(1), 50–66. doi:10.1002/cb.53

Andrade Braga, A. (2009). Netnography: A Naturalistic Approach Towards Online Interaction, book. In B. J. Jansen, A. Spink, & I. Taksa (Eds.), *Handbook of Research on Web Log Analysis* (pp. 488–505). IGI Global. doi:10.4018/978-1-59904-974-8.ch024

Atwal, G., & Williams, A. (2009). Luxury brand marketing – The experience is everything. *Journal of Brand Management*, *16*(5-6), 338–346. doi:10.1057/bm.2008.48

Baker, J., Ashill, N., Amer, N., & Diab, E. (2018). The Internet dilemma: An exploratory study of luxury firms' usage of internet-based technologies. *Journal of Retailing and Consumer Services*, *41*, 37–47. doi:10.1016/j.jretconser.2017.11.007

Bellini, H., Chen, W., Sugiyama, M., Shin, M., Alam, S., & Takayama, D. (2016). *Virtual and Augmented Reality*. https://www.goldmansachs.com/insights/pages/technology-driving-innovation-folder/virtual-and-augmented-reality/report.pdf

Bitner, M. J. (1992). Servicescapes: The impact of physical surroundings on customers and employees. *Journal of Marketing*, *56*(2), 57–71. doi:10.1177/002224299205600205

Blasco-Arcas, L., Holmqvist, J., & Vignolles, A. (2016). Brand Contamination in Social Media: Consumers' Negative Influence on Luxury Brand Perceptions—A Structured Abstract. In *Rediscovering the Essentiality of Marketing. Developments in Marketing Science: Proceedings of the Academy of Marketing Science.* Springer. 10.1007/978-3-319-29877-1_54

Booms, B., & Bitner, M. J. (1981). Marketing strategies and organisation structures for service firms. In J. Donnelly & W. George (Eds.), *Marketing of services: 1981 special educators' conference proceedings* (pp. 46–51). American Marketing Association.

Brakus, J. J., Schmitt, B. H., & Zarantonello, L. (2009). Brand experience: What is it? How is it measured? Does it affect loyalty? *Journal of Marketing*, *73*(3), 52–68. doi:10.1509/jmkg.73.3.052

Carù, A., & Cova, B. (2003). Revisiting consumption experience: A more humble but complete view of the concept. *Marketing Theory*, *3*(2), 259–278. doi:10.1177/14705931030032004

Cearley, D., Walker, M., Burke, B., & Searle, S. (2017, June 23). *Top 10 strategic technology trends for 2017: A Gartner trend insight report.* https://www.gartner.com/doc/3645332?srcId=1-6595640781

Chen, Y., Fay, S., & Wang, Q. (2011). The role of marketing in social media: How online consumer reviews evolve. *Journal of Interactive Marketing*, *25*(2), 85–94. doi:10.1016/j.intmar.2011.01.003

Chung, M., Ko, E., Joung, H., & Kim, S. J. (2020). Chatbot e-service and customer satisfaction regarding luxury brands. *Journal of Business Research*, *117*, 587–595. doi:10.1016/j.jbusres.2018.10.004

Danzinger, P. N. (2019, May 29). 3 ways millennials and gen-z consumers are radically transforming the luxury market. *Forbes.* https://www.forbes.com

Deloitte. (2017). *The 2017 Deloitte millennial survey: Apprehensive millennials: seeking stability and opportunities in an uncertain world.* Author.

Dion, D., & Arnould, E. (2011). Retail Luxury Strategy: Assembling Charisma through Art and Magic. *Journal of Retailing*, *87*(4), 502–520. doi:10.1016/j.jretai.2011.09.001

Dion, D., & Borraz, S. (2015). Managing heritage brands: A study of the sacralization of heritage stores in the luxury industry. *Journal of Retailing and Consumer Services*, *22*, 77–84. doi:10.1016/j.jretconser.2014.09.005

Duncan, E., Fanderl, H., Maechler, N., & Neher, K. (2016). Customer experience: Creating value through transforming customer journeys. McKinsey & Company.

Euromonitor International. (2019). *Luxury Goods: How is Digital Shaping the Industry.* Author.

Fisk, R. P., Grove, S. J., & John, J. (2000). All the websites are a stage, so marketers put on a show. *Marketing News*, *34*(23), 26.

Gentile, C., Spiller, N., & Noci, G. (2007). How to sustain the customer experience: An overview of experience components that co-create value with the customer. *European Management Journal*, *25*(5), 395–410. doi:10.1016/j.emj.2007.08.005

Harris, L. C., & Goode, M. M. H. (2010). Online servicescapes, trust, and purchase intentions. *Journal of Services Marketing*, *24*(3), 230–243. doi:10.1108/08876041011040631

Healy, J. C., & McDonagh, P. (2013). Consumer roles in brand culture and value co-creation in virtual communities. *Journal of Business Research*, *66*(9), 1528–1540. doi:10.1016/j.jbusres.2012.09.014

Helkkula, A. (2011). Characterising the concept of service experience. *Journal of Service Management*, *22*(3), 367–389. doi:10.1108/09564231111136872

Holbrook, M. B., & Hirschmann, E. C. (1982). The experiential aspects of consumption: Consumer fantasies, feelings and fun. *The Journal of Consumer Research*, *9*(2), 132–140. doi:10.1086/208906

Holland, C. P., & Naudé, P. (2004). The metamorphosis of marketing into an information-handling problem. *Journal of Business and Industrial Marketing*, *19*(3), 167–177. doi:10.1108/08858620410531306

Hollebeek, L. D., Srivastava, R. K., & Chen, T. (2019). SD logic- informed customer engagement: Integrative framework, revised fundamental propositions, and application to CRM. *Journal of the Academy of Marketing Science*, *47*(1), 161–185. doi:10.100711747-016-0494-5

Holmqvist, J., Wirtz, J., & Fritze, M. P. (2020, December). Luxury in the digital age: A multi-actor service encounter perspective. *Journal of Business Research*, *121*, 747–756. Advance online publication. doi:10.1016/j.jbusres.2020.05.038

Holzwarth, M., Janiszewski, C., & Neumann, M. M. (2006). The influence of avatars on online consumer shopping behavior. *Journal of Marketing*, *70*(4), 19–36. doi:10.1509/jmkg.70.4.019

Hopkins, C. D., Grove, S. J., Raymond, M. A., & La Forge, M. C. (2009). Designing the e-servicescape: Implications for on-line retailers. *Journal of Internet Commerce*, *8*(1/2), 23–43. doi:10.1080/15332860903182487

Kapferer, J.-N. (2013). *Kapferer on Luxury: How Luxury Brands Can Grow Yet Remain Rare*. Kogan Page.

Kapferer, J.-N., & Bastien, V. (2009). *The Luxury Strategy: Break the rules of marketing to build luxury brands*. Kogan Page.

Kester, J. (2018, October 3). Forbes Travel Guide's 30 Most Luxurious Spas in The World. *Forbes*. https://www.forbes.com

Kim, A. J., & Ko, E. (2012). Do social media marketing activities enhance customer equity? An empirical study of luxury fashion brand. *Journal of Business Research*, *65*(10), 1480–1486. doi:10.1016/j.jbusres.2011.10.014

Kim, J.-H., & Kim, M. (2020). Conceptualization and assessment of E-service quality for luxury brands. *Service Industries Journal*, *40*(5-6), 436–470. doi:10.1080/02642069.2018.1517755

LaSalle, D., & Britton, T. A. (2003). *Priceless: Turning ordinary products into extraordinary experiences*. Harvard Business School Press.

Lemon, K. N., & Verhoef, P. C. (2016). Understanding customer experience throughout the customer journey. *Journal of Marketing*, *80*(6), 69–96. doi:10.1509/jm.15.0420

Mangold, W. G., & Faulds, D. J. (2009). Social media: The new hybrid element of the promotion mix. *Business Horizons*, *52*(4), 357–365. doi:10.1016/j.bushor.2009.03.002

Mangold, W. G., & Smith, K. T. (2012). Selling to Millennials with online reviews. *Business Horizons*, *55*(2), 141–153. doi:10.1016/j.bushor.2011.11.001

Mari, M., & Poggesi, S. (2013). Servicescape cues and customer behavior: A systematic literature review and research agenda. *Service Industries Journal*, *33*(2), 171–199. doi:10.1080/02642069.2011.613934

McKinsey & Company. (2018). *Luxury in the age of digital Darwinism.* https://www.mckinsey.it/idee/luxury-in-the-age-of-digital-darwinism

Nilsson, E., & Ballantyne, D. (2014). Reexamining the place of servicescape in marketing: A service-dominant logic perspective. *Journal of Services Marketing*, *28*(5), 374–379. doi:10.1108/JSM-01-2013-0004

Parasuraman, A., Zeithaml, V. A., & Malhotra, A. (2005). E-S-QUAL: A Multiple-Item Scale for Assessing Electronic Service Quality. *Journal of Service Research*, *7*(3), 213–233. doi:10.1177/1094670504271156

Pine, B. J. II, & Gilmore, J. H. (1999). *The experience economy.* Harvard Business School Press.

Prahalad, C. K., & Ramaswamy, V. (2004). *The future of competition: Co-creating unique value with customers.* Harvard Business School Press.

Pullman, M., & Gross, M. (2004). Ability of experience design elements to elicit emotions and loyalty behaviours. *Decision Sciences*, *35*(3), 551–578. doi:10.1111/j.0011-7315.2004.02611.x

Rather, R. A. (2020). Customer experience and engagement in tourism destinations: The experiential marketing perspective. *Journal of Travel & Tourism Marketing*, *37*(1), 15–32. doi:10.1080/10548408.2019.1686101

Schembri, S. (2006). Rationalizing service logic, or understanding services as experience? *Marketing Theory*, *6*(3), 381–392. doi:10.1177/1470593106066798

Schmitt, B. (1999). Experiential marketing. *Journal of Marketing Management*, *15*(1-3), 53–67. doi:10.1362/026725799784870496

Seraj, M. (2012). We create, we connect, we respect, therefore we are: Intellectual, social, and cultural value in online communities. *Journal of Interactive Marketing*, *26*(4), 209–222. doi:10.1016/j.intmar.2012.03.002

Sonmath, M., Mahmood, M. A., & Joseph, J. L. (2008). Measuring Internet-commerce success: What factors are important. *Journal of Internet Commerce*, *7*(1), 1–28. doi:10.1080/15332860802004113

Thomsen, T. U., Holmqvist, J., von Wallpach, S., Hemetsberger, A., & Belk, R. W. (2020). Conceptualizing unconventional luxury. *Journal of Business Research*, *116*, 441–445. doi:10.1016/j.jbusres.2020.01.058

Toivonen, M., Tuominen, T., & Brax, S. (2007). Innovation process interlinked with the process of service delivery – A management challenge in KIBS. *Economies et Societes*, (3), 355–384.

Tuzovic, S. (2008). Investigating the concept of potential quality: An exploratory study in the real estate industry. *Managing Service Quality*, *18*(3), 255–271. doi:10.1108/09604520810871874

Tynan, C., McKechnie, S., & Chhuon, C. (2010). Co-creating value for luxury brands. *Journal of Business Research, 63*(11), 1156–1163. doi:10.1016/j.jbusres.2009.10.012

Vargo, S. L., & Lusch, R. F. (2008). Service-dominant logic: Continuing the evolution. *Journal of the Academy of Marketing Science, 36*(1), 1–10. doi:10.100711747-007-0069-6

Wiedmann, K.-P., Hennigs, N., & Siebels, A. (2009). Value-based segmentation of luxury consumption behavior. *Psychology and Marketing, 26*(7), 625–651. doi:10.1002/mar.20292

Williams, R., & Dargel, M. (2004). From servicescape to 'cyberscape'. *Marketing Intelligence & Planning, 22*(3), 310–320. doi:10.1108/02634500410536894

Wirtz, J., Holmqvist, J., & Fritze, M. P. (2020). Luxury services. *Journal of Service Management.* ahead-of-print. doi:10.1108/JOSM-11-2019-0342

Zomerdijk, L. G., & Voss, C. A. (2010). Service design for experience-centric services. *Journal of Service Research, 13*(1), 67–82. doi:10.1177/1094670509351960

KEY TERMS AND DEFINITIONS

Case Vignette: Short, written summary of a case study.

Co-Creation: The process of designing a product, service, or experience, in which customer inputs and interactions play a central role throughout the whole process.

Customer Experience: The interaction between firm and customer over the duration of their relationship.

Digital Environment: A setting or place produced through computer technology—including websites, mobile applications, social media, audio and video content, and other web-based resources—that allow social interaction.

E-Servicescape: A service's online environment.

Luxury Service: A high-quality, extraordinary, hedonic service, characterized by exclusivity.

Omnichannel Experience: A holistic, fully integrated shopping experience, drawing on integrated offline and online marketing efforts.

Service Experience: The interaction between provider and customer when service is provided.

Servicescape: The setting or ambience in which the service is delivered and in which the service experience between provider and customer takes place.

Chapter 8

Pivots in the Luxury Business:
Discovering the New Luxury Consumer Through Social Data

Wendy K. Bendoni
Grenoble Ecole de Management, France

Fabio Duma
School of Management and Law, Zurich University of Applied Sciences, Switzerland

ABSTRACT

Consumer behavior is continuously evolving, and with it, so is the business of luxury. Besides other societal and economic changes, digital technology and social networks have affected how people search for information, buy products, and relate to luxury brands. As a growing number of people use social networks, an abundance of social data can be analyzed to detect shifts in perception and behaviors, generating insights that can benefit luxury brands. There is a need for theoretical conceptualizations and, based on these, strategy frameworks to help identify relevant sources of social data and derive actionable insights by using social media intelligence in a strategic, structured, and impact-oriented manner. With their conceptual study, the authors aim to close this gap and contribute towards marketing management literature by proposing a conceptual social listening framework. Their framework highlights the benefits of using social data and explains the basic steps of turning data into valuable insights that drive managerial action based on relevant theory and technology.

INTRODUCTION

The changing global luxury landscape, new competitive dynamics, and rapidly evolving consumer behavior require luxury companies to listen closely to their current and future clientele. Luxury brands must evaluate new ways of studying emerging interests, needs, and preferences to adapt and better connect with their target audiences. This chapter presents a comprehensive framework of the most essential, and frequently overlooked, social data sources and corresponding social listening methods. The

DOI: 10.4018/978-1-7998-5882-9.ch008

framework addresses the disconnect between observed consumer behavior and social data in current marketing theory. It will enable marketers to improve their decision-making processes by applying a more customer-centric approach to their overall marketing strategies. The authors address luxury business pivots - major directional changes in dealing with luxury brands - and show how social listening can provide valuable insights.

The proposed framework is based on relevant theory and the use of social media analytics software. It supports marketers in understanding the possibilities of social listening and helps them identify the changes they need to make to their digital marketing strategies through insights derived from social data related to the brand.

In their framework, the authors structure and explain the attributes of social data and the benefits that can be gained from it. They propose analytical tools to connect with consumers on a deeper level and to improve decision-making that is driven by data. While social data is nothing new to practitioners and researchers seeking to understand consumers' online behavior, the business intelligence available has changed, and related software has dramatically improved along with the ever-growing amount of digital data. However, a gap still exists between data gathering and analysis and, ultimately, marketing decision-making. This is shown by the amount of social data still untapped by luxury companies. According to Forrester, "between 60% and 73% of all data within an enterprise goes unused for analytics" (Gualtieri, 2016, p.1).

Background

Digital transformation presents the world of luxury with new challenges but also countless opportunities. In the beginning, the luxury industry was relatively slow to make use of digital channels. In contrast to the phenomenon of luxury, which can be traced back thousands of years, digitalization is a phenomenon of modern times. It is emblematic of a continuous and accelerating change process that links both the economy and society through information technologies (Laudon, Laudon, & Schoder, 2016, p. 73). The intelligent linking and automation of systems and processes and the smart use of the growing amount of data available make it possible to create new business models or adapt existing business practices, provided a company builds the necessary capabilities to derive relevant insight. Digital value creation processes generate new sources of income and promote new forms of interaction with customers, enabling companies to achieve competitive advantage through data know-how (Bundesministerium für Wirtschaft und Energie, 2015, p. 3).

Technology, however, is only one part of the equation. The value of big data is only as good as a company's ability to gather, structure, and analyze the relevant data, combine it with other, non-digital information, and finally extract actionable insights. This ability affects the way the company interacts with its customers, the control it has over the brand image, and even its corporate culture (Duma, Labati, Brunetti, & Gadgil, 2020). Luxury companies are increasingly forced to transform from a closed entity mode to an ecosystem and network mode, in which the company has to rely on external partners to keep up with the accelerating speed at which its surroundings change (Achille et al., 2013). To succeed, luxury companies need to focus on understanding their audience better through social data, developing the related knowledge and skills, and on integrating tools, processes, and strategies to make most of the sheer mass of information available to them.

To place their research into a larger context - contemporary luxury business and the drivers behind major behavioral shifts - the authors looked at substantial disruptions in the luxury market: the democ-

Pivots in the Luxury Business

ratization of luxury and the role of social networks, the accessibility of luxury products online, and the digital push on both the supply and the demand side of the luxury market, which seems to have intensified.

THE DEMOCRATIC NATURE OF SOCIAL NETWORKS AND INFLUENCE ON CONSUMER INTERACTION

The relationship between luxury brands, digital technology, and the Internet is an intricate one for various reasons (Duma, Labati, Brunetti, & Gadgil, 2020). Kapferer (2015, p.113) described it as rather reserved and conservative. The Internet – including social networks – represents almost the exact opposite of what the concept of luxury stands, or stood, for. The digital sphere is fast-changing, accessible to all, and detached from traditional social hierarchies. In contrast, luxury used to be about timelessness, heritage, or social differentiation and exclusivity (see, e.g., Vigneron & Johnson, 1999). For these reasons, it was initially thought to be ill-suited for the digital domain (Okonkwo, 2009, p. 303).

However, as the online activities of many luxury companies increasingly show, luxury firms ignore the ever-growing pull of the digital universe at their peril. A considerable proportion of the interaction between consumers and luxury brands is shifting online. As one of the digital touchpoints, social networks are gaining in importance. Consumers not only follow their favorite brands and the influencers promoting them, they actively search for information about luxury products and exchange their views of and experiences with coveted goods and services before, finally, purchasing them online, as well. For many decades, the holistic experience associated with the acquisition of a luxury object or a service was staged and controlled solely by the luxury brand. In other words, the brand dominated its customers (Kapferer, 2012). While both the online and the offline experience will remain key to the concept of luxury, total control is no longer possible. The digital communication channels are turning customers into increasingly influential players (Remy et al., 2015, p. 7). Today, luxury exists in a world where consumers gather information from their peers and various other sources; followers on social media and different kinds of influencers share and comment on content, and, by their actions, they co-create the image of a luxury brand. Communities form new subcultures and create their very own narrative around a brand (Okonkwo, 2009, p. 306).

In other words, social networks, e-commerce, and the fast evolution of technology (e.g., virtual reality, augmented reality, or mixed reality) are changing how customers and brands interact, thus forcing luxury companies to adapt and further develop their modus operandi - and to listen to their customers (Duma et al., 2020). Customers no longer want to be perceived as passive observers; they are developing into a dominant market power that obtains information via a growing number of online and offline touchpoints and actively shaping their customer journey (i.e., their information-seeking and purchasing process) (Lay, 2018).

Recent global developments, caused or accelerated in 2020 by the coronavirus pandemic, are driving even more consumers to connect with luxury brands online. The behavioral changes consumers have been forced to undergo as a result of lockdown and other protective measures have led luxury companies to adapt quickly and move their marketing and sales online, offering home delivery, online shops, private viewings, or digital fashion shows. While it remains to be seen which changes will be permanent, the pandemic has acted as a catalyst for the ongoing digital transformation of the luxury business, both in terms of consumer interaction and of brands. For example, French heritage brand Hermès, while reporting a sales drop for the first half of 2020, has seen significant growth of its online channels with rising sales volumes and 75% new online customers since the start of the pandemic. Moreover, as the company has reported, online sales did not decrease once the French luxury house reopened its stores (Hoang, 2020). As data from the Digital Luxury Group shows, English-language searches for Hermès from January to June 2020 increased by 35 percent compared to the previous year, driven principally by searches for the company's iconic Birkin bag (Hoang, 2020). This unprecedented growth in online users now enables marketing managers to gather the social data of its new customers and gain new insights in ways they have not been able to before.

To make the most of this opportunity, luxury brands must adapt their corporate culture and their strategies and processes and need to acquire new resources (Remy et al., 2015, p. 5). Business models today must make use of use digital technologies and e-business concepts to adapt to changing consumer behavior (Abtan et al., 2016, p. 3).

One of the challenges luxury brands must address is how to maintain their integrity and exclusive appeal in the face of influencers and consumers sharing, and even over-sharing, brand-related content on a global scale on social networks. Although brands appreciate the user-generated content, oversharing may affect perceived brand exclusivity and other aspects related to the public perception of the brand.

As mentioned before, Hermès is a prime example of how the rules of luxury management can be followed while embracing the digital world at the same time, without losing any of the brand's cachet. A luxury brand always operates in the intersection between accessibility and exclusivity, and between tradition and innovation (Kapferer & Bastien, 2012). Any imbalance in this respect endangers the brand's value in the eyes of its target groups in the medium to long term. Especially at a time when technology and online channels are increasingly dominating many aspects of life, careful consideration must be given to this, without missing the signs for change. In order to strike the right balance, it is important to understand how exclusivity and luxury evolve and how this changes consumers' perception of a brand and their preferred modes of interaction.

DISCOVERING THE EVOLVING LUXURY CONSUMER THROUGH SOCIAL DATA

Today, luxury consumers have new interests, show different behaviors, and develop a different type of emotional connection to luxury products and experiences. The transformation of luxury brands to build their digital presence (Heine & Berghaus, 2014) continues to gain momentum. In the current environment, the luxury brand is no longer in absolute control of the brand narrative and all the customer touchpoints that form the brand experience. An increasing number of digital interactions generate an abundance of social data that awaits data collection through software tools enabling social listening on a large scale. By tapping into this resource, luxury brands can learn about consumer perceptions and different interpretations of the brand, its products, and their meaning to consumers. Marketers can even gain insight into consumers' non-brand-related interests, evolving preferences, and ultimately about consumers' interactions with the brand, brand-related, and non-brand-related communities and subcultures, as a basis for deep insight and future action. Used strategically, social listening, combined with smart immersive qualitative data gathered in online and offline environments (Batat, 2019), can help luxury brands tell stories, create content, and offer experiences that resonate with their customers – now and in the future. The great potential of utilizing social data, which encompasses information gathered from audiences' online conversations and individual online behavior, makes it possible to discover the digital cultures within different virtual communities. Previous research has focused on luxury brands' use of tools to

Pivots in the Luxury Business

derive more data-driven insights from brand sentiment (Liu, Shin, & Burns, 2019). Social listening tools can enable marketers to identify trends and patterns of consumer insight and provide quality assurance by enabling companies to examine the effect of their digital marketing strategies and outreach campaigns. The ability to search data collected from a specific source in real-time or historical data can help to pinpoint a disruption and react accordingly.

Digital marketers are becoming familiar with the methods of data science for utilizing social listening and monitoring tools. This knowledge, in turn, enables them to understand the process and discover new possibilities for identifying and analyzing social data. A demand for marketing managers who understand data science exists at the "intersection of computer science and social sciences such as computational social science and social computing" (Olteanu, 2019). According to Leganza (2019), organizations realize the importance of "data literacy across all roles" to enable brands to make "critical business decisions based on insights" (p. 1). In order to amplify data to gain business value, it is necessary to analyze and contextualize the data the luxury industry already has available to them. While today, "50% of organizations will lack sufficient AI and data literacy skills to achieve business value" (Panetta, 2019, p.1). The world of luxury needs to adapt quickly and gain more technical and analytical driven marketing positions (Brooke, 2017).

Social Media Virtual Communities

There has been considerable research on understanding why consumers use social media (Hoffman, Novak, & Stein, 2013). Belk's (2016) research on "extended self" in the virtual world, for example, looks at "how the multi-function mobile phone affects our self-presentation and sense of connectedness" (p. 50). Today, consumers can be found on social media networks checking in with their communities by sharing, commenting, and following their consumers and companies (Hennig-Thurau et al., 2010; Kaplan & Haenlein, 2010). These networks have made it possible for like-minded users to connect without borders or biases. Social media communication methods, including "text, audio, photos, and videos, have changed the flow of information between consumers and companies" (Kaiser et al., 2020).

The term "virtual community" was first coined by Rheingold (1993), who classified computer users as a "social aggregations that emerge from the net when enough people carry on (...) public discussions long enough, with sufficient human feeling, to form webs of personal relationships in cyberspace" (cited in Kozinets, 1999). These "communities of interest" (Hagel & Armstrong, 1996) have common interests that bring like-minded individuals together through social networks. Social exchange theory (Emerson, 1976) proposes that individuals perform a mental cost-benefit analysis to determine those behaviors they will engage in, avoiding that which is deemed cost-prohibitive (Pan & Crotts, 2012). The ability to follow, block, and unfollow give social media users the ability to remain in control of their virtual community.

Researchers have looked at these virtual communities through the cultural lens and at a brand-public level (Arvidsson & Caliandro, 2016). McLuhan in 1970 foresaw that the "electric media" would "tribalize" human society into clusters of affiliation (Kozinets, 1999; McLuhan, 1970). These tribalized communities have developed to denote a clustered community of like-minded audiences, which can be referred to as "eTribalized" (Kozinets, 1999). These virtual communities consist of consumers who gather to share their beliefs and interests, and who create a virtual dialogue through videos, text, and photographs. Previous research on virtual communities has focused on "UGC (user-generated content), which emphasizes a consumer's communication behavior based on the dichotomy of contributing (posting) and consumption (lurking)" (Godey, et al. 2016). Social media platforms can serve as potential decision-making platforms

143

through which consumers can exchange opinions and increase their social capital within their tribal community (Munzel & Kunz, 2014). By its nature, social media is dependent upon consumers' co-creation of content. "The existence of united groups of online consumers implies that power is shifting away from marketers and flowing to consumers," states Kozinets in *E-Tribalized Marketing?: The Strategic Implications of Virtual Communities of Consumption* (1999). Through the ability to locate and identify a virtual community connected with the brand's audience, marketers can observe their online social sharing behaviors, allowing brands to better connect with the tribes interested in them.

Social media communities continue to evolve as users find new ways of communicating and discovering other like-minded individuals. In trying to understand virtual communities over time, much research has been conducted on consumers' posting behavior (Berger & Milkman, 2012; Moe & Schweidel, 2012; Toubia & Stephen 2013), eTribalized communities (Kozinets, 1999), and social influence (Aral & Walker 2012; Trusov, Bodapati, & Bucklin 2010), as well as social media as a co-creation tool for brands with UGC (Hughes et al. 2016). The virtual communities gain strength in size and reach with "collaborative consumer-generated content" (Muñiz & Schau, 2011).

EVOLUTION OF HOW MARKETERS UNDERSTAND SOCIAL DATA

Marketers' ability to directly connect with virtual communities is the fundamental reason why social data is a crucial source for social monitoring and social listening. Nonetheless, because of evolving online consumer behavior, new technologies, and changing patterns in algorithms, there are many challenges for marketers. Today, digital marketing teams are responsible for tracking trends and behavior through a large scale of social data. Through this, they have the opportunity to personally connect to their audience, raise awareness, and drive sales and demand for the brand. While most digital teams have their digital analytics specialist, some must use trade tools to gather and mine data (collect, process, and sort). To analyze large amounts of data, it might be necessary to use internal web-based applications, Adobe Analytics, Google Analytics, social media platforms (Facebook, Twitter, Instagram), internal analytics, and commercial social listening tools.

The role of digital marketing managers varies, but ultimately they are part of the teams that develop and execute digital marketing strategies to all the stakeholders within the virtual space to reach the brand's audience through their virtual touchpoints. The digital marketer's role has evolved to include an understanding of the data science (AI) behind translating and curating social data. One of the managerial implications of the proposed social listening framework in this chapter is to enable marketing managers to better understand each technology use stage and analysis behind social listening. New marketing roles have given rise to new expectations on making data-driven decisions and working alongside data teams or external social media analytic teams to make data useful (Kozyrokov, 2019). According to the American Marketing Association, it is necessary for marketing managers to "become fluent in data analytics" and learn how to analyze data and use the resources available (Oh, 2018). The data science element enables a marketer's intuition to be reassured and supported through the data discovered (Whitten, 2020). Given the growth in big data, the evolution in analyzing the data, and the pressure to build on data-driven strategies, more and more marketers are looking to advance in the area of data science. In a recent survey, 77 percent of senior executives stated that an essential part of a successful organization is that marketing managers have knowledge and skillsets involving data science (Gartner, 2019).

Pivots in the Luxury Business

It is essential to understand the possibilities of how data can be used to predict patterns and analyze behavioral and other changes in detail (Raben, 2019). Analytical tools are "an emerging interdisciplinary research field that aims to combine, extend, and adapt methods for the analysis of social media data" (Zeng et al., 2010). These analytical tools enable marketers to derive behavioral insights about consumers based on data. Marketers translate those insights into a market advantage. The recent emergence of new social channels, new and better technology, and digital customer touchpoints have led to an online culture in which marketers strive to understand their customers' expectations or even discover new customer segments. Based on rich, insightful, and current data around their brand and its market, marketing managers have the chance to make better and more accurate decisions by using data analytics. These analytics methods include 'descriptive analytics', 'diagnostic analytics', 'predictive analytics', and 'prescriptive analytics (Mehta, 2017).

In their research, the authors focus on third-party software used to properly analyze and collect social data to get a deeper understanding of their audience's virtual culture. In earlier research, analyzing social data has been defined as a process of evaluating informatics tools and frameworks to "collect, monitor, analyze, summarize, and visualize social media data" (Zeng et al., 2010). The process of social media analytics can be broken down into three stages starting with "capturing" (gathering data), then progressing to "understanding" (executing advance analytics such as opinion mining, trend analytic, etc.), and concluding with "presenting" (summarizing, evaluating, and presenting results) (Ogunmula & Kumar, 2019).

Analyzing Social Data: Social Monitoring and Social Listening

When marketing managers analyze a brand's social data through social monitoring and social listening, it is crucial to understand what they are listening to or monitoring. If utilizing 'social monitoring,' the goal could focus on what is "being said" about the brand, engagement with their campaign(s), or the strength of their social influencers' reach. When looking to understand the brand sentiment, social media monitoring tools enable users to run brand-to-brand comparison, group, and categorize user conversations. When marketing managers want to research the behavior of a brand's virtual community, they need to cast a wider net to understand it. This is when 'social listening' is necessary to gather and reveal actionable data-insight. Social listening tools make it possible for marketing managers to listen to social networks, including blogs, forums, and the web at large. This process analyzes conversations and trends not solely around one brand but also around the industry. Social listening tools enable marketing managers to get insight into "behavior patterns and preferences" (Ab Hamid et al., 2013).

To successfully analyze social data, a company must have the ability to capture, analyze, and translate social listening data into actionable business insights. To ensure that these insights are unbiased and authentic, marketing managers need to use the right lens. They have to understand what methods will be effective to achieve their overall goals. Social monitoring identifies and keeps track of conversations, direct mentions of the brand, discussions related to keywords, trends, topics, and competitors on a brand's social media networks. Traditionally, the process of monitoring a brand's audience was to collect social data through social monitoring such as what a customer said about the brand and related topics, and direct mentions of brand sentiment. Social monitoring enables a brand to measure sentiment metrics around campaigns as well as expanding a brand's reach.

In contrast to social monitoring, social listening enables brands to understand the virtual consumer culture within their online environment to contextualize, analyze and interpret their behavior beyond

145

brand sentiment. Audience intelligence is gained through social listening tools that enable a brand to better understand their audience on a deeper level to provide more personalized strategies. While social listening enables a brand to collect and analyze social data has a broader reach and dives more deeply into the reasons behind online behavior and audience conversations. Through the power of social listening, marketers can learn more about their audience from a customer-centric approach. According to Kozinets, "quantitative data currently collected through online information gathering — i.e., sales, perhaps demographics — tends to be quite unidimensional" (Kozinets, 1999), and social listening will give marketers more actionable insight. Social listening is also not limited to social media from the brand's networks and competitors' social networks and the web. Social listening metrics can enable brands to optimize their real-time social data and implement changes in their digital marketing strategies.

Today, with advances in social listening analytics tools, luxury brands can gather more human-centric marketing insight about their audiences than ever before. Marketers continue to mine data from third-party software such as Adobe Analytics and Google Analytics to track and monitor their audience. Social listening provides a valuable source of knowledge to marketing managers to better understand their audience's interests, opinions, and behaviors, followed by analyzing this data to provide new methods of gaining actionable insights. Social listening enables marketing managers to segment and develop a deeper understanding and provide data-driven insight to apply to the evolving luxury customers.

The use of commercial social media analytics software to collect quantitative data provides valid metrics, but what is needed is a basic framework of social listening attributes to answer digital marketers' essential questions and concerns. Like advances in social media platforms, new AI algorithms continue to advance social listening software and provide more robust tools that enable marketers to analyze millions of posts, conversations, and shares to identify patterns from the datasets collected. Social listening tools, sometimes referred to as social intelligence software, enable users to view visual data charts that monitor social listening insights. The social listening process collects relevant marketing insights and brand-related mentions and filters them to define clear objectives for luxury brand marketing managers.

The global reach of the luxury audience in the digital landscape continues to grow with each new virtual community joining a new network. However, the traditional metrics used in social monitoring are not enough to meet the evolving needs of the luxury audience. It is essential to expand traditional data collection to include a deep dive into the luxury audience's virtual communities and their eTribes (Kozinets, 1999). The vast majority of contemporary luxury brands have embraced social monitoring within their digital marketing strategies.

The evolution of social listening has advanced to better understand audiences at a personal level, from their behaviors to their interests. Social data has grown exponentially, and AI has given social listening tools the power to gather, organize, cluster, develop, and discover new audiences. Since there is limited academic research on the recent advances, the authors relied on secondary data to discover the current business insight platforms and how brands depend on third-party agencies. Through third-party social media analytics software, data insights can be discovered and put into a comprehensive visual data format (dashboards) to enable marketing managers to make data-based decisions. Human-centric knowledge gained from collecting social data improves and personalizes the user experience. Marketers can connect with new, virtual audiences who have a strong affinity with their brand's current audience. Although companies spend millions on collecting and analyzing social data with third-party social data analytics software, most still have trouble using data in an actionable way. This challenge is addressed with a social listening framework to help companies develop a successful business strategy.

Pivots in the Luxury Business

FROM DATA TO INSIGHT: THE SOCIAL LISTENING FRAMEWORK

In this section, the authors elaborate on how to turn questions into data and data into insight by enabling brands to translate social data through the lens of social listening. These industry-based tools enable marketing managers to personalize and engage in cross-promotion, co-branded campaigns, and influencer mapping (Ayodeji & Kumar, 2019). Through social listening analytics tools, marketers can track, collect, and analyze multiple channels to dive deeply into conversations, behavior, and interests of both their brand's and their competitors' audiences. These analytical tools enable brands to communicate and build a personal relationship with the brand's audience to increase reach and engagement and increase the overall return on investment (ROI). Understanding the possibilities that can be achieved with social listening analytics software requires a deep understanding of the brand's audience and utilizing the dashboards to develop engaging data visualization (charts, data tables, word clouds). Using AI and social media analytics, marketers spend much of their time deciphering and analyzing the data and providing the ability to analyze and understand behavioral insights and discover hidden patterns (Erevelles, Fukawa & Swayne, 2016). The process of collecting social data occurs in real time, and historical data enables comparisons and new opportunities.

This audience is connected through shared interests in virtual communities. Their online behavior consists of expressing their personal interests, opinions, and beliefs, which must be understood by marketers to be successful. Social listening goes beyond traditional social monitoring based on engagement such as likes, comments, and mentioning the brand. Utilizing social listening makes it possible to dive deeper into brands' virtual communities to discover their hobbies, interests, and shared affinity with others in the virtual space. The conceptual framework presented here builds on previous work on virtual culture and tribes by Kozinets (2013, 1999) and McLuhan (1970).

The role of social media analytics, according to Zeng et al., is twofold: first in the area of "facilitating conversations and interaction between online communities" and second in "extracting useful patterns and intelligence to serve entities (…) active contributors in ongoing dialogues" (2010). Therefore, it is vital to capture the right social data and use multi-channel data collection software to cover the relevant digital landscape, including, among others, social media, websites, emails, mobile devices, client-server applications, and web-based kiosks.

The following categories (Figure 1) are based on a selection of the most relevant social media analytics tools used today and three divisions of the analytic tools (software). These can be broken down into three categories (Ogunmula & Kumar, 2019): Internal Social Media Network Analytics (ISMNA), Commercial Cross-Platform Social Monitoring Analytics (CCSM), and Commercial Cross-Platform Social Listening Analytics (CPSL). The authors applied social media listening tools to the conceptual, social listening framework that fall under the Commercial Cross-Platform Social Listening Analytics (CPSL) category in the social listening framework.

Conceptualizing the Social Listening Framework

The social listening framework focuses on observing the online behavior of a brand's audience, clustering tribes from like-minded audiences, and developing a deeper connection to their online persona. The social data of the brand's consumers is gathered, analyzed, and curated through data mining techniques along with AI-driven algorithms. The introduction of data mining allows the application of multiple algorithms to extract trends and patterns from large amounts of data. In order to manage the process of social listening, social listening software provides visual data tools on a dashboard that make it possible for marketing managers to analyze data and discover new insights. These dashboards provide marketing managers with the ability to respond to the increasingly complex and diverse market data (Pauwels, 2008), contribute to the discovery of new trends such as, for example, indicated by the online behavior of a brand's social media audience, and also improve the accountability of marketing efforts (La Pointe 2005).

Figure 1. Social Media Analytics Tools (Bendoni and Duma, Illustration 2021)

Tools	Source of Social Data Metrics	Focus	Metric Insight	Company	Free or Paid
Internal Social Media Network Analytics (ISMNA)	Metrics within one social network.	Monitoring the brand's audience engagement from the social platform	• Audience Intelligence within the platform • Content Performance within the platform. • Demographics • Completion Rate • Engagement Day(s) & Time(s) • Customer Variables • Monitor the Audience's Journey	• Snapchat Analytics • Twitter Analytics • Facebook Insights • Instagram Insights • Google Analytics • YouTube Analytics • Pinterest Analytics	Free
Commercial Cross-Platform Social Monitoring Analytics (CCSM)	Metrics from multi-channel social media network and syndicated digital data. Utilizing statistics and social data analytics.	Monitoring the brand's audience engagement across platforms. Monitor mentions of your brand, competitors, industry.	• Audience Intelligence on cross social media platforms. • Measure performance & optimize campaigns. • Content Performance within the platform. • Demographics • Completion Rate • Customer Variables • New customer versus Existing customer. • Engagement Day(s) & Time(s) • Monitor the Audience's Journey • Mentions of your brand, competitors, and industry.	• Hootsuite • TrackMaven (Skyword) • Sprout Social • Brandwatch • Digimind	Paid
Commercial Cross-Platform Social Listening Analytics (CPSL)	Metrics from multi-channel social media networks and syndicated digital data. Utilizing statistics and social data analytics.	Audience segmentation through AI Focusing on audience behavior, attitudes and interests Discover social trends and shared voices.	• Discovers anomalies by comparing historical data through AI • Measuring paid and organic analytics. • Detecting anomalies in behavior and track source. • Discover mentions of your brand, competitors, industry. • Customer Variables • Evolution of behavior that is shared with segmented cluster groups based on affinity analysis	• Khoros • Pulsar Platform • Audiense	Paid

Figure 1 *Social Media Analytics Tools (Bendoni and Duma, Illustration 2021)*

The process of organizing social data on the social listening dashboard includes 1) raw social data 2) the brand's virtual audience 3) data mining techniques including affinity analysis / cluster analysis 4) discovery of virtual communities (see Figure 2). The social listening software begins with the raw data from the brand's virtual audience. It collects, sorts, and segments a brand's audience, enabling marketers to discover new virtual communities and identify the attributes that connect them. The social listening

Pivots in the Luxury Business

analytics software allows marketers to utilize mining techniques that search for correlations among activities, interests, and behaviors. Affinity analysis and cluster analysis are data mining techniques that make it possible for the social listening software to curate the persona of a brand's audience by behavior segmentation (Turcinek, Stastny, & Motycka, 2012). The audience's behavior is then segmented by affinities to group them in clusters and tribes through their shared interests or behavior.

Figure 2. Social listening software process that brings marketing metrics into a single display (Bendoni and Duma Illustration, 2021)

The conceptual social listening framework proposed below (see Figure 3) also consists of four stages: exploration, discovery, learning, and adoption. Through the ability to analyze social data, it combines industry and academic findings. Each stage enables marketing managers to identify clusters to target and explore new audiences. This framework is an integral component of customer-centric marketing initiatives utilizing social data analytics to cluster segments of community tribes through affinity analysis of shared interests, behavior, and beliefs.

Users of the social listening framework must have clear goals and concrete questions. Straightforward questions allow the marketing manager to tap into previously untapped social data and translate it into business decisions. The ability to transform data into business decisions depends on the quality and reliability of the findings and on the marketing manager's ability to address the pain point(s) they want to solve a specific problem or concerns. When conducting audience research with social listening tools, some of the questions that might be addressed are the following:

1. What are some of the mutual interests or goals of the brand audience?
2. In the digital culture surrounding the brand, what are some of the hobbies the audience has in common?
3. What other brands our audience engages with can complement our brand?
4. How many customer segments follow our brand?
5. How does our brand connect with our audience on a personal level?
6. How do we understand the digital culture that follows our brand?
7. How do we find what content from other brands resonates with our audience?
8. Who does our audience identify with as their top influencers and potential brand ambassadors?

Pivots in the Luxury Business

Figure 3. Social listening framework (Bendoni and Duma illustration, 2021)

Stage	Process	Research
Exploration	The first stage is about listening closely to the audience without preconceived biases and exploring new opportunities within the brand audience's virtual community. It is essential at this stage to use a diverse amount of social data without editing manually. The social listening software collects social data, analyzes it, and discovers patterns and trends. In a first stage, the goals are to observe the online community to better understand the virtual culture and shared affinity, preferences, and interests. The digital audience's common attribute for being part of the social listening process is that they follow the brand.	• Virtual Communities: McLuhan (1970), Muiz and Schau (2005)
Discovery	The second stage identifies new audiences, trends within multi-clustered audiences, core values in the context of behaviors and characteristics, and the ability to locate key tastemakers or influencers among the virtual audience of the luxury brand. The discovery stage enables the user to uncover new virtual audience segmentations built around shared interests, beliefs, and engagement. It finds virtual tribes that make up the brand's online audience and enable the learning stage to begin. In turn, this enables marketers to examine the attributes that connect them, such as shared interests, hobbies, and other personal interests.	• E-Tribalized: Kozinets (2014, 2013, 1999) • Viral Sharing: Berger (2012)
Learning	After multiple algorithms have tracked, analyzed, and completed searching through the social data to locate and share visual data through the dashboards, the learning stage begins. This contextualized data shares insights that enable the marketing manager to discover the drivers of change that motivate and build the brand's audience. At the same time, the marketing manager can learn about the audience's connection with competitors in the virtual landscape. This process reveals a more detailed picture of the audience's social behavior and enables marketing managers to learn more about the brand's social and cultural virtual community. This stage can also provide insight that makes it possible for brands to predict how the customer persona shifts and how this could affect the business.	• Neo-Tribalism (Simmons, 2008), • Virtual Communities (Simmons, 2008; Van der Nagel 2013).
Adoption	In the adoption stage, marketing managers can implement the interests and preferences gained to their overall marketing strategies. 1. Critical insights on the online behavior of their brand's audience gives marketing managers the ability to follow a more customer-centric approach. 2. Listening to the audience's language and behavior enables a brand to personalize its content and users' experience from marketing content and communication to the product offering. 3. The adoption stage also makes it possible to collaborate with other teams to maintain a consistent brand voice across all marketing channels.	

Figure 3 - *Social listening framework (Bendoni and Duma illustration, 2021)*

MANAGERIAL IMPLICATIONS

The conceptual framework presented in this chapter explores some of the opportunities for marketers to develop a more customer-centric and integrated marketing plan by utilizing the social data of their current audiences. The fact that the volume of social data continues to grow as more consumers join current and new social media networks makes it imperative for marketing managers to be better prepared for the task of generating valuable insights from their social data. The framework provided here illustrates the basic structure and process of utilizing modern social listening software. Through social listening tools, marketers can dive deeper into luxury consumers' virtual culture and extract relevant insights to create a more personal experience for them.

Seeing the digital landscape through the lens of a brand's virtual communities enables managers to better connect with their audiences. With the changing economy, evolving values concerning the concept

Pivots in the Luxury Business

of luxury, the general transition to online commerce, and the emergence and development of virtual communities, marketers in the luxury industry must be prepared to pivot their strategy. Their challenge is to keep well informed of the ever-changing customer perception with regard to their brands. This is exactly why social data is important to a business to remain aware in the know of their audience and be prepared for change in behavior through real-time data. Disruptions and other unforeseen circumstances can prove challenging, yet marketing managers fail to exploit social data that could provide guidance and lead to actionable insights. By proposing a framework that enables better, data-based decision-making, the authors also take account of the increasing demand for marketing accountability (Rust et al., 2004; Webster, Malter, & Ganesan 2005).

In gathering social data, marketing managers must act responsibly in order not to violate any privacy protection regulations. All social data collected by a brand using third-party social listening software is subject to country-specific laws and restrictions. In many countries, regulators are stepping up privacy protection to reassure consumers that their personal data is safe. Examples include the General Data Protection Regulation (GDPR) of the European Union (EU) (European Commission, 2018) and the California Consumer Privacy Act (CCPA) in the United States.

CONCLUSION

The well-established marketing practice of social monitoring is shifting to include social listening as AI enables social media marketers to become better consumer researchers and consider data across all relevant virtual communities through the advancement of technology listening skills. When uncovering social data insights from analytics reports, it is imperative to create and deliver an analysis that identifies relevant, actionable insights based on emerging data and trends. Understanding consumer behavior, motivations, and affinities shared online with like-minded consumers makes it possible for luxury companies to create better strategies when considering pivots in their business model and adapting their marketing and communication practices.

As has been shown above, social data can enable better customer-centric decision-making through social listening tools, in particular the use of special software. The presented conceptual framework aims to provide a better understanding of how data-driven audience behavior research can contribute to making data-insight-based marketing decisions. Social listening can enable luxury companies to connect more effectively with their customers by using a strategic, structured, and evidence-based approach. While the focus is on social listening, marketers must however not underestimate the value of the human touch in discovering insights from findings generated by social listening software. It is essential to review behavioral segmentation when looking to develop the persona of a brand's virtual. By using the available social listening tools to gather and analyze social data in a structured way, luxury brands can adapt to macroenvironmental changes in a manner that resonates with – and feeds into - their current and future customers' dreams and aspirations

REFERENCES

Ab Hamid, N. R., Akhir, R. M., & Cheng, A. Y. (2013). Social media: An emerging dimension of marketing communication. *The American Journal of Tropical Medicine and Hygiene*, 86(1), 1–8.

Abtan, O., Barton, C., Bonelli, F., Gurzki, H., Mei-Pochtler, A., Pianon, N., & Tsusaka, M. (2016). *Digital or Die: The Choice for Luxury Brands*. The Boston Consulting Group.

Ayodeji, O. G., & Kumar, V. (2019). Social media analytics: A tool for the success of online retail industry. *Int. J. Services Operations and Informatics*, *10*(1), 79–95. doi:10.1504/IJSOI.2019.100630

Batat, W. (2019). Digital Luxury. Transforming Brands & Consumer Experiences. *Sage (Atlanta, Ga.)*.

Berger, J., & Milkman, K. (2012). What Makes Online Content Viral? *JMR, Journal of Marketing Research*, *49*(May), 192–205. doi:10.1509/jmr.10.0353

Brooke, Z. (2017, March 1). *Data Science is the Latest In-Demand Skill Set for Marketing*. American Marketing Association. Retrieved from https://www.ama.org/marketing-news/data-science-is-the-latest-in-demand-skill-set-for-marketing/

Brownlee, J. (2019, August 7). *What is Natural Language Processing? Deep Learning for Natura Language Processing*. Machine Learning Mastery. Retrieved from https://machinelearningmastery.com/natural-language-processing/

Bundesministerium für Wirtschaft und Energie. (2015). *Industrie 4.0 und Digitale Wirtschaft: Impulse für Wachstum*. Beschäftigung und Innovation.

Coste-Manière, I., Panchout, K., & Molas, J. (2012). The Evolution of the Luxury Market: Stairway to Heaven? In J. Hoffmann & I. Coste-Manière (Eds.), *Luxury Strategy in Action*. Palgrave Macmillan. doi:10.1057/9780230361546_2

Denegri-Knott, J., & Molesworth, M. (2010). Concepts and practices of digital virtual consumption. *Consumption Markets & Culture*, *13*(2), 109–132. doi:10.1080/10253860903562130

Dhaoui, C. (2014). An empirical study of luxury brand marketing effectiveness and its impact on consumer engagement on Facebook. *Journal of Global Fashion Marketing*, *5*(3), 209–222. doi:10.1080/20932685.2014.907605

Donzé, P.-Y. (2018). The Birth of Luxury Big Business: LVMH, Richemont and Kering. In P.-Y. Donzé & R. Fujioka (Eds.), *Global Luxury Organizational Change and Emerging Markets since the 1970s*. Palgrave Macmillan. doi:10.1007/978-981-10-5236-1_2

Downey, L. (2019, October 29). What is an Algorithm? *Investopedia*. Retrieved from https://www.investopedia.com/terms/a/algorithm.asp

Duma, F., Labati, F., Brunetti, G., & Gadgil, M. (2020). Mastering the digital transformation as a heritage luxury fashion brand. *Marché et Organisations*, *37*(37), 33–54. doi:10.3917/maorg.037.0033

Duma, F., Popcsev, M., & Seelhofer, D. (2017). Economies of small: niche strategies and success factors of independent luxury brands in a global market dominated by big business. *Global Fashion Management Conference at Vienna Proceedings*, 343-350. 10.15444/GFMC2017.04.08.01

Erevelles, S., Fukawa, N., & Swayne, L. (2016). Big Data consumer analytics and the transformation of marketing. *Journal of Business Research*, *69*(2), 897–904. doi:10.1016/j.jbusres.2015.07.001

Pivots in the Luxury Business

European Commission. (2018, May 23). *Data protection in the EU*. Retrieved from https://ec.europa.eu/info/law/law-topic/data-protection/data-protection-eu_en

Fan, W., & Gordon, M. D. (2014, June). Article. *Communications of the ACM*, *57*(6), 74–81.

Gualtieri, M. (2016). *Hadoop Is Data's Darling For A Reason*. Forrester. Retrieved from https://go.forrester.com/blogs/hadoop-is-datas-darling-for-a-reason/

Hennigs, N., Wiedmann, K.-P., Klarmann, C., & Behrens, S. (2015). The complexity of value in the luxury industry: From consumers' individual value perception to luxury consumption. *International Journal of Retail & Distribution Management*, *43*(10/11), 922–939.

Hermès. (2020). Retrieved from https://finance.hermes.com/en/

Hoang, L. (2020). *Hermès Online Channels Are Booming. Luxury Brands Should Take Note*. Luxury Society.

Jin, S.-A. A. (2012). The potential of social media for luxury brand management. *Marketing Intelligence & Planning*, *30*(7), 687–699.

Kapferer, J.-N. (1999, June). E-Tribalized Marketing? The Strategic Implications of Virtual Communities of Consumption. *European Management Journal*, *17*(3), 252–264.

Kapferer, J.-N. (2015). *Kapferer on Luxury*. How Luxury Brands Can Grow Yet Remain Rare. Kogan Page.

Kapferer, J.-N., & Bastien, V. (2012). *The luxury strategy – break the rules of marketing to build luxury brands*. Kogan Page.

Kemp, S. (1998). Perceiving luxury and necessity. *Journal of Economic Psychology*, *19*(5), 591–606.

Kozinets, R., Patterson, A., & Ashman, R. (2016). Networks of desire: How technology increases our passion to consume. *The Journal of Consumer Research*. Advance online publication. doi:10.1093/jcr/ucw061

Kozinets, R. V., & Arnould, E. J. (2017). *Ruminations on the current state of consumer ethnography*. Routledge Handbook on Consumption, Routledge.

Kozinets, R. V., Dolbec, P.-Y., & Earley, A. (2014). The SAGE handbook of qualitative data analysis. In U. Flick (Ed.), *Netnographic analysis: Understanding culture through social media data*. Sage Publications. doi:10.4135/9781446282243

Krensky, P. Hare, J., Vashisth, S., & Linden, A. (2019, August 6). *Hype Cycle for Data Science and Machine Learning*. Gartner. Retrieved from https://www.gartner.com/en/documents/3955984/hype-cycle-for-data-science-and-machine-learning-2019

Kunz, W., Aksoy, L., Bart, Y., Heinonen, K., Kabadayi, S., Ordenes, F. V., & Theodoulidis, B. (2017). Customer engagement in a Big Data world. *Journal of Services Marketing*, *31*(2), 161–171.

LaPoint, P. (2005). Timken Rolls Out a Marketing Dashboard for Industrial Bearing Group. *Marketing NPV*, *3*(1), 3–6.

Laudon, K., Laudon, J. P., & Schoder, D. (2016). Wirtschaftsinformatik: Eine Einführung (P. Studium, Ed.). Academic Press.

Lay, R. (2018). *Digitale Transformation: Die grösste Herausforderung für die Modebranche*. Deloitte. Retrieved from https://www2.deloitte.com/ch/de/pages/consumerindustrial-products/-articles/ultimate-challenge-fashion-industry-digitalage.html#

Leganza, G. (2019, October 30). *Predictions 2020: Approaches to customer Insights Evolve*. Forrester. Retrieved from https://go.forrester.com/blogs/predictions-2020-customer-insights/

Liu, X., Burns, A. C., & Hou, Y. (2017). An investigation of brand-related user-generated content on Twitter. *Journal of Advertising*, *46*(2), 236–247.

Marr, B. (2016). *What is the difference between artificial intelligence and machine learning?* Retrieved from https://www.forbes.com/sites/bernardmarr/2016/12/06/what-is-the-difference-between-artificial-intelligence-and-machine-learning/#241fc0a72742

McLuhan, M. (1970). *Culture is our Business*. McGraw-Hill.

Mehta, A. (2017, October 13). *Four Types of Business Analytics to Know*. Analytics Insights. Retrieved from https://www.analyticsinsight.net/four-types-of-business-analytics-to-know/

Moe, W. W., & Schweidel, D. A. (2012). Online Product Opinions: Incidence, Evaluation, and Evolution. *Marketing Science*, *31*(3), 372–386.

Moe, W. W., & Schweidel, D. A. (2014, August). Social Media: A Joint Model of Sentiment and Venue Format Choice. *JMR, Journal of Marketing Research*, *LI*, 387–402.

Muller, M., Millen, D. R., Shami, N. S., & Feinberg, J. (2010). *We are all lurkers: Toward a lurker research agenda. Collective Intelligence in Organizations: Toward a Research Agenda Workshop*. CSCW 2010, Savannah, GA. Retrieved from https://www.parc.com/content/events/attachments/Muller-Updated-LurkersInCILurkers-paper3.pdf

Muñiz, A., & Schau, H. J. (2011). How to inspire value-laden collaborative consumer-generated content. *Business Horizons*, *54*(3), 209–217.

Natural Language ProcessingS. A. S. (NLP). (n.d.). Retrieved from https://www.sas.com/en_us/insights/analytics/what-is-natural-language-processing-nlp.html

Ogunmula, G. A., & Kumar, V. (2019, January). Social media analytics; a tool for the success of online retail industry. *International Journal of Services Operation and Informatics*, *10*(1), 79–95.

Oh, A. (2018, July 7). *The Skills Marketers Need to Thrive in the Era of AI*. Retrieved from https://www.ama.org/marketing-news/the-skills-marketers-need-to-thrive-in-the-era-of-ai/

Okonkwo, U. (2009). Sustaining the luxury brand on the Internet. *Brand Management*, *16*(5/6), 302–310.

Pan, B., & Crotts, J. (2012). Theoretical models of social media, marketing implications, and future research directions. In M. Sigala, E. Christou, & U. Gretzel (Eds.), *Social Media in Travel, Tourism and Hospitality: Theory, Practice and Cases* (pp. 73–86). Ashgate.

Pivots in the Luxury Business

Panetta, K. (2019). *Champion data literacy and teach data as a second language to enable data-driven business.* Gartner. Retrieved from https://www.gartner.com/smarterwithgartner/a-data-and-analytics-leaders-guide-to-data-literacy/

Park, H., & Kim, Y. K. (2014). The role of social network websites in the consumer–brand relationship. *Journal of Retailing and Consumer Services, 21*(4), 460–467.

Pauwels, K., Ambler, T., Clark, B., LaPointe, P., Reibstein, D., Skiera, B., Wierenga, B., & Wiesel, T. (2008). Dashboards & Marketing: Why, What, How and Which Research is Needed. *Journal of Service Research, 12*(2), 175–189.

Pavel, Stastny, & Motycka. (2012 August). Usage of cluster analysis in consumer behavior research. *Advances in Applied Information Science*, 172-177.

Pentina, I., Guilloux, V., & Micu, A. C. (2018). Exploring social media engagement behaviors in the context of luxury brands. *Journal of Advertising, 47*(1), 55–69.

Raben, F. (2019, June 7). *American Marketing Association News. What Marketers Need to Know About Innovations in Data.* Retrieved from https://www.ama.org/marketing-news/what-marketers-need-to-know-about-innovations-in-data/

Remy, N., Catena, M., & Durand-Servoingt, B. (2015). *Digital inside: Get wired for the ultimate luxury experience.* McKinsey & Company.

Rust, Ambler, & Carpenter, Kumar, & Srivastave. (2004). Measuring Marketing Productivity: Current Knowledge and Future Directions. *Journal of Marketing, 68*(4), 76–89.

Simmons, G. (2008). Marketing to postmodern consumers: Introducing the internet chameleon. *European Journal of Marketing, 42*(3/4), 299–310.

Techopedia. (2020). *Affinity Analysis.* Retrieved from https://www.techopedia.com/definition/32062/affinity-analysis

Thomas, D. (2007). *Deluxe: How luxury lost its luster.* Penguin Books.

Toubia, O., & Stephen, A. T. (2013). Intrinsic Versus Image-Related Utility in Social Media: Why Do People Contribute Content to Twitter? *Marketing Science, 32*(3), 368–392.

Turngate, M. (2009). *Luxury World: The past, present and future of luxury brands.* Kogan Page.

Van der Nagel, E. (2013). Faceless Bodies: Negotiating Technological and Cultural Codes on reddit gone wild. *Scan: Journal of Media Arts Culture, 10*(2), 1–10.

Vigneron, F., & Johnson, L. W. (1999). A Review and a Conceptual Framework of Prestige-Seeking Consumer Behavior. *Academy of Marketing Science Review, 1999*(1), 51–15.

Webster, Malter, & Ganesan. (2005). The Decline and Dispersion of Marketing Competence. *Sloan Management Review, 46*(4), 35–43.

Whitten, A. (2020, May 14). *With AI and Data Science, Marketers are Maximizing the Power of Customer Data*. Adobe. Retrieved from https://blog.adobe.com/en/2020/05/14/with-ai-and-data-science-marketers-are-maximizing-the-power-of-customer-data.html#gs.i0xhxl

Xia, L., Shin, H., & Burns, A. C. (2019, May 7). Examining the impact of luxury brand's social media marketing on customer engagement: Using big data analytics and natural language processing. *Journal of Business Research*.

Zeithaml, V. A. (2000). Service Quality Profitability and the Economic Worth of Customers: What we Know and What We Need to Learn. *Journal of Academy of Marketing Science, 28*, 67-85.

Zeng, D., Chen, H., Lusch, R., & Li, H. (2010). Social media analytics and intelligence. *IEEE Intelligent Systems*, *25*(6), 13–16.

KEY TERMS AND DEFINITIONS

Social Data: Social data is collected from users' public online activity on social media networks. It can include images, text, location, biographical data, as well as shared and reposted links.

Social Listening: Social listening refers to the mining of social media data, not only in the brand context but across all relevant virtual communities. Social listening is mainly conducted for research purposes and includes listening for brand mentions (positive and negative), trends, and competitive intel.

Social Monitoring: Social monitoring refers to the mining of social data for brand mentions and in order to respond to and engage with a brand's audience. Social monitoring is typically conducted by social media community managers.

Chapter 9
Luxury Brands and Strategic Management Accounting

Peter Clarke
University College Dublin, Ireland

Edoardo Crocco
University of Turin, Italy

ABSTRACT

It is generally accepted that the primary objective of the discipline of management accounting is to provide relevant information, financial and non-financial, to business managers in order to assist in their decision making. This discipline evolved during the Industrial Revolution and it was, initially, referred to as cost accounting due to its emphasis on reporting internally-orientated cost information. The purpose of this chapter is to highlight the current techniques of managerial accounting widely used by business organizations all over the world and to describe the managerial implications of said methods when they are utilized by players operating in the luxury sector.

1. INTRODUCTION

"You gotta have style. It helps you get down the stairs. It helps you get up in the morning. It's a way of life. Without it, you're nobody" (Vreeland, 2016).

According to most of the well-regarded books written in the area of management (or managerial) accounting the primary objective of this discipline is to provide (relevant) information that is useful to the managers in decision making related to the achievement of the stated organizational objectives of a business (Williams, Haka, Bettner and Carcello, 2018). An alternative way of stating this purpose is to argue that management accounting is *not an end in itself* but rather it is a *means towards an end*. In other words, management accounting is a utilitarian discipline designed to facilitate managerial decision-making.

There are three basic principles associated with the discipline of management accounting. Firstly, we must identify which individuals within the management team of the business entity have the appropriate

DOI: 10.4018/978-1-7998-5882-9.ch009

Copyright © 2021, IGI Global. Copying or distributing in print or electronic forms without written permission of IGI Global is prohibited.

decision making responsibilities, although these responsibilities are usually articulated in the manager's job description. Examples of the users of management accounting information within an organization include, for example, plant managers, managers of business units including various departments. Secondly, the management accounting system must be capable of generating and reporting relevant information to internal managers to facilitate their planning decisions. Thirdly, management accounting information must facilitate the monitoring and evaluation of actual performance during a specified accounting period and, where appropriate, reward successful performance. In order to give our contribution to said topics, we ask the following research question: how can management accounting information be reliable and relevant for decision making in the luxury sector? We will explore and respond to that question in the following chapters.

2. FROM COSTING TO MANAGEMENT ACCOUNTING

Before we investigate the role of Management Accounting and the issue of luxury brands and products, it is worthwhile to briefly describe how the discipline of management accounting developed over time. Many accounting historians argue that the development of the discipline of management accounting – known previously as "cost accounting" – was one of the many consequences of the Industrial Revolution which started in Great Britain around the late 1700s and transformed the, then, agrarian society into an industrial one. Prior to the Industrial Revolution there was little incentive to produce finished goods other than those that could be easily distributed using the existing but primitive methods of transport. However, the period of canal construction and the subsequent railway boom greatly improved transportation systems, and this development, which coincided with improved methods of production, encouraged manufacturing firms to increase overall levels of output.

This advent of mass production fueled the need for internal and accurate conversion costs of manufactured goods and this need laid the foundation of the discipline that we, sometimes, refer to as "cost accounting". This product cost information was needed, and used as techniques of planning and control developed during the early 1800s when the textile mills, railroads, the iron, steel and chemical industries and, somewhat later, tobacco companies and metal-making industries became more sophisticated and capital intensive (Kaplan, 1984). The First World War, which stimulated extensive and expensive contracts for munitions, further stimulated the demand for accurate (internal) cost information and the underlying, technical calculations. Thus, by the end of the War the cost accountants of industrial companies had reached sufficient stature, reputation and ability to form their own professional accountancy bodies. In the United Kingdom, what is now referred to as the Chartered Institute of Management Accountants (CIMA) was, initially, founded in 1919 as the Institute of Cost and Works Accountants. In the same year, its American equivalent, the Institute of Management Accountants (IMA) was also formed. Both of these professional management accounting bodies promoted and encouraged developments in cost accounting practice.

However, the application of economic thinking began to change cost accounting practice and resulting information within manufacturing entities. The book *Studies in the Economics of Overhead Costs* by American economist John Maurice Clark (Clark, 1923) was a particularly important contribution. Clark extensively discussed the nature of overhead costs and their use in managerial decision making. He argued that overhead costs – defined as "costs that cannot be traced to particular units of output" – are all-pervasive and he predicted that, in future years, overheads were likely to grow in their importance

Luxury Brands and Strategic Management Accounting

in the overall cost structure of the firm. He coined the phrase "different costs for different purposes" which means that managers require different types of accounting information for different decisions. In this context, Clark was drawing attention to the fact that historical cost information must, necessarily, be revised and amended to make it suitable for managerial decision making. Clark argued that:

"If cost accounting sets out, determined to discover what the cost of everything is and convinced in advance that there is one figure which can be found and which will furnish exactly the information which is required for every possible purpose, it will necessarily fail, because there is no such figure. If it finds a figure which is right for some purpose, it must necessarily be wrong for others."

From the 1930s onwards, the discipline of management accounting further expanded and increased attention was given to using cost information to assist managerial decision making. Moreover, the topic of budgetary control also became more important. Parker (2012) suggests that the growth in the discussion on budgetary control, within the accounting and business management literature, was facilitated by the first *International Conference on Budgetary Control* (1930), held in Geneva by the International Management Institute. Remarkably, for that period, the Conference drew an attendance of some 200 delegates from 27 countries and many different papers were presented to this audience.

Moreover, both American and English cost accountants adopted the engineering ideas of cost standards for production output. Such accounting standards allowed the comparison of actual costs with (predetermined) standard costs, and an analysis of resulting cost variances (Sowell, 1973). In addition, the technique of profit planning, also referred to as cost-volume-profit analysis, based on the concept of cost behaviour relative to volume of production, was increasingly advocated for managerial decision making. Moreover, prompted by the writings of Dean in the 1950s, discounted cash flow techniques were increasingly adopted by firms when making capital expenditure i.e. capital investment decisions. Furthermore, from the 1950s onwards, and arising from the work of Argyris (1952), it was increasingly stressed that there were important behavioural dimensions associated with management accounting information including dysfunctional consequences.

During the 1960's the above (and other) developments received even wider exposure with the publication of two important and well-written management accounting text books written by American professors – Gordon Shillinglaw (1961) and Charles Horngren (1962). The availability of such textbooks facilitated the study of cost/management accounting courses at undergraduate and postgraduate levels at universities. Also, the discipline of management accounting was taught and examined by various professional accountancy bodies. Another influential book appeared in 1965 – *Management Control Systems* - which was authored by Professor Bob Anthony. This text further extended the limits of the management accounting discipline with its emphasis on the implementation and monitoring of strategy within organizations. Anthony (1965) also addressed the behavioural dimension of management accounting together with a discussion of various issues regarding performance measurement. Thus, around the late 1970s/ early 1980s, it appeared to some casual observers, that management accounting could be described as a "perfect discipline" because most of its problem topics and applications had been solved except, perhaps, for some issues dealing with the behavioural aspects of management accounting. However, additional fundamental changes were about to occur in the discipline of management accounting. Underlying these changes were the criticisms of Johnson and Kaplan (1987, p.1) who argued in *Relevance Lost* that:

"management accounting information, driven by the procedures and cycle of the organization's financial reporting system, is too late, too aggregated, and too distorted to be relevant for managers' planning and control decisions"

Thus, in recent times, we see changes in the business environment which have further impacted on the practical discipline of modern management accounting. We now live in a dynamic environment and, in such an environment, organizations must be agile and be able to respond effectively to major environmental forces. Currently, the advent of industrialization has brought dramatic changes to the luxury sector. Two major key elements have affected the recent evolution of the field: an increased emphasis on internalization of the firms and an increased demand of luxury goods from the market, due to the constantly growing purchasing power of consumers (Coste-Maniere et al., 2011). Indeed, all organizations must develop appropriate strategies by identifying the opportunities and threats posed by (a) increased global competition and globalization, (b) advances in manufacturing technologies including information technology and social media, and (c) a greater focus on customers and customer preferences (McWatters and Zimmerman, 2016).

(2a). Increase in Global Competition and Globalization

Globalization represents threats of new competitors entering the market place and these threats require that firms, increasingly, need both financial and non-financial information for decision-making to participate effectively in global markets (Blocher, Stout, Cokins and Chen, 2008). More than ever, in recent times, the business environment is associated with the growth of international markets and the issue of globalization has been a major force affecting trade over the past 50 years. For example, in the early 1960s almost all televisions and cars purchased in the United States were made there. However, to-day most of the televisions and cars purchased in the United States are manufactured elsewhere, which includes Asia. Other examples are provided by shoes which are made in Singapore, T-shirts are made in Guatemala, jeans are made in Cambodia and handbags are made in Italy. Furthermore, the *Internet* has facilitated the creation of a global marketplace.

The opportunity for a growth in sales revenue and overall profitability of a firm lies in the development, and growth, of global markets. The emphasis on global markets and international trade has forced many business organizations, which once faced protected domestic markets, to become more and more cost competitive and adaptive. Instead of making products domestically, business firms now outsource the manufacture of parts and sub-components globally. Moreover, market conditions are changing for a variety of reasons, including changes in government regulations and taxation policies, and one can briefly mention the (anticipated) significant impact of "Brexit" – the exiting of Great Britain from the European Union - to appreciate the favourable and unfavourable financial consequences of international trade, or the lack of it. Globalization increases competition, and will drive inefficient firms out of domestic markets. Thus, increasing globalization requires firms to be efficient producers in order to survive. To be efficient, organizations must know and be able to control their costs. To control costs a firm must have a management accounting system that reports accurate and timely cost management information.

An important factor associated with globalization, and the impact on the profitability of companies, is the issue of transfer pricing. A transfer price is the exchange price for a product or service which one subunit (department or division) of an organization charges for a product or service supplied to another subunit of the same organization (Horngren, Datar, Rajan, 2016). These transfer prices contrast with the

Luxury Brands and Strategic Management Accounting

external price for goods or services which are sold to external customers. The issue of transfer prices becomes complicated for a multinational corporation as transfer prices are impacted by domestic and foreign taxes imposed on profits. There are also important international taxation considerations which are now briefly discussed.

International transfer prices are used when a multinational firm transfers products (or services) between two of the group's units which operate in two countries and these countries have different systems of taxing corporate income. It is also likely that the identified transfer price between these two entities – the buyer and seller – will attract tariffs based on the international transfer price. In such circumstances, the multinational company will try to set a transfer price to minimize its aggregate tax liability generated in the two countries. The use of transfer prices is an effective way for global corporations to shift taxes to lower income tax jurisdictions. Therefore, it is not surprising that government officials and tax authorities, in both the importing and exporting counties around the world, closely monitor firms' (international) transfer pricing methods. These transfer pricing methods are an additional issue in globalization which impact on management accounting information.

(2b). New Manufacturing Technologies

New technology offers opportunities for firms to be more efficient and competitive, but also threatens to make the existing technology of the organization outdated. Therefore, in order to remain competitive in the face of increased global competition, manufacturing firms are adopting new manufacturing technologies such as just-in-time (JIT) systems. JIT is a process of providing products only when an order is received rather than making it and placing it in stock. Thus, under a JIT system customers should not have a long wait for delivery of the ordered product. Rather, the product is manufactured to order. Although the Japanese have been credited with the creation of the idea of JIT, it is not a new concept. Indeed, nearly a century ago, Ford and Crowther (1924) wrote, "if transportation was perfect and an even flow could be assumed, it would not be necessary to carry any stock whatsoever" (Ford and Crowther, 1924). Furthermore, there is no waste product or obsolescence. Another favourable consequence of JIT is that warehousing and insurance costs of holding finished inventory are significantly reduced.

JIT systems can be used for both a raw material purchasing system and/or a finished product production system. The JIT purchasing system aims to coordinate the receipt of raw materials with their expected usage in production so that the holding of raw material inventory is driven towards a zero amount. The JIT production system aims to ensure that the (finished) units produced depends on customer demand and, in the absence of customer demand, no production would, in theory, take place. However, JIT systems are much more than an inventory management system. The philosophy of JIT underpins a commitment to achieve consistently high quality products, partly to obtain competitive advantage in the marketplace, but also to reduce costs associated with the manufacturing process. These manufacturing costs relate to, for example, warehousing, moving inventory within the factory, rework and after-sales rectification. In addition activities such as the response time to customer requests, improves the overall experience of customers when dealing with the firm (Clarke and Brislane, 2000).

(2c). Focus on Customer Preferences and Satisfaction

Increasingly, as part of their strategy, organizations are proclaiming themselves to be "customer driven", and this shift toward customer satisfaction and customer preferences is understandable in the context

161

of strategic thinking. Some implications from unhappy customers can be gleaned from the following rules of thumb, used by some marketing personnel. These underscore the fact that customer satisfaction, customer retention and customer loyalty are crucial issues in determining the long run success of any organization and without which, the financial performance of a firm will be disappointing (Clarke, 2016):

- Only about 5% of unhappy customers will complain directly to the organization involved;
- On average, a customer with a complaint relating to an organization will tell 10 other people;
- It costs, approximately, five times as much to gain new customers than to retain an existing customer.

Changing customer preferences provide opportunities for a production company to develop new products and services, but this could, also, threaten the success of existing products and services. Increasingly, firms are advised by professional experts to better focus on the needs of consumers, and the provision of customer satisfaction because this is the key to long-term success.

While many other authors have also criticised traditional management accounting practice in recent years, it is fair to argue that Johnson and Kaplan have stimulated more debate in the area of management accounting than any other authors. In brief, Johnson and Kaplan (1987) argue that traditional management accounting practice had lost much of its relevance in the modern business environment – hence the title of their pioneering book *"Relevance Lost"*. It is now worthwhile to review some of the suggestions and limitations of traditional management accounting practice, which can now be discussed in the context of developing successful global strategies for the marketing of luxury brands.

3. SOME IMPLICATIONS FOR MANAGEMENT ACCOUNTING

Reflecting the criticisms of the current practices and techniques of management accounting, we can now review some suggestions for improvement. Many of these new techniques and themes are listed by Clarke (2006) and several other authors. These topics are now part of the developing management accounting themes which are an important part of modern management accounting practice and include topics such as "Activity Based Costing", Activity Based Cost Management", "Balanced Scorecard", "Cost Management", "Critical Success Factors", "Customer Profitability Analysis""Key Performance Indicators", "Performance Measures and Key Performance Indicators", "Quality", "Strategy and Strategic Management Accounting". While these terms have different meanings, it is realistic to suggest that they share common implications for the discipline of management accounting. Specifically, they all suggest a broadening of the type of information that is presented by the management accountant to managers for decision making purposes, which includes the monitoring of implementing overall strategy. The growing pressures of global competition and changes in business processes have made these management accounting practices more critical and dynamic than ever before.

(3a). Strategy, Strategic Thinking and Strategic Choice

In order to be effective, business managers are now required to think competitively and creatively in order to develop an appropriate strategy for the company, to translate it into practice and mange it over time. A strategy specifies how an organization matches its own capabilities with the opportunities in

Luxury Brands and Strategic Management Accounting

the marketplace in order to achieve its stated objectives. In other words, a strategy represents a set of decisions by which top business managers plan to achieve the long-term objectives of the business firm. Strategic decisions usually refer to:

- The goods or services to be sold;
- The specific market segments in which the goods and/or services are to be sold;
- The marketing and methodology by which the goods or services will be sold.

In developing a sustainable competitive position, either due to deliberate intention or as a result of market forces, Porter (1980) has defined three generic strategies – cost leadership, product differentiation, and niche or focus (Figure 1). First, it is possible to target the whole market and adopt an "overall cost leadership" strategy with its low cost focus. Secondly, a firm may target the whole market and adopt a "product differentiation" strategy with its emphasis on being different or unique. Thirdly, a firm may focus on a "target market" (also called a segmentation strategy or niche strategy) and adopt either a cost leadership or product differentiation strategy. Thus, Porter (1980) has defined three generic strategies: the industry-wide cost leadership, the industry-wide differentiation and the competitive scope applied to a single market segment. We shall briefly discuss these as a firm succeeds by adopting and effectively implementing one of the above three competitive strategies.

Table 1. Matrix of Strategic Choices

		Strategic Advantage	
		Low cost position	Uniqueness perceived by the customer
Strategic Target	Industry - wide	1. Cost leadership	2. Product differentiation
	Niche of focus, i.e. specific segment only	3. Cost-focused leadership	4. Product- focused differentiation

Source: Porter (1980)

Cost leadership is a strategy in which a firm outperforms competitors in producing products or delivering services at a lower cost than competitors. Based on this strategy, the cost leader makes sustainable profits from products which are sold at lower selling prices, thereby limiting the growth of competition in the industry by success at price wars and undermining the profitability of competitors, which must meet the firm's low price. The cost leader normally has a relatively large market share and tends to avoid niche segment markets by using the price advantage to attract a large portion of a targeted market. A cost leadership strategy will also focus on cost reduction, thereby ensuring a significant cost and price advantage in a competitive market place. However, it should be noted that a potential weakness of the cost leadership strategy is a tendency to reduce costs in a manner that may undermine demand for the product or service due to, for example, the deletion of key features which are required by customers.

The **product differentiation** strategy is implemented by creating a perception among customers that the product or service is unique in some important way, usually by being of higher quality, features or reputation. This perception allows a firm to charge higher prices and outperform competitors in terms of profits generated without reducing costs significantly. Most industries have some "differentiated" firms and the appeal of differentiation is especially strong for product lines for which the perception of quality and image is very important i.e. luxury brands. A possible weakness of the differentiation strategy is the need for the firm to have an aggressive marketing plan in order to reinforce its differentiation strategy. In other words, if the customer begins to believe that the difference between competing products is not significant, then the lower priced products will appear more attractive to the customer.

The "**niche**" or "**focus**" strategy concentrates on a specific niche or segment of the market – as defined, for example, by type of customers, segment of the product line, or geographic area. Strategy is used to identify and choose market niches where competition is the weakest, or where the firm has a strong competitive advantage. The advantage is that the firm succeeds by avoiding direct competition! This firm will have either strong differentiation or low cost advantage (or both) for its market segment.

A luxury branded product can be defined, in economic terms, as a product for which demand increases more than proportionally as overall income rises, so that expenditure on the product for an individual becomes a greater proportion of overall spending. The luxury industry is first and foremost a brand-driven industry: people buy luxury products because they trust and appreciate the brand. Luxury brands are to be found in several product categories, namely fashion, perfumes and cosmetics, wines and spirits, watches and jewellery, automobiles, leisure, banking and home furnishings (Fionda and Moore, 2009).

The world's top 10 most valuable luxury brands are presented in Figure 2 and estimates the value of the leading 10 most luxury brands worldwide in 2019. Although the term "luxury" good is independent of the goods' quality they are generally considered to be goods at the highest end of the market in terms of quality and price. It is interesting to note that most of these firms operate in the fashion industry.

Table 2. Value in dollars of the leading 10 most valuable luxury brands

Rank	Brand/Company	Brand Value US $m	Country	Product
1	Louis Vuitton	$47 m	France	Fashion
2	Chanel	$37 m	France	Fashion
3	Hermes	$31 m	France	Fashion
4	Gucci	$25 m	Italy	Fashion
5	Rolex	$8 m	Switzerland	Watches
6	Cartier	$6 m	France	Fashion
7	Burberry	$4 m	England	Fashion
8	Christian Dior	$4 m	France	Jewellery
9	Yves St. Laurent	$3 m	France	Fashion
10	Prada	$3 m	Italy	Fashion

Source: Statistica 2020, Accessed 1 July 2020

(3b). Strategic Management Accounting

Because strategic issues are increasing in importance to modern business managers, management accountants have moved from their historical and traditional orientation of product costing to the broader issue of strategic cost management. Strategy formation requires information and much of the required information will be derived from the management accounting function, the marketing function, together

Luxury Brands and Strategic Management Accounting

with a knowledge of customers and competitors. Thus, we can broaden out a discussion on "strategy" to the recently developed topic of "strategic management accounting".

Strategic management accounting is concerned with issues, such as market growth and market share, prices of competitors' products, changing customer preferences, spending on research and development, and implementation of technology. (In reality this is a process with elements of inter-firm comparison, continually looking to the future and the firm's external operating environment, and the ability to successfully compete against competitors in a selected market place). It is only with this wider information set that firms can know their true competitive position and appreciate both the threats and opportunities facing the organization. Traditionally, management accounting practice has focused on internal, financial performance (and position). Admittedly, this internally and financially oriented perspective is important to managers in the context of operational planning and control. However, if this is the only information that is generated and provided to managers, then managers will tend to concentrate mainly on operational issues rather than the overall strategic position and direction of the organization. Strategic Management Accounting (SMA) has three main elements, namely environmental scanning, competitive analysis and adopting a strategic perspective on internal data (Clarke, 1995).

i. Environmental Scanning

Environmental scanning involves monitoring the environment for technological developments, changes in customer preferences, significant economic changes and market-based information. In addition, environmental scanning requires information on the demographic, legal, and economic environment in which the firm operates. In an age of fast changing trends, luxury brand companies have identified a new customer class and this class is likely to become increasingly relevant in the future i.e. the HENRYs (i.e. High-Earners-Not-Rich-Yet). Currently, the HENRYs have a significant discretionary income and are highly likely to be wealthy in the future. HENRYs earn between $100,000 and $250,000 per annum, and their average age is about 45 years. They are digital savvy, love online shopping and are big spenders. With HENRYs likely to become some of the wealthiest members of society, the potential benefits of selling luxury brands to this important customer segment, is enormous (Deloitte, 2019).

ii. Competitor Analysis

In order to be successful a company will need to establish its strategies in the context of the firm's position relative to its actual and potential competitors. Competitive aspects such as selling price, quality, durability and after-sales service are important factors in being successful in any competitive market place.

iii. Strategic Perspective on Internal Information

Information about the firm, relating to internal operations, should be viewed from a strategic perspective. For example, the company may report reduced profits for an accounting period, but this profit reduction may be attributable to reduced prices which are expected to build market share. Alternatively, if a firm places too much emphasis on its short-term profitability, it may be reluctant to invest in improving its competitive position and reduce strategic expenditure on essential items, for example, marketing, staff training, research and development. Moreover, an increase in short-term profitability may be attributed

Luxury Brands and Strategic Management Accounting

to increased selling prices which could lead to a future reduction in market share, and this aspect could attract additional competitors into the market.

(3c). Critical Success Factors and Non-Financial Indicators

It is important that managers know the company's financial performance results against budget but also the principal *determinants* of those results. In the context of management accounting these determinants are referred to as critical success factors. In brief, critical success factors are the limited number of key areas in which superior performance is essential for a firm if it is to be competitive and, therefore, successful (Blocher, Stout, Cokins and Chen, 2008). Alternatively stated, Critical Success Factors are the key drivers of successful performance. Thus, in order to successfully implement a selected strategy of the firm, the strategic planning process must identify a set of Critical Success Factors for the business and identify the cause and effect relationship between Critical Success Factors and the firm's related performance. Thus, critical success factors represent the crucial areas to be monitored on a regular basis within the firm since they determine performance. It is obvious to state that an unfavourable performance indicates the need for prompt managerial reaction. Information relating to critical success factors tends to be predominantly of a non-financial nature and, in such a case, these measures can be described as non-financial indicators (NFIs) or key performance indicators (KPIs) which may include financial metrics. A crucial task for management accountants is to develop a range of appropriate key performance metrics which relate to the agreed critical success factors of the firm. Typical non-financial performance indicators will include performance measures, for example, relating to the:

- Production of goods with consistently low defect rates
- Delivery of goods on time to customers
- Provision of reliable and durable products to our customers
- Provision of products and services to satisfy the needs of customers
- Measurement of effective after-sales service to customers.

It should be noted, however, that the identification of key performance indicators or performance measures is not the exclusive role of the accounting system. On the contrary, such performance measures are often collected by Information Technology specialists within the organization. However, since the accounting function within companies has a high degree of expertise in information collection and information reporting within the firm, management accountants are encouraged to become more involved in the collection and reporting of non-financial indicators. As a result, it can be argued that such non-financial indicators should be included with the (regular and frequent) accounting reports that are usually produced within the organization.

(3d). The Balanced Scorecard and Luxury Brands

A number of frameworks for deriving and reporting appropriate performance measures within a firm have been proposed in an attempt to remedy the perceived failings of traditional costing systems. It is realistic to suggest that Kaplan and Norton's *Balanced Scorecard* (1992) is the best known and respected.

The Balanced Scorecard began with the premise that an exclusive reliance on financial measures within the firm's management accounting system may distort managerial decision making. The Balanced

Luxury Brands and Strategic Management Accounting

Scorecard was developed as a result of a research project in the early 1990s into advanced performance measurement techniques carried out by Professor Robert Kaplan, from the Harvard Business School and David Norton (a management consultant). The research project was carried out in 12 US business firms regarding as being at the leading edge of performance measurement. The actual title "Balanced Scorecard" was a variation on the title – Corporate Scorecard – developed by Art Schneiderman, then VP for Quality and Productivity at Analog Devices. The resultant template, the Balanced Scorecard (BSC), became an extension of Schneiderman's presentation and was published in a pioneering article by Kaplan and Norton (1992) in the *Harvard Business Review*. Since that time, the concept of the *Balanced Scorecard* has generated a great deal of interest and practical application. The essential thrust of the *Balanced Scorecard is* based on two fundamental propositions. First, you get what you measure and, secondly, managers need a broad range of performance measures in order to manage their business successfully (Jiambalvo, 2013). The Balanced Scorecard translates the corporate strategy into an action plan that identifies specific objectives and performance measures to help determine if the organization is moving in its required direction. In addition to being linked with the organization's strategy, the Balanced Scorecard provides a comprehensive view of the organization by identifying an appropriate variety of performance measures – both financial and non-financial. It also recognizes the organization's multiple stakeholders who contribute to strategic success. These stakeholders include the shareholders or owners, customers, suppliers, employees and society in general (McWatters and Zimmerman, 2016).

Traditionally, the Balanced Scorecard is divided into four different perspectives and is intended to provide answers to four basic questions which relate to different perspectives as follows (Kaplan and Norton, 1992):

- How does our firm look to shareholders? (the financial perspective)
- How do customers see our firm? (the customer perspective)
- What must our firm excel at? (the internal perspective)
- Can our firm continue to improve and create value? (the learning and growth perspective)

The financial perspective reflects past decisions and represents the historical, financial performance of the firm. The customer and internal process perspectives represent current performance levels. The learning and growth perspective represents what must be done in the future and these actions will have a positive, future impact on the firm. Thus, the Balanced Scorecard is "balanced" in three ways. First, there is a balance between internal and external perspectives. Secondly, the Scorecard is balanced by the use of both financial and non-financial measures. Thirdly, the Scorecard is balanced in terms of time i.e. it reflects the past, the present and the future. Therefore, to be implemented effectively the Balanced Scorecard should, for example:

- Accurately reflect the organization's strategy
- Communicate the organization's strategy to all managers and employees who, in turn, should understand and accept the Balance Scorecard
- Have the support of top management
- Be linked to the reward system – managers and employees should have clear incentives which are linked to the Balanced Scorecard. (Blocher, Stout, Cokins, and Chen, 2008).

The Balanced Scorecard is a relatively modern management tool that can be applied to virtually every type of company. This is because each company, by definition, can incorporate the four aspects of the BSC in some capacity, regardless of sectors and scope. It is important to note, however, that in order to be efficiently implemented, the Balanced Scorecard should be adapted to the company for which it has been applied to. In that regard, it is crucial for a luxury company to fully understand its key components and come up with key performance indicators related to its products and brand.

Intangible assets have always played an important role in the success of any business and now they represent a key factor for success, especially in fashion and luxury brand companies. We define intangible assets as those assets that are not physical in nature, and therefore they are difficult to imitate by competitors. Examples of intangible assets include copyright, brand development or name recognition. For accounting purposes, intangible assets can be assigned monetary values based on arbitrary evaluation procedures, but they are different, in their nature, from tangible assets such as property, plant and equipment.

In luxury brands, the creativity of the designers is usually an important key factor that allows a company to successfully differentiate itself from its competitors and provide its customers with a unique and characterized product. In fashion and luxury brands, competitive advantage is connected to intangible assets such as know-how and creative design, under the watchful eye of the creative director. The main attributes, images and ideas of a firm are represented by the brand through a name, a symbol, a design or various combinations of these (Oliver, Schab, and Holweg, 2007). Thus, luxury brand products are associated with a specific label but also by a combination of elements which have value for consumers (Saviolo and Testa, 2000)

The implementation of the Balanced Scorecard in luxury brand companies is a procedure that requires multiple steps. For example, the first step of the implementation procedure would be the involvement of key managerial individuals representing crucial departments and functions of the company such as the marketing department, the supply chain department or the quality management system. When implementing a corporate strategy and its related management control system, it is important to get as many people involved as possible, in order for them to share their opinions on the general strategic direction and position of the company and work together towards a common goal (Bubbio, Cacciamani, Rubello and Solbiati, 2009). After a generic plan of action is agreed with, the second step of the strategy implementation is to decide how frequently the measurement of the performance indicators, listed in the Balanced Scorecard (Figure 3), will be. Within the luxury brand sector, companies might have very different seasonality patterns, especially when it comes to generating product sales. Therefore, it is important to determine which sales pattern is the most useful for the company in question. For example, a clothing company could experience an increase in sales revenue during the weeks immediately prior to Christmas due to the forthcoming holiday season and should plan their inventory holdings accordingly.

Figure 1. An example of the Balanced Scorecard
Source: Fazzini and Terzani (2006)

		Strategic Advantage	
		Low cost position	Uniqueness perceived by the customer
Strategic Target	Industry - wide	1. Cost leadership	2. Product differentiation
	Niche of focus, i.e. specific segment only	3. Cost-focused leadership	4. Product- focused differentiation

Luxury Brands and Strategic Management Accounting

In addition, once all the strategic initiatives have been determined and agreed in order to achieve the strategic objectives of the business it is important to allocate the appropriate budget resources to each individual activity. An adequate budget not only provides the resources needed in order to achieve the agreed strategy, but it also sets the financial boundaries within which each responsible manager should operate (Bubbio, Cacciamani, Rubello, and Solbiati, 2009).

(3e). Emphasis on Quality

The issue of product quality is now an essential aspect of the contemporary business environment whereas, it is fair to say that, previously, achievements such as economies of scale and standardization were more important. In modern times, customers associate luxury brand products with quality. One reason is that quality is an important aspect of the product differentiation strategy and quality is expected by customers and quality must be delivered to customers. Thus, for luxury brands it can be suggested that, in the future, there will be only two types of businesses – those that practice total quality management and those that are no longer trading! Indeed, in this context it must be stressed that the real judge of quality is the customer. No matter what individuals within the organization believe, it will always be the customer who is the real and ultimate judge of quality.

The recent emphasis on product quality within the discipline of management accounting contrasts with some traditionally held views. In recent times it was generally accepted that there was a desirable balance to be achieved between improved quality and higher costs. Typically, companies would keep large amounts of finished goods and raw materials in stock thus incurring costs of storage, insurance, breakages and, possibly, pilferage. Thus, for many companies, one of the greatest opportunities for effective profit improvement through cost management and overall cost reduction was in managing the cost of quality. The differing views in relation to the issue of quality i.e. the traditional versus the modern approaches are presented in Figure 4 (below).

Table 3. Differing views on Quality

Traditional management view	Modern management view
Improving quality increases overall costs	Improving quality reduces overall costs
A percentage amount of defects is acceptable	The goal of quality is zero defects
Quantity of output is as important as quality	Without quality everything else is irrelevant

Source: Clarke (1996)

It is logical to argue that as luxury brand product companies embrace the quality revolution, they will need to report appropriate performance measures in the area of quality. These "quality measures" can be expressed in non-financial terms and can be part of the Balanced Scorecard. Typical quality performance measures could include the following:

- Number (%) of defective goods delivered by supplier
- Number (%) of production rejects
- Number of rework/overtime hour worked and costs

Luxury Brands and Strategic Management Accounting

- Non-scheduled machine downtown hours
- Number (%) of late deliveries to customers
- Number of accidents in premises
- Number of customer complaints

It has been argued that the financial impact of "quality" should be better highlighted by way of a Cost of Quality (CoQ) report. The Cost of Quality report attempts to compute a single, aggregate financial measure of all explicit costs attributable to preventing and correcting defective products. Sometimes, managers do not realize the significance of the "lack of quality problem" or the potential benefits of good quality until they see the financial consequences (Clarke, 1996). These quality costs are usually divided into four separate categories:

- Prevention costs i.e. actions to reduce or prevent inferior quality output
- Appraisal costs i.e. costs incurred in discovering the condition of raw materials and finished products, including testing procedures
- Internal failure costs i.e. costs incurred when products fail to meet quality standards, before delivery to customers.
- External failure costs i.e. costs incurred because poor quality products were delivered to external customers and now must be rectified.

It should be noted that the above, four categories do not include opportunity costs associated with bad quality output such as the probable loss of future sales and a deteriorating reputation. In addition, it should also be noted that, in many cases, dissatisfied customers do not complain directly to the company. Dissatisfied customers may choose to transfer their trade to a competitor firm. In addition, they may articulate to that competitor their unsatisfactory experiences as a customer of our company.

(3f). Activity-Based Costing (ABC) and Pricing

An important strategic planning decision for an organization is the pricing of its products and services. The pricing decision is complicated because it requires appropriate product cost information. (Such product costs include raw materials, direct labour costs, production and non-production overhead costs). The unit cost calculation serves as a logical and lower boundary for the determination of selling prices. However, it should be noted that customers will only purchase a product or service provided the value derived from the product is considered to be greater than its cost of purchase. In addition, the price which customers are prepared to pay for a product must be estimated. Furthermore, in a global economy, E-Commerce reduces barriers to entry so that new competitors can quickly enter the market place and may set lower selling prices due to a more efficient cost base. Thus, in simple terms, a selling price decision requires knowledge of costs, customers, and competitors and the determination of selling prices is a very important element dimension in the context of strategy and managerial decision making.

Under traditional cost accounting (TCA) overhead costs are assigned to units of output i.e. the absorption of overhead costs, using an overhead absorption base. (For convenience, we shall focus on production overheads, rather than total overheads). The overhead absorption base or cost driver used (i.e. denominator below) is, typically, direct labour hours or machine running hours, because this informa-

Luxury Brands and Strategic Management Accounting

tion is generally available and easy to use, as indicated below, based on budgeted information for the relevant accounting period:

OHAR =	**Production overheads $**	**€100,000**	€5 per DLH
	------------------------------	------------------ =	
	Direct labour hours	*20,000 DLHs*	

However, in the early 1980s, and in the context of a multi-product firm, there developed widespread criticism of this traditional cost accounting method i.e. using direct labour hours (or machine running hours) to absorb production overheads into units of output. This traditional method of cost absorption is acceptable only if a large portion of overheads are proportional to total production volume. This assumption was convenient to calculate and apply but, in many cases, it was an unrealistic assumption. The reason is that, in the modern production environment, an increasing amount of production overhead costs relate to the number of "transactions" or "activities" taking place within the factory. Other examples of "transactions" or "activities" are machine set-ups for a production run, materials handling, and first item inspections. All of these activities are, usually, independent of production volume or machine running hours (Clarke, 1995). For example, the cost of setting up a machine for a production run will be the same for 1 or 1,000 units of output.

Activity based costing (ABC) was initially developed due to perceptions that traditional accounting methods appeared to provide misleading product costs, and therefore, inappropriate unit selling prices. In contrast, ABC is an alternative way of tracing costs to products that, in many cases, leads to very different product costs and therefore different selling prices and product profitability compared to traditional cost accounting. In contrast to the traditional method of overhead absorption, activity-based costing assigns overhead costs to products initially by grouping overhead costs into activity centers or cost pools. The major factor which causes or determines these activity costs is referred is referred to as a "cost driver", for example, the number of inspections undertaken. Finally, cost driver rates are computed and these cost driver rates are used to assign overhead costs to units of output. The development of Activity-Based Costing (ABC), attributed to Cooper and Kaplan, 1988), has received an enormous amount of attention from accounting academics and practitioners around the world since.

The development of Activity Based Costing (ABC) was a response to the increasing amount, and changing pattern, of overhead costs incurred in manufacturing firms, particularly those production overheads that were "transaction" or "activity" driven rather than were incurred due to changes in production volume. Alternatively stated, ABC acknowledges that products consume activities and activities consume overhead costs. This article uses, for simplicity, a three-category hierarchy for a manufacturing firm, unit level activities, transaction based activities and plant level activities, as follows:

- Unit level activities: These costs are incurred each time a unit of output is produced and such costs correspond to the traditional variable production costs.
- Transaction based activities: These are performed each time a transaction or activity occurs, for example machine set-up for a production run, or inspection of finished product.
- Plant level activity: These involve overhead costs which are incurred for a variety of products and can only be assigned to products in an arbitrary manner. A typical example is that of factory rent.

A major difference between traditional product costing (TCA) systems and activity based costing (ABC) is the method by which "transaction" related overheads are assigned for product costing. Traditionally, such overhead costs are assigned to products using either direct labour hours or machine running hours. However, the reality is that many production overhead costs are driven by the number of "transactions" or "activities" which take place within the factory e.g. the cost of setting up a machine for a production run. Such overheads are not related to volume of output. Another example would be first-item inspection of a production run. Thus, in modern factories, an increasing amount of overhead costs which are incurred in the production process relate to the complexity of business operations rather than volume of output. Therefore, it is argued that high-volume, but easy to produce products, may be over-costed using traditional cost accounting, whereas complex and low volume products may be undercosted under traditional cost accounting. Alternatively stated, under TCA, and using direct labour hours as the cost driver, high-volume products are often presented as loss makers. In contrast, low volume products – who receive a low amount of production overheads – are often presented as profitable. In contrast, under ABC, the high-volume products, which may consume only a small amount of activities, are presented as profitable, whereas low volume products, under ABC, are presented as loss-makers. Thus, a product could be presented as a loss maker under TCA but profitable using ABC. Conversely, a product could be presented as profitable under TCA but a loss maker under ABC. As a result of these "distorting" product costs, firms who use TCA may sell their products at lower prices than necessary simply because the product's unit cost information, computed by the firm's management accountant was too low using traditional cost accounting. In such circumstances the (TCA) cost information, was distorted and incorrect and, thus, the supplying firm was subsidizing its customers!

(3g). Activity-based cost management (ABCM)

Another related development in management accounting is that of Activity-Based Cost Management (ABCM) which developed out of Activity Based Costing. ABCM extends ABC and focuses on identifying and better-managing the firm's activities, instead of tracing overhead costs to products. ABCM connects the strategy of the organization with relevant and accurate overhead costs. (It should be remembered that it is argued that high volume products are less costly under ABC, whereas low volume products are more costly compared with ABC. The reason for this is that low volume products are often more complex and costly to produce. In contrast, high volume products, due to, say, large production runs, are less complex to produce, and therefore cheaper to produce. Thus, it is argued that the cost accounting system should reflect this, and this argument favours the use of ABC relative to TCA. However, there are additional considerations in favour of using an ABC system, i.e. ABC information can be further used by managers apart from product-costing purposes. This expanded use of ABC information is referred to as Activity-Based Cost Management (ABCM) and we shall briefly discuss two features of ABCM, namely:

- The identification and elimination on non-value added activities, and
- To perform customer profitability analysis calculations.

(3h). Value added and Non-Value added Costs

The (internal) cost accounting system, based on the recording and reporting of historical costs, may also have to change. Costs have always been an important element in the planning and control of opera-

Luxury Brands and Strategic Management Accounting

tions of a business and it is likely that, with increased competition and globalization, the cost issue will become important in the future, especially if a firm's strategy is based on cost leadership. Traditionally, management accountants were concerned with "counting the costs" i.e. maintaining the cost accumulation system using historical product costs. (As an aside, it is intuitive to say that weighing yourself ten times per day will not, by itself, take off excess weight).

Thus, there was a change in emphasis from "counting costs", as per the traditional historical cost accounting system, to a more focused topic commonly referred to as "Cost Management". This relatively new procedure focuses on methods of reducing a firm's cost base by the identification of the activities which cause costs to be incurred. An organization can be viewed as consisting of a myriad of activities. The important aspect about these activities is to determine whether these activities are necessary to undertake in the first place and whether they are required by customers? If these activities are not required then they represent "wasteful activities" and they should be reduced or eliminated in order to better manage and control costs and, therefore, increase overall profitability.

One way to answer the question of whether activities should be eliminated or not is to classify a firm's activities into either value added or non-value added categories. Value-added activities add to a product's (or service's) desirability in the eyes of the customer and, therefore, it can be said that a customer is prepared to pay for a "value-added" activity. In other words, a customer will pay for an "activity" provided it provides him with value and satisfaction. Non-value added activities do **not** add to the product's desirability and a customer will not be willing to pay for a non-value added activities (Williams, Haka, Bettner and Carcello, 2018). Thus, an organization can decrease its cost base (and increase overall profitability) if a non-value added activity - which consumes resources - is eliminated, provided this does not change the product's desirability in the eyes of the customer. One important example of a non-value added activity is holding large amounts of raw materials, work in progress, or finished goods in inventory If organizations undertake even a crude list of their activities they will uncover many activities that do not add value to customers.

(3i). Customer Profitability Analysis

The technique of Customer Profitability Analysis (CPA) is based on the argument that individual customers place different demands on the selling organization. Thus, understanding the reasons behind the profitability of the customer base should provide additional benefits to a company and also provide a basis for future customer-related decisions. While the topic of Customer Profitability Analysis can be included in "modern developments" in management accounting practice, a discussion of this topic can be traced back to Magee (1933, p. 9) who wrote;

"the total expense for which each product is responsible is determined by a variety of considerations and not by its selling price, and it will be readily appreciated that wide variations in the ratio of expense to selling price, and therefore in the final margin of net profit, may easily occur (and) one product may be sold with a minimum of advertising and sales effort and another may require constant stimulation... the manufacturer should ask where should I sell and to whom" (Magee, 1933, p. 99).

Based on Customer Profitability Analysis information the following questions, inter alia, can be addressed (Clarke, 1994):

- Should the customers who generate low levels of sales revenue and low profit margins be eliminated or should their requirements be reduced?
- Should the organization seek to generate more sales revenue within the more profitable segment of the business?
- Should pricing policy be reviewed?
- Should the company encourage customers to purchase goods in ways that enable efficient production and physical distribution?

The growing interest in the topic of Customer Profitability Analysis has received great publicity due to the Kanthal (Kaplan, 1989) case study. In brief, the Kanthal Company specialized in the production and sale of electrical items and had 10,000 customers and 15,000 items for sale. The Kanthal Company needed a better identification of costs and implemented an Activity Based Costing system. The outcome of the project was a revised cost accounting system that could indicate an individual customer's profitability. Kanthal calculated that only 40% of its customers were profitable but they generated 225% of the company's overall profitability! The least profitable 10% of customers lost 120% of the profits. Even more surprising was that two of the most unprofitable customers turned out to be among the top three in terms of generating total sales revenue.

CONCLUSION

It is here argued that successful organizations are those that adapt quickly to the challenges of globalization and competition, together with the impact of new and more sophisticated technologies in order to become more efficient, with the desired end of satisfying the needs of customers (McWatters and Zimmerman, 2016). This paper argues that (modern) management accounting practices are an integral part of an organization's strategy and subsequent implementation efforts to create customer value. However, in order to be effective, the discipline of management accounting needs to broaden the range of information useful in managerial decision-making. The required managerial accounting information can be classified as either financial or non-financial. In turn, this information can be either historical or future-oriented and, furthermore, can relate to the firm itself or its (competitive) operating environment. Thus, it is fair to argue that modern organizations must continually evaluate and improve their management accounting system, and its orientation with the organization's strategy which is framed in the context of globalization. These aspects will facilitate success in meeting various challenges in a dynamic, global and increasingly competitive business environment. Ultimately, the most important core attributes within a firm are its general management capabilities which include the strategic management and financial management capabilities. The development and practical application of general management, strategic management, and financial management capabilities will require and make important changes to the orientation of a firm's management accounting system. In conclusion, it is important to ask the fundamental question posed by Ferrara (1995, p. 30): "what will the field of management accounting look like in the twenty-first century?" This is a difficult, but important, question to answer with accuracy and authority. In such a context, it can be anticipated, with reasonable certainty, that members of the management team will be more willing to accept innovation and change which is consistent with the organization's strategy to which they have already committed (Young, 1997). Finally, it is inevitable that modern technology,

Luxury Brands and Strategic Management Accounting

together with social media platforms will be used to cultivate important customer relationships in order to influence the purchasing decisions of the new generation of customers for luxury brands (Deloitte, 2019).

REFERENCES:

Anthony, R. (1965). *Management Control Systems: A Framework for Analysis*. Harvard University.

Argyris, C. (1952). *The Impact of Budgets on People*. Controllership Foundation.

Blocher, E., Stout, D., Cokins, G., & Chen, K. (2008). *Cost Management: A Strategic Emphasis* (4th ed.). McGraw-Hill Irwin.

Clark, J. (1923). *Studies in the Economics of Overhead Costs*. University of Chicago Press.

Clarke, P. (1994, October). Activity Based Cost Management. *Accountancy Ireland. Journal of the Institute of Chartered Accountants in Ireland*, *26*(5), 16–17.

Clarke, P. (1995). The Old and New in Management Accounting. *Management Accounting*, *73*(6), 46–51.

Clarke, P. (1995, June). The Old and New in Management Accounting. *Management Accounting, CIMA*, *73*(6), 46–51.

Clarke, P. (1996, May). Putting the Q in TQM. *Management Irish Management Institute*, *43*(2), 12–13.

Clarke, P. (2004, Summer). Footprints in the Sand: Exploring the Evolution of Management Accounting Practices in Ireland. *Irish Accounting Review*, *11*(1), 1–18.

Clarke, P. (2006). *Strategies in Management Accounting: A Series of Essays*. The Institute of Chartered Accountants.

Clarke, P. (2016). *Managerial Accounting: Costing, Decision-making and Control*. Chartered Accountants Ireland.

Clarke, P., & Brislane, C. (2000). Just in Time? Technology Ireland, 32(5), 24 - 25.

Clarke, P., Hill, N., & Stevens, K. (1999). Activity-Based Costing in Ireland: Barriers to and Opportunities for change. *Critical Perspectives on Accounting*, *10*(4), 443–468. doi:10.1006/cpac.1997.0197

Cooper, R., & Kaplan, R. (1988). How Cost Accounting Distorts Product Costs. *Management Accounting*, (April), 20–27.

Coste-Manière, I., Panchout, K., & Molas, J. (2012). *The Evolution of the Luxury Market: Stairway to Heaven?* . doi:10.1057/9780230361546_2

Dean, J. (1951). *Capital Budgeting*. Columbia University Press. doi:10.7312/dean90552

Deloitte Global. (2019). *Global Powers of Luxury Goods: Bridging the gap between the old and the new*. www.deloitte.co.uk

Fazzini, M., & Terzani, S. (2006). *Una proposta di balanced scorecard nelle imprese del sistema moda*. Controllo di Gestione.

Ferrara, W. (1995). Cost/Management Accounting: The Twenty-First Century Paradigm. *Management Accounting*, (December), 30–36.

Fionda, A., & Moore, C. (2009). The anatomy of the luxury fashion brand. *Journal of Brand Management*, *16*(5-6), 347–363. doi:10.1057/bm.2008.45

Ford, H., & Crowther, S. (1924). *My Life and Works*. Heinemann.

Garner, S. P. (1954). *Evolution of Cost Accounting to 1925*. University of Alabama Press.

Grant, R. (2013). *Jeff Immelt and the reinventing of General Electric. In Contemporary Strategy Analysis: Text and Cases*. John Wiley and Sons.

Horngen, C., Datar, S., & Rajan, M. (2016). *Cost Accounting: A Managerial Emphasis* (16th ed.). Pearson Education.

Horngren, C. (1962). *Cost Accounting: A Managerial Emphasis*. Prentice Hall.

International Management Institute. (1930). *International Conference on Budgetary Control*. Geneva: Author.

Jiambalvo, J. (2013). *Management Accounting*. John Wiley and Sons.

Johnson, H. T., & Kaplan, R. (1987). *Relevance Lost: The Rise and Fall of Management Accounting*. Harvard Business School Press.

Kaplan, R. (1984). The evolution of management accounting. *The Accounting Review*, (July), 390–418.

Kaplan, R. (1987, July). The Evolution of Management Accounting. The Accounting Review, 390 – 418.

Kaplan, R. (1989). Kanthal. Harvard Business School Case, ref: 190-002.

Kaplan, R., & Norton, D. (1992, Jan.). The Balanced Scorecard – Measures that Drive Performance. Harvard Business Review, 71 – 79.

Kaplan, R., & Norton, D. (1996). *The Balanced Scorecard: Translating Strategy into Action*. Harvard Business School Press.

Magee, B., (1933, Oct. 7). The practical control of selling expense: an examination of distribution accounting. *The Accountant*.

McWatters, C., & Zimmerman, J. (2016). *Management Accounting in a Dynamic Environment*. Routledge.

Parker, L. (2002). Twentieth Century Textbook Budgetary Discourse: Formalisation, Normalisation and Rebuttal in an Anglo – Saxon Environment. *European Accounting Review*, *11*(2), 305–327. doi:10.1080/09638180220125535

Porter, M. (1980). Competitive Advantage: Techniques for Analysing Industries and Competitors. New York: Free Press, 1980 (and republished in 1998).

Shillinglaw, G. (1961). Cost Accounting: Analysis and Control. Homewood, IL: Academic Press.

Luxury Brands and Strategic Management Accounting

Sowell, E. (1973). *The Evolution of the Theories and Techniques of Standard Costs*. The University of Alabama Press.

Statistica. (2020). Statistica.com/statistics/267948/brand-of-the-leading-10-most-valuable-luxury-brands-worldwide/

Vreeland, D. (2016). *Why accounting is important: A Look inside the Fashion Industry*. https://.grantham.edu/blog/accounting-important-look-inside-fashion-industry/

Williams, J., Haka, S., Bettner, M., & Carcello, J. (2018). *Financial & Managerial Accounting: The Basis for Business Decisions* (18th ed.). McGraw-Hill.

Young, S. M. (1997). Implementing Management Innovations Successfully: Principles for Lasting Change. *Journal of Cost Management*, (September/October), 16–20.

Section 2
Sustainable Development in the Luxury Industry

Chapter 10

Is Luxury Compatible With Corporate Social Responsibility (CSR)?
Models for Sustainable Marketing Strategies

Wided Batat

EM Normandie Business School, Paris, France & Metis Lab, France & University of Lyon 2, France

Inas Khochman

American University of Beirut, Lebanon

ABSTRACT

Luxury as a field of research has attracted many scholars who examined the potential connections and (in) compatibilities between luxury and corporate social responsibility (CSR). While some studies emphasize the incompatibility between luxury and sustainability, others highlight the important efforts of luxury brands in terms of luxury offerings and sustainable marketing strategies to fit eco-friendly consumers. To foster this research stream, this chapter develops a deeper understanding of the rise and evolvement of CSR in the luxury sector and the major marketing strategies implemented by luxury brands to fit with the needs of today's responsible consumers. The authors will first present a chronological literature review through three key periods, including the underground and advancement stages to the consolidation of sustainable luxury marketing as an established research stream. Then, a framework identifying different luxury CSR strategies will be proposed. Finally, opportunities and futures challenges will be discussed at the end of this chapter.

DOI: 10.4018/978-1-7998-5882-9.ch010

Copyright © 2021, IGI Global. Copying or distributing in print or electronic forms without written permission of IGI Global is prohibited.

INTRODUCTION

In the spirit of many, luxury marketing and corporate social responsibility (CSR) practices are especially opposed. While sustainable development often advocates sobriety and simplicity, luxury refers rather to the image of abundance and complexity. Yet the world of luxury is not necessarily antithetical to that of sustainable development. Looking more closely, luxury is also (and perhaps above all) about quality products that are timeless, transmittable, and sustainable over time, and developed from know-how excellence. In a way, luxury is, therefore, an alternative to the logic of disposable and programmed obsolescence, which is in contrast to the overconsumption that characterizes our modern Western societies and their ecological problems. Thus, there are bridges between sustainable development and luxury. To produce additional bridges more sustainably, one can draw inspiration from luxury and its ability to create quality products that are resistant and elegant but functional. Besides, luxury can also be enriched with sustainable development ideas to produce better-rationalized costs, secure supplies, and take advantage of the circular economy. Furthermore, trends show that consumers are increasingly attracted to sustainable development trends. And this is good because the luxury industry is seizing these trends: more and more brands and designers are now combining "luxury marketing" with "sustainable & responsible" development.

In recent years, CSR has become a strategic issue for businesses and a topic of study for researchers in different disciplines (Fombrun, 2005). CSR invites luxury houses and brands to rethink their strategies in the broader perspective of their relations with society as well as the environment in terms of sustainable development. For instance, Rolex, the luxury watchmaker company, stands behind sustainability and because of that, in 1976, it offered a sustainability award program that honors individual acts of courage and kindness. It was created to encourage sustainability by expanding knowledge and improving life. These individual acts improved human lives and preserved cultural heritage as well as protected the nature and environment. The five areas that Rolex Awards support are: environment, science and health, technology, cultural heritage, and exploration. This program boosts improvements in corporate social responsibility through various forms of creative ideas turned into reality and also promotes the idea that Rolex can be environmentally responsible and act sustainably. Present works examining the issues related to sustainability in the luxury sector are scant and mainly focus on promotional actions (e.g., Voyer and Beckham, 2014). Yet many marketing strategies are implemented by luxury companies to rethinking their offerings, positioning, and raise consumers' awareness about the importance of the social and environmental impacts of their consumption and purchase practices. While the majority of prior research examined luxury sustainability from a consumer's perspective (Batat, 2020a), the objective of this chapter is to fill the gap in the literature by taking a managerial perspective to identify, following a chronological approach, CSR practices of luxury brands and the typologies of marketing strategies they implement to promote a new sustainable luxury.

In line with this kind of initiative launched by luxury brands, in this chapter, the authors examine the compatibility between luxury marketing and ethical business practices alongside identifying CSR strategies implemented by luxury firms across different sectors to create sustainable and engaging luxury experiences. The chapter first starts with the theoretical foundations of CSR and sustainability. Then, a chronological approach showing the rise and advancement of sustainable luxury marketing and the examination of the compatibility of CSR with the luxury industry is presented. This perspective provides an in-depth understanding of sustainable luxury production and consumption with guidance on how to promote green and social luxury. This was followed by a methodology section where we introduce a

Is Luxury Compatible With Corporate Social Responsibility (CSR)?

systematic literature review. Finally, the results introducing a framework identifying different luxury CSR strategies implemented by companies will be introduced and explained, followed by the presentation of future challenges to develop green and ethically responsible luxury products and services.

LITERATURE REVIEW

Conceptual Background for CSR and Sustainability

While CSR practices have spread and then become institutionalized, the debates relating to the definition of CSR and its economic values have continued, leading to a fragmentation of theoretical approaches. CSR has been the subject of many theoretical developments since the 1950s, in line with the debates sparked by the works of Friedman, Levitt, and Bowen. Furthermore, in the literature, too many definitions and terms such as sustainability have been proposed to refer to CSR practices. Carroll (1999) listed no less than twenty different definitions, all emphasizing the idea that CSR refers to both the obligations of companies that extend beyond the purely functional, financial, legal, and economic dimension and to the actions of companies that potentially or concretely affect the market and social actors that are in contact with the company. CSR still appears today to a large extent as a concept in the process of being defined, the theorization of which takes place in successive waves, with the introduction of new concepts (Geva, 2008; Dahlsrud, 2006). Traditionally, CSR has been related to sustainability, although the two concepts can be distinguished. Indeed, the concept of CSR refers to the implementation by companies of voluntary actions that integrate social and environmental concerns such as green strategies into the company's commercial activities that guarantee the development of the community (Claydon, 2011). Therefore, we can conclude that CSR includes sustainability and involves key stakeholder groups and the community. Additionally, business ethics and CSR are regularly used to refer to the social and environmental company's reasonability toward the community and different stakeholders (Clarkson, 1999). Although the two concepts appear similar and seem to be overlapping, they are different, since in ethics is it about moral aspect and in CSR, there is the notion of reasonability, which is an obligation of the company toward the community (Clarkson, 1999).

Yet, two main approaches have dominated the conceptual developments. The first raises the question of the definition of CSR and attempts to specify the nature and levels of the concept, the second attempts to analyze market actors towards whom companies should be socially responsible (Freeman et al., 2010). Overall, the most commonly accepted definition of CSR is that the company is required to ensure that its practices are compatible with the societal, economic, and environmental impacts of its activities (Freeman and Phillips, 2002). Almost authors (e.g., Beurden and Gossling, 2008; Freeman et al., 2010; Carroll, 1999) agree on the idea that CSR can be defined according to three perspectives: environmental (compatibility between the company's actions and the ecosystem's preservation), social (social impacts of the company's activity on the community) and economic (financial performance). While a moral perspective of CSR refers to the company's moral responsibility, which should lead it to act in a socially responsible manner because it is its moral duty to do so; the contractual approach assumes that the main idea of CSR comes from the fact that the company is interacting with other stakeholders and is not a separate entity, thus, the company has certain expectations on the activity and appropriate corporate behavior (Wood, 1991). In contrast, the utilitarian approach explores the concept of CSR as a factor of competitive advantage. From this perspective, the company embraces CSR because it is in its interest (Carroll, 1999). Thus, CSR does not serve an ideal, it is simply a means for a given end: the search for a better image and greater profitability.

From the 80s, the stakeholder theory has gradually established itself as a complementary conceptual frame that has identified the groups for which the company should exercise its social responsibilities. Freeman's works (1984) popularized the stakeholder theory, proposing to define as "stakeholder" all the social and organizational actors or groups who are likely to affect or be affected by the unfolding of the strategy. company. This broader approach to the design of the business environment allows the company to include in its strategic analysis groups of actors previously neglected in the business development activities and the management work, such as non-governmental organizations, activist groups, or political institutions. In doing so, the company offers itself as a way to think about its socio-political environment, beyond the purely economic and commercial aspects (Carroll, 2016). Thus, the stakeholder theory aims to examine the normative, descriptive, and instrumental foundations on which the consideration of requests from external groups other than shareholders is based (Masoud, 2017, Donaldson and Preston, 1995).

Drawing on Parmar et al.'s statements (2010), the normative perspective of the stakeholder theory aims to clarify the reasons why requests from groups that are not necessarily in an explicit contractual relationship with companies can be legitimate and must, therefore, be taken into account. This approach is based on the logic of business ethics and philosophical foundations to justify the consideration of stakeholders in business practices. The descriptive perspective attempts to show the empirical relevance of this analytical framework by showing that managers and leaders tend to think of their activity as the management of multiple relationships with internal and external groups. The "stakeholder" approach would already be anchored in the management methods of companies and would, therefore, be more "natural" than an approach centered on shareholders, because it is spontaneously adopted by managers. Finally, the instrumental perspective seeks to examine the economic and financial consequences of stakeholder management and to answer the following question: to what extent taking into account the requests of stakeholders more or less distant from an organization contributes does she improve her performance.

In this research, we rely on Visser's comprehensive definition of CSR as "the way in which business consistently creates shared value in society through economic development, good governance, stakeholder responsiveness, and environmental improvement" (2011, p.1). Visser's definition is appropriate as it allows us to examine the luxury companies' stakeholder reasonability to understand whether their luxury business practices are compatible with social and responsible practices.

Sustainable Luxury Marketing: A Chronological Review

Under institutional and social pressures, the majority of luxury companies are now setting up a range of actions and strategies oriented towards social responsibility with the initial aim of responding to a problem of image vis-à-vis stakeholders as well as their customers. In the marketing field, the definition of CSR relies on two core ideas according to which luxury companies have responsibilities that go beyond the pursuit of profit and the respect of the law that involves, not only shareholders but all parties related to the company's activities. Therefore, the use of CSR in the luxury sector refers to two main approaches that support and justify the positive impact of CSR on luxury houses' profits. While the first approach establishes a positive link between CSR and profit by an increase in total productivity factors, the second justifies this positive link between CSR and profit by the gains in terms of image and brand reputation.

Almost all studies emphasize an ambiguous relationship between two factors: social responsibility and performance (e.g., Salzmann et al., 2005). Yet, some authors indicate that there is no direct link between immediate profit and CSR. Though, CSR could serve as a shock absorber in the event of a negative shock for the company, in particular, a shock that affects its reputation. CSR is, therefore, seen here as a defense against reputational risk. This would explain difficulties in finding a direct connection between profit and CSR, this link being, in fact, very indirect and not immediate.

In the luxury sector, CSR would be linked to the safeguarding of profit in the long term (Batat, 2020a, b). In early 2000, large luxury groups, such as LVMH, Pernod Ricard, and Rothschild Bank, joined the United Nations Global Compact for Development and Responsible Economic Growth. A couple of years later, in 2006, the WWF (World Wide Fund for Nature) published the report "Deeper Luxury," which was based on the survey of 10 luxury companies that emphasized the contradictions of the luxury sector, which should be compatible with the principles of CSR and sustainable development. To understand these contradictions, the chronological examination of sustainable luxury research in marketing revealed three major periods: underground, advancement, and consolidation era of sustainability in luxury marketing research. Table 1 summarized these three periods, which are presented in detail in the next section.

Table 1. The rise and evolution of sustainable luxury marketing

Periods	Underground era	Advancement era	Consolidation era
Main authors	Maycumber (1994), Rowlands (1993), and Gill (1998)	Blevis et al. (2007), Kim et al. (1997), and Kapferer (2010)	Batat (2019, 2020a, 2020b, 2020c)
CSR pillars	Planet and profit	Planet, profit, and people	Planet, people, profit, pleasure, plate, place
Perspective	Good-centric	Good-centric	Consumer-centric
Focus	Luxury product attributes	Luxury product attributes	Luxury as a holistic experience
Sector	Fashion and luxury goods	Fashion and luxury goods	Luxury foodservice, luxury gastronomy sector

The Underground Era of Sustainable Luxury Marketing (1990-2000)

We recall that luxury is a timeless element in the fashion industry, yet it comes with great responsibility, and at a greater price. Previous practices in the underground era (1990-2000) were considered less relevant regarding sustainability and corporate social responsibility, and unconcerned about the consequences of each column holding the luxury industry altogether. However, some exceptional movements defy the aforementioned, where luxury and sustainability coincided in the underground era in particular ways. Eco-fashion has been long addressed by various high-profile luxury brand designers such as Stella Mc-Cartney, Louis Vuitton, and Gucci (Amatulli et al., 2017). Though, misconceptions and incomparable alternatives of sustainable fashion swarmed the industry when Maison Margiela designed a turtleneck made out of second-hand fabric from wool socks. The dilemma here is although this act from Maison Margiela was somewhat eco-friendly, yet sustainability can be measured and implemented in much broader ways and at rather superior terms such as providing healthier material life-cycle analyses, or even more efficient uses and recoveries of certain fabrics (Gill, 1998). Nonetheless, the foundation built by Margiela, which is the concept of deconstructed or recyclable fashion, is above all an undeniable step ahead and not backward. Deconstructionism is also defined as the recreation of certain functions, as it frees the garment from its current function, and manipulates it into different attire. For example, a sleeve could be re-attached as a pocket, or in Margiela's case, a sock could be turned into a fashionable, wearable turtleneck.

On the other hand, the mere outcome behind successful green fashion marketing has proven to build social responsibility and ecological values in fashion consumers. Consumers were more likely to purchase eco-friendly and sustainable products in the United States, where 25-30% of the consumers were more interested in being socially responsible, and 30% willing to buy these products if all apparel, color, and price factors were equal in comparison to non-sustainable products (Tyler, 1993). However, the major consumption that buyers expend from this movement is a reset to their mindset or adding more values to their standards. As previously mentioned, successful marketing can educate consumers on many different levels, regardless of whether the outcome is negative or positive. In this case, however, the outcome is purely positive, since green marketing is deemed to be directly beneficial to both humanity and the planet, which both meet at the midpoint; the sustainability of life. In 1993, Esprit launched its first eco-friendly collection, a sportswear line dedicated to sustainability (Rowlands, 1993), and a year afterward, L.L. Bean based their supplier relationships' criteria on their corporate social responsibility and ecologic mindset (Maycumber, 1994). The business was no longer marketed only through price-to-quality ratio, but also through CSR and green fashion.

In line with these previous studies, a conclusion can be drawn concerning the underground era and sustainable luxury; although very basic acts of eco-friendly fashion and green marketing were made for consumers to digest, yet they paved the way for even larger movements and the green luxury revolution, motivating high-end brands to walk this sustainable path, not only to increase sales but to also target a niche market that was the beginning of the future.

The Advancement of Sustainable Luxury Marketing (2000-2010)

Following the underground era directly enters the advancement era of sustainable luxury marketing (2000-2010), where the price of luxury is recognized and realized by higher-end brands in both the fashion and tourism sectors. Questions become raised as to how cruelty and comfort can coincide in the industry, and more awareness is spread over this particular issue, especially after entering the digital age which overlaps the advancement era of sustainability and luxury.

Furthermore, a study that has examined the terms *luxury* and *new luxury*, as well as *quality* and *equality*, defined the difference between each term (Blevis et al., 2007). According to the authors behind this research, luxury is defined as the mere product or service being designed, new luxury as the making of a business out of luxury, quality as a facilitator for environmental sustainability, and lastly equality in the spirit of sustainable interaction design as the creation of an experience incentivizing CSR. The authors also claim key principles to their study on SID, or sustainable interaction design, which are limited to three points. Firstly, linking invention to disposal, which is a critical idea of creating and inventing new designs that do not necessarily become obsolete easily, and that is by studying the causes and effects of disposal of products. Secondly, promoting renewal and reuse in which the authors suggest that designs that are currently being implemented should be sustainable and endorse their recyclables such as the idea of invention and disposal. Lastly, quality and equality should also be executed because quality promotes longevity and sustainability of products being consumed, which coincides with the idea of granting these consumers a positive equality experience rather than stimulating the disposal of products (Blevis et al., 2007; Kim et al., 1997).

Is Luxury Compatible With Corporate Social Responsibility (CSR)?

Furthermore, author Kapferer (2010) claims that "not all that glitters is green" to demonstrate the hardships of the luxury sector when coming to terms with the new norm of the century; sustainability development. Because sustainability is a mutual challenge that the whole planet has to face, businesses and brands must work together hand in hand to overcome this global obstacle. However, studies show that this challenge might not only affect the environmental health of the planet but also its economic growth, which is why it poses a threat to the direct consumers of natural resources as fuel for their businesses; the luxury sector.

According to Kapferer, durability is the ultimate enemy of the fashion industry and mass market, which plan on the outdatedness of their products prematurely, whereas sustainability is the heart of luxury because it proves every product's lasting worth. For example, 90% of all Porsche's produced are still being driven. Similarly, people still benefit from Louis Vuitton's after-purchase services. For that reason, the luxury sector *must* not overexploit their resources when they are built for durability and sustainability. Also, it must not worry about cost or sale reduction, rather by the creation of value and making the consumer feel very special. For that reason, many brands feel responsible for showcasing more acts of CSR, such as LVMH initiating an Environmental charter in 2001, as well as Tiffany which claims that sustainability is their most important design, and nature being its best designer (Kapferer, 2010).

The Consolidation of Sustainable Luxury Marketing (2010-Present)

In closing, the consolidation period of the sustainable luxury marketing (2010-present) enters the field in our nowadays era, where the luxury sector is a widespread industry amongst its consumers due to penetrating the era of promotional executions (Carrigan et al., 2013), and where marketing and social media presence are a must to every brand to stay relevant. Since sustainability is the main focus of the consolidation era, luxury brands such as LVMH and Kering take the lead in endorsing sustainable development in their luxury practices and making, as well as innovating sustainability-oriented projects as a key strategic priority (Hendriksz, 2018).

LVMH is one of the largest luxury powerhouses and sustainability-driven brands known to date, and they are widely known for their humanitarian acts and sustainable projects. For example, LVMH uses vegetable extracts to tan leather products, rather than using animal extracts. Also, more than 85% of their Hennessy and Hine cognacs are shipped by sea rather than by air. Another sustainability-driven luxury powerhouse is Kering (Gucci and Sergio Rossi), which uses recyclable packaging certified by the Forest Stewardship Council (FSC). Also, a similar example of luxury brands that root for sustainability is Porsche, which uses 85% of recyclable material, as well as 100% recyclable waste from production facilities (Henninger et al. 2016). According to Cervellon and Shammas, sustainability and luxury, in our current times, must co-exist according to the wealthy. The consumers are more inclined to brands that "make luxury" rather than "show luxury;" making luxury is confined to craftsmanship and using rare materials that commit to sustainability procedures and key principles, however showing luxury is limited to overusing the logo and mass production, which shows the consumer a somewhat artificial brand name (Cervellon and Shammas, 2013).

Recent studies from Havas Media show that 86% of buyers amongst 20,000 in ten countries have inspected products from the luxury sector, searching for sustainability aspects, and 35% of them purchased the more sustainable option. However, the vast majority of why consumers choose sustainable luxury over "old-school" luxury is due to the common key values between luxury and sustainability. Although both the former and the latter have very opposite principles (Carrigan et al., 2017), yet Kapferer

(2015) argues that luxury in itself is a sustainable industry, calling it "the business of lasting worth and permanence". Other than that, sustainability and luxury both have become more of a lifestyle, rather than simple key values that consumers look for; a major shift from "conspicuous" to "considered," and from "what you wear" to "who you are." Lastly, some authors argue whether the economic value and luxury go together hand in hand or are opponents, and according to a Nielsen survey (2014) of 30,000 consumers in 60 countries worldwide, 55% of the respondents would be willing to pay a higher price to brands that follow CSR, therefore there is a significant correlation between the economic value and consumer behavior towards sustainable luxury (Jain, 2019). The correlation between subjective social norms and the consumer's attitude towards purchasing luxury products are also related, according to McNeill and Moore, because the consumer's attitude changes based on their knowledge and concern for social and environmental well-being (Batat, 2020a).

METHODOLOGY

This research adopts a qualitative systematic literature review (Gaur and Kumar, 2018), as an approach to limit the bias (Pickering and Byrne, 2014), by considering three main databases, namely Scopus, Web of Science, and Cairn. While we selected Scopus for its largest publication database combining synthesis and citations of academic peer-reviewed articles and Web of Science for its inclusiveness, Cairn was selected because it is a pioneer scientific French database that includes articles written in French — the first author is bilingual French/English — on the topic of luxury, which is dominant in the French academic literature (Batat, 2019).

The systematic review of the literature is an appropriate approach because it provides inclusive, unbiased, and replicable data to be analyzed (Gaur and Kumar, 2018). Besides, this method offers the relevant insight by assisting the researcher in the selection process to order, prioritize, and consolidate the data and thus contribute to the literature on the topic (MacInnis, 2011). This approach allowed us to analyze the multidisciplinary literature related to the topic of luxury and CSR in different fields, including marketing, business and management, and social sciences among others (e.g., Palmatier et al., 2018; Petticrew and Roberts, 2006). To identify both theoretical and practical contributions, our research addresses the following review question: *How can the compatibility between CSR strategies related to luxury contribute to sustainable luxury marketing practices?* Overall, we selected 357 articles following a chronological perspective covering the last 30 years (from 1990 to 2020) published in English and French peer-reviewed academic journals were analyzed.

Despite the growing number of luxury research publications in the area of sustainability and CSR over the last three years (2017 and 2020), systematic literature review as a method is still not extensively utilized in the luxury marketing field (Athwal et al., 2019). To conduct a relevant analysis of the literature, we selected publications featured in peer-reviewed journals following three main criteria: (1) articles written in both French and English; (2) articles indexed in the three databases selected; and (3) articles focusing on CSR and sustainability in the field of luxury. Particularly, we used a mix of keywords to collect data, including concepts such as "sustainable luxury", "sustainable fashion", "eco-friendly luxury", "green luxury" and "responsible luxury" in the search categories "keywords," "title," and "abstract." Additionally, we used these keywords in the subject search fields "social sciences," "marketing," and "business."

Is Luxury Compatible With Corporate Social Responsibility (CSR)?

To analyze the data, we selected the term "sustainable luxury" for its comprehensive scope, since it also encompasses the other concepts used in this research. Primary screening of the 357 articles led to 153 papers identified with the focus on sustainable luxury. In the second phase of the process, the systematic literature review led us to select 35 articles within the scope of our research that focuses on luxury and CSR based on the analysis according to two criteria: (1) the Chartered Association of Business Schools (ABS) ranking and the impact factor of the journal in which the paper was published, and (2) the number of citations received. A content analysis (Kolbe and Burnett, 1991) of the 35 articles was conducted following an interactive process combining both inductive and deductive approaches to develop an in-depth understanding of sustainable and CSR luxury strategies implemented in the marketing field and then the identification of major themes that emerged.

RESULTS AND DISCUSSION

This part frames the results of the systematic literature review about the relationships between luxury and CSR and the marketing sustainable strategies in the luxury sector since 1990. The iterative content analysis of the articles revealed that the implementation of sustainable marketing strategies in the luxury sector has been approached from different perspectives, including one or multiple pillars of CSR. The four strategies are discussed in the next section.

Four Major Models for Luxury Sustainable Marketing Strategies

Several conceptual frameworks have been defined by scholars to explore the relationships companies have with these new actors. Amongst them, Sobczak and Berthoin Antal (2010) identified three main approaches: contractual theory, institutional theory, and stakeholder theory. This last theory has become, today, an essential reference for practitioners when we talk about the operationalization of CSR in the luxury sector (Batat, 2019).

Amongst the examples of luxury brands that embraced CSR and implemented it through different approaches, products, communication campaigns, and strategies, we can cite the following examples: (1) The case of Hermès and the launch of its new Chinese brand Shang Xia to support local craftsmanship in China while offering a modern reinterpretation of authentic know-how; (2) Loewe Madrid, (LVMH Group) with its new ambassador, Pénélope Cruz, who is a member of PETA (NGO that focuses on animals' welfare), organizes for its designers responsible creation workshops to enhance the fact that ecology goes together with creativity. These workshops display new ecological materials, explaining the recycling of fur and the reuse of leather scrap or the use of local materials; or (3) For brands, such as Stella McCartney, Calvin Klein, Vivienne Westwood, Ralph Lauren, Tommy Hilfiger, or Adolfo Dominguez, the introduction of CSR practices is supported by the decision to ban all kinds of animal fur from their collections.

The analysis of CSR practices within different sectors indicated there are four major strategies (Figure 1) implemented by luxury brands to develop and promote sustainable and ethical production and consumption of luxury.

Figure 1. Four major sustainable luxury marketing strategies

Environmentally-Oriented Luxury Marketing Strategies

One of the most important and first world-renowned luxury brands that established an eco-friendly, luxury marketing strategy is Louis Vuitton Moët-Hennessy, or LVMH, prioritizing sustainability, especially in their environmental-friendly operational activities. The company's entire value chain, from sourcing and creating to recycling and waste management is entirely under the name of SD and CSR (Kapferer, 2010). Other than that, luxury leaders and heritage luxury brands are prominent for investing in their brands' R&D and technology to create even newer, more convenient ways to follow sustainability development in their manufacturing procedures, proving their corporate social responsibility and protecting their brand reputation in an era heavily relying on eco-friendly measures.

LVMH is the first to enter the world of sustainability, setting an example and "trend" for other luxury brands as well, by acquiring suppliers of scarce raw materials, where LVMH developed Heng Long reptile skin tannery in 2011, as well as a leather tannery in 2012, Tanneries Roux. To better market their reputation and brand image, LVMH works on integrating sustainability in their brand's DNA, rather than portraying a shift in their business to an eco-friendlier approach, whilst preserving their rare natural resources and materials. LVMH also claims that the environment is what makes them a brand and that it is an undeniably crucial element in their value chain, establishing a commitment to protect these resources in the 1992 Earth Summit in Rio (2015). To consolidate their statement in the latter, LVMH teamed with Central Saint Martins, the number one art and design college in London, by establishing a sustainability fashion program, educating the next generation of fashion designers and creators, as well as motivating these students to further change their purchase behaviors and switch them into more eco-friendly ones (Kim et al., 1997).

Although environmentally-oriented luxury marketing strategies are in line with CSR practices that have a positive impact on the environment, our study highlighted the complexity of luxury's compatibility with sustainability. Almost all scholars who examined consumers' perception of eco-friendly luxury argue that the first criteria to purchase luxury goods is related to the brand name and the quality or the exclusive aspect related to luxury. Our analysis showed that, although luxury companies are implementing and promoting sustainable marketing strategies, their customers more readily associate luxury with unsustainability. This statement is in line with Batat's recent findings (2020a, b, c). Additionally, the

Is Luxury Compatible With Corporate Social Responsibility (CSR)?

results show that eco-friendly luxury goods can be perceived by consumers as less qualitative goods because they are made of recycled materials, which is not the case for non-luxury goods. This finding supports the conclusions of Davies and colleagues (2012). Finally, the analysis of the articles revealed that green and eco-friendly luxury related to environmental-oriented strategies are less desirable and luxurious when labeled eco-friendly (Cavender, 2018) and thus companies should emphasize more the luxury status and exclusivity while promoting sustainable luxury goods.

Community-Oriented Luxury Marketing Strategies

Although luxury gastronomy and Michelin-star restaurants normally target higher social classes, it does not suggest that they are not altruistic or do not give back to the community that made them grow into their leading positions. Going back to the original definition of sustainable luxury, according to Batat, it represents the ability to consume premium products to satisfy one's needs and improve the quality of life without burdening the future generation's needs (Batat, 2019). For that reason, one of the main pillars of consumers of luxury gastronomy is to give back to the local community by buying responsibly. According to Batat et al. (2019), luxury gastronomy is not confined to exceptional cuisine and aesthetically pleasing food experiences, rather it is also linked to social bonds and shared values, by building a community. Tourists are experiential actors that seek meanings through their search for authentic experiences (Holbrook and Hirschman, 1982), and this is achieved by following sustainable culinary experiences and tourism measures such as attending cooking classes, visiting local farmers' markets, and forming solid connections with the food culture of their surrounding community.

Moreover, the "French gastronomic meal" in France, which was labeled as an intangible cultural heritage by UNESCO in 2010, had an important role for French luxury gastronomy, because it helped France connect with its people culturally and traditionally. This allowed tourists from all over the world to experience this cultural gastronomy in both urban and rural areas, minimizing the gap between foreign tourists, and the French community. Similarly, according to Batat (2020a), luxury gastronomy should not be limited to creating exotic recipes and using rare ingredients, rather gastronomy experts should emphasize the relation between the restaurant experiences and cultural heritage. That is by showing both local and international visitors that the restaurant is socially responsible through offering luxury gastronomy that contributes to the local markets, attending local festivals, as well as offering regional cooking.

The present results, however, also underline a more complex picture when it comes to community-oriented strategies that luxury brands can implement to promote CSR practices within the sector. While sustainable practices in luxury goods (products and services) are often related to the tangible features of the goods, in luxury services, especially hospitality and haute gastronomy, focusing on food reachability or food waste management is not enough. This statement is in line with recent works that emphasized the important social role of luxury companies who should endorse the role of the champion in their sector to promote sustainable practices (Batat, 2020a). Thus, playing a role within the society is an important pillar that luxury brands should integrate in their CSR program, especially if they belong to a highly experiential sector such as hospitality or fine dining.

Well-Being-Oriented Luxury Marketing Strategies

Luxury producers too often focus fully on delivering high-end and premium quality products, making them disregard their people's well-being in the process (Batat, 2020a). In that case, luxury brands are no longer considered sustainable since CSR relies heavily on their social responsibility, especially the well-being of their employees. However, some exceptional Michelin-starred chefs are highly concerned about their employees' well-being due to the remarkable workload in the luxury gastronomy sector, which drives these chefs to provide their employees and sous-chefs with the ultimate work/life balance and vacations as time off to de-stress (Athwal et al., 2019).

Primarily, some Michelin-starred chefs encourage their employees to participate in sports activities between each of their shifts, as well as promote a healthier, greener diet to stimulate sustainability. According to one of the chefs interviewed in Batat's research, gastronomy is the only sector in the world of luxury where the main focus is the consumer himself, and not the good (Batat, 2020b, c). For instance, another Michelin-starred chef added that sustainability is the prioritized promotion in our current period; rare ingredients and spices are no longer of the consumer's interest if they were not aligned with sustainability procedures, which includes the health and well-being of the people preparing these exotic foods, such as the local businesses and farms trying to sustain their business and make a profit (Osburg et al., 2020). Conclusively, the EPF or experiential pleasure of the food journey tackles a journey to satisfy both the consumer's food pleasure and food well-being (Batat et al., 2019). In this article, Batat shows the common ground between pleasure and health, by combining the EPF with the EEP (epicurean eating pleasure) to achieve FWB (food well-being), and that is by revealing how gastronomy is perceived to both improve the consumer's emotional well-being by refining food experiences visually and aesthetically, as well as encouraging a healthy living by supporting the adoption of sustainable eating behaviors (Batat, 2019).

The focus on well-being revealed by our analysis of the articles selected shows that luxury brands should redefine their CSR practices by integrating both perspectives: consumer and company. This perspective has recently been discussed in the works that examined CSR and sustainable practices within the luxury gastronomy from a consumer perspective (Batat, 2020b). While most of the literature on sustainable luxury used a managerial perspective to explore substantiality from the company's perspective, we believe that for luxury brands adopting a consumer perspective is a relevant approach to capture the tacit and explicit aspects related to luxury CSR practices (Athwal et al., 2019).

Animal Welfare-Oriented Luxury Marketing Strategies

Regarding animal welfare, luxury brands are notorious for ranking as one of the top industries promoting animal-cruelty. However, in the consolidation period of sustainable luxury marketing, animal-cruelty was replaced by animal-friendliness, prioritizing animal welfare in the fashion industry by using more eco-friendly raw materials that replace exotic skins and leathers. According to Fernandes (2019), consumers believed the theory of "higher-quality fashion coincides with sustainability", thinking that the higher the price, the higher the quality (Fernandes, 2019). However, from what the industry has exhibited, from leather to animal fur, shows that the industry is, in fact, cruel to animals. Two examples that most luxury brands look up to when it comes to sustainable luxury and animal-friendly fashion are the Kering Group and Stella McCartney.

The Kering Group, which is the mother brand of many world-renowned luxury brands and designers such as Gucci, Alexander McQueen, and Bottega Venetta, is both awed by yet optimistic about how the luxury industry is treating animals. For that, Kering decided to make sustainability one of its main concerns, preserving their raw materials, and guaranteeing animal welfare whilst still achieving true craftsmanship. Gucci, by Kering, has followed a strategy to switch into a fur-free luxury brand. Their

Is Luxury Compatible With Corporate Social Responsibility (CSR)?

original statement cited showed Gucci's CSR by striving to do better for the environment and animals, by promising to remove all fur starting from their Spring/Summer 2018 collection. Also, Gucci regenerated their cashmere production by reusing fibers and transforming them into newer fibers, minimizing the phases of wearing animal skin, and proving to be an actual animal-friendly brand by actions, not statements. Lastly, Marchiolo claims how Stella McCartney targets consumers who are not only purchasing high-end products at a luxury price, rather it targets consumers who are also especially environmentally conscious and are looking for fashion that is sustainable and not just appealing (Marchiolo, 2019). Stella McCartney never uses real leather, skins, feathers, nor furs animals, rather they explore alternative raw materials that are both animal and eco-friendly. Also, to accumulate wool in an animal-friendly way, Stella McCartney uses two distinct strategies. Firstly, it only partners with farms that collect wool with the highest animal well-being measures, and secondly, it supports the creators of new alternative ways to form these fibers.

Although, the results show that animal welfare is an integral component of sustainable luxury marketing strategies, in the luxury sector the use of animal leather is associated with the highest quality and the uniqueness of the product (e.g., Kapferer, 2010; 2015). The interpretation of a struggle between comfort/quality provided by the use of animal leather vs. animal welfare may be seen to be supported by the contradictory extant research which has found both positive and negative perceptions related to the use of animal leather and consumer's reactions to sustainable luxury. Indeed, previous studies have emphasized positive reactions as consumers' attitudes were positive toward luxury items made of animal leather (Achabou and Dekhili, 2013) if there is no cruel treatment given to animals.

The Future of Sustainable Luxury: Challenges and Opportunities

In line with all these previous studies, it is difficult to declare luxury as a temporary sector; rather it is a timeless segment that will exist for future generations to benefit from if proven to be sustainable. According to Kapferer (2015), luxury has been a culprit to moral criticism. For that reason, although a somewhat everlasting sector, it is still subject to undeniable challenges to sustain this mass growth of a sector. Judging by the struggle of providing rare skins, ingredients, and fabrics for such mass production, it is easy to suggest that the supply of such raw materials should be increased; however, this procedure does not go in line with sustainability development measures. The increase of supply would encourage killing more alligators and foxes to produce more reptile-skin and fur clothes or shoes, which harms the ultimate pillars of eco-friendly fashion: social harmony and sustainable growth (Carrigan et al., 2013).

Another challenge that threatens the future of sustainable luxury is the fact that it is a profit-driven, consumption-based industry that lacks transparency (Sun, 2018). One of the luxury brands with the least transparency is Michael Kors, which only has a statement on its website of abiding California's Transparency in Supply Chain Act (SB 657). This lack of transparency also reflects the lack of supply chain and human rights transparency, which shows that the disregard of human rights is directly proportional to the disregard of the environment (Sun, 2018), and accusing these brands of greenwashing. On the other hand, opportunities are generated with time, and they exist in diverse sectors of the luxury industry.

As previously mentioned, sustainable luxury is a timeless industry producing premium products without burdening future generations (Batat, 2019), and it is undeniable that social media is the ultimate tool being used to reach out to these generations. According to Osburg et al. (2020), social media is one of the biggest promotional tools luxury brands can make use of to sponsor sustainable and eco-friendly luxury. More specifically, social media influencers are the most fundamental and effective users who can voice luxury brands' mission statements, acting as role models to their followers, and being the secret weapon of any marketer's repertoire. Another important opportunity for the future of sustainable luxury marketing is economic success and competitive advantage. When a luxury brand declares its ethical standards and sustainable production and CSR, it can build a link with customers and stakeholders, locking them in and increasing their sales due to ecological consumption (Osburg et al., 2020). Lastly, the implementation of more multisensory marketing can cause more engaging communication between the brand and the consumer (Cervellon and Shammas, 2013). This can lead to a substantial change in the branding and design of the luxury brand to showcase more ethicality and sustainability in the luxury industry, attracting more conscious consumers (Atwal et al., 2019; Davies et al., 2012).

CONCLUSION

This chapter contributes to the need to take into account the consumer's perspective on CSR and the company's practices aiming to enhance the well-being alongside preserving the environment and helping the community. By rethinking their CSR practices, luxury companies, especially those in the hospitality sector can develop a comprehensive and integrative approach to the way sustainable luxury should be defined to satisfy both the consumer and the community. In this chapter, we proposed an analysis of levels, perspectives, and frameworks related to global sustainable marketing strategies as applied to the luxury sector whether it is about fashion or hospitality. Specifically, a transformative consumer approach such as the focus on consumer well-being and how luxury brands can contribute to the overall well-being of consumers, highlight new consumer perspective, instead of the managerial perspective (three pillars: people, planet, and profit), which is dominant in the marketing of sustainable luxury goods and experiences.

As introduced in this chapter, luxury is a growing sector, and examining its impact in terms of CSR is a relevant field for scholars to focus on. In today's context, scholars should implement a bottom-up approach to develop an in-depth understanding of the dimensions and the perceptions of sustainable luxury products as well as experiences from different perspectives (e.g., consumer, NGOs, brands) and at various levels (e.g., individual, sector, and macro). The literature analyzed in this chapter highlighted the idea of the compatibility between luxury and CSR and the importance of going beyond the three dominant pillars identified in the literature (planet, people, and profit) and focus more on emerging pillars, especially when in the luxury service domain that is highly experiential and subjective in nature. Besides, scholars should also examine the impact of luxury consumption on the individual and collective well-being of people to identify additional marketing strategies and actions to improve consumer well-being. This is in line with Batat and Manika's (2020) call for a new research paradigm by advancing Transformative Luxury Research (TLR) to contribute to marketing theory about the luxury that incorporates ethics and well-being at the center of the research approach to enrich the literature on the topic of luxury and responsible business practices. As recommended by Batat and Manika, there is a need for scholars to expand the research conducted to date, and approach the relationship between luxury and ethical and responsible business practices for well-being through a TLR, which is a comprehensive, critical, and multidisciplinary approach to marketing and business practices in the luxury sector.

Considering sustainable luxury from both consumer and managerial perspectives contributes to redefine CSR practices and integrate new emerging aspects that can improve the luxury brand image while promoting consumer's well-being. This new approach calls companies in the luxury sector and beyond to develop creative approaches to propose sustainable luxury goods and services alongside keeping the prestigious aspect of luxury, and thus develop a strong competitive advantage. There is no doubt that the future of sustainable luxury will be illustrated by the factors identified in this chapter, especially the new one focused on well-being.

REFERENCES

Achabou, M. A., & Dekhili, S. (2013). Luxury and sustainable development: Is there a match? *Journal of Business Research*, *66*(10), 1896–1903. doi:10.1016/j.jbusres.2013.02.011

Amatulli, C., De Angelis, M., Costabile, M., & Guido, G. (2017). *Sustainable luxury brands: Evidence from research and implications for managers*. Springer. doi:10.1057/978-1-137-60159-9

Athwal, N., Wells, V. K., Carrigan, M., & Henninger, C. E. (2019). Sustainable luxury marketing: A synthesis and research agenda. *International Journal of Management Reviews*, *21*(4), 405–426. doi:10.1111/ijmr.12195

Batat, W. (2019). *The New Luxury Experience: Creating the ultimate customer experience*. Springer. doi:10.1007/978-3-030-01671-5

Batat, W. (2020a). The role of luxury gastronomy in culinary tourism: An ethnographic study of Michelin-Starred restaurants in France. *International Journal of Tourism Research*, 1–14. doi:10.1002/jtr.2372

Batat, W. (2020b). Pillars of sustainable food experiences in the luxury gastronomy sector: A qualitative exploration of Michelin-starred chefs' motivations. *Journal of Retailing and Consumer Services*, *57*, 102255. doi:10.1016/j.jretconser.2020.102255

Batat, W. (2020c). How Michelin-starred chefs are being transformed into social bricoleurs? An online qualitative study of luxury foodservice during the pandemic crisis. *Journal of Service Management*. ahead-of-print. doi:10.1108/JOSM-05-2020-

Batat, W., & Manika, D. (2020). Advancing Transformative Luxury Research: Contributions to Marketing Theory About Luxury, Ethics, and Well-Being. *Journal of Macromarketing*, *40*(4), 583–584. doi:10.1177/0276146720954055

Batat, W., Peter, P. C., Moscato, E. M., Castro, I. A., Chan, S., Chugani, S., & Muldrow, A. (2019). The experiential pleasure of food: A savoring journey to food well-being. *Journal of Business Research*, *100*, 392–399. doi:10.1016/j.jbusres.2018.12.024

Beurden, P., & Gossling, T. (2008). The worth of values - a literature review on the relation between corporate social and financial performance. *Journal of Business Ethics*, *82*(2), 407–424. doi:10.100710551-008-9894-x

Blevis, E., Makice, K., Odom, W., Roedl, D., Beck, C., Blevis, S., & Ashok, A. (2007, August). Luxury & new luxury, quality & equality. In *Proceedings of the 2007 conference on Designing pleasurable products and interfaces* (pp. 296-311). 10.1145/1314161.1314188

Carrigan, M., McEachern, M., Moraes, C., & Bosangit, C. (2017). The fine jewellery industry: Corporate responsibility challenges and institutional forces facing SMEs. *Journal of Business Ethics*, *143*(4), 681–699. doi:10.100710551-016-3071-4

Carrigan, M., Moraes, C., & McEachern, M. G. (2013). From conspicuous to considered fashion: A harm-chain approach to the responsibilities of luxury-fashion businesses. *Journal of Marketing Management*, *29*(11-12), 1277–1307. doi:10.1080/0267257X.2013.798675

Carroll, A. B. (1999). Corporate social responsibility: Evolution of a definitional construct. *Business & Society*, *38*(3), 268–295. doi:10.1177/000765039903800303

Carroll, A. B. (2016). Carroll's pyramid of CSR: Taking another look. *International Journal of Corporate Social Responsibility*, *1*(3), 1–8. doi:10.118640991-016-0004-6

Cavender, R. (2018). The Marketing of Sustainability and CSR Initiatives by Luxury Brands: Cultural Indicators, Call to Action, and Framework. In *Sustainability in Luxury Fashion Business* (pp. 29–49). Springer. doi:10.1007/978-981-10-8878-0_3

Cervellon, M.-C., & Shammas, L. (2013). The value of sustainable luxury in mature markets: A customer-based approach. *Journal of Corporate Communications*, *55*(52), 90–101. doi:10.9774/GLEAF.4700.2013. de.00009

Clarkson, M. B. E. (1999). A stakeholder framework for analysing and evaluating corporate social performance. *Academy of Management Review*, *20*(1), 92–117. doi:10.5465/amr.1995.9503271994

Claydon, J. (2011). A new direction for CSR: The shortcomings of previous CSR models and the rationale for a new model. *Social Responsibility Journal*, *7*(3), 405–420. doi:10.1108/17471111111154545

Dahlsrud, A. (2006). How corporate social responsibility is defined: An analysis of 37 definitions. *Corporate Social Responsibility and Environmental Management*, *15*(1), 1–13. doi:10.1002/csr.132

Davies, I. A., Lee, Z., & Ahonkai, I. (2012). Do consumer care about ethical luxury? *Journal of Business Ethics*, *106*(1), 37–51. doi:10.100710551-011-1071-y

Donaldson, T., & Preston, L. E. (1995). The Stakeholder Theory of the Corporation: Concepts, Evidence and Implications. *Academy of Management Review*, *20*(1), 65–91. doi:10.5465/amr.1995.9503271992

Fernandes, C. C. M. S. (2019). *Kering: a path towards sustainable luxury* (Doctoral dissertation).

Fombrun, C. J. (2005). Building corporate reputation through CSR initiatives: Evolving standards. *Corporate Reputation Review*, *8*(1), 7–11. doi:10.1057/palgrave.crr.1540235

Freeman, I., & Sussin, I. (2010). International Cultural Competence in International Business Education: The Need to Respond. *International Journal of Environmental, Cultural, Economic and Social Sustainability*, *6*(1), 355–370. doi:10.18848/1832-2077/CGP/v06i01/54742

Freeman, R. E., & Phillips, R. A. (2002). Stakeholder theory: A libertarian defense. *Business Ethics Quarterly*, *12*(3), 331–350. doi:10.2307/3858020

Freeman, RF. (1984). *Strategic Management: a Stakeholder Approach*. Academic Press.

Gaur, A. S., & Kumar, M. (2018). A systematic approach to conducting review studies: An assessment of content analysis in 25 years of IB research. *Journal of World Business, 53*(2), 280–289. doi:10.1016/j.jwb.2017.11.003

Geva, A. (2008). Three models of corporate social responsibility: Interrelationships between theory, research, and practice. *Business and Society Review, 113*(1), 1–41. doi:10.1111/j.1467-8594.2008.00311.x

Gill, A. (1998). Deconstruction fashion: The making of unfinished, decomposing and re-assembled clothes. *Fashion Theory, 2*(1), 25–49. doi:10.2752/136270498779754489

Hendriksz, V. (2018). *Kering, H&M, Bestseller & more CEOs to tackle 7 crucial sustainable priorities.* Fashion United. Available at: https://fashionunited.uk/news/business/kering-h-m-bestseller-more-ceos-to-tackle-7-crucial-sustainable-priorities/2018032728851

Henninger, C. E., Alevizou, P. J., & Oates, C. J. (2016). What is sustainable fashion? *Journal of Fashion Marketing and Management, 20*(4), 1–19. doi:10.1108/JFMM-07-2015-0052

Holbrook, M., & Hirschman, E. C. (1982). The experimental aspects of consumption: Consumer fantasies, feelings, and fun. *The Journal of Consumer Research, 9*(2), 132–140. doi:10.1086/208906

Jain, S. (2019). Factors affecting sustainable luxury purchase behavior: A conceptual framework. *Journal of International Consumer Marketing, 31*(2), 130–146. doi:10.1080/08961530.2018.1498758

Kapferer, J. N. (2010). All that glitters is not green: The challenge of sustainable luxury. *European Business Review, 2*, 40–45.

Kapferer, J. N. (2015). The future of luxury: Challenges and opportunities. *Journal of Brand Management, 21*(9), 716–726. doi:10.1057/bm.2014.32

Kim, Y. K., Forney, J., & Arnold, E. (1997). Environmental messages in fashion advertisements: Impact on consumer responses. *Clothing & Textiles Research Journal, 15*(3), 147–154. doi:10.1177/0887302X9701500303

Kolbe, R., & Burnett, M. (1991). Content-Analysis Research: An Examination of Applications with Directives for Improving Research Reliability and Objectivity. *The Journal of Consumer Research, 18*(2), 243–250. doi:10.1086/209256

MacInnis, D. J. (2011). A framework for conceptual contributions in marketing. *Journal of Marketing, 75*(4), 136–154. doi:10.1509/jmkg.75.4.136

Marchiolo, E. E. (2019). *Responsible and sustainable luxury: the Stella McCartney case.* Academic Press.

Masoud, N. (2017). How to win the battle of ideas in corporate social responsibility: The International Pyramid Model of CSR. *International Journal of Corporate Social Responsibility, 2*(1), 1–22. doi:10.118640991-017-0015-y

Maycumber, S.G. (1994, April 26). L. L. Bean to ATMI: Environment key factor. *Women's Wear Daily*, p. 14.

Osburg, V. S., Davies, I., Yoganathan, V., & McLeay, F. (2020). Perspectives, Opportunities and Tensions in Ethical and Sustainable Luxury: Introduction to the Thematic Symposium. *Journal of Business Ethics*, 1-10.

Palmatier, R. W., Houston, M. B., & Hulland, J. (2018). Review articles: Purpose, process, and structure. *Journal of the Academy of Marketing Science*, *46*(1), 1–5. doi:10.100711747-017-0563-4

Parmar, B. L., Freeman, R. E., Harrison, J. S., Wicks, A. C., Purnell, P., & de Colle, S. (2010). Stakeholder Theory: The State of the Art. *The Academy of Management Annals*, *4*(1), 403–445. doi:10.5465/19416520.2010.495581

Petticrew, M., & Roberts, H. (2006). *Systematic reviews in the social sciences: a practical guide*. Blackwell Publishing. doi:10.1002/9780470754887

Pickering, C., & Byrne, J. (2014). The benefits of publishing systematic quantitative literature reviews for PhD candidates and other early-career researchers. *Higher Education Research & Development*, *33*(3), 534–548. doi:10.1080/07294360.2013.841651

Rowlands, P. (1993, January 27). Esprit's Ecollection goes to the malls . *Women's Wear Daily*, p. 13.

Salzmann, O., Ionescu-Somers, A., & Steger, U. (2005). The business case for corporate sustainability: Literature review and research options. *European Management Journal*, *23*(1), 27–36. doi:10.1016/j.emj.2004.12.007

Sobczak, A., & Berthoin Antal, A. (2010). Nouvelles perspectives sur l'engagement des parties prenantes: Enjeux, acteurs, recherches. *Revue Management et Avenir*, *33*(3), 117–126. doi:10.3917/mav.033.0116

Sun, O. (2018). *Sustainability Strategies and Challenges in the Luxury Apparel Industry. Diplomski rad*. University of Pennsylvania.

Visser, W. (2011). *The age of responsibility: CSR 2.0 and the new DNA of business*. John Wiley & Sons.

Voyer, B. G., & Beckham, D. (2014). Can Sustainability Be Luxurious? a Mixed-Method Investigation of Implicit and Explicit Attitudes Towards Sustainable Luxury Consumption. In J. Cotte & S. Wood (Eds.), *NA - Advances in Consumer Research* (Vol. 42, pp. 245–250). Association for Consumer Research.

Wood, T. (1991). Corporate social performance revisited. *Academy of Management Review*, *16*(4), 691–718. doi:10.5465/amr.1991.4279616

Chapter 11
Upcycled vs. Recycled Products by Luxury Brands:
Status and Environmental Concern Motives

Feray Adıgüzel
https://orcid.org/0000-0002-5289-1701
LUISS University, Italy

Carmela Donato
https://orcid.org/0000-0002-9301-7498
LUISS University, Italy

ABSTRACT

This chapter aims at covering an important gap, contributing to research in the field of luxury markets as well as sustainable consumption, and focuses on new sustainable products by luxury brands. Through an experimental study 3x1 between-subject design in which the product material (upcycled vs. recycled vs. virgin) of a fictitious luxury product was manipulated, the authors investigated which luxury product (upcycled vs. recycled vs. not sustainable) is preferred by consumers in terms of attitude and purchase intentions. Results of this experimental design can inform luxury product managers and designers about whether consumers react more positively towards upcycle vs. recycle products when consumers' status motives and environmental consciousness increase. In addition, they can understand the reasons and emphasize those in their marketing communications to increase demand for those products with this study.

1. INTRODUCTION

Over the past few years, due the general acknowledgement of the human impact on the environment and of the expected worrying climate changes, the issues concerning the circularity of the economy have become progressively familiar all over the world and words like "Recycling", "Renewable" or "Recovery" have been integrated in the common vocabulary. This, along with the serious measures taken by governments such as the *"Single-Use Plastic Directive"*[1] firstly proposed 2018 by the EU Commission

DOI: 10.4018/978-1-7998-5882-9.ch011

Copyright © 2021, IGI Global. Copying or distributing in print or electronic forms without written permission of IGI Global is prohibited.

which aims to prohibit the utilization of single-use plastic within 2021 and limit plastic waste, or the *"long-term plan"*[2] to reach a "zero climate impact" by 2050 also presented in 2018, led to several structural changes in the market and, as a consequence, has forced the companies to modify their production organization and their business approach in order to respond to the different market requirements. This is quite relevant considering that nowadays consumers, especially millennials, are strongly aware of environmental issues and do support activities such as corporate social responsibility (CSR; Unilever, 2017). Leary et al. (2014) has showed that ethical concerns can have significant impact in terms of consumer behaviors when customers felt their simple action could have a real effect and market influence. Moreover, customers have a tendency to assume that especially luxury brands, due to their prosperous businesses, are exactly the ones more able to make a change towards a greener and more equal world and the ones in charge of leading by example. As a consequence, being sustainable has become an expected and intrinsic element of quality, especially for luxury goods. Expensive products that would not respect the natural and social environment can be negatively perceived by the market, arousing anger among consumers (Kapferer and Michaut, 2015). In that sense several luxury brands are moving their production processes towards a circular perspective, namely a perspective that involves lengthening the life cycle of materials goods. Typical production processes related to a circular perspective are recycling and upcycling. Upcycling can be defined as the reusing of discarded objects or material, just as they are, in such a way as to incorporate them in a totally new product of a higher quality or value than the original ones. On the other hand, recycling is the conversion of waste into reusable material by downgrading it into raw inputs and then using these raw factors in a new industrial process. If an item is being recycled, it goes back into production and is transformed into a completely different one.

For example, Gucci launched an upcycling initiative of waste leather and textiles generated during the production process, adapting its brand name (i.e., Gucci-Up)[3], similarly Prada introduced a handbag line made out of regenerated materials, called Prada re-nylon[4]. Stella McCartney produces bags using fabric made from recycled water bottles and recycled polyester instead of virgin polyester.

Despite a huge number of studies examining the relationship between luxury and sustainability (e.g., Achabou & Dekhili, 2013; Amatulli et al., 2017; Davies et al., 2012; De Angelis et al., 2017; Griskevicius et al., 2010; Janssen et al., 2014) little is known about consumers perceptions about luxury brands producing upcycled vs. recycled products.

The objective of this book chapter is to cover this research gap, shedding light on mechanisms that can lead to a higher vs. lower consumers' evaluation of luxury products using circular economy production processes. In doing that this chapter contributes either to the growth of the stream of research related to luxury consumption and either to luxury brand managers providing them directions about sustainable production processes better fitting to luxury concept.

The remaining of this book chapter is structured as follow. First, a literature review about sustainability and luxury brands will be provided together with the related theoretical framework and hypotheses. Subsequently, in the method section an experimental study aimed at testing the proposed hypotheses will be presented. For concluding a discussion of the findings and presentation of the managerial implications will be offered.

Upcycled vs. Recycled Products by Luxury Brands

2. CONCEPTUAL FRAMEWORK

Fashion represents an important sector in the global economy. Clothing accounts for more than 60% of the total textile used, being a USD 1.3 trillion industry, which employs more than 300 million people along its value chain[5]. The exponential growth of the global middle-class population – with the consequent increase of the demand for goods and consumption pro capita decreed – plus the continuous exposure to social media incessantly showing new trends to imitate, has radically changed the fashion market and its timing: the public request has become more urgent, society has consolidated its unstoppable search for new and revolutionary items, and trends and styles have been renovating faster and faster following one after the other.

Influenced by these radical transformations, fashion industry has started a gradual change towards the fast-fashion model by increasing the number of collections per year and, through the use of inferior quality materials, by lowering the average prices in order to cope with this rising demand.

As a consequence, in the last decade the majority of consumers have developed the idea that due to their perishability and affordability, clothes are "nearly disposal" goods and after wearing them seven or eight times, they can be thrown away. The result is that the clothing production approximately doubled, and sales increased at the same pace while clothing utilization dramatically declined by the same percentage, generating negative environmental impact. To respond to the consumers' unsustainable behavior related to fashion industry, there are rising voices that *luxury fashion* brands should play the leading role in promoting sustainable consumption by encouraging consumers to buy their luxury goods that can be worn for more than one season and reduce the frequency of consumption (Simkus, 2010). Offering long-lasting quality over excessive quantity by luxury brands allows consumers to choose high quality items in a reduced quantity, ultimately leading to minimizing ecological footprint (Kapferer, 2010; Kim and Kim, 2016).

Furthermore, according to Lee et al., (2015) luxury fashion brands can influence consumers' post-consumption behavior promoting the reuse of old products for other purposes or find ways to keep the used products remain in the consumption system for others to use, rather than simply throwing them away (Cho et al., 2015).

Past literature generally converges to associate "luxury" to the top category of prestigious brands (Vigneron and Johnson, 2004), high-quality, scarce, high-priced or rare brands (Kapferer, 1998). Nueno and Quelch (1998) defined luxury brands as *"those whose ratio of functional utility to price is low while the ratio of intangible and situational utility to price is high"*. Previous marketing literature stated that a sustainability-focused strategy adopted by luxury brands might be seen as an improbable event because luxury is typically associated with ostentation, excess and superficiality (De Barnier et al. 2012; Pino et al. 2017), whereas sustainability is typically associated with moderation, sobriety and altruism (Gladwin et al. 1995; Widloecher 2010). As a consequence, these two concepts are perceived as inconsistent. However, there are several contributions that demonstrated the opposite, namely a coherence between luxury and sustainability concepts. For example, according to De Angelis et al., (2017), there are several production processes that a luxury brand can use in order to promote green luxury items, as for instance bamboo, organic cotton, corn resin, cork or recycled fiber. For example, Kering's Bottega Veneta, known for its expertise in high-quality leathers, is introducing the usage of alternatives and greener materials under its new designer, Daniel Lee. An upcoming collection includes pouches and cross-body bags made out of pressed cork and fennel[6]. In addition to the usage of alternative materials, another approach in order to introduce greener luxury items is to focus on a circular economy approach thar strives for the decoupling of production from material inputs. In that sense *recycling* – the conversion of waste into reusable material by downgrading it into raw inputs and then using these raw factors in a new industrial process – seems to be one of the most common production processes used also by luxury brands, for example Armani has recently launched the R-EA, or recycled Emporio Armani, a capsule collection all about regeneration[7]. However incremental gains in efficiency derived from recycling are insufficient to address global concerns related to economic growth, rapid urbanization and climate change (Hobson, 2013; Meadows et al., 2004). One approach to minimize environmental impacts is to combine - instead of downgrade - materials in order to create a completely new item, reducing consequently at the minimum the environmental footprint, according to the so-called upcycling production. The term *upcycling,* originated in the 1990s, means 'reuse (discarded objects or material) in such a way as to create a product of higher quality or value than the original (Bridgens et al., 2018; Wegener, 2016). The usage of such production process implies the creative reuse of materials, as they are, in a way to implicitly increase product perceived quality (Bridgens et al., 2018). In that sense, several luxury brands, as for example Elvis & Kresse, or Reformation, are launching fashion products according to upcycling logic and therefore made by recombining discarded materials, as for example travel bags made by fire hose. However, despite previous research recognizes communalities between luxury and sustainability (e.g., Kapferer, and Michaut, 2015; Amatulli et al., 2017; Amatulli et al., 2018, De Angelis et al., 2017), no previous contributions analyzed and compared consumers' reactions towards recycled and upcycled luxury fashion items.

One of the main motivations explaining luxury brand consumption to display their wealth, and position in the society publicly (O'Cass and Frost, 2002; Fionda and Moore, 2009; Truong et al., 2008). On the other hand, individuals may buy luxury products simply for their inner satisfaction and pleasure (Dubois and Duquesne, 1993; Vickers and Renand, 2003). This means the presence of two possible motivations leading the demand for luxury goods: internalized motives according to which luxury goods are means for expressing their own personal taste and style, and externalized motives according to which luxury goods are means for expressing their own status (Amatulli and Guido, 2011; Eastman and Eastman, 2015). For those consumers high in status motivation the introduction of recycled luxury fashion items could be quite problematic, since one of the main barrier, and therefore concern, related to the introduction of recycled items is the lower perceived quality that implicitly consumers attribute to them (Achabou and Dekhili, 2013). In fact, recycling concept is opposite to the rarity and the prestige concepts that distinguish luxury items (Kapferer and Michaut, 2015). As a consequence, it is possible to suppose that those consumers high in status motives are less willing to buy recycled luxury fashion items compared to traditional (i.e., not sustainable) luxury ones. Formally:

H_1: Recycled luxury products present lower purchase intentions than non-sustainable ones for those customers that present high status motive.

On the other hand, buying a sustainable product might benefit consumers to symbolize how they care about environment and might increase their status when they are environmentally concerned. According to previous literature (e.g., White and Simpson, 2013; McDonald et al., 2015; Roberts and Bacon, 1997) environmental concern (i.e. green motive) is commonly considered to be an immediate antecedent to green consumption intention, which refers to the degree of individual care for ecology and the environment in general.

Upcycled vs. Recycled Products by Luxury Brands

Consequently, being (or not) environmental concerned can influence reaction to upcycle/recycle luxury products. In particular, the authors expect that the willingness to buy sustainable luxury fashion products (recycled and upcycled) compared to traditional (i.e., not sustainable) ones is higher for those consumers environmentally concerned. Formally:

H_2: Recycled and upcycled luxury products present higher purchase intentions than non-sustainable ones for those customers that present high environmental concern motive.

Besides personal motives such as status and environmental concerns, there is a consistent stream of research that shows the pivotal role of emotions in triggering green consumption (Peter and Honea, 2012; Schneider et al., 2017). In particular, pro-environmental behaviors and luxury consumption are both linked to two emotional feelings: guilt and pride. Guilt can be defined as a negative emotion which results from a consumer decision that violates one's values or norms (Burnett and Lunsford, 1994), whereas pride is a positive emotion felt when one succeeds at a socially valued endeavor, and the display of pride may have the function of increasing status within the group (Philippot et al., 2014). Sustainability can be considered as a personal as well as a social standard and anticipated pride and guilt cause individuals to behave in a manner that is in line with their personal norms (Onwezen et. al, 2013). Luxury brand purchases might trigger a sense of guilt due to the expensive prices, whereas a study by Peloza et. Al., (2013) suggested that the desire to avoid anticipated guilt is what drives consumer choice towards ethical consumption. However, the paper stressed also the role of the pleasing feeling of self-accountability, the desire to live up to one's standards, in influencing people preferences towards products with ethical attributes in promoting ethical consumption, in fact, consumers seem to react more positively to offers advertised through ethical appeals rather than explicit guilt framed appeals (Peloza et al., 2013).

On the other hand, also luxury can elicit positive feelings, and in particular pride, in fact according to McFerran et al., (2014), luxury consumption and pride are particularly interrelated. As a consequence, it can be supposed that a possible driver of sustainable fashion luxury items consumption might be pride and not guiltiness. According to Tracy and Prehn (2012), it is possible to distinguish between two facets that characterize pride: authentic and hubristic facets. Authentic pride consists in feelings of self-accomplishment and self-fulfillment and it leads to heightened desire for luxury brands. Hubristic pride is related to an attitude of arrogance, presumptuousness, being needy to show off and it might be the outcome of luxury purchases. The McFerran et al., (2014) contribution, reported that luxury consumption may be considered out of heightened feelings of accomplishment (and not arrogance), signaling the dominance of authentic pride in these purchases.

Additionally, in the context of green behaviors, anticipating one's positive future emotional state just prior to making a decision, leads to higher pro-environmental intentions compared to anticipating one's negative emotional state derived from inaction (Schneider et al., 2017).

In sum, a positive emotion like authentic pride may explain both sustainable and luxury consumption patterns. For instance, pride was claimed to increase consumers' sustainable behavior (Peter and Honea 2012). However, it might be expected that upcycled luxury fashion items can trigger a higher feeling of authentic pride than recycled luxury fashion items due to the fact that upcycle products require creative ideas, perfect craftsman and artisan skills to create unique designs (Bridgens et al., 2018). Then, rarity and social prestige conditions that characterize luxury consumption (Han, Nunes, Dreze 2010) can be verified, and therefore upcycle luxury products might be assessed more positively especially for those consumers high in status motives. That is why, the authors expect that for consumers high in status motives increased authentic pride explains higher purchase intention of upcycled luxury fashion products compared to non-sustainable luxury fashion products, whereas decreased authentic pride explains lower purchase intention of recycled luxury fashion products compared to non-sustainable luxury fashion products. Formally:

H_{3a}: Upcycled luxury products present higher authentic pride than non-sustainable ones when status motive increases, which leads to higher purchase intentions.

H_{3b}: Recycled luxury products present lower authentic pride than non-sustainable ones when status motive increases, which leads to lower purchase intentions.

Conversely, the authors do not expect differences in terms of feelings of authentic pride between upcycled and recycled products for those consumers high in environmental concerns. According to Moser (2015), consumers' attitude toward the protection of the environment positively affects green purchasing behavior, consequently for those consumers, both upcycled and recycled luxury fashion items generate a higher feeling of authentic pride compared to conventional (non-sustainable) luxury ones. Formally:

H_4: Upcycled and recycled luxury products present higher authentic pride than non-sustainable ones when environmental concerns increases, which leads to higher purchase intentions.

The conceptual model was presented in Figure 1 and 2. The hypotheses were examined through one experimental study.

Figure 1.

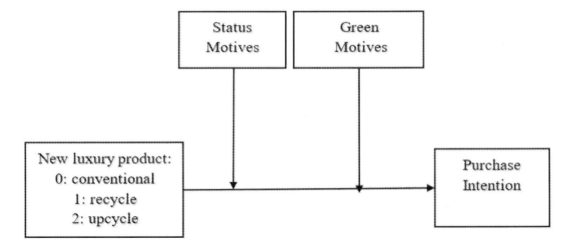

Figure 2.

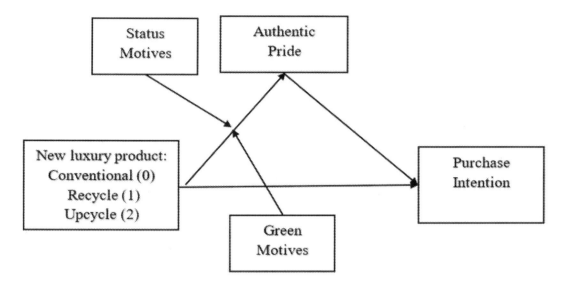

3. METHODOLOGY

155 Mturk workers who live in USA (M_{age} = 37.72 years, SD = 11,74, 48% female) participated in this experiment for monetary compensation. In order to approximate a sample of real luxury buyers, the authors first asked participants' frequency of buying luxury goods (1 = never, 5 = always), and eliminated twenty-one subjects who have never purchased any luxury goods. The final usable sample consisted of 134 participants (M_{age} = 36.54 years, SD = 10.41, 48% female). The authors have conducted 3×1 between-subjects design by manipulating the production process of a new product by a fictitious luxury brand which was upcycled, recycled or conventional. Conventional product was made with virgin material, namely leather and therefore, was non-sustainable. The goal is to investigate which luxury product (upcycled vs. recycled vs. non-sustainable) is preferred by consumers in terms of purchase intentions and how preferences change with two personal factors, namely status and environmental consciousness. Luxury wallet is selected as a product in scenarios; since most of luxury brands contain accessories such as wallet in their product portfolio.

Three scenarios were created for a new fictitious luxury brand. A fictitious luxury brand was preferred to guarantee the absence of any a priori brand knowledge. Depending the condition, participants were randomly exposed to an upcycled vs. recycled vs. non-sustainable luxury wallet. Upcycled product was made with discarded plastic bottle tops as they are (not previously melted), recycled one is made with discarded plastic bottle tops which are previously melted and conventional one is made with superior leather in the scenarios. The discarded plastic bottle tops was selected because the authors found a luxury brand who produce products with this material[8]. The authors also give the definitions of upcycling and recycling because some consumers might not know difference between upcycled and recycled products. The authors opt in not to give any product photo and to have the same scenarios except for the manipulations and definitions to prevent biases in outcomes (see Appendix).

After responding one-item scale of familiarity with upcycled/recycled products, and status motives scale (adapted from Eastman, Goldsmith, and Flynn, 1997, five-items; $\alpha = 0.95$), subjects were exposed one of three scenarios randomly. Subjects has to wait at least ten seconds to move forward with the survey to be sure that they read the scenario carefully. Then respondents were asked about authentic pride (adapted from Tracy and Robins, 2007; seven-items; $\alpha = 0.96$), purchase intention (adapted from Dodds et al., 1991, three-items; $\alpha = 0.92$), and concern for environment (adapted from Haws et al., 2014; six-items; $\alpha = 0.93$). As manipulation checks, subjects assessed two statements "The product I read about is an upcycled/recycled product". Remaining manipulation questions were about sustainability (self-made; three-items: environmentally friendly, sustainable, green; $\alpha = 0.91$), and luxuriousness (one-item) perceptions. Finally, product quality (adapted from Yoo and Donthu, 2001; two-items; $\alpha = 0.80$), durability, contamination perception (I expect: 1 'to be contaminated', 7 'not being contaminated'), product look expectations (I expect: 1 'to be unattractive/to be ugly', 7 'to be attractive/to be beautiful', two-items, $\alpha = 0.95$), and demographics were also measured as control variables. All measurement items were borrowed from previous literature and they were reliable. All scale items were measured with seven-point likert scale, anchoring 1 indicating strongly disagree and 7 indicating strongly agree.

4. RESULTS

Descriptive and Control Variables

To examine whether perceived quality, durability, contamination perception, and product look expectations of a luxury new product type (conventional, recycled, upcycled) significantly differ (or not), one-way ANOVA was ran after setting perceived quality as a dependent variable. There was no significant differences in perceived quality among three ($F(2,131) = 2.03$, p = 0.14, $M_{recycle} = 5.22$, $M_{upcycle} = 5.03$, $M_{nonsustainable} = 5.53$). Similarly, durability perceptions did not significantly differ across three new products ($F(2,131) = 1.33$, $p = 0.27$, $M_{recycle} = 5.23$, $M_{upcycle} = 4.91$, $M_{nonsustainable} = 5.33$). Contamination perceptions also did not significantly differ ($F(2,131) = 2.75$, p = 0.07, $M_{recycle} = 5.68$, $M_{upcycle} = 4.98$, $M_{nonsustainable} = 5.57$). Since a new product was introduced by a luxury brand, consumers did not probably expect any quality, durability and contaminations differences, differing from non-luxury brands. The authors also compared product look expectations for a new product. Interestingly, product look expectations differed significantly ($F(2,131) = 10.05$, $p < 0.001$, $M_{recycle} = 4.78$, $M_{upcycle} = 4.58$, $M_{nonsustainable} = 5.83$). Conventional product was expected to look significantly better than both upcycled ($\Delta = 1.25$, $p < 0.001$) and recycled products ($\Delta = 1.04$, $p < 0.01$). There was no difference in look expectations between recycled and upcycled products ($\Delta = 0.20$, $p = 1.00$).

The respondents were significantly more familiar with recycled products than upcycle ones ($M_{upcycle} = 4.69$, $M_{recycle} = 5.72$, t = -8.24, p < 0.001). Age was not significantly correlated with environmental concern (r = 0.15, $p = 0.08$), but significantly negatively correlated with authentic pride (r = -0.21, $p < 0.05$) and status motives (r = -0.18, $p < 0.05$).

Manipulation Checks

First, one-way ANOVA was conducted to inspect differences in perceptions about being an upcycled/recycled and being sustainable across three conditions (luxury product: non-sustainable, recycled, up-

Upcycled vs. Recycled Products by Luxury Brands

cycled). As intended, upcycled product scenario was significantly perceived as being upcycled (F(2,131) = 20.47, p < 0.001, $M_{upcycle}$ = 5.80, $M_{recycle}$ = 3.75, $M_{non\text{-}sustainable}$ = 3.65) and recycled product scenario was significantly perceived as being recycled ($F(2,131)$ = 15.93, p < 0.001, $M_{recycle}$ = 5.59, $M_{upcycle}$ = 4.45, $M_{nonsustainable}$ = 3.41).

To test whether recycled/upcycled products, indeed, were perceived as being more sustainable than the non-sustainable scenario, one-way ANOVA was conducted after defining sustainability perceptions as a dependent variable. There were significant difference in sustainability perceptions across three new luxury products ($F(2,131)$ = 26.18, p < 0.001). Post-hoc tests indicated no significant differences in sustainability perceptions between recycled and upcycled scenarios ($M_{recycle}$ = 5.68, $M_{upcycle}$ = 5.56, Δ = 0.12, p = 1.00). Recycled product scenario was perceived as being more sustainable than non-sustainable one ($M_{recycle}$ = 5.68, $M_{nonsustainable}$ = 3.82, Δ = 1.86, p < 0.001), and upcycled product scenario was perceived as being more sustainable than non-sustainable one ($M_{upcycle}$ = 5.56, $M_{nonsustainable}$ = 3.82, Δ = 1.74, p < 0.001).

Luxury brand perceptions might change if a luxury brand launch an upcycled, recycled or non-sustainable product. Setting luxury perceptions as a dependent variable, an additional one-way ANOVA was conducted. There were significant differences in luxury perceptions across three scenarios ($F(2,131)$=7.88, p < 0.01): Non-sustainable scenario was significantly perceived as more luxurious than upcycled ($M_{upcycle}$ = 4.95, $M_{nonsustainable}$ = 6.37, Δ = -1.42, p < 0.01) and recycled ($M_{recycle}$ = 5.36, $M_{nonsustainable}$ = 6.37, Δ = -1.00, p < 0.05) conditions; whereas there was no significant difference in luxury perceptions between recycled and upcycled scenarios ($M_{upcycle}$ = 4.95, $M_{recycle}$ = 5.36, Δ = -0.41, p = 0.82).

Testing Hypothesis

The hypotheses were tested with the PROCESS macro for SPSS (Hayes 2018) with the mean composite scores on the items for each construct. To test hypothesis 1 and 2, the authors ran Model 2 by defining status as an moderator W and environmental concern as an moderator Z, new luxury product type as an independent X (0: non-sustainable, 1: recycled, 2: upcycled), purchase intention as a dependent variable Y. Status was positively related to purchase intention (b = 0.59, p < 0.001); but environmental concern was not significantly related (b = 0.18, p = 0.16). When status motive increases, purchase intention of a recycled luxury product was significantly lower compare to non-sustainable one (b = -0.43, p < 0.01). When status motive increases, purchase intention of upcycled luxury product did not significantly differ compare to non-sustainable one (b = -0.20, p = 0.15). Thus, consumers with high status motives might consider upcycled new luxury products, but not recycled ones, confirming H_1. When environmental concern increases, purchase intention of an upcycled new product was significantly higher than non-sustainable one (b = 0.54, p < 0.01). At high values of environmental concern, purchase intention of a recycled new product was not significantly high compare the conventional one (b = 0.35, p = 0.06). Thus, H_2 was confirmed only for upcycled products.

Hypotheses 3a and 3b are about the moderated mediation model. Status motive was considered as a moderator of the relationship between new luxury product type and authentic pride, which, in turn, was considered as a mediator of the relationshp between new luxury product type and the intention to purchase. Before running this model, the authors tested first the mediating role of authentic pride running PROCESS Model 4. Luxury product type was the independent X (0: non-sustainable, 1: recycled, 2: upcycled), purchase intention was the dependent variable Y, and authentic pride was the mediator M. Control variables were environmental concern, status, perceived quality, age, contamination and durability perceptions. When luxury product is being upcycled compare to being non-sustainable, authentic pride was significantly high (b = 0.49, $p < 0.05$). Being recycled product did not lead to significant effect on authentic pride compare to being non-sustainable (b = 0.20, $p = 0.35$). Besides, durability (b = 0.22, $p < 0.05$), status motive (b = 0.53, $p < 0.001$ and environmental concern (b = 0.27, $p < 0.01$) have significant positive effect on authentic pride. Perceived quality and contamination perceptions did not influence authentic pride ($b_{quality}$ = -0.01, p = 0.96; b_{contam} = -0.06, $p = 0.35$). Age has a negative effect on authentic pride (b = -0.02, $p < 0.05$).

When authentic pride was one of antecedents of purchase intention, both upcycled and recycled luxury products did not significantly influence purchase intention. Authentic pride has a significant positive effect on purchase intention (b = 0.55, $p < 0.001$). Among control variables, only perceived quality has a significant positive effect on purchase intention (b = 0.29, $p < 0.05$). More importantly, the indirect effect of upcycled luxury products was significant and positive (c = 0.27, CI [0.04, 0.56]) given that the confidence interval does not contain 0. The indirect effect of recycled luxury products was not significant (c = 0.11, CI [-0.11, 0.37]). Thus, purchase intention of upcycled luxury products was higher than the non-sustainable ones due to increased authentic pride. The same effect was not observed for recycled luxury products.

To test H_{3a}, H_{3b}, and H_4 Process Model 9 was used by setting again status and environmental concern as the moderators W and Z, luxury product type as the independent X (0: non-sustainable, 1: recycled, 2: upcycled), purchase intention as the dependent variable Y and authentic pride as the mediator M. Environmental concern, status, perceived quality, age, contamination and durability perceptions were also added as control variables. While status had a significant positive effect on authentic pride (b = 0.50, $p < 0.001$), environmental concern had not (b = 0.12, $p = 0.35$). Authentic pride for upcycled products was higher than the one for non-sustainable one (b = 0.50, $p < 0.05$). At high values of status motives, only upcycled products have significantly lower authentic pride compare to non-sustainable one ($b_{upcycle}$ = -0.35, $p < 0.05$ $b_{recycle}$ = -0.24, $p = 0.05$). When durability perceptions increase, authentic pride increases (b = 0.22, $p < 0.05$). When age increases, authentic pride decreases (b = -0.02, $p < 0.05$). Contamination and perceived quality perceptions did not significantly influence authentic pride (b_{contam} = 0.03, $p = 0.53$; $b_{quality}$ = -0.02, $p = 0.87$). The effect of upcycled and recycled luxury products on purchase intention were not significant when authentic pride was added as one of predictors ($b_{upcycle}$ = -0.13, $p = 0.48$ $b_{recycle}$ = -0.06, $p = 0.72$), indicating mediating effect of authentic pride again. Moreover, authentic pride and perceived quality influenced positively purchase intention (b_{pride} = 0.60, $p < 0.001$; $b_{quality}$ = 0.30, $p < 0.01$). Contamination (b = 0.08, $p = 0.07$), durability (b = 0.05, $p = 0.53$), and age (b = -0.00, $p = 0.95$) did not significantly influence purchase intention. The indices of partial moderated mediation of upcycled luxury product for status compare to non-sustainable one was significant (index = -0.21, CI(-0.42, -0.02)); however the index for environmental concern was not significant (index = 0.21, CI(-0.04, 0.48)). The indices of partial moderated mediation of recycled luxury product was not significant for status (index = -0.14, CI (-0.33, 0.05)) and environmental concern (index = 0.10, CI(-0.18, 0.34)). Thus, upcycled luxury products have higher purchase intention than non-sustainable one due to increased pride if the authors do not consider status motives as a boundary condition. However, when status motive increases, authentic pride for upcycled products was lower than for non-sustainable ones which is the opposite of H_{3a}. At last, H_{3b} and H_4 were not confirmed.

Upcycled vs. Recycled Products by Luxury Brands

5. CONCLUSION

In one hand, luxury brands in principle target for limited number of "wealthy" elites, and therefore some might think they do not require circular economy practices. On the other hand, recent trends indicate democratization of luxury where middle-income consumers are also selectively looking for goods indicating higher levels of quality, taste, and aspiration and more importantly millennials, the next generation with spending power, are less reluctant buying luxury goods and look for elevated designs, unique pieces indicating their self-identity and brands indicating values on sustainability, environmental and social responsibilities. So, luxury brands might target millennials and niche market of environmentally conscious consumers with their sustainable products made with circular economy practices. However, the goal is first to understand consumers who concern about environment indeed might be more willing to buy upcycle and/or recycle luxury products. Besides, one of the main reasons of why consumer buy luxury goods are status motives. That is why, the authors wanted to understand how status motives might influence purchase intention for upcycle and/or recycle luxury products. To understand the process, the authors have conducted an experiment. Purchase intentions for new luxury products made with upcycled/recycled processes under the circular economy principles was investigated and compared to a traditional luxury product which is not sustainable and made with a virgin material. The authors investigated the role of status and environmental concern on the relationship between a new luxury product made with upcycled/recycled vs non-sustainable material and purchase intentions.

Indeed, consumers with high status motives were more negative about upcycled new luxury products, but not recycled ones. When environmental concern increased, purchase intention of an upcycled new product was significantly higher compare non-sustainable one, but not for recycled ones. Purchase intention for upcycled luxury products were higher compare to traditional ones due to authentic pride. However, when status motive increased, authentic pride for upcycled products was lower than for non-sustainable ones and therefore purchase intentions for upcycle decreased. Environmental concern did not moderate the relationship between new luxury product and authentic pride.

Luxury managers might use environmental concern issues in their marketing communications for upcycled luxury products, but status appeals are not recommended. Status appeals can be more successful for recycled luxury products. Authentic pride theme in marketing communications seems a proper way to sell sustainable luxury products, but especially for upcycled luxury products. Luxury consumers with high status motives are not suitable customers for upcycled products because their authentic pride decreases. Thus, countries who purchase luxury goods to indicate their wealth or ostentatious reasons are not suitable market for upcycled luxury products. When luxury consumers are interested in luxury goods with internal motivations rather than external motivations such as status, they would be more willing to buy upcycled luxury products. For both sustainable new products, product quality should be emphasized given that it is one of significant antecedents for purchase intentions. Older consumers seem feel less authentic pride for sustainable luxury products. Thus, luxury upcycled products are more suitable for younger consumer segments. At last, if luxury managers want to sell upcycled and recycled products more efficiently, they should design good looking and attractive products because product look expectations for upcycled and recycled products were lower than conventional ones. Product look expectations seem to be a barrier to purchase upcycled/recycled luxury products.

These results contributed to two streams of research: luxury marketing and consumer perspectives under circular economy. While luxury and sustainability were discussed as conflicting concepts just a few years ago, this idea is changing with innovative green products, green products with impressive authentic designs, or products made with circular economy practices using creative ideas and high levels of craftsmanship. With more innovative and sustainable production processes over time, luxury brands can inspire fast fashion and premium brands to be more sustainable. Green innovations and innovations with circular economy principles can be a source of competitive advantage and might help to differentiate new luxury brands from others.

Future research should further explore other types of innovative new sustainable luxury products and compare to the circular economy products. The research sample was American consumers and the authors tried to select potential luxury buyers. Future research should test the genaralization of these findings in European and Asian countries and perhaps using real luxury buyers. Finally, status motives are related with external luxury motivations. The relationship between luxury consumers' internal luxury motivations and reaction to upcycled/recycled products are another interesting issue for future.

REFERENCES

Achabou, M. A., & Dekhili, S. (2013). Luxury and sustainable development: Is there a match? *Journal of Business Research*, *66*(10), 1896–1903. doi:10.1016/j.jbusres.2013.02.011

Amatulli, C., De Angelis, M., Costabile, M., & Guido, G. (2017). *Sustainable luxury brands.* Palgrave MacMillan. doi:10.1057/978-1-137-60159-9

Amatulli, C., De Angelis, M., Korschun, D., & Romani, S. (2018). Consumers' perceptions of luxury brands' CSR initiatives: An investigation of the role of status and conspicuous consumption. *Journal of Cleaner Production*, *194*, 277–287. doi:10.1016/j.jclepro.2018.05.111

Amatulli, C., & Guido, G. (2011). Determinants of purchasing intention for fashion luxury goods in the Italian market: A laddering approach. *Journal of Fashion Marketing and Management*, *15*(1), 123–136. doi:10.1108/13612021111112386

Bridgens, B., Powell, M., Farmer, G., Walsh, C., Reed, E., Royapoor, M., Gosling, P., Hall, J., & Heidrich, O. (2018). Creative upcycling: Reconnecting people, materials and place through making. *Journal of Cleaner Production*, *189*, 145–154. doi:10.1016/j.jclepro.2018.03.317

Burnett, M. S., & Lunsford, D. A. (1994). Conceptualizing guilt in the consumer decision-making process. *Journal of Consumer Marketing*, *11*(3), 33–43. doi:10.1108/07363769410065454

Cho, E., Gupta, S., & Kim, Y. K. (2015). Style consumption: Its drivers and role in sustainable apparel consumption. *International Journal of Consumer Studies*, *39*(6), 661–669. doi:10.1111/ijcs.12185

Davies, I. A., Lee, Z., & Ahonkhai, I. (2012). Do consumers care about ethical-luxury? *Journal of Business Ethics*, *106*(1), 37–51. doi:10.100710551-011-1071-y

De Angelis, M., Adıgüzel, F., & Amatulli, C. (2017). The role of design similarity in consumers' evaluation of new green products: An investigation of luxury fashion brands. *Journal of Cleaner Production*, *141*, 1515–1527. doi:10.1016/j.jclepro.2016.09.230

De Barnier, V., Falcy, S., & Valette-Florence, P. (2012). Do consumers perceive three levels of luxury? A comparison of accessible, intermediate and inaccessible luxury brands. *Journal of Brand Management*, *19*(7), 623–636. doi:10.1057/bm.2012.11

Dodds, W. B., Monroe, K. B., & Grewal, D. (1991). Effects of Price, Brand, and Store Information on Buyers' Product Evaluations. *JMR, Journal of Marketing Research, 28*(3), 307.

Dubois, B., & Duquesne, P. (1993). The market for luxury goods: Income versus culture. *European Journal of Marketing, 27*(1), 35–44. doi:10.1108/03090569310024530

Eastman, J. K., & Eastman, K. L. (2015). Conceptualizing a model of status consumption theory: An exploration of the antecedents and consequences of the motivation to consume for status. *Marketing Management Journal, 25*(1), 1–15.

Eastman, J. K., Goldsmith, R. E., & Flynn, L. R. (1999). Status Consumption in Consumer Behavior: Scale Development and Validation. *Journal of Marketing Theory and Practice, 7*(3), 41–52. doi:10.10 80/10696679.1999.11501839

Fionda, A. M., & Moore, C. M. (2009). The anatomy of the luxury fashion brand. *Journal of Brand Management, 16*(5), 347–363. doi:10.1057/bm.2008.45

Gladwin, T. N., Krause, T. S., & Kennelly, J. J. (1995). Beyond eco-efficiency: Towards socially sustainable business. *Sustainable Development, 3*(1), 35–43. doi:10.1002d.3460030105

Griskevicius, V., Tybur, J. M., & Van den Bergh, B. (2010). Going green to be seen: Status, reputation, and conspicuous conservation. *Journal of Personality and Social Psychology, 98*(3), 392–404. doi:10.1037/a0017346 PMID:20175620

Han, Y., Nunes, J., & Drèze, X. (2010). Signaling Status with Luxury Goods: The Role of Brand Prominence. *Journal of Marketing, 74*(4), 15–30. doi:10.1509/jmkg.74.4.015

Haws, K. L., Winterich, K. P., & Naylor, R. W. (2014). Seeing the world through GREEN-tinted glasses: Green consumption values and responses to environmentally friendly products. *Journal of Consumer Psychology, 24*(3), 336–354. doi:10.1016/j.jcps.2013.11.002

Hayes, A. F. (2018). *Introduction to mediation, moderation, and conditional process analysis: A regression-based approach.* Guilford Publications.

Hobson, K. (2013). 'Weak'or 'strong'sustainable consumption? Efficiency, degrowth, and the 10 Year Framework of Programmes. *Environment and Planning. C, Government & Policy, 31*(6), 1082–1098. doi:10.1068/c12279

Janssen, C., Vanhamme, J., Lindgreen, A., & Lefebvre, C. (2014). The Catch-22 of responsible luxury: Effects of luxury product characteristics on consumers' perception of fit with corporate social responsibility. *Journal of Business Ethics, 119*(1), 45–57. doi:10.100710551-013-1621-6

Kapferer, J. N. (1998). Why are we seduced by luxury brands? *Journal of Brand Management, 6*(1), 44–49. doi:10.1057/bm.1998.43

Kapferer, J. N., & Michaut, A. (2015). Luxury and sustainability: A common future? The match depends on how consumers define luxury. *Luxury Research Journal, 1*(1), 3–17. doi:10.1504/LRJ.2015.069828

Kapferer, J. N., & Michaut-Denizeau, A. (2014). Is luxury compatible with sustainability? Luxury consumers' viewpoint. *Journal of Brand Management, 21*(1), 1–22. doi:10.1057/bm.2013.19

Kapferer, N. (2010). All that Glitters is not Green: The Challenge of Sustainable Luxury. *European Business Review*, (November-December), 40–45.

Leary, R. B., Vann, R. J., Mittelstaedt, J. D., Murphy, P. E., & Sherry, J. F. (2014). Changing the market one behavior at a time. *Journal of Business Research, 67*(9), 1953–1958. doi:10.1016/j.jbusres.2013.11.004

Lee, M., Ko, E., Lee, S., & Kim, K. (2015). Understanding Luxury Disposition. *Psychology and Marketing, 32*(4), 467–480. doi:10.1002/mar.20792

McDonald, S., Oates, C. J., Thyne, M., Timmis, A. J., & Carlile, C. (2015). Flying in the face of environmental concern: Why green consumers continue to fly. *Journal of Marketing Management, 31*(13-14), 1503–1528. doi:10.1080/0267257X.2015.1059352

McFerran, B., Aquino, K., & Tracy, J. L. (2014). Evidence for two facets of pride in consumption: Findings from luxury brands. *Journal of Consumer Psychology, 24*(4), 455–471. doi:10.1016/j.jcps.2014.03.004

Meadows, D., Randers, J., & Meadows, D. (2004). *Limits to growth: The 30-year update*. Chelsea Green Publishing.

Nueno, J. L., & Quelch, J. A. (1998). The mass marketing of luxury. *Business Horizons, 41*(6), 61–68. doi:10.1016/S0007-6813(98)90023-4

O'Cass, A. & Frost, H. (2002). Status brands: examining the effects of non-product-related brand associations on status and conspicuous consumption. *Journal of Product & Brand Management, 11*(2), 67-88.

Onwezen, M. C., Antonides, G., & Bartels, J. (2013). The Norm Activation Model: An exploration of the functions of anticipated pride and guilt in pro-environmental behaviour. *Journal of Economic Psychology, 39*, 141–153. doi:10.1016/j.joep.2013.07.005

Peloza, J., White, K., & Shang, J. (2013). Good and guilt-free: The role of self-accountability in influencing preferences for products with ethical attributes. *Journal of Marketing, 77*(1), 104–119. doi:10.1509/jm.11.0454

Peter, P. C., & Honea, H. (2012). Targeting social messages with emotions of change: The call for optimism. *Journal of Public Policy & Marketing, 31*(2), 269–283. doi:10.1509/jppm.11.098

Philippot, P., & Feldman, R. S. (2004). Positive emotion and the regulation of interpersonal relationships. In *The regulation of emotion* (pp. 142–171). Psychology Press. doi:10.4324/9781410610898

Pino, G., Guido, G., & Nataraajan, R. (2017). Iconic art infusion in luxury retail strategies: Unveiling the potential. *Journal of Global Scholars of Marketing Science, 27*(2), 136–147. doi:10.1080/21639159.2017.1283797

Roberts, J. A., & Bacon, D. R. (1997). Exploring the subtle relationships between environmental concern and ecologically conscious consumer behavior. *Journal of Business Research, 40*(1), 79–89. doi:10.1016/S0148-2963(96)00280-9

Schneider, C. R., Zaval, L., Weber, E. U., & Markowitz, E. M. (2017). The influence of anticipated pride and guilt on pro-environmental decision making. *PLoS One, 12*(11), 1–14. doi:10.1371/journal.pone.0188781 PMID:29190758

Simkus, L. (2010). Sustainability within the French luxury consumer-goods market: The role of business and consumer demand. *Best Business Research Papers*, *3*, 71–85.

Tracy, J. L., & Prehn, C. (2012). Arrogant or self-confident? The use of contextual knowledge to differentiate hubristic and authentic pride from a single nonverbal expression. *Cognition and Emotion*, *26*(1), 14–24. doi:10.1080/02699931.2011.561298 PMID:21468998

Tracy, J. L., & Robins, R. W. (2007). The psychological structure of pride: A tale of two facets. *Journal of Personality and Social Psychology*, *92*(3), 506–525. doi:10.1037/0022-3514.92.3.506 PMID:17352606

Truong, Y., Simmons, G., McColl, R., & Kitchen, P. (2008). Status and conspicuousness – are they related? Strategic marketing implications for luxury brands. *Journal of Strategic Marketing*, *16*(3), 189–203. doi:10.1080/09652540802117124

Unilever. (2017, January 1). *Report shows a third of consumers prefer sustainable brands.* https://www.unilever.com/news/Press-releases/2017/report-shows-a-third-of-consumers-prefer-sustainable-brands.html

Vickers, J. S., & Renand, F. (2003). The marketing of luxury goods: An exploratory study – three conceptual dimensions. *The Marketing Review*, *3*(4), 459–478. doi:10.1362/146934703771910071

Vigneron, F., & Johnson, L. W. (2004). Measuring perceptions of brand luxury. *Journal of Brand Management*, *11*(6), 484–506. doi:10.1057/palgrave.bm.2540194

Wegener, C. (2016). Upcycling. In *Creativity—A New Vocabulary* (pp. 181–188). Palgrave Macmillan.

White, K., & Simpson, B. (2013). When do (and don't) normative appeals influence sustainable consumer behaviors? *Journal of Marketing*, *77*(2), 78–95. doi:10.1509/jm.11.0278

Widloecher, P. (2010). *Luxe et développement durable: Je t'aime, moi non plus.* Luxefrancais.

Yoo, B., & Donthu, N. (2001). Developing and validating a multidimensional consumer-based brand equity scale. *Journal of Business Research*, *52*(1), 1–14. doi:10.1016/S0148-2963(99)00098-3

ENDNOTES

[1] https://ec.europa.eu/commission/news/single-use-plastics-2018-may-28_en

[2] https://ec.europa.eu/clima/policies/strategies/2050_en

[3] https://equilibrium.gucci.com/environment/waste-management/gucci-for-circular-economy/

[4] https://www.pradagroup.com/en/sustainability/environment-csr/prada-re-nylon.html

[5] Euromonitor International Apparel & Footwear 2016 Edition (volume sales trends 2005–2015); World Bank, World development indicators, 2017.

[6] https://www.bloomberg.com/news/features/2019-08-20/gucci-and-saint-laurent-face-an-uphill-battle-to-get-green

[7] https://ww.fashionnetwork.com/news/Giorgio-unveils-recycled-emporio-armani-suggests-hiring-prince-harry-as-a-model,1174437.html

[8] https://bottletop.org/

APPENDIX

Scenario 1: Upcycle

The brand X, a new **luxury brand** in the marketplace, has recently launched a new **wallet** model that is **upcycled** and has a timeless design. Indeed, it **is made from plastic bottle tops** with World-class craftmanship and turn into a luxury wallet. In particular, the wallet is made with discarded **plastic bottle tops as they are (not previously melted). Upcycling** is **the process of combining** by-products, waste materials, useless, or unwanted products into new materials or products **without breaking down discarded** materials.

Scenario 2: Recycle

The brand X, a new **luxury brand** in the marketplace, has recently launched a new **wallet** model that is **recycled** and has a timeless design. Indeed, it **is made from plastic bottle tops** with World-class craftmanship and turn into a luxury wallet. In particular, the wallet is made with discarded **plastic bottle tops which are previously melted. Recycling** is the **process of transforming** waste materials useless, or unwanted products into new materials, or products **after breaking down discarded materials.**

Scenario 3: Non-Sustainable

The brand X, a new **luxury brand** in the marketplace, has recently launched a new **wallet** model that has a timeless design. Indeed, it **is made from superior leather** with World-class craftmanship and turn into a luxury wallet.

Section 3
New Trends in Consumer Behaviour

Chapter 12
Generations' Attitudes and Behaviours in the Luxury Sector

Chiara Giachino
University of Turin, Italy

Bernardo Bertoldi
University of Turin, Italy

Augusto Bargoni
University of Turin, Italy

ABSTRACT

The luxury sector needs to adapt its strategies to the digital advent, the online purchasing, and new young customers who have different behaviors and attitudes with respect to older generations. Young generations (Millennials and GenZ) signed a deep change for companies and influenced the way of doing business. They tend to gather information online, they share their opinions, and they pay attention to how companies behave. Since they represent a big part of the market, it is fundamental to understand if the luxury sector is relevant for them and how they consider luxury brands, for example, Moncler. Through an online questionnaire, a comparison between young and old generations has been realized.

INTRODUCTION

In the last decades, the luxury industry has witnessed different shifts in consumer behaviour. The perception of young generations towards the concept of luxury has changed, the awareness towards sustainability has increased steeply and, as a consequence, luxury brands have to constantly intercept those changes to adapt their strategies. For example, the rise of social media communication has led luxury companies to fulfil their need to change their strategies leveraging more on the social media communication (Mosca and Casalegno, 2016), on the adoption of multi-channels' strategy to sell they products (Lee et al., 2020) or to consider the behaviour and needs of new generational cohorts (de Kerviler and Rodriguez, 2016; Rodrigues and Rodrigues, 2019; Kapferer and Denizeau, 2020; Jain and Mishra, 2020).

DOI: 10.4018/978-1-7998-5882-9.ch012

Copyright © 2021, IGI Global. Copying or distributing in print or electronic forms without written permission of IGI Global is prohibited.

It appears neatly that today, more than ever, it is relevant to analyse and identify the different trends in the demand of consumers and how these trends vary from one generation to another. The notion of generation is very important. From a theoretical perspective, generational theorists have well identified the differences that arise in consumer behaviour from one generation to another. Companies, if they want to maintain their competitive advantage in their own market, have to differentiate their strategies to stay relevant to their target market. To do so it is necessary to be acquainted with generational cohorts and generational segmentation.

Usually, the generational cohorts used in market segmentation are four (considering just the population above 18 years old): baby boomers, genX, genY or Millennials and GenZ (McKinsey, 2018). Each of these generations is characterized by specific traits and needs linked to the period they lived in and their past experiences (McKinsey, 2018; Casalegno et al., 2019; Giachino et al., 2019; Forbes, 2019): for this reason many researchers started to analyse attitudes and behaviours of different generational cohorts (Harrington et al., 2012; Chen and Shoemaker, 2014; Kapferer and Denizeau, 2020). GenY and GenZ are the youngest generation but although if Millennials received a lot of attention from scholars and experts (Lama, 2018; Liu et al., 2019; Loureiro & Guerreiro, 2018; Rita et al., 2018; OECD, 2018; Giachino et al., 2019), GenZ has been less analyzed (Robinson & Schanzel, 2019; Skinner et al., 2018; Forbes, 2019).

In the luxury industry, a relevant perspective to consider is the one of the consumer that is highly committed and involved in the purchasing phases of goods and services (Casaburi, 2011): the symbolic dimension and the status symbols that luxury goods and services encompasses influence from a psychological point of view the purchase intention of the consumer. Moreover, considering the product perspective, a number of characteristics are usually associated with luxury products i.e. excellent quality, distinctiveness, craftsmanship, exclusivity and premium prices. But is there any difference between young and old generations in how luxury products are perceived?

In this context, characterized by a fragmented set of generational cohorts and a little known respondence towards luxury, we decided to investigate if there are differences in attitude and behaviours toward luxury between young and old generations. We also investigate how people perceive Moncler, a very well-known luxury brand born in the 50s that, among all, well represents the shifts occurred in the luxury industry and the interception of the changes in consumer behaviour. Moncler, in facts, since its creation has faced the need to change and adapt its concept many times, to face the change in consumer behaviour, in corporate social responsibility or to reposition its brand image.

In order to investigate the point of view of the two groups of generations we made a survey, with closed-ended questions, and we analyse data through a cluster analysis. This allows us to identify four different clusters that put in evidence different level of interest toward luxury, different approach in buying luxury products and a different perception of what luxury products are for people.

This study is a preliminary study that opens to a number of possible future research and with a two-fold contribution: from the theory point of view it contributes to shed new lights on the challenges of the luxury companies to fulfill the need of new demand; from the practical point of view it contributes to give new information to the companies and the industry about new trends and relevant aspects for young generations.

BACKGROUND

Young Generations' Characteristics and Behaviors

Following generational theorists' constructs, belonging to a generational cohort can influence the consumption behaviors of the people belonging to a specific cohort. For this reason, an increasing number of scholars tend to analyze specific industries through the point of view of different generations (Harrington et al., 2012; Chen & Shoemaker, 2014; Manna & Palumbo, 2018; Chen et al., 2019).

Usually, four generational cohorts are taken into consideration: the baby boomers (1940-1959) which are characterized by an idealistic approach molded by the period in which they lived in; GenX (1960-1979) more anchored to a materialistic world; GenY/Millennials generation (1980-1994) which has a global perspective and is usually more open than the previous generations; and, finally, GenZ (1995-2010) or the digital generation (McKinsey, 2018; Lancaster & Stillman, 2003).

The attention of scholars was mainly directed to the study of GenY or the so called Millennials' generation, since they were considered the first generation to use digital tools and directly connected to the external world (Helal et al., 2018). GenY signed also a change with the past generations thanks to their ideas, believes, values and way of taking decision in the purchasing process (Dabija et al., 2018; Smith and Brower, 2012). GenY was considered the first generation that really paid attention to sustainable action and sustainability in general (Giachino et al., 2019; Casalegno et al., 2019) influencing, in this way, the strategy of many companies.

The youngest generation is the GenZ, which includes people born after 1995, which represents the first native digital generation (Forbes, 2019; McKinsey, 2018). The GenZ is still under investigated but together with GenY is fundamental for the future of a lot of industries due to the important size as customers' group. According to a recent study made by Pew Research Center (2020) GenY recently surpassed, in size, the baby boomers that was the biggest living generational cohort andGenZ represents the 32% of the population (Forbes, 2019).

The last two generations are the youngest and there are a number of reasons why the young generations can be relevant to the luxury sector: first of all, they represent a big part of the market, they have money to spend and they sign a drastic change with previous generations in the way they buy and choose products (McKinsey, 2018; Forbes, 2019). In fact, they contributed to modify the approach of companies in doing business since they use digital tools and consider relevant other people's opinions (Oktadiana et al., 2020; Pucciarelli et al., 2019; Tsai & Chen, 2019; Veiga et al., 2017). Moreover, GenZ is considered the first digital generation: it is born with digital devices and internet connection so the way of looking for information, reading articles and sharing opinions is totally different (Forbes, 2019). They seem to be more sensitive and own a strong spirit of entrepreneurship and initiative (Pencarelli et al,2019). On the other hand, people belonging to GenY or Millennials are also associated with the digital era, since they are the first generation that has the chance to live in a digital environment; from this point of view the digital tools influenced a lot their way of living and taking decisions: they want better and more innovative products and want them as quickly and conveniently as possible (Forbes, 2018; Pencarelli et al., 2019). Also for these reasons, some authors started to analyze the relationship between the luxury industry and young generations to identify the potential impact they may have on the sector (Pencarelli et al., 2019; Gazzola et al., 2020; Uche, 2018).

The Luxury Industry

In order to understand how different generations react to luxury and how they approach the buying experience it is important to provide the reader with an overview of what has been said about luxury in the literature and what still has to be said. There is still a lack of consensus in the academic world to define luxury (Ko et al., 2019). Number of scholars have described, across decades, luxury and its meaning, Veblen (2005), for example, wrote that owning or consuming an expensive commodity is a sign of social prestige and, therefore, the possession of a luxury good can be seen as a way to gain respectability. Some other scholars made a distinction among three types of values that can be associated to goods: the first is the functionality or the main purpose that the object has to satisfy; the second is the symbolic value or the value that the consumer assigns to the good; the third is the recognition or what the luxury good symbolizes for the owner. Usually, luxury products or services are defined as those positioned at the highest end of the market, with a higher price and a higher quality that makes the product or the service exclusive. In fact, Corbellini and Saviolo (2007) defined a luxury item as a perfectly calibrated system of attributes: emotion, high price, originality, innovation, quality, durability, selective distribution, qualified service and elite communication. However, the consumption or possession of a luxury good can go far beyond the physical product and reach a symbolic side (Kapferer, 2015).

The concept and perception of luxury goods evolves in parallel with the social context, although if they are traditionally described as products capable of attributing a higher status to consumers. In addition to the primary attributes, such as, for example, functionality, excellent quality and high price, luxury goods are characterized by secondary attributes, which very often become the main motivation for the purchase: emotional component, highly exclusive character, involvement, heritage and many others.

For these reasons, the fashion and luxury goods industry needs to evolve rapidly. For example, it is well known that following a strategy of physical store expansion can be risky due to lowering profitability of retail and, on the other hand, it must be considered that consumers are shifting their approach to buying towards the online channel. In fact, data shows that, until 2025, online luxury purchases will grow from 9% to 25% of sales (BCG-Altagamma, 2019). In this context, it is crucial to better understand the evolution of young generations' attitudes towards fashion and luxury consumption and the impact that these shifts have on the strategies of luxury brands (CFA Institute, 2018).

More CSR and More Digital Instruments in the Luxury Industry

The majority of luxury brands are looking for digital solutions with the objective to increase in-store conversion rates; improve their visibility and rise the customer engagement level; increase marginal revenues contribution while keeping the same invested capital (CFA Institute, 2018). Moncler, among other fashion companies, takes inspiration from these purposes for its communication strategy. According to Remo Ruffini (Moncler) digital platforms must be employed to give customers a real and physical experience able to go beyond the simple allowance of the transaction (Zargani, 2020).

First of all, consumers are now more aware about products in general, more selective, and consequently they pay more attention when they have to decide what to buy and what to do while taking often in consideration the environmental and social consequences of their consumption (Bonadonna et al., 2017). This aspect influenced companies that are always more involved in corporate social responsibility activities (CSR) (Pencarelli et al., 2019; Re and Giachino, 2018; Mosca and Civera, 2017; Mosca et al., 2016). Moreover, a recent research (Nielsen, 2018) confirmed that for 85% of Millennials it is very important that companies implement programs to improve their environmental impact; furthermore, 75% of respondents declared that they definitely or probably would change their purchasing habits to reduce their impact on the environment. GenZ, as well, considers relevant the environment issue and has the necessity to see that brands communicate their CSR involvement, even if CSR activities are not considered a sufficient incentive to buy a specific product (Uche, 2018). Consequently, the question that many companies are trying to solve is: how can luxury fashion be sustainable? In the last years, slow fashion concept is growing in opposition to fast fashion (Pencarelli et al, 2019). Brands need to genuinely implement sustainability and environmentally-friendly models into their practice through transparency and without creating a hype around it (Buckle, 2019).

Beside the role of sustainability, there are some others aspects that the luxury industry has to take into consideration, such as the online shopping, the personalization, the use of smartphones and the role of influencers as well (Gazzola et al, 2020).

The relevance of on-line shopping for every business is quite clear if it is considered that the majority of the internet uses (almost the 60%) experienced an on-line purchase in fashion-related products during the 2018 (Statista, 2018). Recently, on-line platforms such as Amazon or Zalando achieved great results in the selling of luxury-fashion products. This is why companies need to offer a wider range of services, an always higher level of quality and give to customers the possibility to live a unique experience.

Looking at some of the data gathered and analysed by McKinsey in the last years (McKinsey, 2018a; 2019) it emerged that young generations and in particular millennials spend more than three hours/day on the smartphones. Therefore, fashion companies are forced to create apps suitable for mobile phones to give the opportunity to all their customers to visit the brand website both on the desktop or the smart-phone, buy products directly on-line and live a full experience also on the app.

The possibility for customers to be involved on different platforms and in stores is called multichan-nel strategy and it is a quite complex strategy to manage (PC, Tablet, Smartphone, etc.) (Kim, 2019; Bertoldi et al., 2016; Mosca et al., 2015).

Finally, consumers have become more demanding and have high expectations with respect to the quality of products and the customization experiences.

This evolution towards digital platforms is led by the rise of the consumption of new generations. Today Baby-Boomer and Generation X hold the majority of the stake in absolute, and they will make up 45% of the luxury market by 2025 (BCG-Altagamma, 2019).

However, firms face also the challenge to express the premiumness and the buying experience through the online channel and face the need to communicate effectively the history of the brand or its exclusivity.

The image of the brand can be so strong to allow the products to live a second life, just thanks to the connections established with consumers. This connection, as stated before, is even stronger when the founder has the ability to create an essence recognized by customers and used by the company as an asset: a collection must be beautiful, but it is the creative project and the communication that counts to conquer the public (Zargani, 2020).

The consumer's identification process with a company could be defined as an active, selective, volitional act motivated by the satisfaction of one or more self-defined needs (Gistri et al., 2018). The challenge for companies is to implement these strategies maintaining brand consistency.

ARE YOUNGER AND OLDER GENERATION BEHAVING DIFFERENTLY IN THE LUXURY SECTOR?

The luxury world is evolving and at the same time consumers' characteristics are changing. The major issue for the luxury companies is to understand the new needs of the potential customers and their habits.

In order to have a clearer vision on those aspects, it is presented the case of Moncler and then data obtained through a survey are analyzed with a cluster analysis.

Moncler is an interesting case study that well represents the shifts occurred in the luxury industry and the interception of the changes in consumer behaviour. On the other side, with the survey it is possible to gather information on the consumer behaviour in the luxury industry and investigate their awareness about Moncler; the cluster analysis will help to identify clusters of people belonging to young and older generations with similar attitudes and behaviour toward luxury. In the following section is presented the Moncler case and the analysis made on young and old generations.

The History of Moncler

The Moncler brand has French origins and takes its name from the contraction of "Monastier of Clermont", where it was founded in 1952 by Renè Ramillon and André Vincent. The company lived three crucial moments in its history: the first one is linked to the products dedicated to the mountain, the second one to the streetwear and the last one is linked to the transformation into a luxury brand.

The first moment was characterized by the presence of "mountains". The products created by the company were garments and technical tools to camp in the mountains, including tents and sleeping bags. These robust and functional articles immediately had success and its products became the first choice of people that decided to have vacation in the mountains. One of the most important element that contributed to the success of Moncler in this phase was its unique involvement in research and innovation, which allowed the brand to deposit some patents, develop new light and warm materials and become the best supplier for all mountain experts. Some relevant events contributed to its popularity: the expeditions to K2 (above 8.000 meters) and Alaska. Moreover, in the 1968 Moncler became the official supplier of the French Olympic downhill ski team and thanks to the visibility given by the television the brand was recognised as the best product against the cold. Furthermore, it started to acquire also a strong popularity outside of the slopes, getting into fashion magazines and invading the urban streets.

At this moment a second phase started, the "streetwear" phase. Its jackets were the flagship of the Italian subculture "Paninari" and the company decided to take advantage of these trendsetters, reworking the look of the classic down jacket. This positive situation, however, did not last for a long period. In fact, in the 80s Moncler started to suffer and losing market share and audience. The reason was that the company was not ready to that sudden growth and was unable to reposition itself correctly. Moncler was no longer a sport brand but not yet a luxury brand.

The brand awareness was far too weak to let this double identity live and the management was not able to undertake quick choices to recover this negative situation. In the 90s the company took a breath of air thanks to the acquisition of the Italian Group Pepper Company Sarl, whose aim was to restore the brand equity, but the general situation was still really difficult.

In 1998 Finpart SpA bought Moncler with the purpose to create a luxury portfolio of companies and giving new financial resources to the company. However, the turning point for Moncler can be identified in the 2003: Remo Ruffini, already Creative Director, decided to buy the company to re-launch the brand worldwide. The value of the deal was really low compared to the prestige of the brand, but big investments were required to start a new life cycle. Ruffini repositioned the brand in the absolute luxury down jacket segment (CFA Institute, 2018). Moncler's revitalization passed from the development of different lines, characterized by distinct price ranges and materials, to a return to the past, celebrating the marriage between innovation and high quality standards. Remo Ruffini affirmed that the mantra of Moncler was to manage its products as *Technological tools* and this strategy led the company to a new phase of success.

Ten years later, new shareholders arrived, Remo Ruffini was the General Director, CEO and Creative Manager, and the company reached surprising results: Moncler passed from €45 million revenues in 2002 to reach €585 million in 2013; 33% EBITDA margin; it was present in 66 countries and had 107 shops directly managed with 24 openings in 2013, which represented 51% of sales; 1858 wholesales; and, the decision of going public welcomed enthusiastically by the market.

Remo Ruffini was substantially the new *re-founder* of Moncler that tried to relaunch the brand in the luxury world: at the time he controlled the 31.90% of the company through Ruffini Partecipazioni and he took directly the decisions on the business.

Since 2003, Ruffini led Moncler through a repositioning journey moving from the technical mono-product offering (the classic winter down jacket) to a multi-functions/multi-product offering that includes outerwear, knitwear, leather and accessories, avoiding an excessive Autumn/Winter dependence (CFA Institute, 2018). He is the true advocate of Moncler *re-born*. He built the strategy and adopted a strong decision-making process, facing fearless even the most difficult challenges. Mr. Ruffini objective was to create a precise, consistent, coherent, clear and targeted strategy and was able not to lose sight on his goal.

Moreover, Mr. Ruffini firmly believes in the past of the company: the DNA of Moncler was funda-mental in this re-born and the essence given by Ramillon to the brand was to be restored. He bought Moncler because he trusted the history of the brand and the essence created by Ramillon that is the starting point of his construction. He wanted to make the most of the past, but made it happen for the future. About this topic, in an interview with Mr. Rezzonico, Mr. Ruffini said: *With my philosophy and strategy in mind, I decided to try it hard: the icon product was there, the skills were there and the know-how was there too. I needed to make Moncler take off again* (Rezzonico, 2013).

However, in 2014 Moncler had to face another crisis. This time the crisis was not due to a change in consumer behaviour nor led by a change in the demographics but was related to a corporate social responsibility matter. Report, an Italian TV show, denounced how the Ungharian suppliers of duck feath-ers of Moncler exploited the ducks to rip off the feathers from the duck and did not respect the European laws on animal. Without entering into the matter, the impact on the company was similar to the one suffered by Johnson&Johnson during the well-known Tylenol crisis. The company suffered dramatic losses on the stock exchange, the public opinion felt betrayed by the uncovering of the situation as they discovered that the feathers did not come from Italy and that the suppliers of the company used cruelty towards animal. The damage to the brand image was of tremendous entity. Without entering into the details of the crisis nor the crisis management best practices that are not the focus of this chapter, it is important to highlight how the role of information and social media is crucial to transfer a certain brand image and to deploy a correct communication strategy.

Today the society is changing at a very high pace and companies, in order to lead their brands towards a longer life, need to be able to combine long-term strategies (the construction of value takes time) with the capacity to adapt quickly to the changes in the competitive landscape.

Generations' Attitudes and Behaviours in the Luxury Sector

In order to analyse the key factors which brought back Moncler to its path of success, the authors consider necessary to go back to the reasons why the brand was so strong in the 70's, some years after the launch of the company by Renè Ramillon. The triumph of that period open the path to the great crisis of the next two decades.

Moncler, in fact, did not start to get popularity and be acclaimed thanks to a clear and defined strategy. On the contrary, the brand was chosen *by chance* by the Italian subcultural movement of *Paninari* and therefore it became "unconsciously" their symbol. Its awareness did not depend on a precise marketing strategy, or on a communication planning, or a precise positioning. Moncler success was mostly decreed by the contact with this trend, which, like all the currents born from fashion, lasted a few years. The crisis came, therefore, as soon as the movement faded away and found other symbols to express itself. The result of this process was a brand in deep crisis, completely lost, without neither the strong personality of the mountain nor the elegance of the city. In the early 90s there was no more brand identity and the brand associations made by customers were rather negative. The brand did not lose its potential, but it has betrayed itself.

Moncler did not lowered its standards on quality. In fact, quality has always been a key value driver for the Group (CFA Institute, 2018), however, the product was always intact but the consumer did not recognize it anymore.

To summarize, the success period of Moncler was a moment of sales increase and value prestige decrease.

In the 90's, Moncler had not a precise positioning. People found the products in huge retailers' centres as Decathlon and Cisalfa, but the price was far from being aligned with the kind of products sold in these mass-market stores. These shops did not communicate either luxury nor quality or fashion.

Furthermore, the target was too narrow. The brand, without a clear strategy, was focusing on the only category which was still bringing revenues: a female clientele, from 30 to 55, with a passion for winter sports. At this stage, Moncler was presenting all the symptoms of a brand in the last phase of the product life-cycle.

Today, Moncler's objective is to pursue a sustainable and responsible development of its brand in the global luxury sector, in harmony with the uniqueness of its heritage, with a very high focus on generational shift and digitalization as the acquisition of Stone Island represents (see Figure 1). Its strategy could be summarized in five points (CFA Institute, 2018): the continuous innovation and enlargement of the product range; the establishment of a direct control on the value chain; the enlargement of the distribution network with specific focus on digital; the consolidation and expansion of its geographical presence; the creation of a direct relationship with customers.

The history of Moncler is interesting because today, imagining an extremely warm but elegant down-padded garment is synonymous of thinking about Moncler. But, in the past, it has not been always the case: Moncler, in its history, has experienced very difficult and tough times passing through different moments and revolutions.

Attitude and Behavior in the Luxury Market: A First Analysis on Young and Old Generations

An on-line survey was created considering three main topics: luxury products and definition of the luxury sector; attitude and behavior of respondents toward social media and the online shops in the luxury sector; awareness and possession of Moncler products.

Figure 1.
Source: Moncler website; BEYOND FASHION, BEYOND LUXURY - Stone Island joins Moncler 12/7/2020

The survey was managed online and in a three weeks of time 210 answers were collected. All the respondents are Italian, the 59% of the respondents are female and the 76% 18-38 years old (young generations) while the 24% is older than 39 years old. This difference between the % of respondents between young and older generation can be linked to the major attitude of young people in using digital online tools.

The objective of the survey is to compare and eventually identify differences in attitudes and behaviors toward luxury and Moncler among young and old generations. In order to achieve the objective a cluster analysis - which divide the respondents in a partition - was performed and four clusters were identified. R software, FactoMineR (Escofier and Pages, 2008) was used to perform the cluster analysis.

Finding

The majority of respondents to the survey belong to the young generation (76,2%) and specifically to Millennials and GenZ, while the remaining 23,8% belong to older generation. Among the young generation 59% of respondents is female and, in line with expectation, the majority of them do not perceive any income (56%). The older generation included working people i.e. employees, entrepreneurs, managers, etc depicting a quite different social situation: 32% of them is perceiving an income higher than 100.000 euro, 26% has an income ranging from 71 to 100.000 euros while 32% has an income between 16 and 70.000 euro. The income can represent a relevant variable in this context since it can influence the purchasing behavior and knowledge of potential customers.

Through the cluster analysis four main clusters of people with different attitudes and behaviors toward the luxury sector were identified. Here the description of their main characteristics.

Table 1. General information on respondents

		Young generation (18-38)	Previous generation (>39)	Total
Number of Respondents	# (%)	160 (76,2%)	50 (23,8%)	210
Gender	Female # (%)	94 (59%)	32 (64%)	
	Male # (%)	66 (41%)	18 (36%)	
Income	No income	56%	2%	
	<15k euro	11%	8%	
	16-35k euro	5%	16%	
	36-70k euro	17%	16%	
	71-100k euro	8%	26%	
	>100k	3%	32%	

Source: authors' elaboration

Figure 2. Hierarchical clustering on luxury
Source: authors' elaboration

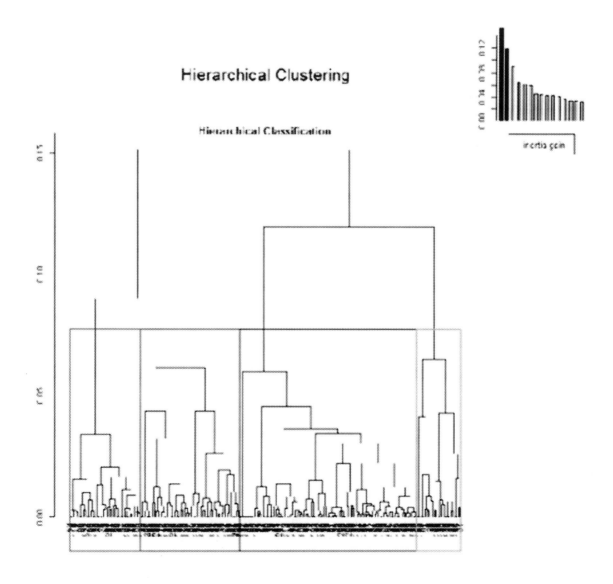

The first cluster is made up by the 45% of respondents and can be describe as the "the social luxury followers". In this cluster people are mainly students, female, without an income and they are between 18-38 years old – young generation. They use social media and they follow a lot of luxury brands online and through their social media pages. When they have to buy luxury products they use multiple channels and mixed forms of channels i.e. they go on the company website to see products but they buy the product in the store or vice versa. They know the Moncler brand and they perceive it as a high luxury brand, however they bought few times products from Moncler.

The second cluster is made up by the 14% of respondents and can be describe as the "luxury what? No, thanks". In this cluster people are worker students, male, with an income lower than 15k euros. They are not interested in luxury brands or, the ones that are interested in, do not have a deep knowledge about luxury brands. They think that luxury goods are characterized by frivolity and superfluity and they prefer to spend for luxury experiences instead of goods. They do not know Moncler and they have not bought products from Moncler, however, they perceive the brand as a streetwear brand.

The third cluster is made up by the 20% of respondents and can be describe as the "I am not interested in". In this cluster people are worker/employee and they have an income between 35k and 70k. They think that luxury can be defined as goods and services of high quality and price but they are not interested in luxury brand. If they have to look for a luxury product they go to the store.

The fourth cluster is made up by the 21% of respondents and can be describe as the "luxury is a part of my life". In this cluster are included entrepreneur and manager with an income higher than 70k euros and more than 39 years old – older generation. They consider luxury products as goods and services characterized by rarity, uniqueness and creativity. They are interested in luxury brand and they often buy luxury products directly in the store. They do not follow any luxury brand on social media. They often buy Moncler products.

The four clusters put in evidence that there is a change in behaviors and attitude toward the luxury sector according to the age of people. In particular, there is the cluster one of young people that can be called "the social luxury followers". They are very interested in luxury and they follow brands on social media although if they are still not buyers of luxury products (they do not have an income). On the contrary, the cluster four "luxury is a part of my life" is made up by older people that are used to buy luxury products and have a traditional approach toward the purchasing process. The difference between the two clusters is also done by the fact that the younger generation do not know Moncler and they do not have products branded by Moncler, while the older generation knows Moncler and often buy its products.

In the middle, there are other two clusters, made up by both young and old generation who are not so interested in luxury. If cluster two can be described as "luxury what? No thanks", the cluster three has a position of indifference toward luxury and can be just named as "I am not interested in". The cluster do not know Moncler while in the cluster three it did not emerge this information.

CONCLUSION AND FUTURE RESEARCH

The luxury market has high potential but it also presents different levels of complexity that need to be managed. First of all, the luxury industry needs to evolve and find the right positioning on the traditional and digital market (BCG-Altagamma, 2019) since that the young generations are more incline to look for goods and information online (Mosca et al., 2015). This aspect has been confirmed by the study that put in evidence that young generations has the habits to follow luxury brands through social media.

Generations' Attitudes and Behaviours in the Luxury Sector

In this context, it is necessary to consider the role of social media and their relevance to communicate with both Millennials and GenZ and to give the right image of the luxury brand. The important point is to identify the shift in the meaning of luxury goods or services for different generational cohorts and, consequently, identify different marketing strategies to satisfy the new requests coming from the market.

Moreover, the emotional aspect seems to play an always more relevant role in the purchase of luxury goods, unlike what happens with the purchase of standard goods. Furthermore, it is a dynamic and constantly moving market both in terms of aesthetic standards and in terms of preferences of consumers. While this dynamism allows for the creation of unique and unrepeatable opportunities and experiences, on the other hand it represents a risk if the company is not able to adapt its strategy to shifting of the external circumstances. According to this point, it emerged that for some people luxury products and service are associated to high quality and price, for some others are unique and creative, while there is a group of people that see those products and services characterized by frivolity and superfluity.

There is another relevant point that can be seen as a further consequence of this continuous change in the external environment and consumers' behavior: the choice of distribution strategies. In fact, it is no longer possible for brands that deal with products and services belonging to the luxury industry to limit themselves to a single sales channel. The integration between online sales and stores and social media is considered a key point for the future of these brands (Kim, 2019; Bertoldi et al., 2016). In particular, through the analysis it clearly emerged how young people tend to look for information and products online, they follow luxury brands on social media and they tend to adopt a mixed approach – on-line and off-line – if they have to buy luxury products. On the contrary, older generations have a more traditional approach and tend to buy luxury products in physical store.

A number of future research directions can be identified. First of all, young generations represent the potential market for the luxury industry – as well as for other industries – and, for this reason going more in depth to understand their perception of luxury is fundamental for fashion companies. Millennials and GenZ have different behaviors and attitudes with respect to older generations. Secondly, the luxury industry needs to find a new equilibrium between digital presence and its traditional business model. On one side there is the shift toward the digital linked to new generations, on the other side there are traditional elements to consider. Identify the right actions to implement digital actions can represent a step forward in research. Finally, the concept of luxury is changing for young generations and according to what it means to them, fashion companies need to reinvent and adapt their communication and product development to the new market requirements. Understanding the key elements that represent value for young generations is important to modify the companies' strategies.

REFERENCES

BCG-Altagamma. (2019). http://media-publications.bcg.com/france/True-Luxury%20Global%20Consumer%20Insight%202019%20-%20Plenary%20-%20vMedia.pdf

Bertoldi, B., Giachino, C., & Pastore, A. (2016). *Strategic pricing management in the omnichannel era.* MERCATI & COMPETITIVITÀ. doi:10.3280/MC2016-004008

Bonadonna, A., Giachino, C., & Truant, E. (2017). Sustainability and mountain tourism: The millennial's perspective. *Sustainability*, *9*(7), 1219. doi:10.3390u9071219

Buckle. (2019). https://blog.globalwebindex.com/chart-of-the-week/luxury-market-2019/

Casaburi, I. (2011). China as a Market: Luxury Brand Consumer Behaviour. *Journal of Marketing*.

Casalegno, C., Giachino, C., & Bertoldi, B. (2019). A New Generation for the Wine Industry. *Micro & Macro Marketing*, *28*(1), 49–70.

CFA Institute. (2018). https://cfasi.it/download/20190124092644.pdf

Chen, H., Ryan, C., & He, H. (2019). Intergenerational differences amongst Chinese visitors to the Terracotta Warriors Museum, Xi'an, China. *Annals of Tourism Research*, *79*, 102682. doi:10.1016/j.annals.2019.01.015

Chen, S. C., & Shoemaker, S. (2014). Age and cohort effects: The American senior tourism market. *Annals of Tourism Research*, *48*, 58–75. doi:10.1016/j.annals.2014.05.007

Dabija, D. C., Bejan, B. M., & Tipi, N. (2018). *Generation X versus millennials communication behaviour on social media when purchasing food versus tourist services*. Economics and Management. doi:10.15240/tul/001/2018-1-013

de Kerviler, G., & Rodriguez, C. M. (2019). Luxury brand experiences and relationship quality for Millennials: The role of self-expansion. *Journal of Business Research*, *102*, 250–262. doi:10.1016/j.jbusres.2019.01.046

Escofier, B., & Pages, J. (2008). *Analyses factorielles simples et multiples: objectifs, m'ethodes et interpr'etation*. Dunod.

Forbes. (2019). https://www.forbes.com/sites/geoffwhitmore/2019/09/13/how-generation-z-is-changing-travel-for-older-generations/

Gazzola, P., Pavione, E., Pezzetti, R., & Grechi, D. (2020). Trends in the Fashion Industry. The Perception of Sustainability and Circular Economy: A Gender/Generation Quantitative Approach. *Sustainability*, *12*(7), 2809. doi:10.3390u12072809

Giachino, C., Truant, E., & Bonadonna, A. (2019). Mountain tourism and motivation: Millennial students' seasonal preferences. *Current Issues in Tourism*, 1–15.

Gistri, G., Corciolani, M., & Pace, S. (2018). The interaction effect between brand identification and personal crisis relevance on consumers' emotional reactions to a fashion brand crisis. *Journal of Global Fashion Marketing*, *9*(3), 252–269. doi:10.1080/20932685.2018.1461021

Harrington, R. J., Ottenbacher, M. C., Staggs, A., & Powell, F. A. (2012). Generation Y consumers: Key restaurant attributes affecting positive and negative experiences. *Journal of Hospitality & Tourism Research (Washington, D.C.)*, *36*(4), 431–449. doi:10.1177/1096348011400744

Helal, G., Ozuem, W., & Lancaster, G. (2018). Social media brand perceptions of millennials. *International Journal of Retail & Distribution Management*, *46*(10), 977–998. doi:10.1108/IJRDM-03-2018-0066

Jain, S., & Mishra, S. (2020). Luxury fashion consumption in sharing economy: A study of Indian millennials. *Journal of Global Fashion Marketing*, *11*(2), 171–189. doi:10.1080/20932685.2019.1709097

Kapferer, J. N. (2015). *Kapferer on luxury: How luxury brands can grow yet remain rare*. Kogan Page Publishers.

Kim, J. (2019). *Luxury fashion goods ownership and collecting behavior in an omni-channel retail environment*. Research Journal of Textile and Apparel. doi:10.1108/RJTA-01-2019-0001

Ko, E., Costello, J. P., & Taylor, C. R. (2019). What is a luxury brand? A new definition and review of the literature. *Journal of Business Research, 99*, 405–413. doi:10.1016/j.jbusres.2017.08.023

Lama, A. V. (2018). Millennial leisure and tourism: The rise of escape rooms [Ocio y turismo millennial: El fenómeno de las salas de escape]. *Cuadernos de Turismo, 41*, 615–636 + 743–746.

Lancaster, L. C., & Stillman, D. (2003). *When generations collide: Who they are, why they clash, how to solve the generational puzzle at work*. HarperBusiness.

Lee, H., Rothenberg, L., & Xu, Y. (2020). Young luxury fashion consumers' preferences in multi-channel environment. *International Journal of Retail & Distribution Management, 48*(3), 244–261. doi:10.1108/IJRDM-11-2018-0253

Liu, H., Wu, L., & Li, X. (2019). Social media envy: How experience sharing on social networking sites drives millennials' aspirational tourism consumption. *Journal of Travel Research, 58*(3), 355–369. doi:10.1177/0047287518761615

Loureiro, S. M. C., & Guerreiro, J. (2018). Psychological behavior of millennials: Living between real and virtual reality. In M. W. Gerhardt & J. Van Eck Peluchette (Eds.), Millennials: Trends, characteristics and perspectives (pp. 67–90). Academic Press.

Manna, R., & Palumbo, R. (2018). What makes a museum attractive to young people? Evidence from Italy. *International Journal of Tourism Research, 20*(4), 508–517. doi:10.1002/jtr.2200

McKinsey. (2018). https://www.mckinsey.com/industries/consumer-packaged-goods/our-insights/true-gen-generation-z-and-its-implications-for-companies

McKinsey. (2018a). https://www.mckinsey.com/~/media/McKinsey/Industries/Retail/Our%20Insights/Renewed%20optimism%20for%20the%20fashion%20industry/The-state-of-fashion-2018-final.ashx

McKinsey. (2019). https://www.mckinsey.com/~/media/mckinsey/industries/retail/our%20insights/the%20state%20of%20fashion%202019%20a%20year%20of%20awakening/the-state-of-fashion-2019-final.ashx

Mosca, F., Bertoldi, B., & Giachino, C. (2015). Development Strategies for International Distribution in luxury industry. *Journal of Management Cases, 4*(4), 4–16.

Mosca, F., & Casalegno, C. (2020). Managing Integrated Brand Communication Strategies in the Online Era: New Marketing Frontiers for Luxury Goods. In Global Branding: Breakthroughs in Research and Practice (pp. 227-242). IGI Global.

Mosca, F., Casalegno, C. G., & Civera, C. (2016). Opportunities and Peculiarities of the Online for Communicating Corporate Social Responsibility. A cross investigation on luxury players and consumers' perceptions. *British Academy of Management Journal, 2016*, 1–26.

Mosca, F., & Civera, C. (2017). The evolution of CSR: An integrated approach. *Symphonya. Emerging Issues in Management*, (1), 16–35.

Nielsen. (2018). https://www.nielsen.com/us/en/insights/report/2018/unpacking-the-sustainability-landscape/

Oake. (2020). https://luxe.digital/business/digital-luxury-trends/millennials-buy-sustainable-luxury/#:~:text=Sustainable%20Luxury%3A%20Millennials%20Buy%20Into%20Socially%20Conscious%20Brands, The%20luxury%20industry&text=A%20study%20from%20Nielsen%20showed,than%20what%20older%20generations%20indicated.

OECD. (2018). https://www.oecd-ilibrary.org/docserver/tour-2018-6-en.pdf?expires=1587111750&id=id&accname=guest&checksum=237A5555558C707C9361698CBB882586

Oktadiana, H., Pearce, P. L., & Li, J. (2020). Let's travel: Voices from the millennial female Muslim travellers. *International Journal of Tourism Research*, *22*(5), 551–563. doi:10.1002/jtr.2355

Pencarelli, T., Ali Taha, V., Škerháková, V., Valentiny, T., & Fedorko, R. (2020). Luxury Products and Sustainability Issues from the Perspective of Young Italian Consumers. *Sustainability*, *12*(1), 245. doi:10.3390u12010245

PewResearch Center. (2020). https://www.pewresearch.org/fact-tank/2020/04/28/millennials-overtake-baby-boomers-as-americas-largest-generation/

Pucciarelli, F., Giachino, C., Bertoldi, B., & Tamagno, D. (2019). A small world experiment in the digital era: Can sWOM be used by start uppers to reach a target? *Mercati & competitività-Open Access*, (1).

Re, P., & Giachino, C. (2018). CSR in Small and Medium Companies and Stakeholder's Relationships. *Symphonya. Emerging Issues in Management*, (1), 76–90.

Re, P., Giachino, C., Bertoldi, B., & Minopoli, M. (2016). The Role of the Founder's DNA throughout Crisis: The Revitalization of Moncler. In *Global Marketing Strategies for the Promotion of Luxury Goods* (pp. 266–283). IGI Global. doi:10.4018/978-1-4666-9958-8.ch012

ReportM. F. (2020). https://www.monclergroup.com/wp-content/uploads/2016/07/Moncler-Half-Year-Financial-Report-as-of-30-June-2020-1.pdf

Rita, P., Brochado, A., & Dimova, L. (2019). Millennials' travel motivations and desired activities within destinations: A comparative study of the US and the UK. *Current Issues in Tourism*, *22*(16), 2034–2050. doi:10.1080/13683500.2018.1439902

Robinson, V. M., & Schänzel, H. A. (2019). A tourism inflex: Generation Z travel experiences. *Journal of Tourism Futures*.

Rodrigues, C., & Rodrigues, P. (2019). Brand love matters to Millennials: The relevance of mystery, sensuality and intimacy to neo-luxury brands. *Journal of Product and Brand Management*, *28*(7), 830–848. doi:10.1108/JPBM-04-2018-1842

Saviolo, S., & Corbellini, E. (2007). *L'esperienza del lusso*. Edizione Ottobre.

Skinner, H., Sarpong, D., & White, G. R. (2018). Meeting the needs of the Millennials and generation Z: Gamification in tourism through geocaching. *Journal of Tourism Futures*, *4*(1), 93–104. doi:10.1108/JTF-12-2017-0060

Smith, K. T., & Brower, T. R. (2012). Longitudinal study of green marketing strategies that influence Millennials. *Journal of Strategic Marketing*, *20*(6), 535–551. doi:10.1080/0965254X.2012.711345

Statista. (2018). https://www.statista.com/statistics/276846/reach-of-top-online-retail-categories-worldwide/#statisticContainer

Tsai, T.-H., & Chen, C.-M. (2019). Mixed logit analysis of trade-off effects between international airline fares and fences: A revenue management perspective. *Current Issues in Tourism*, *22*(1), 265–275. doi:10.1080/13683500.2017.1402869

Uche, S. (2018). *Generation Z and corporate social responsibility*. Academic Press.

Veblen, T. (2005). *The theory of the leisure class: An economic study of institutions*. Aakar Books.

Veiga, C., Santos, M. C., Águas, P., & Santos, J. A. C. (2017). Are millennials transforming global tourism? Challenges for destinations and companies. *Worldwide Hospitality and Tourism Themes*, *9*(6), 603–616. doi:10.1108/WHATT-09-2017-0047

ZarganiL. (2020). https://wwd.com/business-news/financial/monclers-remo-ruffini-on-digital-transformation-keeping-brand-in-top-league-1203688356/

ADDITIONAL READING

Han, Y. J., Nunes, J. C., & Drèze, X. (2010). Signaling status with luxury goods: The role of brand prominence. *Journal of Marketing*, *74*(4), 15–30. doi:10.1509/jmkg.74.4.015

KEY TERMS AND DEFINITIONS

Baby Boomer: 1940-1959, they lived the period of postwar, they are collectivist and revolutionary.

GenX: 1960-1979, they lived a period of political transition and they are materialistic and individualistic.

GenZ: 1995-2010, they are the real digital native and completely live the social networks life, they are realistic and diloguer.

Millennials/GenY: 1980-1994, they lived the period of globalization and economic stability, they are the first generation that learnt to use digital devices and social media.

Multi-Channel: In the retail, the multi-channel is the presence on more than one sales channel.

Paninari: It is a phenomenon born in the 80's in Italy and it is linked with the need to wear luxury clothes.

Chapter 13

There Is No Such Thing as the Millennial:
A Cross-Cultural Analysis of Luxury and Prestige Perception Among Young People in Switzerland and South Korea

Camilla Pedrazzi
School of Management and Law, Zurich University of Applied Sciences, Switzerland

Fabio Duma
School of Management and Law, Zurich University of Applied Sciences, Switzerland

Maya Gadgil
School of Management and Law, Zurich University of Applied Sciences, Switzerland

ABSTRACT

In this chapter, the authors present a cultural comparative study of how millennials in Switzerland and South Korea define and perceive luxury and prestige and how this might influence their luxury consumer behavior. Labels, such as GenX, millennials, GenY, or GenZ, are often used to distinguish cohorts of individuals based on their shared generational experiences and characteristics. However, as previous research shows, mere membership in a generational cohort is not a sufficient explanation for consumption patterns across geographies and cultures. Given the size and importance of the global luxury market and the degree of internationalization of luxury companies, a better understanding of the luxury consumer and the impact of their macro-context is vital. The results of the present study indicate that economic as well as cultural factors have an impact on the definition and perception of luxury among millennials and might also explain differences in consumer behavior.

DOI: 10.4018/978-1-7998-5882-9.ch013

Copyright © 2021, IGI Global. Copying or distributing in print or electronic forms without written permission of IGI Global is prohibited.

INTRODUCTION

Millennials are among the most important luxury consumers globally. Like other generational cohorts, they are frequently treated as if they were a homogeneous group of people and macro-contextual factors, which might lead to different preferences and consumption, are being ignored. Previous studies have shown that there are country-specific differences in evaluating luxury and prestige among millennials. These differences have managerial implications for luxury brands that are active in different countries and cultural contexts. Hence in this chapter the authors suggest taking a more differentiated look at generational cohorts. With Switzerland, well known for its traditional luxury watchmaking industry, and South Korea, one the leading Asian luxury markets, they investigate two countries that in some aspects are similar, but in many others rather different, creating a contrast which might be helpful to illustrate the importance of macro-contextual factors for a differentiated understanding of consumer behavior. The insights gained from this empirical study show that consumers should not merely be segmented by the generational cohort they belong to, but that country-specific, economic and cultural factors should be taken into account by luxury firms, for example, when planning their marketing and communication efforts. These insights can help marketers create better targeted marketing and communications campaigns to address customers with different cultural backgrounds.

BACKGROUND

Luxury: A Global Business

Luxury is one of the most profitable and fastest-growing global markets and spans multiple industries. Central to this phenomenon is a consumer culture that is characterized by an increasing desire for luxury worldwide (Kapferer & Bastien, 2009; D'Arpizio, Levato, Prete & Gault, 2020). While historically luxury has primarily been defined as a means of gaining and maintaining social prestige, nowadays luxury refers to comfort, elegance, and high quality, as well as high expense (Pedrazzi, 2020). Luxury goods have become more affordable and accessible to new customers (Truong, McColl & Kitchen, 2009, p. 2), and more consumers are willing and able to pay a price premium for higher-quality and higher-status products (Gardyn, 2002). Consumers of luxury products come from all different social and income classes and use prestige products because it makes them feel confident and they enjoy wearing well-known brands (Husic & Cicic, 2009), because they express status and membership in or differentiation from social groups (Vigneron & Johnson, 1999). In 2019 the luxury market grew by 4% and reached a global market size of €1.3 trillion. The growing middle class, especially in Asia, will further stimulate the luxury market, especially the entry-level segments. By 2025 market growth is expected to recover from the Covid-19 crisis, resuming gradually and reaching an estimated €320-330 billion (D'Arpizio et al., 2020). As millennials represent the largest global consumer group (DeVaney, 2015, p. 11), it is the generation this study focuses on. But what is the meaning of luxury and prestige among millennials around the world? How do members of one of the world's largest generations define and perceive luxury and prestige in different countries, and what are the determining influences? Consumers demand offerings that correspond with their values and lifestyles (Meredith & Schewe, 2002). Knowing these preferences and satisfying the needs and wants of individual segments still prove to be pivotal to an effective marketing strategy and subsequent business success (Ting, Lim, de Run, Koh & Sahdan, 2016).

There Is No Such Thing as the Millennial

DEFINITION OF LUXURY AND PRESTIGE

What exactly luxury and prestige mean, is still a matter of debate in the literature (Kapferer & Valette-Florence, 2016, p.124). Not only are there multiple definitions of both terms, but they also change over time (Yeoman, 2011; Cristini, Kauppinen-Räisänen, BarthodProthade & Woodside, 2017, p. 102).

The term "luxury" derives from the Latin term "luxus" and refers to a sort of excessive lifestyle (Oxford Latin Dictionary, 1992). Historically, luxury goods are defined as products the simple use or presentation of which bring prestige to the owner (Grossman & Shapiro, 1988, p. 62). Dubois, Czellar & Laurent (2005, p. 121) state that luxury can be described as a combination of the following six features: quality, price, scarcity and uniqueness, heritage, non-utility and superfluity. Luxury goods evoke exclusivity and enjoy high brand awareness. Moreover, luxury is often linked with great product integrity and perceived quality. Other characteristics of luxury brands are culture, history, and focus on customer loyalty (Phau & Prendergast, 2001, p. 124; Beverland, 2004, p.453). In the following table the definitions of luxury that informed the present research are summarized.

Table 1. Definitions of luxury

Definition of luxury	Source	Can it be applied to all categories of luxury?
Luxury is defined by quality, price, scarcity and uniqueness, heritage, non-utility and superfluity.	Dubois, et al. (2005, p. 121)	Yes, Dubois et al. (2005, p. 121) refer to luxury wine, antiques and clothing.
Luxury is a concept based on three spheres: the objective (material: exquisite material and craftsmanship, high functionality, and impressive performance), the subjective (individual: consumers' personal hedonic value), and the collective (social: the value luxury signals to others).	Berthon, et al. (2009, p. 47)	Yes, Berthon et al. (2009, pp. 50-52) refer to luxury fashion products as well as coffee and cars.
Luxury is defined by the following factors: high quality, expensive, non-essential, appears to be rare, exclusive, prestigious, authentic and offers high levels of symbolic and emotional/hedonic values through customer experiences.	Tynan, et al. (2010, p. 1158)	Yes, the dimensions identified by Tynan, et al. (2010) are general and can be applied to many categories of luxury.
Luxury is anything that is desirable and more than necessary or ordinary.	Heine (2012)	Yes, the definition can be applied to many categories of luxury.
Luxury is defined as great comfort, especially as provided by expensive and beautiful things	Cambridge Dictionary, (2014a)	Yes, the definition can be applied to many categories of luxury.

Source: adapted from Ko, Costello and Taylor, 2019

McCarthy and Perreault (1987) define prestige as the relative status of product or service position associated with a brand. In the literature authors mainly refer to prestige as a concept generated from luxury (Vigneron & Johnson, 1999, p. 4). Dubois and Czellar (2002) report that prestige is seen as the subjective categorization of people or inanimate objects such as brands in a high social status. Literature about the definition and perception of prestige is rather scarce (Table 2). Moreover, since this study is not focusing on a specific category of luxury and prestige but is investigating the topic as a general concept, the table also indicates whether the definition of prestige can be applied to all categories or not.

There Is No Such Thing as the Millennial

Table 2. Definitions of Prestige

Definition of prestige	Source	Can it be applied to all categories of prestige?
Prestige is defined as the exhibition of five perceived values relevant to socioeconomic frameworks: conspicuous, unique, social, hedonic and quality.	Vigneron & Johnson (1999, p. 4)	Yes, the identified perceived values can be applied to many categories of prestige.
Prestige is the relative high status of product positioning associated with a brand.	McCarthy and Perreault (1987)	Yes, the definition can be applied to many categories of prestige.
Prestige is defined as respect and admiration given to someone or something, usually because of a reputation for high quality, success, or social influence.	Cambridge Dictonary (2014b)	Yes. the definition can be applied to many categories of prestige.

Source: Pedrazzi, 2020

MILLENNIALS AS GLOBAL LUXURY CONSUMPTION DRIVERS

The influence of younger consumers is gaining importance among luxury brands (D'Arpizio, et al., 2018). In 2019, millennial customers, also known as Generation Y (GenY), already accounted for 35% of luxury consumption; by 2025 they could make up 45% of the market. And the even younger Generation Z (GenZ), born after 2000, could make up 40% of luxury purchases by 2035, up from only 4% today. In 2019, Generations Y and Z represented the entirety of the luxury market's growth (D'Arpizio et al., 2020). It is therefore not surprising, that studies and reports about the expectations, preferences and lifestyles of these generational cohorts abound.

Definition and Characteristics of Millennials

There are many ways to define the generation known as digital natives: millennials, Generation Y, Nexters, or Echo Boomers. In this study, millennials are defined as those born between 1981 and 1996 (Dimock, 2019). Deloitte (2019b) carried out a study based on the views of 13,416 millennials (born between 1983 and 1994) across 42 countries. Among the key findings of the study is, that millennials tend to be disillusioned and have a lack of trust in the traditional social institutions. Moreover, the study's authors point out that millennials value experiences and support companies that align with their values (2019b). Howe & Strauss (2000) reported that millennials tend to think that with success they can get everything they want and therefore see their luxury consumption as a reward for a particular effort in order to enhance personal success. Stępień, Lima, & Hinner (2018, p. 143) report that the slogan "I deserved it" best describes millennials' attitude toward luxury consumption.

Millennials are an important cohort in the luxury industry mainly because of their purchasing power. Moreover from 2018 to 2025, Generations Y and Z will contribute 130% of the market growth, balancing the decline in sales among older generations. Millennial consumers prefer luxury brands that make a positive contribution to society (Deloitte, 2019b). They value transparency and authenticity, therefore millennials are willing to pay a premium price for brand products that make an effort to reflect values that align with theirs (Deloitte, 2019b).

The survey carried out by the Luxury Institute (2019) shows that millennials see brand history and heritage as less relevant decision factors. Quality is seen as the most important factor, followed by customer service, design, craftsmanship and product exclusivity. D'Arpizio et al. (2020) report millennials as critical consumers, driven by experiences, with a new consumption pattern valuing convenience (e.g. rent and share).

The table below summarizes the findings of further studies about the factors influencing the attitude toward luxury among millennials.

Table 3. Factors influencing the attitude toward luxury among millennials

Factors influencing Millennial's attitudes toward luxury	Source	Value
Millennials are more individualistic in nature and need for uniqueness is universally significant among them.	(Burnasheva, et al., 2019, pp. 75-76)	Need for uniqueness
The degree of demonstrated materialism is not related to the score in the Hofstede Cultural Dimension model.	(Burnasheva, et al., 2019, pp. 75-76)	Materialism
Peers and social status have a high influence on the attitude toward fashion luxury brands among Millennials.	(Lachance, et al., 2003, p. 51; Stępień, et al., 2018. p. 149)	Relationships
Parents seem to have a lower influence on the attitude toward fashion luxury brands among Millennials	(Lachance, et al., 2003, p. 51)	Family
Millennials do not value the history and heritage of luxury and only care about what creates value in the last 24 hours.	(Deloitte, 2019b).	Tradition
Quality is the most important factor followed by customer service, design, craftsmanship and product exclusivity shaping the luxury consumption motivation of Millennials.	(Luxury Institue, 2019)	Quality / Service / Design / Exclusivity
The consumption of luxury among Millennials is driven by experience and exclusivity	(D'Arpizio, et al., 2020; Stępień, et al., 2018, p. 148)	Experience/ Exclusivity
Millennials consume luxury in order to reward themselves for success.	(Howe & Strauss, 2000)	Reward/ Prize/ Success

Source: Pedrazzi, 2020

GENERATIONAL COHORTS: A CAUTIONARY TALE

Generational cohorts, such as Baby Boomers, Generation X and Generation Y are defined as "a group of individuals who have shared similar experiences and have unique common characteristics around these experiences" (Beldona, Demicco & Nusair, 2009, p. 407). They are, as shown above in the luxury context, frequently studied in marketing research and segmentation strategies (Lauper, 2020; Meredith & Schewe, 2002, Noble & Schewe, 2003, Yu & Miller, 2003), and thought to provide researchers and business practitioners with a foundation to understand and predict consumer behavior. The respective labels, like GenX or GenY, are used to distinguish cohorts of individuals based on their generational experiences and characteristics (Ting, Lim, de Run, Koh & Sahdan, 2016).

Norum (2003) suggests that generational differences in consumer purchase patterns do exist and need to be further addressed. Eastman & Liu (2012) report significant differences in the level of status consumption by generational cohorts in the United States. To segment and specifically target consumers, marketers and business practitioners have for many years used demographic and psychographic variables (Kotler and Armstrong, 2011, Scardino, 2004). Schewe & Noble (2000, p. 53) suggest that generational cohorts are a more efficient way to segment markets than just by age, as these different cohorts have been impacted in a similar way by external events.

There Is No Such Thing as the Millennial

Kurz et al. further point out that the general narrative seems to be that the consumption behavior of millennials (and now also GenZ) differs so much from that of earlier generations, that the transition of this generation into the prime working-age cohort has induced meaningful changes on macro-economic outcomes. While the narrative sounds plausible, the authors clearly show that distinguishing the shifts in the population's spending patterns, that reflect the unique characteristics of its rising generation, from those that reflect secular trends or cyclical forces, is challenging. In their analysis of the US market, Kurz et al. find that, conditional on age and other factors, millennials do not appear to have preferences for consumption that differ significantly from those of earlier generations (2018). Thus, mere membership in a general generational cohort is not a sufficient explanation for changing consumption patterns.

In order to identify the potential similarities and differences among the luxury consumer behavior across generations and cultures it is important to understand the theoretical underpinnings of luxury consumer behavior.

LUXURY CONSUMER BEHAVIOR: THE ROLE OF VALUES, MACRO-CONTEXTUAL FACTORS & CULTURAL DIFFERENCES

From a consumer point of view, luxury is something that provides personal, as well as social benefits (Theodoridis & Vassou, 2018). Luxury consumption can thus be defined as an individual behavior that to some extent can be adopted in order to obtain a determinate social position (e.g. Vigneron & Johnson, 1999).

Luxury is being interpreted in different ways depending on country of origin, culture, values, knowledge, and social background as well as economic status (Theodoridis & Vassou, 2018). Wong and Ahuvia (1998) were the first to indicate that some consumers focus more on the personal factors influencing their luxury consumer behavior than others. They showed that there are differences between the luxury consumption drivers in Confucian and Western societies. Confucian cultures, as well as other East Asian cultures, are more inclined towards an attitude of self-presentation and consider the context a stronger motivational factor. On the other hand, Western cultures value the independent self and the consumption of luxury is expected to be based on intrinsic motivations such as individual pleasure and personal needs (p. 430). In cross-cultural research, values come up as a core construct used as a moderator, as well as measurement of effects (Fischer & Poortinga, 2012, p. 159). Pozzebon and Ashton (2009) and Schwartz & Rubel (2006, p. 24) have demonstrated that there are substantial differences in values associations among various cultures. Values guide attitudes and are described as what people consider important in life (Boer & Fischer, 2013, p. 1). They are defined as guiding principles in people's lives (Schwartz, 1996), as a belief that selects means, modes and actions (Kluckhon, 1951) or as ongoing patterns of activity that are actively constructed, dynamic and evolving (Wilson, Sandoz, Kit & Roberts, 2010, p. 252).

With a focus on luxury consumption, Vigneron and Johnson (2004) propose an index to classify the two main dimensions of luxury value perception in non-personal perception and personal perception. Vigneron and Johnson's concept is displayed in figure 1.

The *non-personal value perceptions* dimension involves perceived conspicuousness, uniqueness and quality values. The **perceived conspicuousness value** of luxury is important to individuals who value status and social position. Therefore status-conscious consumers tend to see price as an indicator of luxury (Goldsmith, Reinecke, Flynn, & Kim, 2010, p. 326). Wiedmann, Hennigs & Siebels (2009, p. 645) claim that the conspicuousness value is characterized by the importance of the context and public

Figure 1. Framework of luxury brand index
Source: Vigneron & Johnson, 2004, p. 488

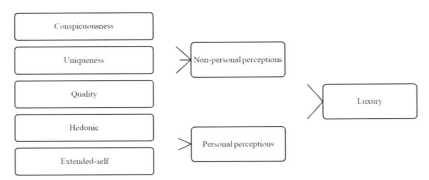

high visibility while consuming luxury. They indicate that it plays an important role in the formation of a positive attitude towards the consumption of luxury. **Uniqueness** refers to the act of seeking differentness in relation to others by purchasing, consuming and displaying something in order to boost one's selfimage and social image (Tian, Bearde, & Hunter, 2001, p. 52). It is commonly expected that luxury offers high **quality** (Vigneron & Johnson, 1999, p. 13; Dubois et al., 2005, p. 121). O'Cass and Frost (2002, p. 82) and Wiedmann et al. (2009, p. 637) claim that high quality is a value that is widely used to differentiate luxury.

The *personal value perceptions* included in the framework by Vigneron & Johnson (2004) entail the perceived hedonic and extended-self values. **Hedonic** is the value that is sought by consumers that value luxury as a personal reward and fulfilment (Vigneron & Johnson, 1999, p. 12). The concept of **extended-self** (Belk, 1988, p. 149) refers to the value of material possessions as part of the individual's own identity. In the literature, there are multiple studies that refer to the consumption of luxury as a motivation to classify or distinguish the self in relation to relevant others (Vigneron & Johnson, 2004; Dubois, et al., 2005, p. 118; Phau & Prendergast, 2001, p. 129).

According to Hennigs et al. (2012) the values driving luxury consumption are similar among different countries, but there are differences in the importance given to the individual values (p. 1018). Shukla (2012) examines the differences in the value perceptions between luxury consumers in developed and in emerging markets. The results show differences in the impact of value perception on luxury consumer behavior among Western developed and Eastern emerging countries.

Macro-Contextual Factors: Focus on Millennials in Switzerland and South Korea

There are several studies related to the attitude of millennials toward luxury. Stępień et al. investigated whether millennials are an internally consistent and distinguishable group with regard to perception of luxury. They explored five countries: Saudi Arabia, Germany, Poland, Turkey and Portugal and identified significant country specific differences (2018, pp. 148-154). Burnasheva et al. (2019) examined the impact of the values of materialism, need for uniqueness, susceptibility to informative influence, and social media usage on millennials' attitudes toward luxury in Russia and South Korea, based on the Hofstede model of cultural dimensions (Hofstede, Minkov, & Minkov, 2010). In both countries, Millennial attitudes toward luxury were strongly affected by a high need for uniqueness. Kim (2005) provided empirical evidence that the most critical factor affecting luxury consumption behavior among South Koreans is the conspicuous value. In the literature there are no studies about the impact of individual values on luxury consumption behavior in Switzerland. However, the results of the previously mentioned studies show that macro-contextual factors should be examined more closely when studying millennial's luxury consumer behavior in different countries.

Macro-contextual variables such as cultural (context and independence), economic (opportunities based on wealth), and ecological (threats due to society, disease and stress) factors impact the overall value system (Boer & Fischer, 2013, p. 2; Rohan, 2000) (figure 2).

Figure 2. Context-sensitive framework of social attitude–value links
Source: Boer & Fisher, 2013, p. 2

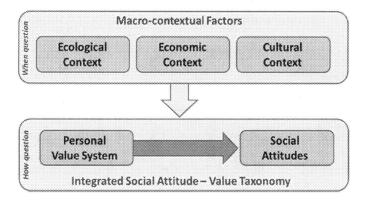

Cultural Context

Cultural orientation is seen as a critical factor in the cross-cultural luxury market (Liao & Wang, 2009). Several authors have examined the impact of different cultures on the luxury consumption attitude and purchase intention (Bian & Forsythe, 2012; Eng & Bogaert, 2010; Watson, Lysonski, Gillan & Raymore, 2002; Zhan & He, 2012). These studies focus on the comparison of Eastern consumers as collectivists and Westerners as individualists. However, the findings about cultural differences in the consumption of luxury seem to be inconsistent. Eng & Bogaert (2010, p. 55) investigate the consumption of Western luxury brands in India, and their results show critical differences between Eastern and Western cultures in the perception of luxury. Others, such as Bian & Forsythe (2012, p. 1449), claim the contrary.

The results of the survey by Hennigs et al. (2012, p. 1024) in ten countries (Brazil, France, Germany, Hungary, India, Italy, Japan, Slovakia, Spain, and the United States) showed that cultural orientation is the factor with the strongest influence on luxury goods consumption. Hennigs et al. (2012, p. 1025) emphasize that Western consumers make decisions based on their individual preference, while Eastern consumers' decisions are more influenced by society.

The potential differences that exist between the Western concept of luxury, such as in Switzerland, and the South Korean definition, have not yet been empirically examined.

Hofstede (1980) defined culture as collective mindsets that differentiate members of categories and groups and identified six cultural dimensions of cultural values: power distance, individualism, masculinity, uncertainty avoidance, long-term orientation and indulgence. Exploring Switzerland and South Korea using the 6-D Model of Hofstede helps to get a deeper understanding of the two cultures (Hofstede, Minkov & Minkov, 2010).

Hofstede's model of cultural dimensions rates each nation on a scale of 0 to 100 for each of the six dimensions and can be used as a basis to compare two cultures. The scores for the two countries Switzerland and South Korea are displayed in figure 3.

Figure 3. The 6 cultural Dimensions by Hofstede – Switzerland and South Korea
Source: Country comparison, 2020, based on Hofstede, Minkov & Minkov, 2010

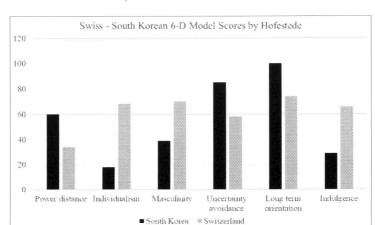

With a score of 60 South Korea is categorized as a country with a lightly hierarchical society. People accept the hierarchical order in which every individual has a place. Switzerland, with a score of 34, is ranked lower and is seen as a society that believes that inequalities amongst people should be minimized. Power in Switzerland is decentralized, and communication is direct and participative among all societal groups.

Individualism, as defined by Hofstede, et al. (2010) suggests the degree of interdependence a society maintains among its members. Individualism also refers to a society in which people are concerned with themselves and with their direct family only (Hofstede & Bond, 1984). By contrast, collectivism is the characteristic of a society by which people feel the need to belong to a group and care for the whole group in exchange for loyalty, with the group caring for the individual (Hofstede & Bond, 1984). Collectivist culture people value the behavioral norm of display of wealth by the possession of luxury (Eng & Bogaert, 2010, p. 59). As reported by Hofstede (2020) at a score of 18, South Korea is classified as a collectivist society in which people have a close long-term commitment to the group and everyone is responsible for other members of their group. Switzerland on the other hand, with a score of 68, is considered an individualistic society.

The third dimension is masculinity. As reported by Eng and Bogaert (2010, pp. 59-60) in a masculine society the consumption and possession of luxury can be attributed to success, assertion and achievement. The Hofstede (2020) country comparison indicates that Switzerland scores 70 in this dimension

There Is No Such Thing as the Millennial

and it is highly success-oriented and driven, and therefore classified as a masculine society in which people "live in order to work". South Korea contrasts with Switzerland, and is categorized as a feminine society (Hofstede, 2020). In South Korea people value equality and solidarity and the focus is on "working in order to live".

The extent to which the members of a culture feel threatened by unknown situations and try to avoid these situations is reflected in the score on uncertainty avoidance (Hofstede, et al., 2010). According to Eng and Bogaert, (2010, p. 58) a high score in uncertainty avoidance indicates a high degree of fellowship and acceptance of norms and reference groups and therefore a preference for famous and well-known luxury brands. In societies with a high score of uncertainty avoidance there is an emotional need for rules. People consider time as money and have an impulse to be busy and work hard. Innovation may resist in those cultures, but precision, punctuality and security have high priority. With a score of 85, South Korea is one of the countries with the highest degree of uncertainty avoidance in the world. The score indicates that South Korea is a country where there are rigid codes of beliefs and behaviors, and a society that is intolerant to unorthodox ideas and behaviors (Hofstede, 2020). Switzerland has a score of 58 in uncertainty avoidance which indicates a well-balanced standing between need for rules and codes and flexibility.

In the dimension "long-term orientation" Switzerland scores 74 and is therefore categorized as a pragmatic society in which people are convinced that truth depends on situation, context and time. Pragmatic societies adapt their traditions easily and tend to be more inclined to save and invest, an attitude in which thriftiness and perseverance are strongly valued. South Korea is, according to Hofstede (2020), one of the most pragmatic and long-term oriented societies. In this dimension South Korea scores 100 and is known to be a society in which people live guided by excellence and morality. Companies in South Korea are driven by the motivation to serve stakeholders and society with a longterm perspective. Long-term oriented cultures value structure in society, such as the perceived status and luxury possessions classes (Eng & Bogaert, 2010, p. 67).

The last dimension of Hofstede's Model (1984) is indulgence. One characteristic of an indulgence society is that people show a positive attitude to and enjoyment of free time (Hofstede, 2020). South Korea scores low on this dimension, at 29, and is therefore categorized as a restraint society. By contrast, Switzerland exhibits a high score. As reported by Hofstede (2020) Switzerland scores 66 in this dimension, which represents the score of an indulgence society. In Switzerland people want to enjoy life and have fun, therefore they tend to exhibit their willingness to achieve their desires and follow their impulses.

Economic Context

From an economic perspective the luxury market increases international competition and therefore sustains economic prosperity (Wiedmann & Hennigs, 2013). Wong & Ahuvia (1998, p. 437) identified a correlation between the economic wealth of a society and luxury consumption drivers. They noted that in societies with a high number of economic class levels, conspicuous consumption of luxury goods is more likely. From a societal perspective, luxury markets provide job opportunities to well-educated people (Wiedmann & Hennigs, 2013). Moreover, effective luxury markets can motivate young people to invest in education and therefore to work hard and be successful in their professional lives in order to earn the money to afford luxury items or services.

According to Lee, E., Edwards, S. M., Youn, S., & Yun, T.. (2018, p. 107), in Asian society social class is mainly determined by economic wellbeing. Therefore, the display of wealth is an important social marker in Asian societies (Lee, et al., 2018, p. 107).

The luxury market in Asia accounts for over 52% of global luxury market sales and South Korea has played an important role in the growth of the luxury market in this world region (Chadha & Husband, 2006). As reported by D'Arpizio, C., Levato, F., Prete, F., Del Fabbro, E., & Gault, C. (2018) the South Korean luxury market is the eighth largest in the world. South Korea reports a per-capita GDP of around USD 31,000 in 2018 (The World Bank, 2020), South Korea's GDP at purchasing power parity (PPP) per capita is forecast to reach USD 46,451.61 by the end of 2020 (CEIC, 2020a). By 2019, South Korea had a High-Net-Worth (HNWI) population of 243,000 individuals, ranking no. 13 in the world (Capgemini, 2020) and a total population of 51.7 million people (The World Bank, 2020). The purchasing power of the South Korean population is on the rise. The average annual household income per capita in South Korea was USD 16,174.49 in 2019 (CEIC, 2020b). As reported by the data published by Santandertrade (2020) the Gini Index is estimated at 0.316 and is expected to remain stable. This implies a moderately good overall income equality. Moreover, Santandertrade (2020) reported that Koreans over 65 are the most affected by poverty. In 2019 the employment rate in South Korea hit a record and was estimated to be 60.9% (Lee & Kim, 2020). According to Kim (2016) the seasonally adjusted jobless rate was 4.1%, and the youth unemployment rate for those aged 15-29 was 12.5%. Lim, Shaw and Liao (2020) carried out research to investigate the effect of income on happiness in South and East Asia. According to them, in South Korea income has the highest and most significant effect on happiness (Lim et al., 2020, p. 408). As stated in the Euromonitor Report (2018) on Consumer Lifestyles in South Korea, the rise of incomes and the accessibility to credit are boosting expenditure among the South Korean population. The Pew Research Center (2015) study shows that compared to the millennials of other countries, South Koreans are doubtful and pessimistic about their future. The survey reveals that only 20% of South Korean millennials claim to be satisfied with the country's government and situation. South Korea was the only country among the countries surveyed where millennials were more negative about the future than the older generations. South Korea has one of the highest percentages of millennials with an undergraduate or college degree (Parker, 2015). The millennial generation in South Korea has been nicknamed the "Given-up Generation" since young South Koreans are forced to give up many things.

Originally the expression was "the 3 Given-up Generation", referring to the fact that young Koreans were starting to give up three things due to financial insecurity: dating, marriage and childbirth. This nickname evolved into "the 5 Given-up Generation", and then "the 7 Given up Generation", and nowadays has become "N Given-up Generation" (Chong, 2016).

Switzerland is one of the most competitive economies worldwide (EDA, 2020). Wellknown as the main exporter of luxury watches in the world (Deloitte, 2019a), the country had a per-capita GDP of around USD 83,000 in 2018 (World Bank, 2020), the second highest worldwide (EDA, 2020) and an HNWI population of 438,000 in 2019, ranking no. 7 worldwide (Capgemini, 2020). The GDP PPP per capita is forecast to be USD 67,557.70 PPP by the end of 2020 (CEIC, 2020c). The highly developed service sector is the basis of Switzerland's robust economy and accounts for 74% of the country's generated GDP. Switzerland's annual household income per capita reached USD 55,422.94 in 2017 (CEIC, 2020d). The Gini Index was estimated to be 0.323 in 2017 (The World Bank, 2019). According to OECD (2020) in Switzerland 80% of people aged 15 to 64 have a paid job, and 84% of men and 75% of women are in paid work. In 2020 the unemployment rate in Switzerland was 3.3% (Trading Economics, 2020).

There Is No Such Thing as the Millennial

Looking at Switzerland overall, the average household net wealth and the employment rate are both much higher than the OECD average (OECD, 2020).

Ecological Context: Lifestyle and Trends

In the present study, the ecological factors are defined as lifestyle and trend. Lifestyle is a long-term construct introduced by Lazer (1964) used to describe and measure activities, interests and opinions. Nowadays lifestyle is a term used to indicate how people utilize their time, financial potential and energy (Ekşi & Candan, 2018). In other words, lifestyle implies how individuals manage their life and what they care about in their environment. People with a similar lifestyle share similar attitudes, beliefs, life patterns and views, as well as needs. According to this, lifestyle is a concept that can be used to classify individuals in more detail than demographic information (Ekşi & Candan, 2018). Lifestyle, defined as a way of life, has a strong influence on consumption behavior (Earl, 1986). Therefore, people with different lifestyles will show different consumption behaviors and patterns.

Among the factors that need to be mentioned when speaking of South Korean consumer lifestyle trends is that Euromonitor (2018) indicates a rapidly ageing population. Currently the median age in South Korea is approximately 48.1 years and life expectancy is approximately 82.5 years (World Population Review, 2020). This phenomenon is producing a highly stressed younger generation trying to cover the needs of the older generations (Chong, 2016). Other trends mentioned are the rise of singletons (The Economist, 2015), a strong desire to achieve work-life balance (Lee, 2019) and a growing obsession with aesthetics (Chang & Thompson, 2014; Kim, 2009).

Shopping tourism and the internet are lifestyle trends shaping consumption behavior in Switzerland, according to Euromonitor. In fact, more than 50% of late-lifers browse the internet. In addition, the Swiss consumer lifestyle is shaped by a greener living trend, especially in the food industry. A large immigrant population creates a demand for more diverse products and services and debt problems are becoming more widespread (2016).

RESEARCH PROBLEM AND AIM OF THE STUDY

Millennials around the world are one of the driving generational cohorts in the international luxury consumption. Despite the fact, that these consumers live in different contexts they are frequently treated as a homogeneous group of people. So far only a limited amount of research has been conducted to explore the impact of cultural, ecological and economic macro-contextual factors (Boer & Fischer, 2013, p. 8) on the personal value system and implications for luxury consumer behavior among millennials. This study focuses on the perception of prestige and luxury among millennials in South Korea and in Switzerland.

As many luxury companies are active internationally and thus in different cultural contexts, for a marketing strategy to be effective and positively received, intercultural differences among target audiences should be taken into account. A lack of sensitivity to cultural codes and identities can lead to inaccurate management decisions (Shukla, Singh & Banerjee, 2015, p. 265) and result in severe business damage and reputational risk, as shown, for example, by the Dolce & Gabbana "PR disaster" in China in fall 2018, where a Chinese woman trying to eat spaghetti and other typical Italian dishes with sticks was thought not at all funny among the brand's Chinese customers and the broader public, and resulted in a major backlash (Friedman & Wee, 2018).

In order to successfully communicate and specifically address their needs and desires, luxury companies must understand how their most important customer groups define and perceive luxury. While numerous studies seem to treat millennials as one coherent generational cohort across borders and cultures, there are country-specific differences (e.g. Stępień, Lima & Hinner, 2018, p. 150).

The aim of this study is to shed light on cultural and macro-contextual differences, deepen our knowledge of the individual reasons for them and determine general implications for strategic and marketing actions of luxury companies active in different geographical and cultural contexts, based on a cultural comparative research between Switzerland and South Korea.

RESEARCH QUESTIONS

Based on the literature review the following research questions are formulated:

- How do South Korean and Swiss millennials define and perceive prestige and luxury?
- What are the differences and similarities in the impact of macro-contextual factors such as culture, economic factors, lifestyle and trends on the definition and perception of luxury among millennials in the two countries of Switzerland and South Korea?
- How does the personal value system influence the intention to buy and/or consume luxury among millennials in the two countries of Switzerland and South Korea?

METHODOLOGY

Approach to Research

The present study is based on a mixed-method research, combining qualitative interviews and a survey. The chosen approach consolidates aspects of qualitative and quantitative methodologies and aimed at enhancing the overall strength of the study (Creswell & Plano Clark, 2007). After a review of the literature and the development of the theoretical and conceptual framework for the present research, the authors formulated interview questions. The interviews were conducted primarily to understand the settings, the values and the lifestyles of the participants in more depth, as well as an understanding of their perception and definition of luxury and prestige. The survey research was applied to define the impact of the personal value construct of the respondents on the intentions' specific action to buy and/or consume luxury. The final step was the evaluation, interpretation and comparison of the collected data in order to derive theoretical insight, as well as formulate recommendations for action.

Theoretical Framework

The following table (table 4) presents the topics that formed the qualitative part of the research and the relevant questions. Through qualitative interviews, the study investigated what influences the definition as well as the perception of luxury and prestige among millennials in the two countries of South Korea and Switzerland.

Table 4. Constructs of the qualitative theoretical framework

Construct	Relevant questions
Individual values	What values are important for Millennials in Switzerland and in South Korea, and what is important for them in relation to their life?
Interpersonal and social values	What values are important for the reference groups or for the society of Swiss and South Korean Millennials?
Cultural values	What cultural values shape the attitudes to luxury among South Korean and Swiss Millennials?
Economic factors	To which degree economic factors such as income and employment shape the attitude toward luxury among South Korean and Swiss Millennials?
Lifestyle and trends	To what degree do lifestyle and trends factors shape the attitude toward luxury among South Korean and Swiss Millennials?
Definition and perception of luxury and prestige	How do South Korean and Swiss Millennials define and perceive luxury and prestige and what are the key characteristics they associate with these two terms?

Source: Pedrazzi, 2020

Conceptual Framework

For the quantitative part, to better understand the impact of the personal values system on the intention to buy luxury among Swiss and South Korean millennials this study examines a number of variables (figure 4). Understanding the impact of these variables and the purchasing intention among millennials in the two countries offers useful insights. Individual values and social values are examined as variables that might influence young South Korean and Swiss consumers purchasing and/or consuming luxury.

As personal values variables this study identifies materialism, conformity, need for uniqueness, and vanity, as well as social recognition. The individual and social values relate to the study by Park et al. (2008). The following framework presents the relationships that were investigated.

The definitions of all constructs of the proposed conceptual quantitative model are listed in table 5.

Figure 4. Conceptual framework of the quantitative research
Source: adapted from Park et al., 2008

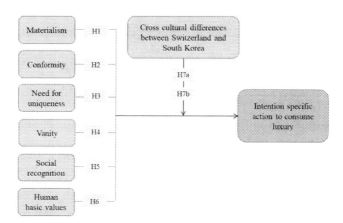

Table 5. Constructs of the quantitative theoretical framework

Construct	Definition
Materialism	Degree to which South Korean and Swiss Millennials value luxury possession and see it as particularly essential to their identity and lives.
Conformity	Degree to which reference groups such as family, friends and society influence the luxury consumption behavior of South Korean and Swiss Millennials.
Need for uniqueness	Represents the opposite of conformity and refers to the degree to which South Korean and Swiss Millennials actively seek to differentiate themselves from others.
Vanity	Extent to which South Korean and Swiss Millennials are concerned with their physical appearance and with their personal achievements.
Social recognition	The likelihood that people close to South Korean and Swiss Millennials are aware of their purchasing and/or consuming luxury products and/or services. People close to can be relatives or friends.
Human basic values	Degree to which the human basic values identified by Schwartz (1992) are anchored across South Korean and Swiss Millennials.
Intention to consume luxury	The likelihood to which South Korean and Swiss Millennials intend to purchase and/or consume luxury products and/or services within the next year period.
Cross cultural differences between Switzerland and South Korea	The impact of the cultural differences of Switzerland and South Korea on the construct that influences the definition of luxury and prestige as well as the intention to purchase and/or consume luxury products and/or services.

Source: Pedrazzi (2020), adapted from Park et al.(2008)

Hypotheses

Again for the quantitative part of the study, it has been hypothesized that individual and social as well as macro-economic factors such as cultural, and economic factors along with lifestyle and trends have an impact on the definition and perception of luxury. Therefore, differences toward the definition of luxury and prestige among the two research groups are being assumed. The following hypotheses have been formulated based on the conceptual framework (figure 4):

H1: Materialism is positively correlated with the individual's intention to purchase luxury.
H2: Conformity is positively correlated with the individual's intention to purchase luxury.
H3: Need for uniqueness is positively correlated with the individual's intention to purchase luxury.
H4: Vanity is positively correlated with the individual's intention to purchase luxury.
H5: Social recognition is positively correlated with the individual's intention to purchase luxury.
H6: The importance of the human basic values is positively correlated with the individual's intention to purchase luxury.

The hypotheses H1 to H6 measure the impact of the personal value system on the intention to buy and/or consume luxury among South Korean and Swiss millennials. The study investigates whether these six values are positively correlated with the intention to buy luxury. Moreover, a cross-cultural comparison of the relationship between values and luxury consumption attitude is examined. Therefore, the following two hypotheses have been formulated:

H7a: Materialism, conformity, need for uniqueness, vanity and social recognition are more pronounced among millennials in South Korea than in Switzerland and therefore have a greater impact on the individual's intention to purchase luxury.

There Is No Such Thing as the Millennial

H7b: There are significant differences toward the importance of the human basic values among Swiss and South Korean millennials; human basic values (HBV) therefore have a greater impact on a South Korean individual's intention to purchase luxury of than that of a Swiss individual.

DATA COLLECTION TECHNIQUES

To collect the data, we applied a concurrent triangulation design, whereby the qualitative and the quantitative data were both collected and analyzed at the same time (Creswell, 2009, p. 213).

Pretest

After developing the interview questions, the interview guide was evaluated in a pretest. The interview guide was tested under field conditions, within the planned target group and under the planned conditions This was to ensure that the interview guide could be used under the defined conditions and would lead to the desired results. After the evaluation of the pretest the structure of the interview guide, the clarity of the questions, and suitability to the participants were assessed as being satisfactory.

Interviews

30 semi-structured interviews were conducted. The interviewees were selected based on two research criteria: nationality (Swiss or South Korean) and age (millennials). To guarantee a differentiated interviewee sample the same amount of female and male interviewees were chosen. The majority of interviews lasted between 30 to 45 minutes. For those interviews, meetings with the interviewee were arranged. In four interviews (two in South Korea and two in Switzerland) the interview guide was shortened, and the interviews lasted between 15 and 20 minutes. Those interviews were taken on the street with a random interviewee.

The interviews were structured in three parts: 1.demographic information including age, nationality, gender, education, employment, income and expenses, 2.ten open-ended questions about the personal values and lifestyle of the participants and 3. 17 openended questions about perception and attitude towards luxury and prestige as well as about luxury consumption. Follow-up questions were asked to gain a deeper understanding of the participants' perspectives, thus improving the qualitative comprehension of the investigated topic and to avoid miscomprehension. The interviews were recorded and transcribed. In a second step the interview transcripts were transferred to the qualitative and mixed methods data analysis tool MAXQDA for evaluation.

Online Survey

To get a deeper understanding of the research field and to gain quantitative information about the values shaping the attitude and consumption of luxury in the two countries of Switzerland and South Korea, a survey questionnaire was developed. In this study the survey was conducted in the form of an online survey, which was widely circulated via social media and email. The online survey questionnaire was programmed with the online tool Questback EFS and widely distributed through Swiss and South Korean social media platforms such as WhatsApp, KaKao Talk and Facebook as well as via email.

There Is No Such Thing as the Millennial

The questionnaire used for the online survey contained measures for personal values (materialism, conformity, need for uniqueness, and vanity), social recognition and specific intention toward purchasing luxury products and/or services. Moreover, the questionnaire included demographics (age, education and employment status, income, expenses and consumption frequency of luxury). To ensure a logical structure, the survey was divided into nine sections. The sections of the online survey and the scales used to measure the values are displayed in table 6.

Table 6. Measured constructs online survey

Construct	Items	Scale	Source
Materialism	18 items	Five-point Likert scale: "strongly disagree – disagree – neutral – agree – strongly agree" correspondent to the numbers "1 to 5"	Richins and Dowson (1992, p.310)
Conformity	12 items	Five-point Likert scale: "strongly disagree – disagree – neutral – agree – strongly agree" correspondent to the numbers "1 to 5"	Bearden et al. (1989, pp. 477-479)
Need for uniqueness	31 items	Five-point Likert scale: "strongly disagree – disagree – neutral – agree – strongly agree" correspondent to the numbers "1 to5"	Tian et al. (2001, pp. 55-56)
Vanity	21 items	Five-point Likert scale: "strongly disagree – disagree – neutral – agree – strongly agree" correspondent to the numbers "1 to 5"	Netemeyer. et al. (1995, p. 624)
Social recognition	1 item	Seven-point Likert scale. "extremely unlikely – very unlikely – unlikely – neutral – likely – very likely – extremely likely" correspondent to the numbers "-3 to 3"	Netemeyer et al. (1995, p. 624)
Intention Specific Action	1 item	Seven-point Likert scale: "extremely unlikely – very unlikely – unlikely – neutral – likely – very likely – extremely likely" correspondent to the numbers "-3 to 3"	Ajzen and Fishbein (1980)
Human basic values	10 items	Nine-point Likert scale: 8 (of supreme importance) - 7 (very important) - 6 (important) - 5 - 4 (important) - 2 - 1 (not important) - 0 (opposed to my values)	Schwartz (1992, p. 17)

Source: Pedrazzi, 2020

Validation Procedures

A mixed methods research approach requires the use of validity procedures for both the qualitative findings and the quantitative data (Creswell, 2009). According to Gibbs (2010) the validity of qualitative findings checks the accuracy and the qualitative reliability indicates the consistency of the collected data.

The key concepts of this study are reported as they are gathered in the field. In order to validate the qualitative findings, the biases that may be brought to the study are displayed and clarified. Another factor that may enhance the validity of qualitative findings is the prolonged time spent in the research field (Creswell, 2009), which results in the development of an in-depth understanding of the research circumstance and of the group studied. Due to an exchange semester, the main author was able to spend a prolonged period in South Korea. This enabled the researcher to establish a relationship with the South Korean target group of the study in the actual setting.

To determine the accuracy of the findings of this study, the member checking method was used. A follow-up interview with one member of the Swiss interview group and one member of the South Korean interview group was conducted. In the follow-up interview the key findings of the research were disclosed and the interviewees had the opportunity to comment on the findings and express whether they think the findings are accurate or not. To determine the consistency and reliability of the collected qualitative data of this study the procedure of the data collection was documented. The quality of the data collection through the quantitative method was evaluated by its objectivity, reliability and validity. The objectiv-

There Is No Such Thing as the Millennial

ity of the survey results is ensured by the fact that the collected data are evaluated using standardized methods. To check the reliability of the measured construct, Cronbach's alpha scores were evaluated.

The internal validity of the model includes content and construct validity. For the present research model, constructs and items are adapted from previous published studies, therefore the content and construct internal validity are ensured. The external validity grasps the extent of generalizability of the results (Hussy & Echterhoff, 2013, p. 137). Since the survey of this study was conducted in Switzerland and in South Korea, the results cannot be generalized and the external validity of this study is therefore limited.

The validation criteria for the qualitative and the quantitative data collection were followed during the whole research process. The interview guide and the questionnaire were corrected and translated by Korean native speakers to guarantee reliability. Moreover, pretests, as displayed above, were implemented to test the interview guide as well as the questionnaire for the online survey.

Data Interpretation Techniques

For the interpretation and analysis of the collected qualitative data in this study a qualitative contents analysis (Ryan & Bernard, 2000) using MAXQDA was used. For the interpretation and analysis of the quantitative data collected using the online survey method, SPSS Statistics software was used. All the interviews conducted were recorded and documented in audio recording form and field notes and postscripts were written by the interviewer immediately after each interview. The postscripts were meant to include the particularities of each interview. To ensure a systematic interpretation of the collected qualitative data all the interviews were transcribed by the researcher. At the start of the process the entire interview records were transcribed to avoid an unconscious preselection of the collected material. After that, the transcribed material was analyzed and then arranged using a selective method and using the interview guide as a template to reduce and categorize the data. To categorize the data a codebook was developed. The analysis of the interviews that are relevant to the response of the research questions of this study are presented in the results section.

The data from both surveys (the one in English and the one in Korean) were downloaded directly, merged and saved in SPSS-compatible files. The incomplete samples were identified and coded with SPSS. Partial samples and samples considered to be invalid were excluded from the data analysis. To ensure clean data, the variable names, types and scales were adjusted to the measured constructs.

Analysis of the quantitative results were divided into descriptive and inferential analyses. The characteristics of the variables as well as of the data sample were analyzed following descriptive analysis methods. The main descriptive techniques adopted to analyze the quantitative data of this study are correlation and cross-tabulation. To reduce the scale of the variable items an exploratory factor analysis was executed in SPSS. A confirmatory factor analysis was done to test the unidimensionality of the variable and create factor scores in order to do the correlation and regression analysis. In addition, other inferential analysis was generated in order to gain insights from the collected data. T-test, Anova and regression and variance analysis are presented in the following chapters. The collected data, their analysis and findings are described in the results section. In a final step, both qualitative insights and the survey results were compared to determine any convergence or differences, or possible combinations thereof (Creswell, 2009).

RESEARCH FINDINGS

Definition and Perception of Prestige

Prestige is defined by high quality, social influence, achievement and material possessions. Accordingly, prestige is perceived as a form of exclusivity and acknowledgment. The findings show that South Korean millennials refer to influence much more than Swiss millennials when talking about the definition and perception of prestige.

Both groups of respondents refer to prestige as something that is admired, that not everyone can get but that everyone would like to have. They underline the fact that prestige is admiration given by doing something special or being something extraordinary. High quality, special, success, social influence, noble and precious are words that were used by the respondents to describe prestige. The respondents mainly reported that prestige is strongly correlated with social recognition and admiration. In the following tables (7 and 8) the most relevant definitions of prestige of the two groups are reported.

Table 7. Interview Quotes about the definition of Prestige – Swiss sample

Interview quotes – definition of prestige – Swiss millennials
"If I describe something or somebody as prestigious that means that they are regarded by others as being the best or of the best." (Interview CH2, personal communication, 04.04.2020)
"I mean prestige is kind of a positive reputation that someone or something has." (Interview CH5, personal communication, 05.04.2020)
"I would say that prestige is external, externally generated. You can't tell yourself you have prestige; it has to be other people looking at a person and holding them in high regard." (Interview CH8, personal communication, 18.04.2020)

Source: Pedrazzi, 2020

Table 8. Interview Quotes about the definition of Prestige – South Korean sample

Interview quotes – definition of prestige – South Korean millennials
"For me being prestigious means being famous in a positive way. If someone has prestige people around them admire them." (Interview SK2, personal communication, 04.02.2020)
"Prestige requires good reputation too, even though people think it means only money." (Interview SK2, personal communication, 05.02.2020)
"For me prestige means social success." (Interview SK11, personal communication, 08.02.2020)
"Prestige is something that people get when they show off" (Interview SK14, personal communication, 09.02.2020)

Source: Pedrazzi, 2020

The definition of prestige presented by the respondents are in line with the definition of prestige found in the literature. The overall perception of prestige can be assessed as positive particularly because of the strong association of prestige with admiration and respect presented by the respondents. Some differences are identified among the Swiss and South Korean respondents. South Korean millennials tend to define and perceive prestige according to the group. Moreover, the analysis reveals that the associating factor of a personal experience and prestige is mainly based on acknowledgment. Those findings reflect

There Is No Such Thing as the Millennial

the characteristics of the collectivist South Korean culture. On the other hand, Swiss millennials seem to be more concerned about themselves than about the group. Indeed, they describe prestige as a pleasant feeling as well as exclusive experience and skills.

Definition and Perception of Luxury

One difference towards the definition of luxury among the two groups of respondents is that the Swiss often referred to luxury as something that is not necessary, something that is above the basic individual needs. Some examples are shown in table 9.

Table 9. Interview Quotes about the definition of Luxury – Swiss sample

Interview quotes – definition of luxury - Swiss millennials
"Luxury is something that goes above our basic needs. I would say it is like an add-on." (Interview CH1, personal communication, 27.03.2020)
"So, I would say luxury is everything above necessary and functional." (Interview CH2, personal communication, 02.04.2020)
"Luxury is not necessary, but it is nice to have." (Interview CH4, personal communication, 02.04.2020)
"Luxury cars are for me the best example of luxury, if someone needs a car it makes sense to buy a car, but like buying a Ferrari or Porsche is definitely a luxury. Because the car is necessary, the luxury car is an excess. For bags it's actually the same. If you need a bag you can buy an H&M bag, you don't have to buy an expensive Hermes bag." (Interview CH5, personal communication, 03.04.2020)
"For me, luxury is everything above what you need. If you need two pairs of shoes the third pair of shoes is a luxury." (Interview CH7, personal communication, 04.04.2020)
"I don't think that luxury has to be expensive, for me luxury is what you don't need." (Interview CH7, personal communication, 04.04.2020)

Source: Pedrazzi, 2020

By contrast, the South Korean respondents only sporadically refer to the unnecessary aspect of luxury and seemingly focus more on the expensive aspect of luxury, as the following quotes show (table 10).

Table 10. Interview Quotes about the definition of Luxury – South Korean sample

Interview quotes – definition of luxury - South Korean millennials
"For me luxury is something that is over my budget." (Interview SK1, personal communication, 04.02.2020)
"Luxury products are expensive. You can usually have similar products that are cheaper, have maybe inferior quality but still good products, not everything that is not luxurious is trash." (Interview SK2, personal communication, 04.02.2020)
"When I think about luxury the first thing that comes to my mind is something expensive and special." (Interview SK9, personal communication, 07.02.2020)

Source: Pedrazzi, 2020

When talking about the definition and perception of luxury the differences among the two groups of respondents are more marked. Swiss millennials refer to luxury as something that is not necessary, something above their basic needs. On the other hand, South Korean millennials focus more on the monetary value aspect of luxury and refer to it as something that is very expensive and typically over their budget. South Koreans perceive uncertainty about the future, while in contrast, Swiss millennials demonstrate a very positive attitude to luxury and report being regular luxury consumers.

The cultural aspects, in particular South Korean collectivism, seem to have an impact on the definition and perception of luxury among millennials. Moreover, the South Korean millennials show insecurities about the future and this results in a skeptical perception of luxury, as illustrated with the interview quote below.

"Being rich doesn't always make you happy but being poor always makes you sad." (Interview SK3, personal communication, February 5, 2020).

In Switzerland, the most marked luxury aspect was related to the fact that luxury is something that is not necessary. This said, Swiss millennials seem to know how to enjoy life and thanks to their working and financial stability they suggest being positive and confident about luxury.

"I think it is very important to be happy about the little things before starting to consume luxury." (Interview CH7, personal communication, April 4, 2020).

Macro-Contextual Impact

Economic as well as cultural factors seem to influence the perception of luxury especially among the South Korean respondents. The collectivistic aspects of South Korean culture have a strong influence on the definition and perception of luxury. Respondents in South Korea repeatedly report being very concerned about how society judges them, or more precisely about being aware of the importance of others' views. Social recognition has high importance among South Korean millennials.

Another aspect that has an impact on the definition and perception of luxury is their economic situation. South Korean millennials with stable incomes report consuming luxury regularly. On the other hand, respondents who are still studying and don't have substantial incomes seem to be skeptical about the future and about being able to consume luxury on a regular basis. Swiss millennials consume luxury based on hedonistic motivational factors. South Korean millennials seem to enjoy more conspicuous and recognition factors linked to the consumption of luxury. Achieving and progressing in a career is very important among millennials in the two countries. This can be explained by the fact that both countries have a strong economy and the quality of life is on average good. Therefore, a career is seen as the way to attain certain status in life and society.

The Swiss respondents in particular reported a career being very important in their lives, *"I can't imagine my life without work because it is such a big part in our lives."* (Interviewee CH2, personal communication, April 2, 2020).

Personal Values

The values that are most positively correlated with the consumption of luxury are conformity and social recognition. This applies to both groups of respondents. The qualitative results indicate that social recognition has a strong impact on the definition and perception of luxury and prestige. In contrast to the qualitative results, the quantitative results show that conformity has a stronger impact than social recognition and both factors have a stronger impact among South Korean millennials than among Swiss

There Is No Such Thing as the Millennial

millennials. The variables materialism, need for uniqueness and vanity do not have a statistically significant impact on the intention to buy and/or consume luxury. On average the variables materials, need for uniqueness, vanity and social recognition have higher importance among the South Korean respondents.

Surprisingly, the conformity variable is reported as being more important for the Swiss respondents, but the result is not statistically significant. The only result that demonstrated statistical significance is the difference in the social recognition value. Therefore, the social recognition is positively related to the intention to buy and/or consume luxury for both research groups. It has a higher importance among South Korean millennials than Swiss millennials. This result supports the qualitative findings.

CONCLUSION

The luxury industry is growing and the meaning of luxury and prestige is not static across countries and generations. The influence of younger consumers is gaining importance among luxury brands. Millennials are expected to account for 50% of the spending in the personal luxury market by 2025. The ability to communicate to customers is extremely important. In order to develop marketing campaigns that specifically address millennials, it is paramount to understand how they define and perceive luxury and prestige. Moreover, divergences among different countries must be clarified in order to assess the need for country or culture-specific marketing campaigns.

Based on the presented empirical study with Swiss and South Korean respondents, a variety of factors have been shown to influence the definition and perception of luxury and prestige. There are clearly different perceptions and intentions towards luxury among Swiss and South Korean millennials. The differences are explained through several factors, including the macro-contextual factors of economic and cultural as well as lifestyle and trends.

Swiss and South Korean millennials tend to define luxury and prestige in a way that corresponds with the definitions presented in the existing literature. A shift in the perception of luxury from a material concept to an experience is marked among the groups of respondents. Luxury is mainly perceived as something exclusive and special, that not everyone can get. Swiss millennials, however, tend to define luxury more as something that is not necessary and that represents something that cannot be attained readily. On the other hand, South Korean millennials refer to luxury as something expensive and something than not everyone can afford.

Prestige is seen as acknowledgment and respect based on perceived qualities and/or performance. Both groups define prestige as respect and admiration and something that has a higher importance than luxury, but that is also more abstract. South Korean millennials define prestige as respect and social influence whereas Swiss millennials refer to prestige as something exclusive. Social recognition has a significant positive impact on the intention to consume luxury and is perceived more strongly among South Korean millennials than Swiss millennials. Swiss millennials, on the contrary, tend to value freedom and the individual self.

RECOMMENDATIONS

The results of this study indicate a managerial need to develop country-specific marketing campaigns in order to address millennials and stimulate their luxury consumption. The collectivistic South Korean culture has an impact on how millennials in South Korea define and perceive luxury and luxury companies must address potential customers there differently from their target customers in Switzerland. In Switzerland millennials are more focused on themselves and on their own needs. The insights gained from this study demonstrate, that even if the world appears to be globalized and cultures and traditions seem to be slowly losing importance among younger generations, there are still significant differences which should be taken into account by companies selling their products and services internationally. The relevance of understanding intercultural differences and life contexts of target groups has been demonstrated by the major negative repercussions of marketing activities by major luxury and fashion brands that lacked a sufficient understanding of culture and context, especially when addressing millennials. While due to the ongoing globalization and digitalization of cultures there might indeed be some similarities across generational cohorts with different cultural backgrounds, macro-contextual factors and, based on this, differences in preferences and consumer behavior, must be understood by marketers to tailor global campaigns to the persisting and continuously evolving cultural diversity of consumers and their relative life contexts.

LIMITATIONS

With regards to the research methods used, several limitations need to be addressed. The online questionnaire sample size is significantly too small and the results thus not generalizable. The findings based on the questionnaire cannot be considered statistically significant. Moreover, the distribution of the participants among the two research groups cannot be considered representative. Since only 43 South Korean millennials completed the online questionnaire, the results cannot be generalized and/or transferred. The online questionnaire was translated into Korean in order to raise participant numbers. In order to generate more responses to the survey used in the study, the researchers suggest shortening the survey and investigating the included constructs separately. By investigating a single construct, the online survey would be much shorter, which might have a positive influence on the response rate. Moreover, to add depth and contextual insight, ethnographic research methods should be included. This would potentially reduce weaknesses of the chosen methodology, such as biases that can occur during interview and in surveys.

The Cronbach's Alpha of the materialism variable is not satisfactory, therefore the items used to measure the value seemed to be non-applicable. The items were adapted from previous published studies and no changes were made to their structure. Moreover, the human basic values are shown to not be a valid variable for the presented conceptual model. The SSVS (The short Schwartz's value survey) was not adapted to be measured as an independent value. Therefore, the use of human basic values as measurement to rate their impact on an intention value is not recommended.

FUTURE RESEARCH DIRECTIONS

This study contributes to the literature of luxury consumer behavior considering the macro-contextual factors, specifically in the cohort of millennials. The understanding of cultural and macro-contextual factors and their impact on consumer behavior, also among specific generational cohorts, is a relevant insight for future research in this field.

In this study, luxury and prestige are investigated as generalized constructs, not addressing potential differences among specific luxury categories. In future studies, the chosen study methodology could be adopted and applied to specific categories of luxury, in order to generate insights with a closer link to a particular context and different product categories. Furthermore, the research design underlying the study could be adopted to study other countries, cultural contexts or different generational cohorts.

Macro-contextual factors, as researched in this study, can have an impact on the personal value system before other influencing factors. Therefore, as a first step, the impact of cultural, economic and lifestyle factors on the personal value system and, by extension, on status and prestige consumption, should be further investigated. Moreover, the impact of product or brandspecific values could be included. Further research could aim to investigate the impact of cultural values and respective value perceptions on the image of luxury brands, enabling marketers to employ a more differentiated way of targeting and addressing this generational group and building a key element in a marketing strategy to address millennials and younger cohorts such as Generation Z in an appropriate and profitable way.

REFERENCES

Beldona, S., Demicco, F., & Nusair, K. (2009). Online travel purchase behavior of generational cohorts: A longitudinal study. *Journal of Hospitality Marketing & Management*, *18*(4), 406–420. doi:10.1080/19368620902799627

Belk, R. W. (1988). Possessions and the extended self. *The Journal of Consumer Research*, *15*(2), 139–168. doi:10.1086/209154

Beverland, M. (2004). Uncovering 'theories-in-use': Building luxury wine brands. *European Journal of Marketing*, *38*(3/4), 446–466. doi:10.1108/03090560410518648

Bian, Q., & Forsythe, S. (2012). Purchase intention for luxury brands: A cross cultural comparison. *Journal of Business Research*, *65*(10), 1443–1451. doi:10.1016/j.jbusres.2011.10.010

Blackwell, R. D., Paul, W. M., & James, F. E. (2005). *Consumer behavior* (10th ed.). Thomson Learning.

Boer, D., & Fischer, R. (2013). How and when do personal values guide our attitudes and sociality? Explaining cross-cultural variability in attitude–value linkages. *Psychological Bulletin*, *139*(5), 1113–1147. Advance online publication. doi:10.1037/a0031347 PMID:23339521

Burnasheva, R., Gusuh, Y., & Villalobos-Moron, K. (2019). Factors affecting millennials' attitudes toward luxury fashion brands: A cross cultural study. *International Business Research*, *12*(6), 69–81. doi:10.5539/ibr.v12n6p69

Capgemini Financial Services Analysis. 2018,) -. Retrieved 25 September 2020 from https:// https:// asiapacificwealthreport.com/reports/population/asia-pacific/south-korea/

CEIC. (2020a). *South Korea forecast GDP PPP per capita*. Retrieved 29 April 2020 from https://www. ceicdata.com/en/indicator/korea/forecast-gdp-ppp-per-capita

CEIC. (2020b). *South Korea household income per capita*. Retrieved 29 April 2020 from https://www. ceicdata.com/en/indicator/korea/annual-household-income-per-capita

CEIC. (2020c). *Switzerland forecast GDP PPP per capita.* Retrieved 29 April 2020 from https://www.ceicdata.com/en/indicator/switzerland/forecast-gdp-ppp-per-capita

CEIC. (2020d). *Switzerland household income per capita.* Retrieved 29 April 2020 from https://www.ceicdata.com/en/indicator/switzerland/annual-household-income-per-capita

Chadha, R., & Husband, P. (2006). *The cult of the luxury brand: inside Asia's love affair with luxury.* Nicholas Brealey International.

Chang, J., & Thompson, V. (2014). *South Korea's Growing Obsession with Cosmetic Surgery.* abcNews. Retrieved 13 October 2020 from https://abcnews.go.com/Lifestyle/south-koreas-growing-obsession-cosmetic-surgery/story?id=24123409

Chong, K. (2016). *South Korea's troubled millennial generation.* Retrieved 29 April 2020 from https://cmr.berkeley.edu/blog/2016/4/south-korea/

Creswell, J. W. (2009). *Research design qualitative, quantitative, and mixed mehtods approaches* (3rd ed.). SAGE.

Creswell, J. W., & Plano Clark, V. L. (2007). *Designing and conducting mixed method research.* SAGE.

Cristini, H., Kauppinen-Räisänen, H., Barthod-Prothade, M., & Woodside, A. (2017). Toward a general theory of luxury: Advancing from workbench definitions and theoretical transformations. *Journal of Business Research, 2017*(70), 101–107. doi:10.1016/j.jbusres.2016.07.001

D'Arpizio, C., Levato, F., Prete, F., Del Fabbro, E., & Gault, C. (2018). *Luxury goods worldwide market study fall–winter 2018 - The future of luxury: A look into tomorrow to understand today.* Boston: Bain and Company.

D'Arpizio, C., Levato, F., Prete, F., & Gault, C. (2020). *Eight themes that are rewriting the future of luxury goods.* Bain & Company.

Deloitte. (2019a). Global Powers of Luxury Goods 2019. Shaping the future of the luxury industry. Milan: Deloitte Italy S.p.A.

Deloitte. (2019b). *The Deloitte global millennial survey 2019: Societal discord and technological transformation create a "generation disrupted".* Deloitte AG.

DeVaney, S. A. (2015). Understanding the millennial generation. *Journal of Financial Service Professionals, 69*(6), 11–14.

Dimock, M. (2019). *Defining generations: Where millennials end and generation z begins.* Pew Research Center. Retrieved 13 April 2020 from https://www.pewresearch.org/fact-tank/2019/01/17/where-millennials-end-and-generation-z-begins/

Doss, F., & Robinson, T. (2013). Luxury perceptions: Luxury brand vs counterfeit for young US female consumers. *Journal of Fashion Marketing and Management, 17*(4), 424–439. doi:10.1108/JFMM-03-2013-0028

Dubois, B., & Czellar, S. (2002). *Prestige brands or luxury brands? An exploratory inquiry on consumer perceptions.* University of Geneva.

There Is No Such Thing as the Millennial

Dubois, B., Czellar, S., & Laurent, G. (2005). Consumer segments based on attitudes toward luxury: Empirical evidence from twenty countries. *Marketing Letters, 16*(2), 115–128. doi:10.100711002-005-2172-0

Earl, P. E. (1986). *Lifestyle economics: Consumer behaviour in a turbulent world*. Palgrave Macmillan.

EDA. (2020). *Swiss Economy – Facts and Figures*. Retrieved 29 April 2020 from https://www.eda.admin.ch/aboutswitzerland/en/home/wirtschaft/uebersicht/wirtschaft---fakten-und-zahlen.html

Ekşi, O., & Candan, F. B. (2018). The effect of lifestyle on conspicuous consumption. In F. B. C. & H. Kapucu (Eds.), Current debates in business studies (pp. 109-125). London: OPEC Art Design.

Eng, T.-Y., & Bogaert, J. (2010). Psychological and cultural insights into consumption of luxury Western brands in India. *Journal of Consumer Behaviour, 9*(1), 55–75. doi:10.1362/147539210X497620

Euromonitor. (2016). *Consumer Lifestyles in Switzerland*. Retrieved 29 April 2020 from https://www.euromonitor.com/consumer-lifestyles-in-switzerland/report

Euromonitor. (2018). *Consumer Lifestyles in South Korea*. Retrieved 29 April 2020 from https://www.euromonitor.com/consumer-lifestyles-in-south-korea/report

Fischer, R., & Poortinga, Y. H. (2012). Are cultural values the same as the values of individuals? *International Journal of Cross Cultural Management, 12*(2), 157–170. doi:10.1177/1470595812439867

Gibbs, G. R. (2010). *Analyzing qualitative data*. SAGE.

Godey, B., Pederzoli, D., Aiello, G., Donvito, R., Wiedmann, K.-P., & Hennigs, N. (2012). An Intercultural Comparison of the perception of Luxury by Young Consumers. In K.-P. Wiedmann & N. Hennigs (Eds.), *Luxury Marketing* (pp. 59–76). Springer.

Goldsmith, R. E., Reinecke Flynn, L., & Kim, D. (2010). Status consumption and price sensitivity. *Journal of Marketing Theory and Practice, 18*(4), 323–338. doi:10.2753/MTP1069-6679180402

Grossman, G. M., & Shapiro, C. (1988). Counterfeit-product trade. *The American Economic Review, 78*(1), 59–75.

Hennigs, N., Wiedmann, K.-P., Klarmann, C., Strehlau, S., Godey, B., Pederzoli, D., Neulinger, A., Kartik, D., Aiello, G., Donvito, R., Taro, K., Tàboreckà-Petrovicovà, J., Rodrìguez Santos, C., Jung, J., & Oh, H. (2012). What is the Value of Luxury? A cross-cultural consumer perspective. *Psychology and Marketing, 29*(12), 1018–1034. doi:10.1002/mar.20583

Herawati, H., Prajanti, S. D. W., & Kardoyo, K. (2019). Predicted purchasing decisions from lifestyle, product quality and price through purchase motivation. *The Journal of Economic Education, 8*(1), 1–11.

Hofstede, G. (1980). *Culture's consequences: International differences in work-related values*. SAGE.

Hofstede, G., & Bond, H. M. (1984). Hofstede's culture dimensions: An independent validation using Rokeach's value survey. *Journal of Cross-Cultural Psychology, 15*(4), 417–433. doi:10.1177/0022002184015004003

Hofstede, G. H., Minkov, G. J., & Minkov, M. (2010). *Cultures and organizations: Software for the mind* (3rd ed.). McGraw-Hill Professional.

Hofstede. (2020). *Country comparison.* Retrieved 05 May 2020 from https://www.hofstede-insights.com/country-comparison/south-korea,switzerland/

Howe, N., & Strauss, B. (2000). *Millennials rising: The next great generation.* Vintage.

Hussy, W., Schreier, M., & Echterhoff, G. (2013). *Forschungsmethoden in Psychologie und Sozialwissenschaften für Bachelor* (2nd ed.). Springer. doi:10.1007/978-3-642-34362-9

Kapferer, J.-N., & Bastien, V. (2009). *The Luxury Strategy: Break the Rules of Marketing to Build Luxury Brands.* Kogan Page.

Kapferer, J.-N., & Valette-Florence, P. (2016). Beyond rarity: The paths of luxury desire. How luxury brands grow yet remain desirable. *Journal of Product and Brand Management, 25*(2), 120–133. doi:10.1108/JPBM-09-2015-0988

Kim, C. (2016). *South Korea unemployment rate jumps to six-year high at 4.1%.* Bloomberg. Retrieved 25. May 2020 from https://www.bloomberg.com/news/articles/2016-03-16/south-korea-unemployment-rate-jumps-to-six-year-high-at-4-1

Kim, H. (2009). *The Plastic Surgery Obsession in South Korea.* Syracuse University Honors Program Capstone Projects, 485.

Kim, S.-S. (2005). The study about masstige high-end products (Part I) - Focusing on values. *Journal of Korean Society of Clothing and Textiles, 29*(11), 1381–1388.

Kluckhohn, C. (1951). Values and value-orientations in the theory of action: an exploration in definition and classification. In T. S. E. Parsons (Ed.), *Toward a General Theory of Action* (pp. 388–433). Harvard University Press. doi:10.4159/harvard.9780674863507.c8

Ko, E., Costello, J. P., & Taylor, C. R. (2019). What is a luxury brand? A new definition and review of the literature. *Journal of Business Research, 2019*(99), 405–413. doi:10.1016/j.jbusres.2017.08.023

Lauper, J. (2020). *Evolving Luxuriousness. A Cross-Generational Analysis of the Swiss Value Perception and Consumer Behavior of Luxury* (Bachelor Thesis). Zurich University of Applied Sciences, School of Management and Law.

Lazer, W. (1964). Lifestyle concepts and marketing. In S. A. Greyser (Ed.), *Toward scientific marketing* (pp. 243–252). American Marketing Association.

Lee, E., Edwards, S. M., Youn, S., & Yun, T. (2018). Understanding the moderating effect of motivational values on young consumers' responses to luxury brands: A cross-cultural study of South Korea and the USA. *Journal of Marketing Communications, 24*(2), 103–124. doi:10.1080/13527266.2014.975830

Lee, J., & Kim, S. (2020). *Record South Korean employment leans on part-timers.* Bloomberg. Retrieved 29 April 2020 from https://www.bloomberg.com/news/articles/2020-01-14/

Lee, K. (2019). More Koreans pursuing work-life balance. *Korea Times.* Retrieved 13 October 2020 from https://www.koreatimes.co.kr/www/biz/2020/04/367_280533.html

Liao, J., & Wang, L. (2009). Face as a mediator of the relationship between material value and brand consciousness. *Psychology and Marketing*, *26*(11), 987–1001. doi:10.1002/mar.20309

Lim, H., Shaw, D., Liao, P., & Duan, H. (2020). The effects of income on happiness in east and south Asia: Societal values matter? *Journal of Happiness Studies*, *2020*(21), 391–415. doi:10.100710902-019-00088-9

Luxury Institute. (2019). *Luxury institute's 'state of the luxury industry' survey shows wealthy shoppers around the world crave emotional and human connections with luxury brands.* Retrieved 26 April 2020 from https://www.globenewswire.com/news-release/2019/01/22/1703335/0/en/Luxury-Institute-s-State-Of-The-Luxury-Industry-Survey-Shows-Wealthy-Shoppers-Around-The-World-Crave-Emotional-and-Human-Connections-With-Luxury-Brands.html

McCarthy, E. J., & Perreault, W. D. (1987). *Basic Marketing: A Managerial Approach* (9th ed.). R.D. Irwin.

Müller-Stewens, G., & Berghaus, B. (2018). The market and business of luxury: An introduction. In K. Page (Ed.), *The management of luxury* (pp. 3–53). Kogan Page.

O'Cass, A., & Frost, H. (2002). Status brands: Examining the effects of non-product-related brand associations on status and conspicuous consumption. *Journal of Product and Brand Management*, *11*(2), 67–88. doi:10.1108/10610420210423455

OECD. (2017). *The pursuit of gender equality: An uphill battle.* Retrieved 15. April 2020 from https://www.oecd.org/publications/the-pursuit-of-gender-equality-9789264281318-en.htm

OECD. (2020). *Switzerland.* Retrieved 15 April 2020 from http://www.oecdbetterlifeindex.org/countries/switzerland/

Park, H.-J., Rabolt, N. J., & Jeon, K. S. (2008). Purchasing global luxury brands among young Korean consumers. *Journal of Fashion Marketing and Management*, *12*(2), 244–259. doi:10.1108/13612020810874917

Parker, B. (2015). *South Korea's millennials downbeat about payoff of education, future.* Retrieved 29. April 2020 from https://www.pewresearch.org/fact-tank/2015/02/25/south-koreas-millennials-downbeat-about-payoff-of-education-future/

Pedrazzi, C. (2020). *How do millennials define and perceive luxury and prestige and how does it influence their luxury consumer behaviour? A cultural comparative study between Switzerland and South Korea* (Bachelor Thesis). Zurich University of Applied Sciences, School of Management and Law.

Phau, I., & Prendergast, G. (2001). Consuming luxury brands: The relevance of the "rarity" principle. *Journal of Brand Management*, *8*(2), 122–138. doi:10.1057/palgrave.bm.2540013

Pozzebon, J. A., & Ashton, M. C. (2009). Personality and values as predictors of self-and peer-reported behavior. *Journal of Individual Differences*, *30*(3), 122–129. doi:10.1027/1614-0001.30.3.122

Richins, M. L., & Dowson, S. (1992). A consumer values orientation for materialism and its measurement: Scale development and validation. *The Journal of Consumer Research*, *19*(3), 303–316. doi:10.1086/209304

Rohan, M. J. (2000). A rose by any name? The values construct. *Personality and Social Psychology Review*, *4*(3), 255–277. doi:10.1207/S15327957PSPR0403_4

Ryan, G. W., & Bernard, H. R. (2000). Data management and analysis methods. In N. K. Denzin & Y. S. Lincoln (Eds.), Handbook of qualitative research (2nd ed., pp. 769-802). Academic Press.

Santandertrade. (2020). *South Korea: Reaching the consumer*. Retrieved 29 April 2020 from https://santandertrade.com/en/portal/analyse-markets/south-korea/reaching-the-consumers?&actualiser_id_banque=oui&id_banque=17&memoriser_choix=memoriser

Schwartz, S. H. (1996). *Value Priorities and Behavior: Applying a theory of integrated value systems*. Lawrence Erlbaum.

Schwartz, S. H. (2012). An overview of the Schwartz theory of basic values. *Online Readings in Psychology and Culture*, *2*(1), 2–20. doi:10.9707/2307-0919.1116

Schwartz, S. H., & Rubel, T. (2006). Sex differences in value priorities: Cross-cultural and multi-method studies. *Journal of Personality and Social Psychology*, *89*(6), 1010–1028. doi:10.1037/0022-3514.89.6.1010 PMID:16393031

Shukla, P. (2012). The influence of value perceptions on luxury purchase intentions in developed and emerging markets. *International Marketing Review*, *29*(6), 574–596. doi:10.1108/02651331211277955

Shukla, P., Singh, J., & Banerjee, M. (2015). They are not all same: Variations in Asian consumers' value perception of luxury brands. *Marketing Letters*, *2015*(26), 265–278. doi:10.100711002-015-9358-x

Stępień, B., Lima, A. P., & Hinner, M. (2018). Are millennials a global cohort? Evidence from the luxury good sector. *Journal of Intercultural Management*, *10*(2), 139–158. doi:10.2478/joim-2018-0012

The Economist. (2015, July 23). *I don't*. Retrieved 13 October 2020 from https://www.economist.com/asia/2015/07/23/i-dont

The World Bank. (2019). *GINI index (World Bank estimate) - Switzerland*. Retrieved 29 April 2020 from https://data.worldbank.org/indicator/SI.POV.GINI?locations=CH&name_desc=false

The World Bank. (2019). *GDP per capita (current US – Korea.Rep)*. Retrieved 25 September 2020 from https:// https://data.worldbank.org/indicator/NY.GDP.PCAP.CD?locations=KR

Theodoridis, P., & Vassou, S. (2018). Exploring luxury consumer behaviour. In B. Berghaus, M. Gunter, & S. Reinecke (Eds.), *The management of luxuy: An international guide* (pp. 76–86). Kogan Page.

Tian, K. T., Bearde, N. W., & Hunter, G. (2001). Consumers' need for uniqueness: Scale. *The Journal of Consumer Research*, *28*(1), 50–66. doi:10.1086/321947

Trading Economics. (2020). *Switzerland Youth Unemployment Rate*. Retrieved 25 May 2020 from https://tradingeconomics.com/switzerland/youth-unemployment-rate

Truong, Y., McColl, R., & Kitchen, P. J. (2009). New luxury brand positioning and the emergence of masstige brands. *Journal of Brand Management*, *16*(5-6), 375–382. doi:10.1057/bm.2009.1

Vigneron, F., & Johnson, L. W. (1999). A review and a conceptual framework of prestige-seeking consumer behavior. *Academy of Marketing Science Review*, *2*(1), 1–15.

Vigneron, F., & Johnson, L. W. (2004). Measuring perceptions of brand luxury. *Brand Management*, *11*(6), 484–506. doi:10.1057/palgrave.bm.2540194

Watson, J., Lysonski, S., Gillan, T., & Raymore, L. (2002). Psychological and cultural insights into consumption of luxury. *Journal of Business Research*, *9*(1), 923–931. doi:10.1016/S0148-2963(01)00212-0

Wiedmann, K.-P., & Hennigs, N. (2013). Placing luxury marketing on the research agenda not only for the sake of luxury - An introduction. In N. Hennigs (Ed.), *Luxury Marketing* (pp. 5–17). Springer. doi:10.1007/978-3-8349-4399-6_1

Wiedmann, K.-P., Hennigs, N., & Siebels, A. (2009). Value-based segmentation of luxury consumption behavior. *Psychology and Marketing*, *26*(7), 625–651. doi:10.1002/mar.20292

Wilson, K. G., Sandoz, E. K., Kit, J., & Roberts, M. (2010). The value living questionnaire: Defining and measuring valued action within a behavioral framework. *The Psychological Record*, *60*(2), 249–272. doi:10.1007/BF03395706

Wong, N. Y., & Ahuvia, A. C. (1998). Personal taste and family face: Luxury consumption in Confucian and Western societies. *Psychology and Marketing*, *15*(5), 423–442. doi:10.1002/(SICI)1520-6793(199808)15:5<423::AID-MAR2>3.0.CO;2-9

World Population Review. (2020). *South Korea Population 2020*. Retrieved 29 April 2020 from https://worldpopulationreview.com/countries/south-korea-population/

Yeoman, I. (2011). The changing behaviours of luxury consumption. *Journal of Revenue and Pricing Management*, *2011*(10), 47–50. doi:10.1057/rpm.2010.43

Zhan, L., & He, Y. (2012). Understanding luxury consumption in China: Consumer perceptions of best-known brands. *Journal of Business Research*, *2012*(65), 1452–1460. doi:10.1016/j.jbusres.2011.10.011

KEY TERMS AND DEFINITIONS

Generational Cohort: A group of individuals, e.g. Baby Boomers, GenX, GenY or GenZ, born in a certain period, who have shared similar experiences and have unique common characteristics around these experiences.

Luxury: Term with Latin origins, that stems from the word "lux" for light or brightness, but also "luxuria" meaning intemperance or debauchery, and "luxus" for opulence, lusciousness and pomp. Historically, luxury has primarily been defined as a means of gaining and maintaining social prestige, nowadays luxury refers to comfort, elegance, and high quality, as well as high expense.

Luxury Goods: Products typically offered at a price that exceeds their functional value, wrapped in a holistic hedonistic experience, and often tied to a heritage, unique know-how, and culture. Luxury goods are often social markers and bought to display status and a certain position in society or a specific social group.

Macro-Contextual Factor: Defined as cultural (context and independence), economic (opportunities based on wealth), and ecological (threats due to society, disease, and stress) factors that impact the overall value system of consumers. Macro-contextual factors shape personal values.

Personal Value System: Determines what a person regards as desirable or not, it has an impact on the preferences and consumer behavior. The personal value system is defined by individual values, social related values, and human basic values.

Prestige: Subjective categorization of people or objects such as brands in a high social status.

Social Value: Characterized by a desire of differentiation within a non-prestigious or non-reference group in order to relate to a prestigious group. Social value arouses consumption based on the purpose of display of wealth and increase to the ego in an ostentatious way.

Chapter 14
Designing Luxurious Food Experiences for Millennials and Post-Millennials

Monica Mendini
University of Applied Sciences and Arts of Southern Switzerland (SUPSI), Switzerland

Wided Batat
EM Normandie Business School, Paris, France & Metis Lab, France & University of Lyon 2, France

Paula C. Peter
San Diego State University, USA

ABSTRACT

The relationship between young generations (Millennials and Gen Z), luxury, and food is a current and complex subject. Millennials and Gen Z are the first digital native generations to be very comfortable with technology devices and interested at an early stage in luxury food experiences. By exploring youth food culture and current luxury food experiences and practices, the authors identify three trends (digitalization, extended realities, and cause-related marketing) as key areas food brands and food actors (e.g., restaurants) should capitalize on to educate, facilitate, and promote the adoption of pleasurable, healthy, and sustainable food consumptions. The authors provide an overview of these three new key trends together with examples Millennials and Gen Z consumers are attracted to considering luxurious food consumption and experiences. This chapter contributes to the need to look at contexts of application (food) where sustainability and the digital transformation highlights the present and future for the promotion of luxury goods and experiences.

DOI: 10.4018/978-1-7998-5882-9.ch014

Copyright © 2021, IGI Global. Copying or distributing in print or electronic forms without written permission of IGI Global is prohibited.

1. INTRODUCTION

The relationship between Millennials, Gen Z, luxury, and food is a subject that is both very current and particularly complex. Gen Y, or Millennials, are commonly characterized as individuals born approximately between 1985 and 2005. Gen Z, or Post-Millennials, is the demographic cohort succeeding Millennials, including individuals born between 1995 and 2015. These young people are among the first digital native generations to be very comfortable with technology devices, being concerned about healthy and sustainable (food) choices, and being extremely interested in luxury (food) experiences.

For luxury brands in the food sector, each generation advent raises new questions about the transmission, continuity, and breakdown of social behaviors (work, food consumption, daily life, etc.). Referring to Millennials and Gen Z, the technological revolution has had a powerful impact in terms of food values and characteristics of luxury food consumption of this youth generation. Today, in fact, the youngest generations are confronted with digital experiences, such as the ones facilitated by social media, physical and virtual influencers, and extended reality technologies (XR) aimed at creating immersive experiences, which need to be authentic and entertaining. For instance, the advent of extended reality technologies is opening new doors to luxury food brands for delivering compelling customer experiences in the luxury food market. XR makes individuals feel as if they are in an entirely new digital world (O'Donnell, 2018), augmenting hedonic value, such as entertainment and shopping/experience enjoyment, leading to higher customer satisfaction at the end (Childers et al. 2001). Therefore, all these digital tools can potentially influence and shape the relationship Millennials and Gen Z have with food, luxury food consumption, and experiences.

Furthermore, Gen Y and Gen Z are also defined as the "empathetic generation" (Arnett, 2010). They seem to be the most receptive to corporate social responsibility activities and above all to cause-related marketing activities, i.e. the partnering of a for-profit company with relevant social causes (CM, e.g. Bucic et al, 2012). These generations are looking for an emotional connection with companies and brands, as they are deeply concerned about social issues (Howe & Strauss, 2000; Youn & Kim, 2008). Millennials demand companies be socially responsible, and companies recognize the power of these consumers not as merely buyers and users of their products, services, experiences, or ideas, but also as allies to change and make a positive impact on society at large.

In thinking about how the broader area of food, luxury food, and well-being might be promoted in society, learning more about the motivations and trends of young adults is important as they are learning to be consumers and are the future main consumers of luxury brands. There is the opportunity for long-term positive effects if the research can understand them better at the point that they begin to take on more responsibility for their own food consumption and the relationship between luxury food and experiences.

By exploring youth food culture and current luxury food experiences and practices, the authors wish to identify trends that luxury food brands can potentially use to educate, facilitate and promote the adoption of pleasurable, luxurious, and sustainable food consumption, which can contribute to the well-being of youth by offering them unique and exclusive luxury food experiences.

Moreover, the aim of the chapter is also to investigate and provide details on what are the new key trends Millennials or Gen Z consumers are interested in when they look for luxurious, healthy, and sustainable food consumption and experiences.

In particular, the trends identified, which are going to be discussed in detail in the chapter pertaining to the luxury food industry are the following:

Designing Luxurious Food Experiences for Millennials and Post-Millennials

i)   Social media and the importance of influencers
ii) Extended Realities (XR), such as augmented reality and virtual reality
iii) Cause-related Marketing (CM), as the partnership with social related causes

The authors review each of these trends and provide connections and examples as related to luxury food consumption and pleasurable and healthy food experience.

2. LUXURY FOOD CONSUMPTION AND EXPERIENCES

Luxury foods are foods that are characterized by sophistication and often complexity in textures, are creative in their presentation, and often offer new and original tastes. Luxury foods stimulate a consumer's five senses and provide social status distinction. Luxury food consumption is more of an experience than high-quality products (Batat, 2020a). It can be defined by its experiential aspects such as hedonism, symbolism, and social status instead of its functional and utilitarian purposes such as the fulfillment of biological needs of hunger (Batat, 2020b). In the luxury food industry, therefore, refers to foods that are often scarce and consumed primarily for the sensory and emotional pleasure they provide (Batat et al., 2019; Marcilhac, 2013). For a food product to be considered luxurious, it must be culturally desirable and socially distinctive (Batat, 2019a). It is above all consumed as a sign, which reflects the social status of the person who consumes it (Batat, 2020a; Batat and De Kerviler, 2020). The consumption of luxury food arises by virtue — and not a necessity — of a prior specific desire (Berry, 1994). Multiple luxury food cultures feature the highest quality products. These cultures of luxury food have emerged since Antiquity in Asia and Europe before spreading to other parts of the world (Marcilhac and Pitte, 2012). Yet, luxury food is considered as a French singularity and the French luxury food culture has dominated and influenced luxury food consumption and production worldwide (Batat and De Kerviler, 2020). This French singularity is based on the production of a discourse on the rarity and originality of the product, which transforms its consumption into an exceptional moment, a "luxury of sensations and pleasures." (Marcilhac and Pitte, 2012). According to Batat, this singularity can be explained by the fact that "few cultures have pushed gastronomy to the level of the sophistication reached by the French" (2019a, p. 4). In France, luxury gastronomy signifies a "heritage proudly claimed by all individuals who belong to the French food culture, regardless of their social position" (2019a, p. 4). Furthermore, the French Michelin Guide used to rank gastronomic high-end restaurants by stars from one to three according to various criteria (e.g., quality of food ingredients, chefs' creativity, service excellence, restaurant décor, and staging) is a highly influential guide used worldwide. It is also considered to be the most consistent and broadly referred to restaurant guide in the world, valued by both chefs and customers (Batat, 2020b; Lane, 2010). Although luxury gastronomy is nowadays a growing market, from an academic perspective, it is an emerging field of research and there are limited studies that examine the attitudes and perceptions of consumers towards luxury foods, especially, younger generations, namely GenY and GenZ consumers, who belong to a fast food consumption culture. Indeed, the nature of eaters' relationship to luxury food is complex and it is not limited to the exacerbation of the economic value of the products offered (or of the service, the setting, and its staging), but also in its psychological, sociocultural, ideological, experiential, and symbolic dimensions (Batat et al., 2019; Marcilhac, 2013).

3. NEW LUXURY CONSUMERS (MILLENNIALS AND POST-MILLENNIALS)

Younger generations of consumers, who are part of Gen Y (1980-1994) and Gen Z, (1995-present) do not have the same relationship to luxury as the previous generation such as Gen X (earlier than 1980). More cautious, thoughtful, and committed than previous generational cohorts, generations Y and Z are nowadays pushing luxury brands to reinvent themselves to attract these young consumers. Among the features that differentiate the relationship of younger generations to luxury compared to Gen X, three major trends should be considered, namely ethical values, gender-dilution, and authenticity (Batat, 2019a). While ethical values refer to a luxury brand's actions towards the protection of the environment (e.g. the use of recycled material) and animal welfare (e.g., banning animal leather), authenticity emphasizes luxury brand transparency about the price and its embeddedness within the local context (e.g., luxury items should be manufactured locally). These two values are critical to connect with youth generations and share common values with them. Besides, when targeting these generations, luxury brands should consider gender-fluidity in its offerings and communication actions as these generations do not limit themselves to one gender whether it is a male or female (Batat, 2017).

These generations (Y and Z) have been a blessing for the luxury industry, and the reason for its digital growth. Considering the food industry, Millennials and post-Millennials are considered as "food lovers" and real food fans thanks to Instagram that features food aesthetics and trendy food experiences. Their interest in food luxury can be translated through following Michelin-starred chefs on social media where they can discover the creative meal of the week or comment on the chefs' creations. For these younger generations, luxury food is not only related to eating but it is considered as a domain for artistic creations that enhance consumers' emotions and food experience. Also, culinary shows have contributed to raising the awareness of youth generations regarding luxury gastronomy by featuring inspiring young Michelin-starred chefs as rock stars.

For young people, luxury food is perceived as a highly experiential domain charged with emotions that allows them to define a social status (Batat, 2017a). The relationship between young generations and luxury food also depends on the local food culture in which young consumers' eating behaviors are embedded and shaped (Batat et al. 2019). For instance, young people in France are born in a gastronomic culture transmitted across generations, are more eager to appreciate gastronomic experiences, and develop an interest in luxury food consumption and thus healthy and pleasurable eating behaviors. Besides, the adoption of healthy and sustainable eating behaviors, which constitute an integral part of luxury food consumption, is an ongoing process affected by day-to-day social interactions, which can shape our relationship with food. In thinking about how luxury food experiences can be promoted and facilitated, learning more about the motivations of young adults is important as they are learning to be consumers. Moreover, there is an opportunity for long-term positive effects if researchers can understand them better to the point that they begin to take on more responsibility for their own food choices and experiences.

By exploring youth food culture and current luxury food experiences and practices in consideration within a particular at-risk and vulnerable group, the authors identified three key factors that luxury food brands and services can potentially use to educate and facilitate the adoption of pleasurable, luxurious, healthy, and sustainable food consumption and thus contribute to the well-being of youth by offering them unique and exclusive luxury food experiences. In the following chapters, the trends will be described in detail.

Designing Luxurious Food Experiences for Millennials and Post-Millennials

4. NEW KEY TRENDS

4.1. Trend 1: Social Media and Influencers

The food world has been colonized by an array of new digital devices, online content, and communication technologies (Lewis, 2018). The youngest generations are confronted today with a new digital world and with new digital experiences, i.e. the combination of technology and enjoying a meal to create a new level of engagement between consumers and food brands or restaurants/food providers. In general, Gen Y and Z look for authentic and entertaining experiences when they interact with new digital devices, such as social media.

Social media platforms have become powerful social tools for online communication, allowing individuals to interact, to share their views, to collaborate, and to contribute on developing, extending, rating, and commenting on foods and food experiences (Canhoto and Padmanabhan, 2015). In current years, the realm of digital media has been invaded by food related-content, such as food snapshots on Facebook and Instagram or cooking and food channels on YouTube. As a matter of fact, social media allows for connections between consumers, heightening food pleasure, and facilitating healthy food consumption (Coary and Poor, 2016). Generally, social media is also used by young consumers to show off their consumption (Wang and Griskevicius, 2014). This happens with no exception also in the food field, where consumers tend to show off their luxury food consumption or at least to make it more visible (Wilcox, Kim, & Sen, 2009). Examples of this are dining at famous restaurants or cafes and showing off quality pictures or videos on social media to be shared with loved ones, families, friends, or colleagues (e.g. at famous Michelin-star restaurants or in branded bistros or cafes).

In addition, the growing use of mobile photo-sharing services, such as Instagram, has seen a rise in everyday amateur food photography, where consumers act as photographers of different food plates (Hu, Manikonda, & Kambhampati, 2014). According to research, 18-35-year-olds spend five whole days a year browsing food images on Instagram, and 30 percent would avoid a restaurant if their Instagram presence was weak (Hosie, 2017). Previous research by Holmberg and colleagues (2016) analyzed how adolescents communicate food images using Instagram and discovered that users often imitated the aesthetics of food advertising and cookbooks. Millennials and Gen Z are used to personally craft and curate food images as a sign that represents both a kind of conspicuous culinary consumption and performance of artisanal craft labor, a double mastery of the crafting of food and the shaping of associated imagery (Lewis, 2018). The focus on the interest in and the high circulation of highly aestheticized food images on different social media and blogs is strongly connected to what is currently happening in the food field, with the introduction of globally popular reality-style cookery TV formats such as MasterChef.

Further, new digital tools have also seen the rise of different typologies of influencers, such as the rise of celebrity chefs as a major popular cultural phenomenon. For instance, many are the top gourmet food influencers that can be mentioned and can be found on the web and on social media, such as Molly Tavoletti or well-known chefs such as Iginio Massari or Jamie Oliver. Antonino Cannavacciuolo, an Italian Michelin-star renowned chef and TV presenter are other examples of famous food influencers (https://www.antoninocannavacciuolo.it/). He owns the famous 2-Michelin star restaurant Villa Crespi in Northern Italy and several other bistros around the country, and he is one of the most appreciated judges in the Italian versions of programs such as Masterchef, Celebrity Masterchef, and Family Food Fight. Currently, his Instagram profile counts 2.7 million followers (https://www.instagram.com/antoninochef/), and he is considered to be the king of gourmet food influence in Italy. Interestingly, food influencers cannot only be physical but also virtual. Mentioning several examples, Colonel Sanders is the new computer-generated virtual-influencer created by KFC, who personifies the avatar of its famous founder (1.5m like; Steland, 2019). Noonoouri (https://www.instagram.com/noonoouri/; 365k followers), the famous virtual fashion blogger, has also started posting on food luxury experiences, e.g. in luxury restaurants (Le Royal Monceau-Raffles in Paris), bistros (e.g. Kioske Cartier in Munich) or with gourmet/luxury food products such as the pastry products of Pierre Hermè, implying this trend is here to stay in the food world.

4.2. Trend 2: Extended Reality (XR)

Extended reality (XR), as characterized by the continuum from augmented reality to virtual reality, has only recently started to find fertile ground in the food industry and represents one of the biggest promises for the luxury food experience. Virtual reality (VR), a 3D computer-generated simulation, has been explored and tested in different industries for years such as art, gaming, real estate, and tourism. Augmented reality (AR), a technology allowing companies to introduce products/services in consumers' reality, has offered new means for marketers in different industries to communicate with consumers (e.g. Baratali et al., 2016). These technologies have allowed for greater engagement of consumers when the experience is the focal point of the product and/or service offered.

In the general food industry, AR has been used to engage consumers and offer in-depth information about their food and beverage products, while VR has been mainly adopted in food research and training. From a food menu offered with a 3D view with no language barrier (e.g. www.kabaq.io) to theme-based entertainment provided while waiting for the food, restaurants/bars are starting to increase their technology offering and service to complement the food experience. For example, in 2012 Absolut launched their Absolut Truths campaign where AR allowed users to explore the where, what, how, when related to the production of this liquor (Eleftheriou-Smith 2012). The campaign provided Absolut consumers with unique experiences that strengthened their associations with the brand. Considering VR, the technology has been used primarily for employer training and food product development research. VR can provide training when training and experimentation appear particularly expensive and ineffective (Brinkley 2020). Research indicates that VR-based employee training has an 80% retention rate a year after training while only a 20% retention rate using traditional training (Brinkley 2020). From a research standpoint, it is easier to test new and expensive food arrangements based on food position, size, shape, and color in the virtual world than in the real world. Research indicates that the experience in the virtual world vs. the real world is perceived to be almost identical giving confidence in the usefulness of the technology for research and experimentation (Gouton et al., 2020). This can be particularly beneficial for luxury restaurants who wish to test the arrangement and combination of menu items without using the actual expensive and often scarce food ingredients. The simulated environment has also been recognized as a great motivator for actual consumption since subjects who are exposed to the product in the virtual environment are more inclined to try it in reality (Ruppert, 2011).

It is clear that AR and VR can be particularly beneficial in the luxury food industry where consumers already have high expectations for the experience and are looking forward to elements of surprise and long-lasting engagement. According to the latest trends shared online, chefs and marketers of fine dining experiences have been asked to engage in collaborative and entrepreneurial work in order to identify new food-related experiences that might appeal to the new generations of foodies. Where the

Designing Luxurious Food Experiences for Millennials and Post-Millennials

experience needs to be memorable and is often shared through social media accounts (Mendini, Pizzetti, Peter 2019), AR and VR offer the greatest potential.

A very interesting case is offered by the Japanese-based restaurant Tree by Naked in Tokyo which offers a 360-degree high-end technology-based dining experience. The restaurant is the brainchild of the director of the design firm Naked Inc. and offers an immersive dining experience which is now structured according to the waiting room, birth, spur, expansion, phantasm, unity, and rebirth (https://tree. naked.works/yoyogi/course/). The restaurant redefines fine-food gastronomy by adding multi-layers of sensory experiences in order to immerse the customer in a memorable journey around tasty foods and fancy drinks. Specifically, the environment is characterized by projection mapping, VR sensors, lights, smoke, scents, music, and performances. The experience-based art restaurant accepts booking only for eight people with a set course menu of eight different meals and paired drinks (https://tree.naked.works/ yoyogi/course/). The experience combines traditional Japanese culture and entertainment with the latest cutting-edge technologies and advanced expressions. The dinner includes a VR headset that aims to create new associations in the mind of consumers while tasting the experience. The result is the creation of new and memorable associations that have the potential to reshape taste perceptions forever and help understand how senses operate in creating the food experience.

4.3. Trend 3: Cause Related Marketing (CM)

Cause related marketing (CM) underlines the intersection between business and society, and the opportunity to communicate the concept of "doing well by doing good." According to a general definition of CM, in cause related marketing, a firm contributes to a cause, "linked to customers' engaging in revenue-producing transactions with the firm" (Varandarajan & Menon, 1988, p. 60). However, cause related marketing today is much more than a pure transaction which might limit its beneficial impact on the company, consumers, and society at large. Cause related marketing is in fact often considered marketing of and for a cause and underlines the intersection between business and society, and the opportunity to communicate the concept of "doing well by doing good" (Mendini and Peter, 2018).

Currently, CM is increasingly used by companies worldwide. In 2017, cause-sponsorship spending amounted to $62.7 billion globally and is projected to increase more in the course of the upcoming years (IEG, 2018). Cause related marketing activities have been used to create differential advantage, "by building an emotional and spiritual bond with consumers" (Meyer, 1999, p. 29).

Today, CM is very often the result of the demand from new generations of consumers to create successful business models that contribute to the wellbeing of society and its members. As emphasized in the literature, Millennials and Post-Millennials seem to be the most receptive to cause marketing activities (e.g. Bucic et al, 2012) and are often the main target audience (i.e., the "empathic generation"; Arnett, 2010), as they view CM in a positive light (Youn & Kim, 2008). New generations are looking for an emotional connection with companies and brands, and companies can properly gain their trust by partnering with relevant social causes (Furlow, 2011).

Evidence shows that these consumers are tolerant and trustworthy and are willing to pay more for products that have a social benefit, as they are deeply concerned about social issues (Howe & Strauss, 2000). For instance, Nielsen (2014) reported that 42% of North American shoppers would pay extra for products and services from companies committed to positive social and environmental impact. Cone (2015) reported that when choosing between two brands of equal quality and price, 90% of U.S. shoppers are likely to switch to a cause branded product. Further, according to the Deloitte Millennial Survey of 2017, six out of ten Millennials say "a sense of purpose" is part of the reason they chose to work for their current employer as the belief that your work can have a positive impact on individuals and society remains important to them. Consequently, for a for-profit company, having an active CM program leads to higher sales and more purchases (Barone, Miyazaki, & Taylor, 2000; Lichtenstein et al., 2004). This results in an enhanced corporate image (Koschate-Fischer, Stefan, & Hoyer, 2012) and larger brand equity (Hoeffler & Keller, 2002). Creating an alliance in which the company donates to a charitable cause provides evidence of the firm's good corporate citizenship, which may enhance the corporate image and brand equity (Hoeffler & Keller, 2002; Lafferty & Goldsmith, 2005; Rim, Yang, & Lee, 2016).

Millennials demand companies be socially responsible, and companies recognize the power of consumers not as merely buyers and users of their products, services, experiences, or ideas, but also as allies to change and make a positive impact on society at large. This is also true in the food field. As food consumers, we like the idea of trying restaurants where individuals with a turbulent past are given a second chance to become responsible citizens (e.g. Rob de Matt restaurant, Milan, Italy; Interno restaurant in Cartagena) or brands that use the power of food and gastronomy to address social inequality, fight hunger, and improve nutrition education.

An interesting case is offered by the premium chocolate brand, GODIVA Chocolatier, which partnered years ago with the non-profit association "Toys for Tots." With a Belgian heritage dating back to 1926, GODIVA is considered as the global leader in premium chocolate and during the years, became a universal symbol of luxury, quality, and delicious chocolate. The company owns more than 600 shops in the United States, Canada, Europe, and Asia and is available via over 10,000 specialty retailers (https://www.godiva.com).

A few years ago, Godiva launched the campaign "Hot Chocolate for a Cause" during Christmas time. In particular, the company partnered with the non-profit association Toys for Tots helping children in need. In this occasion, GODIVA donated $1.00 to Toys for Tots for every GODIVA Hot Chocolate beverage sold in their retail stores from Giving Tuesday, December 1st, through December 15th (https://www.prnewswire.com/news-releases/godiva-launches-hot-chocolate-for-a-cause
-in-partnership-with-toys-for-tots-foundation-300185650.html). Why was this successful? Consumers, especially Millennials and Gen Z, like to experience the pleasure derived from "feeling well by doing good," where engaging in cause related marketing activities and purchasing products implies "caring," i.e. creating feelings of solidarity and bonding (Belk, 2009).

5. DISCUSSION

This chapter examined the connection between youth generations of consumers, namely Millennials and Post-Millennials, along with food luxury consumption within a highly digitized and socially engaged Western food culture. The authors revealed three key trends (digitization, extended realities, and cause related marketing) that marketers should integrate into their targeting strategies to design suitable luxury food experiences that help young consumers improve their individual and social food well-being. In order to design efficient luxury food experiences that enhance young people's food well-being, luxury brand managers and scholars should examine not food as the act of ingesting, but experiencing, as a system of social values, actions, know-how, symbolism, norms, and representations (Garabuau-Moussaoui, 2001) that constitute an integral part of the identity construction and the socialization process adopted by youth within their food culture (Batat & Tanner, 2019; Batat, 2014) shaped by digital and experi-

Designing Luxurious Food Experiences for Millennials and Post-Millennials

ential aspects. As a result, luxury food brands should engage in a shift in their strategies by embracing "food transformation 3.0" as a new strategy when targeting Millennials and Post-Millennials. Indeed, the food sector is undergoing a transformation digitally, socio-culturally, and environmentally. This food transformation can be implemented following the emergence of new food consumption practices among youth and desired by professionals in the luxury and food sector following the integration of technologies and various innovations in the production and distribution of food luxury products. Thus, the axes of the food transformation 3.0 encompass three major pillars to support luxury food for young generations: The importance of food well-being linked to the pleasure generated by the culinary experience (Batat et al., 2019), the role of phygital (physical and digital) in eating habits, and the rise of alternative food consumption practices (Batat et al., 2017). Therefore, the importance of food well-being linked to the pleasure generated by the luxury culinary experience today marks the transition in the way of doing and thinking of professionals in the luxury food sector (Batat, 2020b). This new logic encourages the luxury food sector to adopt a bottom-up approach that is more focused on youth and their culinary experience with its functional, social, sensory, and cultural dimensions. Thus, thinking that a pleasant culinary experience contributes to the nutritional well-being of individuals leads to rethinking the very popular pyramid of nutritional needs introduced in 1993 by the Harvard School of Public Health which encourages a healthy diet by recommending the consumption of adapted portions of five food categories. Although the nutrition pyramid is an effective tool, it has been the subject of some criticism that limits its scope (Batat, 2019c). From now on, it is a question of a new pyramid "Pyramid of the dietary food experience," as recommended by Batat (2019c) as it is more in line with the real needs of young consumers. It puts young people and their tangible and intangible needs at the center for the apprehension of their nutritional well-being through culinary experiences that are both healthy and enjoyable.

6. CONCLUSIONS, IMPLICATIONS AND FUTURE RESEARCH

In the luxury food industry, where the focus is primarily on the food experience (Batat 2019), chefs and food designers have been called to explore new ways to enhance their offerings by providing audiences with new sensory and communication experiences: the next-generation food gastronomy. As globalization advances and luxury gastronomy starts to belong to all individuals regardless of their social position, we find in the new generations' interest in luxurious experiences, the advent of new technologies (social media and XR) and business narratives (cause related marketing), fertile ground for the food luxury industry to be a potential new propeller for society and consumer well-being. Interestingly enough, no research to our knowledge has really considered these areas as potential for research. As mentioned above, the nature of eaters' relationship to luxury food is complex, and it is not limited to the exacerbation of the economic value of the products offered (or of the service, the setting, and its staging). Instead, it calls for the considerations of the psychological, sociocultural, ideological, experiential, and symbolic dimensions (Batat et al., 2019; Marcilhac, 2013) of the luxury food experience. Our chapter underlines details in the role of new factors that need to be taken into account such as authenticity as facilitated (or hindered) by social media, the potential for contribution to society and the environment through the consumption of luxury foods as associated to a cause, and the advent of extended realities as way to enhance the luxury food experience. Consuming luxury foods go beyond the pure and private act of ingesting delicacy. It calls for entrepreneurs to come up with creative ideas, for cross-pollinations among fields of studies (such as culinary sciences, industrial and product design, and marketing) to create experiences that are fulfilling and contributing to society at large. A focus on these areas contributes also to the understanding of the phygital consumption and how to best serve consumers who still want the physical experience but benefit from the digital experience. There is no doubt that the future of the luxury food experience will be characterized by these factors. What is surprising and promising is that it will also contribute to consumer well-being and the society they live in.

REFERENCES

Arnett, J. J. (2010). *Adolescence and emerging adulthood: A cultural approach* (4th ed.). Prentice Hall.

Baratali, E., Abd, R. M., Parhizkar, B., & Gebril, Z. M. (2016). Effective of augmented reality (AR) in marketing communication; a case study on brand interactive advertising. *International Journal of Management and Applied Science*, 2(4), 133–137.

Barkin, S. L., Heerman, W. J., Warren, M. D., & Rennhoff, C. (2010). Millennials and the world of work: The impact of obesity on health and productivity. *Journal of Business and Psychology*, 25(2), 239–245. doi:10.100710869-010-9166-5 PMID:20502510

Barone, M. J., Miyazaki, A. D., & Taylor, K. A. (2000). The influence of cause-related marketing on consumer choice: Does one good turn deserve another? *Journal of the Academy of Marketing Science*, 28(2), 248–262. doi:10.1177/0092070300282006

Batat, W. (2014). How do adolescents define their own competencies in the consumption field? A portrait approach. *Recherche et Applications en Marketing*, 29(1), 27–60. doi:10.1177/0767370113505946

Batat, W. (2017a). *Les nouvelles youth cultures*. Editions EMS. doi:10.3917/ems.batat.2017.01

Batat, W. (2017b). *Comprendre et séduire la génération Z. Comportements de consommation et relations des postmillennials avec les marques*. Ellipses.

Batat, W. (2019a). *Food and experiential marketing. Pleasure, wellbeing and consumption*. Routledge. doi:10.4324/9781351182201

Batat, W. (2019b). *The new luxury experience: creating the ultimate customer experience*. Springer. doi:10.1007/978-3-030-01671-5

Batat, W. (2019c). Eating for pleasure: An introduction of the healthy food experience pyramid. *Qualitative Market Research*, 22(4), 530–543. doi:10.1108/QMR-09-2019-190

Batat, W. (2020a). The role of luxury gastronomy in food tourism. *International Journal of Tourism Research*.

Batat, W. (2020b). Pillars of sustainable food experiences in the luxury gastronomy sector: A qualitative exploration of Michelin-starred chefs' motivations. *Journal of Retailing and Consumer Services*, 57, 102255. doi:10.1016/j.jretconser.2020.102255

Batat, W., & De Kerviler, G. (2020). How can the art of living (art de vivre) make the French luxury industry unique and competitive? *Marché & Organisations*, 37(37), 17–34. doi:10.3917/maorg.037.0015

Designing Luxurious Food Experiences for Millennials and Post-Millennials

Batat, W., Peter, P., Vicdan, H., Manna, V., Ulusoy, E., Ulusoy, E., & Hong, S. (2017). Alternative food consumption (AFC): Idiocentric and allocentric factors of influence among low socio-economic status (SES) consumers. *Journal of Marketing Management, 33*(7-8), 580–601. doi:10.1080/026725 7X.2017.1289974

Batat, W., Peter, P. C., Moscato, E. M., Castro, I. A., Chan, S., Chugani, S., & Muldrow, A. (2019). The experiential pleasure of food: A savoring journey to food well-being. *Journal of Business Research, 100*, 392–399. doi:10.1016/j.jbusres.2018.12.024

Batat, W., & Tanner, J. Jr. (2019). Unveiling (in)vulnerability in an adolescent's consumption subculture: A framework to understand adolescents' experienced (in)vulnerability and ethical implications. *Journal of Business Ethics*, 1–18. doi:10.100710551-019-04309-2

Belk, R. (2009). Sharing. *The Journal of Consumer Research, 36*(5), 715–734. doi:10.1086/612649

Berry, C. J. (1994). *The idea of luxury: A conceptual and historical investigation.* Cambridge University Press. doi:10.1017/CBO9780511558368

Brinkley, R. (2020, March 22). *I ate a meal in virtual reality. Here's what it tasted like.* https://www.cnbc.com/2020/03/21/virtual-reality-dining-explained.html

Bucic, T., Harris, J., & Arli, D. (2012). Ethical consumers among the millennials: A cross-national study. *Journal of Business Ethics, 110*(1), 113–131. doi:10.100710551-011-1151-z

Canhoto, A. I., & Padmanabhan, Y. (2015). 'We (don't) know how you feel'–a comparative study of automated vs. manual analysis of social media conversations. *Journal of Marketing Management, 31*(9-10), 1141–1157. doi:10.1080/0267257X.2015.1047466

Childers, T. L., Carr, C. L., Peck, J., & Carson, S. (2001). Hedonic and utilitarian motivations for online retail shopping behavior. *Journal of Retailing, 77*(4), 511–535. doi:10.1016/S0022-4359(01)00056-2

Coary, S., & Poor, M. (2016). How consumer-generated images shape important consumption outcomes in the food domain. *Journal of Consumer Marketing, 33*(1), 1–8. doi:10.1108/JCM-02-2015-1337

Cone Communications. Ebiquity global CSR study. (2015). Report retrieved from http://www.cone-comm.com

Deloitte. The Deloitte millennial survey 2017. (2017). Report retrieved from https://www2.deloitte.com/global/en/pages/about- deloitte/articles/millennialsurvey.html

Eleftheriou-Smith, L.-M. (2012). *Absolut Vodka launches augmented reality app.* Retrieved from https://www.campaignlive.co.uk/article/absolut-vodka-launchesaugmented-reality-app/1113514

Eves, A., & Gesch, B. (2003). Food provision and the nutritional implications of food choices made by young adult males, in a young offenders' institution. *Journal of Human Nutrition and Dietetics, 16*(3), 167–179. doi:10.1046/j.1365-277X.2003.00438.x PMID:12753110

Furlow, N. E. (2011). Find us on Facebook: How cause marketing has embraced social media. *Journal of Marketing Development and Competitiveness, 5*(6), 61.

Garabuau-Moussaoui, I. (2001) La cuisine des jeunes: désordre alimentaire, identité générationnelle et ordre social. *Anthropology of Food.*

Gouton, M.-A., Dacremont, C., Trystram, G., & Blumenthal, D. (2020). *Validation of food visual attribute perception in virtual reality. Food quality and preference.* https://www.sciencedirect.com/science/article/abs/pii/S0950329320302858?via=ihub

Harker, D., Sharma, B., Harker, M., & Reinhard, K. (2010). Leaving home: Food choice behavior of young German adults. *Journal of Business Research, 63*(2), 111–115. doi:10.1016/j.jbusres.2009.02.007

Hoeffler, S., & Keller, K. L. (2002). Building brand equity through corporate societal marketing. *Journal of Public Policy & Marketing, 21*(1), 78–89. doi:10.1509/jppm.21.1.78.17600

Holmberg, C., Chaplin, J. E., Hillman, T., & Berg, C. (2016). Adolescents' presentation of food in social media: An explorative study. *Appetite, 99*, 121–129. doi:10.1016/j.appet.2016.01.009 PMID:26792765

Hosie, R. (2017). How instagram has transformed the restaurant industry for millennials. *The Independent.* Retrieved from https://www.independent.co.uk/life-style/food-and-drink/millenials-restaurant-how-choose-instagram-social-media-where-eat-a7677786.html

Howe, N., & Strauss, W. (2000). *Millennials rising: The next great generation.* Vintage.

Hu, Y., Manikonda, L., & Kambhampati, S. (2014, June). What we instagram: A first analysis of instagram photo content and user types. ICWSM.

Koschate-Fischer, N., Stefan, I. V., & Hoyer, W. D. (2012). Willingness to pay for cause-related marketing: The impact of donation amount and moderating effects. *JMR, Journal of Marketing Research, 49*(6), 910–927. doi:10.1509/jmr.10.0511

Lafferty, B. A., & Goldsmith, R. E. (2005). Cause–brand alliances: Does the cause help the brand or does the brand help the cause? *Journal of Business Research, 58*(4), 423–429. doi:10.1016/j.jbusres.2003.07.001

Lane, C. (2010). The Michelin-Starred Restaurant Sector as a Cultural Industry, Food. *Cultura e Scuola, 13*(4), 493–519.

Lewis, T. (2018). Digital food: From paddock to platform. *Communication Research and Practice, 4*(3), 212–228. doi:10.1080/22041451.2018.1476795

Marcilhac, V., & Pitte, J. R. (2012). Le luxe alimentaire - Une singularité française. Presses Universitaires de Rennes.

Memery, J., Megicks, P., & Williams, J. (2005). Ethical and social responsibility issues in grocery shopping: A preliminary typology. *Qualitative Market Research, 8*(4), 399–412. doi:10.1108/13522750510619760

Mendini, M., & Peter, P. C. (2018). Marketing for social change. Marketing and Humanity: Discourses in the Real World, 206.

Mendini, M., Pizzetti, M., & Peter, P. C. (2019). Social food pleasure: When sharing offline, online, and for society amplifies a pleasurable and healthy food experiences and well-being. *Qualitative Market Research, 22*(4), 544–556. doi:10.1108/QMR-06-2018-0067

Meyer, H. (1999). When the cause is just. *The Journal of Business Strategy, 20*(6), 27–31. doi:10.1108/eb040042 PMID:10230315

Nelson, M. C., Larson, N. I., Barr-Anderson, D., Neumark-Sztainer, D., & Story, M. (2009). Disparities in dietary intake, meal patterning, and home food environments among young adult nonstudents and 2-and 4-year college students. *American Journal of Public Health, 99*(7), 1216–1219. doi:10.2105/AJPH.2008.147454 PMID:19443824

O'Donnell, D. (2018). *Driving immersive experiences in virtual and augmented reality.* https://blog.westerndigital.com/driving-immersive-experience-virtual-augmented-reality/

Pendergast, D. (2010). Getting to Know the Y Generation. In P. Benckendorff & G. Moscardo (Eds.), *Tourism and Generation Y*. CABI Publisher.

Ruppert, B. (2011). New directions in the use of virtual reality for food shopping: Marketing and education perspectives. *Journal of Diabetes Science and Technology, 5*(2), 315–318. doi:10.1177/193229681100500217 PMID:21527099

Steland, A. (2019). *Top 10 Virtual Influencers – Understanding the latest trend and 10 great examples.* Influencerdb. Retrieved from https://influencerdb.com/blog/top-10-virtual-influencers/

Van der Veen, M. (2003). When is food a luxury? *World Archaeology, 34*(3), 405–427. doi:10.1080/0043824021000026422

Varadarajan, P. R., & Menon, A. (1988). Cause-related marketing: A coalignment of marketing strategy and corporate philanthropy. *Journal of Marketing, 52*(3), 58–74. doi:10.1177/002224298805200306

Wang, Y., & Griskevicius, V. (2014). Conspicuous consumption, relationships, and rivals: Women's luxury products as signals to other women. *The Journal of Consumer Research, 40*(5), 834–854. doi:10.1086/673256

Wilcox, K., Kim, H. M., & Sen, S. (2009). Why do consumers buy counterfeit luxury brands? *JMR, Journal of Marketing Research, 46*(2), 247–259. doi:10.1509/jmkr.46.2.247

Youn, S., & Kim, H. (2008). Antecedents of consumer attitudes toward cause-related marketing. *Journal of Advertising Research, 48*(1), 123–137. doi:10.2501/S0021849908080136

Chapter 15

Influence of Celebrity Endorsement on Mature Female Luxury Cosmetic Consumers

Leonor Alberola Amores
Universitat Jaume I, Spain

Susana Miquel Segarra
Universitat Jaume I, Spain

Irene García Medina
Glasgow Caledonian University, UK

Zahaira Fabiola González Romo
Universitat Internacional de Catalunya, Spain

ABSTRACT

A 'celebrity endorser' is any individual easily recognisable by the general public who leverages this visibility and goodwill to either appear alongside the product in an ad or endorse the product. This helps cosmetics brands to architect a strong brand image in the eyes of end users, a result due in large to the transference of the endorser's trustworthiness to the brand she/he backs. The study revealed that mature female consumers were more likely to relate to an ad featuring celebrities of similar age as themselves and who are actual users of the product rather than armchair or hands-off endorsers.

INTRODUCTION

This study primarily aims to perform a critical examination of whether or not the purchasing decisions of "mature women" in the 40-60 demographic around luxury cosmetics are influenced by celebrity endorsements and, if so, to what extent. The study is set in the context of UK's luxury cosmetic industry pegged at £7,6 billion (IBIS, 2019) and easily one of the country's largest markets. In the United Kingdom, income in 2018 was £ 14.2 billions (GlobalData, 2019). The market participants include the who's who of the

DOI: 10.4018/978-1-7998-5882-9.ch015

Copyright © 2021, IGI Global. Copying or distributing in print or electronic forms without written permission of IGI Global is prohibited.

luxury cosmetics space like Chanel, Dior and Gyvenchy (GlobalData, 2019), all vying for the mindspace and wallets of à la mode and image conscious consumers. The offerings include a miscellany ranging from foundations and mascara to haircare products like shampoo and dye. And, in a hypercompetitive market, marketers are making an ongoing effort to improve their formula and ingredients.

A 'celebrity endorser' is any individual easily recognisable by the general public and leverages this visibility and goodwill to either appear alongside the product in an ad or furthermore endorse the product. Celebrity endorsement over the years has emerged as a widespread and firmly implanted marketing strategy in the cosmetic industry (McCracken, 1989). The past decades have seen several products being endorsed by celebrities on television and in print ads. Hollywood icon Monica Bellucci' endorsement for Dior and actress Liv Tyler's for Gyvenchy are just some of the notable instances. In more recent times, there has been a virtual explosion of celebrity endorsements of every possible kind and across a plethora of social media platforms including Facebook, and Instagram (García, 2016).

As mentioned earlier, previous research (Tantiseneepong, et al., 2012) has limited itself for the most part to the influence of celebrity endorsement on relatively younger consumers. Celebrity marketing campaigns are known to exercise a positive influence on their buying decisions, not quite surprising since younger consumers build their self image after celebrities and their style and appearance are more often than not influenced by megastars (Kastanakis et al., 2012). By contrast, with limited research in literature on mature female consumers, the extent of the influence exerted by celebrity endorsement on this segment is a matter of conjecture.

What are the plausible distinguishing features of a certain celebrity that might cause these buyers to move one step closer in their cognitive journey towards the brand? What kind of celebrities carry more credibility and vibe better with mature female consumers? This is a fairly sizable target market and therefore it becomes all the more important for brands to lift the current fog and develop a coherent understanding of it in order to be able to tailor an effective celebrity endorsement strategy, a key element of which consists in picking the "right" endorser who can successfully engage the market (Sharma, et al., 2019).

Background

Back in 1989, McCracken defined 'celebrity' as someone who has become popular by virtue of being occupied in domains like for example cinema, or television. With time, advent of social media, and a general shift of social interests in general, the term has broadened in meaning so much so that there are now alternative routes to becoming a celebrity. The result is that even someone who is not a high-profile actor or sportsperson or without any other 'special achievement' can turn into a celebrity provided she/he can garner public interest (Marshall & Redmond, 2016). Due to changes in the terminology, businesses can now pick and choose from a large and rather mixed bag of celebrities to endorse diverse brands (Hollensen & Schimmelpfennig, 2013).

Celebrity endorsement is the promotion of a product or service by a person who is widely known and uses such public recognition to appear with service or a product in an ad, in effect, giving it her/his seal of approval (Dwivedi et al., 2015). Seno & Lukas, (2007); explained that there are different types of celebrity endorsement: explicit, implicit, co-representational and imperative.

In explicit celebrity endorsement, the endorsers call out the brand or product they are supporting. Implicit endorsement throws hints that the celebrity pictured in the ad is in the habit of using the endorsed product without directly expressing the same (Wang et al., 2017). Such tacit endorsement encourages consumers into trying the product to benefit from the same privileged experience as the celebrity, according to Seno and Lukas (2007). In this class of endorsement, consumers see the celebrity using the product, which seems their preferred option as evidenced by extensive research carried out by Knoll and Matthes (2016). Even so, more research is still needed to figure out what type of celebrity endorsement is more influential vis-a-vis different types of brands and when advertising to various demographics (Pradahan, et al., 2016).

Celebrities are also in the practice of telling consumers to utilize certain products, a method termed as imperative celebrity endorsement. Last but no less important is co-representational advertisement where the celebrity appears only alongside the endorsed product (Seno & Lukas, 2007).

The mileage celebrity endorsement gives brands has been highlighted time and again by several authors (Sääksjärvi et al., 2015). In comparison with the competition, brands that employ celebrity endorsement can enhance their products' standing, improve consumers' product and brand recall, and, in the final analysis, trigger good consumer attitudes towards the brand (Sääksjärvi et al., 2015).

COSMETICS CONSUMER BEHAVIOUR

Consumer behaviour may be defined as the series of actions, starting with the consumer's awareness of a brand, her/his response to information flowing from the brand about its products, as well as how she/he processes such information and makes it a baseline for making buying decisions (Boon-Long & Wongsurawat, 2015). Salomon et al. (2006) offers another definition and explain the consumer behaviour consist in studding the process involve when individuals purchase, use or dispose of products, services, ideas or experiences in order to satisfy needs and desires. Kotler and Keller (2011), in their definition change the needs and desires of Salomon for needs and wants as Enis (1974).

Kumart (2010) refers to the consume of goods and services for personal consumption. Another valuable argument is provided by Egen (2007) regarding understanding consumer behaviour. According to him, awareness of consumer behaviour is a positive contribution to the country's economic state.

With the advent of social media, brands are well-placed to deliver bespoke messages to their target audiences. Besides, they can also keep a closet tab on online buying trends and behaviour (Neti, 2011). This literature examines UK's market for female cosmetics, a fairly large one, and gives some thought to the demographics, market shifts, and factors influencing purchase decisions.

British women are less inclined to buy beauty products online as compared to shopping offline at beauty counters. This is a key insight for brands since footfalls in stores means they must engage customers with highly persuasive instore ads (Mintel 2019). Female consumers aged 16 and above, when they run out of cosmetics stocks, are more likely to buy the same brand to replenish the stock rather than try a new brand. Also, product preferences vary with age groups. Lipsticks are most popular with women aged 65 and above; The biggest buyers of eye-shadow pallets are 16-24-year-olds since this is the stage of life when females feel the need for colour the most and show an urge to try out new shades and dazzling colours (Mintel, 2019).

Another of Mintel's (2019) findings was that women in the 40-60 age group like to spruce up their appearance much like younger women. More than a third of women in this demographic were fond of experimenting with new cosmetic brands while a marginally higher fraction of women in fact felt it is important to dabble in different brands in accordance with their bodily changes . However, it is still not amply clear whether this cosmetics takeup by women helps in boosting their ideal self or in achieving a sense of harmony with their actual self (Nasir, 2016).

SELF CONCEPT

The self-concept comprises a whole bunch of attributes that consumers assign to themselves. The self-concept takes its life from the consumer's self-esteem, their estimation of their overall competences, and how they think they appear to others around them (Matzler et al., 2015). The last factor, in fact, contributes a lion share to a person's self concept . After all, consumers gain an understanding of their self concept while involving with other individuals and their habitat in general (Goldsmith et al., 1999). The self-concept carries a lot of significance for brands because past studies have drawn attention to its preeminent role in influencing market takeup (Goldsmith et al., 1999).

Soneji et al (2015) have performed further research on the self concept, with emphasis on the Self concept Clarity (SCC) model, which helps ascertain whether or not a individual's self concept has been defined confidently and consistently, and exhibits a certain stability. This model postulates that higher the SCC score, the more clarity a consumer will have about who she/he is. Conversely, consumers who score low on SCC could be expected to lack that clarity about who they are and lack the belief in themselves . More importantly, such individuals look to informed and credible external sources (e.g., celebrities) for guidance and counsel. Brands can turn this to good advantage provided they are sufficiently aware and have enough understanding of the self concept (Soneji et al., 2015).

Onkvisit and Shaw (1987) have historically defined the self concept along four key dimensions (namely, real self, self image, ideal self, and looking-glass self) in their attempt to decode the consumer's self image and its influence on purchasing decisions. However, more recent studies have narrowed it down to two dimensions: actual self and ideal self. The actual self is how individuals actually see themselves; ideal self is how persons would like to see themselves and be seen and interpreted by others (Peters et al., 2011).

Castro and Marquez (2017) posit that brands must target the type of self concept (ideal or actual) based on the nature of their product. For instance, offerings belonging in the 'communicating product' category are openly consumed in public and have the objective of boosting the user's self-esteem. Since augmented self-esteem is the ideal image of her/his self that the user wants to convey to others, the brand in question should target the user's ideal self as different from the actual self.

The self concept has a bearing on how consumers perceive and interact with celebrity endorsement, so it is imperative that brands carefully select a celebrity endorser who closely corresponds to the target user's self concept (Goldsmith et al., 2012). Onkvisit and Shaw (1987) think a brand's awareness of the self concept will enable it to tailor effective celebrity-endorsed marketing strategies that are spot-on.

The younger crop of consumers are still in the process of building out their ideal self; therefore, it is only natural that they look to celebrities for inspiration in matters like style, values, and attributes. They are more likely to buy an offering that was endorsed by a celebrity who they thought was an inspiration. When it comes to the mature market, there is scant research about the effectiveness and influence of celebrity endorsers. It remains a matter of speculation whether a mature market does indeed turn for inspiration to celebrities who potentially match their ideal or actual selves (Boon & Lonmore, 2001).

By purchasing products backed by celebrities, consumers probably stand to acquire the desirable associations represented by the celebrity and augment their own ideal self image, a viewpoint underscored by Choi and Rifon (2012). They further hypothesise that consumers will develop a positive attitude toward a brand once they believe there is a great deal of similarity between their the celebrity concerned and their own ideal self.

For the same reason, people typically relate better to an endorser who they consider 'normal-looking,' with a greater perceived similarity with themselves, compared to another celebrity who comes across as highly attractive. This could also be a case of brands effectively targeting consumers' actual self and, in the process, allowing the truth to sink in that matching or attempting to match the looks of the celebrity featured in the ad is an unrealistic and meritless pursuit (Tantiseneepong et al., 2012).

Choi and Rifon (2012) often talk about the self-image/product-image congruence model that lays emphasis on how congruence between consumers' ideal self and the product influences affects their orientation towards both the ad and the brand. Consumers develop positive belief sets about the brand where it is congruent with their self-image. A fit between a brand image and the consumer's actual self is termed 'self-congruity' while a fit between a brand image and the consumer's ideal self goes by the name 'ideal-congruity'.

The customer's positive feeling towards the ad, by extension, results in a positive connection with the featured brand, and this attitude, in turn, directly links to the customer's buying decisions. This model, however, has limited research underpinning it; besides, it may not be in a position to account for the sentiments of consumers belonging to all age groups (Hood, 2012;). Nevertheless, this model can tell if the congruence between the celebrity and consumers' ideal self can influence their outlook on the brand under consideration. Besides, this model could potentially help determine whether negative vibes given off by the consumer to the celebrity can give rise to negative attitudes towards the brand, which could come in the way of the purchase intention (Jain & Roy, 2016).

IDEAL SELF

Choi and Rifon (2012) explained some strains in consumer behaviour that seem to indicate that people settle for brands that represent a right-fit for or correspond to their ideal self, a relationship referred to as consumer-product congruence. So far as the meaning-transfer model is concerned, people subconsciously think that the positive qualities ingrained in the product and brand will move to them, and, by so doing, further improve their image of their ideal self (Lea-Greenwood, 2012). Along the same lines, Choi and Rifon (2012) presume that buyers consume, purchase, and re-purchase products from brands that they have reason to believe will augment their ideal self and correspond closely with their ideal self. Most research finds that brands tend to derive the most value from targeting people' actual self or ideal self (Solomon & Ralbot, 2013).

It has been suggested that wherever a consumer's ideal self conforms to a brand's personality (human characteristics that are often extended to a brand), it drives up the consumer's satisfaction levels. Hence, it is crucial for brands to engage their target consumers effectively and intelligently via celebrity endorsement (Kumar, 2010). Businesses must put the finger on their consumer's understanding of her/his actual and ideal self and define which of these selves will sit well with their ad. The marketing communication should not only be in synch with consumers' aspirations around how they want to appear on the outside but also match their values and attributes (Seno & Lukas, 2007).

While credibility represents an important arsenal in the endorser's armour, this credibility comprised different aspects, and these were valued differently by various demographics. Research has also identified a clear match or chemistry between brand and endorser on one hand, and between endorser and consumer on the other. This means it is crucially important to pick the right-fit celebrity capable of nurturing in consumers favourable attitudes towards the brand. There are also interesting insights on

Influence of Celebrity Endorsement on Mature Female Luxury Cosmetic Consumers

how various nuances of how consumers make decisions about cosmetics purchase can also affect how celebrities influence them. All the same, there is no data on the various influences on the mature female market, which makes a case for research on celebrity endorsement in the cosmetics sector and market for mature females.

LUXURY COSMETIC INDUSTRY AND CELEBRITY ENDORSEMENT

In the sector of cosmetic, a luxury brand can be defined as an impression in the mind of the consumer that could associate the brand with high levels of price, quality, aesthetics and exclusivity (Heine, 2009).

The market for makeup is a burgeoning one, providing a wide and evergrowing portfolio of products (Mintel, 2019). The market has grown by 9% in 2018 in the UK, buoyed by makeup trends like colour-correction, The top luxury brands in the UK market are, not surprisingly, global giants like Chanel, Dior, Gyvenchy, Yves Saint Laurnt, Estee Lauder.

Celebrity endorsement is well-established advertising tool method used by a quarter of all advertisers worldwide. Top-of-the-pack luxury brands in cosmetic industry (the likes of Chanel, Dior and Gyvenchy) lavishly indulge in celebrity endorsement (Ingavale, 2016). This helps them architect a strong brand image in the eyes of end users, a result due in large to the transference of the endorser's trustworthiness to the brand she/he backs (Hodge et al., 2015). Studies show that multiple factors, like the celebrity's attractiveness, trustworthiness, and perceived expertise, tend to weigh with buyers, which makes it all the more important that brands exercise a lot of care to handpick the right endorser who can carry the message effectively and cogently to consumers (Choi & Rifon, 2012).

In the current century, people are aware of image manipulation techniques, like photoshop and editing, widely used to make celebrities look unblemished and unrealistic (Smit et al., 2007). Since customers are more informed than ever before, brands are increasingly choosing a whole new path, namely, running highly realistic campaigns that celebrate age rather than anti-ageing as well as natural appearances and beauty. L'Oréal Paris (2016) was among the first to taste success with a campaign of this kind. Such endorsements vibe much better with women in the 40-60 age group as these urge them to embrace their age and be proud of their mature looks. . This brings focus and discussion on whether luxury cosmetics brands should choose celebrity endorsers whose age correspond to that of their target market, which would make them more relatable for these consumers (LaWare & Moutsatsos, 2013).

On the contrary, a greater part of research indicates that it is with younger audiences that celebrity endorsement produces the most result (Hugosson, Matthys & Phung, 2014). According to this author, the celebrity's attractiveness works better with the younger age groups while older demographics lay more stress on the expertise level and credibility of the endorser. Celebrity-endorsed cosmetics create a more positive feeling with consumers in the 15-34 demographic, and they are more likely to buy the brand as a consequence.

CREDIBILITY, CONGRUENCE AND TRANSFERENCE

The credibility (quality of being trusted) of a celebrity step up her/his effectiveness as an endorser. Source credibility is the people's perception of the expertise, trustworthiness and attractiveness of the celebrity in question (Mannukka et al., 2016).

Spry et al. (2011) are of the view that a credible celebrity endorser can have a good impact on the endorsed product. In their view, consumers believe the credibility of the celebrity and this credibility transfers to the product, thus making the product credible in their eyes, in turn helping to augment the consumers' valuation of the brand and building brand equity. On the contrary, a celebrity endorser who fails to convince the end audience could potentially drive consumers away from the brand, and this can possibly happen in instances where more than one product is endorsed by the selfsame celebrity (Farrell et al., 2000).

Consumers believe the celebrity has sufficient understanding and experience of the product she/he is endorsing and this is termed as (perceived) expertise. And trustworthiness is the quantum of confidence and honesty that people associate with the celebrity endorser (Dwivedi et al., 2015).

Brands frequently pick celebrities from the product job or who are in the habit of using the product to impart the distinctive image of an expert or an opinion leader. Opinion leaders are believed to have the ability to influence opinions or beliefs of others; they also liaise between brands and their consumers. To sound credible, brands ought to choose effective opinion leaders (Hoyer et al., 2008).

However, Valente et al (2014) point to tennist player Rafa Nadal as an example of an endorser whose lack of expertise in recommending a financial services provider, namely, Sabadell, failed the credibility test with consumers. The results found consumers failed to view a sportsman as having the expertise to be able to recommend a financial company compared to his hugely successful endorsement of sports as for example Nike. Mannukka et al (2016) sounds a cautionary note saying that consumers are going to draw the inference, based on a celebrity endorser's occupation and likely use of the product, that a certain celebrity is perhaps not going to be fully experienced in the products she/he is endorsing.

As a result, brands have to factor in their long-term aims and interests when choosing a celebrity for their product in order for consumers to deem the celebrity as credible and feel confident about the messaging that reaches them.

Sääksjärvi et al. (2016) opines that the attractiveness of a celebrity endorser is important in terms of exercising a positive influence. Research indicates that attractiveness determines a celebrity endorser's perceived credibility and quality. Attractiveness includes appealing physical appearance, facials, as well as body features, besides personal style. Endorsers who consumers considered as physically attractive were more successful in driving appreciable changes to consumers' purchase decisions than, say, by less attractive or "unattractive" comparisons (Spry et al., 2011).

Lee and Park (2014) say that attractiveness holds within its definition other factors such as personal characteristics (personality or social status for example). A celebrity's admirers typically 'pick' characteristics of their object of admiration since it is their very aspiration to be like them.

In a world with ever-changing public interests, it is therefore critically necessary for marketers to identify the right kind of celebrity endorsers who people can find credible to provide an impetus to consumer buying process (Marshall & Redmond, 2016).

The compatibility of the celebrity endorser with the brand (congruence) is another factor that influences the endorser's effectiveness (Silvera & Austad, 2004). Congruence is essentially the perceived affinity between the brand, and the endorser. In commentaries about brand congruence, authors consider the logic and consistency between a celebrity endorser's characteristics and that of the products she/he endorses (Seno & Lukas, 2007). As illustration of a successful celebrity endorsement we can use the example of the actor George Cloony who was endorsing Omega´s luxury watch collection. Backed by Cloony's physical attraction, Omega was able to make people belive that the celebrity were ideal, so celebrity brand congruence is important.

Influence of Celebrity Endorsement on Mature Female Luxury Cosmetic Consumers

Halonen-Knight and Hurmerinta (2010) feel a celebrity-brand mismatch might turn off people from buying the endorsed product. However small degree of incongruence in celebrity endorsement might stimulate buying behaviour. Compared to ads with a high degree of such congruence, those with little to moderate incongruence might actually end up generating more attention for the ad (Lee & Thorson, 2008).

It is still not clear whether brands intentionally choose a celebrity to create incongruence and generate any interest thereof (Lee & Thorson, 2008). Also, there is very little research regarding consumers preferring endorsement by a matching celebrity. Given this scenario, it is necessary to identify brands that might benefit from congruent endorsement and others that might stand to conversely benefit from incongruent endorsement (Halonen Knight et al., 2010)

Research models such as the "meaning transfer model" have drawn the conclusion that a transfer of associations occurs between the celebrity endorser and the endorsed product (Lea-Greenwood, 2012). These include the reputation and associated attributes the celebrity endorser has obtained externally from her/his film roles or in publicised personal life; all of these associations transfer to the endorsed brand and product (Halonen-Knight & Humerinta, 2010).

The final stage of the model consists of a transfer of characteristics from the celebrity and the brand to the consumer through consumption, gifting or other possession of the brand. This model is particularly significant in that it tries to ascertain whether or not consumers believe the desired characteristics of the endorser and brand got transferred to them and, in addition, attempts to ascertain if the celebrity indirectly influenced them or not (Jain & Roy, 2016; Halonen-Knight & Humerinta, 2010).

Nevertheless, Jain and Roy (2016) also point to some negative connotation of the "transfer" process. Consumer studies indicate negative connections with the celebrity were more likely to be transferred to the brand than positive ones. What's more, negative associations with a brand can damage their brand image and reputation (Hood, 2012). Celebrities embroiled in sensational scandals can act as a drag on the effectiveness of their endorsements (White et al., 2007). As an example have reaction of Dior with Sharon Stone. On May 12 of 2008 over 69,000 people lost their lives when a massive earthquake hit southwest China. Sharon Stone took the news as an opportunity to get political, suggesting that the earthquake was "karma" because of Beijing's treatment of Tibet. Stone later apologized, but the backlash against the actress led luxury brand Christian Dior to cancel Stone's endorse contract (Xiao & Li, 2012)

There is not research that prove if a negative event, such as a scandal, would have a direct influence on the "meaning transfer model," especially on the final phase of transference from brand to consumer. Even if we were to admit the possibility of such transfer, it is still not clear if negative associations are transferred to the same degree as positive associations or if consumers would still want to buy a brand endorsed by a tainted celebrity (Jain & Roy, 2016).

In sum, celebrity endorsement serves as a potent marketing tool wherever end users think the endorser is credible with regard to her/his expert skills, trustworthiness, and attractiveness. In this regard, it is important to develop an indepth understanding of key concepts around consumer behaviour associated with the purchase of celebrity-endorsed products in order to reach the inference that celebrity endorsement influences such buying (Wallace, 2014).

SOCIAL MEDIA AND CELEBRITY ENDORSEMENT

Maturing of technology and rise to prominence of social media in particular have played a key role in redefining 'celebrity'. Celebrities increasingly connect with consumers/followers on Facebook, Instagram,

Twitter and Snapchat, giving them a sneak-peak of their personal space, including of the products they use (Turner, 2014).A study of online celebrity presence by Kowalczyk and Pounders (2016), reveals that consumers felt motivated to buy products that celebrities endorsed via their social platforms, either implicitly or explicitly. People got the feeling of being able to connect with celebrities on a personal level and felt product recommendations they made were authentic.

However, participants in the above study were younger females, and other similar studies have also invariably centred on the same public.. The UK boasts around 7 million female users on Facebook aged 40-60, as per Statisa (2019). This large populace on the social networking site certainly evokes keen interest and represents a compelling business opportunity to research how and to what extent this group is influenced by online celebrity endorsements (BrandFinance, 2019).

MAIN FOCUS OF THE CHAPTER

This research aims to examine the way buying behaviour of mature female consumers aged 40 to 60 in the matter of luxury cosmetics is influenced by celebrity endorsement. The objectives are to:

- Examine the awareness or recognition level of mature female consumers with respect to celebrity endorsement campaigns by luxury cosmetic brands.
- Identify the features that they deem most credible in a celebrity endorser.
- Examine how mature female consumers perceive their own ideal self and whether the luxury cosmetic brands they buy are in synch with this ideal self.
- Analyse, using aspects of the match-up hypothesis, from the standpoint of mature female consumers, whether luxury cosmetic brands are successfully choosing appropriate celebrities to endorse their brand.
- Provide actionable recommendations, which will help stimulate further research to possibly improve the potential of celebrity endorsement as an efficient marketing tool for luxury cosmetic brands now and in the future.

Methodology

In order that the research is effective and meaningful, it is important to understand what kind of data needs to be collected to fulfil the research objectives (Wilson, 2014). The following research rationale gives an indication of primary and secondary data and explain which of these is advantageous to the study.

Primary data is typically gathered r using surveys, interviews, and other collection methods keeping in mind the specific requirements of the research topic. Basically, primary research is independent of any pre-existing data collected by a previous researcher. Primary data has historically been expensive from a cost and time perspective but the arrival of social media and other relatively newer crop of technologies has enabled easy sharing of, say, questionnaires, with a large sample of consumers without having to worry about cost (Zikmund et al., 2010). At the time of this research, there is no pre-existing secondary data that considers the awareness level of mature female consumers in the cosmetics market about their ideal self and further correlates the same with celebrity endorsement. Besides, a major chunk of contemporary research is centred on the awareness of relatively younger female consumers about celebrity endorsement and the attributes of celebrity endorsers that they consider important. Therefore, collecting primary data, which involves gathering fresh responses from mature female consumers, a segment not sampled by any past study, will precisely address the aims of this current research (Bryman & Bell, 2011).

Regarding the research approach on which the methodology of this study is predicated, alternative approaches are critically considerate in order to establish the most relevant for this particular research. Positivism and interpretivism are popular epistemological research paradigms. Epistemology is the nature of knowledge the researcher has about the external environment as well as her/his outlook on the external environment (Saunders et al., 2009).

A paradigm exerts a certain influence on the research and the same is chosen as basis when conducting a study based on the outlook and attitude of the researcher as well as her/his conviction of how data should be collected, examined, and leveraged (Bryman & Bell, 2011).

Positivism concerns itself only with the application of science to authenticate a certain social phenomenon. It is essentially a fundamental study that applies existing theory to the analysis of a situation with a view to validate it and, in the course of it, the researcher remains objective (Saunders et al., 2009).

Interpretivism is basically the belief that social features of the world of business are too complex to be validated through the application of natural sciences. By extension, in order to understand social phenomena, the researcher must participate in the social environment in which it takes place. This philosophy calls on the researcher to be subjective and holds the belief that individuals experience phenomena in different ways (Wilson, 2014).

The following research seeks to follow the positivist route. The philosophical paradigm of positivism sits well with this research because of the application of existing celebrity endorsement theories. Wilson (2014) opines that positivism is centred around whether or not the social word can be researched using natural science as a basis and regards as important the application of literature to the study of a social phenomenon. The interpretivists believe that every single participant has her/his individual experience that theory cannot generalize.

The positivists state that the researcher is the person who is being objective to the phenomenon under research. The researcher is objective about how celebrity endorsement impacts mature females; therefore, the research is independent of any hypothesis (Hugosson, 2014).

Identifying the research approach is the next logical step, and this could be either inductive or deductive. The key influence here is the positivist research philosophy (Wilson, 2014). In the inductive approach, the research is centred on collecting data and, based on its conclusions, evolving a theory. On the other hand, the focal point of a deductive approach is the relationship between theory and research, and, furthermore, application of theoretical frameworks to the research. It is considered an element of the positivist philosophical theory (Ghauri and Gronhaug, 2005).

This study embraces the deductive approach since theoretical frameworks like the self concept and the match-up hypothesis are both put to use in this research to develop an understanding of how they affect the mature female user market. The other overarching reason why the deductive approach is best suited to this study is that it underscores the relationship between research and theory by drawing on preexisting literature on celebrity endorsement to realise the objectives. An inductive approach is ruled out since the study doesn't aim to develop a new theory around celebrity endorsement as a marketing strategy (Saunders et al., 2009).

The philosophy and approach underlying a research is responsible for shaping its design. Any study could choose to follow one of three research designs: exploratory, descriptive, and explanatory. (Burns & Burns, 2008)

Exploratory study interrogates what is happening in the context of the research by employing inquisitive research methods and seeks to frame new theories and push the envelope of knowledge (Wilson, 2014).

Descriptive involves carrying out research around contemporary or past phenomena and employs various interview methods to collect data (Gill & Johnson, 2010).

Explanatory research concerns itself with uncovering relationships between different variables responsible for causing a certain phenomenon. In general, it endeavours to establish a cause-and-effect relationship between a phenomenon and the reason that provocated it (Blumberg et al., 2014).

As seen in above, since an exploratory design works towards developing a new theory, it has little or no relevance to the current study whose intent and purpose is to relate contemporary writings on celebrity endorsement to the understanding by mature female consumers of celebrity endorsement as well as their own interpretation of their ideal selves. And because this study doesn't seek to contribute to any new theory by putting to use inquisitive research tools, exploratory design can be eliminated from its scope (Dick et al 2008).

The study fundamentally aims to perform a systematic inquiry into how celebrity endorsement influences the purchasing choices of mature female consumers with a view to establish the facts of the case. Therefore, by adopting a descriptive approach, complete with structured interviews and questionnaires, the research can hope to gain an accurate and deep understanding of the characteristics they think are important in a celebrity endorser (Blumberg et al., 2014).

Data Collection

Research will use the mixed-method strategy, which employs quantitative and qualitative methods for gathering primary data. Quantitative research can be general when it comes to analysing the awareness level of consumers and the attributes of celebrity endorsers that consumers deem relevant. This means the researcher can use a large sample to take stock of any common themes in the data (Wilson, 2014).

This research is deductive, so it is worthwhile to get qualitative data as well, via interviews, and this will provide further granularity and detail to the questionnaire responses. Qualitative research imparts more depth, overall, when it comes to interrogating literature concepts unlike numerical data generated via quantitative tools that fail to bring out people's perspectives around their own ideal self (Baxter, 2015).

Key data method use in quantitative data collection is the questionnaire (Zikmund, 2009). A questionnaire comprises of structured questions designed to realize the objectives outlined by a study. Postal and online questionnaire are some variants of this tool. Questionnaires help in obtaining information Web-based questionnaires can be administered free of cost and in a timely manner to a large population. In this approach, respondents get enough time to answer the questions without feeling any undue pressure (Baxter, 2015). Sometimes, respondents interpret questions wrongly, leading to incorrect and invalid responses. A lot of care should go into framing structured questions needed to elicit the right responses and valid data. There is the possibility of the questionnaire being administered to the wrong persons or sample, and the result is inaccurate representation of the sample. Mailing out questionnaires can be a tedious and time-consuming exercise (Saunders et al., 2009).

This study aims to reach out to a large number of female consumers aged 40-60, so an online questionnaire is most appropriate. Also, as previously stated, the positivist theory and approach that typifies this research involves generalising within the study based on results gathered from a large sample.

Needless to say, sending and receiving individual postal questionnaires is a time-consuming and wasteful process while online questionnaires are faster to administer and process (Jankowicz, 2000).

Influence of Celebrity Endorsement on Mature Female Luxury Cosmetic Consumers

This study also makes use of interviews as a data collection method to supplement data provided by online questionnaires as well as explore in depth the perspectives of mature female consumers on various literature concepts in celebrity endorsement. In addition, small focus groups were brought together to discuss specific themes, and while they were at it, the participants were observed for their verbal and non-verbal communication, besides gathering their feedback (Zikmund, 2009).

As observed by Wilson (2014) face-to-face interviews have the advantage of letting the author talk at length with respondents and flesh out more details about the individual's attitudes and beliefs with respect to a subject, rather than banking simply on non-verbal communication. The researcher can ensure she/he is on the same page as the respondent by explaining the concept of celebrity endorsement in more detail before plunging into the interview (Sekaran & Bougie, 2013).

The online questionnaire must include questions that are well-structured and sufficiently open-ended while being specific enough to capture precise data that maps to the research objectives (Baxter, 2015).

The online questionnaire developed for this research meets two of the objectives of the study. Questionnaires typically include different types of questions (Baxter et al., 2015). The table below highlights the key features of each type of questions: Open, Closed, Multiple choice, Likert scale and Rank order questions (Wilson, 2014).

For this study, closed questions with fixed responses are the most appropriate. Also multiple choice options and ranking scales are suitable.

The online questionnaire returns quantitative data; therefore, responses from the questionnaire needs be simple and easy to slice and dice. As mentioned above, if participants are allowed to answer however they please, the result could be lengthy and digressive answers that are going to be difficult to decode (Bryman & Bell, 2011). Since trustworthiness, attractiveness and expertise have been identified as the attributes that contribute to the endorser's credibility, it is only appropriate to let participants rank them in their order of priority and establish levels of importance. A ranking scale method is utiliced to get a handle on which factors are the most valuable for consumers in the cosmetics market.

Closed questions have the advantage of returning succinct and simple responses and can be easily administered to a fairly large sample. According to Baxter et al., (2015), questions tend to attract participants' interest than, say, statements on a Likert scale; the latter often suffers from 'acquiescence bias,' which causes respondents to agree with or positively answer the questions posed. On the other hand, when faced with a 'Yes' or 'No' answers, respondents have to necessarily choose one and only one that connects with their specific scenario. In addition, open-ended questions are also included in this research to provide them with enough latitude to develop answers of their choice. When considering the awareness level of mature female consumers about celebrity endorsement in the luxury cosmetics market, they are encouraged to name celebrity endorsers they are aware of. This gives the researcher a sneak-peek into the kind of celebrities this market segment is more likely to recognize (Blumberg et al., 2011).

In a structured interview, respondents are provided with identical questionnaires, which facilitates a comparative analysis of responses. By contrast, the unstructured interviews with opens up a field of questions, which are triggered by the interviewees' initial responses (Jankowicz, 2000).

So far as the current study is concerned, the interviews will have open-ended questions whose focus is on consumer behaviour and celebrity endorsement; however, there is no provision to allow interviewees to expand their initial answers any further. But the interviews certainly provide a window for the author to show any concept that the interviewee is not aware of. Terms like 'self concept', or "congruence" are explained to dispel any ambiguity in the respondent's mind as would result in unclear answers. The interviews will show images to interviewees and then proceed to ask them to identify attributes they

Influence of Celebrity Endorsement on Mature Female Luxury Cosmetic Consumers

would typically relate to the celebrity and brands they endorse. They are also quizzed about whether they believe the celebrity is indeed a right-fit for the brand she is endorsing (Blumberg et al., 2011).

Sampling

The focus of the current research is on mature female luxury cosmetic consumers in the 40-60 demographic. As it is impossible to collate data from the entire universe of the females in the age of the study, a representative sample that sums up the population in a nutshell would have to be considered.

This research makes use of non-probability sampling to understand the view of point of mature female luxury consumers aged 40-60. Snowball sampling technique comes across as the most effective method for the current study based on the evaluation of competing sampling methods. Snowball sampling carries the clear advantage that it can be conveniently shared by the researcher online with female luxury consumers aged 40-60 within her/his family and friends circle as opposed to convenience sampling in which just about anyone who is available on hand can readily participate. Furthermore, with the snowball approach, the researcher's family and friends can share the same questionnaire with their online friends who answer the same criteria and get them to participate. In effect, 'snowballing' the sample size with little effort. Quota sampling was ruled out as the study doesn't call for representing the entire population, given the unique criteria of the samples (Ticehurst & Veal, 2000).

RESULTS

Recongnition Level

All the people participant in the study knew what celebrity endorsement mean, and 90 percent of them manage to recognize celebrities who endorse various cosmetic products. Claudia Schiffer, Nicole Kidman and Penelope Cruz, endorsers of Chanel, were celebrities recognise very easily by interviewees. Every single interviewee had watched celebrity endorsed products advertised on television, and a majority of them were mindful of their presence in stores.

The following question of the interview quizzed interviewees as to whether their purchase of any product had been influenced by celebrity endorsers, and 90% of respondents answered in the negative. Knoll and Matthes' (2016) opine that implicit advertising, wherein a celebrity subtly suggests that they use a certain brand, is capable of persuading a consumer to use the product. Interviewee #1 and #7 responded that they would be willing to try a celebrity-backed product:

"I'd be very keen to find out if they [celebrity endorsers] really use the product and aren't just doing it just for the sake of money." Interviewee #1

"I don't think I am going to be excited though. If I saw someone [a celebrity] I liked or admired I might try out the product they are using. But I'd like to believe that they indeed use it." Interviewee #7

Interviewee #1 and #7 said they would like to presume that celebrity endorsers are also users of the product in question, an indication that implicit celebrity endorsement was more effective vis-a-vis explicit endorsement. In addition, six out of seven respondents who said celebrity endorsement was influential

Influence of Celebrity Endorsement on Mature Female Luxury Cosmetic Consumers

in persuading them to buy a certain brand seemed to believe that the celebrity used the luxury brand and derived the benefits endorsed by her/him. This is very much in line with Seno and Lukas (2007) view that implicit endorsement is more effective.

The questionnaire also asked participants to rank factors (price, packaging, quality and celebrity endorser) they thought were critical to cosmetics buying on a scale of 1 to 4, "1" being most important and "4" being least important. A majority of female consumers aged 40-60 ranked quality as the most important factor, and celebrity endorsers the least important, in their choice of a luxury cosmetic brand.

Hence, it can be inferred that celebrity endorsement is not significantly important for this cosmetics segment even where they know who is endorsing a certain product.

An overwhelming majority of 98 participants out of 100 participants were active on one social networking site at the very least. However, a massive majority of 98 percent of them answered in the negative when asked if ever a celebrity endorser had influenced them to buy a cosmetic brand.

Potential buyers watch celebrities endorsing online products online they are more likely to be persuaded into buying them. Respondents in the current study did not seem to have been swayed by celebrity endorsement though a majority of them were active on at least one social media networking site. The reason could be their low recognition level about celebrity endorsers on social media, which is borne out by the fact that 85 percent of respondents acknowledged that they were not cognisant of celebrities endorsing luxury cosmetic brands via social networks (Kowalczyk & Pounders 2016).

Only 20% of respondents didn't have a presence on any social network, with one saying:

"I'm not very active on social networks, so probably I miss out a lot of stuff, like online celebrity endorsements. But let me tell you this, I don't think I am going to be influenced even if I get to see these endorsers a lot on social media." Interviewee #4

The person who was interviewed was deadset that if she had a social networks presence, she would not have been persuaded by a celebrity endorser into buying a certain product. Since this respondent pool had a low awareness level with respect to celebrity endorsed ads on social networks, the sample is not particularly suited to the application of Kowalczyk and Pounders' (2016) findings.

Another theme that popped in the course of the study was that interviewees' children were playing a key role in increasing their parents' awareness of celebrity endorsement. When they were questioned to cite some names of celebrity endorsers of luxury cosmetic products, 20% respondents said they were conscious of the younger crop of celebrity endorsers thanks to their children's recognition of them:

"And because of my daughter I know about Zoella and she gets paid to endorse cosmetic products." Interviewee #1

"Lily-Rose Deep, Johnny Depp's daughter, it seems, backs a perfume or so, my daughter tells me. So wanted me to buy her that for birthday. And, yes, I did." Interviewee #2

Respondents admitted that celebrity endorsers were indeed an influence on their children and, further, that they were in the habit of purchasing such endorsed products for their children. It was stated earlier, pre-existing studies reveal younger people were more disposed to let themselves influence by celebrity endorsers. Even so, the current research suggests that their children's recognition of celebrity endorsers does exert some influence on the buying decisions of mature female consumers in the 40-60 demographic though in all certainty they themselves were not directly influenced (Chan, 2013).

Features of Celebrity Endorsement

The online survey and interview were framed with the idea of identifying the various characteristics or features of a celebrity endorser of luxury cosmetic brands that consumers thought were important to their buying decision. The survey posed the question 'Which attributes in a celebrity endorser would you consider as most important for a luxury cosmetics brand?' and asked respondents to rank these qualities on a scale of 1 to 3, "1" being most important and "3", least important'. Seno & Lukas (2007) point to expertise, physical attractiveness, and trustworthiness as some of the most critical attributes of a celebrity endorser.

A majority of respondents identified expertise as the most important feature that a celebrity endorser ought to have in order to be effective and successful. Luxury cosmetics brands select celebrities who utilise the product, such that the target market deems them credible or is influenced by the endorser's expertise. (Hoyer et al., 2008) Respondents to the online survey were also questioned – 'Which kind of profession in a celebrity [model, singer, actress, or reality television star] would you be more disposed to trust when endorsing a luxury cosmetic product?'

The above findings are in sync with the theory set forth by Hoyer et al., (2008) as well as Seno and Lukas (2007) that a credible endorser is one whose persona effectively intersects expertise and trust-worthiness. The researchers discovered consumers are more likely to trust celebrities with a certain level of perceived expertise in relation to the product under consideration. This expertise was deemed by respondents to come from the celebrities' practical contact with the product in their professional role.

An oft-recurring theme in the interviews was the appropriateness of the celebrity endorser's age to the product she/he was backing. Three of the people who were interviewed showed a preference of celebrities with an appropriate age:

"Supposing they are endorsing a cosmetic brand then I feel they ought to be appropriate, age-wise I mean, to the kind of audience they are aimed. What is the point otherwise?" Interviewee #2

"From my perspective, brands should show consider a certain age range when it comes to picking stars endorsers. A lot of times, people get too caught up with wishing to be younger than they are. They should probably accept the age they are. And brands should egg them on to do that." Interviewee #4

"I think that is important the age like a parameter, and brands should bring in more older endorsers." Interviewee #6

The study reveal on the fact that people rather prefer to see famouses who are closer to their age range endorsing luxury cosmetics. Another conclusion is that brands are increasingly prevailing on consumers to accept their age, rather than obscuring it. Jane and Roy (2016) have narrowed the trust, experience and appeal as key attributes associated with creating a reliable celebrity supporter. Even so, respondents felt the celebrity's age was also a key attribute and endorsers must be age appropriate to the target audience. Alternatively, brands should feature a range of endorsers from different age groups. This means that a celebrity of the same age or belonging to the same age group as they can affect this sample.

Influence of Celebrity Endorsement on Mature Female Luxury Cosmetic Consumers

Self Concept and Ideal Self

The structured interview comprised questions aimed at capturing the perception of the ideal self of the people who were interviewed and whether or not they purchase luxury cosmetic brands that correlate their ideal self. The terms 'self concept' and 'ideal self' were defined for the benefit of the participants prior to the interview.

90 percent of respondents seemed confident that they were able to identify their ideal self. A pivotal theme that emerged from this discourse was that the respondents' ideal self consisted in appearing younger in the eyes of others:

"Yes, I think I buy cosmetics mostly to look younger than what I am, I must admit. Therefore I think my ideal self is to be a younger. Because I am conscious that I am getting older and want to show a younger image." Interviewee #1

"Certainly, I would like to look younger than what I am. To feel youthful and look nicer, I do my makeup and hairstyle every day and once a week I'm going to a professional stylist." Interviewee #8

Authors think luxury cosmetic brands stand to gain the most value by targeting their promotionals at consumers' ideal self. Quite many respondents in the current study acknowledged that they were desirous of appearing younger in the eyes of friends and colleagues and their luxury cosmetics purchases were driven by this intent. They purchase cosmetics that correspond to their ideal self. People who were interviewed declare that purchased lotions to keep their skin younger- and healthier-looking. One of the respondents said:

"Because they are kind of rejuvenating brands, I buy Dior and Guerlain. And yes, I do want to look and feel younger deep inside than what I am. Having young daughters does impact my selections." Interviewee #7

This is very much in step with literature as interviewee #7 was quite conscious that she buys the luxury cosmetic products that resonate with her ideal self. Hence, it can be inferred that this pool of mature women buy cosmetics that relate to the image they want to build and nurture in others' eyes. Only one interviewee bought a brand that related to her ideal self, namely, Dior and Guerlain. By contrast, the other respondents bought products – like anti-wrinkle formulas and moisturisers that they thought were in synch with ideal selves.

Self Concept Clarity Model

A new theme surfaced from the responses to the interview question – 'When it comes to buying cosmetic products or following makeup trends, do you look to celebrities for inspiration? Or is there any other reason why you follow celebrities?' and this was in line with much of the literature around the self concept clarity model Consumers who score low in the SCC model tend to be younger and still working on developing their own style and appearance. Such low scorers are inclined to be less confident about their self (Soneji et al, 2015). The responses of many interviews corresponded with this body of literature:

"I think new generations are more likely to keep a tab on celebrity trends compared to older people my age. As a matter of course, I don't follow celebrities but just in case, I come across a style and that catches my eye, I would try it out for sure." Interviewee #3

"No I don't. Though my daughters do." Interviewee #7

Through close association and contact ("ruboff effect") with younger members in their family, the interviews realize that younger people are increasingly inspired in the matter of appearances and styles by celebrities. This having been said, all ten interviewees, when asked if they search celebrities for inspiration in relation to luxury cosmetics, answered in the negative:

"I don't, I like to believe I have my own style. On television or in a magazine, if I see a celebrity with a lovely look, I might think of trying it out. That doesn't mean I go out my way to get draw inspiration from them." Interviewee #6

This leads to the belief that this women would mark high in the self-concept clarity model since they don't seem to look to celebrities for cues or inspiration when it comes to their own appearance. Far from being influenced by celebrity trends, they seem confident with their own evolved style. (Soneji et al., 2015).

Positive Associations

An overwhelming number of respondents assigned the most favourable features to Nicole Kidman and Monica Bellucci. They tended to focus more on the positive personality characteristics, like 'trustworthy, caring, approachable and intelligent,' rather than the outward form in case of Nicole Kidman and Monica Bellucci. By contrast, they chose to associate negative characteristics with Liv Tyler probably because her father is Steven Tayler singer of rock group Aerosmith, and maybe there is a transfer between father and daughter.

These responses closely correspond to Choi and Rifon's (2012) congruence model, which proposes that consumers who are in harmony with the celebrity have tendency to also be favourably disposed to the brand. When asked - "Which famous would you identify to the most (in terms of style, characteristics, etc.) and why?" – all of the respondents said they believe that it is to Nicole Kidman and Monica Bellucci that they relate the most:

"I identify most to, eh...Nicole Kidman. At least, I think so. And, she's more or less my age." Interviewee #8

"I probably identify most to Monica Bellucci. Have seen many of her movies, so I think I know her a little better than the others." Interviewee #4

"I'd probably identify most to Nicole Kidman. We are exactly the same age. And have a similar style too.". Interviewee #10

When questioned to define their ideal self, more than 50 percent of respondents said their ideal self consists in appearing younger; so, respondents in the current study find common ground with celebri-

Influence of Celebrity Endorsement on Mature Female Luxury Cosmetic Consumers

ties of the same age. In addition, they associate positively ('trustworthy, professional and intelligent') with a celebrity they relate to the most, which is further indication that they consider such celebrities as credible endorsers (Solomon et al., 2015).

CONCLUSION

In its essence, celebrity endorsement does not exert a great deal of influence on the buying decisions of mature female consumers in the luxury cosmetics market under consideration.

The current research shows that mature females in the 40-60 demographic are more likely to approve of celebrity endorsers who they can clearly connect with. Therefore, luxury cosmetic brands in this buyer segment would stand to benefit if they increasingly target their promotionals towards the actual self rather than the ideal self of their intended audience. And while they are at it, brands are recommended to bring such celebrity endorsers into play who are in the same or similar age group as the target market. In addition, in order that the endorser is perceived as credible, brands must strive to imply (implicit advertising) that she/he is also a user of the product under consideration.

The research was carried out on a small sample comprising 10 interviewees and 100 online questionnaire participants; it is now proposed that the same study be conducted on a larger scale to frame application-oriented general concepts around how celebrity endorsers influence mature female buyers. Mature female consumers have a significant presence on various social media platforms, so it is recommended that conclusions of this study be used as a beach head to launch further studies on how to amplify the effect of celebrity endorsement on social media users in this age group.

The small sample size of this research proved a key limitation since it resulted in rather weak generalisations around how celebrity endorsers influence the buying behaviour of mature female consumers in the luxury cosmetics market. Also, the structured and standardised interviews didn't provide room for further exploratory questions that might have helped gather more indepth and granular data on respondents' opinions and values. Hence, there was no scope for any further exploration of existing literature on celebrity endorsement.

By using descriptive design methods that enable collection of comprehensive and thorough data around the interpretations of self concept and congruence, the study presents real-world and large-scale indications of how celebrity endorsers influence consumers.

Recognition

Implicit celebrity endorsement was considered most effective and influential with consumers, as per the research. The focus of others studies has been younger people; this opened up the possibility to study the recognition level and preferences of older demographics in the matter of celebrity endorsement.

The respondents were acutely conscious of in-store and journal ads, though the major part of them didn't seem to have been persuaded by celebrity endorsers into buying luxury cosmetics. A few respondents acknowledged there were more conscious of celebrity endorsers, something attributable to celebrity endorsers' influence on respondents' children. The result was that such respondents bought celebrity-endorsed products for their children. A key finding here was that respondents were indeed buying celebrity-endorsed products though they themselves were not directly influenced by the celebrity.

In addition, responses to the online survey revealed that product quality was the factor respondents overwhelmingly weighed in when buying a cosmetic; in stark contrast, the celebrity endorser was considered the least important factor. Also, responses in several earlier research on younger people indicate participants would like to see more of implicit advertising, particularly where the celebrity endorser suggests that she/he is also a user of the said product.

Respondents scored low in terms of their awareness of celebrity endorsers, quite surprising since a few of them were on social media and quite engage at that. This calls for more research to identify the causes of low recognition of celebrity-endorsed ads on social networks and ways luxury cosmetic brands can fine-tune their targeting of mature female consumers on social networking sites.

Features

According to existing literature, expertise, trustworthiness and attractiveness were the key characteristics that informed the credibility of the celebrity endorser. Nevertheless, the relative importance of these characteristics might vary from one consumer to another. The aim of the current study was to establish the features of celebrity endorsers that mature female consumers deemed important, as well as any additional attributes that they thought were relevant. The online survey served as an effective tool for bringing these characteristics to light.

The questionnaire found that mature female consumers had a greater chance of trusting celebrities, given their experience with luxury cosmetic brands, a discovery that matched the observation in current literature that credible endorsers often came with a mix of expertise and trustworthiness.

Apart from expertise, consumers also thought the endorser's age was a key feature, as revealed by interviews and questionnaires. Consumers' favourable disposition toward the Dior ad featuring Monica Bellucci, who was in the same age group as them, mirrored this sentiment. The broader implication is that it's time luxury brands began considering including multiple celebrity endorsers belonging to different age groups in their ads, so as to be able to appeal to more numbers of mature consumers.

Self Concept

According to Castro & Marquez (2017), luxury brands stand to benefit the most by targeting a consumer's ideal self. The interviews used in the current study helped flesh out the respondents' perception of their ideal self.

The answers of the interviews gave rise to another theme that helped fathom out the female consumers' ideal self. It appears that their ideal self was a younger and fresh look they desired to show to others, which, in turn, influenced their luxury cosmetics choices and purchases.

As stated earlier, the research sample also believed that they were more likely to be swayed by a celebrity endorsers belonging in the same age group as themselves. So age appropriateness also figured as an important feature of the celebrity endorser, a feature that corresponded to the consumers' actual self rather than their ideal self.

REFERENCES

Baxter, K., Courage, C., & Caine, K. (2015). *Understanding Your Users* (2nd ed.).

Influence of Celebrity Endorsement on Mature Female Luxury Cosmetic Consumers

Blumberg, B., Cooper, R., & Schindler, P. (2014). *Business Research Methods* (4th ed.). McGraw-Hill Education.

Boon, S., & Lomore, C. (2001). Admirer-celebrity relationships among young adults: Explaining perceptions of celebrity influence on identity. *Human Communication Research, 27*(3), 432–465. doi:10.1111/j.1468-2958.2001.tb00788.x

Boon-Long, S., & Wongsurawat, W. (2015). Social media marketing evaluation using social network comments as an indicator for identifying consumer purchasing decision effectiveness. *Journal of Direct, Data and Digital Marketing Practice, 17*(2), 130–149. doi:10.1057/dddmp.2015.51

Bryman, A., & Bell, E. (2011). *Business Research Methods* (3rd ed.). Oxford University Press.

Burns, B., & Burns, A. (2008). *Business Research Methods and Statistics using SPSS* (1st ed.). SAGE Publications Ltd.

Castro, L., & Marquez, J. (2017). The use of Facebook to explore self-concept: Analysing Colombian consumers. *Qualitative Market Research, 20*(1), 43–59. doi:10.1108/QMR-12-2015-0086

Chan, K., Leung Ng, Y., & Luk, E. K. (2013). Impact of Celebrity Endorsement in Advertising on Brand Image Among Chinese Adolescents. *Young Consumers, 14*(2), 167–179. doi:10.1108/17473611311325564

Choi, M., & Rifon, N. (2012). It Is a Match: The Impact of Congruence between Celebrity Image and Consumer Ideal Self on Endorsement Effectiveness. *Psychology and Marketing, 29*(9), 639–650. doi:10.1002/mar.20550

Dwivedi, A., Johnson, W., & McDonald, E. (2015). Celebrity endorsement, self-brand connection and consumer-based brand equity. *Journal of Product and Brand Management, 24*(5), 449–461. doi:10.1108/JPBM-10-2014-0722

Easterby-Smith, M., Thorpe, R., & Jackson, P. (2012). *Management Research* (4th ed.). SAGE Publications Ltd.

Farrell, A., Karels, V., Montfort, W., & McClatchey, A. (2000). Celebrity performance and endorsement value: The case of Tiger Woods. *Managerial Finance, 26*(7), 1–15. doi:10.1108/03074350010766756

García, I. (2016). *Estudios sobre el impacto de las comunidades de redes sociales en el consumo de productos de belleza de lujo*. Glasgow Caledonian University.

Ghauri, P., & Gronhaug, K. (2005). *Research Methods in Business Studies: A Practical Guide* (3rd ed.). Pearson Education Limited.

Gill, J., & Johnson, P. (2010). *Research Methods for Managers* (4th ed.). SAGE Publications Ltd.

GlobalData. (2016). *TrendSights Analysis: Image Consciousness; Exploring consumers' attitudes towards image and beauty*. Available at: https://www.globaldata.com/store/report/cs0053ts--trendsights-analysis/

Goldsmith, E., Moore, M., & Beaudoin, P. (1999). Fashion innovativeness and self-concept: A replication. *Journal of Product and Brand Management, 8*(1), 7–18. doi:10.1108/10610429910257904

Halonen-Knight, E., & Hurmerinta, L. (2010). Who endorses whom? Meanings transfer in celebrity endorsement. *Journal of Product and Brand Management, 19*(6), 452–460. doi:10.1108/10610421011085767

Hodge, A., Romo, Z., Medina, I., & Fionda-Douglas, A. (2015). Consumer–brand relationships within the luxury cosmetic domain. *Journal of Brand Management, 22*(8), 631–657. doi:10.1057/bm.2015.36

Hollensen, S., & Schimmelpfennig, C. (2013). Selection of celebrity endorsers: A case approach to developing an endorser selection process model. *Marketing Intelligence & Planning, 31*(1), 88–102. doi:10.1108/02634501311292948

Hood, M. (2012). The Tiger Woods scandal: A cautionary tale for event studies. *Managerial Finance, 38*(5), 543–558. doi:10.1108/03074351211217850

Hoyer, W., & MacInnis, D. (2008). *Consumer Behaviour* (5th ed.). South-Western Cengage Learning.

Hugosson, O., Matthys, C., & Phung, L. (2014). *Perception of the Celebrity Endorser: A study of how age and gender influences the consumer perception.* Jonkoping International Business School.

Jankowicz, A. D. (2000). *Business Research Projects* (3rd ed.). Thomson Learning.

Kowalczyk, C., & Pounders, R. (2016). Transforming celebrities through social media: The role of authenticity and emotional attachment. *Journal of Product and Brand Management, 25*(4), 345–356. doi:10.1108/JPBM-09-2015-0969

LaWare, M., & Moutsatsos, C. (2013). For Skin That's Us, Authentically Us: Celebrity, Empowerment, and the Allure of Antiaging Advertisements. *Women's Studies in Communication, 36*(2), 189–208. doi:10.1080/07491409.2013.794753

Lea-Greenwood, G. (2013). *Fashion Marketing Communications* (1st ed.). John Wiley & Sons.

Matzler, K., Bauer, A., & Mooradian, A. (2015). Self-esteem and transformational leadership. *Journal of Managerial Psychology, 30*(7), 815–831. doi:10.1108/JMP-01-2013-0030

McCracken, G. (1989). Who is the Celebrity Endorser? Cultural Foundations of the Endorsement Process. *The Journal of Consumer Research, 13*(3), 310–321. doi:10.1086/209217

Nasir, N. (2016). Celebrity Endorsement and Consumer Buying Intention with the Mediating Role of Brand Performance: An Empirical Consumer Perception Study in FMCG Sector of Pakistan. *Science International Journal, 8*(1), 617–624.

Neti, S. (2011). Social Media and Its Role in Marketing. *International Journal of Enterprise Computing and Business Systems, 1*(2), 1–15.

Onkvisit, S., & Shaw, J. (1987). Self-concept and image congruence: Some research and managerial implications. *Journal of Consumer Marketing, 4*(1), 13–23. doi:10.1108/eb008185

Peters, C., Shelton, A., & Thomas, B. (2011). Self-concept and the fashion behavior of women over 50. *Journal of Fashion Marketing and Management, 15*(3), 291–305. doi:10.1108/13612021111151905

Sääksjärvi, M., Hellén, K., & Balabanis, G. (2016). Sometimes a celebrity holding a negative public image is the best product endorser. *European Journal of Marketing, 50*(3/4), 421–444. doi:10.1108/EJM-06-2014-0346

Saunders, M., Philip, L., & Thornhill, A. (2009). *Research Methods for Business Students* (5th ed.). Pearson Education Limited.

Sekaran, U., & Bougie, R. (2013). *Research Methods for Business* (6th ed.). John Wiley & Sons Ltd.

Seno, D., & Lukas, A. (2007). The equity effect of product endorsement by celebrities. *European Journal of Marketing, 41*(1/2), 121–134. doi:10.1108/03090560710718148

Silvera, H., & Austad, B. (2004). Factors predicting the effectiveness of celebrity endorsement advertisements. *European Journal of Marketing, 38*(11/12), 1509–1526. doi:10.1108/03090560410560218

Solomon, M., & Rabolt, N. (2013). *Consumer Behaviour in Fashion*. Pearson Education, Inc.

Soneji, D., Riedel, A., & Martin, B. (2015). How Gordon Ramsay appeals to consumers: Effects of self-concept clarity and celebrity meaning on celebrity endorsements. *Journal of Strategic Marketing, 23*(5), 457–468. doi:10.1080/0965254X.2014.991349

Spry, A., Pappu, T., & Cornwell, B. (2011). Celebrity endorsement, brand credibility and brand equity. *European Journal of Marketing, 45*(6), 882–909. doi:10.1108/03090561111119958

Tantiseneepong, N., Gorton, M., & White, J. (2012). Evaluating responses to celebrity endorsements using projective techniques. *Qualitative Market Research, 15*(1), 57–69. doi:10.1108/13522751211191991

Ticehurst, G., & Veal, A. (2005). *Business Research Methods: A Managerial Approach* (2nd ed.). Pearson Education Australia.

Wallace, E., Buil, I., & de Chernatony, L. (2014). Consumer engagement with self-expressive brands: Brand love and WOM outcomes. *Journal of Product and Brand Management, 23*(1), 33–42. doi:10.1108/JPBM-06-2013-0326

Wang, S., Hsiu-Ying, K., & Ngamsiriudom, W. (2017). Consumers' attitude of endorser credibility, brand and intention with respect to celebrity endorsement of the airline sector. *Journal of Air Transport Management, 60*, 10–17. doi:10.1016/j.jairtraman.2016.12.007

Wilson, J. (2014). *Essentials of Business Research: A Guide to Doing Your Research Project* (2nd ed.). SAGE Publications Ltd.

World, I. B. I. S. (2016). Cosmetics & Toiletries Retailers in the UK: Market Research Report. *IBISworld*. Available at: https://www.ibisworld.co.uk/market-research/cosmetics-toiletries-retailers.html

Xiao, J., & Li, H. (2012). Online Discussion of Sharon Stone's Comment on China Earthquake. *China Media Research, 8*(1), 25–39.

Zikmund, G., Babin, J., Carr, C., & Griffin, M. (2010). *Business Research Methods* (8th ed.). Cengage Learning.

Compilation of References

Aaker, D. A. (1996). *Building Strong Brands*. Free Press.

Ab Hamid, N. R., Akhir, R. M., & Cheng, A. Y. (2013). Social media: An emerging dimension of marketing communication. *The American Journal of Tropical Medicine and Hygiene*, *86*(1), 1–8.

Abtan, O., Barton, C., Bonelli, F., Gurzki, H., Mei-Pochtler, A., Pianon, N., & Tsusaka, M. (2016). *Digital or Die: The Choice for Luxury Brands*. Retrieved from: https://www.bcg.com/it-it/publications/2016/digital-or-die-choice-luxury-brands

Abtan, O., Barton, C., Bonelli, F., Gurzki, H., Mei-Pochtler, A., Pianon, N., & Tsusaka, M. (2016). *Digital or Die: The Choice for Luxury Brands*. The Boston Consulting Group.

Accenture. (2020). *A., & Accenture*. Altagamma Social Luxury Index.

Achabou, M. A., & Dekhili, S. (2013). Luxury and sustainable development: Is there a match? *Journal of Business Research*, *66*(10), 1896–1903. doi:10.1016/j.jbusres.2013.02.011

Achille, A. (2017). *Digital Luxury Experience 2017*. Altagamma–McKinsey Online Observatory.

Addis, M., & Holbrook, M. B. (2001). On the conceptual link between mass customisation and experiential consumption: An explosion of subjectivity. *Journal of Consumer Behaviour*, *1*(1), 50–66. doi:10.1002/cb.53

Agarwal, M.V. (2020). *Importance of User Generated Content as a part of Social Media Marketing that drives Customer's Brand Awareness and Purchase Intentions*. doi:10.13140/RG.2.2.33503.61609

Aguinis, H., Villamor, I., & Ramani, R. S. (2020). MTurk Research: Review and Recommendations. *Journal of Management*. Advance online publication. doi:10.1177/0149206320969787

Ahuja, V. (2014). Louis Vuitton: Using Digital Presence for Brand Repositioning and CRM. In Handbook of Research on Effective Marketing in Contemporary Globalism (pp. 315–324). IGI Global.

Aiolfi, S., & Sabbadin, E. (2019). Fashion and New Luxury Digital Disruption: The New Challenges of Fashion between Omnichannel and Traditional Retailing. *International Journal of Business and Management*, *14*(8), 41. doi:10.5539/ijbm.v14n8p41

Allen, M. W., Walker, K. L., & Brady, R. (2012). Sustainability Discourse with a Supply Chain Relationship: Mapping Convergence and Divergence. *Journal of Business Communication*, *49*(3), 210–236. doi:10.1177/0021943612446732

Altagamma & Accenture. (2020). *Altagamma Social Luxury Index 2020*. Author.

Amatulli, C., De Angelis, M., Costabile, M., & Guido, G. (2017). *Sustainable luxury brands: Evidence from research and implications for managers*. Springer. doi:10.1057/978-1-137-60159-9

Compilation of References

Amatulli, C., De Angelis, M., Korschun, D., & Romani, S. (2018). Consumers' perceptions of luxury brands' CSR initiatives: An investigation of the role of status and conspicuous consumption. *Journal of Cleaner Production, 194*, 277–287. doi:10.1016/j.jclepro.2018.05.111

Amatulli, C., & Guido, G. (2001). Determinants of purchasing intention for fashion luxury goods in the Italian market: A laddering approach. *Journal of Fashion Marketing and Management, 15*(1), 123–136. doi:10.1108/13612021111112386

Amatulli, C., & Guido, G. (2012). Externalised vs. internalised consumption of luxury goods: Propositions and implications for luxury retail marketing. *International Review of Retail, Distribution and Consumer Research, 22*(2), 189–207. doi:10.1080/09593969.2011.652647

Amatulli, C., Guido, G., & Caputo, T. (2011). Strategic Analysis through the General Electric/McKinsey Matrix: An Application to the Italian Fashion Industry. *International Journal of Business and Management, 5*(6), 61–75. doi:10.5539/ijbm.v6n5p61

Amatulli, C., Mileti, A., Speciale, V., & Guido, G. (2016). The Relationship between Fast Fashion and Luxury Brands: An Exploratory Study in the UK Market. In *Global marketing strategies for the promotion of luxury goods* (pp. 244–265). IGI Global. doi:10.4018/978-1-4666-9958-8.ch011

Andrade Braga, A. (2009). Netnography: A Naturalistic Approach Towards Online Interaction, book. In B. J. Jansen, A. Spink, & I. Taksa (Eds.), *Handbook of Research on Web Log Analysis* (pp. 488–505). IGI Global. doi:10.4018/978-1-59904-974-8.ch024

Anthony, R. (1965). *Management Control Systems: A Framework for Analysis.* Harvard University.

Argyris, C. (1952). *The Impact of Budgets on People.* Controllership Foundation.

Armani. (2015). *40 Years of Armani.* Retrieved June 15, 2015, from http://atribute.armani.com/it/atribute–to–history/

Arnett, J. J. (2010). *Adolescence and emerging adulthood: A cultural approach* (4th ed.). Prentice Hall.

Arrigo, E. (2018). Social media marketing in luxury brands: A systematic literature review and implications for management research. *Management Research Review, 41*(6), 657–679. doi:10.1108/MRR-04-2017-0134

Assouly, O., & Bergé, P. (2005). *Le luxe: essais sur la fabrique de l'ostentation. Institut français de la mode.* Editions du regard.

Athwal, N., Wells, V. K., Carrigan, M., & Henninger, C. E. (2019). Sustainable luxury marketing: A synthesis and research agenda. *International Journal of Management Reviews, 21*(4), 405–426. doi:10.1111/ijmr.12195

Atwal, G., & Williams, A. (2009). Luxury brand marketing – The experience is everything. *Journal of Brand Management, 16*(5-6), 338–346. doi:10.1057/bm.2008.48

Atwal, G., & Williams, A. (2017). Luxury brand marketing–the experience is everything! In *Advances in luxury brand management* (pp. 43–57). Palgrave Macmillan. doi:10.1007/978-3-319-51127-6_3

Ayodeji, O. G., & Kumar, V. (2019). Social media analytics: A tool for the success of online retail industry. *Int. J. Services Operations and Informatics, 10*(1), 79–95. doi:10.1504/IJSOI.2019.100630

Bain & Company. (2020). *Eight Themes That Are Rewriting the Future of Luxury Goods.* Luxury Goods Worldwide Market Study, Fall-Winter 2019.

Baker, J., Ashill, N., Amer, N., & Diab, E. (2018). The internet dilemma: an exploratory study of luxury firms' usage of internet-based technologies. *Journal of Retailing and Consumer Services, 41*, 37-47. doi: 10.1016/j.jretconser.2017.11.007

Baker, J., Ashill, N., Amer, N., & Diab, E. (2018). The internet dilemma: An exploratory study of luxury firms' usage of internet-based technologies. *Journal of Retailing and Consumer Services, 41*, 37–47. doi:10.1016/j.jretconser.2017.11.007

Banathy, H. B. (1996). *Designing social systems in a changing world.* Plenum Press. doi:10.1007/978-1-4757-9981-1

Banister, E., Roper, S., & Potavanich, T. (2020). Consumers' practices of everyday luxury. *Journal of Business Research, 116*, 458–466. doi:10.1016/j.jbusres.2019.12.003

Baratali, E., Abd, R. M., Parhizkar, B., & Gebril, Z. M. (2016). Effective of augmented reality (AR) in marketing communication; a case study on brand interactive advertising. *International Journal of Management and Applied Science, 2*(4), 133–137.

Barkin, S. L., Heerman, W. J., Warren, M. D., & Rennhoff, C. (2010). Millennials and the world of work: The impact of obesity on health and productivity. *Journal of Business and Psychology, 25*(2), 239–245. doi:10.100710869-010-9166-5 PMID:20502510

Barlow, A. K., Siddiqui, N. Q., & Mannion, M. (2004). Developments in information and communication technologies for retail marketing channels. *International Journal of Retail & Distribution Management, 32*(3), 157–163. doi:10.1108/09590550410524948

Barnes, L., & Lea–Greenwood, G. (2010). Fast fashion in the retail store environment. *International Journal of Retail & Distribution Management, 10*(38), 760–772. doi:10.1108/09590551011076533

Barone, M. J., Miyazaki, A. D., & Taylor, K. A. (2000). The influence of cause-related marketing on consumer choice: Does one good turn deserve another? *Journal of the Academy of Marketing Science, 28*(2), 248–262. doi:10.1177/0092070300282006

Barron, L. (2019). The Return of the Celebrity Fashion Muse: Brand Endorsement, Creative Inspiration and Celebrity-Influenced Design Communication. *Fashion Theory*, 1–20. doi:10.1080/1362704X.2019.1656946

Bastos, W., & Levy, S. J. (2012). A history of the concept of branding: Practice and theory. *Journal of Historical Research in Marketing, 4*(3), 347–368. doi:10.1108/17557501211252934

Batat, W. (2020c). How Michelin-starred chefs are being transformed into social bricoleurs? An online qualitative study of luxury foodservice during the pandemic crisis. *Journal of Service Management.* ahead-of-print. doi:10.1108/JOSM-05-2020-

Batat, W. (2014). How do adolescents define their own competencies in the consumption field? A portrait approach. *Recherche et Applications en Marketing, 29*(1), 27–60. doi:10.1177/0767370113505946

Batat, W. (2017). *Luxe et expérience client.* Dunod.

Batat, W. (2017a). *Les nouvelles youth cultures.* Editions EMS. doi:10.3917/ems.batat.2017.01

Batat, W. (2017b). *Comprendre et séduire la génération Z. Comportements de consommation et relations des postmillennials avec les marques.* Ellipses.

Batat, W. (2019). Digital Luxury. Transforming Brands & Consumer Experiences. *Sage (Atlanta, Ga.).*

Batat, W. (2019). *Experiential Marketing: Consumer Behavior, Customer Experience and The 7Es.* Routledge. doi:10.4324/9781315232201

Batat, W. (2019). *The New Luxury Experience: Creating the Ultimate Customer Experience.* Springer International Publishing. doi:10.1007/978-3-030-01671-5

Compilation of References

Batat, W. (2019a). *Food and experiential marketing. Pleasure, wellbeing and consumption.* Routledge. doi:10.4324/9781351182201

Batat, W. (2019c). Eating for pleasure: An introduction of the healthy food experience pyramid. *Qualitative Market Research, 22*(4), 530–543. doi:10.1108/QMR-09-2019-190

Batat, W. (2020a). The role of luxury gastronomy in culinary tourism: An ethnographic study of Michelin-Starred restaurants in France. *International Journal of Tourism Research,* 1–14. doi:10.1002/jtr.2372

Batat, W. (2020a). The role of luxury gastronomy in food tourism. *International Journal of Tourism Research.*

Batat, W. (2020b). Pillars of sustainable food experiences in the luxury gastronomy sector: A qualitative exploration of Michelin-starred chefs' motivations. *Journal of Retailing and Consumer Services, 57,* 102255. doi:10.1016/j.jretconser.2020.102255

Batat, W., & De Kerviler, G. (2020). How can the art of living (art de vivre) make the French luxury industry unique and competitive? *Marché & Organisations, 37*(37), 17–34. doi:10.3917/maorg.037.0015

Batat, W., & Manika, D. (2020). Advancing Transformative Luxury Research: Contributions to Marketing Theory About Luxury, Ethics, and Well-Being. *Journal of Macromarketing, 40*(4), 583–584. doi:10.1177/0276146720954055

Batat, W., Peter, P. C., Moscato, E. M., Castro, I. A., Chan, S., Chugani, S., & Muldrow, A. (2019). The experiential pleasure of food: A savoring journey to food well-being. *Journal of Business Research, 100,* 392–399. doi:10.1016/j.jbusres.2018.12.024

Batat, W., Peter, P., Vicdan, H., Manna, V., Ulusoy, E., Ulusoy, E., & Hong, S. (2017). Alternative food consumption (AFC): Idiocentric and allocentric factors of influence among low socio-economic status (SES) consumers. *Journal of Marketing Management, 33*(7-8), 580–601. doi:10.1080/0267257X.2017.1289974

Batat, W., & Tanner, J. Jr. (2019). Unveiling (in)vulnerability in an adolescent's consumption subculture: A framework to understand adolescents' experienced (in)vulnerability and ethical implications. *Journal of Business Ethics,* 1–18. doi:10.100710551-019-04309-2

Baxter, K., Courage, C., & Caine, K. (2015). *Understanding Your Users* (2nd ed.).

Bazi, S., Filieri, R., & Gorton, M. (2020). Customers' motivation to engage with luxury brands on social media. *Journal of Business Research, 112,* 223–235. doi:10.1016/j.jbusres.2020.02.032

BCG & Altagamma. (2020). *True-Luxury Global Consumer Insight.* Author.

BCG. (2019). *2019 True-Luxury Global Consumer Insight.* BCG.

BCG. (2019). *2019 True-Luxury Global Consumer Insight.* Retrieved from: http://media-publications.bcg.com/france/TrueLuxury%20Global%20Consumer%20Insight%202019%20-%20Plenary%20-%20vMedia.pdf

BCG. (2020). *Transform customer journeys at scale—and transform your business.* Retrieved from: https://image-src.bcg.com/Images/BCG-Transform-Customer-Journeys atScale%E2%80%94and-Transform-Your-Business-Nov-2019_tcm9-233853.pdf

BCG-Altagamma. (2019). http://media-publications.bcg.com/france/True-Luxury%20Global%20Consumer%20Insight%202019%20-%20Plenary%20-%20vMedia.pdf

Beldona, S., Demicco, F., & Nusair, K. (2009). Online travel purchase behavior of generational cohorts: A longitudinal study. *Journal of Hospitality Marketing & Management, 18*(4), 406–420. doi:10.1080/19368620902799627

Belghiti, S., Ochs, A., Lemoine, J. F., & Badot, O. (2018). The Phygital Shopping Experience: An Attempt at Conceptualization and Empirical Investigation. In P. Rossi & N. Krey (Eds.), *Marketing Transformation: Marketing Practice in an Ever-Changing World. AMSWMC 2017*. doi:10.1007/978-3-319-68750-6_18

Belk, R. (2009). Sharing. *The Journal of Consumer Research*, *36*(5), 715–734. doi:10.1086/612649

Belk, R. W. (1975). Situational variables and consumer behavior. *The Journal of Consumer Research*, *2*(3), 157–164. doi:10.1086/208627

Belk, R. W. (1988). Possessions and the extended self. *The Journal of Consumer Research*, *15*(2), 139–168. doi:10.1086/209154

Belk, R. W., Ger, G., & Askegaard, S. (2003). The fire of desire: A multisited inquiry into consumer passion. *The Journal of Consumer Research*, *30*(3), 326–351. doi:10.1086/378613

Bellini, H., Chen, W., Sugiyama, M., Shin, M., Alam, S., & Takayama, D. (2016). *Virtual and Augmented Reality*. https://www.goldmansachs.com/insights/pages/technology-driving-innovation-folder/virtual-and-augmented-reality/report.pdf

Berger, J., & Milkman, K. (2012). What Makes Online Content Viral? *JMR, Journal of Marketing Research*, *49*(May), 192–205. doi:10.1509/jmr.10.0353

Berry, C. J. (1994). *The idea of luxury: A conceptual and historical investigation*. Cambridge University Press. doi:10.1017/CBO9780511558368

Bertoldi, B., Giachino, C., & Pastore, A. (2016). *Strategic pricing management in the omnichannel era*. MERCATI & COMPETITIVITÀ. doi:10.3280/MC2016-004008

Beurden, P., & Gossling, T. (2008). The worth of values - a literature review on the relation between corporate social and financial performance. *Journal of Business Ethics*, *82*(2), 407–424. doi:10.100710551-008-9894-x

Beverland, M. (2004). Uncovering 'theories-in-use': Building luxury wine brands. *European Journal of Marketing*, *38*(3/4), 446–466. doi:10.1108/03090560410518648

Bhardwaj, V., & Fairhurst, A. (2010). Fast fashion: Response to changes in the fashion industry. *International Review of Retail, Distribution and Consumer Research*, *1*(20), 5–173. doi:10.1080/09593960903498300

Bian, Q., & Forsythe, S. (2012). Purchase intention for luxury brands: A cross cultural comparison. *Journal of Business Research*, *65*(10), 1443–1451. doi:10.1016/j.jbusres.2011.10.010

Bijmolt, T., Leeflang, P., Block, F., Eisenbeiss, M., Hardie, B., Lemmens, A., & Saffert, P. (2010). Analytics for Customer Engagement. *Journal of Service Research*, *13*(3), 341–356. doi:10.1177/1094670510375603

Binz, C., Hair, J. F. Jr, Pieper, T. M., & Baldauf, A. (2013). Exploring the effect of distinct family firm reputation on consumers' preferences. *Journal of Family Business Strategy*, *4*(1), 4–11. doi:10.1016/j.jfbs.2012.12.004

Bitner, M. J. (1992). Servicescapes: The impact of physical surroundings on customers and employees. *Journal of Marketing*, *56*(2), 57–71. doi:10.1177/002224299205600205

Bjørn–Andersen, N., & Hansen, R. (2011). The adoption of Web 2.0 by luxury fashion brands. *Proceedings of CONFIRM*, 34.

Blackden, E. (2016). 6 key luxury trends that will make or break brands in 2016. *Luxury Society*. Retrieved April 25, 2020, from https://www.luxurysociety.com/en/articles/2016/01/6-key-luxury-trends-that-will-make-or-break-brands-in-2016/

Blackwell, R. D., Paul, W. M., & James, F. E. (2005). *Consumer behavior* (10th ed.). Thomson Learning.

Compilation of References

Blasco-Arcas, L., Holmqvist, J., & Vignolles, A. (2016). Brand Contamination in Social Media: Consumers' Negative Influence on Luxury Brand Perceptions—A Structured Abstract. In *Rediscovering the Essentiality of Marketing. Developments in Marketing Science: Proceedings of the Academy of Marketing Science*. Springer. 10.1007/978-3-319-29877-1_54

Blevis, E., Makice, K., Odom, W., Roedl, D., Beck, C., Blevis, S., & Ashok, A. (2007, August). Luxury & new luxury, quality & equality. In *Proceedings of the 2007 conference on Designing pleasurable products and interfaces* (pp. 296-311). 10.1145/1314161.1314188

Blocher, E., Stout, D., Cokins, G., & Chen, K. (2008). *Cost Management: A Strategic Emphasis* (4th ed.). McGraw-Hill Irwin.

Blumberg, B., Cooper, R., & Schindler, P. (2014). *Business Research Methods* (4th ed.). McGraw-Hill Education.

Boer, D., & Fischer, R. (2013). How and when do personal values guide our attitudes and sociality? Explaining cross-cultural variability in attitude–value linkages. *Psychological Bulletin*, *139*(5), 1113–1147. Advance online publication. doi:10.1037/a0031347 PMID:23339521

Bolton, R. N., McColl-Kennedy, J. R., Cheung, L., Gallan, A., Orsingher, C., Witell, L., & Zaki, M. (2018). Customer experience challenges: Bringing together digital, physical and social realms. *Journal of Service Management*, *29*(5), 776–808. doi:10.1108/JOSM-04-2018-0113

Bonadonna, A., Giachino, C., & Truant, E. (2017). Sustainability and mountain tourism: The millennial's perspective. *Sustainability*, *9*(7), 1219. doi:10.3390u9071219

Booms, B., & Bitner, M. J. (1981). Marketing strategies and organisation structures for service firms. In J. Donnelly & W. George (Eds.), *Marketing of services: 1981 special educators' conference proceedings* (pp. 46–51). American Marketing Association.

Boon-Long, S., & Wongsurawat, W. (2015). Social media marketing evaluation using social network comments as an indicator for identifying consumer purchasing decision effectiveness. *Journal of Direct, Data and Digital Marketing Practice*, *17*(2), 130–149. doi:10.1057/dddmp.2015.51

Boon, S., & Lomore, C. (2001). Admirer-celebrity relationships among young adults: Explaining perceptions of celebrity influence on identity. *Human Communication Research*, *27*(3), 432–465. doi:10.1111/j.1468-2958.2001.tb00788.x

Borden, N. H. (1964). The Concept of the Marketing Mix. *Journal of Advertising Research*, *24*(4), 7–12.

Bourdieu, P. (1984). *Distinction: A Social Critique of the Judgement of Taste*. Harvard University Press.

Braccini, A. M., & Spinelli, R. (n.d.). *Empowering Organizations* (Vol. 11). Springer International Publishing. doi:10.1007/978-3-319-23784-8_23

Brakus, J. J., Schmitt, B. H., & Zarantonello, L. (2009). Brand experience: What is it? How is it measured? Does it affect loyalty? *Journal of Marketing*, *73*(3), 52–68. doi:10.1509/jmkg.73.3.052

Bridgens, B., Powell, M., Farmer, G., Walsh, C., Reed, E., Royapoor, M., Gosling, P., Hall, J., & Heidrich, O. (2018). Creative upcycling: Reconnecting people, materials and place through making. *Journal of Cleaner Production*, *189*, 145–154. doi:10.1016/j.jclepro.2018.03.317

Brinkley, R. (2020, March 22). *I ate a meal in virtual reality. Here's what it tasted like*. https://www.cnbc.com/2020/03/21/virtual-reality-dining-explained.html

Brogi, S., Calabrese, A., Campisi, D., Capece, G., Costa, R., & Di Pillo, F. (2013). The Effects of Online Brand Communities on Brand Equity in the Luxury Fashion Industry. *International Journal of Engineering Business Management*, *5*, 32. doi:10.5772/56854

Brooke, Z. (2017, March 1). *Data Science is the Latest In-Demand Skill Set for Marketing*. American Marketing Association. Retrieved from https://www.ama.org/marketing-news/data-science-is-the-latest-in-demand-skill-set-for-marketing/

Brooks, A. (2015). *Clothing Poverty: The Hidden World of Fast Fashion and Second–hand Clothes*. Zed Books Ltd. doi:10.5040/9781350219243

Brownlee, J. (2019, August 7). *What is Natural Language Processing? Deep Learning for Natura Language Processing*. Machine Learning Mastery. Retrieved from https://machinelearningmastery.com/natural-language-processing/

Brownlie, D., Hewer, P., & Stewart, R. (2013, July). Keeping fashionable company: ASOS and the collective logic of online spaces. *Academy of Marketing Conference 2013*.

Brown, T. (2011). Are you a digital native or a digital immigrant? Being client centred in the digital era. *British Journal of Occupational Therapy*, *74*(7), 313–314. doi:10.4276/030802211X13099513660992

Bruce, M., & Hines, T. (2007). *Fashion Marketing. Contemporary Issues*. Elsevier Ltd.

Brun, A., Castelli, C. M., Kluge, P. N., & Fassnacht, M. (2015). Selling luxury goods online: Effects of online accessibility and price display. *International Journal of Retail & Distribution Management*, *43*(10-11), 1065–1082.

Brun, A., Castelli, C., & Karaosman, H. (2016). See now buy now: A revolution for luxury supply chain management. In R. Rinaldi & R. Bandinelli (Eds.), *Business Models and ICT Technologies for the Fashion Supply Chain* (pp. 33–46). Springer.

Bruner, G. C. II. (1988). The marketing mix: A retrospective and evaluation. *Journal of Marketing Education*, *10*(1), 29–33. doi:10.1177/027347538801000104

Bucic, T., Harris, J., & Arli, D. (2012). Ethical consumers among the millennials: A cross-national study. *Journal of Business Ethics*, *110*(1), 113–131. doi:10.100710551-011-1151-z

Buckle. (2019). https://blog.globalwebindex.com/chart-of-the-week/luxury-market-2019/

Bundesministerium für Wirtschaft und Energie. (2015). *Industrie 4.0 und Digitale Wirtschaft: Impulse für Wachstum*. Beschäftigung und Innovation.

Burnasheva, R., Gusuh, Y., & Villalobos-Moron, K. (2019). Factors affecting millennials' attitudes toward luxury fashion brands: A cross cultural study. *International Business Research*, *12*(6), 69–81. doi:10.5539/ibr.v12n6p69

Burnett, M. S., & Lunsford, D. A. (1994). Conceptualizing guilt in the consumer decision-making process. *Journal of Consumer Marketing*, *11*(3), 33–43. doi:10.1108/07363769410065454

Burns, B., & Burns, A. (2008). *Business Research Methods and Statistics using SPSS* (1st ed.). SAGE Publications Ltd.

Business of Fashion. (2011). BoF Exclusive: Getting The Luxury Fashion Business Model Right. *The Business of Fashion*. Retrieved September 15, 2013, from http://www.businessoffashion.com/2011/01/bof–exclusive–getting–the–luxury–fashion–business–model–right.html

Cailleux, H., Mignot, C., & Kapferer, J.-N. (2009). Is CRM for luxury brands? *Journal of Brand Management*, *16*(5–6), 406–412. doi:10.1057/bm.2008.50

Compilation of References

Canhoto, A. I., & Padmanabhan, Y. (2015). 'We (don't) know how you feel'–a comparative study of automated vs. manual analysis of social media conversations. *Journal of Marketing Management, 31*(9-10), 1141–1157. doi:10.1080/0267257X.2015.1047466

Capgemini Financial Services Analysis. 2018,) -. Retrieved 25 September 2020 from https:// https://asiapacificwealthreport.com/reports/population/asia-pacific/south-korea/

Carrigan, M., McEachern, M., Moraes, C., & Bosangit, C. (2017). The fine jewellery industry: Corporate responsibility challenges and institutional forces facing SMEs. *Journal of Business Ethics, 143*(4), 681–699. doi:10.100710551-016-3071-4

Carrigan, M., Moraes, C., & McEachern, M. G. (2013). From conspicuous to considered fashion: A harm-chain approach to the responsibilities of luxury-fashion businesses. *Journal of Marketing Management, 29*(11-12), 1277–1307. doi:10.1080/0267257X.2013.798675

Carroll, A. B. (1999). Corporate social responsibility: Evolution of a definitional construct. *Business & Society, 38*(3), 268–295. doi:10.1177/000765039903800303

Carroll, A. B. (2016). Carroll's pyramid of CSR: Taking another look. *International Journal of Corporate Social Responsibility, 1*(3), 1–8. doi:10.118640991-016-0004-6

Carù, A., & Cova, B. (2003). Revisiting consumption experience: A more humble but complete view of the concept. *Marketing Theory, 3*(2), 259–278. doi:10.1177/14705931030032004

Casaburi, I. (2011). China as a Market: Luxury Brand Consumer Behaviour. *Journal of Marketing Trends, 1*(6), 47–56.

Casaburi, I. (2011). China as a Market: Luxury Brand Consumer Behaviour. *Journal of Marketing.*

Casalegno, C., Giachino, C., & Bertoldi, B. (2019). A New Generation for the Wine Industry. *Micro & Macro Marketing, 28*(1), 49–70.

Casalegno, C., & Li, Y. (2012). *Tendenze evolutive in atto: la comunicazione integrata.* Academic Press.

Castro, L., & Marquez, J. (2017). The use of Facebook to explore self-concept: Analysing Colombian consumers. *Qualitative Market Research, 20*(1), 43–59. doi:10.1108/QMR-12-2015-0086

Catry, B. (2003). The Great Pretenders: The Magic of Luxury Goods. *Business Strategy Review, 14*(3), 10–17. doi:10.1111/1467-8616.00267

Cavender, R. (2018). The Marketing of Sustainability and CSR Initiatives by Luxury Brands: Cultural Indicators, Call to Action, and Framework. In *Sustainability in Luxury Fashion Business* (pp. 29–49). Springer. doi:10.1007/978-981-10-8878-0_3

Cearley, D., Walker, M., Burke, B., & Searle, S. (2017, June 23). *Top 10 strategic technology trends for 2017: A Gartner trend insight report.* https://www.gartner.com/doc/3645332?srcId=1-6595640781

CEIC. (2020a). *South Korea forecast GDP PPP per capita.* Retrieved 29 April 2020 from https://www.ceicdata.com/en/indicator/korea/forecast-gdp-ppp-per-capita

CEIC. (2020b). *South Korea household income per capita.* Retrieved 29 April 2020 from https://www.ceicdata.com/en/indicator/korea/annual-household-income-per-capita

CEIC. (2020c). *Switzerland forecast GDP PPP per capita.* Retrieved 29 April 2020 from https://www.ceicdata.com/en/indicator/switzerland/forecast-gdp-ppp-per-capita

CEIC. (2020d). *Switzerland household income per capita*. Retrieved 29 April 2020 from https://www.ceicdata.com/en/indicator/switzerland/annual-household-income-per-capita

Cervellon, M.-C., & Shammas, L. (2013). The value of sustainable luxury in mature markets: A customer-based approach. *Journal of Corporate Communications*, *55*(52), 90–101. doi:10.9774/GLEAF.4700.2013.de.00009

CFA Institute. (2018). https://cfasi.it/download/20190124092644.pdf

Chadha, R., & Husband, P. (2006). *The cult of the luxury brand: inside Asia's love affair with luxury*. Nicholas Brealey International.

Chaffey, D., Hemphill, T., & Edmundson–Bird, D. (2019). *Digital business and e–commerce management*. Pearson.

Chaffey, D., & Smith, P. R. (2017). *Digital marketing excellence: planning, optimizing and integrating online marketing*. Taylor & Francis. doi:10.4324/9781315640341

Chailan, C. (2013). The role of Art in Luxury Management. In Proceedings of 6th Euromed Conference of the Euromed Academy of Business, 'Confronting Contemporary Business Challenges through Management Innovation (pp. 569-574). Academic Press.

Chailan, C. (2018). Art as a means to recreate luxury brands' rarity and value. *Journal of Business Research*, *84*, 414–423. doi:10.1016/j.jbusres.2017.10.019

Chandon, J., Laurent, G., & Valette-Florence, P. (2016). Pursuing the concept of luxury: Introduction to the JBR Special Issue on "Luxury Marketing from Tradition to Innovation". *Journal of Business Research*, *69*(1), 299–303. doi:10.1016/j.jbusres.2015.08.001

Chang, J., & Thompson, V. (2014). *South Korea's Growing Obsession with Cosmetic Surgery*. abcNews. Retrieved 13 October 2020 from https://abcnews.go.com/Lifestyle/south-koreas-growing-obsession-cosmetic-surgery/story?id=24123409

Chan, K., Leung Ng, Y., & Luk, E. K. (2013). Impact of Celebrity Endorsement in Advertising on Brand Image Among Chinese Adolescents. *Young Consumers*, *14*(2), 167–179. doi:10.1108/17473611311325564

Chaudhuri, H. R., & Majumdar, S. (2006). Of Diamonds and Desires: Understanding Conspicuous Consumption from a Contemporary Marketing Perspective. *Academy of Marketing Science Review*, *11*, 1–18.

Chen, H., Ryan, C., & He, H. (2019). Intergenerational differences amongst Chinese visitors to the Terracotta Warriors Museum, Xi'an, China. *Annals of Tourism Research*, *79*, 102682. doi:10.1016/j.annals.2019.01.015

Chen, S. C., & Shoemaker, S. (2014). Age and cohort effects: The American senior tourism market. *Annals of Tourism Research*, *48*, 58–75. doi:10.1016/j.annals.2014.05.007

Chen, Y., Fay, S., & Wang, Q. (2011). The role of marketing in social media: How online consumer reviews evolve. *Journal of Interactive Marketing*, *25*(2), 85–94. doi:10.1016/j.intmar.2011.01.003

Chevalier, M., & Gutsatz, M. (2012). *Luxury retail management: How the world's top brands provide quality product and service support*. Wiley. http://public.eblib.com/choice/publicfullrecord.aspx?p=818410

Chevalier, M., & Mazzalovo, G. (2008). *Luxury brand management*. Franco Angeli.

Childers, T. L., Carr, C. L., Peck, J., & Carson, S. (2001). Hedonic and utilitarian motivations for online retail shopping behavior. *Journal of Retailing*, *77*(4), 511–535. doi:10.1016/S0022-4359(01)00056-2

Cho, E., Gupta, S., & Kim, Y. K. (2015). Style consumption: Its drivers and role in sustainable apparel consumption. *International Journal of Consumer Studies*, *39*(6), 661–669. doi:10.1111/ijcs.12185

Compilation of References

Choi, M., & Rifon, N. (2012). It Is a Match: The Impact of Congruence between Celebrity Image and Consumer Ideal Self on Endorsement Effectiveness. *Psychology and Marketing, 29*(9), 639–650. doi:10.1002/mar.20550

Choi, T. M. (2011). *Fashion supply chain management: industry and business analysis.* IGI Global.

Chong, K. (2016). *South Korea's troubled millennial generation.* Retrieved 29 April 2020 from https://cmr.berkeley.edu/blog/2016/4/south-korea/

Chung, M., Ko, E., Joung, H., & Kim, S. J. (2020). Chatbot e-service and customer satisfaction regarding luxury brands. *Journal of Business Research, 117*, 587–595. doi:10.1016/j.jbusres.2018.10.004

Clarke, P., & Brislane, C. (2000). Just in Time? Technology Ireland, 32(5), 24 - 25.

Clarke, P. (1994, October). Activity Based Cost Management. *Accountancy Ireland. Journal of the Institute of Chartered Accountants in Ireland, 26*(5), 16–17.

Clarke, P. (1995). The Old and New in Management Accounting. *Management Accounting, 73*(6), 46–51.

Clarke, P. (1995, June). The Old and New in Management Accounting. *Management Accounting, CIMA, 73*(6), 46–51.

Clarke, P. (1996, May). Putting the Q in TQM. *Management Irish Management Institute, 43*(2), 12–13.

Clarke, P. (2004, Summer). Footprints in the Sand: Exploring the Evolution of Management Accounting Practices in Ireland. *Irish Accounting Review, 11*(1), 1–18.

Clarke, P. (2006). *Strategies in Management Accounting: A Series of Essays.* The Institute of Chartered Accountants.

Clarke, P. (2016). *Managerial Accounting: Costing, Decision-making and Control.* Chartered Accountants Ireland.

Clarke, P., Hill, N., & Stevens, K. (1999). Activity-Based Costing in Ireland: Barriers to and Opportunities for change. *Critical Perspectives on Accounting, 10*(4), 443–468. doi:10.1006/cpac.1997.0197

Clark, J. (1923). *Studies in the Economics of Overhead Costs.* University of Chicago Press.

Clarkson, M. B. E. (1999). A stakeholder framework for analysing and evaluating corporate social performance. *Academy of Management Review, 20*(1), 92–117. doi:10.5465/amr.1995.9503271994

Claydon, J. (2011). A new direction for CSR: The shortcomings of previous CSR models and the rationale for a new model. *Social Responsibility Journal, 7*(3), 405–420. doi:10.1108/17471111111154545

Coary, S., & Poor, M. (2016). How consumer-generated images shape important consumption outcomes in the food domain. *Journal of Consumer Marketing, 33*(1), 1–8. doi:10.1108/JCM-02-2015-1337

Coelho, P. S., Rita, P., & Santos, Z. (2018). On the relationship between consumer-brand identification, brand community, and brand loyalty. *Journal of Retailing and Customer Services, 43*, 101–110. doi:10.1016/j.jretconser.2018.03.011

Cone Communications. Ebiquity global CSR study. (2015). Report retrieved from http://www.conecomm.com

Constantinides, E. (2006). The Marketing Mix Revisited: Towards the 21st Century Marketing. *Journal of Marketing Management, 22*(3), 407–438. doi:10.1362/026725706776861190

Cooper, R., & Kaplan, R. (1988). How Cost Accounting Distorts Product Costs. *Management Accounting,* (April), 20–27.

Corbellini, E., & Saviolo, S. (2015). *Managing Fashion and Luxury Companies.* ETAS.

Correa, T., Hinsley, A. W., & De Zúñiga, H. G. (2010). Who interacts on the web? The inter-section of users' personality and social media use. *Computers in Human Behavior, 26*(2), 247–253. doi:10.1016/j.chb.2009.09.003

305

Coste-Manière, I., Panchout, K., & Molas, J. (2012). The Evolution of the Luxury Market: Stairway to Heaven? In J. Hoffmann & I. Coste-Manière (Eds.), *Luxury Strategy in Action*. Palgrave Macmillan. doi:10.1057/9780230361546_2

Creswell, J. W. (2009). *Research design qualitative, quantitative, and mixed mehtods approaches* (3rd ed.). SAGE.

Creswell, J. W., & Plano Clark, V. L. (2007). *Designing and conducting mixed method research*. SAGE.

Cristini, H., Kauppinen-Räisänen, H., Barthod-Prothade, M., & Woodside, A. (2017). Toward a general theory of luxury: Advancing from workbench definitions and theoretical transformations. *Journal of Business Research, 2017*(70), 101–107. doi:10.1016/j.jbusres.2016.07.001

Cuomo, M. T., Mazzucchelli, A., Chierici, R., & Ceruti, F. (2020). Exploiting online environment to engage customers: Social commerce brand community. *Qualitative Market Research, 23*(3), 339–361. doi:10.1108/QMR-12-2017-0186

Cuty, R. G., & Zhang, P. (2011). Social Commerce: Looking Back and Forward. *Proceedings ASIST*.

D'Arpizio, C., Levato, F., Fenili, S., Colacchio, F., & Prete, F. (2020). *Luxury after Covid-19: Changed for (the) Good?* Bain & Company. Retrieved from: https://www.bain.com/insights/luxury-after-coronavirus/

D'Arpizio, C., Levato, F., Prete, F., Del Fabbro, E., & Gault, C. (2018). *Luxury goods worldwide market study fall–winter 2018 - The future of luxury: A look into tomorrow to understand today*. Boston: Bain and Company.

D'Arpizio, C., Levato, F., Prete, F., & Gault, C. (2020). *Eight themes that are rewriting the future of luxury goods*. Bain & Company.

Dabija, D. C., Bejan, B. M., & Tipi, N. (2018). *Generation X versus millennials communication behaviour on social media when purchasing food versus tourist services*. Economics and Management. doi:10.15240/tul/001/2018-1-013

Dahlsrud, A. (2006). How corporate social responsibility is defined: An analysis of 37 definitions. *Corporate Social Responsibility and Environmental Management, 15*(1), 1–13. doi:10.1002/csr.132

Dall'Olmo Riley, F., & Lacroix, C. (2003). Luxury branding on the Internet: Lost opportunity or impossibility? *Marketing Intelligence & Planning, 21*(2), 96–104. doi:10.1108/02634500310465407

Danziger, P. N. (2018). 4 Mega-Trends ahead for the luxury market in 2019: expect turmoil and slowing sales. *Forbes*. Retrieved April 25, 2020, from https://www.forbes.com/sites/pamdanziger/2018/12/18/whats-ahead-for-the-luxury-market-in-2019-expect-turmoil-and-slowing-sales/#35352dd86578

Danzinger, P. N. (2019, May 29). 3 ways millennials and gen-z consumers are radically transforming the luxury market. *Forbes*. https://www.forbes.com

Daugherty, T., Eastin, M. S., & Bright, L. (2008). Exploring Consumer Motivations for Creating User-Generated Content. *Journal of Interactive Advertising, 8*(2), 16–25. doi:10.1080/15252019.2008.10722139

Davies, I. A., Lee, Z., & Ahonkai, I. (2012). Do consumer care about ethical luxury? *Journal of Business Ethics, 106*(1), 37–51. doi:10.100710551-011-1071-y

De Angelis, M., Amatulli, C., & Zaretti, M. (2020). The Certification of Luxury: how art can affect perceived durability and purchase intention of luxury products. *Sustainable Luxury and Craftsmanship*, 61-84. doi:10.1007/978-981-15-3769-1_4

De Angelis, M., Adıgüzel, F., & Amatulli, C. (2017). The role of design similarity in consumers' evaluation of new green products: An investigation of luxury fashion brands. *Journal of Cleaner Production, 141*, 1515–1527. doi:10.1016/j.jclepro.2016.09.230

Compilation of References

De Barnier, V., Falcy, S., & Valette-Florence, P. (2012). Do consumers perceive three levels of luxury? A comparison of accessible, intermediate and inaccessible luxury brands. *Journal of Brand Management, 19*(7), 623–636. doi:10.1057/bm.2012.11

De Chernatony, L. (2001). *From Brand Vision to Brand Evaluation. Strategically Building and Sustain- ing Brands.* Butterworth Heinemann.

De Kerviler, G., & Rodriguez, C. M. (2019). Luxury brand experiences and relationship quality for Millennials: The role of self-expansion. *Journal of Business Research, 102,* 250–262. doi:10.1016/j.jbusres.2019.01.046

De Lassus, C., & Anido Freire, N. (2014). Access to the luxury brand myth in pop-up stores: A netnographic and semiotic analysis. *Journal of Retailing and Consumer Services, 21*(1), 61–68. doi:10.1016/j.jretconser.2013.08.005

Dean, J. (1951). *Capital Budgeting.* Columbia University Press. doi:10.7312/dean90552

Deloitte Global. (2019). *Global Powers of Luxury Goods: Bridging the gap between the old and the new.* www.deloitte.co.uk

Deloitte. (2017). *The 2017 Deloitte millennial survey: Apprehensive millennials: seeking stability and opportunities in an uncertain world.* Author.

Deloitte. (2019). *Global Powers of Luxury Goods 2019 Bridging the gap between the old and the new.* Retrieved from: https://www2.deloitte.com/content/dam/Deloitte/ar/Documents/Consumer_and_Industrial_Products/Global-Powers-of-Luxury-Goods-abril-2019.pdf

Deloitte. (2019a). Global Powers of Luxury Goods 2019. Shaping the future of the luxury industry. Milan: Deloitte Italy S.p.A.

Deloitte. (2019b). *The Deloitte global millennial survey 2019: Societal discord and technological transformation create a "generation disrupted".* Deloitte AG.

Deloitte. The Deloitte millennial survey 2017. (2017). Report retrieved from https://www2.deloitte.com/global/en/pages/about- deloitte/articles/millennialsurvey.html

Demirkan, H., & Spohrer, J. (2014). Developing a framework to improve virtual shopping in digital malls with intelligent self–service systems. *Journal of Retailing and Consumer Services, 21*(5), 860–868. doi:10.1016/j.jretconser.2014.02.012

Denegri-Knott, J., & Molesworth, M. (2010). Concepts and practices of digital virtual consumption. *Consumption Markets & Culture, 13*(2), 109–132. doi:10.1080/10253860903562130

DeVaney, S. A. (2015). Understanding the millennial generation. *Journal of Financial Service Professionals, 69*(6), 11–14.

Dhaoui, C. (2014). An empirical study of luxury brand marketing effectiveness and its impact on consumer engagement on Facebook. *Journal of Global Fashion Marketing, 5*(3), 209–222. doi:10.1080/20932685.2014.907605

Dholakia, R. R., & Uusitalo, O. (2002). Switching to electronic stores: Consumer characteristics and the perception of shopping benefits. *International Journal of Retail & Distribution Management, 30*(10), 459–469. doi:10.1108/09590550210445335

Diallo, M. F., DahmaneMouelhi, N.B., Gadekar, M., & Schill, M. (2020). CSR actions, brand value, and willingness to pay a premium price for luxury brands: Does long-term orientation matter? *Journal of Business Ethics.* Advance online publication. doi:10.100710551-020-04486-5

Dimitrova, L. I., Björck, L., & Fregne, A. (2018). Limited edition: Collaborations between luxury brands. *LBMG Strategic Brand Management-Masters Paper Series.*

Dimock, M. (2019). *Defining generations: Where millennials end and generation z begins*. Pew Research Center. Retrieved 13 April 2020 from https://www.pewresearch.org/fact-tank/2019/01/17/where-millennials-end-and-generation-z-begins/

Dion, D., & Arnould, E. (2011). Retail Luxury Strategy: Assembling Charisma through Art and Magic. *Journal of Retailing, 87*(4), 502–520. doi:10.1016/j.jretai.2011.09.001

Dion, D., & Borraz, S. (2015). Managing heritage brands: A study of the sacralization of heritage stores in the luxury industry. *Journal of Retailing and Consumer Services, 22*, 77–84. doi:10.1016/j.jretconser.2014.09.005

Dixon, D. F., & Blois, K. J. (1973). Some Limitations of the 4 Ps as a Paradigm of Marketing. In *Proceedings of the Marketing Education Group* (pp. 92-107). Academic Press.

Dodds, W. B., Monroe, K. B., & Grewal, D. (1991). Effects of Price, Brand, and Store Information on Buyers' Product Evaluations. *JMR, Journal of Marketing Research, 28*(3), 307.

Donaldson, T., & Preston, L. E. (1995). The Stakeholder Theory of the Corporation: Concepts, Evidence and Implications. *Academy of Management Review, 20*(1), 65–91. doi:10.5465/amr.1995.9503271992

Donovan, R. J., Rossiter, J. R., Marcoolyn, G., & Nesdale, A. (1994). Store atmosphere and purchasing behavior. *Journal of Retailing, 70*(3), 283–294. doi:10.1016/0022-4359(94)90037-X

Donzé, P. Y. (2018). The birth of luxury big business: LVMH, Richemont and Kering. In P. Donzé & R. Fujioka (Eds.), *Global Luxury* (pp. 19–38). Palgrave. doi:10.1007/978-981-10-5236-1_2

Donzé, P. Y., & Wubs, B. (2019). Storytelling and the making of a global luxury fashion brand: Christian Dior. *International Journal of Fashion Studies, 6*(1), 83–102. doi:10.1386/infs.6.1.83_1

Doss, F., & Robinson, T. (2013). Luxury perceptions: Luxury brand vs counterfeit for young US female consumers. *Journal of Fashion Marketing and Management, 17*(4), 424–439. doi:10.1108/JFMM-03-2013-0028

Downey, L. (2019, October 29). What is an Algorithm? *Investopedia*. Retrieved from https://www.investopedia.com/terms/a/algorithm.asp

Dubois, B., & Czellar, S. (2002). *Prestige brands or luxury brands? An exploratory inquiry on consumer perceptions*. University of Geneva.

Dubois, B., Czellar, S., & Laurent, G. (2005). Consumer segments based on attitudes toward luxury: Empirical evidence from twenty countries. *Marketing Letters, 16*(2), 115–128. doi:10.100711002-005-2172-0

Dubois, B., & Duquesne, P. (1993). The market for luxury goods: Income versus culture. *European Journal of Marketing, 27*(1), 35–44. doi:10.1108/03090569310024530

Duesenberry, J. S. (1949). *Income, Saving and the Theory of Consumer Behaviour*. Harvard University Press.

Duma, F., Labati, F., Brunetti, G., & Gadgil, M. (2020). Mastering the digital transformation as a heritage luxury fashion brand. *Marché et Organisations, 37*(37), 33–54. doi:10.3917/maorg.037.0033

Duma, F., Popcsev, M., & Seelhofer, D. (2017). Economies of small: niche strategies and success factors of independent luxury brands in a global market dominated by big business. *Global Fashion Management Conference at Vienna Proceedings*, 343-350. 10.15444/GFMC2017.04.08.01

Duncan, E., Fanderl, H., Maechler, N., & Neher, K. (2016). Customer experience: Creating value through transforming customer journeys. McKinsey & Company.

Duncan, T., & Mulhern, F. (2004). *A White Paper on the Status, Scope and Future of IMC*. New York: McGraw-Hill.

Compilation of References

Dwivedi, A., Johnson, W., & McDonald, E. (2015). Celebrity endorsement, self-brand connection and consumer-based brand equity. *Journal of Product and Brand Management, 24*(5), 449–461. doi:10.1108/JPBM-10-2014-0722

Dwivedi, A., & McDonald, R. E. (2020). Examining the efficacy of brand social media communication: A consumer perspective. *Journal of Marketing Theory and Practice, 28*(4), 373–386. doi:10.1080/10696679.2020.1768870

Earl, P. E. (1986). *Lifestyle economics: Consumer behaviour in a turbulent world*. Palgrave Macmillan.

Easterby-Smith, M., Thorpe, R., & Jackson, P. (2012). *Management Research* (4th ed.). SAGE Publications Ltd.

Eastman, J. K., & Eastman, K. L. (2011). Perceptions of status consumption and the economy. *Journal of Business & Economics Research, 9*(7), 9–20. doi:10.19030/jber.v9i7.4677

Eastman, J. K., & Eastman, K. L. (2015). Conceptualizing a model of status consumption theory: An exploration of the antecedents and consequences of the motivation to consume for status. *Marketing Management Journal, 25*(1), 1–15.

Eastman, J. K., Goldsmith, R. E., & Flynn, L. R. (1999). Status Consumption in Consumer Behaviour: Scale Development and Validation. *Journal of Marketing Theory and Practice, 7*(3), 41–52. doi:10.1080/10696679.1999.11501839

EDA. (2020). *Swiss Economy – Facts and Figures*. Retrieved 29 April 2020 from https://www.eda.admin.ch/aboutswitzerland/en/home/wirtschaft/uebersicht/wirtschaft---fakten-und-zahlen.html

Ekşi, O., & Candan, F. B. (2018). The effect of lifestyle on conspicuous consumption. In F. B. C. & H. Kapucu (Eds.), Current debates in business studies (pp. 109-125). London: OPEC Art Design.

Eleftheriou-Smith, L.-M. (2012). *Absolut Vodka launches augmented reality app*. Retrieved from https://www.campaign-live.co.uk/article/absolut-vodka-launchesaugmented-reality-app/1113514

Eng, T.-Y., & Bogaert, J. (2010). Psychological and cultural insights into consumption of luxury Western brands in India. *Journal of Consumer Behaviour, 9*(1), 55–75. doi:10.1362/147539210X497620

Erevelles, S., Fukawa, N., & Swayne, L. (2016). Big Data consumer analytics and the transformation of marketing. *Journal of Business Research, 69*(2), 897–904. doi:10.1016/j.jbusres.2015.07.001

Erner, G. (2004). *Victimes de la mode?* La Découverte.

Ertekin, Z. O., & Atik, D. (2015). Sustainable Markets: Motivating Factors, Barriers, and Remedies for Mobilization of Slow Fashion. *Journal of Macromarketing, 35*(1), 53–69. doi:10.1177/0276146714535932

Escofier, B., & Pages, J. (2008). *Analyses factorielles simples et multiples: objectifs, m'ethodes et interpr'etation*. Dunod.

Euromonitor International. (2019). *Luxury Goods: How is Digital Shaping the Industry*. Author.

Euromonitor. (2016). *Consumer Lifestyles in Switzerland*. Retrieved 29 April 2020 from https://www.euromonitor.com/consumer-lifestyles-in-switzerland/report

Euromonitor. (2018). *Consumer Lifestyles in South Korea*. Retrieved 29 April 2020 from https://www.euromonitor.com/consumer-lifestyles-in-south-korea/report

European Commission. (2018, May 23). *Data protection in the EU*. Retrieved from https://ec.europa.eu/info/law/law-topic/data-protection/data-protection-eu_en

Evans, N. J., Phua, J., Lim, J., & Jun, H. (2017). Disclosing Instagram influencer advertising: The effects of disclosure language on advertising recognition, attitudes, and behavioral intent. *Journal of Interactive Advertising, 17*(2), 138–149. doi:10.1080/15252019.2017.1366885

Eves, A., & Gesch, B. (2003). Food provision and the nutritional implications of food choices made by young adult males, in a young offenders' institution. *Journal of Human Nutrition and Dietetics*, *16*(3), 167–179. doi:10.1046/j.1365-277X.2003.00438.x PMID:12753110

Fabris, G., & Minestroni, L. (2004). *Valore e valori della marca*. Franco Angeli.

Fan, W., & Gordon, M. D. (2014, June). Article. *Communications of the ACM*, *57*(6), 74–81.

Farrell, A., Karels, V., Montfort, W., & McClatchey, A. (2000). Celebrity performance and endorsement value: The case of Tiger Woods. *Managerial Finance*, *26*(7), 1–15. doi:10.1108/03074350010766756

Fazzini, M., & Terzani, S. (2006). *Una proposta di balanced scorecard nelle imprese del sistema moda*. Controllo di Gestione.

Feitelberg, R. (2010). Mix and match. Sportswear houses are playing the versatility card. *Women's Wear Daily*, *2*, 10.

Fernandes, C. C. M. S. (2019). *Kering: a path towards sustainable luxury* (Doctoral dissertation).

Fernie, J., Moore, C. M., & Lawrie, A. (1998). A tale of two Cities: An Examination of Fashion Designer Retailing within London and New York. *Journal of Product and Brand Management*, *7*(5), 366–378. doi:10.1108/10610429810237637

Ferrara, W. (1995). Cost/Management Accounting: The Twenty-First Century Paradigm. *Management Accounting*, (December), 30–36.

Fionda, A. M., & Moore, C. M. (2009). The anatomy of the luxury fashion brand. *Journal of Brand Management*, *5*(16), 347–363. doi:10.1057/bm.2008.45

Fischer, R., & Poortinga, Y. H. (2012). Are cultural values the same as the values of individuals? *International Journal of Cross Cultural Management*, *12*(2), 157–170. doi:10.1177/1470595812439867

Fisk, R. P., Grove, S. J., & John, J. (2000). All the websites are a stage, so marketers put on a show. *Marketing News*, *34*(23), 26.

Fombrun, C. J. (2005). Building corporate reputation through CSR initiatives: Evolving standards. *Corporate Reputation Review*, *8*(1), 7–11. doi:10.1057/palgrave.crr.1540235

Forbes. (2019). https://www.forbes.com/sites/geoffwhitmore/2019/09/13/how-generation-z-is-changing-travel-for-older-generations/

Ford, H., & Crowther, S. (1924). *My Life and Works*. Heinemann.

Frasquet, M., & Miquel, M. J. (2017). Do channel integration efforts pay–off in terms of online and offline customer loyalty? *International Journal of Retail & Distribution Management*, *45*(7/8), 859–873. doi:10.1108/IJRDM-10-2016-0175

Freeman, RF. (1984). *Strategic Management: a Stakeholder Approach*. Academic Press.

Freeman, I., & Sussin, I. (2010). International Cultural Competence in International Business Education: The Need to Respond. *International Journal of Environmental, Cultural, Economic and Social Sustainability*, *6*(1), 355–370. doi:10.18848/1832-2077/CGP/v06i01/54742

Freeman, R. E., & Phillips, R. A. (2002). Stakeholder theory: A libertarian defense. *Business Ethics Quarterly*, *12*(3), 331–350. doi:10.2307/3858020

Friedman, V. (2015). Balenciaga Names Demna Gvasalia, Vetements Designer, as Artistic Director. *New York Times*. Retrieved April 25, 2020, from https://www.nytimes.com/2015/10/08/fashion/balenciaga-names-demna-gvasalia-vetements-designer-as-artistic-director.html

Compilation of References

Fukai, A. (2002). *Fashion: the collection of the Kyoto Costume Institute: a history from the 18th to the 20th century.* Taschen.

Furlow, N. E. (2011). Find us on Facebook: How cause marketing has embraced social media. *Journal of Marketing Development and Competitiveness, 5*(6), 61.

Gabrielli, V., Baghi, I., & Codeluppi, V. (2013). Consumption practices of fast fashion products. *Journal of Fashion Marketing and Management, 17*(2), 206–224. doi:10.1108/JFMM-10-2011-0076

Gallaugher, J., & Ransbotham, S. (2010). Social media and customer dialog management at Starbucks. *MIS Quarterly Executive, 9*(4), 197–212.

Garabuau-Moussaoui, I. (2001) La cuisine des jeunes: désordre alimentaire, identité générationnelle et ordre social. *Anthropology of Food.*

García, I. (2016). *Estudios sobre el impacto de las comunidades de redes sociales en el consumo de productos de belleza de lujo.* Glasgow Caledonian University.

Gardetti, M. A. (2020). The Basic Aspects of Luxury and Its Relations with Sustainability. In *Sustainability: Is it Redefining the Notion of Luxury?* (pp. 17–64). Springer. doi:10.1007/978-981-15-2047-1_2

Garner, S. P. (1954). *Evolution of Cost Accounting to 1925.* University of Alabama Press.

Gaur, A. S., & Kumar, M. (2018). A systematic approach to conducting review studies: An assessment of content analysis in 25 years of IB research. *Journal of World Business, 53*(2), 280–289. doi:10.1016/j.jwb.2017.11.003

Gazzola, P., Pavione, E., Pezzetti, R., & Grechi, D. (2020). Trends in the Fashion Industry. The Perception of Sustainability and Circular Economy: A Gender/Generation Quantitative Approach. *Sustainability, 12*(7), 2809. doi:10.3390u12072809

Geerts, A. (2013). Cluster Analysis of Luxury Brands on the Internet. *International Journal of Management and Marketing Research, 6*(2), 79–82.

Gentile, C., Spiller, N., & Noci, G. (2007). How to sustain the customer experience: An overview of experience components that co-create value with the customer. *European Management Journal, 25*(5), 395–410. doi:10.1016/j.emj.2007.08.005

Geva, A. (2008). Three models of corporate social responsibility: Interrelationships between theory, research, and practice. *Business and Society Review, 113*(1), 1–41. doi:10.1111/j.1467-8594.2008.00311.x

Ghauri, P., & Gronhaug, K. (2005). *Research Methods in Business Studies: A Practical Guide* (3rd ed.). Pearson Education Limited.

Giachino, C., Truant, E., & Bonadonna, A. (2019). Mountain tourism and motivation: Millennial students' seasonal preferences. *Current Issues in Tourism,* 1–15.

Giacosa, E. (2011). *L'economia della aziende di abbigliamento.* Giappichelli.

Giacosa, E. (2012). *Mergers and Acquisitions (M&As) in the Luxury Business.* McGraw-Hill.

Giacosa, E. (2014). *Innovation in Luxury Fashion Family Business.* MacMillan. doi:10.1057/9781137498663

Gibbs, G. R. (2010). *Analyzing qualitative data.* SAGE.

Giertz-Mårtenson, I. (2012). H&M–documenting the story of one of the world's largest fashion retailers. *Business History, 54*(1), 108–115. doi:10.1080/00076791.2011.617203

Gill, A. (1998). Deconstruction fashion: The making of unfinished, decomposing and re-assembled clothes. *Fashion Theory*, *2*(1), 25–49. doi:10.2752/136270498779754489

Gill, J., & Johnson, P. (2010). *Research Methods for Managers* (4th ed.). SAGE Publications Ltd.

Gistri, G., Corciolani, M., & Pace, S. (2018). The interaction effect between brand identification and personal crisis relevance on consumers' emotional reactions to a fashion brand crisis. *Journal of Global Fashion Marketing*, *9*(3), 252–269. doi:10.1080/20932685.2018.1461021

Gladwin, T. N., Krause, T. S., & Kennelly, J. J. (1995). Beyond eco-efficiency: Towards socially sustainable business. *Sustainable Development*, *3*(1), 35–43. doi:10.1002d.3460030105

Glaser, B., Bailyn, L., Fernandez, W., Holton, J. A., & Levina, N. (2015). What Grounded Theory Is...A Critically Reflective Conversation Among Scholars. *Organizational Research Methods*, *18*(4), 581–599. doi:10.1177/1094428114565028

GlobalData. (2016). *TrendSights Analysis: Image Consciousness; Exploring consumers' attitudes towards image and beauty.* Available at: https://www.globaldata.com/store/report/cs0053ts--trendsights-analysis/

Godey, B., Manthiou, A., Pederzoli, D., Rokka, J., Aiello, G., Donvito, R., & Singh, R. (2016). Social media marketing efforts of luxury brands: Influence on brand equity and consumer behavior. *Journal of Business Research*, *69*(12), 5833–5841. doi:10.1016/j.jbusres.2016.04.181

Godey, B., Pederzoli, D., Aiello, G., Donvito, R., Wiedmann, K.-P., & Hennigs, N. (2012). An Intercultural Comparison of the perception of Luxury by Young Consumers. In K.-P. Wiedmann & N. Hennigs (Eds.), *Luxury Marketing* (pp. 59–76). Springer.

Goldsmith, E., Moore, M., & Beaudoin, P. (1999). Fashion innovativeness and self-concept: A replication. *Journal of Product and Brand Management*, *8*(1), 7–18. doi:10.1108/10610429910257904

Goldsmith, R. E., Reinecke Flynn, L., & Kim, D. (2010). Status consumption and price sensitivity. *Journal of Marketing Theory and Practice*, *18*(4), 323–338. doi:10.2753/MTP1069-6679180402

Gouton, M.-A., Dacremont, C., Trystram, G., & Blumenthal, D. (2020). *Validation of food visual attribute perception in virtual reality. Food quality and preference.* https://www.sciencedirect.com/science/article/abs/pii/S0950329320302858?via=ihub

Grant, R. (2013). *Jeff Immelt and the reinventing of General Electric. In Contemporary Strategy Analysis: Text and Cases.* John Wiley and Sons.

Grassi, A. (2020). Art to enhance consumer engagement in the luxury fashion domain. *Journal of Fashion Marketing and Management*, *24*(3), 327–341.

Grewal, D., Roggeveen, A. L., & Nordfält, J. (2017). The future of retailing. *Journal of Retailing*, *93*(1), 1–6. doi:10.1016/j.jretai.2016.12.008

Griffioen, A. (2011). *Creating Profit Through Alliances: How collaborative business models can contribute to competitive advantage.* Retrieved October 10, 2013, from http://www.allianceexperts.com/images/documents/creating–profit–through–alliances–sq.pdf

Griskevicius, V., Tybur, J. M., & Van den Bergh, B. (2010). Going green to be seen: Status, reputation, and conspicuous conservation. *Journal of Personality and Social Psychology*, *98*(3), 392–404. doi:10.1037/a0017346 PMID:20175620

Grossman, G. M., & Shapiro, C. (1988). Counterfeit-product trade. *The American Economic Review*, *78*(1), 59–75.

Gualtieri, M. (2016). *Hadoop Is Data's Darling For A Reason.* Forrester. Retrieved from https://go.forrester.com/blogs/hadoop-is-datas-darling-for-a-reason/

Compilation of References

Guercini, S., Ranfagni, S., & Runfola, A. (2020). E-commerce internationalization for top luxury fashion brands: Some emerging strategic issues. *Journal of Management Development*. ahead-of-print. doi:10.1108/JMD-10-2019-0434

Guercini, S., & Ranfagni, S. (2012). Social and Green Sustainability and the Italian Mediterranean Fashion Brands. In *Proceedings of Euromed Congress* (pp. 1-15). Nicosia: Euromed Press.

Guercini, S., & Ranfagni, S. (2013). Sustainability and luxury: The Italian case of a supply chain based on native wools. *Journal of Corporate Citizenship*, *52*(52), 76–89. doi:10.9774/GLEAF.4700.2013.de.00008

Guercini, S., & Woodside, A. G. (2012). A strategic supply chain approach: Consortium marketing in the Italian leatherwear industry. *Marketing Intelligence & Planning*, *30*(7), 700–716. doi:10.1108/02634501211273814

Guido, G., Amatulli, C., Peluso, A. M., De Matteis, C., Piper, L., & Pino, G. (2020). Measuring internalized versus externalized luxury consumption motivations and consumers' segmentation. *Italian Journal of Marketing*, 1–23.

Gurzki, H., Schlatter, N., & Woisetschlager, D. M. (2019). Crafting extraordinary stories: Decoding luxury brand communication. *Journal of Advertising*, *48*(4), 401–414. doi:10.1080/00913367.2019.1641858

Hagtvedt, H., & Patrick, V. M. (2009). The broad embrace of luxury: Hedonic potential as a driver of brand extendibility. *Journal of Consumer Psychology*, *19*(4), 608–618. doi:10.1016/j.jcps.2009.05.007

Hall, E. T., & Hall, M. R. (1990). *Understanding Cultural Differences*. Intercultural Press.

Halonen-Knight, E., & Hurmerinta, L. (2010). Who endorses whom? Meanings transfer in celebrity endorsement. *Journal of Product and Brand Management*, *19*(6), 452–460. doi:10.1108/10610421011085767

Han, Y., Nunes, J., & Drèze, X. (2010). Signaling Status with Luxury Goods: The Role of Brand Prominence. *Journal of Marketing*, *74*(4), 15–30. doi:10.1509/jmkg.74.4.015

Harker, D., Sharma, B., Harker, M., & Reinhard, K. (2010). Leaving home: Food choice behavior of young German adults. *Journal of Business Research*, *63*(2), 111–115. doi:10.1016/j.jbusres.2009.02.007

Harrington, R. J., Ottenbacher, M. C., Staggs, A., & Powell, F. A. (2012). Generation Y consumers: Key restaurant attributes affecting positive and negative experiences. *Journal of Hospitality & Tourism Research (Washington, D.C.)*, *36*(4), 431–449. doi:10.1177/1096348011400744

Harris, L. C., & Goode, M. M. H. (2010). Online servicescapes, trust, and purchase intentions. *Journal of Services Marketing*, *24*(3), 230–243. doi:10.1108/08876041011040631

Harrisson, L., & Huntington, S. (2000). *Culture Matters: How values shape human progress*. Basic Books.

Hasbullah, N. N., Sulaiman, Z., & Mas'od, A. (2020). User-Generated Content Sources: The Use Of Social Media In Motivating Sustainable Luxury Fashion Consumptions. *International Journal of Scientific & Technology Research*, *9*(3), 5208-5214.

Hauck, W. E., & Stanforth, N. (2007). Cohort perception of luxury goods and services. *Journal of Fashion Marketing and Management*, *11*(2), 175–188. doi:10.1108/13612020710751365

Hawkins, D. I., Best, R. J., & Coney, K. A. (2004). *Consumer Behavior: Building Marketing Strategy*. McGraw-Hill Irwin.

Haws, K. L., Winterich, K. P., & Naylor, R. W. (2014). Seeing the world through GREEN-tinted glasses: Green consumption values and responses to environmentally friendly products. *Journal of Consumer Psychology*, *24*(3), 336–354. doi:10.1016/j.jcps.2013.11.002

Hayes, A. F. (2018). *Introduction to mediation, moderation, and conditional process analysis: A regression-based approach*. Guilford Publications.

Healy, J. C., & McDonagh, P. (2013). Consumer roles in brand culture and value co-creation in virtual communities. *Journal of Business Research, 66*(9), 1528–1540. doi:10.1016/j.jbusres.2012.09.014

Heine, K., & Berghaus, B. (2014). Luxury goes digital: How to tackle the digital luxury brand–consumer touchpoints. *Journal of Global Fashion Marketing, 5*(3), 223–234. doi:10.1080/20932685.2014.907606

Helal, G., Ozuem, W., & Lancaster, G. (2018). Social media brand perceptions of millennials. *International Journal of Retail & Distribution Management, 46*(10), 977–998. doi:10.1108/IJRDM-03-2018-0066

Helkkula, A. (2011). Characterising the concept of service experience. *Journal of Service Management, 22*(3), 367–389. doi:10.1108/09564231111136872

Hemphill, C. S., & Suk, J. (2009). The Law, Culture, and Economics of Fashion. *Stanford Law Review*, 61.

Hendriksz, V. (2018). *Kering, H&M, Bestseller & more CEOs to tackle 7 crucial sustainable priorities*. Fashion United. Available at: https://fashionunited.uk/news/business/kering-h-m-bestseller-more-ceos-to-tackle-7-crucial-sustainable-priorities/2018032728851

Hennigs, N., Wiedmann, K.-P., & And Klarmann, C. (2012). Luxury brands in the digital age – exclusivity versus ubiquity. *Marketing Review St. Gallen, 29*(1), 30–35. doi:10.100711621-012-0108-7

Hennigs, N., Wiedmann, K.-P., Klarmann, C., & Behrens, S. (2015). The complexity of value in the luxury industry: From consumers' individual value perception to luxury consumption. *International Journal of Retail & Distribution Management, 43*(10/11), 922–939.

Hennigs, N., Wiedmann, K.-P., Klarmann, C., Strehlau, S., Godey, B., Pederzoli, D., Neulinger, A., Kartik, D., Aiello, G., Donvito, R., Taro, K., Tàboreckà-Petrovicovà, J., Rodrìguez Santos, C., Jung, J., & Oh, H. (2012). What is the Value of Luxury? A cross-cultural consumer perspective. *Psychology and Marketing, 29*(12), 1018–1034. doi:10.1002/mar.20583

Henninger, C. E., Alevizou, P. J., & Oates, C. J. (2016). What is sustainable fashion? *Journal of Fashion Marketing and Management, 20*(4), 1–19. doi:10.1108/JFMM-07-2015-0052

Herawati, H., Prajanti, S. D. W., & Kardoyo, K. (2019). Predicted purchasing decisions from lifestyle, product quality and price through purchase motivation. *The Journal of Economic Education, 8*(1), 1–11.

Herhausen, D., Binder, J., Schoegel, M., & Herrmann, A. (2015). Integrating bricks with clicks: Retailer–level and channel–level outcomes of online–offline channel integration. *Journal of Retailing, 91*(2), 309–325. doi:10.1016/j.jretai.2014.12.009

Hermès. (2020). Retrieved from https://finance.hermes.com/en/

Hine, C. (2015). *Ethnography for the internet: Embedded, embodied and everyday*. Bloomsbury Publishing.

Hoang, L. (2020). *Hermès Online Channels Are Booming. Luxury Brands Should Take Note*. Luxury Society.

Hobson, K. (2013). 'Weak'or 'strong'sustainable consumption? Efficiency, degrowth, and the 10 Year Framework of Programmes. *Environment and Planning. C, Government & Policy, 31*(6), 1082–1098. doi:10.1068/c12279

Hodge, A., Romo, Z., Medina, I., & Fionda-Douglas, A. (2015). Consumer–brand relationships within the luxury cosmetic domain. *Journal of Brand Management, 22*(8), 631–657. doi:10.1057/bm.2015.36

Compilation of References

Hoecklin, L. (1996). *Managing Cultural Differences: Strategies for Competitive Advantage* (2nd ed.). Addison-Wesley Publishers.

Hoeffler, S., & Keller, K. L. (2002). Building brand equity through corporate societal marketing. *Journal of Public Policy & Marketing, 21*(1), 78–89. doi:10.1509/jppm.21.1.78.17600

Hoffmann, J., & Coste–Manière, I. (2012). *Luxury Strategy in Action.* Palgrave Macmillan. doi:10.1057/9780230361546

Hofstede. (2020). *Country comparison.* Retrieved 05 May 2020 from https://www.hofstede-insights.com/country-comparison/south-korea,switzerland/

Hofstede, G. (1980). *Culture's consequences: International differences in work-related values.* SAGE.

Hofstede, G. H., Minkov, G. J., & Minkov, M. (2010). *Cultures and organizations: Software for the mind* (3rd ed.). McGraw-Hill Professional.

Hofstede, G., & Bond, H. M. (1984). Hofstede's culture dimensions: An independent validation using Rokeach's value survey. *Journal of Cross-Cultural Psychology, 15*(4), 417–433. doi:10.1177/0022002184015004003

Holbrook, M. B., & Anand, P. (1990). Effects of tempo and situational arousal on the listener's perceptual and affective responses to music. *Psychology of Music, 18*(2), 150–162. doi:10.1177/0305735690182004

Holbrook, M. B., & Hirschmann, E. C. (1982). The experiential aspects of consumption: Consumer fantasies, feelings and fun. *The Journal of Consumer Research, 9*(2), 132–140. doi:10.1086/208906

Holland, C. P., & Naudé, P. (2004). The metamorphosis of marketing into an information-handling problem. *Journal of Business and Industrial Marketing, 19*(3), 167–177. doi:10.1108/08858620410531306

Hollebeek, L. D., Srivastava, R. K., & Chen, T. (2019). SD logic- informed customer engagement: Integrative framework, revised fundamental propositions, and application to CRM. *Journal of the Academy of Marketing Science, 47*(1), 161–185. doi:10.100711747-016-0494-5

Hollensen, S., & Schimmelpfennig, C. (2013). Selection of celebrity endorsers: A case approach to developing an endorser selection process model. *Marketing Intelligence & Planning, 31*(1), 88–102. doi:10.1108/02634501311292948

Holmberg, C., Chaplin, J. E., Hillman, T., & Berg, C. (2016). Adolescents' presentation of food in social media: An explorative study. *Appetite, 99*, 121–129. doi:10.1016/j.appet.2016.01.009 PMID:26792765

Holmqvist, J., Diaz Ruiz, C. A., & Penaloza, L. (2019). Moments of luxury: Hedonic escapism as a luxury experience. *Journal of Business Research, 116*, 503–513. doi:10.1016/j.jbusres.2019.10.015

Holmqvist, J., Wirtz, J., & Fritze, M. P. (2020, December). Luxury in the digital age: A multi-actor service encounter perspective. *Journal of Business Research, 121*, 747–756. Advance online publication. doi:10.1016/j.jbusres.2020.05.038

Holzwarth, M., Janiszewski, C., & Neumann, M. M. (2006). The influence of avatars on online consumer shopping behavior. *Journal of Marketing, 70*(4), 19–36. doi:10.1509/jmkg.70.4.019

Hood, M. (2012). The Tiger Woods scandal: A cautionary tale for event studies. *Managerial Finance, 38*(5), 543–558. doi:10.1108/03074351211217850

Hopkins, C. D., Grove, S. J., Raymond, M. A., & La Forge, M. C. (2009). Designing the e-servicescape: Implications for on-line retailers. *Journal of Internet Commerce, 8*(1/2), 23–43. doi:10.1080/15332860903182487

Horngen, C., Datar, S., & Rajan, M. (2016). *Cost Accounting: A Managerial Emphasis* (16th ed.). Pearson Education.

Hosie, R. (2017). How instagram has transformed the restaurant industry for millennials. *The Independent*. Retrieved from https://www.independent.co.uk/life-style/food-and-drink/millenials-restaurant-how-choose-instagram-social-media-where-eat-a7677786.html

Howell, M., & Prevenier, W. (2001). *From Reliable Sources: An Introduction to Historical Methods*. Cornell University Press.

Howe, N., & Strauss, B. (2000). *Millennials rising: The next great generation*. Vintage.

Hoyer, W., & MacInnis, D. (2008). *Consumer Behaviour* (5th ed.). South-Western Cengage Learning.

Hughes, M. U., Bendoni, W. K., & Pehlivan, E. (2016). Storygiving as a co-creation tool for luxury brands in the age of internet: A love story by Tiffany and thousands of lovers. *Journal of Product and Brand Management, 25*(4), 357–364. doi:10.1108/JPBM-09-2015-0970

Hugosson, O., Matthys, C., & Phung, L. (2014). *Perception of the Celebrity Endorser: A study of how age and gender influences the consumer perception*. Jonkoping International Business School.

Hussy, W., Schreier, M., & Echterhoff, G. (2013). *Forschungsmethoden in Psychologie und Sozialwissenschaften für Bachelor* (2nd ed.). Springer. doi:10.1007/978-3-642-34362-9

Hu, Y., Manikonda, L., & Kambhampati, S. (2014, June). What we instagram: A first analysis of instagram photo content and user types. ICWSM.

Interbrand. (2020). *Best Global Brands 2019*. Retrieved at: https://www.interbrand.com/best–brands/

International Management Institute. (1930). *International Conference on Budgetary Control*. Geneva: Author.

Jahn, B., Kunz, W. H., & Meyer, A. (2013). The Role of Social Media for Luxury-Brands – Motives for Consumer Engagement and Opportunities for Businesses. SSRN *Electronic Journal*. doi:10.2139srn.2307106

Jain, S. (2019). Factors affecting sustainable luxury purchase behavior: A conceptual framework. *Journal of International Consumer Marketing, 31*(2), 130–146. doi:10.1080/08961530.2018.1498758

Jain, S., & Mishra, S. (2020). Luxury fashion consumption in sharing economy: A study of Indian millennials. *Journal of Global Fashion Marketing, 11*(2), 171–189. doi:10.1080/20932685.2019.1709097

Jankowicz, A. D. (2000). *Business Research Projects* (3rd ed.). Thomson Learning.

Janssen, C., Vanhamme, J., Lindgreen, A., & Lefebvre, C. (2014). The Catch-22 of responsible luxury: Effects of luxury product characteristics on consumers' perception of fit with corporate social responsibility. *Journal of Business Ethics, 119*(1), 45–57. doi:10.100710551-013-1621-6

Jiambalvo, J. (2013). *Management Accounting*. John Wiley and Sons.

Jin, B., & Cedrola, E. (2017). *Fashion Branding and Communication: Core Strategies of European Luxury Brands*. Springer. doi:10.1057/978-1-137-52343-3

Jin, S.-A. A. (2012). The potential of social media for luxury brand management. *Marketing Intelligence & Planning, 30*(7), 687–699.

Johnson, H. T., & Kaplan, R. (1987). *Relevance Lost: The Rise and Fall of Management Accounting*. Harvard Business School Press.

Jones, G. G., & Pouillard, V. (2009). Christian Dior: A New Look for Haute Couture. Harvard Business School Case no. 809-159. Harvard Business School Publishing.

Compilation of References

Jones, C., Makri, M., & Gomez-Mejia, L. R. (2008). Affiliate directors and perceived risk bearing in publicly traded, family-controlled firms: The case of diversification. *Entrepreneurship Theory and Practice*, *32*(6), 1007–1026. doi:10.1111/j.1540-6520.2008.00269.x

Jones, R. (2002). *The apparel industry*. Blackwell.

Joy, A., Sherry, J. F. Jr, Venkatesh, A., Wang, J., & Chan, R. (2012). Fast Fashion, Sustainability, and the Ethical Appeal of Luxury Brands. *Fashion Theory*, *3*(16), 273–296. doi:10.2752/175174112X13340749707123

Joy, A., Wang, J. J., Chan, T. S., Sherry, J. F. Jr, & Cui, G. (2014). M (Art) worlds: Consumer perceptions of how luxury brand stores become art institutions. *Journal of Retailing*, *90*(3), 347–364. doi:10.1016/j.jretai.2014.01.002

Kalakota, R., & Whinston, A. B. (1997). *Electronic commerce: a manager's guide*. Addison–Wesley Professional.

Kapferer, J.-N., & Bastien, V. (2012). *The Luxury Strategy: Break the Rules of Marketing to Build Luxury Brands*. Academic Press.

Kapferer, J. N. (1997). Managing luxury brands. *Journal of Brand Management*, *4*(4), 251–260. doi:10.1057/bm.1997.4

Kapferer, J. N. (1998). Why are we seduced by luxury brands? *Journal of Brand Management*, *6*(1), 44–49. doi:10.1057/bm.1998.43

Kapferer, J. N. (2002). *Ce qui va changer les marques*. Editions d'Organisation.

Kapferer, J. N. (2008). *The new strategic brand management: Creating and sustaining brand equity long term*. Kogan Page Publishers.

Kapferer, J. N. (2010). All that glitters is not green: The challenge of sustainable luxury. *European Business Review*, *2*, 40–45.

Kapferer, J. N. (2012). All That Glitters is not Green: The Challenge of Sustainable Luxury. *European Business Review*, (November/December), 40–45.

Kapferer, J. N. (2015). *Kapferer on luxury: How luxury brands can grow yet remain rare*. Kogan Page Publishers.

Kapferer, J. N. (2017). *Lusso. Nuove sfide, nuovi sfidanti*. Franco Angeli.

Kapferer, J. N., & Bastien, V. (2009). *Luxury Strategy*. Franco Angeli.

Kapferer, J. N., & Bastien, V. (2009). The specificity of luxury management: Turning marketing upside down. *Journal of Brand Management*, *16*(5-6), 311–322. doi:10.1057/bm.2008.51

Kapferer, J. N., & Bastien, V. (2012). *The Luxury Strategy: Break The Rules of Marketing to Build Luxury Brands* (2nd ed.). Kogan Page Ltd.

Kapferer, J. N., & Bastien, V. (2012). *The luxury strategy: Break the rules of marketing to build luxury brands*. Kogan Page Publishers.

Kapferer, J. N., & Michaut, A. (2015). Luxury and sustainability: A common future? The match depends on how consumers define luxury. *Luxury Research Journal*, *1*(1), 3–17. doi:10.1504/LRJ.2015.069828

Kapferer, J. N., & Michaut-Denizeau, A. (2014). Is luxury compatible with sustainability? Luxury consumers' viewpoint. *Journal of Brand Management*, *21*(1), 1–22. doi:10.1057/bm.2013.19

Kapferer, J. N., & Michaut-Denizeau, A. (2020). Are millennials really more sensitive to sustainable luxury? A cross-generational international comparison of sustainability consciousness when buying luxury. *Journal of Brand Management*, *27*, 35–47. doi:10.105741262-019-00165-7

Kapferer, J.-N. (1999, June). E-Tribalized Marketing? The Strategic Implications of Virtual Communities of Consumption. *European Management Journal*, *17*(3), 252–264.

Kapferer, J.-N. (2013). *Kapferer on Luxury: How Luxury Brands Can Grow Yet Remain Rare*. Kogan Page.

Kapferer, J.-N. (2014). The future of luxury: Challenges and opportunities. *Journal of Brand Management*, *21*(9), 716–726. doi:10.1057/bm.2014.32

Kapferer, J.-N. (2015). *Kapferer on Luxury*. How Luxury Brands Can Grow Yet Remain Rare. Kogan Page.

Kapferer, J.-N., & Bastien, V. (2009). *The Luxury Strategy: Break the rules of marketing to build luxury brands*. Kogan Page.

Kapferer, J.-N., & Bastien, V. (2009). *The Luxury Strategy: Break the Rules of Marketing to Build Luxury Brands*. Kogan Page.

Kapferer, J.-N., & Bastien, V. (2012). *The luxury strategy – break the rules of marketing to build luxury brands*. Kogan Page.

Kapferer, J.-N., & Valette-Florence, P. (2016). Beyond rarity: The paths of luxury desire. How luxury brands grow yet remain desirable. *Journal of Product and Brand Management*, *25*(2), 120–133. doi:10.1108/JPBM-09-2015-0988

Kapferer, N. (2010). All that Glitters is not Green: The Challenge of Sustainable Luxury. *European Business Review*, (November-December), 40–45.

Kaplan, R. (1987, July). The Evolution of Management Accounting. The Accounting Review, 390 – 418.

Kaplan, R. (1989). Kanthal. Harvard Business School Case, ref: 190-002.

Kaplan, R., & Norton, D. (1992, Jan.). The Balanced Scorecard – Measures that Drive Performance. Harvard Business Review, 71 – 79.

Kaplan, A. M., & Haenlein, M. (2010). Users of the world, unite! The challenges and opportunities of Social Media. *Business Horizons*, *53*(1), 59–68. doi:10.1016/j.bushor.2009.09.003

Kaplan, R. (1984). The evolution of management accounting. *The Accounting Review*, (July), 390–418.

Kaplan, R., & Norton, D. (1996). *The Balanced Scorecard: Translating Strategy into Action*. Harvard Business School Press.

Kastanakis, M., & Balabanis, G. (2012). Between the mass and the class: Antecedents of the "bandwagon" luxury consumption behavior. *Journal of Business Research*, *65*(10), 1399–1407. doi:10.1016/j.jbusres.2011.10.005

Kauppinen-Raisanen, H., Gummerus, J., VonKoskull, C., & Cristini, H. (2017). The new wave of luxury: The meaning and value of luxury to the contemporary consumer. *Qualitative Market Research*, *12*(3), 229–249. doi:10.1108/QMR-03-2016-0025

Kaur, G. (2011). Traditional Commerce Vs. E–Commerce. *International Research Journal of Management Science and Technology*, *2*(3), 334–340.

Kemp, S. (1998). Perceiving luxury and necessity. *Journal of Economic Psychology*, *19*(5), 591–606.

Kemp, S. (1998). Perceiving Luxury and Necessity. *Journal of Economic Psychology*, *19*(5), 591–606. doi:10.1016/S0167-4870(98)00026-9

Compilation of References

Kennedy, E., & Guzman, F. (2017). When perceived ability to influence plays a role: Brand co-creation in Web 2.0. *Journal of Product and Brand Management, 26*(4), 342–350. doi:10.1108/JPBM-04-2016-1137

Kent, A., Vianello, M., Cano, M. B., & Helberger, E. (2016). Omnichannel fashion retail and channel integration: The case of department stores. In *Handbook of research on global fashion management and merchandising* (pp. 398–419). IGI Global. doi:10.4018/978-1-5225-0110-7.ch016

Kester, J. (2018, October 3). Forbes Travel Guide's 30 Most Luxurious Spas in The World. *Forbes.* https://www.forbes.com

Kim, C. (2016). *South Korea unemployment rate jumps to six-year high at 4.1%.* Bloomberg. Retrieved 25. May 2020 from https://www.bloomberg.com/news/articles/2016-03-16/south-korea-unemployment-rate-jumps-to-six-year-high-at-4-1

Kim, H. (2009). *The Plastic Surgery Obsession in South Korea.* Syracuse University Honors Program Capstone Projects, 485.

Kim, A. J., & Ko, E. (2012). Do social media marketing activities enhance customer equity? An empirical study of luxury fashion brand. *Journal of Business Research, 65*(10), 1480–1486. doi:10.1016/j.jbusres.2011.10.014

Kim, A., & Ko, E. (2010). Impacts of Luxury Fashion Brand's Social Media Marketing on Customer Relationship and Purchase Intention. *Journal of Global Fashion Marketing, 1*(3), 164–171. doi:10.1080/20932685.2010.10593068

Kim, H., Choi, Y. J., & Lee, Y. (2015). Web atmospheric qualities in luxury fashion brand web sites. *Journal of Fashion Marketing and Management, 19*(4), 384–401. doi:10.1108/JFMM-09-2013-0103

Kim, J. (2019). *Luxury fashion goods ownership and collecting behavior in an omni-channel retail environment.* Research Journal of Textile and Apparel. doi:10.1108/RJTA-01-2019-0001

Kim, J. E., Lloyd, S., & Cervellon, M. C. (2016). Narrative-transportation storylines in luxury brand advertising: Motivating consumer engagement. *Journal of Business Research, 69*(1), 304–313. doi:10.1016/j.jbusres.2015.08.002

Kim, J.-H. (2019). Imperative challenge for luxury brands: Generation Y consumers' perceptions of luxury fashion brands' e-commerce sites. *International Journal of Retail & Distribution Management, 47*(2), 220–244. doi:10.1108/IJRDM-06-2017-0128

Kim, J.-H., & Kim, M. (2020). Conceptualization and assessment of E-service quality for luxury brands. *Service Industries Journal, 40*(5-6), 436–470. doi:10.1080/02642069.2018.1517755

Kim, S.-S. (2005). The study about masstige high-end products (Part I) - Focusing on values. *Journal of Korean Society of Clothing and Textiles, 29*(11), 1381–1388.

Kim, Y. K., Forney, J., & Arnold, E. (1997). Environmental messages in fashion advertisements: Impact on consumer responses. *Clothing & Textiles Research Journal, 15*(3), 147–154. doi:10.1177/0887302X9701500303

Kitchen, P. J. (2017). Integrated Marketing Communications: Evolution, Current Status, Future Developments. *European Journal of Marketing, 51*(3), 394–405. doi:10.1108/EJM-06-2016-0362Kitchen, P. J., Tourky, M. E. A., Petrescu, M., & Rethore, C. (2020). (in press). Globalisation, Marketing, Sustainability, Tourism and the Hand Mirror of COVID-19. *Academy of Business Research.*

Kitchen, P. J., Brignell, J., Li, T., & Jones, G. S. (2004). The Emergence Of IMC: A Theoretical Perspective. *Journal of Advertising Research, 44*(1), 19–30. doi:10.1017/S0021849904040048

Klaus, P. P. (2020). The end of the world as we know it? The influence of online channels on the luxury customer experience. *Journal of Retailing and Consumer Services, 57.* Advance online publication. doi:10.1016/j.jretconser.2020.102248

Klaus, P., & Manthiou, A. (2020). Applying the EEE customer mindset in luxury: Reevaluating customer experience research and practice during and after corona. *Journal of Service Management, 31*(6), 1175–1183. doi:10.1108/JOSM-05-2020-0159

Kluckhohn, C. (1951). Values and value-orientations in the theory of action: an exploration in definition and classification. In T. S. E. Parsons (Ed.), *Toward a General Theory of Action* (pp. 388–433). Harvard University Press. doi:10.4159/harvard.9780674863507.c8

Knowledge@Wharton. (2020). *Can Luxury Retail Attract a New Generation of Shoppers?* Author.

Ko, E., Costello, J. P., & Taylor, C. R. (2019). What is a luxury brand? A new definition and review of the literature. *Journal of Business Research, 99*, 405–413. doi:10.1016/j.jbusres.2017.08.023

Koivisto, E., & Mattila, P. (2020). Extending the luxury experience to social media – User-Generated Content co-creation in a branded event. *Journal of Business Research, 117*, 570–578. doi:10.1016/j.jbusres.2018.10.030

Kolbe, R., & Burnett, M. (1991). Content-Analysis Research: An Examination of Applications with Directives for Improving Research Reliability and Objectivity. *The Journal of Consumer Research, 18*(2), 243–250. doi:10.1086/209256

Koschate-Fischer, N., Stefan, I. V., & Hoyer, W. D. (2012). Willingness to pay for cause-related marketing: The impact of donation amount and moderating effects. *JMR, Journal of Marketing Research, 49*(6), 910–927. doi:10.1509/jmr.10.0511

Kotler, P. (1973). Atmospherics as a marketing tool. *Journal of Retailing, 49*(4), 48–64.

Kotler, P., & ... . (2016). *Marketing management*. Pearson.

Kotler, P., Adam, S., Denize, S., & Armstrong, G. (2009). *Principles of Marketing* (4th ed.). Pearson Education.

Kowalczyk, C., & Pounders, R. (2016). Transforming celebrities through social media: The role of authenticity and emotional attachment. *Journal of Product and Brand Management, 25*(4), 345–356. doi:10.1108/JPBM-09-2015-0969

Kozinets, R. V., & Arnould, E. J. (2017). *Ruminations on the current state of consumer ethnography*. Routledge Handbook on Consumption, Routledge.

Kozinets, R. V., de Valck, K., Wojnicki, A. C., & Wilner, S. (2010). Networked narratives: Understanding Word-of-Mouth Marketing in Online Communities. *Journal of Marketing, 74*(2), 71–89. doi:10.1509/jm.74.2.71

Kozinets, R. V., Dolbec, P.-Y., & Earley, A. (2014). The SAGE handbook of qualitative data analysis. In U. Flick (Ed.), *Netnographic analysis: Understanding culture through social media data*. Sage Publications. doi:10.4135/9781446282243

Kozinets, R. V., Sherry, J. F., DeBerry-Spence, B., Duhacheck, A., Nuttavuthisi, K., & Storm, D. (2002). Themed Flagship Brand Stores in the new Millenium: Theory, Practice, Prospect. *Journal of Retailing, 78*(1), 17–29. doi:10.1016/S0022-4359(01)00063-X

Kozinets, R., Patterson, A., & Ashman, R. (2016). Networks of desire: How technology increases our passion to consume. *The Journal of Consumer Research*. Advance online publication. doi:10.1093/jcr/ucw061

Kozlova, O. A., Sukhostav, E. V., Anashkina, N. A., Tkachenko, O. N., & Shatskaya, E. (2017, December). Consumer model transformation in the digital economy era. In *Perspectives on the use of New Information and Communication Technology (ICT) in the Modern Economy* (pp. 279–287). Springer.

Krensky, P. Hare, J., Vashisth, S., & Linden, A. (2019, August 6). *Hype Cycle for Data Science and Machine Learning*. Gartner. Retrieved from https://www.gartner.com/en/documents/3955984/hype-cycle-for-data-science-and-machine-learning-2019

Compilation of References

Krugman, D. M., Reid, L. N., Dunn, S. W., & Barban, A. M. (1994). *Advertising: Is Role in Modern Marketing.* Dryden Press.

Kunz, W., Aksoy, L., Bart, Y., Heinonen, K., Kabadayi, S., Ordenes, F. V., & Theodoulidis, B. (2017). Customer engagement in a Big Data world. *Journal of Services Marketing, 31*(2), 161–171.

La Ferla, R. (2000). Cheap Chic'Draws Crowds on 5th Ave. *New York Times.* Retrieved April 25, 2020, from https://www.nytimes.com/2000/04/11/style/cheap-chic-draws-crowds-on5thave.htmUpagewanted= all

Lafferty, B. A., & Goldsmith, R. E. (2005). Cause–brand alliances: Does the cause help the brand or does the brand help the cause? *Journal of Business Research, 58*(4), 423–429. doi:10.1016/j.jbusres.2003.07.001

Lama, A. V. (2018). Millennial leisure and tourism: The rise of escape rooms [Ocio y turismo millennial: El fenómeno de las salas de escape]. *Cuadernos de Turismo, 41*, 615–636 + 743–746.

Lancaster, L. C., & Stillman, D. (2003). *When generations collide: Who they are, why they clash, how to solve the generational puzzle at work.* HarperBusiness.

Lane, C. (2010). The Michelin-Starred Restaurant Sector as a Cultural Industry, Food. *Cultura e Scuola, 13*(4), 493–519.

Langlade, É. (1913). *Rose Bertin: The Creator of Fashion at the Court of Marie-Antoinette.* Charles Scribner's Sons.

LaPoint, P. (2005). Timken Rolls Out a Marketing Dashboard for Industrial Bearing Group. *Marketing NPV, 3*(1), 3–6.

Larraufie, A.-F. M., & Kourdoughli, A. (2014). The e-semiotics of luxury. *Journal of Global Fashion Marketing, 5*(3), 197–208. doi:10.1080/20932685.2014.906120

LaSalle, D., & Britton, T. A. (2003). *Priceless: Turning ordinary products into extraordinary experiences.* Harvard Business School Press.

Laudon, K., Laudon, J. P., & Schoder, D. (2016). Wirtschaftsinformatik: Eine Einführung (P. Studium, Ed.). Academic Press.

Lauper, J. (2020). *Evolving Luxuriousness. A Cross-Generational Analysis of the Swiss Value Perception and Consumer Behavior of Luxury* (Bachelor Thesis). Zurich University of Applied Sciences, School of Management and Law.

LaWare, M., & Moutsatsos, C. (2013). For Skin That's Us, Authentically Us: Celebrity, Empowerment, and the Allure of Antiaging Advertisements. *Women's Studies in Communication, 36*(2), 189–208. doi:10.1080/07491409.2013.794753

Lawry, C. A., & Choi, L. (2013). The Omnichannel luxury retail experience: Building mobile trust and technology acceptance of quick response (QR) codes. *Marketing ZFP, 35*(2), 144–154. doi:10.15358/0344-1369_2013_2_144

Lay, R. (2018). *Digitale Transformation: Die grösste Herausforderung für die Modebranche.* Deloitte. Retrieved from https://www2.deloitte.com/ch/de/pages/consumerindustrial-products/-articles/ultimate-challenge-fashion-industry-digitalage.html#

Lazer, W. (1964). Lifestyle concepts and marketing. In S. A. Greyser (Ed.), *Toward scientific marketing* (pp. 243–252). American Marketing Association.

Lea-Greenwood, G. (2013). *Fashion Marketing Communications* (1st ed.). John Wiley & Sons.

Leary, R. B., Vann, R. J., Mittelstaedt, J. D., Murphy, P. E., & Sherry, J. F. (2014). Changing the market one behavior at a time. *Journal of Business Research, 67*(9), 1953–1958. doi:10.1016/j.jbusres.2013.11.004

Lee, J., & Kim, S. (2020). *Record South Korean employment leans on part-timers.* Bloomberg. Retrieved 29 April 2020 from https://www.bloomberg.com/news/articles/2020-01-14/

Lee, K. (2019). More Koreans pursuing work-life balance. *Korea Times*. Retrieved 13 October 2020 from https://www.koreatimes.co.kr/www/biz/2020/04/367_280533.html

Lee, E., Edwards, S. M., Youn, S., & Yun, T. (2018). Understanding the moderating effect of motivational values on young consumers' responses to luxury brands: A cross-cultural study of South Korea and the USA. *Journal of Marketing Communications*, *24*(2), 103–124. doi:10.1080/13527266.2014.975830

Lee, H., Rothenberg, L., & Xu, Y. (2019). Young luxury fashion consumers' preferences in multichannel environment. *International Journal of Retail & Distribution Management*, *48*(3), 244–261. doi:10.1108/IJRDM-11-2018-0253

Lee, M., Ko, E., Lee, S., & Kim, K. (2015). Understanding Luxury Disposition. *Psychology and Marketing*, *32*(4), 467–480. doi:10.1002/mar.20792

Leganza, G. (2019, October 30). *Predictions 2020: Approaches to customer Insights Evolve*. Forrester. Retrieved from https://go.forrester.com/blogs/predictions-2020-customer-insights/

Lemon, K. N., & Verhoef, P. C. (2016). Understanding customer experience throughout the customer journey. *Journal of Marketing*, *80*(6), 69–96. doi:10.1509/jm.15.0420

Lewis, T. (2018). Digital food: From paddock to platform. *Communication Research and Practice*, *4*(3), 212–228. doi:10.1080/22041451.2018.1476795

Lewnard, J. A., & Lo, N. C. (2020). Scientific and ethical basis for social–distancing interventions against COVID–19. *The Lancet Infectious Diseases*.

Liao, J., & Wang, L. (2009). Face as a mediator of the relationship between material value and brand consciousness. *Psychology and Marketing*, *26*(11), 987–1001. doi:10.1002/mar.20309

Lim, H., Shaw, D., Liao, P., & Duan, H. (2020). The effects of income on happiness in east and south Asia: Societal values matter? *Journal of Happiness Studies*, *2020*(21), 391–415. doi:10.100710902-019-00088-9

Lissitsa, S., & Kol, O. (2016). Generation X vs. Generation Y–A decade of online shopping. *Journal of Retailing and Consumer Services*, *31*, 304–312. doi:10.1016/j.jretconser.2016.04.015

Liu, H., Wu, L., & Li, X. (2019). Social media envy: How experience sharing on social networking sites drives millennials' aspirational tourism consumption. *Journal of Travel Research*, *58*(3), 355–369. doi:10.1177/0047287518761615

Liu, X., Burns, A. C., & Hou, Y. (2017). An investigation of brand-related user-generated content on Twitter. *Journal of Advertising*, *46*(2), 236–247.

Liu, X., Shin, H., & Burns, A. C. (2019). Examining the impact of luxury brand's social media marketing on customer engagement: Using big data analytics and natural language processing. *Journal of Business Research*. Advance online publication. doi:10.1016/j.jbusres.2019.04.042

Loonam, J., Eaves, S., Vikas, K., & Parry, G. (2017). Towards Digital Transformation: Lessons learned from Traditional Organisations. *Strategic Change*.

Lou, C., & Yuan, S. (2019). Influencer marketing: How message value and credibility affect consumer trust of branded content on social media. *Journal of Interactive Advertising*, *19*(1), 58–73. doi:10.1080/15252019.2018.1533501

Loureiro, S. M. C., & Guerreiro, J. (2018). Psychological behavior of millennials: Living between real and virtual reality. In M. W. Gerhardt & J. Van Eck Peluchette (Eds.), Millennials: Trends, characteristics and perspectives (pp. 67–90). Academic Press.

Compilation of References

Loureiro, S. M. C., Maximiano, M., & Panchapakesan, P. (2018). Engaging fashion consumers in social media: The case of luxury brands. International Journal of Fashion Design. *Technology and Education, 11*(3), 310–321. doi:10.10 80/17543266.2018.1431810

Lutz, C. A., & Collins, J. L. (1993). *Reading National Geographic.* University of Chicago Press.

Luxury Institute. (2019). *Luxury institute's 'state of the luxury industry' survey shows wealthy shoppers around the world crave emotional and human connections with luxury brands.* Retrieved 26 April 2020 from https://www.globenewswire. com/news-release/2019/01/22/1703335/0/en/Luxury-Institute-s-State-Of-The-Luxury-Industry-Survey-Shows-Wealthy-Shoppers-Around-The-World-Crave-Emotional-and-Human-Connections-With-Luxury-Brands.html

Lynch, S., & Barnes, L. (2020). Omnichannel fashion retailing: Examining the customer decision–making journey. *Journal of Fashion Marketing and Management, 24*(3), 471–493. doi:10.1108/JFMM-09-2019-0192

MacInnis, D. J. (2011). A framework for conceptual contributions in marketing. *Journal of Marketing, 75*(4), 136–154. doi:10.1509/jmkg.75.4.136

Magee, B., (1933, Oct. 7). The practical control of selling expense: an examination of distribution accounting. *The Accountant.*

Magnelli, A., Pizziol, V., & Manzo, M. (2020). Innovative in-store ICT marketing solutions for an enhanced luxury shopping-experience. *Marche et organisations, 37*(1), 165–183.

Mandler, T., Johnen, M., & Gräve, J.-F. (2020). Can't help falling in love? How brand luxury generates positive consumer affect in social media. *Journal of Business Research, 120,* 330–342. doi:10.1016/j.jbusres.2019.10.010

Mangold, W. G., & Faulds, D. J. (2009). Social media: The new hybrid element of the promotion mix. *Business Horizons, 52*(4), 357–365. doi:10.1016/j.bushor.2009.03.002

Mangold, W. G., & Smith, K. T. (2012). Selling to Millennials with online reviews. *Business Horizons, 55*(2), 141–153. doi:10.1016/j.bushor.2011.11.001

Manna, R., & Palumbo, R. (2018). What makes a museum attractive to young people? Evidence from Italy. *International Journal of Tourism Research, 20*(4), 508–517. doi:10.1002/jtr.2200

Marchiolo, E. E. (2019). *Responsible and sustainable luxury: the Stella McCartney case.* Academic Press.

Marcilhac, V., & Pitte, J. R. (2012). Le luxe alimentaire - Une singularité française. Presses Universitaires de Rennes.

Mari, M., & Poggesi, S. (2013). Servicescape cues and customer behavior: A systematic literature review and research agenda. *Service Industries Journal, 33*(2), 171–199. doi:10.1080/02642069.2011.613934

Marr, B. (2016). *What is the difference between artificial intelligence and machine learning?* Retrieved from https:// www.forbes.com/sites/bernardmarr/2016/12/06/what-is-the-difference-between-artificial-intelligence-and-machine-learning/#241fc0a72742

Masoud, N. (2017). How to win the battle of ideas in corporate social responsibility: The International Pyramid Model of CSR. *International Journal of Corporate Social Responsibility, 2*(1), 1–22. doi:10.118640991-017-0015-y

Matzler, K., Bauer, A., & Mooradian, A. (2015). Self-esteem and transformational leadership. *Journal of Managerial Psychology, 30*(7), 815–831. doi:10.1108/JMP-01-2013-0030

Maycumber, S.G. (1994, April 26). L. L. Bean to ATMI: Environment key factor. *Women's Wear Daily*, p. 14.

McCharty, E. J. (1964). *Basic Marketing: A Managerial Approach* (2nd ed.). Irwin, Homewood.

McCracken, G. (1989). Who is the Celebrity Endorser? Cultural Foundations of the Endorsement Process. *The Journal of Consumer Research*, *13*(3), 310–321. doi:10.1086/209217

McDonald, S., Oates, C. J., Thyne, M., Timmis, A. J., & Carlile, C. (2015). Flying in the face of environmental concern: Why green consumers continue to fly. *Journal of Marketing Management*, *31*(13-14), 1503–1528. doi:10.1080/02672 57X.2015.1059352

McFerran, B., Aquino, K., & Tracy, J. L. (2014). Evidence for two facets of pride in consumption: Findings from luxury brands. *Journal of Consumer Psychology*, *24*(4), 455–471. doi:10.1016/j.jcps.2014.03.004

McKinsey & Company. (2018). *Luxury in the age of digital Darwinism*. https://www.mckinsey.it/idee/luxury-in-the-age-of-digital-darwinism

McKinsey. (2018). https://www.mckinsey.com/industries/consumer-packaged-goods/our-insights/true-gen-generation-z-and-its-implications-for-companies

McKinsey. (2018a). https://www.mckinsey.com/~/media/McKinsey/Industries/Retail/Our%20Insights/Renewed%20 optimism%20for%20the%20fashion%20industry/The-state-of-fashion-2018-final.ashx

McKinsey. (2019). https://www.mckinsey.com/~/media/mckinsey/industries/retail/our%20insights/the%20state%20of%20 fashion%202019%20a%20year%20of%20awakening/the-state-of-fashion-2019-final.ashx

McKinsey. (2020), *It's time to rewire the fashion system: State of Fashion coronavirus update*. McKinsey and Company. https://www.mckinsey.com/industries/retail/our–insights/its–time–to–rewire–the–fashion–system–state–of–fashion–coronavirus–update

McKinsey. (2020). *The luxury industry during—And after—Coronavirus*. Retrieved on 31st July 2020, Retrieved from: https://www.mckinsey.com/industries/retail/our-insights/a-perspective-for-the-luxury-goods-industry-during-and-after-coronavirus

McLuhan, M. (1970). *Culture is our Business*. McGraw-Hill.

McWatters, C., & Zimmerman, J. (2016). *Management Accounting in a Dynamic Environment*. Routledge.

Meadows, D., Randers, J., & Meadows, D. (2004). *Limits to growth: The 30-year update*. Chelsea Green Publishing.

Megehee, C. M., & Spake, D. F. (2012). Consumer enactments of archetypes using luxury brands. *Journal of Business Research*, *65*(10), 1434–1442. doi:10.1016/j.jbusres.2011.10.009

Mehta, A. (2017, October 13). *Four Types of Business Analytics to Know*. Analytics Insights. Retrieved from https://www.analyticsinsight.net/four-types-of-business-analytics-to-know/

Memery, J., Megicks, P., & Williams, J. (2005). Ethical and social responsibility issues in grocery shopping: A preliminary typology. *Qualitative Market Research*, *8*(4), 399–412. doi:10.1108/13522750510619760

Mendini, M., & Peter, P. C. (2018). Marketing for social change. Marketing and Humanity: Discourses in the Real World, 206.

Mendini, M., Pizzetti, M., & Peter, P. C. (2019). Social food pleasure: When sharing offline, online, and for society amplifies a pleasurable and healthy food experiences and well-being. *Qualitative Market Research*, *22*(4), 544–556. doi:10.1108/QMR-06-2018-0067

Meyer, H. (1999). When the cause is just. *The Journal of Business Strategy*, *20*(6), 27–31. doi:10.1108/eb040042 PMID:10230315

Compilation of References

Miller, D., & Le Breton-Miller, I. (2005). *Managing for the Long Run: Lessons in Competitive Advantage from Great Family Businesses.* Harvard Business Press.

Miller, K. (2013). Hedonic customer responses to fast fashion and replicas. *Journal of Fashion Marketing and Management, 2*(17), 160–174. doi:10.1108/JFMM-10-2011-0072

Miller, L. E. (1993). *Cristóbal Balenciaga.* Batsford.

Moe, W. W., & Schweidel, D. A. (2012). Online Product Opinions: Incidence, Evaluation, and Evolution. *Marketing Science, 31*(3), 372–386.

Moe, W. W., & Schweidel, D. A. (2014, August). Social Media: A Joint Model of Sentiment and Venue Format Choice. *JMR, Journal of Marketing Research, LI,* 387–402.

Moore, C. M., Doherty, A. M., & Doyle, S. A. (2010). Flagship Stores as a Market Entry Method: the Perspective of Luxury Fashion Retailing. *European Journal of Marketing, 44*(1(2), 139-161

Moore, K., & Reid, S. (2008). The birth of brand: 4000 years of branding. *Business History, 50*(4), 419–432. doi:10.1080/00076790802106299

Morra, M. C., Gelosa, V., Ceruti, F., & Mazzucchelli, A. (2018). Original or counterfeit luxury fashion brands? The effect of social media on purchase intention. *Journal of Global Fashion Marketing, 9*(1), 24–39. doi:10.1080/2093268 5.2017.1399079

Mosca, F., & Casalegno, C. (2020). Managing Integrated Brand Communication Strategies in the Online Era: New Marketing Frontiers for Luxury Goods. In Global Branding: Breakthroughs in Research and Practice (pp. 227-242). IGI Global.

Mosca, F., & Casalegno, C. (2020). Managing Integrated Brand Communication Strategies in the Online Era: New Marketing Frontiers for Luxury Goods. In Global Branding: Breakthroughs in Research and Practice (pp. 227–242). IGI Global.

Mosca, F., & Chiaudano, V. (2020). Digital channels and distribution in luxury market. *Marché et organisations, 37*(1), 147-163.

Mosca, F., & Chiaudano, V. (2020). Digital channels and distribution in luxury market. *Marchè et organisations, 37*(1), 147–163.

Mosca, F., & Civera, C. (2018). *Digital channels and social media management in luxury markets.* Academic Press.

Mosca, F., & Giacosa, E. (2016), Old and New Distribution Channels in the Luxury Sector. IGI Global. doi:10.4018/978-1-4666-9958-8.ch010

Mosca, F., Casalegno, C., & Rosso, C. (2017). *Luxury Brands and Social Media: Implications around New Trends in Selling Luxury Products. A study across different product categories.* Global Fashion Management Conference at Vienna 2017, Vienna, Austria. 10.15444/GFMC2017.01.01.01

Mosca, F., Casalegno, C., &Feffin A. (2013, October). *Nuovi modelli di comunicazione nei settori dei beni di lusso: un'analisi comparata.* Paper X Convegno della Scuola Italiana di Marketing, Milano.

Mosca, F. (2010). *Il marketing dei beni di lusso.* Pearson Italia.

Mosca, F. (2014). *Distribution Strategies in Luxury Markets: emerging trends.* McGraw-Hill.

Mosca, F. (2017). *Strategie nei mercati del lusso. Marketing, digitalizzazione, sostenibilità.* Egea.

Mosca, F., Bertoldi, B., & Giachino, C. (2015). Development Strategies for International Distribution in luxury industry. *Journal of Management Cases, 4*(4), 4–16.

Mosca, F., Casalegno, C. G., & Civera, C. (2016). Opportunities and Peculiarities of the Online for Communicating Corporate Social Responsibility. A cross investigation on luxury players and consumers' perceptions. *British Academy of Management Journal, 2016,* 1–26.

Mosca, F., Casalegno, C., & Feffin, A. (2014, September). Last Marketing Communication Challenges In Luxury Brand Markets: A Comparative Analysis. *7th Annual Conference of the EuroMed Academy of Business.*

Mosca, F., & Civera, C. (2017). *Digital channels and social media management in luxury markets.* Routledge. doi:10.4324/9780203702048

Mosca, F., & Civera, C. (2017). The evolution of CSR: An integrated approach. *Symphonya. Emerging Issues in Management,* (1), 16–35.

Mosquera, A., Olarte–Pascual, C., Ayensa, E. J., & Murillo, Y. S. (2018). The role of technology in an omnichannel physical store. *Spanish Journal of Marketing–ESIC.*

Muller, M., Millen, D. R., Shami, N. S., & Feinberg, J. (2010). *We are all lurkers: Toward a lurker research agenda. Collective Intelligence in Organizations: Toward a Research Agenda Workshop.* CSCW 2010, Savannah, GA. Retrieved from https://www.parc.com/content/events/attachments/Muller-Updated-LurkersInCILurkers-paper3.pdf

Müller-Stewens, G., & Berghaus, B. (2018). The market and business of luxury: An introduction. In K. Page (Ed.), *The management of luxury* (pp. 3–53). Kogan Page.

Mulyanegara, R. C., & Tsarenko, Y. (2009). Predicting brand preferences: An examination of the predictive power of personality and values in the Australian fashion market. *Journal of Fashion Marketing and Management, 13*(3), 358–371. doi:10.1108/13612020910974492

Mundel, J., Huddleston, P., & Vodermeier, M. (2017). An exploratory study of consumers' perceptions: What are affordable luxuries? *Journal of Retailing and Consumer Services, 35,* 68–75. doi:10.1016/j.jretconser.2016.12.004

Muniz, A. M. Jr, & O'Guinn, T. C. (2001). Brand Community. *The Journal of Consumer Research, 27*(4), 412–432. doi:10.1086/319618

Muñiz, A., & Schau, H. J. (2011). How to inspire value-laden collaborative consumer-generated content. *Business Horizons, 54*(3), 209–217.

Nambiar, R. (2018). Storytelling long-format Ads – A better way for effective consumer engagement. *International Journal of Research and Scientific Innovation, 5*(3), 8–13.

Nasir, N. (2016). Celebrity Endorsement and Consumer Buying Intention with the Mediating Role of Brand Performance: An Empirical Consumer Perception Study in FMCG Sector of Pakistan. *Science International Journal, 8*(1), 617–624.

Natural Language ProcessingS. A. S. (NLP). (n.d.). Retrieved from https://www.sas.com/en_us/insights/analytics/what-is-natural-language-processing-nlp.html

Nelson, M. C., Larson, N. I., Barr-Anderson, D., Neumark-Sztainer, D., & Story, M. (2009). Disparities in dietary intake, meal patterning, and home food environments among young adult nonstudents and 2-and 4-year college students. *American Journal of Public Health, 99*(7), 1216–1219. doi:10.2105/AJPH.2008.147454 PMID:19443824

Neti, S. (2011). Social Media and Its Role in Marketing. *International Journal of Enterprise Computing and Business Systems, 1*(2), 1–15.

Compilation of References

Neto, M. J. P. (2018). Charles Frederick Worth and the birth of Haute Couture: Fashion design and textile renewal in the times of conspicuous consumption. In G. Montagna & C. Carvalho (Eds.), *Textiles, Identity and Innovation: Design the Future: Proceedings of the 1st International Textile Design Conference*. CRC Press.

Nielsen. (2018). https://www.nielsen.com/us/en/insights/report/2018/unpacking-the-sustainability-landscape/

Nilsson, E., & Ballantyne, D. (2014). Reexamining the place of servicescape in marketing: A service-dominant logic perspective. *Journal of Services Marketing, 28*(5), 374–379. doi:10.1108/JSM-01-2013-0004

Novak, T. P., & MacEvoy, B. (1990). On comparing alternative segmentation schemes: The list of values (LOV) and values and life styles (VALS). *The Journal of Consumer Research, 17*(1), 105–109. doi:10.1086/208541

Nueno, J. L., & Quelch, J. A. (1998). The Mass Marketing of Luxury. *Business Horizons, 41*(November- December), 61–68. doi:10.1016/S0007-6813(98)90023-4

Nwankwo, S., Hamelin, N., & Khaled, M. (2014). Consumer values, motivation and purchase intention for luxury goods. *Journal of Retailing and Consumer Services, 21*(5), 735–744. doi:10.1016/j.jretconser.2014.05.003

O'Cass, A. & Frost, H. (2002). Status brands: examining the effects of non-product-related brand associations on status and conspicuous consumption. *Journal of Product & Brand Management, 11*(2), 67-88.

O'Cass, A., & Frost, H. (2002). Status brands: Examining the effects of non-product-related brand associations on status and conspicuous consumption. *Journal of Product and Brand Management, 11*(2), 67–88. doi:10.1108/10610420210423455

O'Donnell, D. (2018). *Driving immersive experiences in virtual and augmented reality.* https://blog.westerndigital.com/driving-immersive-experience-virtual-augmented-reality/

Oake. (2020). https://luxe.digital/business/digital-luxury-trends/millennials-buy-sustainable-luxury/#:~:text=Sustainable%20Luxury%3A%20Millennials%20Buy%20Into%20Socially%20Conscious%20Brands,The%20luxury%20industry&text=A%20study%20from%20Nielsen%20showed,than%20what%20older%20genera-tions%20indicated.

OECD. (2017). *The pursuit of gender equality: An uphill battle.* Retrieved 15. April 2020 from https://www.oecd.org/publications/the-pursuit-of-gender-equality-9789264281318-en.htm

OECD. (2018). https://www.oecd-ilibrary.org/docserver/tour-2018-6-en.pdf?expires=1587111750&id=id&accname=guest&checksum=237A5555558C707C9361698CBB882586

OECD. (2020). *Switzerland.* Retrieved 15 April 2020 from http://www.oecdbetterlifeindex.org/countries/switzerland/

Ogunmula, G. A., & Kumar, V. (2019, January). Social media analytics; a tool for the success of online retail industry. *International Journal of Services Operation and Informatics, 10*(1), 79–95.

Oh, A. (2018, July 7). *The Skills Marketers Need to Thrive in the Era of AI.* Retrieved from https://www.ama.org/marketing-news/the-skills-marketers-need-to-thrive-in-the-era-of-ai/

Okonkwo, U. (2007). *Luxury Fashion Branding. New York Palgrave.* Macmillan. doi:10.1057/9780230590885

Okonkwo, U. (2009). Sustaining Luxury Brands on the Internet. *Journal of Brand Management, 16*(5/6), 302–310. doi:10.1057/bm.2009.2

Okonkwo, U. (2009). Sustaining the luxury brand on the Internet. *Brand Management, 16*(5/6), 302–310.

Okonkwo, U. (2010). *Luxury Online.* Palgrave, MacMillan. doi:10.1057/9780230248335

Oktadiana, H., Pearce, P. L., & Li, J. (2020). Let's travel: Voices from the millennial female Muslim travellers. *International Journal of Tourism Research*, *22*(5), 551–563. doi:10.1002/jtr.2355

Olds, L. (2001). World War II and fashion: The birth of the new look. *Constructing the Past*, *2*(1), 47–64.

Onkvisit, S., & Shaw, J. (1987). Self-concept and image congruence: Some research and managerial implications. *Journal of Consumer Marketing*, *4*(1), 13–23. doi:10.1108/eb008185

Onwezen, M. C., Antonides, G., & Bartels, J. (2013). The Norm Activation Model: An exploration of the functions of anticipated pride and guilt in pro-environmental behaviour. *Journal of Economic Psychology*, *39*, 141–153. doi:10.1016/j.joep.2013.07.005

Orton, J., & Weick, K. (1990). Loosely Coupled Systems: A Reconceptualization. *Academy of Management Review*, *15*(2), 203–223. doi:10.5465/amr.1990.4308154

Osburg, V. S., Davies, I., Yoganathan, V., & McLeay, F. (2020). Perspectives, Opportunities and Tensions in Ethical and Sustainable Luxury: Introduction to the Thematic Symposium. *Journal of Business Ethics*, 1-10.

Osmonbekov, T., Bello, D. C., & Gilliland, D. I. (2009). The impact of e-business infusion on channel coordination, conflict and reseller performance. *Industrial Marketing Management*, *38*(7), 778–784. doi:10.1016/j.indmarman.2008.03.005

Ozuem, W., & Azemi, Y. (Eds.). (2017). *Digital Marketing Strategies for Fashion and Luxury Brands*. IGI Global.

Palmatier, R. W., Houston, M. B., & Hulland, J. (2018). Review articles: Purpose, process, and structure. *Journal of the Academy of Marketing Science*, *46*(1), 1–5. doi:10.100711747-017-0563-4

Pan, B., & Crotts, J. (2012). Theoretical models of social media, marketing implications, and future research directions. In M. Sigala, E. Christou, & U. Gretzel (Eds.), *Social Media in Travel, Tourism and Hospitality: Theory, Practice and Cases* (pp. 73–86). Ashgate.

Panetta, K. (2019). *Champion data literacy and teach data as a second language to enable data-driven business*. Gartner. Retrieved from https://www.gartner.com/smarterwithgartner/a-data-and-analytics-leaders-guide-to-data-literacy/

Pantano, E., & Dennis, C. (2019). The Case of Tommy Hilfiger. In *Smart Retailing* (pp. 91–97). Palgrave Pivot. doi:10.1007/978-3-030-12608-7_8

Parasuraman, A., Zeithaml, V. A., & Malhotra, A. (2005). E-S-QUAL: A Multiple-Item Scale for Assessing Electronic Service Quality. *Journal of Service Research*, *7*(3), 213–233. doi:10.1177/1094670504271156

Parker, B. (2015). *South Korea's millennials downbeat about payoff of education, future*. Retrieved 29. April 2020 from https://www.pewresearch.org/fact-tank/2015/02/25/south-koreas-millennials-downbeat-about-payoff-of-education-future/

Parker, L. (2002). Twentieth Century Textbook Budgetary Discourse: Formalisation, Normalisation and Rebuttal in an Anglo – Saxon Environment. *European Accounting Review*, *11*(2), 305–327. doi:10.1080/09638180220125535

Park, H.-J., Rabolt, N. J., & Jeon, K. S. (2008). Purchasing global luxury brands among young Korean consumers. *Journal of Fashion Marketing and Management*, *12*(2), 244–259. doi:10.1108/13612020810874917

Park, H., & Kim, Y. K. (2014). The role of social network websites in the consumer–brand relationship. *Journal of Retailing and Consumer Services*, *21*(4), 460–467.

Park, M., Im, H., & Kim, H.-Y. (2018). "You are too friendly!" The negative effects of social media marketing on value perceptions of luxury fashion brands. *Journal of Business Research*, *117*, 529–542. doi:10.1016/j.jbusres.2018.07.026

Compilation of References

Parmar, B. L., Freeman, R. E., Harrison, J. S., Wicks, A. C., Purnell, P., & de Colle, S. (2010). Stakeholder Theory: The State of the Art. *The Academy of Management Annals, 4*(1), 403–445. doi:10.5465/19416520.2010.495581

Parrott, G. R., Danbury, A. H., & Kanthavanich, P. (2015). Online behavior of luxury fashion brand advocates. *Journal of Fashion Marketing and Management, 19*(4), 360–383. doi:10.1108/JFMM-09-2014-0069

Parry, Z. (2018). *From hood to haute: the luxurification of streetwear* [Unpublished doctoral dissertation]. Hogeschool van Amsterdam.

Passavanti, R., Pantano, E., Priporas, C. V., & Verteramo, S. (2020). The use of new technologies for corporate marketing communication in luxury retailing: Preliminary findings. *Qualitative Market Research, 23*(3), 503–521. doi:10.1108/QMR-11-2017-0144

Pauwels, K., Ambler, T., Clark, B., LaPointe, P., Reibstein, D., Skiera, B., Wierenga, B., & Wiesel, T. (2008). Dashboards & Marketing: Why, What, How and Which Research is Needed. *Journal of Service Research, 12*(2), 175–189.

Pavel, Stastny, & Motycka. (2012 August). Usage of cluster analysis in consumer behavior research. *Advances in Applied Information Science*, 172-177.

Payne, E. M., Peltier, J. W., & Barger, V. A. (2017). Omni–channel marketing, integrated marketing communications and consumer engagement. *Journal of Research in Interactive Marketing*.

Pedrazzi, C. (2020). *How do millennials define and perceive luxury and prestige and how does it influence their luxury consumer behaviour? A cultural comparative study between Switzerland and South Korea* (Bachelor Thesis). Zurich University of Applied Sciences, School of Management and Law.

Peloza, J., White, K., & Shang, J. (2013). Good and guilt-free: The role of self-accountability in influencing preferences for products with ethical attributes. *Journal of Marketing, 77*(1), 104–119. doi:10.1509/jm.11.0454

Pencarelli, T., Ali Taha, V., Škerháková, V., Valentiny, T., & Fedorko, R. (2020). Luxury Products and Sustainability Issues from the Perspective of Young Italian Consumers. *Sustainability, 12*(1), 245. doi:10.3390u12010245

Pendergast, D. (2010). Getting to Know the Y Generation. In P. Benckendorff & G. Moscardo (Eds.), *Tourism and Generation Y*. CABI Publisher.

Pentina, I., Guilloux, V., & Micu, A. C. (2018). Exploring social media engagement behaviors in the context of luxury brands. *Journal of Advertising, 47*(1), 55–69.

Perrey, J., & Spillecke, D. (2012). *Principles of successful brand management: art, science, craft. Retail Marketing and Branding: A Definitive Guide to Maximizing ROI*. John Wiley & Sons.

Peter, J. P., Donnelly, J. H., Pratesi, C. A., & Aliverti, G. (2018). *Marketing*. McGraw Hill.

Peter, P. C., & Honea, H. (2012). Targeting social messages with emotions of change: The call for optimism. *Journal of Public Policy & Marketing, 31*(2), 269–283. doi:10.1509/jppm.11.098

Peters, C., Shelton, A., & Thomas, B. (2011). Self-concept and the fashion behavior of women over 50. *Journal of Fashion Marketing and Management, 15*(3), 291–305. doi:10.1108/13612021111151905

Petticrew, M., & Roberts, H. (2006). *Systematic reviews in the social sciences: a practical guide*. Blackwell Publishing. doi:10.1002/9780470754887

PewResearch Center. (2020). https://www.pewresearch.org/fact-tank/2020/04/28/millennials-overtake-baby-boomers-as-americas-largest-generation/

Phau, I., & Prendergast, G. (2000). Consuming luxury brands: The relevance of the 'Rarity Principle'. *Journal of Brand Management*, *8*(2), 122–138. doi:10.1057/palgrave.bm.2540013

Philippot, P., & Feldman, R. S. (2004). Positive emotion and the regulation of interpersonal relationships. In *The regulation of emotion* (pp. 142–171). Psychology Press. doi:10.4324/9781410610898

Pickering, C., & Byrne, J. (2014). The benefits of publishing systematic quantitative literature reviews for PhD candidates and other early-career researchers. *Higher Education Research & Development*, *33*(3), 534–548. doi:10.1080/07294360.2013.841651

Pine, B. J. II, & Gilmore, J. H. (1999). *The experience economy*. Harvard Business School Press.

Pini, F. M., & Pelleschi, V. (2017). Creating a Seamless Experience for Luxury Consumers Integrating Online and Offline Communication. In E. Rigaud-Lacresse & F. Pini (Eds.), *New Luxury Management* (pp. 217–237). Palgrave Macmillan. doi:10.1007/978-3-319-41727-1_12

Pino, G., Guido, G., & Nataraajan, R. (2017). Iconic art infusion in luxury retail strategies: Unveiling the potential. *Journal of Global Scholars of Marketing Science*, *27*(2), 136–147. doi:10.1080/21639159.2017.1283797

Popomaronis, T. (2017). Luxury Brands Are Becoming Big Players In The E-Commerce Game. *Forbes*. Retrieved April 25, 2020, from https://www.forbes.com/sites/tompopomaronis/2017/02/28/luxury-brands-are-becoming-big-players-in-the-growing-ecommerce-game/#4fb635d22079

Porter, M. (1980). Competitive Advantage: Techniques for Analysing Industries and Competitors. New York: Free Press, 1980 (and republished in 1998).

Poza, E. (2007). *Family business* (2nd ed.). Thompson.

Pozzebon, J. A., & Ashton, M. C. (2009). Personality and values as predictors of self-and peer-reported behavior. *Journal of Individual Differences*, *30*(3), 122–129. doi:10.1027/1614-0001.30.3.122

Prahalad, C. K., & Ramaswamy, V. (2004). *The future of competition: Co-creating unique value with customers*. Harvard Business School Press.

Pucciarelli, F., Giachino, C., Bertoldi, B., & Tamagno, D. (2019). A small world experiment in the digital era: Can sWOM be used by start uppers to reach a target? *Mercati & competitività-Open Access*, (1).

Pullman, M., & Gross, M. (2004). Ability of experience design elements to elicit emotions and loyalty behaviours. *Decision Sciences*, *35*(3), 551–578. doi:10.1111/j.0011-7315.2004.02611.x

Raben, F. (2019, June 7). *American Marketing Association News. What Marketers Need to Know About Innovations in Data*. Retrieved from https://www.ama.org/marketing-news/what-marketers-need-to-know-about-innovations-in-data/

Rangaswamy, A., & Van Bruggen, G. (2005). Opportunities and challenges in multichannel marketing: An introduction to the special issue. *Journal of Interactive Marketing*, *19*(2), 5–11. doi:10.1002/dir.20037

Rather, R. A. (2020). Customer experience and engagement in tourism destinations: The experiential marketing perspective. *Journal of Travel & Tourism Marketing*, *37*(1), 15–32. doi:10.1080/10548408.2019.1686101

Reinartz, W., Wiegand, N., & Imschloss, M. (2019). The impact of digital transformation on the retailing value chain. *International Journal of Research in Marketing*, *36*(3), 350–366. doi:10.1016/j.ijresmar.2018.12.002

Remaury, B. (2004). *Marques et récits: La marque face à l'imaginaire culturel contemporain*. Institut Français de la Mode-Editions du Regard.

Compilation of References

Remy, N., Catena, M., & Durand–Servoingt, B. (2015). *Digital inside: Get wired for the ultimate luxury experience.* McKinsey & Company.

Re, P., & Giachino, C. (2018). CSR in Small and Medium Companies and Stakeholder's Relationships. *Symphonya. Emerging Issues in Management*, (1), 76–90.

Re, P., Giachino, C., Bertoldi, B., & Minopoli, M. (2016). The Role of the Founder's DNA throughout Crisis: The Revitalization of Moncler. In *Global Marketing Strategies for the Promotion of Luxury Goods* (pp. 266–283). IGI Global. doi:10.4018/978-1-4666-9958-8.ch012

Report Digital 2020: I dati global. (2020). *We Are Social Italia.* https://wearesocial.com/it/blog/2020/01/report-digital-2020-i-dati-global

ReportM. F. (2020). https://www.monclergroup.com/wp-content/uploads/2016/07/Moncler-Half-Year-Financial-Report-as-of-30-June-2020-1.pdf

Richins, M. L., & Dowson, S. (1992). A consumer values orientation for materialism and its measurement: Scale development and validation. *The Journal of Consumer Research*, *19*(3), 303–316. doi:10.1086/209304

Rigby, D. (2011). The future of shopping. *Harvard Business Review*, *89*(12), 65–76.

Rios, A. E. (2016). The impact of the digital revolution in the development of market and communication strategies for the luxury sector (fashion luxury). *Central European Business Review*, *5*(2), 17–36. doi:10.18267/j.cebr.149

Rita, P., Brochado, A., & Dimova, L. (2019). Millennials' travel motivations and desired activities within destinations: A comparative study of the US and the UK. *Current Issues in Tourism*, *22*(16), 2034–2050. doi:10.1080/13683500.2018.1439902

Ritzer, G. (1999). *Enchanting and disenchanted world: revolutionizing the means of consumption.* Pine Forge Press.

Roberts, J. A., & Bacon, D. R. (1997). Exploring the subtle relationships between environmental concern and ecologically conscious consumer behavior. *Journal of Business Research*, *40*(1), 79–89. doi:10.1016/S0148-2963(96)00280-9

Robinson, V. M., & Schänzel, H. A. (2019). A tourism inflex: Generation Z travel experiences. *Journal of Tourism Futures.*

Rodrigues, C., & Rodrigues, P. (2019). Brand love matters to Millennials: The relevance of mystery, sensuality and intimacy to neo-luxury brands. *Journal of Product and Brand Management*, *28*(7), 830–848. doi:10.1108/JPBM-04-2018-1842

Roggeveen, A. L., & Sethuraman, R. (2020). How the COVID-19 Pandemic May Change the World of Retailing. *Journal of Retailing*, *96*(2), 169–171. doi:10.1016/j.jretai.2020.04.002

Rohan, M. J. (2000). A rose by any name? The values construct. *Personality and Social Psychology Review*, *4*(3), 255–277. doi:10.1207/S15327957PSPR0403_4

Rollet, M., Hoffmann, J., Coste–Manière, I., & Panchout, K. (2013). The concept of creative collaboration applied to the fashion industry. *Journal of Global Fashion Marketing*, *1*(4), 57–66. doi:10.1080/20932685.2012.753337

Rose, G. (2012). Visual methodologies: An introduction to researching with visual methods. *Sage (Atlanta, Ga.).*

Rosenblum, P. (2015). Fast Fashion Has Completely Disrupted Apparel Retail. *Forbes.* Retrieved June 30, 2015, from http://www.forbes.com/sites/paularosenblum/2015/05/21/fast–fashion–has–completely–disrupted–apparel–retail/

Ross, J., & Harradine, R. (2011). Fashion value brands: The relationship between identity and image. *Journal of Fashion Marketing and Management*, *15*(3), 306–325. doi:10.1108/13612021111151914

Rovai, S. (2014). The evolution of luxury consumption in China. In G. Atwal & D. Bryson (Eds.), *Luxury Brands in Emerging Markets* (pp. 130–134). Palgrave Macmillan. doi:10.1057/9781137330536_12

Rowlands, P. (1993, January 27). Esprit's Ecollection goes to the malls . *Women's Wear Daily*, p. 13.

Ruppert, B. (2011). New directions in the use of virtual reality for food shopping: Marketing and education perspectives. *Journal of Diabetes Science and Technology*, 5(2), 315–318. doi:10.1177/193229681100500217 PMID:21527099

Rust, Ambler, & Carpenter, Kumar, & Srivastave. (2004). Measuring Marketing Productivity: Current Knowledge and Future Directions. *Journal of Marketing*, 68(4), 76–89.

Ryan, G. W., & Bernard, H. R. (2000). Data management and analysis methods. In N. K. Denzin & Y. S. Lincoln (Eds.), Handbook of qualitative research (2nd ed., pp. 769-802). Academic Press.

Ryu, S. (2020). Online luxury goods with price discount or onsite luxury goods with luxury services: Role of situation-specific thinking styles and socio-demographics. *Journal of Retailing and Consumer Services*, 57. Advance online publication. doi:10.1016/j.jretconser.2020.102253

Sääksjärvi, M., Hellén, K., & Balabanis, G. (2016). Sometimes a celebrity holding a negative public image is the best product endorser. *European Journal of Marketing*, 50(3/4), 421–444. doi:10.1108/EJM-06-2014-0346

Sachs, J. (2012). *Winning the Story Wars*. Harvard Business Review Press.

Salzmann, O., Ionescu-Somers, A., & Steger, U. (2005). The business case for corporate sustainability: Literature review and research options. *European Management Journal*, 23(1), 27–36. doi:10.1016/j.emj.2004.12.007

Santandertrade. (2020). *South Korea: Reaching the consumer*. Retrieved 29 April 2020 from https://santandertrade.com/en/portal/analyse-markets/south-korea/reaching-the-consumers?&actualiser_id_banque=oui&id_banque=17&memoriser_choix=memoriser

Sashi, C. M. (2012). Customer engagement, buyer-seller relationships, and social media. *Management Decision*, 50(2), 253–272. doi:10.1108/00251741211203551

Saunders, M., Philip, L., & Thornhill, A. (2009). *Research Methods for Business Students* (5th ed.). Pearson Education Limited.

Saviolo, S., & Corbellini, E. (2007). *L'esperienza del lusso*. Edizione Ottobre.

Schembri, S. (2006). Rationalizing service logic, or understanding services as experience? *Marketing Theory*, 6(3), 381–392. doi:10.1177/1470593106066798

Schiffman, L. G., Hansen, H., & Kanuk, L. L. (2008). *Consumer Behaviour: A European Outlook*. Prentice Hall FT.

Schivinski, B., Christodoulides, G., & Dabrowski, D. (2016). Measuring Consumers' Engagement With Brand-Related Social-Media Content: Development and Validation of a Scale that Identifies Levels of Social-Media Engagement with Brands. *Journal of Advertising Research*, 56(1), 64–80. doi:10.2501/JAR-2016-004

Schmitt, B. (1999). Experiential marketing. *Journal of Marketing Management*, 15(1-3), 53–67. doi:10.1362/026725799784870496

Schneider, C. R., Zaval, L., Weber, E. U., & Markowitz, E. M. (2017). The influence of anticipated pride and guilt on pro-environmental decision making. *PLoS One*, 12(11), 1–14. doi:10.1371/journal.pone.0188781 PMID:29190758

Scholz, J., & Smith, A. N. (2016). Augmented reality: Designing immersive experiences that maximize consumer engagement. *Business Horizons*, 59(2), 149–161. doi:10.1016/j.bushor.2015.10.003

Compilation of References

Schüller, S., Dietrich, D., & Spielmann, L. (2018). The Future Role of Physical Touchpoints in Luxury Retailing. *Marketing Review St. Gallen*, *35*(6).

Schultz, D. E., Tannenbaum, S. I., & Lauterborn, R. F. (1993). *Integrated Marketing Communications*. NTC Business.

Schwartz, S. H. (1996). *Value Priorities and Behavior: Applying a theory of integrated value systems*. Lawrence Erlbaum.

Schwartz, S. H. (2012). An overview of the Schwartz theory of basic values. *Online Readings in Psychology and Culture*, *2*(1), 2–20. doi:10.9707/2307-0919.1116

Schwartz, S. H., & Rubel, T. (2006). Sex differences in value priorities: Cross-cultural and multimethod studies. *Journal of Personality and Social Psychology*, *89*(6), 1010–1028. doi:10.1037/0022-3514.89.6.1010 PMID:16393031

Sekaran, U., & Bougie, R. (2013). *Research Methods for Business* (6th ed.). John Wiley & Sons Ltd.

Seno, D., & Lukas, A. (2007). The equity effect of product endorsement by celebrities. *European Journal of Marketing*, *41*(1/2), 121–134. doi:10.1108/03090560710718148

Seo, Y., & Buchanan-Oliver, M. (2019). Constructing a typology of luxury brand consumption practices. *Journal of Business Research*, *99*, 414–421. doi:10.1016/j.jbusres.2017.09.019

Seo, Y., Buchanan-Oliver, M., & Cruz, A. (2015). Luxury brand markets as confluences of multiple cultural beliefs. *International Marketing Review*, *32*(2), 141–159. doi:10.1108/IMR-04-2013-0081

Sepe, G., & Anzivino, A. (2020). Guccification: Redefining Luxury Through Art—The Gucci Revolution. In M. Massi & A. Turrini (Eds.), *The Artification of Luxury Fashion Brands* (pp. 89–112). Springer International.

Seraj, M. (2012). We create, we connect, we respect, therefore we are: Intellectual, social, and cultural value in online communities. *Journal of Interactive Marketing*, *26*(4), 209–222. doi:10.1016/j.intmar.2012.03.002

Seringhaus, F. R. (2005). Selling luxury brands online. *Journal of Internet Commerce*, *4*(1), 1–25. doi:10.1300/J179v04n01_01

Sestino, A., Amatulli, C., Peluso, A. M., & Guido, G. (2020b). *New technologies in luxury consumption experiences: The role of individual differences*. Conference Italian Society of Marketing, LIUC University of Castellanza. Retrieved at: https://www.researchgate.net/publication/344994033_New_technologies_in_luxury_consumption_experiences_The_role_of_individual_differences

Sestino, A., Prete, M. I., Piper, L., & Guido, G. (2020a). Internet of Things and Big Data as enablers for business digitalization strategies. *Technovation*, *98*, 102173. doi:10.1016/j.technovation.2020.102173

Settembrini, L. (1994). *From haute couture to prêt-à-porter*. Guggenheim Museum.

Shillinglaw, G. (1961). Cost Accounting: Analysis and Control. Homewood, IL: Academic Press.

Shim, B., Choi, K., & Suh, Y. (2012). CRM strategies for a small–sized online shopping mall based on association rules and sequential patterns. *Expert Systems with Applications*, *39*(9), 7736–7742. doi:10.1016/j.eswa.2012.01.080

Shi, S., Wang, Y., Chen, X., & Zhang, Q. (2020). Conceptualization of omnichannel customer experience and its impact on shopping intention: A mixed–method approach. *International Journal of Information Management*, *50*, 325–336. doi:10.1016/j.ijinfomgt.2019.09.001

Shukla, P. (2012). The influence of value perceptions on luxury purchase intentions in developed and emerging markets. *International Marketing Review*, *29*(6), 574–596. doi:10.1108/02651331211277955

Shukla, P., Singh, J., & Banerjee, M. (2015). They are not all same: Variations in Asian consumers' value perception of luxury brands. *Marketing Letters, 2015*(26), 265–278. doi:10.100711002-015-9358-x

Silvera, H., & Austad, B. (2004). Factors predicting the effectiveness of celebrity endorsement advertisements. *European Journal of Marketing, 38*(11/12), 1509–1526. doi:10.1108/03090560410560218

Simkus, L. (2010). Sustainability within the French luxury consumer-goods market: The role of business and consumer demand. *Best Business Research Papers, 3*, 71–85.

Simmons, G. (2008). Marketing to postmodern consumers: Introducing the internet chameleon. *European Journal of Marketing, 42*(3/4), 299–310.

Skinner, H., Sarpong, D., & White, G. R. (2018). Meeting the needs of the Millennials and generation Z: Gamification in tourism through geocaching. *Journal of Tourism Futures, 4*(1), 93–104. doi:10.1108/JTF-12-2017-0060

Smith, K. E. (2002). *The influence of Audrey Hepburn and Hubert de Givenchy on American fashion, 1952–1965* [Unpublished master's thesis]. Michigan State University.

Smith, K. T., & Brower, T. R. (2012). Longitudinal study of green marketing strategies that influence Millennials. *Journal of Strategic Marketing, 20*(6), 535–551. doi:10.1080/0965254X.2012.711345

Sobczak, A., & Berthoin Antal, A. (2010). Nouvelles perspectives sur l'engagement des parties prenantes: Enjeux, acteurs, recherches. *Revue Management et Avenir, 33*(3), 117–126. doi:10.3917/mav.033.0116

Solis, B. (2013). *WTF? What's the Future of Business? Changing the Way Businesses Create Experiences*. John Wiley & Sons.

Solomon, M., & Rabolt, N. (2013). *Consumer Behaviour in Fashion*. Pearson Education, Inc.

Soneji, D., Riedel, A., & Martin, B. (2015). How Gordon Ramsay appeals to consumers: Effects of self-concept clarity and celebrity meaning on celebrity endorsements. *Journal of Strategic Marketing, 23*(5), 457–468. doi:10.1080/09652 54X.2014.991349

Sonmath, M., Mahmood, M. A., & Joseph, J. L. (2008). Measuring Internet-commerce success: What factors are important. *Journal of Internet Commerce, 7*(1), 1–28. doi:10.1080/15332860802004113

Sowell, E. (1973). *The Evolution of the Theories and Techniques of Standard Costs*. The University of Alabama Press.

Spence, C., Puccinelli, N. M., Grewal, D., & Roggeveen, A. L. (2014). Store atmospherics: A multisensory perspective. *Psychology and Marketing, 31*(7), 472–488. doi:10.1002/mar.20709

Spillecke, D., & Perrey, J. (2012). *Retail Marketing and Branding: A Definitive Guide to Maximizing ROI*. Wiley.

Sproles, G. B. (1981). Analyzing fashion life cycles—Principles and perspectives. *Journal of Marketing, 45*(4), 116–124.

Spry, A., Pappu, T., & Cornwell, B. (2011). Celebrity endorsement, brand credibility and brand equity. *European Journal of Marketing, 45*(6), 882–909. doi:10.1108/03090561111119958

Sreejesh, S. (2012). Consumers' Evaluation of Co–Brand Extensions: The Effects of Concept Congruity on the Evaluation of Co–Branded Products, Analyzing the Moderating Role of Task Involvement. *International Management Review, 1*(8).

Stadiem, W. (2014). *Jet Set: The People, the Planes, the Glamour, and the Romance in Aviation's Glory Years*. Ballantine Books.

Statista Digital Market Outlook. (2020). *Fashion eCommerce Report 2020*. Stastista. Retrieved at: https://www.statista.com/study/38340/ecommerce–report–fashion

Compilation of References

Statista. (2018). https://www.statista.com/statistics/276846/reach-of-top-online-retail-categories-worldwide/#statisticContainer

Statistica. (2020). Statistica.com/statistics/267948/brand-of-the-leading-10-most-valuable-luxury-brands-worldwide/

Steele, V. (2017). *Paris fashion: a cultural history*. Bloomsbury Publishing. doi:10.5040/9781474269711

Stein, A., & Ramaseshan, B. (2016). Towards the identification of customer experience touch point elements. *Journal of Retailing and Consumer Services*, *30*, 8–19. doi:10.1016/j.jretconser.2015.12.001

Steland, A. (2019). *Top 10 Virtual Influencers – Understanding the latest trend and 10 great examples*. Influencerdb. Retrieved from https://influencerdb.com/blog/top-10-virtual-influencers/

Stephen, A. T. (2016). The role of digital and social media marketing in consumer behavior. *Current Opinion in Psychology*, *10*, 17–21. doi:10.1016/j.copsyc.2015.10.016

Stępień, B., Lima, A. P., & Hinner, M. (2018). Are millennials a global cohort? Evidence from the luxury good sector. *Journal of Intercultural Management*, *10*(2), 139–158. doi:10.2478/joim-2018-0012

Stokburger-Sauer, N. E., & Teichmann, K. (2013). Is luxury just a female thing? The role of gender in luxury brand consumption. *Journal of Business Research*, *66*(7), 889–896. doi:10.1016/j.jbusres.2011.12.007

Sun, O. (2018). *Sustainability Strategies and Challenges in the Luxury Apparel Industry. Diplomski rad*. University of Pennsylvania.

Tantiseneepong, N., Gorton, M., & White, J. (2012). Evaluating responses to celebrity endorsements using projective techniques. *Qualitative Market Research*, *15*(1), 57–69. doi:10.1108/13522751211191991

Taplin, I. M. (2014). Who is to blame? A re-examination of Fast Fashion after the 2013 factory disaster in Bangladesh. *Critical Perspectives on International Business*, *10*(1/2), 72–83. doi:10.1108/cpoib-09-2013-0035

Taube, J., & Warnaby, G. (2017). How brand interaction in pop-up shops influences consumers' perceptions of luxury fashion retailers. *Journal of Fashion Marketing and Management*, *21*(3), 385–399. doi:10.1108/JFMM-08-2016-0074

Techopedia. (2020). *Affinity Analysis*. Retrieved from https://www.techopedia.com/definition/32062/affinity-analysis

Thamm, A., Anke, J., Haugk, S., & Radic, D. (2016, July). Towards the omni–channel: Beacon–based services in retail. In *International Conference on Business Information Systems* (pp. 181–192). Springer. 10.1007/978-3-319-39426-8_15

The Economist. (2015, July 23). *I don't*. Retrieved 13 October 2020 from https://www.economist.com/asia/2015/07/23/i-dont

The State of Fashion. (2021) Retrieved from: https://www.mckinsey.com/~/media/McKinsey/Industries/Retail/Our%20Insights/State%20of%20fashion/2021/The-State-of-Fashion-2021-vF.pdf

The World Bank. (2019). *GDP per capita (current US – Korea.Rep)*. Retrieved 25 September 2020 from https:// https://data.worldbank.org/indicator/NY.GDP.PCAP.CD?locations=KR

The World Bank. (2019). *GINI index (World Bank estimate) - Switzerland*. Retrieved 29 April 2020 from https://data.worldbank.org/indicator/SI.POV.GINI?locations=CH&name_desc=false

Theodoridis, P., & Vassou, S. (2018). Exploring luxury consumer behaviour. In B. Berghaus, M. Gunter, & S. Reinecke (Eds.), *The management of luxuy: An international guide* (pp. 76–86). Kogan Page.

Thomas, D. (2007). *Deluxe: How luxury lost its luster*. Penguin Books.

Thompson, C. J., Rindfleisch, A., & Zeynec, A. (2006). Emotional branding and the strategic value of the doppelganger brand image. *Journal of Marketing*, *70*(1), 50–64. doi:10.1509/jmkg.70.1.050.qxd

Thomsen, T. U., Holmqvist, J., von Wallpach, S., Hemetsberger, A., & Belk, R. W. (2020). Conceptualizing unconventional luxury. *Journal of Business Research*, *116*, 441–445. doi:10.1016/j.jbusres.2020.01.058

Tian, K. T., Bearde, N. W., & Hunter, G. (2001). Consumers' need for uniqueness: Scale. *The Journal of Consumer Research*, *28*(1), 50–66. doi:10.1086/321947

Ticehurst, G., & Veal, A. (2005). *Business Research Methods: A Managerial Approach* (2nd ed.). Pearson Education Australia.

Toivonen, M., Tuominen, T., & Brax, S. (2007). Innovation process interlinked with the process of service delivery – A management challenge in KIBS. *Economies et Societes*, (3), 355–384.

Toktali, N. (2008). Global Sourcing Insights from the Clothing Industry: The Case of Zara, a Fast Fashion Retailer. *Journal of Economic Geography*, (8), 21–38.

Toubia, O., & Stephen, A. T. (2013). Intrinsic Versus Image-Related Utility in Social Media: Why Do People Contribute Content to Twitter? *Marketing Science*, *32*(3), 368–392.

Tracy, J. L., & Prehn, C. (2012). Arrogant or self-confident? The use of contextual knowledge to differentiate hubristic and authentic pride from a single nonverbal expression. *Cognition and Emotion*, *26*(1), 14–24. doi:10.1080/02699931. 2011.561298 PMID:21468998

Tracy, J. L., & Robins, R. W. (2007). The psychological structure of pride: A tale of two facets. *Journal of Personality and Social Psychology*, *92*(3), 506–525. doi:10.1037/0022-3514.92.3.506 PMID:17352606

Trading Economics. (2020). *Switzerland Youth Unemployment Rate*. Retrieved 25 May 2020 from https://tradingeconomics.com/switzerland/youth-unemployment-rate

Trochim, W. M. (1989). Outcome pattern matching and program theory. *Evaluation and Program Planning*, *12*(4), 355–366. doi:10.1016/0149-7189(89)90052-9

Truong, Y., McColl, R., & Kitchen, P. J. (2009). New luxury brand positioning and the emergence of masstige brands. *Journal of Brand Management*, *16*(5-6), 375–382. doi:10.1057/bm.2009.1

Truong, Y., Simmons, G., McColl, R., & Kitchen, P. (2008). Status and conspicuousness – are they related? Strategic marketing implications for luxury brands. *Journal of Strategic Marketing*, *16*(3), 189–203. doi:10.1080/09652540802117124

Tsai, T.-H., & Chen, C.-M. (2019). Mixed logit analysis of trade-off effects between international airline fares and fences: A revenue management perspective. *Current Issues in Tourism*, *22*(1), 265–275. doi:10.1080/13683500.2017.1402869

Turban, E., Outland, J., King, D., Lee, J. K., Liang, T. P., & Turban, D. C. (2017). *Electronic commerce 2018: a managerial and social networks perspective*. Springer.

Turner, N. (2011). Deprivation Fashion. *Duck: Journal for Research in Textiles and Textile Design, 2*.

Turngate, M. (2009). *Luxury World: The past, present and future of luxury brands*. Kogan Page.

Turunen, L. L. M. (2018). *Interpretations of Luxury. Exploring the customer perspective*. Palgrave Advances in Luxury.

Tuzovic, S. (2008). Investigating the concept of potential quality: An exploratory study in the real estate industry. *Managing Service Quality*, *18*(3), 255–271. doi:10.1108/09604520810871874

Compilation of References

Tynan, C., McKechnie, S., & Chuon, C. (2010). Co-creating Value for Luxury Brands. *Journal of Business Research*, *63*(11), 1156–1163. doi:10.1016/j.jbusres.2009.10.012

Uche, S. (2018). *Generation Z and corporate social responsibility*. Academic Press.

Unilever. (2017, January 1). *Report shows a third of consumers prefer sustainable brands*. https://www.unilever.com/news/Press-releases/2017/report-shows-a-third-of-consumers-prefer-sustainable-brands.html

Van der Nagel, E. (2013). Faceless Bodies: Negotiating Technological and Cultural Codes on reddit gone wild. *Scan: Journal of Media Arts Culture*, *10*(2), 1–10.

Van der Veen, M. (2003). When is food a luxury? *World Archaeology*, *34*(3), 405–427. doi:10.1080/0043824021000026422

Varadarajan, P. R., & Menon, A. (1988). Cause-related marketing: A coalignment of marketing strategy and corporate philanthropy. *Journal of Marketing*, *52*(3), 58–74. doi:10.1177/002224298805200306

Vargo, S. L., & Lusch, R. F. (2008). Service-dominant logic: Continuing the evolution. *Journal of the Academy of Marketing Science*, *36*(1), 1–10. doi:10.100711747-007-0069-6

Veblen, T. (2005). *The theory of the leisure class: An economic study of institutions*. Aakar Books.

Veiga, C., Santos, M. C., Águas, P., & Santos, J. A. C. (2017). Are millennials transforming global tourism? Challenges for destinations and companies. *Worldwide Hospitality and Tourism Themes*, *9*(6), 603–616. doi:10.1108/WHATT-09-2017-0047

Venkatesan, R., Kumar, V., & Ravishanker, N. (2007). Multichannel Shopping: Causes and Consequences. *Journal of Marketing*, *71*(2), 114–132. doi:10.1509/jmkg.71.2.114

Venus Jin, S., Muqaddam, A., & Ryu, E. (2019). Instafamous and social media influencer marketing. *Marketing Intelligence & Planning*, *37*(5), 567–579. doi:10.1108/MIP-09-2018-0375

Verhoef, P. C., Kannan, P. K., & Inman, J. J. (2015). From multi–channel retailing to omni–channel retailing: Introduction to the special issue on multi–channel retailing. *Journal of Retailing*, *91*(2), 174–181. doi:10.1016/j.jretai.2015.02.005

Vickers, J. S., & Renand, F. (2003). The marketing of luxury goods: An exploratory study – three conceptual dimensions. *The Marketing Review*, *3*(4), 459–478. doi:10.1362/146934703771910071

Vigneron, F., & Johnson, L. W. (1999). A review and a conceptual framework of prestige–seeking consumer behavior. *Academy of Marketing Science Review*, *1*(1), 1–15.

Vigneron, F., & Johnson, L. W. (1999). A Review and a Conceptual Framework of Prestige-Seeking Consumer Behavior. *Academy of Marketing Science Review*, *1999*(1), 51–15.

Vigneron, F., & Johnson, L. W. (1999). A review and a conceptual framework of prestige-seeking consumer behavior. *Academy of Marketing Science Review*, *9*(1), 1–14.

Vigneron, F., & Johnson, L. W. (2004). Measuring perceptions of brand luxury. *Journal of Brand Management*, *11*(6), 484–506. doi:10.1057/palgrave.bm.2540194

Villanueva, J., Yoo, S., & And Hanssens, D. M. (2008). The Impact of Marketing-Induced Versus Word-of-Mouth Customer Acquisition on Customer Equity Growth. *JMR, Journal of Marketing Research*, *45*(1), 48–59. doi:10.1509/jmkr.45.1.48

Visser, W. (2011). *The age of responsibility: CSR 2.0 and the new DNA of business*. John Wiley & Sons.

Vithayathil, J., Dadgar, M., & Osiri, J. K. (2020). Social media use and consumer shopping preferences. *International Journal of Information Management*, *54*, 102117. doi:10.1016/j.ijinfomgt.2020.102117

Voyer, B., & Tran, V. (2013). *Risks and benefits in selling luxury goods online: should Chanel, the icon of timeless fashion, open an e-boutique?* ESCP Europe, case study 3. Retrieved from www.casecenter.org

Voyer, B. G., & Beckham, D. (2014). Can Sustainability Be Luxurious? a Mixed-Method Investigation of Implicit and Explicit Attitudes Towards Sustainable Luxury Consumption. In J. Cotte & S. Wood (Eds.), *NA - Advances in Consumer Research* (Vol. 42, pp. 245–250). Association for Consumer Research.

Vreeland, D. (2016). *Why accounting is important: A Look inside the Fashion Industry.* https://.grantham.edu/blog/accounting-important-look-inside-fashion-industry/

Wallace, E., Buil, I., & de Chernatony, L. (2014). Consumer engagement with self-expressive brands: Brand love and WOM outcomes. *Journal of Product and Brand Management, 23*(1), 33–42. doi:10.1108/JPBM-06-2013-0326

Wang, S., Hsiu-Ying, K., & Ngamsiriudom, W. (2017). Consumers' attitude of endorser credibility, brand and intention with respect to celebrity endorsement of the airline sector. *Journal of Air Transport Management, 60*, 10–17. doi:10.1016/j.jairtraman.2016.12.007

Wang, T., & Lee, F.-Y. (2020). Examining customer engagement and brand intimacy in social media context. *Journal of Retailing and Consumer Services, 54*, 10. doi:10.1016/j.jretconser.2020.102035

Wang, Y., & Griskevicius, V. (2014). Conspicuous consumption, relationships, and rivals: Women's luxury products as signals to other women. *The Journal of Consumer Research, 40*(5), 834–854. doi:10.1086/673256

Ward, J. L. (1997). Growing the family business: Special challenges and best practices. *Family Business Review, 10*(4), 323–337. doi:10.1111/j.1741-6248.1997.00323.x

Washburn, J. H., Till, B. D., & Priluck, R. (2004). Brand alliance and customer-based brand-equity effects. *Psychology and Marketing, 21*(7), 487–508. doi:10.1002/mar.20016

Watson, J., Lysonski, S., Gillan, T., & Raymore, L. (2002). Psychological and cultural insights into consumption of luxury. *Journal of Business Research, 9*(1), 923–931. doi:10.1016/S0148-2963(01)00212-0

Webster, Malter, & Ganesan. (2005). The Decline and Dispersion of Marketing Competence. *Sloan Management Review, 46*(4), 35–43.

Wegener, C. (2016). Upcycling. In *Creativity—A New Vocabulary* (pp. 181–188). Palgrave Macmillan.

Weick, K. (1976). Educational Organizations as Loosely Coupled Systems. *Administrative Science Quarterly, 21*(1), 1–19. doi:10.2307/2391875

Wetzlinger, W., Auinger, A., Kindermann, H., & Schönberger, W. (2017, July). Acceptance of personalization in omni-channel retailing. In *International Conference on HCI in Business, Government, and Organizations* (pp. 114–129). Springer. 10.1007/978-3-319-58484-3_10

White, K., & Simpson, B. (2013). When do (and don't) normative appeals influence sustainable consumer behaviors? *Journal of Marketing, 77*(2), 78–95. doi:10.1509/jm.11.0278

Whitten, A. (2020, May 14). *With AI and Data Science, Marketers are Maximizing the Power of Customer Data.* Adobe. Retrieved from https://blog.adobe.com/en/2020/05/14/with-ai-and-data-science-marketers-are-maximizing-the-power-of-customer-data.html#gs.i0xhxl

Widloecher, P. (2010). *Luxe et développement durable: Je t'aime, moi non plus.* Luxefrancais.

Wiedmann, K.-P., & Hennigs, N. (2013). Placing luxury marketing on the research agenda not only for the sake of luxury - An introduction. In N. Hennigs (Ed.), *Luxury Marketing* (pp. 5–17). Springer. doi:10.1007/978-3-8349-4399-6_1

Compilation of References

Wiedmann, K.-P., Hennigs, N., & Siebels, A. (2009). Value-based segmentation of luxury consumption behavior. *Psychology and Marketing, 26*(7), 625–651. doi:10.1002/mar.20292

Wilcox, K., Kim, H. M., & Sen, S. (2009). Why do consumers buy counterfeit luxury brands? *JMR, Journal of Marketing Research, 46*(2), 247–259. doi:10.1509/jmkr.46.2.247

Willems, K., Brengman, M., & Van De Sanden, S. (2017). In–store proximity marketing: Experimenting with digital point–of–sales communication. *International Journal of Retail & Distribution Management, 45*(7/8), 910–927. doi:10.1108/IJRDM-10-2016-0177

Williams, J., Haka, S., Bettner, M., & Carcello, J. (2018). *Financial & Managerial Accounting: The Basis for Business Decisions* (18th ed.). McGraw-Hill.

Williamson, J. (1978). *Decoding advertisements: ideology and meaning in advertising.* Marion Boyers.

Williams, R., & Dargel, M. (2004). From servicescape to 'cyberscape'. *Marketing Intelligence & Planning, 22*(3), 310–320. doi:10.1108/02634500410536894

Wilson, J. (2014). *Essentials of Business Research: A Guide to Doing Your Research Project* (2nd ed.). SAGE Publications Ltd.

Wilson, K. G., Sandoz, E. K., Kit, J., & Roberts, M. (2010). The value living questionnaire: Defining and measuring valued action within a behavioral framework. *The Psychological Record, 60*(2), 249–272. doi:10.1007/BF03395706

Winter, R. S., Dahar, R., & Mosca, F. (2011). *Marketing Management.* Milano Apogeo.

Wirtz, J., Holmqvist, J., & Fritze, M. P. (2020). Luxury services. *Journal of Service Management.* ahead-of-print. doi:10.1108/JOSM-11-2019-0342

Wong, N. Y., & Ahuvia, A. C. (1998). Personal taste and family face: Luxury consumption in Confucian and Western societies. *Psychology and Marketing, 15*(5), 423–442. doi:10.1002/(SICI)1520-6793(199808)15:5<423::AID-MAR2>3.0.CO;2-9

Wood, T. (1991). Corporate social performance revisited. *Academy of Management Review, 16*(4), 691–718. doi:10.5465/amr.1991.4279616

World Population Review. (2020). *South Korea Population 2020.* Retrieved 29 April 2020 from https://worldpopulationreview.com/countries/south-korea-population/

World, I. B. I. S. (2016). Cosmetics & Toiletries Retailers in the UK: Market Research Report. *IBISworld.* Available at: https://www.ibisworld.co.uk/market-research/cosmetics-toiletries-retailers.html

Xiang, Z., & Gretzel, U. (2010). Role of social media in online travel information search. *Tourism Management, 31*(2), 179–188. doi:10.1016/j.tourman.2009.02.016

Xiao, J., & Li, H. (2012). Online Discussion of Sharon Stone's Comment on China Earthquake. *China Media Research, 8*(1), 25–39.

Yazdanian, N., Ronagh, S., & Laghaei, P. (2019). The mediation roles of purchase intention and brand trust in relationships between social marketing activities and brand loyalty. *International Journal of Business Intelligence and Data Mining, 15*(4), 371–387. doi:10.1504/IJBIDM.2018.10008661

Yeoman, I. (2007). Pricing trends in Europe's fashion industry. *Journal of Revenue and Pricing Management, 6*(4), 287–290. doi:10.1057/palgrave.rpm.5160099

Yeoman, I. (2011). The Changing Behaviour of Luxury Consumption. *Journal of Revenue and Pricing Management, 10*(1), 47–50. doi:10.1057/rpm.2010.43

Yin, R. K. (2003). *Design and methods. Case study research.* Sage.

Yoo, B., & Donthu, N. (2001). Developing and validating a multidimensional consumer-based brand equity scale. *Journal of Business Research, 52*(1), 1–14. doi:10.1016/S0148-2963(99)00098-3

Yoo, B., Donthu, N., & Lee, S. (2000). An Examination of Selected Marketing Mix Elements and Brand Equity. *Journal of the Academy of Marketing Science, 28*(2), 195–211. doi:10.1177/0092070300282002

Young, S. M. (1997). Implementing Management Innovations Successfully: Principles for Lasting Change. *Journal of Cost Management,* (September/October), 16–20.

Youn, S., & Kim, H. (2008). Antecedents of consumer attitudes toward cause-related marketing. *Journal of Advertising Research, 48*(1), 123–137. doi:10.2501/S0021849908080136

Zafarani, R., Abbasi, M. A., & Liu, H. (2014). *Social Media Mining: An Introduction.* Cambridge University Press. https://books.google.it/books?id=fVhzAwAAQBAJ doi:10.1017/CBO9781139088510

ZarganiL. (2020). https://wwd.com/business-news/financial/monclers-remo-ruffini-on-digital-transformation-keeping-brand-in-top-league-1203688356/

Zeithaml, V. A. (2000). Service Quality Profitability and the Economic Worth of Customers: What we Know and What We Need to Learn. *Journal of Academy of Marketing Science, 28,* 67-85.

Zeng, D., Chen, H., Lusch, R., & Li, H. (2010). Social media analytics and intelligence. *IEEE Intelligent Systems, 25*(6), 13–16.

Zhan, L., & He, Y. (2012). Understanding luxury consumption in China: Consumer perceptions of best-known brands. *Journal of Business Research, 2012*(65), 1452–1460. doi:10.1016/j.jbusres.2011.10.011

Zollo, L., Filieri, R., Rialti, R., & Yoon, S. (2020). Unpacking the relationship between social media marketing and brand equity: The mediating role of consumers' benefits and experience. *Journal of Business Research, 117,* 256–267. doi:10.1016/j.jbusres.2020.05.001

Zomerdijk, L. G., & Voss, C. A. (2010). Service design for experience-centric services. *Journal of Service Research, 13*(1), 67–82. doi:10.1177/1094670509351960

About the Contributors

Fabrizio Mosca is a Bachelor of Business Management (University of Torino, Italy), MBA (University of Torino, Italy) and took a PhD in Economics and Business Administration at Luigi Bocconi University, Milano, Italy. Fabrizio Mosca has written several articles and books on Strategic Luxury Management and Luxury Marketing. This topic is the main field of his research. Fabrizio Mosca is, presently, a professor at the Business Management Department of the University of Torino, where he teaches Marketing, Marketing Advanced and Strategic Management. He is also involved in many different postgraduate and International Master programs, in the Luxury Master of Il Sole24Ore and in the doctoral program. He is also part of the Scuola di Amministrazione Aziendale, the Turin Business School of Management.

Cecilia Casalegno is PhD in business administration, researcher and lecturer at the Department of Management, University of Turin. She teaches Marketing, Strategy and Communication. Her main fields of research concern the integrated marketing communication and the leadership development strategy. She is the author of national and international publications. She is co-founder and CEO of the University spin off Spin Lab - Laboratorio di impresa Srl.

Rosalía Gallo is Bachelor of Arts (hons), MBA (IESE, Barcelona) and a Doctor in Economics and Business administration (UPC, Universidad Politécnica de Cataluña). Rosalía Gallo has written several articles and cases on Family Business. She has also contributed to different books. She has published articles on Marketing and teaching methodology and innovation, and has contributed to different congresses and seminars both with presentations and participating in discussion panels. Rosalía Gallo works as a consultant for companies (frequently Family Businesses) in marketing and Management. Rosalía Gallo is, presently, a professor at the Business Economics Department at Universitat Autònoma de Barcelona, where she teaches at the BBA program, in different postgraduate and International Master programs , and in the doctoral program "Culture production and consumption" where she has taught the course "Marketing arts and culture", as well the IDEM doctoral program where she has taught the course "Family business" She has also been part of the management the Economics and Business School at Universitat Autònoma de Barcelona.

***

Feray Adıgüzel is professor of Marketing and have working experience at various universities: Luiss University, Erasmus University Rotterdam, VU University Amsterdam. Her main research interests are market research methodology, marketing models, cross cultural marketing and Sustainability. She has published in journals such as Journal of Marketing Research, International Journal of Research in Marketing, Journal of Business Research, Journal of Cleaner Production, Journal of Economic Psychology and Journal of Consumer Affairs. The paper that she collaborated with Michalek, J., Ebbes, P., Feinberg, R.E. & Papalambros, P. was received 2011 IJRM Best paper award.

Cesare Amatulli is Associate Professor of Marketing at the University of Bari, Italy.

Augusto Bargoni is a PhD student in Business and Management at the Department of Management of the University of Turin where he focuses his research in the field of strategic marketing, entrepreneurship and family business. He holds a Master in Business Administration obtained at Collège des Ingénieurs in Paris.

Wided Batat is Professor of marketing at EM Normandie Business School in Paris and the University of Lyon 2. Her research broadly examines marketing theory, consumer and employee experience, behaviors and well-being in different sectors (e.g. food, luxury, tourism, digital, etc.) with an ethnographic focus on consumption cultures and how policy makers and businesses can adopt responsible initiatives that help consumers to achieve their well-being. Dr. Batat has been the guest editor of multiple top leading journals in business, ethics, management, and marketing such as Journal of Marketing Management, Journal of Strategic Marketing, European Journal of Marketing, etc. Her research has been published in academic journals such as: Journal of Business Ethics, Journal of Business Research, Marketing Theory, Journal of Marketing Management, Journal of Macromarketing, Journal of Services Marketing, Journal of retailing and Consumer Services, Journal of Consumer Marketing, amongst others.

Wendy Bendoni is the Chair of the Marketing & Fashion Marketing department and an Assistant Professor in the School of Business at Woodbury University. She is established as a consumer and market researcher for the past three decades focusing on cultural shifts discovered through the power of social data. Currently, she is a doctorate candidate at Grenoble École de Management. Leveraging her marketing reputation, Wendy continues to explore market research by adding to her portfolio research in the area of predictive marketing. Currently, she is working on research in Digital Consumer Culture, Innovation, Social Data, A.I., Analytics, and insight through the new machine age. She has presented at major international conferences and published research with her colleagues in the Journée International du Marketing, Marketing EDGE, Academy of Marketing Science, Global Marketing Conference, Journal of Product and Brand Management, The Marketing Educators' Association Conference, and Consumer Culture Theory Conference.

Bernardo Bertoldi, Ph.D. in Business Administration, is an Associate Professor at the Department of Management, University of Turin (Italy). He teaches competitive analysis, family business strategy, and marketing. He published journal articles, contributed chapters and books and cases with Harvard Business Publishing, and regularly contributes to Italian newspapers and participates in public debates about management and family capitalism.

Giulia Bonelli graduated in Marketing Management at the University of Turin in 2019. She gained a Postgraduate Certificate in Digital Marketing in The Luxury Sector at Condé Nast College of Madrid in 2018. Her research interests are in digital marketing and luxury brand management.

About the Contributors

Valentina Chiaudano is a PhD fellow in Business and Management and adjunct professor of Brand Management and Marketing at the University of Turin, Italy. Her research interests are in digital marketing, social media, and digital transformation with a specific focus on the luxury market.

Chiara Civera holds a Ph.D. in Business and Management from the University of Turin, Department of Management and is currently a researcher at the Department of Management, University of Turin (IT), qualified as Associate Professor and adjunct pro- fessor of Strategic Marketing at SAA School of Management. She has published in top-tier international journals such as British Food Journal, Business Ethics: a European Review, and Psychology and Marketing around the topics of Corporate Social Responsibility, Sustainability, Communication, Stakeholder Engagement and Empowerment applied to various industries with a focus on the food and beverage industry and its sectors, such as the coffee chain.

Peter Clarke (Chartered Accountant, B. Comm., Higher Diploma in Education, Masters in Economics, PhD) is Emeritus Professor of Accounting in the Smurfit School of Business at University College Dublin (UCD), Ireland. He has lectured both managerial accounting, and financial reporting at undergraduate and postgraduate levels. In addition, he has lectured on notable MBA and executive programmes on various aspects of accounting and financial management for the China Europe International Business School (CEIBS) in Shanghai, Cyprus International Institute of Management (CIIM), ESCP/ EAP (Paris), the University of Rhode Island (USA), the University of Lethbridge (Canada), the S. P. Jain School of Global Management (Dubai), and the World Academy of Sport (London and Malaysia). Peter has authored three main accounting books entitled: Managerial Accounting: Costing, Decision Making & Control (2016, 3rd edition), Accounting Information for Managers (2002) and Financial Accounting (2000) and is, currently, writing a book entitled "Financial Management in Organisations". His main research interests focus on the design and use of accounting information within businesses, and the impact of International Financial Reporting Standards (IFRSs) on such information and decision making. In addition, Peter has actively researched various aspects of accounting history. In total, he has published over 150 papers in both peer-reviewed academic and professional journals. Some of these papers were originally presented at conferences of the American, European and Irish Accounting Associations. Furthermore, he authored case studies for the Institute of Management Accountants (USA) for the 2009 Student Management Accounting Case Competition, and the 2010 Chinese Student Management Accounting Case Competition... He was the founder Director of the (full-time) MBA programme at UCD and, subsequently, the UCD Sports Management programme. Furthermore, he was a founder member and past Chairman of the Irish Accounting and Finance Association, in addition to being the first editor of the Irish Accounting Review. He has served on the Editorial Boards of the European Accounting Review, Accounting Education, the Irish Accounting Review and the IMA Educational Case Journal. He was the recipient, on two occasions (1992 and 2004), of the Accountancy Ireland award, which gives recognition, annually, to the author who has made the most valuable contribution to Accountancy Ireland journal during the preceding calendar year. In addition, he was the first recipient of the Professor Edward Cahill prize (in 2006) for the outstanding article in the Irish Accounting Review for the period 2003 – 2005. He has also received acknowledgment from Chartered Accountants Ireland for this teaching excellence.

About the Contributors

Laura I. M. Colm, who earned her M.Sc in Marketing Management from Bocconi University (Milan, Italy) and her Ph.D. in Marketing Management from the University of Stuttgart (Germany), is Junior Lecturer in Marketing and Sales at SDA Bocconi School of Management. Her topics of interest, both in research and teaching, are Services Marketing, Business-to-Business Marketing, the Interface of Marketing and Sales, International Marketing, and Digital Marketing, with a focus on Qualitative Inquiry.

Edoardo Crocco graduated from the Business Administration postgraduate program in 2018 at the university of Turin, Italy. He worked as a researcher for the university of Turin for one year, before enrolling in the Business & Management PHD programme. His main research field is Accounting Education, however he has been researching the digitalization of accounting in Italian SMEs as well. He is currently enrolled in the second year of the Turin PHD programme and works as a TA for several Accounting courses.

Matteo De Angelis is a Full Professor of marketing at LUISS University.

Carmela Donato is lecturer of Marketing at LUISS Guido Carli University. Her main research interests are consumer behavior, sustainability, emotions and sensory marketing. She has published in journals such as Psychology & Marketing, Journal of Consumer Behaviour, Journal of Consumer Marketing.

Fabio Duma is an expert in the field of luxury management and marketing and has been researching the phenomenon of luxury for several years. His current research focus lies on intercultural aspects of luxury consumption, connoisseurship consumption, management specifics of independent, privately-owned luxury companies and start-ups, luxury ecosystems and the specifics of customer experience and personal interaction in luxury. He works as a senior lecturer and Head Competence Team Luxury Management at the Zurich University of Applied Sciences, School of Management and Law (ZHAW SML), one of the leading universities of applied sciences in Switzerland. For his contributions to excellence in the education of business, Fabio Duma has been awarded faculty membership in the international business honor society of Beta Gamma Sigma. He has earned his PhD from the internationally renowned University of St. Gallen (HSG) in Switzerland with a thesis on the management of personal interaction in luxury retail for which he got support from numerous renowned Swiss manufacturers and retailers of luxury timepieces. Throughout his academic career, Fabio Duma has published numerous articles, books and book chapters and presented his research at conferences in the luxury capitals of the world. As a speaker, Fabio Duma is often being invited to luxury- and fashion-related events and conferences. He serves as an advisor and board member in various organizations, such as the Academic board of the Luxury Venture Group in Switzerland or the Swiss-Arab Network. He is the co-founder and president of Orbis Excellentiae, an international cross-industry association of independent, privately owned purveyors of excellence. As an entrepreneur, Fabio Duma has successfully founded and co-founded two companies in the premium and luxury segment of different industries.

Maya Gadgil works as a Senior Research Associate /Lecturer with the function Deputy Head of the Competence Team Luxury Management at the Zurich University of Applied Sciences, School of Management and Law (ZHAW SML), Switzerland. She has earned her MLaw degree at the University of Zurich, has numerous years of working experience in the field of Marketing and is head supervisor of international student business projects for luxury companies. She has published various articles and

344

About the Contributors

papers. Her research interests include sustainable luxury, cross-cultural perspectives of luxury, luxury ecosystems and Transformative luxury/Luxury Foresights.

Irene García Medina is a lecturer in Marketing at the Glasgow Caledonian University (Glasgow, United Kingdom). She is bachelor of Communication Sciences (Complutense University of Madrid, Spain) and Ph.D. in Marketing (University of Sophia - Antipolis, France) and International Relations (University of Vienna, Austria). As a teacher, García Medina has previously taught Marketing and International Business Management at graduate level and master's degree in the Faculty of Business and Economics at the University of Madeira (Portugal), at the University of Vic (Spain) and at the University Pompeu Fabra (Spain). As a professional, she has worked, among others, as Marketing Director of the French company VTDIM, as Consultant for the Portuguese Chamber of Commerce, as Head of Communication and Promotion of CORDIS (European Commission, DGXIII, Luxembourg). She has given lectures, seminars and workshops in the field of marketing and advertising in several countries and has published numerous articles and books. Her main areas of interest in research are mobile marketing, digital marketing, digital communication, social media and e-branding.

Chiara Giachino, PhD, is Associate Professor in Marketing at the Department of Management, University of Turin, Italy. Her most recent researches concern the consumer behaviors with particular focus on young generations, tourism marketing and strategy. Recently, she started to research on machine learning and its application in cultural institution. She teaches marketing, industrial marketing and business management and she is involved also in some masters' courses. She is a member of the Consulta in the SIM (Italian Marketing Association) and she recently was visiting researcher at the Columbia Business School.

Elisa Giacosa received the PhD Degree in Business Administration in 2003 in the University of Turin, Italy. She is Full Professor of Business Administration in the Department of Management, University of Turin, Italy. She teaches Financial Accounting and International Financial Accounting courses in the University of Turin, Italy. Her main areas of research include family businesses, food business, food business, crisis management and universities missions, on which several international publications have been focused. She's Associate Fellow of the EuroMed Academy of Business.

Zahaira Fabiola González Romo is a Lecturer, Universitat Internacional de Catalunya. Ph.D. in Advertising and Public Relations from the AUB, Spain. Professor of Advertising, Marketing and Public Relations at several universities (UIC, UVIC, UOC, UPC CITM, UEMC, Tecnocampus, Mediterrani and ESERP). She has given lectures, seminars and workshops in the field of marketing and advertising in several countries and has published numerous articles and books. At the moment her research is about consumer behaviour, digital marketing and fashion.

Gianluigi Guido (Ph.D., University of Cambridge, UK) is Full Professor of Marketing at the University of Salento, Lecce (Italy). His research is about consumer behavior and marketing strategies. He has published more than twenty books and 200 papers in scholarly journals.

Inas Khochman is a Research Assistant specialized in luxury at the business School of the American University of Beirut.

Philip J. Kitchen, PhD - Professor of Marketing, ICN-Artem School of Business, Nancy, France. Emeritus Professor University of Salford, UK and Brock University, Canada. Editor - Journal of Marketing Communications and Founder of the International Conference on Corporate and Marketing Communications (held annually since 1996). Has served as guest editor for the European Journal of Marketing formerly. Published over 170 papers in journals including Journal of Business Research, European Journal of Marketing, Journal of Advertising Research, International Journal of Advertising, International Journal of Human Resource Management among others, together with 20 published books on marketing communications, corporate communications, marketing management and marketing theory. Listed as one of the 'The Top 50 Gurus who influenced the Future of Marketing', Marketing Business, December 2003, 12-16. Fellow of CIM, RSA, HEA, IOD; and Member of the ALCS and Institute of Marketing Science (USA). He recently was the keynote speaker at the Italian Institute of Management Conference in Rome, July 2019, and at the University of Salford, UK, also in 2019,

Monica Mendini is Lecturer-researcher in Marketing at the Department of Business Economics, Health and Social Care of the University of Applied Sciences and Arts of Southern Switzerland, SUPSI. Before joining SUPSI, she obtained her Ph.D. in Marketing (sponsored by the Swiss National Science Foundation, Doc.CH) at the Università della Svizzera italiana in Lugano, where she still teaches in graduate programs. Her research focuses mainly on consumer behavior, with particular reference to consumer-brand relationships, cause-marketing, design thinking, food consumption and consumer well-being. Her work has been published in the Journal of Business Research, Journal of Consumer Behaviour, Qualitative Market Research and Marketing Education Review.

Susana Miquel has been Assistant Professor since 2018 in the Department of Communication of the Universitat Jaume I de Castelló (UJI) and accredited to access tenure by ANECA since 2017. She holds a degree in Information Sciences, specialising in Advertising and Public Relations, from CEU San Pablo (attached to the Universidad Politécnica de Valencia). She received her PhD in 2016 from the Universidad de Alicante (UA) through the Business, Economics and Society programme. Since 2018, after 16 years as an associate professor, she has taught on the Degree in Advertising and Public Relations, mainly on the subject of Account Management, and on the Degree in Journalism, on the subject of Communication Management.

Camilla Pedrazzi earned a BSc in Business Administration with a major in General Management and an MSc in Marketing from the Zurich University of Applied Sciences, School of Management and Law. She completed her studies both, in Switzerland and in South Korea. Camilla Pedrazzi currently works as a Customer Marketing Manager at a major European consumer goods company and has held different positions at her family's jewelry business in Switzerland.

Paola Peretti is a known leader bringing a broad international experience and a deep knowledge of marketing and digital strategy combined with a passion for innovation and transformation. Paola's skills cover a wide spectrum ranging from marketing to eCommerce, analytics and omnichannel strategies. Paola is also the author of several publications, a sought-after speaker at major conferences as well as a lecturer at key institutions like Columbia University, Bocconi University and Kellogg School of Management. She has a vast experience across different industries, from Media, Spirits, Major appliances, Confectionery and Food (MARS) and luxury fashion brand experience wherein her previous role she

About the Contributors

was the Chief Digital Officer of Moncler. She is well known for her bold thinking, her positive "can do" leadership style and her ability to make things happen. Paola now based in Italy, she lived in the US for 11 years and also Stockholm, Paris and Barcelona. Outside of work, on top of running & cooking, Paola is active in volunteering and she is organizing a crowdfunding campaign every year to support a local non-profit association. She thinks "the best way to predict the future is to build it" and she is happy to work at Mars as Global Customers, VP.

Paula C. Peter is Full Professor of Marketing at San Diego State University (SDSU). Her research interests are on experiential marketing, new technologies (AR/VR), and consumer psychology as they relate to effective integrated marketing communications and marketing education. Her most recent work focuses on the area of alternative food consumptions, design thinking, and extended realities (AR/VR). Dr. Peter's research has been published in academic journals such as: Journal of Public Policy and Marketing, Journal of Business Research, Marketing Theory, Journal of Marketing Management, Journal of Marketing Education, Journal of Consumer Affairs, Journal of Consumer Marketing, Journal of Research for Consumers, Journal of Applied Social Psychology, etc.

Fabrizio Pini is currently co-director of the International Master in Luxury Management (IMLUX), Director of marketing programs and adjunct professor of marketing and communications at MIP school of Management, Politecnico of Milan. He is professor of business model innovation and digital marketing in the "Master on digital entrepreneurship" at HDBW - Hochschule der Bayerischen Wirtschaft, Munich. He collaborates with Neoma Business School, Reims Campus (France) for the corporate programmes on the subjects of digital marketing and business model innovation.

Stefano Prestini, Ph.D., is Academic Fellow at the Marketing Department at Bocconi University in Milan, Italy, where he is coordinator of the specialized Master in Marketing and Communication. His current research interests are in consumer behavior, luxury experience, arts marketing and advertising.

Mohanbir Sawhney is a globally recognized scholar, teacher, consultant and speaker in strategic marketing, innovation and new media. His research and teaching interests include marketing and media in the digital world, process-centric marketing, collaborative marketing, organic growth and network-centric innovation. He has been widely recognized as a thought leader. Business Week named him as one of the 25 most influential people in e-Business. Crain's Chicago Business named him a member of "40 under 40", a select group of young business leaders in the Chicago area. He is a Fellow of the World Economic Forum. Prof. Sawhney is the co-author of five books. His most recent books are Collaborating with Customers to Create (2008) and The Global Brain: Your Roadmap for Innovating Smarter and Faster in the Networked World (2007). His research has been published in leading journals like California Management Review, Harvard Business Review, Journal of Interactive Marketing, Management Science, Marketing Science, MIT Sloan Management Review, and Journal of the Academy of Marketing Science. He has also written several influential trade articles in publications like the Financial Times, CIO Magazine, and Business 2.0. He has won several awards for his teaching and research, including the 2006 Sidney Levy Award for Teaching Excellence at the Kellogg School, the 2005 runner-up for Best Paper in Journal of Interactive Marketing, the 2001 Accenture Award for the best paper published in California Management Review in 2000 and the Outstanding Professor of the Year at Kellogg in 1998. Students have nominated him as one of the top 5 professors at Kellogg in 2008 and 2009. He was awarded the Distinguished Alumni Award by the Indian Institute of Management, Calcutta in 2011 and he received the Light of India Award in 2011. Prof. Sawhney advises and speaks to Global 2000 firms and governments worldwide. His speaking and consulting clients include Accenture, Adobe Systems, Alticor, Banco Real, Boeing, Celanese, Cisco Systems, Dell, DuPont, Ericsson, Fidelity Investments, General Mills, Goldman Sachs, HCL Technologies, Honeywell, IBM Consulting Services, Infosys, Johnson & Johnson, Juniper Networks, Kellogg Company, Kraft Foods, McDonald's, Microsoft, Motorola, MTV Networks, Nissan Motor, Nomura Research Institute, Raytheon Missile Systems, SAP, Sony, Teradata and Thomson Corporation. He serves on the boards and advisory boards of several technology startup companies, including EXLservice, Bahwan Cybertek, mock, Cross-Tab Group, Firescope and Page well. Prof. Sawhney holds a PhD in marketing from the Wharton School of the University of Pennsylvania; a Master's degree in management from the Indian Institute of Management, Calcutta; and a Bachelor's degree in Electrical Engineering from the Indian Institute of Technology, New Delhi.

Andrea Sestino is Ph.D. Candidate in Management and Marketing, at University of Bari (Italy), and Assistant Researcher at University of Salento, Lecce (Italy). He holds a M.Sc. in Business Management at Sapienza University, Rome (Italy). He is R&D Specialist for an Italian consulting company in the field of Applied Research to technology, involved in private and national research projects. His research interests fall in the areas of technology, business innovation and digital transformation and related impact to companies and consumers. He published in major academic journals such as Technovation, technology Analysis and Strategic Management, British Food Journal, Int. J. of Learning and Intellectual Capital, J. of Financial Service Marketing.

Dinara Timergaleeva is a junior consultant in the practice of Digital Marketing and Business Model Innovation. Formerly Junior Brand Manager at Cashmere and Silk, Moscow. MSc Degree in Luxury Management from Mip School of Management, Politecnico of Milan and NEOMA Busoiness School, Reims.

Luca Matteo Zagni is a beneficiary of a grant in Marketing Management at the University of Turin. He is graduated in Marketing Management at the University of Turin in 2019.

Index

A

accounting 157-162, 164-166, 168-177
Activity Based Costing 162, 171-172, 174
amplification 119, 131-134
analytics 16, 45, 88, 99, 139-140, 144-149, 151-152, 154, 156
artificial intelligence 28, 45, 139, 154
augmented reality 30-31, 36, 42, 72, 119, 126, 128, 134, 141, 263, 266, 270-271, 273
authentic pride 197, 201-202, 204-207, 211

B

Baby Boomer 229
Balanced Scorecard 157, 162, 166-169, 175-176
brand communication archetypes 101, 113
brand equity 13, 17, 24, 45, 63, 66, 81, 83, 87, 89-92, 94-98, 100, 113, 116, 211, 219, 268, 272, 280, 293, 295
brand narratives 101, 107, 110-113

C

campaign 30, 62, 64, 73-75, 93, 96, 106, 145, 266, 268, 279
case vignette 126, 138
celebrity endorsement 23, 274-288, 291, 293-295
channel integration 1, 6, 39-40, 65
co-creation 19, 78-79, 111, 113-114, 119, 122, 125, 131-133, 136, 138, 144
consumer behavior 17, 21, 38, 43, 98, 120, 139-140, 142, 144, 151, 155, 186, 209-210, 230-231, 234-237, 241, 252-253, 256, 259-260
content 2, 19, 23, 32, 40, 56, 59, 62-64, 66-67, 69, 71, 73-74, 76-79, 81, 83-85, 87-88, 90-97, 99-102, 108-114, 122-123, 127, 138, 141-144, 149, 152, 154-155, 187, 195, 247, 265, 272
COVID-19 crisis 66, 101, 106-108, 112, 231

CSR 78, 179-192, 194-196, 198, 208, 217-218, 228, 271
CULTURAL-COMPARATIVE STUDY 230
customer engagement 16, 45, 60, 66, 99-100, 107, 113-114, 121, 125, 131, 133, 136, 153, 156, 217
customer experience 19, 30, 33, 38, 42-43, 45, 47, 51, 56-59, 61, 72, 79, 103, 119-121, 124, 127-129, 131, 135-138, 193, 270
Customer-Based Brand Equity (CBBE) 100
Customer-Centricity 46, 61

D

digital 1-15, 18-19, 23-25, 27-49, 51-62, 64-67, 69-70, 72-77, 81-91, 93-94, 96, 99, 101, 106, 108-109, 113-115, 119-120, 122-147, 149-150, 152, 155, 165, 184, 214, 216-218, 221-222, 224-225, 228-229, 233, 261-262, 264-265, 268-270, 272, 293
digital channel 1-5, 8-10, 12-15, 28, 61, 65, 70, 76
digital environment 2, 67, 119, 131-132, 138, 216
digital marketing 30, 38, 41, 53, 73, 101, 113, 122, 140, 143-144, 146, 293
digital world 29, 36, 120, 142, 261-262, 265
digitalisation 44-45, 47-48, 52-53, 56-57, 81-82, 96
digitization 1, 3, 55-56, 268
distribution strategies 1-3, 5, 7, 9, 11, 19, 67, 96, 225

E

e-commerce 1, 3-4, 9-10, 12, 14-15, 45, 47, 50-52, 54, 59, 82, 98, 101, 106, 117, 122-123, 125, 141, 170
engagement 5, 16, 19, 40-42, 45-47, 51, 53, 57, 60, 62, 65-67, 69-73, 78-79, 98-100, 102, 104, 106-108, 110-114, 121, 125, 127, 131, 133, 136-137, 145, 147, 152-153, 155-156, 196, 217, 265-266, 295
Environamental Concerns 197
e-servicescape 119, 124-126, 128, 130-133, 136, 138
exclusivity 3-4, 8, 14, 18, 23-26, 28-29, 34, 39, 45-46, 50, 66, 71, 73, 82, 84, 89, 96, 101, 104, 106-107, 119, 121-122, 124, 132, 138, 141-142, 189, 215,

218, 232, 234, 248, 279
extended reality technologies 262

F

fashion 2, 6, 8, 11-12, 16-20, 22-43, 47, 59-60, 65, 69, 72-73, 78-80, 82, 85, 88, 92, 97-99, 101-117, 122, 136, 141, 152, 164, 168, 176-177, 183-186, 188, 190-192, 194-195, 197, 199-202, 208-209, 217-219, 221-222, 225-227, 252-254, 257, 266, 293-295
fast fashion brands 22-28, 33-37
Firm-Created Content (FCC) 100
Forte Village 119, 126-128, 131-132

G

generational cohort 216, 230-231, 235, 242, 259
GenX 215-216, 229-230, 234, 259
GenZ 214-216, 218, 222, 225, 229-230, 233, 235, 259, 263

I

inclusivity 62, 64, 73
Instagram 39, 53, 63, 66, 89, 92, 96, 102, 107-114, 144, 264-266, 272, 275, 281
integration 1, 3, 6-7, 15, 23-24, 27, 35, 39-40, 44-45, 47-49, 51-54, 56-58, 65-67, 69-70, 86, 96, 114, 119, 131-134, 225, 269
interactive technologies 22, 30, 33
INTERNATIONAL LUXURY MANAGEMENT 230

K

key performance indicators 162, 166, 168

L

luxuriousness 22, 37, 204, 256
luxury 1-60, 62-67, 69-99, 101-117, 119-129, 131-143, 146, 150-158, 160, 162, 164-166, 168-169, 175-176, 179-212, 214-246, 249-259, 261-266, 268-271, 273-275, 279-282, 285-292, 294
luxury brand communication 78, 81, 83, 86, 89, 96
luxury brands 1, 3-6, 8, 10, 12-15, 17-18, 20-24, 26-29, 32-37, 39-41, 45-47, 49-59, 62-65, 71, 74, 76-78, 81-82, 84-85, 88-89, 91-92, 96-99, 101-102, 104-107, 109-111, 114-117, 121-123, 126, 134-136, 138-142, 146, 151-153, 155, 157-158, 162, 164-166, 168-169, 175, 179-180, 185, 187-194,

197-201, 203, 207-211, 214, 217, 224-225, 227, 231-233, 237, 239, 251, 253-254, 256-258, 262, 264, 273, 279, 292
luxury consumer behavior 139, 230, 235-237, 241, 252
luxury consumption 6, 21, 25, 28, 39-40, 42, 117, 138, 153, 192, 196, 198, 201, 217, 233, 235-237, 239, 241, 244-245, 251, 259, 268
luxury cosmetic 274, 279, 282, 286-289, 291-292, 294
luxury experiences 126, 180, 224, 261, 266
luxury fashion 17-20, 23-24, 26-28, 31, 38-39, 41, 59-60, 69, 78-79, 88, 97-99, 101-115, 117, 122, 136, 152, 176, 194, 199-202, 208-209, 218, 226-227, 253
luxury food consumption 261-265
luxury goods 1-4, 6, 12-16, 18, 20, 23, 25, 27-29, 37-38, 51, 59, 62-65, 67, 69-73, 76-77, 80, 89, 91-92, 103, 116, 125, 135, 160, 175, 188-189, 192-193, 198-200, 203, 207-209, 211, 215, 217, 224-225, 227-229, 231-232, 237, 239, 254, 259, 261
luxury service 119-124, 126, 132-134, 138, 192

M

macro-context 230
Macro-Contextual Factor 260
Management 1, 4, 7-11, 14-21, 24, 29-30, 34-35, 37-44, 57-60, 63, 65, 67, 71, 78-79, 97-102, 104, 109, 111, 113-117, 119-120, 127-128, 130, 132, 134-139, 142, 152-155, 157-162, 164-169, 172-177, 182, 186, 188-189, 193-196, 208-211, 219-220, 225-230, 241, 253-259, 270-271, 293-295
Managerial Accounting 157, 174-175, 177
Mercedes Club 119, 126, 129-132
millennials 3, 17, 30, 78, 92, 101, 105-107, 123, 127, 135, 137, 198, 207, 214-218, 222, 225-231, 233-236, 240-245, 248-254, 256-258, 261-262, 264-265, 267-272
Moncler 109, 214-215, 217, 219-222, 224, 228
multichannel 36, 65-66, 68-70, 77, 79-80, 214, 218
multi-channel 13, 147, 227, 229

N

new luxury consumers 46, 261, 264

O

offline 6, 9-10, 22, 24, 28-30, 35-36, 39, 47-49, 51-54, 56-57, 62-63, 65-67, 69-70, 75, 80, 86-87, 93, 102, 116, 123-126, 128, 132-133, 138, 141-142, 272, 276

Index

omnichannel 2-3, 6, 12, 14, 22-24, 28-37, 40-43, 46-47, 52, 57, 61-62, 64, 119-121, 123, 125, 131, 134, 138, 225
omnichannel experience 24, 35-36, 61, 138
omnichannel strategies 22, 28-29, 32-33, 35-36, 120, 125
Online Brand Community (OBC) 100
online channel 15, 29, 69-70, 214, 217-218
online marketing 22, 28, 38, 138

P

Paninari 219, 221, 229
personal value system 241-242, 244, 253, 260
Post-Millennials 261-262, 264, 267-269
prestige 7, 14, 23, 25, 27-28, 43, 46, 84, 200-201, 217, 220-221, 230-233, 241-242, 244-245, 248-251, 253-254, 257, 259-260
prestige-seeking consumer behavior 21, 155, 259

R

recycle 197, 201, 207, 212

S

service experience 121-124, 126, 128, 130, 132-134, 136, 138
servicescape 123-124, 126, 133, 137-138
social data 139-140, 142-151, 156
social listening 139-140, 142-151, 156
Social Luxury 76-77, 85, 97, 180, 214, 224
social media 3-5, 11, 17-19, 23, 29-30, 34, 40-41, 43, 46, 50, 52-53, 56, 58-60, 63, 66-67, 69, 73-75, 77-92, 96-102, 105-116, 122-125, 127, 131, 135-136, 138-141, 143-148, 150-156, 160, 175, 185, 191, 199, 214, 220-221, 224-227, 229, 236, 245,

262-265, 267, 269, 271-272, 274-276, 281-282, 287, 291-294
social media platform 108, 112
social monitoring 139, 144-147, 151, 156
social network 63, 73-74, 81, 87-88, 92, 155, 287, 293
Social value 132, 260
Sotheby's International Realty 126, 128-129, 132
status 17, 24-28, 31, 39, 45, 63, 78, 98, 121, 189, 197, 200-211, 215, 217, 229, 231-232, 234-235, 239, 246, 250, 253, 255, 257, 259-260, 263-264, 271, 280
status consumption 17, 28, 39, 209, 234, 255
Strategic Management Accounting 157, 162, 164-165
substitution 119, 131-134
sustainability 15, 18, 40, 62, 64, 78, 98, 179-181, 183-186, 188, 190-192, 194, 196, 198-201, 204-205, 207, 209, 211, 214, 216, 218, 225-226, 228, 261
sustainable luxury marketing 179-180, 182-186, 188, 190-193
sustainable marketing strategies 179, 187-188, 192

U

upcycle 197, 201, 204, 207, 212
User-Generated Content (UGC) 63, 100

V

virtual platforms 44, 47-51, 53, 56-57
virtual relationship platforms 45, 47, 49-51, 56, 61

Y

young generations 75, 85, 214-218, 222, 224-225, 261, 264, 269

Recommended Reference Books

IGI Global's reference books are available in three unique pricing formats:
Print Only, E-Book Only, or Print + E-Book.

Shipping fees may apply.

www.igi-global.com

ISBN: 978-1-7998-1048-3
EISBN: 978-1-7998-1049-0
© 2020; 605 pp.
List Price: US$ **285**

ISBN: 978-1-5225-8933-4
EISBN: 978-1-5225-8934-1
© 2020; 667 pp.
List Price: US$ **295**

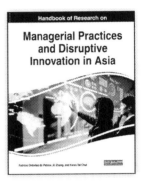

ISBN: 978-1-7998-0357-7
EISBN: 978-1-7998-0359-1
© 2020; 451 pp.
List Price: US$ **235**

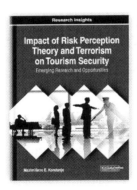

ISBN: 978-1-7998-0070-5
EISBN: 978-1-7998-0071-2
© 2020; 144 pp.
List Price: US$ **175**

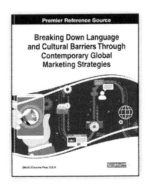

ISBN: 978-1-5225-6980-0
EISBN: 978-1-5225-6981-7
© 2019; 339 pp.
List Price: US$ **235**

ISBN: 978-1-5225-5390-8
EISBN: 978-1-5225-5391-5
© 2018; 125 pp.
List Price: US$ **165**

Do you want to stay current on the latest research trends, product announcements, news, and special offers?
Join IGI Global's mailing list to receive customized recommendations, exclusive discounts, and more.
Sign up at: **www.igi-global.com/newsletters**.

Publisher of Peer-Reviewed, Timely, and Innovative Academic Research

www.igi-global.com Sign up at www.igi-global.com/newsletters facebook.com/igiglobal twitter.com/igiglobal linkedin.com/igiglobal

Ensure Quality Research is Introduced to the Academic Community

Become an Evaluator for IGI Global Authored Book Projects

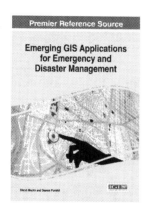 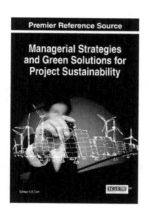  

The overall success of an authored book project is dependent on quality and timely manuscript evaluations.

Applications and Inquiries may be sent to:
development@igi-global.com

Applicants must have a doctorate (or equivalent degree) as well as publishing, research, and reviewing experience. Authored Book Evaluators are appointed for one-year terms and are expected to complete at least three evaluations per term. Upon successful completion of this term, evaluators can be considered for an additional term.

If you have a colleague that may be interested in this opportunity, we encourage you to share this information with them.

IGI Global Author Services

Providing a high-quality, affordable, and expeditious service, IGI Global's Author Services enable authors to streamline their publishing process, increase chance of acceptance, and adhere to IGI Global's publication standards.

Benefits of Author Services:

- **Professional Service:** All our editors, designers, and translators are experts in their field with years of experience and professional certifications.
- **Quality Guarantee & Certificate:** Each order is returned with a quality guarantee and certificate of professional completion.
- **Timeliness:** All editorial orders have a guaranteed return timeframe of 3-5 business days and translation orders are guaranteed in 7-10 business days.
- **Affordable Pricing:** IGI Global Author Services are competitively priced compared to other industry service providers.
- **APC Reimbursement:** IGI Global authors publishing Open Access (OA) will be able to deduct the cost of editing and other IGI Global author services from their OA APC publishing fee.

Author Services Offered:

English Language Copy Editing
Professional, native English language copy editors improve your manuscript's grammar, spelling, punctuation, terminology, semantics, consistency, flow, formatting, and more.

Scientific & Scholarly Editing
A Ph.D. level review for qualities such as originality and significance, interest to researchers, level of methodology and analysis, coverage of literature, organization, quality of writing, and strengths and weaknesses.

Figure, Table, Chart & Equation Conversions
Work with IGI Global's graphic designers before submission to enhance and design all figures and charts to IGI Global's specific standards for clarity.

Translation
Providing 70 language options, including Simplified and Traditional Chinese, Spanish, Arabic, German, French, and more.

Hear What the Experts Are Saying About IGI Global's Author Services

"Publishing with IGI Global has been *an amazing experience* for me for sharing my research. The *strong academic production* support ensures quality and timely completion." – **Prof. Margaret Niess, Oregon State University, USA**

"The service was *very fast, very thorough, and very helpful* in ensuring our chapter meets the criteria and requirements of the book's editors. I was *quite impressed and happy* with your service." – **Prof. Tom Brinthaupt, Middle Tennessee State University, USA**

Learn More or Get Started Here:

For Questions, Contact IGI Global's Customer Service Team at cust@igi-global.com or 717-533-8845

www.igi-global.com

Celebrating Over 30 Years of Scholarly Knowledge Creation & Dissemination

InfoSci®-Books

A Database of Nearly 6,000 Reference Books Containing Over 105,000+ Chapters Focusing on Emerging Research

GAIN ACCESS TO **THOUSANDS** OF REFERENCE BOOKS AT **A FRACTION** OF THEIR INDIVIDUAL LIST **PRICE**.

InfoSci®-Books Database

The **InfoSci®-Books** is a database of nearly 6,000 IGI Global single and multi-volume reference books, handbooks of research, and encyclopedias, encompassing groundbreaking research from prominent experts worldwide that spans over 350+ topics in 11 core subject areas including business, computer science, education, science and engineering, social sciences, and more.

Open Access Fee Waiver (Read & Publish) Initiative

For any library that invests in IGI Global's InfoSci-Books and/or InfoSci-Journals (175+ scholarly journals) databases, IGI Global will match the library's investment with a fund of equal value to go toward **subsidizing the OA article processing charges (APCs) for their students, faculty, and staff** at that institution when their work is submitted and accepted under OA into an IGI Global journal.*

INFOSCI® PLATFORM FEATURES

- Unlimited Simultaneous Access
- No DRM
- No Set-Up or Maintenance Fees
- A Guarantee of No More Than a 5% Annual Increase for Subscriptions
- Full-Text HTML and PDF Viewing Options
- Downloadable MARC Records
- COUNTER 5 Compliant Reports
- Formatted Citations With Ability to Export to RefWorks and EasyBib
- No Embargo of Content (Research is Available Months in Advance of the Print Release)

*The fund will be offered on an annual basis and expire at the end of the subscription period. The fund would renew as the subscription is renewed for each year thereafter. The open access fees will be waived after the student, faculty, or staff's paper has been vetted and accepted into an IGI Global journal and the fund can only be used toward publishing OA in an IGI Global journal. Libraries in developing countries will have the match on their investment doubled.

To Recommend or Request a Free Trial:
www.igi-global.com/infosci-books

eresources@igi-global.com • Toll Free: 1-866-342-6657 ext. 100 • Phone: 717-533-8845 x100

www.igi-global.com

Printed in the United States
by Baker & Taylor Publisher Services